THINK
AMERICAN GOVERNMENT

NEAL TANNAHILL
Houston Community College

Longman

New York   San Francisco   Boston
London   Toronto   Sydney   Tokyo   Singapore   Madrid
Mexico City   Munich   Paris   Cape Town   Hong Kong   Montreal

W9-BAQ-929

Editor-in-Chief: Eric Stano
Assistant Development Manager: David Kear
Associate Development Editor: Donna Garnier
Marketing Manager: Lindsey Prudhomme
Media Supplements Editor: Regina Vertiz
Production Manager: Eric Jorgensen
Project Coordination, Development, Text Design, Photo Research, and Electronic Page Makeup: Pre-Press PMG
Cover Design Manager: John Callahan
Cover Designer: Kay Petronio
Cover Photo: Courtesy of Veer and iStock
Manufacturing Manager: Mary Fischer
Printer and Binder: Quebecor World/Dubuque
Cover Printer: Lehigh-Phoenix Color/Hagerstown

For permission to use copyrighted material, grateful acknowledgment is made to the copyright holders on pp. 456–457, which are hereby made part of this copyright page.

Library of Congress Cataloging-in-Publication Data

Tannahill, Neal, 1949-
    Think American Government / Neal Tannahill. -- 1st ed.
        p. cm.
    ISBN 0-205-63673-X
    1. United States--Politics and government. I. Title.
    JK275.T36 2009
    320.473--dc22

                                    2009000255

1 2 3 4 5 6 7 8 9 10—QWD—12 11 10 09

Longman
is an imprint of

www.pearsonhighered.com

ISBN-13: 978-0-205-63673-0
ISBN-10:   0-205-63673-X

>brief CONTENTS

intro

GOVERNMENT, POLITICS, AND THE POLICYMAKING PROCESS 2
How do government policies affect your daily life?

1 A CHANGING AMERICA 14
What is the face of America today?

2 AMERICAN CONSTITUTION 34
What are the ground rules of government and the policymaking process?

3 THE FEDERAL SYSTEM 58
How is power distributed among the levels of government?

4 PUBLIC OPINION 76
How do Americans develop their attitudes about government?

5 POLITICAL PARTICIPATION 100
Who voted (and who didn't) in the last election?

6 THE MEDIA 116
Where do Americans get their news?

7 INTEREST GROUPS 132
How do people make their voices heard in government?

8 POLITICAL PARTIES 152
What are the differences between Democrats and Republicans?

9 CAMPAIGNS AND ELECTIONS 170
How do public officials get elected?

10 CONGRESS 202
What do members of Congress do?

11 THE PRESIDENCY 228
What makes a president successful?

12 FEDERAL BUREAUCRACY 256
How does the government implement federal programs?

13 THE FEDERAL COURTS 284
How do the courts influence public policy?

14 ECONOMIC POLICYMAKING 310
How does government affect the economy?

15 CIVIL LIBERTIES POLICYMAKING 338
What are the limits of freedom?

16 CIVIL RIGHTS POLICYMAKING 362
How does a government protect the rights of its citizens?

17 FOREIGN AND DEFENSE POLICYMAKING 386
What is America's role on the global stage?

p. 188 Complete Election Coverage:
How the White House Was Won

The Bush Legacy
p. 311 The Current State of the Economy
p. 401 U.S. Involvement in Iraq
p. 357 Civil Liberties in the U.S.

▶ **on the cover:**

p. 259 The Next Administration:
An Insider's Look at the New Players in Washington

p. 104 College Students: How They Voted and What Lies Ahead

>detailed
CONTENTS

acknowledgments x | about the author xi

intro

GOVERNMENT, POLITICS, AND THE POLICYMAKING PROCESS   2

The Importance of Government 4

Government and Politics 5

The Public Policy Approach 6

The Policymaking Environment 6 • Agenda Building 6 • Policy Formulation 7 • Policy Adoption 8

take action> Government and You 8

Policy Implementation 9 • Policy Evaluation 9

Looking Forward 10

In the Know | Why American Youth Will Vote 11

1

A CHANGING AMERICA   14

Political Culture 16

The International Environment 18

The Demographic Environment 18

Immigration 19 • Illegal Immigration 19

Around the World: Immigration Policy and Politics in France 21

Population Diversity 22

take action> A Changing Nation, Changing Communities 23

The Economic Environment 24

Global Economy 25 • Income Distribution 26

Taking Sides / Changing Faces of Republican and Democratic Parties 27

In the Know | An Older and More Diverse Nation by Midcentury 28

Poverty 29

Conclusion: The Cultural, International, & SocioEconomic Context for Policymaking 30

Agenda Building 30 • Policy Formulation and Adoption 30 • Policy Implementation and Evaluation 31

2

AMERICAN CONSTITUTION   34

Background of the Constitution 36

Historical Setting 36 • American Political Thought 39

Constitutional Principles 40

Representative Democracy 40 • Rule of Law 41 • Limited Government 43 • Separation of Powers with Checks and Balances 44

take action> Service Learning 45

Federalism 46

Around the World: The British Parliamentary System 47

Bicameralism 48

The Living Constitution 49

Constitutional Change through Practice and Experience 49 • Constitutional Change through Amendment 50 • Constitutional Change through Judicial Interpretation 51

The Constitution, Politics, and Public Policy 52

Taking Sides / Constitutional Principles 53

Conclusion: Constitutional Environment for Policymaking 55

Agenda Building 55 • Policy Formulation and Adoption 55 • Policy Implementation and Evaluation 55

3

THE FEDERAL SYSTEM   58

The Constitutional Basis of Federalism 60

Powers of the National Government 60 • The Constitutional Status of the States 62 • The States' Rights/National Government

Supremacy Controversy 63 • The Federal System and the Supreme Court 63

Taking Sides / Federalism and the States 65

Federal Grant Programs 67

take action> Federal Programs and You 67

Program Adoption 67 • Types of Federal Programs 68

Around the World: Education Policy and Federalism in Germany 69

Grant Conditions 70

In the Know | Binge Drinking 71

Conclusion: Federalism & Public Policy 73

Agenda Building 73 • Policy Formulation and Adoption 73 • Policy Implementation and Evaluation 73

4 PUBLIC OPINION 76

Political Socialization 78

Process of Socialization 78 • Agents of Socialization 78 • Can Political Attitudes Be Genetically Transmitted? 80

Measuring Public Opinion 81

Sampling 81 • Question Wording 83

In the Know | Is There a "Bradley Effect?" 84

Question Sequencing 85 • Attitudes, Non-Attitudes, and Phantom Opinions 85 • Interviewer-Respondent Interaction 85 • Timing 85

Political Knowledge 86

Support for Democratic Principles 86 • Political Trust and Political Legitimacy 88

Around the World: Civil Unions in Denmark 89

Political Efficacy 90

take action> Family Politics 90

Political Philosophy 91

Are Americans Liberal or Conservative? 92 • Opinion Differences Among Groups 93

Taking Sides / Media and Public Opinion 95

Conclusion: Public Opinion & Public Policy 96

Agenda Building 96 • Policy Formulation and Adoption 96 • Policy Implementation and Evaluation 97

5 POLITICAL PARTICIPATION 100

Forms of Participation 102

Explaining Participation 103

Personal Resources 103 • Psychological Engagement 103 • Voter Mobilization 103 • Community Involvement 104

Patterns of Participation 104

Income 104 • Age 104 • Race/Ethnicity 105

take action> Registering to Vote 106

Gender 106

Trends in Voter Turnout 106

Participation Rates in Comparative Perspective 107

Around the World: Compulsory Voting in Australia 109

Participation Bias 110

Conclusion: Political Participation & Public Policy 111

Agenda Building 111 • Policy Formulation and Adoption 111 • Policy Implementation and Evaluation 112

Taking Sides / Electronic Voting: Helpful or Harmful? 113

6 THE MEDIA 116

The Media Landscape 118

Around the World: Government Control of the Media in Cuba 121

Covering the News 122

Taking Sides / Media 6.0 vs. the Typewriter 124

Media Biases 126

take action> Favorite News and Information
Links 127

Conclusion: The Media & Public Policy 128

Agenda Building 128 • Policy Formulation
and Adoption 128 • Policy Implementation
and Evaluation 129

7 INTEREST GROUPS 132

Types of Interest Groups 134

Business Groups 134 • Labor Unions 135
• Professional Associations 136 • Racial
and Ethnic Minority Rights Groups 137
• Religious Groups 137 • Citizen,
Advocacy, and Cause Groups 138

Around the World: Church and State
in Mexico 139

Interest Group Tactics 140

Electioneering 140 • Lobbying 143
• Creating Public Pressure 144
• Protest Demonstrations 144

Taking Sides / Interest Groups and Politics 145

Litigation 146 • Political Violence 146

take action> Politics at the Movies 145

The Strength of Interest Groups 147

Alliances with Political Parties 147
• Alliances with Members of Congress
and Executive Branch Officials 147 • Public
Opinion 147 • Unity among Groups
Representing the Same Cause 147
• Opposition from Other Groups 147

Conclusion: Interest Groups & Public
Policy 147

Agenda Building 147 • Policy Formulation
and Adoption 148 • Policy Implementation
and Evaluation 148

In the Know | Small Texas School District Lets
Teachers, Staff Pack Pistols 149

8 POLITICAL PARTIES 152

The Party System 154

Around the World: The Israeli Party
System 156

Party Organization 157

The Party Balance: Democrats, Republicans,
and Independents 158

Taking Sides / Are Party Conventions
Irrelevant? 159

Voting Patterns 160

Income 160 • Race and Ethnicity 160
• Education 160

take action> Party Politics at
the Grassroots 161

Gender 161 • Age 162 • Family and
Lifestyle Status 162 • Region 162 • Political
Ideology 162 • Religion 163 • Place of
Residence 163 • Issue Orientation 163

Divided Government 164

Conclusion: Political Parties & Public Policy 166

Agenda Building 166 • Policy Formulation
and Adoption 166 • Policy Implementation
and Evaluation 167

9 CAMPAIGNS AND ELECTIONS 170

Types of Elections 172

Election Districts and Redistricting 173

Reapportionment 174 • Voting Rights Act
(VRA) 175 • Gerrymandering 176

Election Campaigns 176

The Role of Money 176 • Campaign
Organization and Strategy 179

Taking Sides / The Internet and Campaign
Revolution 180

Congressional Elections 182

• House Elections 182 • Senate
Elections 183

take action> In-Person Politics 183

Presidential Elections 184

The Presidential Nomination Phase 184

Around the World: Legislative Elections in
Brazil 185

The Road to the Nomination 188

Pre-Primary Positioning Stage 188 • Iowa
and New Hampshire: Narrowing the Field
188 • Super Tuesday 189 • The Post–Super
Tuesday Contests 189 • The Transition 190
• The National Party Conventions 190

General Election Phase 191

The Electoral College 191 • The Fall
Campaign 194 • Blue States, Red States, and
the 2008 Election 195

The Voters Decide 196

Party Identification 196 • Issues 196
• Campaigns 196 • Retrospective and
Prospective Voting 197

Conclusion: Elections & Public Policy 198

Agenda Building 198 • Policy Formulation
and Adoption 198 • Policy Implementation
and Evaluation 199

10 CONGRESS 202

Bicameralism 204

Membership 206

Profile of the Membership 206 • Compensation 207 • Personal Styles 207 • Home
Styles 208 • Membership Turnover 209

Organization 210

Organization of the Floor 210

Around the World: The Indian Parliament 214
Committee and Subcommittee
Organization 215

take action> In-Person Learning 216

The Legislative Process 217

Introduction 218 • Committee and
Subcommittee Action 218

Taking Sides / Congressional War Power 219

Floor Action 221 • Conference Committee
Action 223 • Presidential Action 224

Conclusion: Congress & Public Policy

Agenda Building 225 • Policy Formulation
and Adoption 225 • Policy Implementation
and Evaluation 225

11 THE PRESIDENCY 228

The Constitutional Presidency 230

Qualifications and Backgrounds 230
• Term of Office 230 • Impeachment and
Removal 231 • Presidential Succession and
Disability 232 • The Vice Presidency 233

Presidential Powers 235

Diplomatic Powers 235 • Military
Powers 236

Around the World: The Russian
Presidency 237

Inherent Powers 239 • Judicial Powers 240
• Executive Powers 240

Taking Sides / Judicial Selection and Partisan
Politics 241

Legislative Powers 242

The Organization of the Presidency 243

The White House Staff 243 • The Executive
Office of the President 244 • The
Presidential Bureaucracy and Presidential
Influence 244

Theories of Presidential Leadership 246

Presidential Character 246

take action> Why Do They Run? 247

The Power to Persuade 248 • Going
Public 248 • Unilateral Tools of Presidential
Power 249

Presidential Popularity 250

Conclusion: The Presidency & Public Policy 252

Agenda Building 252 • Policy Formulation
and Adoption 252 • Policy Implementation
and Evaluation 253

12 FEDERAL BUREAUCRACY 256

Organization of the Bureaucracy 258

Cabinet Departments 258 • Independent Executive Agencies 260 • Government Corporations 262 • Foundations and Institutes 263 • Independent Regulatory Commissions 263 • Quasi-Governmental Companies 264

Personnel 264

Employment Practices 265

Rulemaking 269

take action> Working for Uncle Sam 270

Politics and Administration 270

The President 270 • Congress 271 • Interest Groups 272 • Bureaucrats 273

Taking Sides / 9/11 Commission 274

Subgovernments and Issue Networks 275

Around the World: The Egyptian Bureaucracy 277

In the Know | New Offshore Drilling Not a Quick Fix, Analysts Say 279

Conclusion: The Federal Bureaucracy & Public Policy 280

Agenda Building 280 • Policy Formulation and Adoption 280 • Policy Implementation and Evaluation 281

13 THE FEDERAL COURTS 284

Judicial Policymaking 286

The Federal Court System 287

District Courts 288 • Courts of Appeals 290

Around the World: Islamic Law in Nigeria 292

Supreme Court 293

In the Know | Justice Kennedy Casts Decisive Vote 299

take action> A Day in Court 302

Power, Politics, and the Courts 302

Taking Sides / Congressional Control over the Judiciary 305

Conclusion: The Courts & Public Policy 306

Agenda Building 306 • Policy Formulation and Adoption 306 • Policy Implementation and Evaluation 307

14 ECONOMIC POLICYMAKING 310

The Goals of Economic Policy 312

Fund Government Services 312 • Encourage/Discourage Private Sector Activity 313 • Redistribute Income 313 • Economic Growth with Stable Prices 314

Tax Revenues 314

Individual Income Tax 314

take action> Tax Breaks for College Students 316

Payroll Taxes 316 • Corporate Income Taxes and Other Revenue Sources 316 • Issues in Government Finance 316 • The Bush Tax Reforms 318

Taking Sides / Tobacco Regulation 320

Budget Deficits and Surpluses 321

Government Expenditures 322

Healthcare 322

Around the World: Healthcare in Canada 323

Social Security 324 • National Defense 326 • Income Security 326

In the Know | Raise Retirement Age to Save Social Security? 328

Interest on the Debt 329

Fiscal Policymaking 329

Ground Rules for Budgeting 329 • The Budget Process 330

Monetary Policymaking 332

Conclusion: Economic Policymaking 333

Agenda Building 334 • Policy Formulation
and Adoption 334 • Policy Implementation
and Evaluation 335

15 CIVIL LIBERTIES POLICYMAKING 338

The Constitutional Basis of Civil Liberties
Policymaking 340

The U.S. Constitution 340 • State
Constitutions 341

Civil Liberties Issues and Policies 342

Government and Religion 342 • Freedom
of Expression 345 • Privacy Rights 347

Taking Sides / Flag-Burning Amendment 348

Due Process of Law and the Rights of the
Accused 350

Around the World: Population Policy
in China 351

take action> Talking About Miranda 353

Executive Authority, Civil Liberties, and the
War on Terror 356

Conclusion: Civil Liberties Policymaking 358

Agenda Building 359 • Policy Formulation
and Adoption 359 • Policy Implementation
and Evaluation 359

16 CIVIL RIGHTS POLICYMAKING 362

The Constitutional Basis of Civil Rights
Policymaking 364

Civil Rights Issues and Policies 365

Equality Before the Law 365 • Voting
Rights and Representation 370

Taking Sides / Hate-Crimes Legislation 371

Freedom from Discrimination 373 • Sexual
Harassment 375

Around the World: Women's Rights in
Saudi Arabia 376

Affirmative Action 377

take action> Voices from the Past 378

Conclusion: Civil Rights Policymaking 380

Agenda Building 380 • Policy Formulation
and Adoption 382 • Policy Implementation
and Evaluation 382

17 FOREIGN AND DEFENSE POLICYMAKING 386

The International Community 388

The Ends and Means of American Policy 392

Foreign Policy 395

Taking Sides / The "Clash of Civilizations" 399

Defense Policy 400

Defense Spending 400 • Defense Forces
and Strategy 400

take action> America in the Eyes of
the World 401

Around the World: Nuclear Weapons in
Pakistan 405

Conclusion: Foreign and Defense
Policymaking 406

Agenda Building 406 • Policy Formulation
and Adoption 406 • Policy Implementation
and Evaluation 408

In the Know | Congress Should Repeal
"Don't Ask, Don't Tell" 409

appendix 412 | glossary 432 | notes 445 | credits 456 | index 458

>acknowledgments

Many people contributed to the writing and production of this book. Eric Stano, Donna Garnier, Eric Jorgensen, and the whole team at Pre-Press PMG gave me sympathetic and professional help from the beginning of work on the edition to its completion.

I am grateful to my friends and colleagues among the government faculty at Houston Community College for their friendship and support. I have learned most of what I know about teaching from them. Finally, I wish to dedicate this book to the people who are close to me personally, especially Anup Bodhe, Anderson Brandao, Jason Orr, and Kim Galle.

NEAL TANNAHILL

>about the
AUTHOR

NEAL TANNAHILL has taught courses in American government and politics at Houston Community College for more than 30 years. The primary focus of his career has been helping students to master course content, successfully complete courses, earn degrees, and achieve their academic goals. He is the author of a series of textbooks including *American Government, Texas Government,* and *American and Texas Government.*

Neal Tannahill welcomes your comments and suggestions about this *Think American Government* text at neal.tannahill@hccs.edu or ntannahill@aol.com.

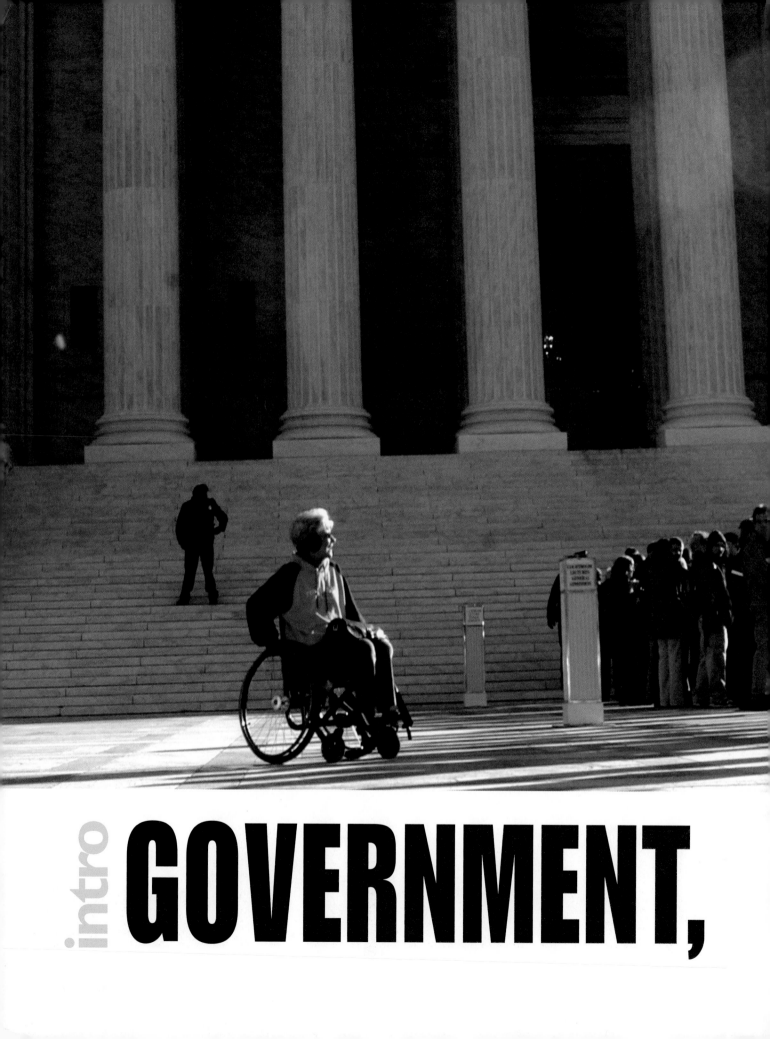

intro **GOVERNMENT,**

> **WHAT'S AHEAD**

The Importance of Government
Government and Politics
The Public Policy Approach
Looking Forward

The Americans with Disabilities Act of 1990 (ADA) is a federal law designed to end discrimination against persons with disabilities and to eliminate barriers to their full participation in American society. The ADA protects people with disabilities from discrimination in all employment practices, including hiring, firing, promotions, and compensation. The ADA does not force employers to hire unqualified individuals who happen to be disabled, but it does require companies to make "reasonable accommodation" for otherwise qualified job applicants or current employees who happen to be disabled unless the business can show that the accommodation would put an "undue hardship" on its operation. The ADA also requires that private businesses that are open to the public—such as restaurants, hotels, theaters, retail stores, funeral homes, healthcare offices, pharmacies, private schools, and daycare centers—be accessible to persons with disabilities. Business owners may have to modify their premises or change their ways of doing business so long as these changes do not unduly burden the business or force business owners to alter the fundamental nature of the goods or services they provide.[1]

POLITICS, AND THE POLICYMAKING PROCESS

the importance
OF GOVERNMENT

the ADA illustrates the importance of government. For millions of Americans with disabilities, the act offers the promise of opportunity to compete in the workplace without discrimination. It guarantees access to restaurants, hotels, shops, and clinics. The ADA forces employers to review their employment practices to ensure compliance with the law and to take reasonable steps to accommodate the needs of workers and customers with disabilities. For society as a whole, the ADA gives millions of people with disabilities the opportunity to become full participants in the nation's economy, both as workers and as consumers.

Government affects individual Americans through regulations, services, and taxes. Government regulates many aspects of daily life, either directly or indirectly. The government sets speed limits and other driving regulations, determines a minimum age to purchase and consume alcoholic beverages, and establishes the educational and technical qualifications required for practicing many occupations and professions. Government regulations affect the quality of air and water, gasoline mileage performance of automobiles, and working conditions in factories. In addition, regulation attempts to protect consumers from unsafe products, untested drugs, misleading package labels, and deceptive advertising.

Government services provide benefits to all Americans. Public hospitals, schools, and transportation networks serve millions of people. Many college students receive financial aid and attend institutions that benefit from public funding. Government welfare programs assist millions of low-income families. Elderly people and many individuals with disabilities receive Social Security and Medicare benefits.

Rebuilding New Orleans.

Government regulations and services cost money. Federal, state, and local taxes combined represent 29 percent of the nation's **Gross Domestic Product (GDP),** which is the total value of goods and services produced by a nation's economy in a year, excluding transactions with foreign countries.[2] Workers pay income and payroll taxes on the wages they earn. Consumers pay sales taxes on retail purchases, and excise taxes on tobacco, alcohol, tires, gasoline, and other products. Homeowners and business owners pay property taxes on their homes and businesses.

Government not only touches the lives of individual Americans, but also affects the quality of life of the nation as a whole. Few people would want to live, work, or run a business in a country without a fully functioning government. Government regulations and services help ensure safe neighborhoods, a healthy environment, an efficient transportation system, and an educated workforce. The tax system provides a mechanism for government to spread the cost of its operation across a broad range of individuals and groups in society. In times of emergency, such as a terrorist attack or a natural disaster, people expect government to respond to the crisis, assist the victims, and rebuild damaged communities.

> These statements have NOT BEEN EVALUATED by the Food and Drug Administration (FDA). These products ARE NOT INTENDED TO DIAGNOSE, TREAT, CURE, OR PREVENT ANY DISEASE.

gross domestic product (GDP) the total value of goods and services produced by a nation's economy in a year, excluding transactions with foreign countries.

government
AND POLITICS

government and *politics* are distinct but closely related terms. **Government** is the institution with authority to set policy for society. Congress, the president, courts, and government agencies, such as the Social Security Administration (SSA) and the Food and Drug Administration (FDA), are all structures of American national government. Each state has a governor, legislature, court system, and administrative departments, in addition to a series of local governments, such as municipalities, townships, counties, and school districts.

Government is an *institution*, but politics is a *process*. One political scientist says that **politics** is the way in which decisions for a society are made and considered binding most of the time by most of the people.[3] Another scholar declares that the study of politics is "the attempt to

government the institution with authority to set policy for society.

politics the process that determines who shall occupy the roles of leadership in government and how the power of government shall be exercised.

explain the various ways in which power is exercised in the everyday world and how that power is used to allocate resources and benefits to some people and groups, and costs and burdens to other people and groups."[4] We could add a third definition: Politics is the process that determines who shall occupy the roles of leadership in government and how the power of government shall be exercised.

think

Do you favor a small government that provides relatively modest services but holds down taxes, or an active government that provides more services but costs more?

the public
POLICY APPROACH

the public policy approach is one of the models that political scientists use for studying government and politics. **Public policy** is the response, or lack of response, of government decision-makers to an issue. Government policies can take the form of laws, executive orders, regulations, court decisions, or, in some cases, no action at all. The decision by government decision-makers *not* to act is just as much a policy decision as the choice to take a particular action.

The **public policy approach** is a comprehensive method for studying the process through which issues come to the attention of government decision-makers and through which policies are formulated, adopted, implemented, and evaluated. The public policy approach goes beyond an examination of the content of laws and regulations to consider the broader scope of policymaking. A study of government policy toward persons with disabilities would begin by examining the legal, cultural, socioeconomic, and political factors shaping the environment for the policy. It would consider how the rights of people with disabilities became an issue of public concern, and it would examine the process through which the government formulated and adopted the ADA. The study would also consider the policy's implementation and evaluation.[5]

The Policymaking Environment

The **policymaking environment** is the complex of factors outside of government that has an impact, either directly or indirectly, on the policymaking process. The types of issues that the government addresses, the set of policy alternatives that government decision-makers are willing to consider, and the resources available to the government depend on the international, cultural, demographic, economic, constitutional, and political environments.

Agenda Building

Agenda building is the process through which problems become matters of public concern and government action. The politics of agenda building involves government officials and groups outside of the government competing to determine which problems government will address. Whereas some interests want to promote the consideration of certain issues, other forces that oppose change work to block discussion by denying that a problem exists or by arguing that the government either cannot or should not address it.[6]

Agenda building not only identifies problems for government attention but also defines the nature of those problems, and therefore the eventual thrust of a policy solution.[7] Consider the issue of disability rights. During the debate in Congress on the ADA, spokespersons for advocacy groups for the disabled, such as the Disability Rights Education and Defense Fund (DREDF) and the Americans Disabled for Attendant Programs Today (ADAPT), noted that the employment rate for persons with severe disabilities was only 23 percent, compared to an employment rate for adults without disabilities of nearly 80 percent.[8] The supporters

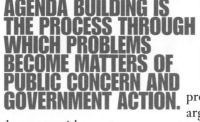

AGENDA BUILDING IS THE PROCESS THROUGH WHICH PROBLEMS BECOME MATTERS OF PUBLIC CONCERN AND GOVERNMENT ACTION.

public policy the response or lack of response of government decision-makers to an issue.

public policy approach a comprehensive method for studying the process through which issues come to the attention of government decision-makers and through which policies are formulated, adopted, implemented, and evaluated.

policymaking environment the complex of factors outside of government that has an impact, either directly or indirectly, on the policymaking process.

agenda building the process through which problems become matters of public concern and government action.

of disability rights argued that discrimination or a lack of access to public facilities prevented many persons with disabilities from working. They proposed passage of federal legislation prohibiting discrimination against people with disabilities and ensuring access to business facilities as a solution to the problem. In contrast, business groups opposed government regulation. They denied that employment discrimination against people with disabilities was a major problem, suggesting instead that the employment rate for people with disabilities was low because many people with disabilities either cannot work or do not want to work. Furthermore, they claimed, individuals with disabilities who have few skills can make more money from government disability payments than they can earn in low-wage jobs.

Policy Formulation

Policy formulation is the development of strategies for dealing with the problems on the official policy agenda. Government officials as well as individuals and organizations outside of government, such as interest groups, political parties, policy experts, and the media, participate in policy formulation. The formulation of ADA legislation, for example, involved negotiations among members of Congress, executive branch officials, business interests, and advocacy groups for people with disabilities. Although most business groups supported the goals of the ADA, they were concerned that the law would require businesses to hire unqualified applicants or make extensive (and expensive) physical modifications to their facilities. Business owners also worried that the new law would subject them to lawsuits and the possibility of expensive jury settlements.

The wording of the ADA reflects a compromise between the supporters of people with disabilities and business interests. The advocacy groups succeeded in writing a broad definition of disability into the law. The ADA declares that an individual with a disability is "a person who

policy formulation the development of strategies for dealing with the problems on the official policy agenda.

Disability rights activists crawl across the plaza of the U.S. Supreme Court building to protest court rulings limiting the scope of the ADA.

SUTTON V. UNITED AIRLINES (1999):
The U.S. Supreme Court has weakened the ADA by limiting its applicability and interpreting its provisions narrowly. *Sutton v. United Airlines* involved a lawsuit filed by twin sisters against United Airlines. The airline refused to consider them for employment as pilots because their uncorrected eyesight did not meet the company's minimum standard of 20/100. The sisters could see well with glasses, so they sued the airlines, charging that it discriminated against them because of their disability. The U.S. Supreme Court rejected their lawsuit because, the Court said, their vision was correctable with glasses and they were therefore no longer disabled under the law.

MURPHY V. UNITED PARCEL SERVICE (1999):
The case of *Murphy v. United Parcel Service* concerned a UPS mechanic who was fired because the company thought that his high blood pressure might interfere with his ability to safely operate a motor vehicle. Murphy said that he was not a safety risk because his blood pressure was controlled by medication. He filed suit under the ADA, but the Supreme Court ruled that he was not covered by the law because doctors testified that his hypertension could be completely controlled by medication. He was therefore not disabled under the law.

CONGRESS AMENDS THE ADA:
In 2008, Congress passed, and President George W. Bush signed, legislation to make it clear that the courts should interpret the civil rights guarantees of the ADA broadly and that mitigating factors should not be considered in determining whether an individual has a disability. The measure explicitly reversed the Supreme Court's interpretation of the ADA in *Sutton* and *Murphy*.

has a physical or mental impairment that substantially limits one or more major life activities, a record of such an impairment, or is regarded as having such an impairment."[9] Major life activities include the ability of individuals to care for themselves, perform manual tasks, walk, see, hear, speak, breathe, learn, work, sit, stand, lift, and reach. Under the law, persons with learning disabilities, epilepsy, mental illness, muscular dystrophy, HIV infection, cancer, diabetes, mental retardation, alcoholism, and cosmetic disfigurement are considered disabled.

Business groups succeeded in limiting the scope of the law. Although the ADA prohibits discrimination, it does not establish a quota system for hiring people with disabilities. It requires only that employers hire and promote qualified candidates without regard to disability. Furthermore, the ADA declares that a business need make only "reasonable accommodations" for employees and customers with disabilities that do not place an "undue hardship" on its operations.

Political scientists use the term **issue network** to describe a group of political actors actively involved with policymaking in a particular issue area. Issue networks vary from issue to issue. The issue network for disabilities includes advocacy groups for people with disabilities, business organizations, individual spokespersons for disability rights, journalists who focus on disability issues, members of Congress and the executive branch who are involved with the issue, and the courts. Although not all participants in an issue network are equally influential, generally no one individual or group is able to dominate policymaking on the issue. Instead, policy reflects the result of conflict, and occasionally compromise, among the participants.

Policy Adoption

Policy adoption is the official decision of a government body to accept a particular policy and put it into effect. The ADA, for example, was enacted through the legislative process. Congress passed the measure and the president signed it into law.

Not all policies are drafted into formal legislation and adopted through the legislative process. Courts adopt policies when they decide cases. Government agencies, such as the Environmental Protection Agency (EPA), adopt policies

issue network a group of political actors that is actively involved with policymaking in a particular issue area.

policy adoption the official decision of a government body to accept a particular policy and put it into effect.

takeaction

GOVERNMENT AND YOU >>

Government policies affect each of us every day in ways that are obvious and in ways that may not always be readily apparent. If a police officer stops you for speeding on your way to class, the government has touched you in a fashion that is direct and clear. In contrast, when you pick up a relative at the airport for a holiday visit, it may not occur to you that tax dollars paid to build the airport.

An important goal of this course is for students to recognize the relevance of government to their own lives and to the life of their community. To help achieve that goal, your assignment is to keep a journal documenting the impact of government on your life throughout the semester. You can write in longhand in a notebook or create your journal entries in a computer file to be submitted at the end of the term. Each entry will identify and discuss a daily event in your life that involved your interaction with government, either directly or indirectly.

Your instructor will grade your journal on the following criteria:

- Number and frequency of entries. Your journal must include at least four dated entries for each week of the course.

- Evidence of growth in your understanding of American government. As the course progresses, your journal entries should reveal a higher level of sophistication than entries made in the first few weeks of the term.

- Quality of journal entries. Some of your entries should identify a connection to course materials, citing concepts discussed in your textbook or in the classroom. At least one entry a week should include a personal evaluation of the role of government. You will not be graded on your point of view, but you should display evidence that you have thought critically about the role of government in your life and in society as a whole.

by issuing regulations. The president can adopt policy by issuing executive orders. Government officials also make policy when they decide either to take no action or to continue policies already in place.

Policy Implementation

Policy implementation is the stage of the policy process in which policies are carried out. Implementation involves not just government officials but also individuals and groups outside of the government. Private businesses, individual with disabilities, the Equal Employment Opportunity Commission (EEOC), and the courts participate in the implementation of the ADA. The law requires private businesses to take reasonable steps to accommodate employees and customers with disabilities. If individuals with disabilities believe they have suffered discrimination, the law allows them to file a lawsuit against the offending business and/or file a complaint with the EEOC. Penalties for violators can be as high as $110,000 for repeat offenders.[10] During 2006, the EEOC, which also hears charges of racial, ethnic, gender, and age discrimination, handled 15,575 complaints based on the ADA, more than a fifth of the total complaints filed with the agency.[11]

The implementation process often involves supplying details and interpretations of policy that are omitted, either intentionally or unintentionally, during policy formulation. The ADA, as noted, requires

In 1969, the Cuyahoga River in northeastern Ohio gained national attention when the debris and chemical runoff from industrial pollution caught fire. The images of the burning river were so spectacular that Congress passed the Clean Water Act. The Environmental Protection Agency (EPA) was put in charge of the Cuyahoga River cleanup program. The river drains over 800 square miles and empties into Lake Erie, which it was helping to pollute at an alarming rate. Today, the Cuyahoga River supports 62 species of fish, where there were none in 1962. Several of the Cuyahoga's tributaries have already met some, or all, of the requirements of the Clean Water Act. In spite of this really encouraging progress, the river system still fails to meet many of the mandates of the Clean Water Act. And most environmentalists agree that a complete river recovery is at least 20 years in the future. The EPA and volunteer organizations continue to work for a complete recovery for the Cuyahoga River.

businesses to make "reasonable accommodations" for employees and customers with disabilities that do not place an "undue hardship" on their operations. How these terms apply to hundreds of specific circumstances depends on their interpretation by the EEOC and the courts. The EEOC, for example, has ruled that employers may not refuse to hire people with disabilities because of concerns about their impact on health insurance costs.[12] More often than not, the courts have sided with employers, narrowing the scope of the ADA and making it difficult for individuals to prevail in disability discrimination lawsuits filed against businesses. Employers win more than 90 percent of the workplace discrimination cases filed under the ADA.[13]

Has the ADA been a success or failure? What is the basis for your answer?

Policy Evaluation

Policy evaluation is the assessment of policy. It involves questions of equity, efficiency, effectiveness, and political feasibility. Equity is the concept that similarly situated people should be treated equally. Efficiency is a comparison of a policy's costs with the benefits it provides. Effectiveness is the extent to which a policy achieves its goals. Political feasibility refers to the ability of a policy to obtain and hold public support. Equitable policies are not always efficient. Similarly, some policies that are effective are not politically feasible, and vice versa.[14]

policy implementation the stage of the policy process in which policies are carried out.

policy evaluation the assessment of policy.

normative analysis a method of study that is based on certain values.

Evaluation can be either normative or empirical. A **normative analysis** is a method of study based on certain values. A normative evaluation of the ADA, for example, might consider the merits of the goals of the law or the wisdom of trying to achieve those goals through government regulation. In contrast, an **empirical analysis** is a method of study that relies on experience and scientific observation. An empirical evaluation might focus on changes in the employment rate for people with disabilities, the number of lawsuits filed under the law, or the average cost of compliance to employers and business owners.

Evaluation studies show that the ADA has had a mixed impact:

- A survey of corporate executives found that the median cost of making the workplace more accessible was only $223 per individual with disabilities. Two-thirds of the executives surveyed reported that the ADA had not spawned an increase in lawsuits.[15]
- A majority of ADA complaints filed with the EEOC have involved issues that members of Congress did not discuss in drafting the law, such as back problems and psychological stress. Only 10 percent of the complaints have come from people with spinal cord injuries or other neurological problems—the conditions most frequently mentioned when the ADA was written.[16]
- Despite the ADA, the employment rate for people with disabilities actually declined between 1992 and 2000.[17]

The impact of the results of policy evaluation on the policy process is known as **feedback**. If a policy is judged successful and the problem solved, officials may terminate the policy. Should the problem persist, the policy process may begin anew as groups and individuals once again push the issue to the forefront of the policy agenda. Evaluation studies frequently result in initiatives to modify policies or improve their implementation. In 1999, for example, Congress passed, and President Bill Clinton signed, legislation making it easier for people with disabilities to keep their government-funded healthcare coverage after taking a job. Despite the ADA, thousands of people with disabilities had been kept out of the job market, because of fear of losing their health coverage. The supporters of the act hoped it would enable them to take jobs.

Evaluation studies frequently result in initiatives to modify policies or improve their implementation.

empirical analysis a method of study that relies on experience and scientific observation.

feedback the impact of the results of policy evaluation on the policy process.

looking FORWARD

The public policy approach provides the basis for the organization of this textbook. The book's first three chapters deal with the international, socioeconomic, and constitutional environments for policymaking. Chapter 1 focuses on the cultural, international, demographic, and economic backgrounds of policymaking in America, whereas the next two chapters explore the constitutional environment for policymaking. Chapter 2 deals with the U.S. Constitution; Chapter 3 focuses on the federal system.

Chapter 4 through Chapter 9 focus on the various elements of the political environment for policymaking: Chapter 4 examines political socialization and public opinion. Chapter 5 discusses individual participation. Chapter 6 considers the media, whereas Chapter 7 looks at interest groups. Chapter 8 deals with political parties, and Chapter 9 discusses political campaigns and elections.

The next four chapters profile the policymaking institutions of American national government: Chapter 10 examines Congress; Chapter 11, the president. The federal bureaucracy is the subject of Chapter 12. Chapter 13 focuses on the federal courts.

The last four chapters of the text deal with the nature of policy and policymaking in four substantive areas: Chapter 14 examines economic policymaking. In Chapter 15, the focus is on civil liberties policymaking, whereas civil rights policymaking is the subject of Chapter 16. Finally, Chapter 17 examines foreign and defense policymaking.

Why American Youth Will Vote

The American Prospect
By COURTNEY E. MARTIN
NOVEMBER 4, 2008

LET'S JUST CLEAR THE AIR. There are a lot of reasons to be skeptical about electoral politics. Especially if you, like me, have only voted in two presidential elections that were both highly contested, dragged-out affairs involving hanging chads, smug Bushes, and a cowardly Congress.

But this, all you hipsters and hip-hop heads, Rock Band addicts and radical libertarians, 18- and 28-year-olds, is why we will vote today.

We will vote because we were raised on a lot of rhetoric about the American Dream, but rarely have a chance to participate in it so directly. Hang out in this sprawling, strip-malled land of opportunity long enough, and you learn that "bootstraps" is code for "you're on your own," and the legacy of slavery and sexism is invisible only to those who benefit from it.

It's hard to counter the deeply entrenched notion that all hard work is equally rewarded in the good ol' U. S. of A. But on this day, November 4, Election Day, every single person who walks in that booth is granted equal say in our shared destiny. We will vote because it is time to show—with fierce and united force— just what our generation is made of. We will vote because it's an opportunity to provide skeptical pundits who have written us off as apathetic with statistics that will shut them up, once and for all.

We will vote because those of us who are female know that women were beaten, ostracized, divorced, and threatened for our privilege. It's hard to even imagine that there was a time when our politics were considered irrelevant simply because of our sex. We will vote in honor of our own blissful amnesia of these preposterous times.

We will vote because those of us who are youth of color know that our ancestors not only endured economic oppression, physical and verbal abuse, and humiliation, but died for our privilege. And for the first time in American history, many of us have the opportunity to elect a leader who looks like us, doesn't demonize or condescend to us, who has shared some of our most intimate experiences of growing up in a country with an unfinished racial revolution.

We will vote because we want to be a part of history. We want to sit down with our children and grandchildren as they hit the history books and tell them colorful stories about the election of '08 with all its unprecedented twists and turns.

We will vote because we dreamed that we would someday "make a difference" in the world, and then our rent was hard to afford and our cigar-smoking uncles kept asking us what we were going to do with our lives and we got drunk and forgot.

We will vote because, though we are sometimes too cool for our own good, we're also young and naïve enough to hope. And as Barack Obama himself has told us, "In the unlikely story that is America, there has never been anything false about hope."

↗ CRITICAL THINKING QUESTIONS:

- How do your friends feel about voting?
- Why is it important for young people to vote?
- According to the author, why did young people vote in large numbers in the 2008 presidential election?

>> END

1 Which of the following is not a provision of the Americans with Disabilities Act (ADA)?

A. Employers are required to hire any disabled person who applies for a job as long as that person meets the minimum qualifications.

B. Private businesses that are open to the public must be accessible to people with disabilities.

C. Employers must make "reasonable accommodations" for disabled employees who are otherwise qualified for their jobs.

D. Employers may not discriminate against disabled persons in hiring and promotions.

2 The institution with authority to set policy for society is known as which of the following?

A. Politics

B. Political science

C. Government

D. Congress

3 Congress, the president, the Federal Communications Commission, and the Supreme Court are all part of which of the following institution?

A. Politics

B. Policymaking environment

C. Government

D. Feedback

4 The way in which decisions for a society are made and considered binding most of the time by most of the people is a definition of which of the following?

A. Politics

B. Political science

C. Government

D. Public policy

5 A city council refuses to adopt an ordinance (local law) designed to regulate smoking in public places. Is this decision an example of a public policy?

A. No. Public policies require the adoption of a policy and the city council rejected the policy proposal.

B. No. This proposal would have violated the ADA.

C. Yes. This is an example of a public policy because it would have regulated public places.

D. Yes. A public policy is the response, or lack of response, by government decision-makers to an issue.

6 Is the ADA an example of a public policy?

A. Yes, because it is the response of government decision–makers to the issue of discrimination against people with disabilities.

B. Yes, because it was not done secretly.

C. Yes, because it affects a lot of people.

D. No, because it does not involve an election.

7 Which of the following is NOT an example of a public policy?

A. The decision of the United States government not to grant diplomatic recognition to the nation of Cuba.

B. The decision of *CBS Nightly News* to name Katie Couric as the anchor of its network evening news.

C. The decision of the Federal Communications Commission (FCC) to adopt a rule concerning the joint ownership of a newspaper, television, and radio station in the same market.

D. The decision of the Senate to confirm a presidential appointment to the Fifth Circuit Court of Appeals.

8 "The complex of factors outside of government that has an impact, either directly or indirectly, on the policymaking process" is a definition of which of the following terms?

A. Agenda building

B. Policymaking environment

C. The public policymaking process

D. Politics

9 "The process through which problems become matters of public concern and government action" is a definition of which of the following terms?

A. Policy adoption

B. Policy implementation

C. Agenda building

D. Policy formulation

10 Which of the following is a good example of agenda building?

A. The president meets with advisors to discuss how best to respond to North Korea testing a nuclear weapon.

B. The Supreme Court rules that the execution of convicted murderers who are mentally retarded violates the U.S. Constitution.

C. A group of concerned scientists publish a report on the problem of global warming.

D. An economist publishes a study showing the impact of minimum wage laws on the unemployment rate of low-skilled workers.

11 The development of strategies for dealing with the problems on the official policy agenda is a definition for which of the following?

A. Policy formulation
B. Policy adoption
C. Policy implementation
D. Policy evaluation

12 A congressional committee meets to discuss the details of proposed legislation to improve automobile mileage standards. The action best illustrates which of the following stages of the policymaking process?

A. Agenda building
B. Policy formulation
C. Policy adoption
D. Policy evaluation

13 A group of political actors that is actively involved with policymaking in a particular issue area is known as which of the following?

A. Interest group
B. Issue network
C. Feedback
D. Political party

14 The official decision of a government body to accept a particular policy and put it into effect is a definition for which of the following?

A. Policy evaluation
B. Policy formulation
C. Policy implementation
D. Policy adoption

15 The president issues an executive order imposing U.S. sanctions on Sudan, a North African country whose government is accused of human rights violations. This act illustrates which stage of the policymaking process?

A. Agenda setting
B. Policy adoption
C. Policy evaluation
D. Policy implementation

16 The stage of the policy process in which policies are carried out is a definition for which of the following?

A. Agenda setting
B. Policy adoption
C. Policy evaluation
D. Policy implementation

17 The president signs legislation establishing a process for trying individuals accused of plotting terror attacks against the United States. This action best illustrates which of the following stages of the policymaking process?

A. Agenda setting
B. Policy adoption
C. Policy formulation
D. Policy implementation

18 Medicare beneficiaries register for prescription drug benefits. This action illustrations which of the following?

A. Agenda setting
B. Policy adoption
C. Policy evaluation
D. Policy implementation

19 In which stage of the policymaking process are policies assessed to determine their impact and effectiveness?

A. Agenda setting
B. Policy adoption
C. Policy evaluation
D. Policy implementation

20 Congress changes the Medicare prescription drug benefit program in response to complaints about coverage. This event best illustrates which of the following?

A. Feedback
B. Issue networks
C. Normative analysis
D. Empirical analysis

1. A; 2. C; 3. C; 4. D; 5. D; 6. A; 7. B; 8. B; 9. C; 10. C; 11. A; 12. B; 13. B; 14. D; 15. D; 16. D; 17. B; 18. D; 19. C; 20. A

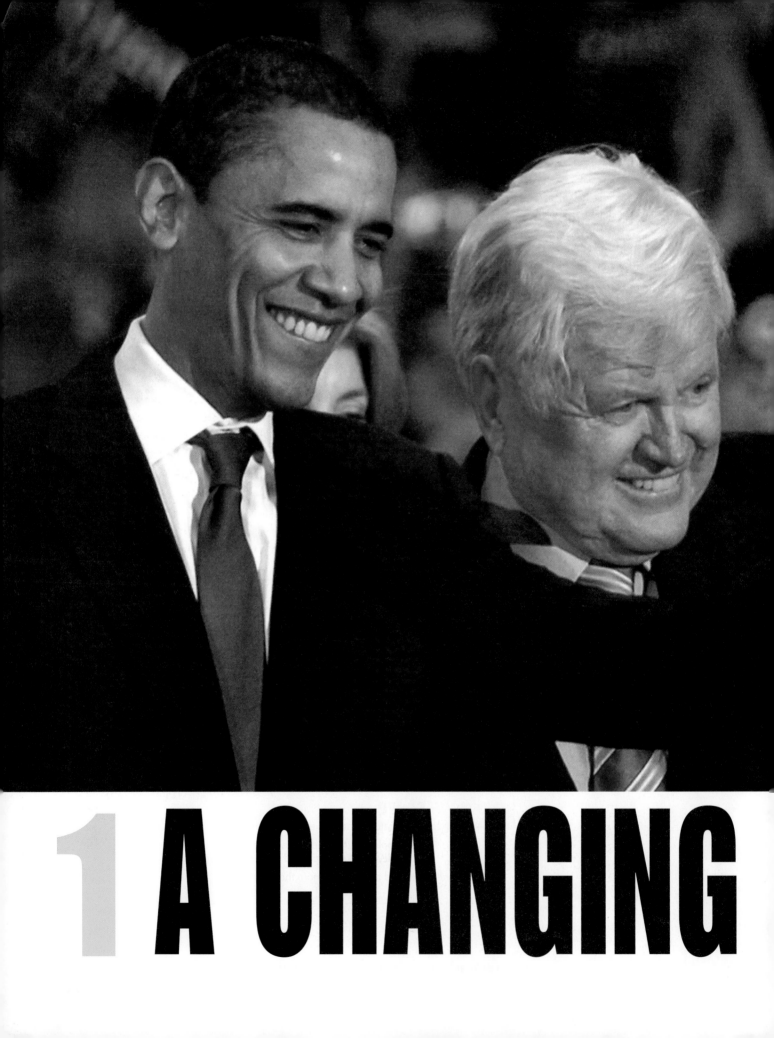

1 A CHANGING

> **WHAT'S AHEAD**

Political Culture

The International Environment

The Demographic Environment

The Economic Environment

Conclusion: The Cultural, International, & Socioeconomic Context for Policymaking

The population of the United States is aging. In 2005, 36.8 million Americans were age 65 or older. The U.S. Census Bureau estimates that the number of older Americans will increase steadily for at least the next two decades. While the older population is increasing rapidly, the number of people between 16 and 64 years of age, the prime working years, is growing slowly (actually falling as a percentage of the total population).[1]

The aging of the population threatens the financial solvency of the government's major healthcare and pension programs—Medicare, Medicaid, and Social Security. Medicare and Medicaid are healthcare programs. **Medicare** is a federally funded health insurance program for the elderly. As the population ages, the number of people eligible for Medicare will climb and the cost of the program will grow. **Medicaid** is a federal program designed to provide health insurance coverage to low-income persons, people with disabilities, and elderly people who are impoverished. Although older people are a minority of Medicaid recipients, the cost of their healthcare is greater than it is for other groups of beneficiaries. **Social Security** is a federal pension and disability insurance program funded through a payroll tax on workers and their employers. Its costs will rise as an increasing number of people reach retirement age and begin collecting benefits. Because the traditional working age population is growing slowly, payroll tax revenues will be unable to keep up with program expenditures.

Demographic change, such as the aging of the population, is an important element of the policymaking environment. This complex of factors outside of government has an impact, either directly or indirectly, on the policymaking process. The policymaking environment influences the types of issues that appear on the policy agenda, the policy options government

AMERICA

decision-makers consider during policy formulation, the policy alternatives selected during policy adoption, the resources available for policy implementation, and the values that influence policy evaluation. Chapter 1 is the first of a series of chapters that deals with the environment for policymaking. This chapter examines some of the more important aspects of the cultural, international, and socioeconomic environments for policymaking in America. Subsequent chapters address the legal/constitutional environment and the political environment.

ESSENTIALS...

after studying Chapter 1, students should be able to answer the following questions:

> How would you describe America's political culture?

> How does the global economy affect policymaking in the United States?

> How has the population of the United States changed in terms of size, growth rate, race and ethnicity, and geographic distribution? How do these changes affect the policymaking environment?

> What are the patterns of wealth and poverty in America, and how does the economic status of families and individuals vary based on race, ethnicity, gender, residence, region, and family composition?

> What is the relationship between the cultural, international, demographic, and economic environments and the policymaking process?

political CULTURE

political culture refers to the widely held, deeply rooted political values of a society. America's political culture can be characterized as a capitalistic democracy. A **democracy** is a system of government in which ultimate political authority is vested in the people. In the box on the following page, political scientist Robert A. Dahl identifies eight criteria of a democratic society. **Capitalism** is an economic system characterized by individual and corporate ownership of the means of production, and a market economy based on the supply and demand of goods and services. Under capitalism, the marketplace, in which buyers and sellers freely exchange goods and services, determines what goods and services

Medicare a federally funded health insurance program for the elderly.

Medicaid a federal program designed to provide health insurance coverage to low-income persons, people with disabilities, and elderly people who are impoverished.

Social Security a federal pension and disability insurance program funded through a payroll tax on workers and their employers.

political culture the widely held, deeply rooted political values of a society.

democracy a system of government in which ultimate political authority is vested in the people.

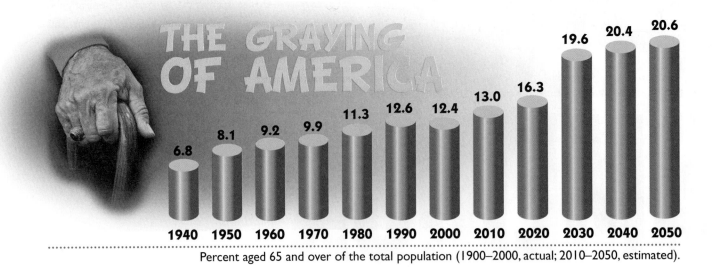

THE GRAYING OF AMERICA

1940	1950	1960	1970	1980	1990	2000	2010	2020	2030	2040	2050
6.8	8.1	9.2	9.9	11.3	12.6	12.4	13.0	16.3	19.6	20.4	20.6

Percent aged 65 and over of the total population (1900–2000, actual; 2010–2050, estimated).

8 CRITERIA OF DEMOCRACY

ROBERT A. DAHL POLITICAL SCIENTIST

1 THE RIGHT TO VOTE. All or nearly all citizens enjoy the right to vote and have their votes counted equally. In the United States, every adult citizen has the right to vote except people who have lost their voting rights because they have been convicted of a serious crime. Significant restrictions on the right to vote are undemocratic. For example, Saudi Arabia held elections for the first time in 2006 to select members of municipal councils but only allowed men to cast ballots. Although holding an election is a step toward democracy, excluding women is undemocratic.

2 THE RIGHT TO BE ELECTED. Citizens have the right to compete for elective office, including people who oppose the policies of the current government. In 2002, Vietnam held elections for the National Assembly with 759 candidates competing for 498 positions. The election fell short of democracy, however, because the only candidates who were allowed to compete were either members of the Communist Party or had been approved by the party organization.[2]

3 THE RIGHT OF POLITICAL LEADERS TO COMPETE FOR SUPPORT AND VOTES. Candidates have an opportunity to conduct campaigns in order to win support. If candidates cannot campaign, voters are unable to make informed choices.

4 FREE & FAIR ELECTIONS. All candidates compete under the same set of rules, without legal advantage or disadvantage. Democratic governments respect the outcomes of elections, peacefully stepping down from office and allowing opposition political parties and leaders to take power.

5 FREEDOM OF ASSOCIATION. Citizens have the right to form political parties and organize groups. They can attend meetings, participate in political rallies, and take part in peaceful demonstrations.

6 FREEDOM OF EXPRESSION. People living in a democracy have the right to express their political views without censorship or fear of government retaliation. Governments that jail their critics are not democracies. For example, an Egyptian court sentenced an opposition political leader to five years in prison at hard labor for allegedly forging the signatures on the petition he used to create his own political party, including those of his wife and father.[3]

7 ALTERNATIVE SOURCES OF INFORMATION. The citizens in a democracy have access to information sources that are not controlled by the government. Elections cannot be free and fair if the only information voters have about government policies and candidates is information supplied and controlled by the government.

8 INSTITUTIONS FOR MAKING PUBLIC POLICIES DEPEND ON VOTES & OTHER EXPRESSIONS OF CITIZEN PREFERENCE. In a democracy, citizens elect policymakers. Free and fair elections are meaningless if military leaders or religious figures that do not answer to the voters are the real policymakers.[4]

are produced, how they are produced, and for whom they are produced. The proponents of capitalism argue that it is good for consumers because businesses compete to provide quality goods and services at prices that consumers are willing to pay. They believe that capitalism promotes economic growth because only the most efficient business enterprises survive the competition of the marketplace.

capitalism an economic system characterized by individual and corporate ownership of the means of production and a market economy based on the supply and demand of goods and services.

the international
ENVIRONMENT

the United States is the preeminent nation in the world, militarily, economically, and culturally. Since the collapse of the Soviet Union in 1991, the United States has become the world's only military superpower. The United States alone accounts for 45 percent of world military expenditures, which in 2007 were estimated at $1.34 trillion. The United Kingdom, China, France, and Japan were the countries with the next largest defense budgets, with each accounting for 4 to 5 percent of total world military expenditures."[5]

The United States is also the foremost economic power with the world's largest and most productive economy, which is more closely tied to the global economy than ever before. Furthermore, American culture permeates the world. American fashion, music, and entertainment are pervasive.

A newsstand in Beijing displays the Chinese version of *Rolling Stone* magazine, demonstrating the pervasiveness of American culture around the world.

the demographic
ENVIRONMENT

the United States has more than 300 million people. The figure on page 19 traces the population growth rate of United States during the twentieth century. The nation's population increased rapidly in the early decades of the century. Then the Depression years of the 1930s slowed the growth rate sharply. The population growth rate accelerated in the late 1940s and 1950s with the birth of **the baby boom generation**, which is the exceptionally large number of Americans born during the late 1940s, 1950s, and early 1960s.

baby boom generation the exceptionally large number of Americans born during the late 1940s, 1950s, and early 1960s.

Many American families delayed having children during the Great Depression of the 1930s and also during World War II in the early 1940s. After the war, the birthrate soared because families reunited and people were optimistic about the future. With the end of the baby boom, the rate of population growth slowed in each subsequent decade until the 1990s, when the nation's population increased more rapidly than it had in any decade since the 1950s. Even though birthrates fell during the 1990s, the population growth rate climbed because of increased immigration.

Immigration

Immigrants constitute an eighth of the nation's population.[6] Whereas earlier waves of immigration to the United States were primarily from Europe, most recent immigrants come from Latin America or Asia. The primary countries of origin for recent legal immigrants to the United States are, in descending order, Mexico, India, Philippines, and China. The states in which immigrants most frequently settle are California, New York, Texas, Florida, New Jersey, and Illinois.[7]

Illegal Immigration

More than 11 million people live in the United States illegally. The undocumented population is evenly divided between people who entered the country legally but overstayed temporary visas, such as student visas and tourist visas, and people who crossed the border illegally. More than half of the unauthorized immigrants are from Mexico. One of every nine Mexicans now lives in the United States. A quarter of illegal immigrants are from other Latin American countries, particularly Honduras, El Salvador, Guatemala, Nicaragua, and Brazil. The rest come from Canada and various countries in Europe, Africa, and Asia. The Center for Immigration Studies believes that the population of illegal immigrants in the United States has been falling recently be-

Average Annual Growth Rate of the American Population — percent annual growth

POPULATION GROWTH RATES WERE DEPRESSED DURING THE GREAT DEPRESSION.

THE BIRTHRATE BOOMED AFTER WORLD WAR II.

A SURGE OF IMMIGRANTS LED TO A RESURGENCE IN THE POPULATION GROWTH RATE.

1900–1910 1.9
1910–1920 1.4
1920–1930 1.5
1930–1940 0.7
1940–1950 1.3
1950–1960 1.7
1960–1970 1.3
1970–1980 1.1
1980–1990 0.9
1990–2000 1.2

cause of stepped-up immigration law enforcement and because of a slump in the U.S. economy.[8]

People migrate to the United States primarily for economic reasons. Unauthorized workers account for 5 percent of the civilian workforce. They are concentrated in low-wage occupations such as farming, cleaning, construction, and food preparation. Although unauthorized workers in the United States earn only about half as much per person as do American

Should U.S. immigration policies favor people from English-speaking countries?

citizens and permanent residents, they make substantially more money than they would earn in their home countries. Nonetheless, most unauthorized families live at or near the poverty level and lack health insurance.[9]

Illegal immigration is controversial. Critics charge that undocumented workers drive down wages for American citizens while overcrowding schools and hospital emergency rooms. They argue that unauthorized immigrants undermine the nation's cultural integrity because they create cultural enclaves that resemble their home countries instead of learning English and adopting the customs of the United States. The opponents of illegal immigration favor tighter border controls, strict enforcement of immigration laws, and punishment for American citizens who provide unauthorized im-

IMMIGRATION ADVOCATES CONTEND THAT THE UNITED STATES BENEFITS FROM IMMIGRATION, EVEN ILLEGAL IMMIGRATION

migrants with jobs, housing, healthcare, and other services.

Immigration advocates contend that the United States benefits from immigration, even illegal immigration. They argue that undocu-mented workers take jobs that citizens do not want and that they pay more in taxes than they receive in government services. An influx of hard-working, well-motivated manual workers enhances the competitiveness of American industry and provides additional jobs for citizens as managers. The defenders of immigration believe that today's immigrants enrich the nation's culture just as did earlier waves of immigrants from Great Britain, Germany, Ireland, Italy, and Poland. Furthermore, the proponents of immigration contend that most recent immigrants are quick to learn English and eager to become citizens so they can participate in the nation's political life. Immigration advocates believe that the United States should grant legal status to undocumented workers who have helped build the nation's economy while enacting a realistic immigration system to enable foreign workers to enter the country legally to find jobs.

Illegal immigrants are concentrated in low-wage occupations such as farming, cleaning, construction, and food preparation.

Immigration Policy and Politics in France

After World War II, the government of France encouraged immigration to provide labor for postwar reconstruction. France was experiencing a postwar labor shortage because it suffered 600,000 casualties during the war. It also had the lowest birthrate in Europe between World War I and World War II. The steel, mining, and electric power industries, in particular, needed foreign workers to meet the postwar demand. Many foreign workers took jobs in service industries as well. Over the next 30 years, millions of foreign workers migrated to France. Sometimes they were joined by their families. Immigrants came to France from Southern Europe, especially Italy and Portugal, and from North Africa. Algeria, which had been a French colony prior to its independence in 1962, was the most common North African nation of origin.[10]

The presence in France of a large number of North African immigrants has been controversial. Some French see North Africans as a threat to social cohesion and even national security. North Africans, most of whom are Arab Muslims, are ethnically and culturally different from the French European majority, most of which is non-observant Catholic. Some French also consider North Africans a threat to national security because of the association of some European Islamic immigrants with 9/11 and other terrorist acts. Nonetheless, many European French reject anti-immigrant appeals because they believe that anti-immigrant sentiments contradict the fundamental principles of French democracy, which are *Liberté, Égalité, Fraternité* (liberty, equality, and brotherhood). They believe that France should embrace the cultural diversity of immigrant populations rather than forcing their assimilation.[11]

France has adopted a series of laws and regulations aimed at addressing the issue of non-European immigration. France has halted the immigration of non-European workers but continues to allow family reunification, which has increased the number of North Africans living in France. The government has threatened to fine employers who use illegal workers. To reduce the size of its immigrant population, France has also offered financial incentives for immigrants to return home, but the program has had little success. France has also attempted to pressure North African immigrants to assimilate into French culture. A 2004 law, for example, bans religious symbols from public schools. This law effectively prevents Muslim girls from covering their heads in French classrooms.[12]

> **THIS LAW EFFECTIVELY PREVENTS MUSLIM GIRLS FROM COVERING THEIR HEADS IN FRENCH CLASSROOMS**

Muslim schoolgirls gather in Strasbourg to protest a ruling banning headscarves in French public schools.

Questions

1. How important is it for immigrants to adopt the culture of the majority of people in their new country?

2. Are Mexican immigrants in the United States as culturally different as North African immigrants in France?

3. Is opposition to non-European immigration in France (and the United States) racist?

Population Diversity

The United States is a multiracial/multiethnic society. A 2008 U.S. census report found that the nation's population was 65 percent non-Hispanic white, 15 percent Hispanic, 13 percent African American, 5 percent Asian American, 1.6 percent American Indian and Alaska Native, and 0.4 percent Native Hawaiian and other Pacific Is-

The Face of AMERICA

65% NON-HISPANIC WHITE
15% HISPANIC
13% AFRICAN AMERICAN
5% ASIAN AMERICAN
1.6% AMERICAN INDIANS AND ALASKA NATIVE
0.4% NATIVE HAWAIIAN AND OTHER PACIFIC ISLANDERS

landers.[13] Nearly 15 percent of the nation's population identified as Hispanic (who may be of any race). Hispanics were the most rapidly growing American ethnic group during the 1990s, increasing by more than 50 percent. Demographers predict that Hispanics will make up a fourth of the nation's population by 2050.[14]

The population of the United States has been shifting to the South and the West, the region known as the **Sunbelt**, and away from the Northeast and Midwest, the **Frostbelt**. In 1970, a majority of the nation's population, 52 percent, lived in the Frostbelt. The population has subsequently shifted steadily to the South and West. In 2000, 58 percent of Americans lived in the Sunbelt.[15] The Sunbelt population is growing because of relatively higher birthrates in the region, immigration from abroad, and intrastate migration from the Frostbelt.

Population changes have affected the political balance in the U.S. House of Representatives. Because the Northeast and Midwest have lost population, they have lost seats in the House. After the 2000 U.S. Census, New York and Pennsylvania each lost two House seats, and eight other Frostbelt states lost one seat each. In contrast, the South and West gained seats. Arizona, Texas, Florida, and Georgia gained two seats each in the House. Four other Sunbelt states added one seat apiece.

Sunbelt the southern and western regions of the United States.

Frostbelt the northeastern and midwestern regions of the United States.

Sunbelt politicians have also dominated the race for the White House; every elected president from 1964–2004 has been from the Sunbelt.

Ronald Reagan (1980 and 1984)

Richard Nixon (1968 and 1972)

Lyndon Johnson (1964)

George H.W. Bush (1988)

Bill Clinton (1992 and 1996)

George W. Bush (2000 and 2004)

Jimmy Carter (1976)

takeaction

A CHANGING NATION, CHANGING COMMUNITIES >>

Data from the 2000 U.S. Census show that the United States is changing. The population is both aging and growing more diverse. Whereas the huge baby boom generation is aging, immigration, especially from Latin America and Asia, is transforming the face of America. The economy is changing as well. "Smokestack industries," such as automobile manufacturing and steel production, are in decline; high-tech industries, such as biotechnology and robotics, are expanding.

Is your local community changing as well? Your assignment is to research the ways in which your community has changed by interviewing one or more people who are longtime residents. The individuals you interview should be persons who have lived in the community for at least 15 or 20 years. They can be relatives, friends, coworkers, or classmates. Your questions should cover the following topics:

1. **Population change.** Has the population of your area grown? Have people immigrated to your community from other states or other nations? How has the racial/ethnic makeup of the population changed? Has the population as a whole grown younger or older?

2. **Economic change.** Has the mix of businesses and industries changed? Have any major employers gone out of business? Are there new industries?

3. **Cultural change.** Does the community have places of worship for religious faiths new to the area? Are there new types of restaurants? Do grocery stores carry different varieties of produce to match the tastes of new residents? Does the community celebrate different or additional holidays and festivals?

Take careful notes on what you are told because your instructor plans to organize a class discussion around the research that you and other students have completed. The instructor will ask students to relate the information from their interviews and then analyze the impact of socioeconomic change on the policymaking process. Prepare for the discussion by considering the following questions:

1. Would you expect different issues to appear on the policy agenda today as compared with 20 years ago because of the changes that have taken place in your community?

2. Do you think the capacity of government to respond to policy demands has changed?

3. Would you expect that the community's standard for evaluating government performance has changed?

1980–2006
GROWTH OF HISPANIC POPULATION
HISPANIC POPULATION AND PERCENTAGE OF TOTAL POPULATION

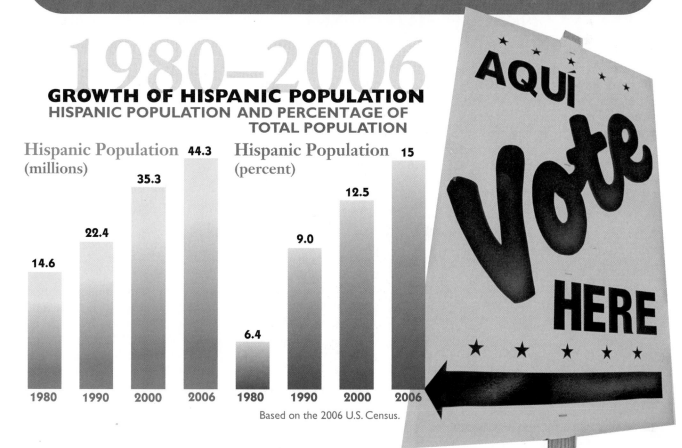

Hispanic Population (millions)

1980	1990	2000	2006
14.6	22.4	35.3	44.3

Hispanic Population (percent)

1980	1990	2000	2006
6.4	9.0	12.5	15

Based on the 2006 U.S. Census.

AQUI Vote HERE

Stock markets in Japan and around the world tumbled during the American financial crisis of late 2008.

the economic
ENVIRONMENT

the United States has the largest economy in the world. The **gross domestic product (GDP)** is the total value of goods and services produced by a nation's economy in a year, excluding transac-

U.S. Census Bureau, "Gross Domestic Product (GDP) by Country: 1990-2004," 2008 Statistical Abstract, available at www.census.gov.

tions with foreign countries. The U.S. GDP stood at $13.8 trillion at the end of 2007. No other country's economy is nearly as large. Even though the United States contains only 4.6 percent of the world's population, it generates 21.1 percent of world economic output.[16]

The figure at left shows GDP **per capita** (per person) adjusted for purchasing power differences for Canada, Germany, Japan, Mexico, the United Kingdom, and the United States. Because the cost of goods and services varies from country to

gross domestic product (GDP) the total value of goods and services produced by a nation's economy in a year, excluding transactions with foreign countries.

per capita per person.

standard of living the goods and services affordable to and available to the residents of a nation.

country, the same amount of money does not purchase the same quantity of goods and services from one nation to another. Adjusting GDP per capita to reflect differences in purchasing power is a good measure of a nation's **standard of living**, which is

AVERAGE ANNUAL PER CAPITA PURCHASING POWER

USA	$39,732
Canada	$31,828
UK	$30,806
Japan	$29,567
Germany	$28,605
Mexico	$10,139

a term that refers to the goods and services affordable by, and available to, the residents of a nation. As the figure indicates, the average American enjoys greater purchasing power than people living in the other countries listed in the table. Meanwhile, the standard of living in the United States is substantially higher than it is in Mexico and other **developing countries**, which are nations with relatively low levels of per capita income.

Global Economy

The United States is part of a **global economy**, which is the integration of national economies into a world economic system in which companies compete worldwide for suppliers and markets. International treaties and agreements have reduced the barriers to trade among the world's countries. The move toward free trade has allowed American companies to compete for business abroad, but it has also forced them to compete at home against overseas competitors.

Some American companies and workers have prospered in the global economy. American agriculture and major retailers such as Wal-Mart have benefited from international trade because their markets (and profits) have grown.[17] Companies that have lowered their cost of doing business through outsourcing or the

use of modern technology have also done well. Their investors have profited from higher stock prices, and their managers and executives have reaped the reward in higher salaries and bonuses. Skilled workers who understand and can operate the latest technology in their fields are in high demand, especially workers who have the ability to adapt quickly as technology changes.

In contrast, international trade has been a disaster for workers in fields that have been unable to compete against low-wage competition from abroad. Less expensive transportation and communication systems

"American companies have begun to cut costs by outsourcing" make it possible to produce goods in countries where production costs are low and then transport those goods to markets worldwide. How can an American manufacturer afford to pay $15 an hour to low-skill assembly workers in the United States if low-skill workers in Indonesia, China, or the Caribbean will do the same work for less than $2 an hour? The American firm must either move its production process to a country with lower wage costs or lose market share because it cannot compete. American companies have also begun to cut costs by outsourcing information technology work and some business process functions to India, China, and Russia—countries that have a large number of college-educated workers who work for much lower wages

developing countries nations with relatively low levels of per capita income.

global economy the integration of national economies into a world economic system in which companies compete worldwide for suppliers and markets.

btw...

Outsourcing may be more prevalent in your daily life than you realize. In 2006, about 50 McDonald's restaurants began experimenting with "remote order-taking." Customers at drive-through windows from Hawaii to Mississippi were, in fact, placing their orders to a call center in California. The call centers take advantage of ever-cheaper communications technology and specially trained minimum-wage employees to field and place the orders over the Internet. Saving just a few seconds on each order can add up in the volume of extra sales, and, thus far, the system appears to be improving accuracy and cutting costs.

than their counterparts in the United States. Computer programming jobs that pay $60,000 to $80,000 a year in the United States can be performed for as little as $9,000 a year in China, $6,000 in India, and $5,000 in Russia.[18]

Low-skill, poorly educated American workers have also been damaged by technological change. Modern technology has enabled companies to replace low-skill workers with machines, which generate the same output, or more, with fewer workers. Between 1979 and 2000, U.S. factory output nearly doubled even though the number of manufacturing jobs fell by more than 2 million. A quarter century ago, General Motors (GM) employed 454,000 workers to manufacture 5 million vehicles. Today, GM produces the same number of cars and trucks, but its payroll has shrunk to 118,000 employees.[19] American workers who lose their jobs because of international trade and technological change usually find new positions, but these new jobs often come without benefits

and typically pay $2 or more an hour less than their old jobs.[20]

Income Distribution

As the U.S. economy has changed, the gap between the rich and other income groups has widened. The figure below shows the share of national income earned by each of five income groups, from the poorest fifth of American families through the wealthiest fifth. Over a 26-year period from 1980 through 2006, the proportion of national income received by the wealthiest fifth of the population increased from 41.4 percent to 50.5 percent. The rich got richer. In the meantime, the share of national income earned by the four other groups of families declined. In particular, the share of income earned by the poorest families fell by more than 35 percent, from 5.3 percent of the total in 1980 to 3.4 percent in 2006. The poor got poorer.

Economist Robert H. Frank attributes the growth of income inequality to changes in the economy and in tax policy. Professor Frank says that the United States has a

"THE WEALTHIEST 4,000 AMERICANS EARNED MORE MONEY IN 2000 THAN MORE THAN HALF A MILLION RETAIL CLERKS EARNED COMBINED"

DONALD L. BARLETT & JAMES B. STEELE,
"HAS YOUR LIFE BECOME A
GAME OF CHANCE?"
TIME, FEBRUARY 2, 2004, P. 42.

winner-take-all economy in which small differences in performance often translate into huge differences in economic reward. Corporate executives, sports stars, and well-known entertainers earn huge paychecks, many times greater than the earnings of ordinary workers, average athletes, and entertainers without "star power." In the meantime, income tax reductions adopted during the Ronald Reagan and George W. Bush administrations significantly reduced income tax rates for upper-income earners, effectively shifting wealth toward the top of the income ladder.[21]

Household income in the United States varies, depending on race, ethnicity, residence, region, and gender. Whites and Asian Americans/Pacific Islanders are better off than Latinos and African Americans. Incomes vary depending on whether families live in metropolitan or non-metropolitan areas. In 2006, the average household income for families living in metropolitan areas was higher than it was for families located outside big cities. Suburban households had higher incomes than families living in the inner city. Family incomes differ based on region. In 2006, household income was lower in the South than

DATE	POOREST 5TH	SECOND 5TH	THIRD 5TH	FOURTH 5TH	WEALTHIEST 5TH
1980	5.3 %	11.6 %	17.6 %	24.4 %	41.4 %
1985	4.8 %	11.0 %	16.9 %	24.3 %	43.1 %
1990	4.6 %	10.8 %	16.6 %	23.8 %	44.3 %
1995	4.4 %	10.1 %	15.6 %	23.2 %	46.5 %
2000	4.3 %	9.8 %	15.5 %	22.8 %	47.4 %
2006	3.4 %	8.6 %	14.5 %	22.9 %	50.5 %

SHARE OF NATIONAL INCOME RECEIVED BY EACH FIFTH OF FAMILIES, 1980–2006

U.S. Census Bureau, *2008 Statistical Abstract*, available at www.census.gov; U.S. Census Bureau, "Income and Earnings Summary Measures by Selected Characteristics: 2005 and 2006," *Income, Poverty, and Health Insurance Coverage in the United States: 2006*, available at www.census.gov.

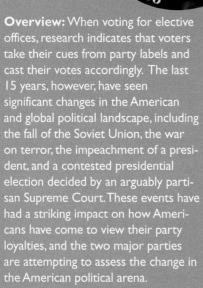

Changing Faces of Republican and Democratic Parties

Do the parties still represent their mid- to late-twentieth-century constituencies? How have they adapted to meet technological and political change?

Whom do the parties truly represent? Is there really significant change in whom the parties actually represent and, if so, what is the reason?

Overview: When voting for elective offices, research indicates that voters take their cues from party labels and cast their votes accordingly. The last 15 years, however, have seen significant changes in the American and global political landscape, including the fall of the Soviet Union, the war on terror, the impeachment of a president, and a contested presidential election decided by an arguably partisan Supreme Court. These events have had a striking impact on how Americans have come to view their party loyalties, and the two major parties are attempting to assess the change in the American political arena.

Generally speaking, certain groups of voters are associated with either one of the two major parties, and the parties themselves claim to represent these same voters. Voting studies demonstrate that there is truth to this contention. For example, in the 2006 midterm election, the Joint Center for Political and Economic Studies reports that 89 percent of black Americans who voted, voted for the Democratic Party; and Pew Research shows that 55 percent of those who attend worship services regularly voted for the Republican Party. But with the momentous changes in global and American politics, can office-seekers continue to count on the support of traditional voting blocs?

American politics is now considered to be polarized between the "blue" (Democratic-leaning) and "red" (Republican-leaning) states and precincts, and the country is understood to be in the middle of a historic national dialogue concerning its future and values. The 2006 midterm election is instructive. The Democratic Party ran on a traditional Republican platform of earmark reform and less government spending, and the Republicans ran on a traditional Democratic party platform of benefit provisions, such as the prescription drug bill. With changes such as these, how is a voter to take his or her cue?

supporting a demographic shift in party affiliation

research indicates that American youth may be changing party affiliation. For example, a 2003 Harvard University poll shows that 31 percent of college students consider themselves Republicans, whereas 27 percent consider themselves Democrats, a reversal of trends over the last 30 years.

the parties have modified their policy position to represent changes in American political values. For instance, the Democratic Party's support of welfare reform, limited government, and middle-class tax cuts are much different than the Democratic policies created in Lyndon Johnson's Great Society of the mid-1960s.

american voters are responding to changes in global and domestic politics. For example, the war on terror has focused the electorate on foreign affairs, and the results of the 2006 midterm elections may be viewed as a referendum of the Bush administration's management of international policy.

against a demographic shift in party affiliation

in politics, it is normal for there to be temporary shifts in voter allegiance. Take, for example, the "Reagan Democrats." President Reagan was supported by most Americans—both Republicans and Democrats—in his attempt to end the Cold War, but once the Cold War ended, Reagan Democrats began to vote for the Democratic Party out of concern for domestic politics.

once the rhetoric used by the major parties is swept aside, one finds that the parties still represent their traditional post–World War II constituencies. The parties do represent their respective voting blocs. For example, the Democratic Party still champions minority rights, and the Republican Party is still considered to represent religious values.

an examination of the party platforms shows that the parties are concerned with representing the issue and policy preferences of their members. For example, the Democratic Party platform advocates the use of international institutions and allies in the prosecution of the war on terror, and the Republican Party platform advocates keeping the Bush administration tax cuts while cutting government spending.

An Older and More Diverse Nation by Midcentury

U.S. CENSUS BUREAU

AUGUST 14, 2008

THE NATION will be more racially and ethnically diverse, as well as much older, by midcentury, according to projections released today by the U.S. Census Bureau.

Minorities, now roughly one-third of the U.S. population, are expected to become the majority in 2042, with the nation projected to be 54 percent minority in 2050. By 2023, minorities will comprise more than half of all children.

In 2030, when all of the baby boomers will be 65 and older, nearly one in five U.S. residents is expected to be 65 and older. This age group is projected to increase to 88.5 million in 2050, more than doubling the number in 2008 (38.7 million).

Similarly, the 85 and older population is expected to more than triple, from 5.4 million to 19 million between 2008 and 2050.

By 2050, the minority population—everyone except for non-Hispanic, single-race whites—is projected to be 235.7 million out of a total U.S. population of 439 million. The nation is projected to reach the 400 million population milestone in 2039.

The non-Hispanic, single-race white population is projected to be only slightly larger in 2050 (203.3 million) than in 2008 (199.8 million). In fact, this group is projected to lose population in the 2030s and 2040s and comprise 46 percent of the total population in 2050, down from 66 percent in 2008.

Meanwhile, the Hispanic population is projected to nearly triple, from 46.7 million to 132.8 million during the 2008–2050 period. Its share of the nation's total population is projected to double, from 15 percent to 30 percent. Thus, nearly one in three U.S. residents would be Hispanic.

The black population is projected to increase from 41.1 million, or 14 percent of the population in 2008, to 65.7 million, or 15 percent in 2050.

The Asian population is projected to climb from 15.5 million to 40.6 million. Its share of the nation's population is expected to rise from 5.1 percent to 9.2 percent.

Among the remaining race groups, American Indians and Alaska Natives are projected to rise from 4.9 million to 8.6 million (or from 1.6 to 2 percent of the total population). The Native Hawaiian and other Pacific Islander population is expected to more than double, from 1.1 million to 2.6 million. The number of people who identify themselves as being of two or more races is projected to more than triple, from 5.2 million to 16.2 million.

↗ CRITICAL THINKING QUESTIONS:

- Why is the minority population growing more rapidly than the white population?
- Why do you think the white population is expected to decline in size during the 2030s and 2040s?
- What government programs will be affected by the various changes noted in the press release? Explain the connection.

>> END

Americans and Latinos. Women often fall behind their male counterparts on the career ladder because many women leave the workforce for years to raise children. Jobs that are traditionally held by women, such as nursing and education, typically pay less than jobs that are traditionally male. Finally, many observers believe that the incomes of women and minorities lag behind those of white males because of employment discrimination.

Poverty

The government measures poverty on a subsistence basis. The **poverty threshold** is the amount of money an individual or family needs to purchase basic necessities, such as food, clothing, healthcare, shelter,

poverty threshold the amount of money an individual or family needs to purchase basic necessities, such as food, clothing, healthcare, shelter, and transportation.

it was in any other region of the country. Household income was highest in the Northeast. Income also varies by gender. In 2006, the average income of male, full-time, year-round workers was $42,261 compared to $32,515 for women.[22]

Income differences among racial and ethnic groups, and between men and women, reflect disparities in education and training, social factors, and discrimination. As a group, Asian Americans and whites are better educated than African

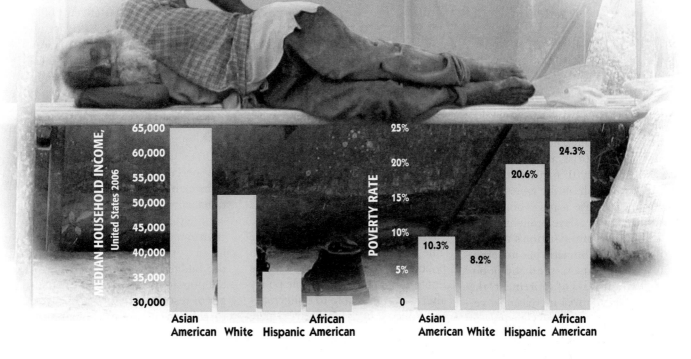

INCOME AND POVERTY RATE IN THE UNITED STATES, BY ETHNICITY

MEDIAN HOUSEHOLD INCOME, United States 2006

POVERTY RATE

Asian American — White — Hispanic — African American

Poverty rate: Asian American 10.3%, White 8.2%, Hispanic 20.6%, African American 24.3%

and transportation. The actual dollar amount varies with family size and rises with inflation. In 2008, the official government poverty threshold was $21,200 for a family of four.[23] Nearly 37 million Americans lived in poverty in 2006, or 12.3 percent of the population.[24]

Although the poverty rate for racial and ethnic minority groups and for families headed by women has declined over the last 50 years, it is still higher than for other groups. In 2006, the poverty rate for Latinos, African Americans, and Asian Americans stood at 20.6 percent, 24.3 percent, and 10.3 percent, respectively, compared with 8.2 percent for whites. Poverty also affects children and families headed by women in disproportionate numbers. In 2006, more than 17 percent of the nation's children under 18 lived in families that were poor. The poverty rate for families headed by women was 28.3 percent.[25]

Nearly 47 million Americans, 15.8 percent of the population, lack health insurance coverage. Government funded health insurance programs—Medicare, Medicaid, and military healthcare—cover about a fourth of the population. Almost 60 percent of the population enjoy health insurance through their employers, although that figure has been falling because some companies have dropped coverage for existing employees or have chosen not to offer coverage to new employees.[26] Most of the people who lack health insurance work in jobs that do not provide coverage. These people also have too much income to be eligible for Medicaid and are too young to qualify for Medicare. Without health insurance, they and their families must do without healthcare, pay for health services out of pocket, or go to hospital emergency rooms.

think **What could the government do to reduce poverty?**

CONCLUSION
the cultural, international, & SOCIOECONOMIC CONTEXT FOR POLICYMAKING

the cultural, international, demographic, and economic environments affect every stage of the policymaking process.

Agenda Building

The policymaking environment creates the context in which individuals and groups raise issues to the policy agenda. Dramatic events can have an immediate impact on the policy agenda. For example, the startling terrorist attacks of September 11, 2001 focused the nation's attention on the issues of national defense and homeland security. Other developments, such as the aging of the nation's population, are less dramatic but nonetheless important. As the baby boom generation reaches retirement, the policy agenda will increasingly reflect the interests and demands of older adults. Healthcare and retirement income security will claim a higher place on the policy agenda. Patterns of income distribution have an impact on attitudes about government programs. African Americans and Latinos are more likely to favor government healthcare and income security programs than are whites and Asian Americans because the former are more in need of government assistance.

Policy Formulation and Adoption

The environment has an impact on policy formulation. Political culture limits the range of acceptable policy alternatives available to policymakers. Policy solutions that are widely perceived as undemocratic or contrary to the nation's capitalist traditions are not politically feasible. The nation's economy affects policy formulation as well. A healthy economy generates tax revenues that can be used to tackle policy problems, whereas a stagnant economy reduces the options of policymakers. Defense spending reflects the perceived level of threat to American interests in the international environment.

POLITICAL CULTURE LIMITS THE RANGE OF ACCEPTABLE POLICY ALTERNATIVES

Policy adoption is affected by environmental factors. Consider the impact of the population aging on the budget process. The aging of the population is draining the budget of resources that could be used to support new government programs. When the baby boom generation retires, the cost of programs targeting the elderly will consume so much of the budget that they will crowd out most other spending.

Policy Implementation and Evaluation

Cultural, international, demographic, and economic factors affect policy implementation. The ability of the government to implement expensive policies successfully may depend on long-term economic growth sufficient to generate revenue. For example, illegal immigration from Mexico may slow in the next few years because the Mexican economy is growing, while the size of the Mexican population is increasing more slowly. [27]

Environmental factors also influence policy evaluation. Americans evaluate policies from the perspectives of the broad political culture—capitalism and democracy. Groups of Americans that are numerous and groups that are economically advantaged are better positioned to make their voices heard in evaluating policies than smaller groups with relatively fewer resources.

New Yorkers flee as the World Trade Center collapses on September 11, 2001. These events quickly brought issues of national defense and homeland security to the top of the nation's policy agenda.

the THINK SPOT
www.thethinkspot.com

TEST yourself

1 Why is the average age of the American population increasing?

A. The immigration rate is increasing.

B. The large baby boom generation is nearing retirement age.

C. The birthrate is increasing.

D. All of the above

2 A system of government in which ultimate political authority is vested in the people is the definition of which of the following terms?

A. Policymaking environment

B. Political culture

C. Democracy

D. Capitalism

3 According to Robert A. Dahl, which of the following is a criterion of democracy?

A. Candidates have the opportunity to conduct political campaigns in order to win political support.

B. All businesses and industry are privately owned.

C. All citizens enjoy a minimum standard of living, including access to healthcare.

D. All of the above

4 According to Robert A. Dahl's criteria of democracy, which of the following nations would NOT be considered a democracy?

A. In Country A, the government controls the news media and ensures that information damaging to the government is suppressed.

B. In Country B, the government owns and operates the airlines and the railroads.

C. In Country C, the income gap between the wealthiest and poorest sectors of society is huge.

D. All of the above

5 Which of the following is characteristic of a democracy?

A. People have the right to criticize the government.

B. People have the right to join unions and other interest groups.

C. People have the right to run against current officeholders.

D. All of the above

6 An economic system characterized by individual and corporate ownership of the means of production, and a market economy based on the supply and demand of goods and services is a definition of which of the following?

A. Constitutional monarchy

B. Capitalism

C. Democracy

D. Absolute monarchy

7 Which of the following nations spends the most on its military?

A. The United States

B. China

C. Russia

D. India

8 Which of the following nations has the largest economy?

A. The United States

B. China

C. Russia

D. India

9 Which of the following statements is true about the baby boom generation?

A. The baby boom generation is smaller than preceding or succeeding generations.

B. The baby boom generation retired just before 2000.

C. The baby boom generation was born during the late 1940s, 1950s, and early 1960s.

D. None of the above

10 Which of the following statements is true about population growth in the 1990s?

A. The population growth rate increased during the decade largely because of immigration.

B. The population growth rate increased during the decade largely because the birthrate increased.

C. The population growth rate fell during the decade because the baby boom generation began to die off.

D. The population growth rate fell during the decade because the birthrate declined.

11 Which of the following countries is NOT an important source of recent immigration to the United States?

A. Mexico

B. China

C. Great Britain

D. India

12 Which racial/ethnic group grew the most rapidly during the 1990s?

A. Latinos

B. Whites

C. African Americans

D. Asian Americans

13 After the 2000 Census, California gained seats in the U.S. House of Representatives. Knowing that fact, which of the following statements must therefore be true?

A. California is the most populous state in the nation.

B. The population of California increased at a faster rate in the 1990s than did the population of the United States as a whole.

C. California is in the Sunbelt.

D. All of the above

14 The integration of national economies into a world economic system in which companies compete worldwide for suppliers and markets is the definition for which of the following terms?

A. Capitalism

B. Gross domestic product

C. Democracy

D. Global economy

15 How have low-skilled workers been affected by the global economy?

A. They have been harmed because global competition has led to price increases for many of the products that they purchase.

B. They have been harmed because American companies cannot afford to pay high wages to low-skill workers and still compete effectively against foreign competitors with lower wage costs.

C. They have been helped because the number of good jobs available to low-skill workers has increased.

D. All of the above

16 Which of the following statements is true about income distribution in the United States?

A. Since 1980, the proportion of national income received by the wealthiest fifth of the population has increased.

B. Since 1980, the proportion of income received by the poorest fifth of the population has fallen.

C. The income gap between the wealthiest and poorest families has been increasing.

D. All of the above

17 Median household income in the United States is highest for which of the following groups?

A. Asian Americans

B. Whites

C. African Americans

D. Latinos

18 Which of the following statements is true?

A. Household income is higher in the South than it is in any other region.

B. On average, women earn more than men.

C. The average income for people living in metropolitan areas is lower than it is for people living outside metropolitan areas.

D. None of the above

19 How is the official poverty threshold determined?

A. The poverty threshold is set at 30 percent of the average household income. Anyone earning less than 30 percent of the average is considered poor.

B. The official poverty rate was set in 1950 at $8,000 and changes each year based on the inflation rate.

C. The poverty threshold is based on the amount of money an individual or family needs to purchase basic necessities.

D. People declare whether they are poor based on their perception of their ability to buy the things they need.

20 Which of the following statements is true about poverty in America?

A. Nearly half of African Americans and Latinos live in poverty.

B. Nearly a third of all Americans have incomes below the official poverty level.

C. More than a fourth of families headed by women are below the official poverty level.

D. All of the above

KNOW *the* **score**

18–20 correct: Congratulations! You are well informed!

15–17 correct: Your political knowledge is a bit low—be sure to review the key terms and visit TheThinkSpot.

<14 correct: Reread the chapter more thoroughly.

1. B; 2. C; 3. A; 4. A; 5. D; 6. B; 7. A; 8. A; 9. C; 10. A; 11. C; 12. A; 13. B; 14. D; 15. B; 16. D; 17. A; 18. D; 19. C; 20. C

test yourself **33**

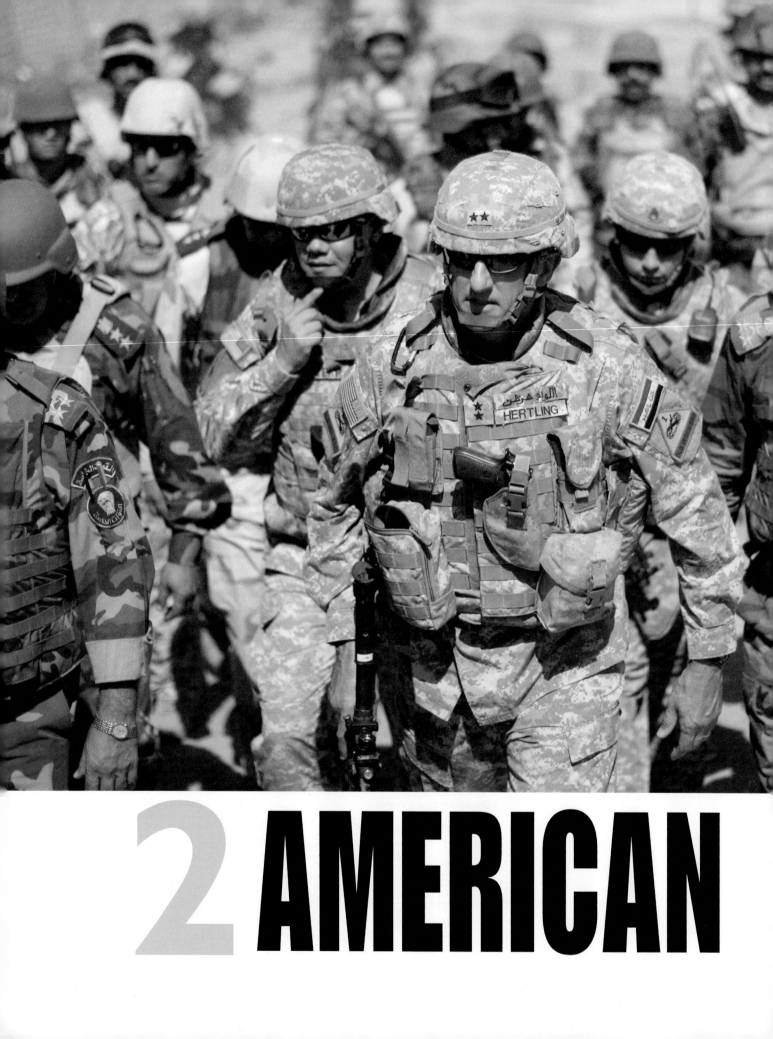

2 AMERICAN

> WHAT'S AHEAD

Background of the Constitution

Constitutional Principles

The Living Constitution

The Constitution, Politics,
and Public Policy

Conclusion: The Constitutional
Environment for Policymaking

The Democratic Party won the 2006 congressional election, capturing narrow majorities in both the U.S. House and Senate. When the 110th session of Congress convened in January 2007, Democrats outnumbered Republicans in the House, 233–202. The margin in the Senate was 51–49, counting two independents as Democrats because they voted with the Democrats to organize the chamber.

The foremost goal for the new Democratic majority in Congress was ending the war in Iraq. Public opinion polls registered strong opposition to the war, especially among Democratic voters, and most Democratic members of Congress had campaigned on the issue. In May 2007, Congress passed a funding bill for the wars in Iraq and Afghanistan that included a provision requiring the president to begin withdrawing troops in October with the goal of getting all U.S. combat forces out of Iraq by the end of March 2008. The measure failed to become law, however, because President George W. Bush vetoed it and Congress was unable to override the veto.

The Constitution erects a buffer between short-term public opinion and public policy, especially if opinion is closely divided on an issue. The Constitution specifies that legislation cannot pass Congress unless both the House and Senate approve identical measures. Furthermore, legislation cannot become law without presidential support or acquiescence, unless both houses of Congress are able to override a presidential veto by a two-thirds vote of each chamber. Democrats won control of Congress in 2006 because they opposed the war, but their margin of control was too narrow to force a change in policy.

CONSTITUTION

English colonists advertised opposition to the hated Stamp Act on everyday items, such as this teapot.

background
OF THE CONSTITUTION

a **Constitution** is the fundamental law by which a state or nation is organized and governed, and to which ordinary legislation must conform. It establishes the framework of government, assigns the powers and duties of government bodies, and defines the relationship between the people and their government. The U.S. Constitution, which is more than 220 years of age, is the oldest written national constitution still in effect in the world today.

Historical Setting

The Americans who wrote the Constitution of 1787 had lived through two difficult periods: the late colonial period under British rule and the period under the government created by the Articles of Confederation. To a considerable degree, the Constitution was a reaction to these two experiences.

The Colonial Period. The American colonists were initially satisfied with the political relationship with Great Britain. Preoccupied with matters at home, the British authorities allowed the Americans a substantial measure of self-government. Each colony had a governor, appointed by the king, and a legislative assembly whose members were locally elected. The colonial assemblies could levy taxes, appropriate money, approve or reject the governor's appointments, and pass laws for their colony. Although the governor had the power to veto legislation, the assemblies exercised considerable leverage over the governor by virtue of their control of the budget. This **power of the purse**, which is the authority to raise and spend money, made the locally elected legislative assemblies the dominant bodies of colonial government.

After 1763, the British chose to reorganize their colonial system. The French and Indian War (1756–1763), in which the British and the Americans fought against the French and their Indian allies for control of North America, left the British with a sizable war debt. The British also faced the problem of governing Canada and enforcing treaties with the Indians, which limited westward expansion by the colonists.

British officials decided that the American colonists should pay part of the cost of defending and administering the empire in North America. The British imposed new taxes, and to enforce their policies, they increased the number of officials in North America and permanently stationed troops in the colonies.

To the surprise of the British, the Americans were outraged. Over the years, the colonists had grown accustomed to self-government and they were unwilling to surrender the privilege. They regarded the new policies as a violation of local traditions and an abridgment of their rights as British citizens. Before 1763, the only taxes the Americans paid to London were duties on trade, and the colonists interpreted the duties as measures to regulate

constitution the fundamental law by which a state or nation is organized and governed, and to which ordinary legislation must conform.

power of the purse the authority to raise and spend money.

commerce rather than taxes. Now, however, London attempted to impose levies that were clearly taxes. The Americans argued that as English citizens they could be taxed only by their own elected representatives and not by the British Parliament. No taxation without representation, they declared. This argument made no sense to the British. In their view, every member of Parliament represented every British citizen; it was irrelevant that no Americans sat in Parliament. The dispute over taxation and other issues worsened, leading eventually to revolution and American independence.

During the Revolutionary War, the American colonies became the United States, loosely allied under the leadership of the Continental Congress, which was a **unicameral** (one-house) **legislature** in which each state had a single vote. Although the Continental Congress had no official governing authority, it declared America's independence, raised an army, appointed George Washington commander in chief,

Alexander Hamilton, the first secretary of the Treasury, was one of the strongest critics of the weak central government of the Articles of Confederation. He was one of the leaders of the movement to strengthen the national government.

coined money, and negotiated with foreign nations. The Continental Congress also drafted a plan for national union. This plan, known as the Articles of Confederation, went into effect in 1781, upon approval by the 13 states.

The Articles of Confederation. The Articles of Confederation created a league of friendship, a "perpetual union" of states, with a unicameral congress. Although state legislatures could send as many as seven delegates to the Confederation Congress, each state possessed a single vote, and 9 states (of 13) had to approve decisions. Amending the Articles required unanimous approval of the states. The Articles provided for no independent national executive or national judiciary.

unicameral legislature a one-house legislature.

btw...

While residents of the District of Columbia do vote in the presidential election, they have only a non-voting delegate in the House of Representatives and no representation in the Senate.

The slogan "Taxation Without Representation" was added to D.C. license plates in 2000 to protest the District's lack of representation in Congress. In 2008, the District also attempted to incorporate the slogan into its design for the 50 State Quarters program, but it was rejected by the U.S. Mint. Do you think the half million residents of the District of Columbia are fairly represented in Congress?

Washington, D.C.

D.C. GOVT.
★★★
Fleet

DC 2368

TAXATION WITHOUT REPRESENTATION

The states were the primary units of government in the new nation rather than the Confederation government. Each of the 13 states had its own state constitution that established a framework for state government. These state constitutions typically provided for a **bicameral** (two-house) **legislature**, a governor, and a court system. Because Americans feared executive power as a source of tyranny, they adopted state constitutions that limited the powers of state governors, making legislatures the dominant branch of state government.[1]

The Americans who wrote the Articles of Confederation were determined to create a government whose powers would be strictly limited. Having just freed themselves from British rule, they did not want to create a strong national government that might become as oppressive as the British colonial government. The Americans who wrote the Articles apparently went too far, however, because the Confederation proved too weak to deal effectively with the new nation's problems. It lacked the power to collect taxes from individuals, having to rely instead on contributions from the states. When state governments failed to pay—as many did—the Confederation government was left without financial support. The Confederation also lacked authority to regulate commerce, prohibit states from printing worthless currency, enforce the provisions of the peace treaty with Great Britain, or even defend itself against rebellion. When small farmers in western Massachusetts engaged in an armed uprising against the government over debt and taxes in 1786–1787, the Confederation government failed to respond. After a private army finally crushed the insurrection, which was known as Shay's Rebellion after its leader, Daniel Shay, public opinion began to coalesce in favor of a stronger national government than the one provided by the Articles of Confederation.

Popular protest in the United States did not end with Shay's Rebellion. Ironically, a strong central government became the protector of the right to protest. Consider the modern cause of animal rights. Animal rights activists have protested at fashion shows, dumped dead animals on fashionable restaurant tables, and thrown red paint on fur coats. Fashion magazine editors have also been taken to task for encouraging the wearing of furs. A stronger national government has been able to suppress armed rebellions, but it has also taken on the cause of protecting people's right to protest.

bicameral legislature a two-house legislature.

"HERE'S THE REST OF YOUR FUR COAT."

Singer Shirley Manson and other high-profile celebrities, such as Alicia Silverstone and Pamela Anderson, embrace their constitutional right to protest by engaging in public demonstrations or creating controversial advertisements to protest the wearing of furs.

John Locke & American Political Thought

The colonists used Locke's theories to justify their revolution and inform the creation of their new government.

THE REVOLUTION

Locke's theory of revolution offered the perfect theoretical rationale for the American Revolution. In the Declaration of Independence, which is reprinted in the Appendix of this text, the founders used Locke's theory to justify independence from Great Britain. The Americans were justified in revolting against the king, the founders declared, because the king deprived them of their rights to "Life, Liberty, and the pursuit of Happiness."

THE NEW GOVERNMENT

Locke provided a theoretical basis for the creation of a national government that could be a positive force in society instead of just a necessary evil. According to Locke, the people create government in order to accomplish certain goals, that is, to protect life, liberty, and property from the dangers inherent in a state of nature. In theory, then, government can play an active, positive role in society.

THE BILL OF RIGHTS

Locke's concept of natural rights offered a theoretical foundation for limiting government authority over the individual. The doctrine of natural rights is the belief that individual rights transcend the power of government. People create government to protect their rights, not to abridge them. Locke's theory of natural rights provided a basis for a bill of rights, which is a constitutional document guaranteeing individual rights and liberties.

Actor Heath Ledger portrayed an American soldier caught up in the issues of the American Revolution in the film *The Patriot*.

American Political Thought

The Americans who wrote the Constitution were educated people who studied the important political writings of their day. The work of Englishman John Locke (1632–1704) was particularly influential. In his *Second Treatise on Government* (1689), Locke declared that people in their natural state were born free and equal, and possessed certain natural rights, which were life, liberty, and property. Unfortunately, Locke said, evil people disrupt the good life of the state of nature by conspiring to deprive others of their life, liberty, or property. In order to protect their rights, people voluntarily join together to form governments. The power of government, then, stems from the consent of the governed, who entrust the government with responsibility for protecting their lives, liberty, and possessions. Should government fail in this task, Locke declared, the people have the right to revolt and institute a new government.

Although the nation's founders frequently cited the writings of European philosophers such as Locke, they did more than just apply the theories developed in Europe to the United States. They created a nation and wrote a Constitution that was also based on American events, experiences, and ideas.[2]

The most important element of American political thought was the changing conception of the nature of politics and government. At the time of the Revolution, American political theorists believed that politics was a never-ending struggle between the people and the government. In their view, the people were virtuous and united in support of the public good. In contrast, the government, personified by the king, was corrupt and oppressive. After declaring their independence, the Americans knew that they needed a national government, but they did not want a strong one. The government established by the Articles of Confederation fit the bill nicely.

After a few years of independence, many Americans recognized that they were wrong about the nature of the people and the role of government. Instead of society being united behind a common perception of the public good, they saw that it was composed of a variety of interests or factions, which opposed each other on a number of policy issues. Furthermore, practical political experience in the states demonstrated that the people were not so virtuous after all. When one faction gained control of the government of a particular state or locality, it would often use its power to enforce its will over opposing interests.

By 1787, many Americans had decided that a strong national government could play a positive role in society. First, the national government could reconcile the divergent concerns of various groups in society to

A LARGE NATION, SUCH AS THE UNITED STATES, INCLUDES A **WIDE** RANGE OF INTERESTS COMPETING FOR POWER.

produce policies designed to achieve the public good. A large nation, such as the United States, includes a wide range of interests competing for power. Although a particular group or faction might be strong enough to control the government in one state or a local area, no single group would be able to dominate nationwide. A strong national government would provide a forum in which groups would be able to reconcile their differences. The result would be policies that would be acceptable to a broad range of interests.

Second, a strong national government could protect individual liberty and property from the power of

oppressive majorities. At the state or local level, a dominant faction could adopt policies designed to advance its own religious or economic interests at the expense of the minority.

At the national level, however, no one group or faction would be powerful enough to enforce its will on the entire nation. Because every group held minority status in one state or another, it would be in each group's interest to protect minorities against the power of oppressive local majorities.[3] For example, the framers of the Constitution included a provision prohibiting a state-supported church because of the multiplicity of religious sects in America. Although many of the early American religious groups would have liked nothing better than to establish their faith as the official state religion, they lacked the power to achieve that goal. Consequently, they preferred an official government policy of religious freedom to risking the possibility that another religious group would gain official recognition.[4]

constitutional
PRINCIPLES

to understand the American Constitution, we must study the principles behind it. Let's look in detail at some of the constitution's most important themes.

Representative Democracy

A **democracy** is a system of government in which the people hold ultimate political power. Although the framers of the Constitution favored a government that would answer to the people, they did not

want to give too much power to majority opinion. The framers were particularly wary of **direct democracy**, which is a political system in which the citizens vote directly on matters of public concern. The framers of the Constitution worried that ordinary citizens lacked the information to make intelligent policy decisions. They feared that direct democracy would produce policies reflecting hasty, emotional decisions rather than well-considered judgments.

The framers also worried that direct democracy would enable a majority of the people to enact policies

democracy a system of government in which ultimate political authority is vested in the people.

direct democracy a political system in which the citizens vote directly on matters of public concern.

that would silence, disadvantage, or harm the minority point of view, thus producing a **tyranny of the majority**, which is the abuse of the minority by the majority. The danger of majority rule is that the majority may vote to adopt policies that unfairly disadvantage the minority. The challenge for the framers of the Constitution was to create a form of government that would provide for majority rule while protecting the rights and liberties of minorities.

Instead of a direct democracy, the framers created a **representative democracy** or a **republic**, which is a political system in which citizens elect representatives to make policy decisions on their behalf. The framers believed that elected representatives would act as a buffer between the people and government policies. Representatives would be more knowledgeable than ordinary citizens about policy issues. They would also be more likely than the general public to recognize the legitimate interests of different groups in society and to seek policy compromises designed to accommodate those interests.

To further guard against the tyranny of the majority, the framers provided that some policy actions could be taken only with the consent of a **supermajority**, a voting margin which is greater than a simple majority. Constitutional amendments must be proposed by two-thirds of the members of both the House and the Senate and ratified by three-fourths of the states. Treaties must be approved by two-thirds of the Senate. Presidential vetoes can be overridden only by a two-thirds vote of each chamber of Congress. Executive and judicial officials can be removed from office only by a two-thirds vote of the Senate. In each of these cases, a simple majority of 50 percent plus one does not prevail. Instead, policy actions require the support, or at least acceptance, of a supermajority of two-thirds or more.

Rule of Law

The **rule of law** is the constitutional principle that holds that the discretion of public officials in dealing with individuals is limited by the law. The very existence of a written constitution implies the rule of law, but certain constitutional provisions deserve special notice. In Article I, Section 9, the Constitution guarantees the privilege of the writ of *habeas corpus* except in cases of invasion, rebellion, or threat to public

The Fifth Amendment allows private property to be seized for public purposes if compensation is made. In 2005, the Supreme Court's 5–4 ruling in *Kelo v. New London* stretched the definition of eminent domain by allowing a city to seize private property (Susette Kelo's house in New London, Connecticut, as pictured above) to sell to a private real estate developer, with the hopes that tax revenues would benefit the city.

tyranny of the majority the abuse of the minority by the majority.

representative democracy/republic a political system in which citizens elect representatives to make policy decisions on their behalf.

supermajority a voting margin that is greater than a simple majority.

rule of law the constitutional principle that holds that the discretion of public officials in dealing with individuals is limited by the law.

think

Should the government be allowed to arrest American citizens and hold them without charges and without trial if it believes that they are involved in planning terrorist attacks against the United States?

safety. A **writ of *habeas corpus*** is a court order requiring that government authorities either release a person held in custody or demonstrate that the person is detained in accordance with law. *Habeas corpus* is designed to prevent arbitrary arrest and imprisonment. The Constitution protects Americans from being held in custody by the government unless they are charged and convicted in accordance with the law.

The Constitution prohibits the passage of bills of attainder and *ex post facto* laws. A **bill of attainder** is a law declaring a person or a group of persons guilty of a crime and providing for punishment without benefit of a judicial proceeding. An ***ex post facto* law** is a retroactive criminal statute that operates to the disadvantage of accused persons. It makes a crime out of an act that was not illegal when it was committed.

Due process of law is the constitutional principle holding that government must follow fair and regular procedures in actions that could lead to an individual's suffering loss of life, liberty, or property. In both the Fifth and Fourteenth Amendments, the Constitution provides that neither Congress (the Fifth Amendment) nor the states

writ of *habeas corpus* a court order requiring government authorities either to release a person held in custody or demonstrate that the person is detained in accordance with law.

bill of attainder a law declaring a person or a group of persons guilty of a crime and providing for punishment without benefit of a judicial proceeding.

***ex post facto* law** a retroactive criminal statute that operates to the disadvantage of accused persons.

due process of law the constitutional principle holding that government must follow fair and regular procedures in actions that could lead to an individual's suffering loss of life, liberty, or property.

PROTECTIONS GUARANTEED BY THE
Bill of RIGHTS

FIRST AMENDMENT Protects freedom of speech, press, assembly, and petition, and prohibits Congress from creating an established religion or restricting the free exercise of religion.

SECOND AMENDMENT Guarantees the right to keep and bear arms.

THIRD AMENDMENT Prohibits forced quartering of troops during time of peace.

FOURTH AMENDMENT Protects against unreasonable searches and seizures.

FIFTH AMENDMENT Guarantees due process, the use of a grand jury for serious crimes, protects against double jeopardy and self-incrimination, and prohibits seizure of private property without compensation.

SIXTH AMENDMENT Protects the rights of the accused, including the right to a speedy and public trial and to an impartial jury, the right to be informed of charges, face accusers, and obtain witnesses, and the right to counsel.

SEVENTH AMENDMENT Guarantees the right to a civil trial by jury.

EIGHTH AMENDMENT Prohibits excessive bail and cruel and unusual punishment.

NINTH AMENDMENT Declares that individual rights are not limited to those rights specifically enumerated in the Constitution.

TENTH AMENDMENT Stipulates that the powers not delegated to the national government or denied to the states are reserved for the states or the people.

THE CREATION AND INCORPORATION OF THE BILL OF RIGHTS

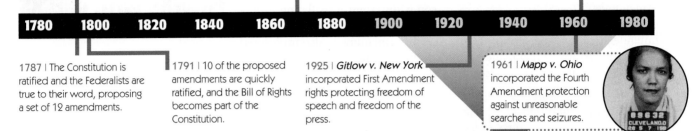

1787 | In order to promote the ratification of the Constitution written in 1787, the Federalists promise to add a bill of rights once the Constitution is approved.

1868 | The Fourteenth Amendment is ratified, declaring that states may not "deprive any person of life, liberty, or property, without due process of law."

1963 | *Gideon v. Wainwright* incorporated the Sixth Amendment requirement for courts to provide counsel in criminal cases for indigent defendants.

1780	1800	1820	1840	1860	1880	1900	1920	1940	1960	1980

1787 | The Constitution is ratified and the Federalists are true to their word, proposing a set of 12 amendments.

1791 | 10 of the proposed amendments are quickly ratified, and the Bill of Rights becomes part of the Constitution.

1925 | *Gitlow v. New York* incorporated First Amendment rights protecting freedom of speech and freedom of the press.

1961 | *Mapp v. Ohio* incorporated the Fourth Amendment protection against unreasonable searches and seizures.

20th Century | Throughout the twentieth century, the Supreme Court began selective incorporation of the Bill of Rights against the states.

(the Fourteenth Amendment) may deprive any person of "life, liberty, or property, without due process of law." Due process of law generally protects individuals from the arbitrary actions of public officials. Before individuals may be imprisoned, fined, or executed, they must be given their day in court in accordance with law. Among other rights, the Constitution guarantees accused persons the right to a speedy, public trial by an impartial jury, the right to confront witnesses, and the right to legal counsel.

Limited Government

Limited government is the constitutional principle that government does not have unrestricted authority over individuals. The government of the United States is not a dictatorship with absolute authority; its power is limited. Perhaps the most important constitutional restriction on the authority of government is the **Bill of Rights**, the first 10 amendments to the Constitution.

The Bill of Rights was not part of the original Constitution because a majority of the framers of the Constitution believed that such a provision was unnecessary, redundant, useless, and possibly even dangerous. The framers thought that a bill of rights would be unnecessary be-

cause each state constitution had a bill of rights, and the national government lacked sufficient power to threaten individual liberty. They considered a bill of rights redundant because the Constitution already contained a number of provisions designed to protect individual liberty, such as the prohibition against *ex post facto* laws and bills of attainder, and the guarantee of due process of law. They thought that a bill of rights would be useless because they believed that a paper guarantee of individual liberty would mean little in the face of public pressure. Finally, the framers resisted the inclusion of a bill of rights in the Constitution because they worried that some rights might be inadvertently left out and that any right omitted from the document would be lost.[5]

After the Constitution was written in 1787, it still had to be approved (or ratified) by 9 of the 13 states. The failure to include a bill of rights became a political issue during the debate over ratification of the proposed Constitution. The **Antifederalists** opposed the ratification of the new Constitution because they thought it gave too much power to the national government. They raised the issue of a bill of rights in hopes of defeating the Constitution and to force the con-

A BILL OF RIGHTS BECAME A POLITICAL ISSUE DURING THE DEBATE OVER RATIFICATION

vening of a new constitutional convention. The **Federalists** supported the ratification of the Constitution. Although most Federalists had opposed inclusion of a bill of rights in the constitution, they switched sides in order to secure ratification and to prevent a new convention. They promised to add a bill of rights once the Constitution was ratified and the new government took office.[6]

The Federalists kept their promise. In 1789, the First Congress of the United States proposed 12 amendments, 10 of which were

limited government the constitutional principle that government does not have unrestricted authority over individuals.

Bill of Rights the first ten amendments to the U.S. Constitution.

Antifederalists Americans opposed to the ratification of the new Constitution because they thought it gave too much power to the national government.

Federalists Americans who supported the ratification of the Constitution.

ratified by a sufficient number of states to become part of the Constitution by 1791. One of the rejected amendments was a provision that a congressional pay raise could not go into effect without an intervening election. It was finally ratified in 1992 as the Twenty-seventh Amendment.

The authors of the Bill of Rights intended that it would apply only to the national government and not the states because the states already

James Madison is called "Father of the Constitution."

had bills of rights. The U.S. Constitution and the national Bill of Rights would protect individual rights against abuse by the national government. State constitutions and state bills of rights would secure individual rights from infringement by state governments.

The Fourteenth Amendment, which was added to the Constitution immediately after the Civil War, provided the constitutional basis for applying the national Bill of Rights to the states. Congress proposed the Fourteenth Amendment in 1866 to protect the rights of former slaves from infringement by state governments. The amend-

ment defined U.S. citizenship, making it clear that all Americans are citizens of both the United States and the state in which they live. The amendment declared that state governments could not take life, liberty, or property without "due process of law," or deny to any person within their jurisdiction "equal protection of the laws." The Fourteenth Amendment also prohibited states from making laws abridging the "privileges or immunities" of citizens.

The Fourteenth Amendment did not play a major role in the protection of individual rights until the twentieth century. Initially, the Fourteenth Amendment had little impact on individual rights because the Supreme Court of the United States refused to interpret its provisions to protect individual rights. Not until the twentieth century did the Court begin the process known as the selective incorporation of the Bill of Rights against the states. This is the process through which the U.S. Supreme Court interpreted the Due Process Clause of the Fourteenth Amendment of the U.S. Constitution to apply most of the provisions of the national Bill of Rights to the states. Although the Supreme Court has never ruled that the Bill of Rights as a whole applies to the states, it has selectively held that virtually all of its key provisions apply against the states through the Due Process Clause of the Fourteenth Amendment. As a result, the national Bill of Rights now protects individual rights against infringement by both the national government and state governments as well.

Separation of Powers with Checks and Balances

The framers of the U.S. Constitution adopted separation of powers

JAMES MADISON WAS THE PRINCIPAL ARCHITECT OF AMERICA'S SYSTEM OF SEPARATION OF POWERS WITH CHECKS AND BALANCES

with checks and balances to control the power of the Federal government. The roots of these concepts went back a century, but they were more fully developed by Baron de Montesquieu, an eighteenth-century French political philosopher. Montesquieu identified three kinds of political power: the power to make laws (**legislative power**), to enforce laws (**executive power**), and to interpret laws (**judicial power**). Montesquieu warned against allowing one person or a single group of people to exercise all three powers because that person or group would pose a threat to individual liberty. Montesquieu advocated **separation of powers**, that is, the division of political power among executive, legislative, and judicial branches of government. He called for a system of checks and balances to prevent any one of the three branches from becoming too strong. **Checks and balances** refer to the

legislative power the power to make laws.

executive power the power to enforce laws.

judicial power the power to interpret laws.

separation of powers the division of political power among executive, legislative, and judicial branches.

checks and balances the overlapping of the powers of the branches of government designed to ensure that public officials limit the authority of each other.

overlapping of the powers of the branches of government to ensure that public officials limit the authority of each other.

James Madison was the principal architect of America's system of separation of powers with checks and balances. In fact, scholars sometimes refer to the nation's constitutional apparatus as the Madisonian system. Madison and two other proponents of the new constitution, Alexander Hamilton and John Jay, wrote a series of essays known as the **Federalist Papers** to advocate the ratification of the new Constitution. In *The Federalist* No. 51, Madison identified two threats to liberty: 1) **factions**, which are special interests who seek their own good at the expense of the common good, and 2) the excessive concentration of political power in the hands of government officials. Madison's remedy for these dangers was the creation of a strong national government with separation of powers and checks and balances.

Madison believed that the nation needed a strong national government to control the power of factions. In this regard, Madison noted the advantage of a large nation with many diverse interests. At the local or state level, he said, a single faction might be powerful enough to dominate. It could unfairly force its will on the minority, creating a tyranny of the majority. Over the breadth of the entire nation, however, the narrow perspectives of that faction would be checked by the

Federalist Papers a series of essays written by James Madison, Alexander Hamilton, and John Jay advocating the ratification of the Constitution.
factions special interests who seek their own good at the expense of the common good.

take action
SERVICE LEARNING >>

Service learning is based on the concept that students can learn more about a subject through participation and experience combined with traditional coursework than they can through classroom instruction alone. Students will gain valuable knowledge and skills from the experience beyond those normally acquired in a classroom.

Use the following checklist to guide you through your service-learning project:

1. Identify a government office or agency that welcomes student volunteers. You may wish to begin with the mayor's office, a county commissioner or county supervisor, school district, hospital district, or state legislator. They can give you suggestions or referrals to agencies that deal with issues related to your career goals.

2. Call the agency or department that interests you and ask to speak to the volunteer coordinator. Explain that you are completing a service-learning project for your college and want to know about volunteer opportunities. You will want to arrange a placement that matches your interests and the needs of the agency.

3. Your instructor will set the number of hours you should volunteer over the course of the term. Normally, students should expect to work from 20 to 40 hours over a long semester to receive full benefit from the activity.

4. As you complete your assignment at the agency, ask the volunteer coordinator to provide you with documentation of the hours of your work to present to your instructor.

You will be required to keep a reflective journal documenting your service. Journal entries should discuss your work on the project and your reaction to the experience. Your journal should cover the following topics:

1. What you did for the organization.
2. What you thought of the clients served by the organization.
3. What you thought of the other people working for the organization.
4. What you thought of the work done by the organization.
5. How your experience relates to course materials.
6. How your experience relates to topics in the news.

Write at least one journal entry for every two hours you spend at your placement. Each journal entry should be at least four sentences long. You will be evaluated on the amount of time you spent at your placement, the number and length of your journal entries, and the quality of your entries.

THE CONNECTICUT COMPROMISE

The precise organization of America's bicameral Congress was the product of an agreement between large-state and small-state forces known as the Connecticut Compromise. Members of the House of Representatives would be chosen by direct popular election to serve two-year terms with the number of representatives from each state based on population. (This pleased large states.) Each state would have two senators chosen by their state legislatures to serve six-year terms. This pleased small states. The adoption of the Seventeenth Amendment in 1913 provided for direct popular election of senators.

interests of other factions entrenched in other areas. A strong national government would provide an arena in which factions would counterbalance each other. National policies, therefore, would reflect compromise among a range of interests.

Madison also favored separation of powers with checks and balances as a means to control the power of government officials. Madison said that the goal of the system was "to divide and arrange the several offices [of government] in such a manner as that each may be a check on the other."[7] In this fashion, the selfish, private interests of office-holders would counterbalance each other to the public good. "Ambition," Madison wrote, "must be made to counteract ambition."[8]

The Constitution contains an elaborate network of checks and balances. The executive branch, for example, checks the judicial branch through the power of the president to appoint members of the Supreme Court and other federal courts. Congress, in turn, checks the president and the courts in that the Senate must confirm judicial appointments. Similarly, the Constitution declares that Congress has the authority to declare war, but it names the president commander in

chief of the armed forces. The president negotiates treaties, but the Senate must ratify them.

Federalism

The framers of the Constitution set out to establish a government that would be capable of effective administration but would not undermine the American tradition of local control. Their solution was to create a federation. A **federation** or **federal system** is a political system that divides power between a central government, with authority over the whole nation, and a series of state governments.

A federation is a compromise between unitary government and a confederation. In a unitary system, the national government is sovereign. **Sovereignty** is the authority of a state to exercise its legitimate powers within its boundaries, free from external interference. The powers of state and local governments (if they exist) are granted to them by the national government. In a confederation, the states are sov-

ereign. The national government's authority flows from the states. In a federal system, both the national (or federal) government and the state governments are sovereign. They derive their authority not from one another but from the Constitution. Both levels of government act directly on the people through their officials and laws, both are supreme within their proper sphere of authority, and both must consent to constitutional change.

A federation offers Americans several advantages. A federal system provides a means of political representation that can accommodate the diversity of American society. Individual Americans are citizens of their states and the nation, and participate in the selection of representatives to both levels of government. In a federal system, local interests shape local policy. The national government, meanwhile, is an arena in which local interests from different regions can check and balance each other, permitting the national interest to prevail.

Federalism can help protect against the tyranny of the majority. The federal system creates a series of overlapping state and district election systems that select both members of congress and the

> **Which do you think is the best form of government—a unitary government, a confederation, or a federal government?**

federation/federal system a political system that divides power between a central government, with authority over the whole nation, and a series of state governments.

sovereignty the authority of a state to exercise its legitimate powers within its boundaries, free from external interference.

The British Parliamentary System

Most of the world's democracies are patterned after the British parliamentary system rather than the checks and balances system of the United States. A **parliamentary system** is a system of government in which political power is concentrated in a legislative body and a cabinet headed by a prime minister. The British legislature, which is called the **Parliament**, has two chambers, a House of Commons and a House of Lords. Real power is in the hands of the House of Commons, which is composed of 660 members elected from districts. The House of Lords, which includes the bishops of the Church of England and other members appointed for life by the king or queen, is now little more than a debating society with the power only to delay legislation, not to defeat it.

British voters understand that when they vote for members of Parliament that they are also choosing a government. At election time, each British political party presents the voters with a detailed set of policy proposals that it promises to implement. Voters know that a vote for a particular parliamentary candidate is also a vote for the policies offered by that candidate's political party and a vote for the election of that party's leader as prime minister.

In the 1997 national election, the Labour Party won a majority of seats in Commons, ending 18 years of rule by the Conservative Party. The new Parliament elected Tony Blair, the Labour Party leader, prime minister, to replace John Major, the Conservative prime minister. With a majority in Parliament, the Labour government was able to enact its program without worrying about constitutional checks and balances.

The primary check on the government in Great Britain is the electorate. The government must hold a new parliamentary election within five years, giving voters the opportunity to keep the current government in power or to turn the government over to the opposition. Labour has continued in office because it has been able to maintain its parliamentary majority, winning elections in both 2001 and 2005. When Blair resigned as prime minister in 2007, the Labour members of Parliament chose Gordon Brown as their new leader and he became prime minister.

Questions

1. Which political system is more responsive to citizen demands—the American or the British system?

2. Which political system is more likely to produce dramatic policy change?

3. Which political system is better equipped to protect the rights of minorities?

parliamentary system a system of government in which political power is concentrated in a legislative body and a cabinet headed by a prime minister.

Parliament the British legislature.

Britain's Queen Elizabeth II named Labor Party leader Gordon Brown (inset) prime minister in June 2007.

president. The federal election system gives minorities of all kinds—racial, ethnic, religious, regional, local, occupational, social, and sexual—the opportunity to be part of a majority because they may comprise the swing vote in a closely divided state or district. Consequently, they must be consulted; their interests must be considered.[9]

Nonetheless, a federal system imposes certain disadvantages. Local variations confuse citizens and hinder business. Traveling Americans face different traffic laws in each state. People who move from one state to another must adapt to different laws regarding such matters as marriage, divorce, wills, and occupational licensing. A couple approved as foster parents in one state may have to go through the approval process again if they move to another state. Businesses must adjust to variations in tax laws and regulations. Federalism also sets the stage for conflict. American history is filled with examples of disputes between states and the national government; the Civil War was the most serious. Issues such as the 55-mile-per-hour speed limit requirement and the 21-

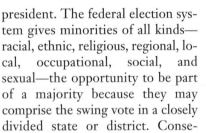

A FEDERAL SYSTEM IMPOSES CERTAIN DISADVANTAGES

year-old minimum legal drinking age are contemporary examples of conflicts between states and the national government.

Bicameralism

The framers of the Constitution expected the legislative branch to be the dominant institution of American national government because it was the dominant branch of state governments. To prevent the national legislature from becoming too powerful, the framers divided Congress into two houses with different sizes, terms of office, responsibilities, and constituencies.

The framers expected that the popularly elected House would be constrained by a more conservative Senate. With a two-year term, members of the House would be closer to the people and more likely to act hastily in accordance with short-term popular sentiment. In contrast, senators, chosen by state legislatures and serving longer terms, would be insulated from popular pressures, thus enabling them to act more cautiously and to put the national interest ahead of short-term political gain.[10]

the living CONSTITUTION

the Constitution has not merely survived for more than 220 years. It has grown and matured with the nation, serving as the fundamental framework for policymaking to this day. The genius of the Constitution lies in its ability to adapt to changing times while maintaining adherence to basic principles. The Constitution is a brief, generalized document that is full of phrases lacking clear definition. The Eighth Amendment, for example, prohibits "cruel and unusual punishments." Article I, Section 8 gives Congress the power to regulate "commerce." Article II, Section 4 declares that the president may be impeached and removed from office for "treason, bribery, or other high crimes and misdemeanors." The Fourth Amendment prohibits "unreasonable searches and seizures." What do these terms mean? What punishments are "cruel and unusual?" What is "commerce?" What are "high crimes and misdemeanors"? Which searches and seizures are "reasonable" and which are "unreasonable"?

The Constitution is often vague, and this is what the framers intended. They set down certain basic, fundamental principles, but omitted details in order to allow succeeding generations to supply specifics in light of their own experiences. The basic idea behind the concept of "cruel and unusual punishments," for example, is that government must not go too far in punishing criminals. The prohibition against "unreasonable searches and seizures" places limits on the police. Had the framers of the Constitution decided to spell out everything in detail, they would have produced a document far longer and less satisfactory than the one we have. Eventually, the nation would have outgrown it and either cast it aside or been forced to amend it repeatedly.

Constitutional Change through Practice and Experience

The Constitution has adapted to changing times through practice and experience. Consider the role of the presidency. The historical development of the office has given definition to the powers of the presidency beyond the scope of that office as foreseen by the framers. Other elements of American government have developed despite slight mention in the Constitution. The federal bureaucracy, for example, is barely discussed in the Constitution. Yet its importance in American government has grown to the point that some observers refer to it as the fourth branch of government. Furthermore, some important contemporary features of American government are not mentioned in the Constitution at all, including the committee system in Congress, the executive cabinet, and the political party system. To an important extent, the meaning of the Constitution

In 2002, in *Atkins v. Virginia*, the Supreme Court reversed its previous course and said that the execution of the mentally retarded was cruel and unusual punishment. The ruling benefited Daryl Renard Atkins (shown here) who was convicted of the slaying of an airman from Langley Air Force Base.

CONSTITUTIONAL CHANGE

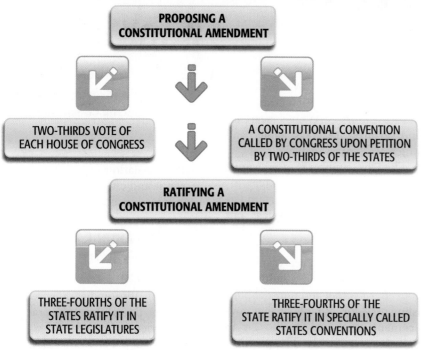

PROPOSING A CONSTITUTIONAL AMENDMENT

TWO-THIRDS VOTE OF EACH HOUSE OF CONGRESS

A CONSTITUTIONAL CONVENTION CALLED BY CONGRESS UPON PETITION BY TWO-THIRDS OF THE STATES

RATIFYING A CONSTITUTIONAL AMENDMENT

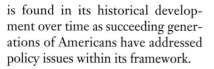

THREE-FOURTHS OF THE STATES RATIFY IT IN STATE LEGISLATURES

THREE-FOURTHS OF THE STATE RATIFY IT IN SPECIALLY CALLED STATES CONVENTIONS

called by Congress upon petition by two-thirds of the states. The first method has been used many times; Congress proposed all 27 amendments that have been added to the Constitution. The convention procedure has never been used.

After an amendment is proposed, by either Congress or a convention, three-fourths of the states must ratify it. Ratification can be accomplished either by vote of the state legislatures or by specially called state conventions. The former method has been used successfully 26 times, the latter only once, to ratify the Twenty-first Amendment repealing Prohibition.

Constitutional Change

constitutional amendment a formal, written change or addition to the nation's governing document.

is found in its historical development over time as succeeding generations of Americans have addressed policy issues within its framework.

Constitutional Change through Amendment

A **constitutional amendment** is a formal, written change or addition to the nation's governing document. A major flaw of the Articles of Confederation was that the articles could be amended only by unanimous vote. In practice, this made change impossible because of the obstinacy of only one or a few states. In 1787, then, the Constitution's framers were careful to include a reasonable method of amendment that permitted change but was difficult enough to preclude hasty, ill-conceived changes.

The Constitution provides two methods for proposing amendments and two methods for their ratification. An amendment may be proposed by either a two-thirds vote of each house of Congress or by a constitutional convention

(From left to right) George E.C. Hayes, Thurgood Marshall, and James M. Nabrit, were the NAACP Legal Defense Fund attorneys who represented the Brown family in *Brown v. Board of Education* (1954), the great school desegregation case.

through Judicial Interpretation

A final means of constitutional change is judicial interpretation. In fact, it may be no exaggeration to say that what counts most in constitutional law is the interpretation of the Constitution by the courts, particularly the U.S. Supreme Court, rather than the words of the document itself. Many phrases important to constitutional law are not even in the Constitution, including "war power," "clear and present danger," "separation of church and state," "right of privacy," "separate but equal," and "police power." These famous words appear not in the Constitution but in judicial opinions.

Judicial interpretation of the Constitution is inevitable because of the document's generalized nature. Many of the phrases of the Constitution are purposely ambiguous, requiring continuous reinterpretation and adaptation. Indeed, one constitutional scholar says that we have an unwritten constitution, whose history is the history of judicial interpretation.[11]

The power of courts to declare unconstitutional the actions of the other branches and units of government is known as **judicial review**. Although the Constitution is silent about the power of judicial review, many historians believe that the founders expected the courts to exercise the authority. Ironically, the Supreme Court assumed the power of judicial review through constitutional interpretation, first holding an act of Congress unconstitutional in 1803 in the case of *Marbury v. Madison*.[12]

Judicial review is an instrument of constitutional change because the process involves constitutional interpretation. Professor Richard H. Fallon, Jr., says that today's justices interpret the Constitution in light of history, precedent (that is, earlier

judicial review the power of courts to declare unconstitutional the actions of the other branches and units of government.

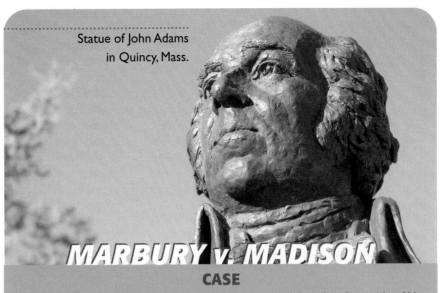

Statue of John Adams in Quincy, Mass.

MARBURY v. MADISON

CASE

In 1800, President John Adams and his Federalist Party were defeated. In the months of his remaining presidency, Adams appointed a number of loyal Federalists to the judicial branch of government. One of these judicial appointments went to William Marbury, who was named justice of the peace for the District of Columbia.

President Adams signed and sealed Marbury's commission the day before he left office, but the secretary of state neglected to deliver it. The new president, Thomas Jefferson, ordered his secretary of state, James Madison, not to deliver the commission. Marbury sued, asking the Supreme Court to issue a writ of *mandamus* to force Madison to deliver his commission. A writ of *mandamus* is a court order directing a public official to perform a specific act or duty.

DECISION

The Supreme Court had a problem. Chief Justice John Marshall and the other members of the Court were Federalists. They would have liked to force Madison to deliver the commission. However, Jefferson might well have defied the order, damaging the Court's prestige.

Judicial review provided Marshall and the Court with their way out of the dilemma. Marshall used the Court's opinion to scold Jefferson and Madison for refusing to deliver the commission. Marbury was entitled to his commission, said Marshall, and a writ of *mandamus* was in order.

However, Marshall also ruled that the Supreme Court lacked authority to issue the writ. Marshall pointed out that the Constitution lists the types of cases that may be tried before the Supreme Court in Article III, Section 2. The list does not include the power to issue writs of *mandamus* to federal officials. Congress had given the Court the authority to issue the writ in the Judiciary Act of 1789, but Marshall argued that Congress had no constitutional authority to do this. Therefore, the section of the Judiciary Act that gave the Court the power to issue writs of *mandamus* was unconstitutional. By this means, Marshall was able to attack Jefferson but keep the president from defying the Court.

SIGNIFICANCE

Marbury v. Madison is the first case in which the Supreme Court ruled that acts of Congress can be unconstitutional. In his ruling, Marshall stated that the Constitution is the "fundamental and paramount law of the nation" and that it is the duty of the courts to interpret the law.

"Thus," Marshall continued, "the particular phraseology of the Constitution of the United States confirms and strengthens the principle . . . that a law repugnant to the Constitution is void."

Marshall concluded that it was the Court's duty to enforce the Constitution by refusing to uphold the act of Congress.

interpretations), and considerations of moral desirability and practical workability.[13] Consider the history of judicial interpretation of the **Equal Protection Clause**, which is the provision found in the Fourteenth Amendment of the U.S. Constitution that declares that "No State shall . . . deny to any person within its jurisdiction the equal protection of the laws." Historians believe that Congress proposed this phrase to safeguard the civil rights of former slaves and their offspring by requiring states to treat all of their residents equally under state law, regardless of race.

The U.S. Supreme Court's initial interpretation of the Equal Protection Clause came in 1896 in *Plessy v. Ferguson.* The case centered on the constitutionality of a Louisiana law that required racial segregation (separation) in passenger railcars. Could a state government prohibit African American travelers from sharing a railcar with white passengers without violating the Equal Protection Clause? The Supreme Court answered that it could as long as the accommodations were equal. "Separate but equal" facilities, said the Court, were sufficient to satisfy the requirements of the Fourteenth Amendment.[14] Almost 60 years later, the Supreme Court addressed a similar issue in the case of *Brown v. Board of Education of Topeka* (1954). The *Brown* case involved a constitutional challenge to a Kansas law requiring racial segregation in public schools. Could a state government prohibit African American youngsters from sharing a school with white children without violating the Equal Protection Clause? In this case, the Supreme Court overruled *Plessy,* holding that the Equal Protection Clause of the Fourteenth Amendment prohibits state laws requiring racial segregation in public schools. The Court declared that "separate but equal" was a contradiction because the legal requirement of separation placed the stamp of inferiority on the black race.[15] And so the Constitution was changed, not through the adoption of a constitutional amendment (the wording of the Equal Protection Clause remained the same), but because of changing judicial interpretation.

Equal Protection Clause a provision of the Fourteenth Amendment of the U.S. Constitution that declares that "No State shall . . . deny to any person within its jurisdiction the equal protection of the laws."

the constitution, politics,
AND PUBLIC POLICY

the U.S. Constitution affects the policymaking process by fragmenting political power. Separation of powers divides power at the national level among legislative, executive, and judicial branches. Bicameralism splits power between the House and Senate. Federalism distributes power between the national government and the states.

The fragmentation of political power in the United States produces slow, incremental change. Presidents need the cooperation of Congress to have their programs enacted. In turn, Congress has difficulty acting without presidential initiative. Both the president and Congress need the support of the bureaucracy if their policies are to be faithfully executed. Frequently, they require the cooperation of state and local officials as well. The courts, meanwhile, can reverse or delay policies adopted at other levels or by other branches of

California Governor Arnold Schwarzenegger asked the federal government for financial aid during a state budget crisis in 2008.

Constitutional Principles

What is the best way of understanding the Constitution? Does it embody universal values, or should it be understood in terms of contemporary society?

Is there a difference between the founding conceptions of equality and those of today? Does a natural rights understanding assume more individual freedom?

Overview: When the Constitution was ratified in June 1788, the United States had a population of roughly 3.9 million, with an urban population of less than 500,000 citizens (approximately 11 percent). The overwhelmingly dominant religion was Protestantism, and the right to vote was held principally by those who owned property. In 2005, the United States had a population of nearly 300 million, with an urban population of roughly 225 million (75.2 percent). How is it that the Constitution can incorporate the differing social and political views of a multicultural and diverse nation?

Some scholars argue that the Constitution has been a successful document because it is based upon the principles of natural law and natural rights—principles holding that all human beings are created equal and endowed with certain inalienable rights, that these principles do not change over time, and that political institutions can be created to reflect natural equality and human dignity.

Others argue that the Constitution is a flexible instrument created to adapt to social, historical, and political change. This view—positivism—holds that constitutions and laws should reflect prevailing social convention and thought, and it is in this way that the Constitution has been able to be interpreted to allow for equality and social justice.

Just what does the Constitution mean, and how will this question determine the near future of American history?

supporting a natural rights interpretation of the Constitution

natural rights theory assumes a higher moral law. The founders were correct in their supposition that it is through liberty and justice that individuals can realize their potential and approach happiness, and the Constitution was created to embody these values. These values do not change over time.

a natural rights interpretation assumes the use of reason. Alexander Hamilton argues in the *Federalist Papers* that the Constitution represents "good government" created by "reflection and choice." The founders used reflection and reason to create a new form of government based on the natural rights principle that all political power is derived from the people exercising their right to create government and to live under laws of their own choosing.

natural rights theory embodies the principle of political equality. The Constitution should be interpreted as incorporating the principle found in the Declaration of Independence that "all men are created equal" and should have equal political rights. This allows the rich and the poor, the highly educated and the ignorant, the secular and the religious, and the interested and the apathetic to have a say and a share in government.

against a natural rights interpretation of the Constitution

the founders simply used the prevailing philosophies of their times. There is no way to determine if natural rights theory is true. The founders lived in a certain moment in history and they had no way of knowing what the future held in the way of new philosophies and science of government. For example, they did not consider that government could be used for social purposes, such as ensuring social welfare through government policy.

the Constitution must be interpreted in light of advances in technology and social organization. The United States of 2008 is a different nation than the America of 1788. It is highly unlikely that the founders could envision the complex evolution of human society and technology—how could they consider freedom-of-speech issues and the Internet? To apply constitutional law to Internet speech issues necessarily means interpreting the Constitution in a way undreamed of by the founders.

natural rights theory as understood by the founders leads to inequality. For example, the Declaration of Independence declares all men are equal, yet it allowed for slavery and unregulated free markets. The Constitution must be interpreted with a view to new understandings of social and political equality.

government. When policy changes occur, they are generally incremental and gradual, reflecting compromise among the various political actors involved in the process.

The framers of the U.S. Constitution were cautious people, wary of rapid change and none too confident about the judgment of popular majorities. Consequently, they created a constitutional apparatus that would work slowly. The founders feared that rapid, major change would too often produce more harm than good.

The Constitution promotes policy stability.[16] The election of a new president or a change in control of Congress is unlikely to produce dramatic policy change. A new president with bold new ideas must convince both Congress and the federal courts that the policy ideas are not only wise but constitutional.

President John F. Kennedy confers with his brother, Attorney General Robert Kennedy, during the 1962 Cuban Missile Crisis.

The framers of the Constitution wanted to ensure that the diversity of political interests in American society would be represented in the policy process. During the debates at the constitutional convention of 1787, one of the major issues was how best to protect the small states from large-state domination. The authors of the Constitution established a system that would provide opportunity for the varied groups and interests of American society to participate in policymaking.

America's constitutional arrangements have their critics. The oldest complaint is that the Constitution favored the rich and wellborn over the common people. In the early twentieth century, historian Charles Beard argued that the framers of the Constitution had been members of a small group of wealthy Americans who set out to preserve and enhance the economic and political opportunities of their class.[17] Although modern historians have refuted most of Beard's research, a number of contemporary observers nonetheless believe that the Constitution benefits special interests. The constitutional fragmentation of power that presents a range of forums in which different groups may be heard also provides a series of power centers that interest groups can control. Entrenched groups can frequently muster the influence to halt policy changes, sometimes overriding the wishes of a majority in Congress and the nation.

The most basic criticism of the Constitution is that it is a blueprint for political deadlock among the branches and units of government. By dividing government against itself, the founders ensured that all proposals for policy change must pass through a maze of power centers. The complexity of the arrangement not only slows the policymaking process but also gives most of the trump cards to the forces opposing whatever measure is under consideration. It is easier to defeat policy proposals than to pass them.

Professor James Sundquist believes that American history is filled with the failures of the system to respond effectively to policy crises. Consider the dilemma of the Vietnam War. Congress and the president were unable to agree either to withdraw American forces or do what was necessary to win the war. As a result, the nation was condemned to a half-in, half-out compromise policy that satisfied no one. Sundquist says the same constitutional paralysis hindered the nation's ability to deal with secession in the 1860s, the Great Depression in the 1930s, and federal budget deficits of the 1980s.[18]

Nonetheless, constitutional stalemate is not inevitable. The nation did eventually rise to the challenge of secession and preserved the Union. The constitutional deadlock over the Great Depression ended. The budget deficit of the 1980s was finally eliminated. Furthermore, we can point to national crises such as World War II and the Cuban Missile Crisis that the American government was able to address in a forthright, spirited manner.

Policy deadlocks are as much political as they are constitutional. The Constitution structures the policy process by setting the ground rules. It does not dictate the outcome of the policy process. The failure of American government to resolve the Vietnam War reflected a lack of political consensus rather than a constitutional breakdown.[19] We could say the same about the failure of Congress to dictate the withdrawal of American combat forces from Iraq. Whereas public opinion polls showed that a majority of Americans believed that the war was a mistake, they found the public conflicted on the best course to end American involvement.[20]

constitutional
ENVIRONMENT FOR POLICYMAKING

the U.S. Constitution has an impact on every stage of the policymaking process.

Agenda Building

Constitutional principles often define issues during the agenda setting stage of the policymaking process. Because of the Constitution, Americans debate the role of religion in public life from the perspectives of the First Amendment, considering both the constitutional guarantee of free exercise of religion and the prohibition against an establishment of religion. Discussions of the wisdom of state-sponsored prayers in public-school classrooms inevitably revolve around issues of constitutionality. Constitutional considerations frame the abortion controversy as well, with a constitutional "right to life" counterbalanced against a "right to choose."

Policy Formulation and Adoption

The Constitution limits the policy options available to policymakers during the policy formulation stage to those policy approaches that are consistent with the Constitution. A policy aimed at shielding children from offensive materials on the Internet must be formulated with the Constitution in mind because it will likely face legal challenge from critics who believe that it violates the free speech provision of the First Amendment. Similarly, policies designed to control illegal immigration must be formulated to pass constitutional scrutiny because the Constitution protects all *persons* in the United States, not just citizens.

The Constitution sets the ground rules for policy adoption. Legislative policies require passage by both houses of Congress and the signature of the president. If the president vetoes a measure, the Constitution provides that it dies unless the House and Senate pass it again by a two-thirds margin. Not all policies are adopted through the legislative process. The Constitution also establishes procedures, either explicitly or implicitly, for the adoption of policies through treaties, constitutional amendments, executive orders, judicial decisions, and rulemaking by government agencies.

The Constitution sets the ground rules for policymaking

Policy Implementation and Evaluation

The Constitution influences the implementation of policy. At the national level of government, policy implementation is primarily the responsibility of the executive branch. State and local governments also participate in policy implementation because of the federal system.

Finally, the Constitution affects policy evaluation. The separation of powers system with checks and balances ensures that each branch of government can evaluate policies adopted by the other branches. Congress oversees policy implementation by the executive branch. The judicial branch evaluates policies adopted by the other branches by interpreting laws and reviewing the constitutionality of executive and legislative policies.

Congressional supporters of the bill watch as President George W. Bush signs the No Child Left Behind bill into law.

1 The fundamental law by which a state or nation is organized and governed, and to which ordinary legislation must conform, is the definition of which of the following?

A. Bicameralism

B. Separation of powers

C. Constitution

D. Federalism

2 Which of the following can be defined as a political system in which the citizens vote directly on matters of public concern?

A. Representative democracy

B. Direct democracy

C. Republic

D. Confederation

3 Suppose that the majority of the people of a particular political district adhere to the same religion. The majority uses its control of government to adopt policies that limit public office to members of that religion, and they seriously disadvantage people who do not share their belief. The framers of the Constitution would use which of the following terms or phrases to describe that situation?

A. Tyranny of the majority

B. Representative democracy

C. Direct democracy

D. Separation of powers with checks and balances

4 Which of the following can be defined as a political system in which citizens elect representatives to make policy decisions on their behalf?

A. Federalism

B. Direct democracy

C. Unitary government

D. Representative democracy

5 Congress passes a law that criminalizes past actions that were taken before the law was passed. This law would be an example of which of the following?

A. *Ex post facto* law

B. Bill of attainder

C. *Habeas corpus*

D. Separation of powers

6 The Constitution guarantees accused persons the right to a speedy, public trial by an impartial jury, the right to confront witnesses, and the right to legal counsel. These provisions embody which of the following constitutional principles?

A. Separation of powers

B. Tyranny of the majority

C. Checks and balances

D. Due process of law

7 The constitutional principle that government does not have unrestricted authority over individuals is the definition for which of the following terms?

A. Limited government

B. Due process of law

C. Separation of powers

D. Bicameralism

8 The first 10 amendments to the Constitution are known as which of the following?

A. Declaration of Independence

B. Articles of Confederation

C. Bill of Rights

D. Bill of attainder

9 Do the provisions of the Bill of Rights apply to state governments?

A. No. The Bill of Rights applies only to the actions of the federal government.

B. Yes. The Supreme Court has ruled that the entire Bill of Rights applies to state governments as well as the national government.

C. Yes. The Supreme Court has ruled that the Bill of Rights applies to the states but not to the national government.

D. Yes, for the most part. The Supreme Court has ruled that most of the provisions of the Bill of Rights apply to the states.

10 The selective incorporation of the Bill of Rights to the states is based on which of the following constitutional provisions?

A. The Due Process Clause of the Fourteenth Amendment

B. The Equal Protection Clause of the Fourteenth Amendment

C. The Privileges and Immunities Clause of the Fourteenth Amendment

D. The Thirteenth Amendment

11 The political thought of Baron de Montesquieu is associated most closely with which of the following constitutional principles?

A. Bill of Rights

B. Separation of powers

C. Federalism

D. Due process of law

12 According to James Madison, what constitutional principle was designed to prevent the concentration of power in the hands of one government official or set of officials?

A. Separation of powers with checks and balances

B. Federalist Papers

C. Tyranny of the majority

D. Bill of Rights

13 The president nominates Person A to the U.S. Supreme Court, but the Senate rejects the nomination. This scenario is an example of which of the following?

A. Federalism

B. Bicameralism

C. Checks and balances

D. Tyranny of the majority

14 The state of California has tougher automobile emissions standards than the national government. This situation reflects which of the following constitutional principles?

A. Representative democracy

B. Bicameralism

C. Separation of powers with checks and balances

D. Federalism

15 Why did the framers of the Constitution create a bicameral legislative branch?

A. They wanted to ensure that the executive branch would be the dominant branch of government.

B. They wanted to prevent the legislative branch from becoming too powerful.

C. They wanted to prevent the judicial branch from becoming too powerful.

D. They wanted to strengthen the legislative branch.

16 Which of the following statements is true of the British parliamentary system?

A. It is undemocratic because it does not have separation of powers.

B. The House of Lords and the House of Commons are equally powerful.

C. The prime minister is chosen by the queen.

D. None of the above

17 Which of the following is a means through which the Constitution changes?

A. Practice and experience

B. Constitutional amendment

C. Judicial interpretation

D. All of the above

18 Which of the following is NOT a step in the process of amending the Constitution?

A. The House votes to propose the amendment by a two-thirds vote.

B. The Senate votes to propose the amendment by a two-thirds vote.

C. The president signs the proposed amendment.

D. Three-fourths of the states ratify the proposed amendment.

19 What was the significance of *Marbury v. Madison?*

A. It was the first case in which the U.S. Supreme Court declared an act of Congress unconstitutional.

B. The U.S. Supreme Court ruled that racial segregation was constitutional.

C. The U.S. Supreme Court ruled that state laws requiring racially segregated schools were unconstitutional.

D. The U.S. Supreme Court ruled that federal law takes precedence over state law.

20 How does the U.S. Constitution affect the policymaking process?

A. Change often comes slowly because the Constitution fragments political power.

B. Public policies often reflect compromise among various interests and groups.

C. Drastic policy changes are unlikely to occur.

D. All of the above

1. C; 2. B; 3. A; 4. D; 5. A; 6. D; 7. A; 8. C; 9. D; 10. A; 11. B; 12. A; 13. C; 14. D; 15. B; 16. D; 17. D; 18. C; 19. A; 20. D

3 THE FEDERAL

> **WHAT'S AHEAD**

The Constitutional Basis
of Federalism

Federal Grant Programs

Conclusion: Federalism
& Public Policy

o Child Left Behind (NCLB) is a federal law that
requires state governments and local school
districts to institute basic skills testing in reading and mathematics for students in grades
three through eight, and to use the results to
assess school performance. Schools must assess student
progress not just for the entire school but also by subgroups
based on race/ethnicity, income level, English proficiency, and
special education status. Even if a school's overall performance
is good, it will receive a failing grade under the law if, for example, the performance of Latino or special-education students
lags.[1] The goal of NCLB is to make schools regularly improve
their performance so all students, including low-income and
minority students and students with disabilities or with limited
English proficiency, will be proficient in reading and math by
2014.

NCLB, which was named for a slogan used by the George W.
Bush presidential campaign, substantially increases the role of
the federal government in public education.[2] Historically, state
and local governments operated the nation's public education
system and provided more than 90 percent of education
money.[3] NCLB forces states to neglect their own education
reform plans to concentrate instead on creating an intricate
system of high-stakes basic skills testing. Instead of learning to
read, write, and do math, students will learn how to take mul-
tiple-choice exams to pass a particular test. The school may
even pressure weak students to drop out of school before the
test is administered in order to inflate school test scores.[4]

The controversy over the federal role in public education
demonstrates the relevance of the federal system to the policymaking process.

SYSTEM

ESSENTIALS...

after studying Chapter 3, students should be able to answer the following questions:

> What powers does the Constitution delegate to each of the three branches of the federal government, and what powers are implied? What is the status of the federal system in light of both *McCulloch v. Maryland* and recent Supreme Court rulings?

> How are federal programs adopted? What are the different kinds of grants, and what are the restrictions Congress places on the receipt of federal money?

> What is the impact of the federal system on each stage of the policymaking process?

the constitutional
BASIS OF FEDERALISM

the United States has a **federal system**, which is a political system that divides power between a central government with authority over the whole nation and a series of state governments.

Powers of the National Government

The powers explicitly granted to the national government by the Constitution are known as the **delegated** or **enumerated powers**. The Constitution grants each branch of the national government certain powers. It gives the legislative branch the most extensive list of powers and the judicial branch the least extensive.

Powers of the Legislative Branch. The Constitution vests the **legislative power**, the power to make laws, in Congress. In Article I, Section 8, the Constitution gives Congress broad legislative authority. Congress has the **power of the purse**, the authority to raise and spend money.

The Constitution charges Congress with providing for the "common defense and general welfare." It authorizes Congress to borrow money and to repay the nation's debt. Congress can regulate commerce among the states and trade with other nations. It can coin money, enact laws governing bankruptcy, set standards for weights and measures, provide for

federal system a political system that divides power between a central government, with authority over the whole nation, and a series of state governments.

delegated or enumerated powers the powers explicitly granted to the national government by the Constitution.

legislative power the power to make laws.

power of the purse the control of the finances of government.

SEPARATION OF POWERS AND CHECKS AND BALANCES

EXECUTIVE BRANCH

Checking Judicial
- Appoint federal judges
- Enforce federal laws and court orders
- Grant reprieves and pardons

Checking Executive
- Declare executive branch actions unconstitutional

JUDICIAL BRANCH

Checking Legislative
- Propose legislation to Congress
- Negotiate foreign treaties
- Serve as commander in chief of the armed forces
- Veto bills

Checking Legislative
- Declare acts of Congress unconstitutional

Checking Executive
- Pass all federal laws
- Pass the federal budget
- Declare war
- Ratify treaties and confirm presidential appointments
- Override presidential vetoes
- Impeachment

LEGISLATIVE BRANCH

Checking Judicial
- Establish courts and set the number of judges
- Amend the Constitution
- Impeachment

An Army recruiting center in New York City. In Article I, Section 8, the Constitution gives Congress the authority to "raise…Armies."

the punishment of counterfeiters, create post offices and post roads, and establish rules for copyright and patent protection. The Constitution also gives Congress an important role in foreign affairs and the nation's defense. Congress can suppress insurrection and repel invasion. It can declare war, raise and support armies, and maintain a navy.

Article I, Section 8 concludes with the **Necessary and Proper Clause or Elastic Clause**. "[Congress shall have the power] to make all laws which shall be necessary and proper for carrying into execution the foregoing powers, and all other powers vested by this Constitution in the government of the United States, or

> THE NECESSARY AND PROPER CLAUSE IS THE BASIS FOR MUCH OF THE LEGISLATION PASSED BY CONGRESS BECAUSE IT GIVES CONGRESS THE MEANS TO EXERCISE ITS DELEGATED AUTHORITY

in any department or office thereof." The Necessary and Proper Clause is the basis for much of the legislation passed by Congress because it gives Congress the means to exercise its delegated authority.

The Necessary and Proper Clause is the constitutional basis for the doctrine of **implied powers**, which are those powers of Congress not explicitly mentioned in the Constitution but derived by implication from the delegated powers. Because the Constitution explicitly grants Congress the authority to raise armies, for example, the power to draft men and women into the armed forces would be an example of an implied power. The authority to draft is not explicitly granted as a delegated power, but it can be inferred as an action "necessary and proper" for carrying out one of the delegated powers—raising armies.

Powers of the Executive Branch. The Constitution grants **executive power**, the power to enforce laws, to the president, declaring that the

Necessary and Proper Clause/Elastic Clause the Constitutional provision found in Article I, Section 8 that declares that "[Congress shall have the power] to make all laws which shall be necessary and proper for carrying into execution the foregoing powers, and all other powers vested by this Constitution in the government of the United States, or in any department or office thereof." It is the basis for much of the legislation passed by Congress because it gives Congress the means to exercise its delegated authority.

implied powers those powers of Congress not explicitly mentioned in the Constitution, but derived by implication from the delegated powers.

executive power the power to enforce laws.

president should "take Care that Laws be faithfully executed." In Article II, the Constitution says that the president shall be commander in chief of the nation's armed forces. It states that the president may require reports from the heads of the executive departments, grant pardons and reprieves, make treaties with "the Advice and Consent" of the Senate, and appoint ambassadors, judges, and other officials. The president may make policy recommendations to Congress, receive ambassadors, and convene special sessions of Congress.

Powers of the Judicial Branch. The Constitution vests **judicial power**, the power to interpret laws, in a Supreme Court and whatever other federal courts Congress sees

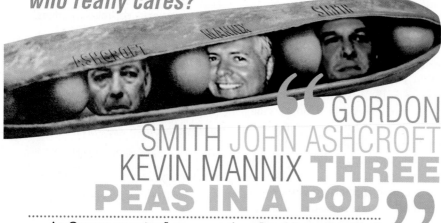

"we know we're unfair ...but if Oregon's angry, who really cares?"

GORDON SMITH JOHN ASHCROFT KEVIN MANNIX THREE PEAS IN A POD

An Oregon campaign flyer groups three Republicans, claiming all three would end Oregon's Death With Dignity Law and undermine the Tenth Amendment to the Constitution.

fit to create. In Article III, the Constitution declares that the judicial power extends to all cases arising under the Constitution, federal law, and treaties. The Constitution gives the Supreme Court of the United States the authority to try a limited range of cases, such as cases affecting ambassadors and cases in which a state is a party. Congress determines the types of cases that may be appealed to the Court.

National Supremacy. The Constitution addresses the question of the relative power of the national and state governments in Article VI in a passage known as the **National Supremacy Clause**. This is the constitutional provision that declares that the Constitution and laws of the United States take precedence over the constitutions and laws of the states. The U.S. Constitution is superior to national law, state constitutions, and state laws. National law is superior to state constitutions and state laws.

The Constitutional Status of the States

The Constitution discusses the relationship of states with one another and with the national government. The **Full Faith and Credit Clause** is the constitutional provision requiring that states recognize the official acts of other states, such as marriages, divorces, adoptions, court orders, and other legal decisions. The **Privileges and Immunities Clause** is a constitutional provision prohibiting state governments from discriminating against the citizens of other states. This provision ensures that visitors to a state are accorded the same legal protection, travel rights, and property rights as a state's own citizens. **Extradition** is the return from one state to another of a person accused of a crime. A person charged with a crime in California who flees to

judicial power the power to interpret laws.

National Supremacy Clause the constitutional provision that declares that the Constitution and laws of the United States take precedence over the constitutions and laws of the states.

Full Faith and Credit Clause the constitutional provision requiring that states recognize the official acts of other states, such as marriages, divorces, adoptions, court orders, and other legal decisions.

Privileges and Immunities Clause the constitutional provision prohibiting state governments from discriminating against the citizens of other states.

extradition the return from one state to another of a person accused of a crime.

republic a representative democracy in which citizens elect representatives to make policy decisions on their behalf.

Nevada, for example, could be extradited back to California.

The Constitution prohibits states from taking certain actions. States may not negotiate international treaties, form alliances with foreign countries, or engage in war unless they are invaded. States may not create their own currency or levy taxes on commerce with other states or foreign nations.

The Constitution includes a number of guarantees to the states. It declares that states may not be divided or consolidated without their permission. The Constitution also promises states defense against invasion, protection from domestic violence when requested, equal representation in the U.S. Senate, and a republican form of government. A **republic** is a representative democracy in which citizens elect representatives to make policy decisions on their behalf. The Eleventh Amendment prohibits foreign residents or the citizens of other states from suing a state in federal court.

The best-known constitutional guarantee given the states is the Tenth Amendment: "The powers not delegated to the United States by the Constitution, nor prohibited by it to the states, are reserved to

reserved/residual powers the powers of government left to the states.

states' rights an interpretation of the Constitution that favors limiting the authority of the federal government while expanding the powers of the states.

Which side more closely reflects your point of view: the supporters of a strong national government or the advocates of states' rights? Why?

the states respectively, or to the people." The powers of the national government are enumerated in the Constitution—the delegated powers. According to the Tenth Amendment, the powers not delegated to the national government are reserved to the states or to the people. **Reserved,** or **residual powers**, then, are the powers of government left to the states. In other words, the national government may exercise only those powers granted to it by the Constitution, whereas state governments possess all the powers not given to the national government, except those that are prohibited to the states by the Constitution.

The States' Rights/ National Government Supremacy Controversy

The supporters of states' rights and the proponents of national government supremacy have long debated the role of the states and the national government in the federal system. The doctrine of **states' rights** is an interpretation of the Constitution that favors limiting the authority of the federal government while expanding the powers of the states. The advocates of states' rights believe that the Constitution is a compact among the states that restricts the national government to those powers explicitly granted to it

by the Constitution, that is, to the delegated powers. They would question, for example, whether the federal government should be involved in public education at all. The advocates of states' rights argue that the scope of the implied powers should be strictly limited. In contrast, the supporters of national government supremacy contend that the Constitution is a contract among the people rather than the states. They note that the document begins with the following phrase: "We the people…" The supporters of a strong national government believe that the implied powers should be construed broadly in order to further the interests of the people. The federal government has a role to play in public education, they say, because it has a duty to "promote the general Welfare."

The Federal System and the Supreme Court

The Supreme Court of the United States first addressed the controversy over the relationship between the states and the national government in the famous case of *McCulloch v. Maryland* (1819), when the Court ruled that states do not have the right to interfere in the constitutional operations of the national government. (See box on next page.)

NATIONAL POWERS (ENUMERATED)

- COIN MONEY
- CONDUCT FOREIGN RELATIONS
- REGULATE COMMERCE WITH FOREIGN NATIONS AND AMONG THE STATES
- RAISE AND SUPPORT ARMIES
- PROVIDE AND MAINTAIN A NAVY
- DECLARE AND CONDUCT WAR
- ESTABLISH A NATIONAL COURT SYSTEM
- MAKE LAWS NECESSARY AND PROPER TO CARRY OUT THE DELEGATED POWERS

CONCURRENT POWERS (SHARED)

- TAX
- BORROW MONEY
- MAKE AND ENFORCE LAWS
- CHARTER BANKS AND CORPORATIONS
- SPEND MONEY FOR THE GENERAL WELFARE
- TAKE PRIVATE PROPERTY FOR PUBLIC PURPOSES, WITH JUST COMPENSATION

STATE POWERS (RESERVED)

- ESTABLISH LOCAL GOVERNMENTS
- REGULATE COMMERCE IN THE STATE
- CONDUCT ELECTIONS
- RATIFY AMENDMENTS TO THE FEDERAL CONSTITUTION
- TAKE MEASURES FOR PUBLIC HEALTH, SAFETY, AND MORALS
- EXERCISE POWERS THE CONSTITUTION DOES NOT DELEGATE TO THE NATIONAL GOVERNMENT OR PROHIBIT THE STATES FROM USING

THE GROWTH OF FEDERAL POWER
MCCULLOCH V. MARYLAND (1819)

BACKGROUND

In 1791, Congress chartered a national bank, the First Bank of the United States, amid great controversy. Secretary of State Thomas Jefferson opposed the bank because the authority to create it was not among the powers specifically enumerated by the Constitution. In contrast, Secretary of the Treasury Alexander Hamilton supported the bank and the power of Congress to establish it. He believed that the action of Congress was justified as an exercise of authority reasonably implied by the delegated powers. Despite the controversy, no legal challenge to the bank arose, and it operated until its charter expired in 1811.

CASE

Congress chartered the Second Bank of the United States in 1816. It, too, became the object of controversy, particularly in the West and South. Critics accused the bank of corruption and inefficiency. The most serious charge was that the bank was responsible for an economic downturn that ruined thousands of investors. Several states responded to the public outcry against the bank by adopting restrictions on it or levying heavy taxes against it. Maryland, for example, required payment of an annual tax of $15,000 on the bank's Baltimore branch, which, in those days, was a sum large enough to drive the bank out of business in the state. When James W. McCulloch, the bank's cashier, refused to pay the tax, Maryland sued. The case presented two important constitutional issues: 1) Does the national government have authority to charter a bank?; and 2) Does a state have the power to tax an arm of the national government?

DECISION

Chief Justice John Marshall wrote the unanimous opinion of the U.S. Supreme Court, answering both questions. First, the Court upheld the authority of Congress to charter a bank on the basis of the doctrine of implied powers. Marshall noted that although the Constitution does not specifically grant Congress the power to incorporate a bank, the Constitution does say that Congress may lay and collect taxes, borrow money, and raise and support armies. What if, Marshall asked, tax money collected in the North is needed in the South to support an army? The creation of a national bank to transport that money would be a "necessary and proper" step to that end. The power to charter the bank, Marshall held, was implied by the Necessary and Proper Clause.[5] Second, the Court ruled that Maryland's tax was unconstitutional. The power to tax, said Marshall, is the power to destroy because a high tax can drive the object of the taxation out of existence. If Maryland or any state has the authority to tax an arm of the national government, it could effectively shut it down and that would be contrary to the nature of the federal union as stated in the National Supremacy Clause.

IMPLICATIONS

The Supreme Court's decision in *McCulloch v. Maryland* supported the position of those who favored national government supremacy. By giving broad scope to the doctrine of implied powers, the Court provided the national government with a vast source of power. By stressing the importance of the National Supremacy Clause, the Court denied states the right to interfere in the constitutional operations of the national government.

The Supreme Court has not always been as receptive to the exercise of federal power as it was in *McCulloch v. Maryland*. In 1857, a few years before the outbreak of the Civil War, the infamous *Dred Scott* decision held that the national government lacked authority to regulate slavery in the territories.[6] Similarly, in the early 1930s, the Supreme Court limited the power of the national government to respond to the Great Depression by striking down much of the **New Deal**, the legislative package of reform measures proposed by President Franklin Roosevelt for dealing with the economic crisis.

> The Supreme Court's decisions in *Dred Scott* and its anti–New Deal rulings were all eventually reversed.

The Supreme Court's decisions in *Dred Scott* and its anti–New Deal rulings were all eventually reversed. Congress and the states overturned the *Dred Scott* decision by ratifying the Thirteenth, Fourteenth, and Fifteenth Amendments. The Supreme Court reversed itself in the late 1930s, eventually holding New Deal legislation constitutional. For half a century thereafter, the Supreme Court found few constitutional limitations on the exercise of federal power.

In recent years, however, the Supreme Court has issued a series of states' rights rulings. In 1995, the Supreme Court ruled that Congress had overstepped its authority when it enacted the Gun-Free School Zones Act of 1990, banning firearms within 1,000 feet of a school. The Court found the act unconstitutional, ruling that Congress can regulate only the economic activity that "substantially affects" interstate commerce, and that the possession of a firearm in the

New Deal a legislative package of reform measures proposed by President Franklin Roosevelt for dealing with the Great Depression.

Taking Sides

Federalism and the States

What level of government is best equipped to determine and enforce individual rights and obligations?

Is Madison correct in his belief that the authority of both the federal and state governments should be allowed to fluctuate in response to historical events?

Overview: The doctrine of federalism was meant to be a flexible mechanism within which to address the needs and desires of the American people. James Madison contends in the *Federalist Papers* that, over time, the American people will themselves determine which level of government should have primary law and policymaking authority, and that this authority will alternate between the federal and state governments in response to historical events.

Over the past few years, the proper role of both federal and state governments in determining social policy has been front and center in the domestic policy debates surrounding marriage rights, though with an unusual turn of events. Many social conservatives, typically linked to a limited-government philosophy which holds that the states should have significant authority over individual citizens, now argue for a constitutional amendment to define marriage rights. Social liberals, who have long held that the federal government has the primary role in protecting reproductive rights, now make the argument that it is up to the states to determine marriage rights. What gives?

Neither side is being hypocritical; they are simply pursuing political strategies within the framework of the Constitution that promote their conception of American life. The question being posed, however, raises a fundamental constitutional issue: Who determines the rights of the people? Is it the federal government—particularly the judiciary—or the state governments who have the Tenth Amendment authority to inform the American people of their rights?

supporting an increased policymaking role for the states

state governments are closer to the people and are better suited to represent their needs. For example, the people of the state of California have determined that marriage is defined by the union of a man and a woman, whereas the states of Massachusetts and Connecticut have held that homosexuals cannot be denied marriage licenses.

the founders were correct in their assessment that the states could be "laboratories" in which there will be policy innovation. Take, for instance, global warming policy. The state of California enacted legislation in 2006 that mixes innovative market and regulatory mechanisms that may be copied by other states to help reduce carbon discharge.

the Tenth Amendment gives the states the authority to determine the specific rights of their citizens. The recent decisions of the Supreme Court that have restored the right of the states to govern individual citizens are simply the return to proper constitutional principles.

against an increased policymaking role for the states

the states have demonstrated that they are incapable of enforcing significant policy. For example, the state of Louisiana demonstrated it could not effectively undertake disaster preparedness in the aftermath of Hurricane Katrina. Later policy analysis showed that most states lack the means to handle significant disasters.

some state governments, due to their small size, do not have the means to adequately address the policy needs of their citizens, and this creates *de facto* inequality that may violate the Fourteenth Amendment. For example, the state of Texas on its own has the world's eighth-largest economy and is thus better positioned to address the needs of its citizens than Arkansas, one of the poorest states in the country.

changes in technology and social mores make it imperative that the federal government increase its regulatory control. For example, the American founders could not foresee such technological and communications innovation as the computer and the Internet. Only an institution with the resources of the federal government can regulate the use and content of the Internet equitably and fairly.

vicinity of a school does not meet that criterion.[7] In 1997, the Supreme Court overturned a provision in the **Brady Act**, a federal gun control law that requires a background check on an unlicensed purchaser of a firearm. The Court ruled unconstitutional a provision in the bill that required local law enforcement agencies to conduct background checks on potential gun purchasers. The Court said that the national government did not have the authority to force state governments to carry out its regulatory policies.[8] In 2000, the Supreme Court threw out a provision in the federal Violence Against Women Act that gave the victims of sexual assault the right to sue their attackers for damages. Congress based the measure on its constitutional power to regulate interstate commerce, but the Court ruled that violent crime is insufficiently connected to interstate commerce to justify Congress taking action.[9]

Brady Act a federal gun control law that requires a background check on an unlicensed purchaser of a firearm in order to determine whether the individual can legally own a weapon.

Congress took advantage of the Supreme Court's broad interpretation of the doctrine of implied powers to exercise authority in a wide range of policy areas. In particular, Congress made frequent use of the Commerce Clause to justify legislation. The Commerce Clause is the constitutional provision giving Congress authority to "regulate commerce … among the several states." Congress used the Commerce Clause as a basis for legislation dealing with such diverse subjects as child labor, agricultural price supports, and racial discrimination in public places. In each instance, Congress argued that the particular activity it sought to regulate was part of interstate commerce, which Congress is empowered to regulate, and in each instance, the Supreme Court eventually accepted the argument.

Under the Umbrella of the Commerce Clause

Supreme Court Decisions:
National Supremacy vs. States' Rights

■ Decisions for National Supremacy
■ Decisions for States' Rights

1819 | McCulloch v. Maryland Determined that Maryland had no power to interfere with the Second Bank of the United States.

1958 | Ableman v. Booth Held that state courts cannot issue rulings that contradict the decisions of federal courts.

1997 | Printz v. United States Ruled unconstitutional provision of the Brady Handgun Violence Prevention Act that would compel local officers to conduct background checks.

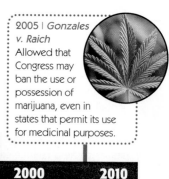

2005 | Gonzales v. Raich Allowed that Congress may ban the use or possession of marijuana, even in states that permit its use for medicinal purposes.

| 1820 | 1930 | 1940 | 1950 | 1960 | 1990 | 2000 | 2010 |

1824 | Gibbons v. Ogden Held that the power to regulate interstate navigation was granted to Congress by the Commerce Clause.

1857 | Dred Scott v. Sanford Declared that Congress had no authority to abolish slavery in federal territories.

1932 | Worcester v. Georgia Ruled that Native Americans were entitled to federal protection from state governments' actions that would infringe on their sovereignty.

2000 | U.S. v. Morrison Struck down parts of the Violence Against Women Act as unconstitutional because they exceeded congressional power.

2006 | Gonzales v. Oregon Ruled that the Federal Justice Department cannot block physician-assisted suicides, as permitted by an Oregon law.

federal grant
PROGRAMS

a **federal grant program** is a program through which the national government gives money to state and local governments to spend in accordance with set standards and conditions. NCLB is an example of a federal program that deals with public education. Other federal programs address such policy areas as transportation, childhood nutrition, healthcare, public housing, vocational education, airport construction, hazardous waste disposal, job training, law enforcement, scientific research, neighborhood preservation, mental health, and substance abuse prevention and treatment.

functions of
FEDERAL GRANTS

health 232.3

income security 94.9

education/employment 57.2

transportation 56.1

**community and regional
development 17.1**

environment 5.9

**administration
of justice 4.2**

general government 4.2

other 3.3

agriculture 0.9

total: $462 Billion

···

The national government provides state and local governments with more than $450 billion in grant funding. Medicaid is the largest federal grant program, accounting for more than 43 percent of federal grant funding.

www.gpoaccess.gov/usbudget/fy09/bis.html

takeaction
FEDERAL PROGRAMS
AND YOU >>

Federal grants and loans are important for students and the institutions they attend. Many students depend on federal financial aid to complete their degrees. Furthermore, federal grant and loan programs effectively subsidize higher education by making it possible for students to go to college. Institutions that lose their accreditation must often close their doors because they forfeit their ability to award federal financial aid to their students.

Federal financial assistance to students comes in the form of grants and loans. Students need not repay grant money, but loans must be repaid. Pell Grants provide federal financial assistance to students based on their financial need. The amount of money that students can receive depends on the cost of their education and their available financial resources. Federal Family Education Loans (FFEL) and the Stafford Loan Program enable students to borrow money to attend college. Depending on their financial need, students may be eligible for subsidized federal loans, which do not begin assessing interest until recipients begin repayment.

Your assignment is to complete the paperwork to apply for federal financial aid. Visit your college's financial aid office or go to its website to obtain the appropriate documents. You may wish to attend a financial aid seminar to learn what aid is available and whether you are eligible. Complete the paperwork and submit the original or a copy to your instructor to document that you have completed the assignment.

HOW YOU'RE FOOTING THE BILL:
UNDERGRADUATE FINANCIAL AID

FEDERAL LOANS ($39.1)

INSTITUTIONAL GRANTS ($20.6)

PELL GRANTS ($12.9)

STATE GRANTS ($7.5)

PRIVATE & EMPLOYER GRANTS ($7.3)

**EDUCATION TAX CREDITS &
DEDUCTIONS ($5.1)**

**FEDERAL GRANT PROGRAMS
OTHER THAN PELL ($3.6)**

Undergraduate student aid (in billions) in 2007.

Program Adoption

Congress and the president adopt federal programs through the legislative process. Both houses of Congress must agree to establish a program and the president must either sign the legislation or allow it to become law without signature. If the president vetoes the measure, it can become law only if Congress votes to override the veto by a two-thirds margin in each house. Congress passed the No Child Left Behind Act in late 2001 and President Bush signed it into law in early 2002.

federal grant program a program through which the national government gives money to state and local governments to spend in accordance with set standards and conditions.

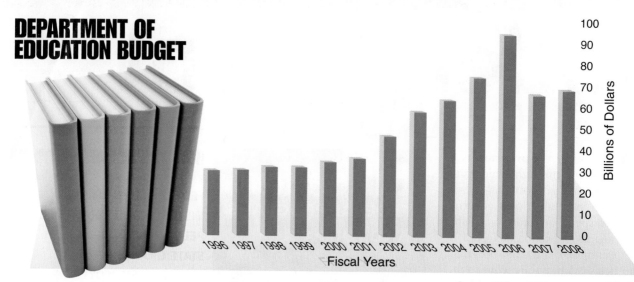

DEPARTMENT OF EDUCATION BUDGET

Fiscal Years

Billions of Dollars

100 90 80 70 60 50 40 30 20 10 0

1996 1997 1998 1999 2000 2001 2002 2003 2004 2005 2006 2007 2008

Source: Office of Management and Budget

Federal programs must be authorized and funds appropriated for their operation. The **authorization process** is the procedure through which Congress legislatively establishes a program, defines its general purpose, devises procedures for its operation, specifies an agency to implement the program, and indicates an approximate level of funding for the program but does not actually provide money. Although Congress authorizes some federal programs on a permanent basis, it stipulates that other programs must be re-authorized periodically. NCLB is the re-authorizing legislation for the Elementary and Secondary Education Act (ESEA) of 1965, which was the authorization legislation for most federal education programs.

The **appropriations process** is the procedure through which Congress legislatively allocates money for a particular purpose. The appropriations process takes place annually. Federal programs do not function unless Congress authorizes them *and* appropriates money for their operation. Without money, programs go out of business or, if they are new programs, never begin functioning. Even if opponents of a federal program cannot prevent its authorization, they can accomplish the same goal by cutting or eliminating the program's funding.

Types of Federal Programs

Federal programs come in a variety of forms.

Categorical and Block Grants. A **categorical grant program** is a federal grant program that provides funds to state and local governments for a narrowly defined purpose, such as removing asbestos from school buildings or acquiring land for outdoor recreation. In this type of program, Congress allows

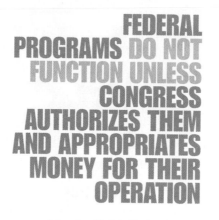

FEDERAL PROGRAMS DO NOT FUNCTION UNLESS CONGRESS AUTHORIZES THEM AND APPROPRIATES MONEY FOR THEIR OPERATION

state and local officials little discretion as to how the money is spent. Categorical grants comprise more than 90 percent of all federal grants and provide nearly 90 percent of federal grant money to state and local governments.[10] A **block grant program** is a federal grant program that provides money for a program in a broad, general policy

authorization process the procedure through which Congress legislatively establishes and defines a program, but does not actually provide funding for it.

appropriations process the procedure through which Congress legislatively allocates money for a particular purpose.

categorical grant program a federal grant program that provides funds to state and local governments for a fairly narrow, specific purpose.

block grant program a federal grant program that provides money for a program in a broad, general policy area.

area, such as childcare or job training. State and local governments have more discretion in spending block grant funds than they have in spending categorical grant money.

Officials at different levels of government hold contrasting views about categorical and block grants. Most state officeholders favor block grants because they allow states more discretion in implementation. In contrast, members of Congress usually prefer categorical grants because they enable Congress

Education Policy and Federalism in Germany

Encouraged by the Allied powers, Germany created a federal system after World War II. Having fought two world wars against Germany, the allies wanted the Germans to create a political system that would disperse power among the national government and a series of states, rather than concentrate it in a central government. The German federal system divides power between a national government and 16 states called *länder*.[11]

Although the German Constitution grants the *länder* exclusive jurisdiction over education policy, the German public supports a uniform national approach to education. Unlike the American states, the *länder* are more accurately described as administrative units rather than historically or culturally distinct regions. Public opinion favors centralized education policymaking with a uniform national policy because German society is culturally homogeneous, and the public wants the schools to promote national unity. The German public also believes that a consistent national educational policy promotes academic excellence, whereas educational diversity produces mediocrity.

The *länder* use the Standing Conference of Ministers of Culture (KMK) to circumvent the constitutionally required decentralization of educational policy. The KMK has negotiated an agreement to standardize the curriculum, establish uniform educational assessment criteria, and coordinate the timing and duration of the school year among the *länder*. Consequently, Germany has a uniform national education policy despite the constitutional requirement of decentralization.[12]

Questions

1. Would the German public favor or oppose an educational initiative such as No Child Left Behind? Why or why not?

2. Why do Americans, unlike the Germans, resist a national set of educational policies?

3. Do you believe states should be able to set their own education policies or should education policy be determined at the national level?

Students in German schools follow a national curriculum.

to exercise more control over implementation. Members of the U.S. House, in particular, like categorical grants because they entail special projects that can be targeted to individual congressional districts.[13]

Project and Formula Grants. Federal grants differ in the criteria by which funding is awarded. A **project grant program** requires state and local governments to compete for available federal money. State and local governments make detailed grant applications which federal agencies evaluate to make funding decisions. A **formula grant program** awards funding on the basis of a formula established by Congress. In contrast to project grants, formula grants provide money for every state and/or locality that qualifies under the formula. Most formulas are based on state population with modifications designed to focus on areas of greater need and to ensure that every state receive at least a minimal amount of money.[14] Formula grants outnumber project grants by a four-to-one ratio. Most federal money is awarded through formula grants as well.[15]

think

If you were a member of Congress, would you prefer block grants or categorical grants?

Grant Conditions

Federal grants usually come with conditions. A **matching funds requirement** is the legislative provision that the national government will provide grant money for a particular activity only on condition that the state or local government supplies a certain percentage of the total money required for the project or program. For example, the federal government covers only 75 percent of the cost of highway construction projects, requiring states to provide a 25 percent match. About half of all federal grant programs require funding participation by the recipient.[16]

project grant program a grant program that requires state and local governments to compete for available federal money.

formula grant program a grant program that awards funding on the basis of a formula established by Congress.

matching funds requirement the legislative provision that the national government will provide grant money for a particular activity only on the condition that the state or local government involved supplies a certain percentage of the total money required for the project or program.

Medicaid a federal program designed to provide health insurance to low-income persons, people with disabilities, and elderly people who are impoverished.

federal GRANTS

	Purpose	Discretion given to state and local governments	Example
Categorical Grant	Narrowly defined purpose	Very little flexibility	Food Stamp Program
Block Grant	For a broad, general policy area	Some flexibility	Community Development Program
	How is money allocated?		**Example**
Project Grant	• State and local governments compete for available federal money • Doesn't provide money for every state/locality that qualifies		National Sciences Foundation grants for biological sciences
Formula Grant	• Funding awarded based on formula established by Congress to focus on areas of greater need • Provides money for every state/locality that qualifies		School Lunch Program, Unemployment Insurance, Temporary Assistance for Needy Families (TANF)

Binge Drinking

COLLEGE PRESIDENTS WANT DRINKING AGE LOWERED TO 18

By Jennifer Maloney

AUGUST 19, 2008

COLLEGE PRESIDENTS from more than 100 schools across the country are calling on lawmakers to do something about binge drinking: Consider lowering the drinking age from 21 to 18.

"Twenty-one is not working," says the group's statement, signed by presidents from prominent colleges such as Dartmouth, Duke and Syracuse. "A culture of dangerous, clandestine 'binge drinking'–often conducted off-campus–has developed."

Even before the presidents begin the public phase of their efforts, which might include newspaper ads in the coming weeks, they face sharp criticism.

Mothers Against Drunk Driving says lowering the drinking age would lead to more fatal car crashes. It accuses the presidents of misrepresenting research and looking for an easy way out of an inconvenient problem, and urges parents to think carefully about safety at colleges whose presidents have signed on.

The current law, Duke University president Richard Brodhead said, "pushes drinking into hiding, heightening its risks, including risks from drunken driving, and it prevents us from addressing drinking with students as an issue of responsible choice."

The two sides agree alcohol abuse by college students is a huge problem, but disagree on whether raising the legal drinking age to 21 has saved lives.

In 1984, Congress voted to penalize any state that set its legal drinking age lower than 21 by rescinding 10 percent of that state's federal highway funding. Here are some pros and cons of lowering the drinking age, according to organizations that have studied the issue.

PROS

The United States has the oldest drinking age in the world. Most nations allow alcohol consumption at 16 or 18, and some have no minimum drinking age at all.

A lower drinking age could lead to less binge drinking, experts say, since 18- to 20-year-olds won't have to imbibe surreptitiously.

At 18, Americans can marry, serve in the military, vote and enter into legally binding contracts.

CONS

Safer roads. Laws setting the drinking age at 21 cut traffic fatalities involving drivers age 18–20 by 13 percent, according to a National Highway Traffic Safety Administration study.

Since states' laws differ on the drinking age, the result could be 18- to 20-year-olds traveling across state lines to buy or consume alcohol with sometimes disastrous results.

Adolescents' brains, some studies say, are still developing past the age of 18 and significant alcohol use can interfere in that process.

↗ CRITICAL THINKING QUESTIONS:

- Why do you think college presidents rather than college students are taking the lead on this issue?
- From your personal experience, does the 21-year minimum legal drinking age work to reduce drunken driving by young adults?
- Do you think that state legislatures would even consider reducing the minimum legal drinking age until Congress repeals the legislation that penalizes (with a loss of highway funding) states which have a lower-than-21 drinking age?

>> END

Matching funds requirements sometimes force states and localities to devote ever-growing sums of money to particular programs. Consider the impact on state budgets of **Medicaid**, a federal program designed to provide health insurance coverage to low-income persons, people with disabilities, and elderly people who are impoverished. The federal government and the states split the cost of Medicaid, with the federal government pick-

Congress also imposes mandates on recipients of federal funds. A **federal mandate** is a legal requirement placed on a state or local government by the national government requiring certain policy actions. Some mandates apply to grants recipients in general. These include provisions in the area of equal rights, equal access for the disabled, environmental protection, historic preservation, and union wage rates for contractors' person-

Grant conditions and federal mandates impose substantial costs on state and local governments. The National Conference on State Legislatures estimates the annual cost of federal mandates to states at $30 billion.[19] The most expensive federal programs for states and localities are federally mandated special education programs, NCLB, and prescription drug costs for people eligible for both Medicare and Medicaid.[20]

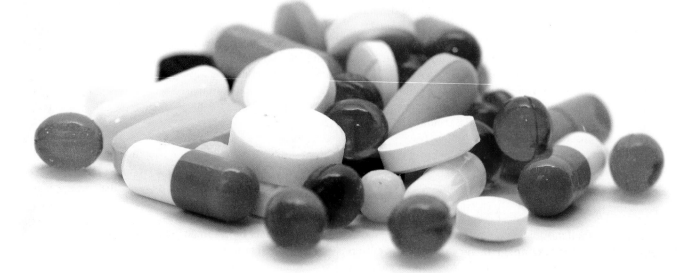

ing up 50 to 80 percent of the cost, depending on a state's wealth. Healthcare costs, especially the cost of prescription drugs, are rapidly rising. Medicaid is the most rapidly growing item in most state budgets, accounting for 13 percent of state general fund expenditures.[17]

nel. Individual programs often have particular strings attached as well. In order to receive federal law enforcement grants, for example, states must collect data on sex offenders, include DNA samples, and prepare a statewide sex offender registry database.[18]

federal mandate a legal requirement placed on a state or local government by the national government requiring certain policy actions.

the THINK SPOT
www.thethinkspot.com

CONCLUSION
federalism
& PUBLIC POLICY

the federal system is a fundamental part of the legal/constitutional environment for policymaking, affecting every stage of the policy process.

Agenda Building

The United States does not have a single government but rather thousands of interconnected governments. Each level of government has its own policy agenda and procedures for policy adoption.

State and local governments have adopted legislation to address some policy issues because the federal government has failed to act. Frustrated with a lack of federal action on illegal immigration, for example, many states have adopted measures designed to address the issue. Several states have passed legislation to prevent illegal immigrants from obtaining driver's licenses.[21]

Policy Formulation and Adoption

The federal system affects policy formulation. To a degree, each state is a policy laboratory. Both the federal government and other states draw from the experiences of particular states in formulating their own policies. For example, policymakers across the nation are closely watching the implementation of a healthcare program in Massachusetts aimed at providing universal health insurance coverage. The government subsidizes the cost of health insurance for lower-income people.[22] If the Massachusetts plan proves successful, it could be the basis of a national program.

The federal system influences policy adoption. Most policy issues in the United States are addressed by policies adopted by more than one unit and level of government. The national government, state governments, and local governments all adopt policies concerning issues such as education, healthcare,

> **Most policy issues in the United States are addressed by policies adopted by more than one unit and level of government.**

the environment, resource development, and law enforcement.

The national government affects state and local policy adoption through mandates and preemption. Federal mandates require states and localities to take certain actions. The National Voter Registration Act (also known as the Motor Voter Act) forces state governments to make it easier for people to register to vote. The Asbestos Hazard Emergency Response Act requires state and local governments to remove asbestos from all public buildings.

The federal government prevents state and local governments from making policy in some policy areas. An act of Congress adopting regulatory policies that overrule state policies in a particular regulatory area is known as **federal preemption of state authority.** Since 1965, Congress and the president have adopted more than 350 laws preempting state regulation, including

preemptions of state policies dealing with cellular phone rates, nuclear power safety, nutrition labeling, and private pension plans.[23] States may not regulate airlines, bus and trucking companies, mutual funds, or the telecommunications industry. For example, federal law prevents cities and other units of local government from banning the construction of cell towers even though many local residents would like to keep the towers out of their neighborhoods because they are unsightly and negatively affect property values.[24]

Policy Implementation and Evaluation

Federalism affects policy implementation. Many of the policies adopted by the national government require implementation by state and local officials. NCLB is a federal education program that must be implemented by state and local governments. Federal regulations also affect the implementation of public policies adopted at the state level.

Finally, the federal system influences policy evaluation. Public officials at all levels of government evaluate policy and give feedback. State and local officials frequently communicate their evaluations of federal programs to members of Congress and senators from their states. Federal officials often evaluate the effectiveness of federal programs by assessing their implementation at the state and local level. Congress uses feedback from evaluation reports to redesign federal programs.

TEST yourself

1 Which of the following is the foremost goal of the No Child Left Behind Act (NCLB)?

A. To ensure that students with disabilities have access to educational opportunities

B. To ensure that all public schools are racially integrated

C. To make public school systems accountable for the progress of all students

D. To provide free or reduced rate meals for school children from low-income families

2 A political system that divides power between a central government with authority over the whole nation and a series of state governments is known as which of the following?

A. Federal system of government

B. Confederation

C. Unitary government

D. Republic

3 Article I, Section 8 of the U.S. Constitution declares that Congress has the authority to coin money. Coining money is an example of which of the following?

A. Delegated powers

B. Implied powers

C. Checks and balances

D. Concurrent powers

4 Which of the following is true about Congress?

A. The Constitution vests legislative power in Congress.

B. Congress has the power of the purse.

C. The Constitution delegates certain powers to Congress in Article I, Section 8.

D. All of the above

5 Which of the following statements is accurate about the powers of Congress?

A. Congress can exercise any power it wishes to exercise because it is a sovereign body.

B. Congress can exercise any power except those powers prohibited by the U.S. Constitution.

C. Congress can exercise only those powers delegated to it by the U.S. Constitution or implied through the application of the Necessary and Proper Clause.

D. Congress can exercise only those powers given to it in the Bill of Rights.

6 In Article I, Section 8, the Constitution grants Congress authority to "regulate commerce among the several states." Congress passes legislation establishing regulations for interstate trucking, including safety standards for trucks and drivers. Which of the following constitutional provisions or principles gives Congress the authority to set standards for trucks and truck drivers?

A. National Supremacy Clause

B. Implied powers

C. Concurrent powers

D. Equal Protection Clause

7 The Elastic Clause is another name for which of the following constitutional provisions?

A. National Supremacy Clause

B. Equal Protection Clause

C. Necessary and Proper Clause

D. Commerce Clause

8 The Constitution delegates which of the following powers to the president?

A. The power to regulate commerce among the states

B. The power to command the armed forces

C. The power to declare war

D. All of the above

9 Suppose Congress passes a law which conflicts with the state constitution of Georgia. Which takes precedence—the U.S. law or the Georgia Constitution?

A. The Georgia Constitution, because of the Tenth Amendment

B. The Georgia Constitution, because all constitutions take precedence over all laws

C. The U.S. law, because of the delegated powers

D. The U.S. law, because of the National Supremacy Clause

10 A person wanted for a crime in New York flees to Florida where he is arrested. The procedure for returning the accused person to New York to face criminal charges is known as which of the following?

A. Full Faith and Credit

B. Privileges and Immunities

C. Extradition

D. Delegated powers

11 The Tenth Amendment is the constitutional basis for which of the following?

A. Reserved powers
B. Delegated powers
C. Implied powers
D. Concurrent powers

12 Both state governments and the national government have the constitutional authority to tax and spend. Therefore, the power to tax and spend is an example of which of the following?

A. Reserved powers
B. Delegated powers
C. Implied powers
D. Concurrent powers

13 Which of the following statements would be most likely to come from an advocate of a strong national government as opposed to a supporter of states' rights?

A. National control makes for better public policies.
B. The Constitution is a compact among the states and the powers of the national government should be narrowly interpreted.
C. The powers of the national government should be closely limited to the delegated powers.
D. All of the above

14 Would states' rights advocates favor or oppose the NCLB?

A. They would favor the law because it provides federal money to support state education programs.
B. They would favor the law because a Republican president was behind the adoption of the measure.
C. They would oppose the law because it increased federal involvement in education policy, which is traditionally an area of state responsibility.
D. They would oppose the law because it didn't provide enough money to support public education.

15 Which of the following was part of the Supreme Court's ruling in *McCulloch v. Maryland*?

A. The Supreme Court ruled that Congress lacked the constitutional authority to charter a bank.
B. The Supreme Court ruled that the powers of Congress were limited to the delegated powers.
C. The Supreme Court upheld the Maryland tax on the bank.
D. None of the above

16 A federal grant program that provides funds to state and local governments for a fairly narrow, specific purpose is known as which of the following?

A. Block grant
B. Formula grant
C. Categorical grant
D. Program grant

17 A federal grant program that provides money for a program in a broad, general policy area, such as childcare or job training, is known as which of the following?

A. Block grant
B. Formula grant
C. Categorical grant
D. Program grant

18 A grant program that requires state and local governments to compete for available federal money is known as which of the following?

A. Block grant
B. Formula grant
C. Categorical grant
D. Project grant

19 A grant program that awards funding on the basis of a formula established by Congress is known as which of the following?

A. Block grant
B. Formula grant
C. Categorical grant
D. Program grant

20 NCLB requires that states meet certain goals in order to continue receiving federal funds. This requirement is an example of which of the following?

A. Federal mandate
B. Matching funds requirement
C. Federal preemption of state authority
D. Project grant

KNOW *the* **score**

18–20 correct: Congratulations! You are well informed!

15–17 correct: Your political knowledge is a bit low—be sure to review the key terms and visit TheThinkSpot.

<14 correct: Reread the chapter more thoroughly.

---

1. C; 2. A; 3. A; 4. D; 5. C; 6. B; 7. C; 8. B; 9. D; 10. C; 11. A; 12. D; 13. A; 14. C; 15. D; 16. C; 17. A; 18. D; 19. B; 20. A

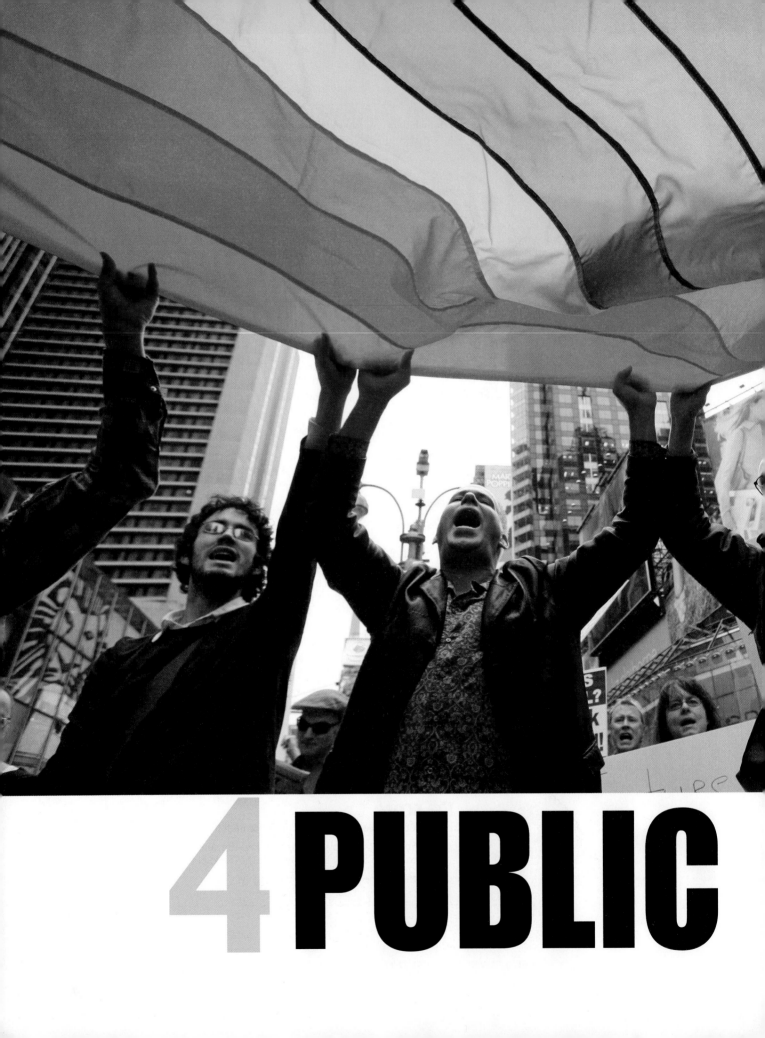

4 PUBLIC

> WHAT'S AHEAD

Political Socialization

Measuring Public Opinion

Political Knowledge

Political Philosophy

**Conclusion: Public Opinion
& Public Policy**

A controversial issue provides a good way to study public opinion. Gay and lesbian rights are among the most controversial and emotional subjects in American politics. The supporters of gay and lesbian rights define the issue in terms of civil rights and human dignity. They believe that gay men and lesbians should be afforded the same rights and privileges under the law as all other Americans. Opponents regard the issue as a matter of traditional family values and social permissiveness. They are against granting civil rights protections to gay men and lesbians, and oppose any legal recognition of homosexual relationships.

A large majority of Americans (89 percent) believe that gay men and lesbians "should have equal rights in terms of job opportunities," but the nation is divided on other gay and lesbian rights issues. While a majority of Americans (57 percent) believe that homosexuality is an acceptable alternative lifestyle, Americans are almost evenly divided on whether homosexuality is morally acceptable. Furthermore, a majority of Americans (53 percent) tell researchers that same-sex unions should not be recognized by law.[1]

The topic of gay and lesbian rights provides a good introduction to the study of public opinion by raising a number of questions:

• How do scholars measure public opinion? How accurate are opinion surveys, especially on controversial or complex subjects?

• Why do different groups of Americans hold different views? What factors account for individual attitudes and beliefs?

• What is the nature of public opinion in America? What can public opinion tell us about the democratic principles of majority rule and minority rights? Does public opinion vary in intensity and among different groups?

• Finally, to what extent does public opinion influence policy?

OPINION

ESSENTIALS...

after studying chapter 4, students should be able to answer the following:

> What is the process of political socialization, and what are the roles played by genetics, family, school, peer groups, religious institutions, and the media?

> What is the theory and practice of survey research, and how do sampling, question wording, sequencing, phantom opinions, interviewer-respondent interaction, and timing affect the measurement of public opinion?

> What is the level of political knowledge in the United States, and how does this impact the policymaking process? What is the level of political trust and political efficacy in the United States?

> What are liberalism and conservatism? How do the political views of Americans break down based on social class, race and ethnicity, religion, generation, region, and gender?

> What is the role of public opinion in the policymaking process?

political SOCIALIZATION

the process through which individuals acquire political knowledge, attitudes, and beliefs is called **political socialization**. Socialization is a learning process, but it does not always take place in a classroom. Informal learning, filling out an income tax return, serving on a jury, and standing for the National Anthem also provide opportunities for political socialization.

Process of Socialization

Grade-school students recognize terms such as *Congress*, *political party*, and *democracy*, but they do not understand their meanings. Many youngsters can name the political party their family supports, but they are unable to distinguish between the two major parties on issues. Almost all young children have a positive attitude toward government and its symbols. Most can distinguish the American flag from other flags, for example, and say they like it best.

In adolescence, young people begin to separate individuals from institutions. They understand, for example, that one can criticize the president while supporting the presidency. Adolescents are aware of processes such as voting and lawmaking, and their general understanding of these processes is more sophisticated.

Attitudes begin to diverge in the adolescent years. For example, many African American children grow less trustful of authority figures, especially police officers.[2] Political events can also drive adolescent socialization. For example, young people gain knowledge and develop party attachments during a presidential campaign. The more intense the po-litical event, the more enduring the political views it creates. The Civil War and the Great Depression had a lifelong impact on generations of Americans.[3]

Political socialization continues in adulthood. Attitudes and basic political knowledge crystallize during early adulthood and tend to persist throughout life.[4] Nonetheless, as adults go to work, start families, and retire, they may change their views on specific political issues.

Agents of Socialization

Agents of socialization contribute to political socialization by shaping formal and informal learning.

political socialization the process whereby individuals acquire political knowledge, attitudes, and beliefs.

agents of socialization those factors that contribute to political socialization by shaping formal and informal learning.

Family. Children acquire attitudes toward politics from their families. Voters, for example, are usually the children of voters.[5] Children of politically knowledgeable parents are themselves more likely to be well-informed about government and politics.[6]

Families influence at least the initial development of political party affiliation. As parents talk with one another and with their children, they are unconsciously

think

Should schools teach youngsters to be patriotic Americans?

constructing a "family identity" that may include party identification.[7] A study of fourth graders found that 60 percent of the youngsters identified with a party even though they had virtually no knowledge of party history, issues, or candidates.

Political similarities between parents and children diminish over time. Young adults frequently change their political and party affiliation in response to new socializing experiences. By the age of 25, young adults often adjust their political party identification to place it in line with the party they prefer on the issues about which they care.[8]

School. Civics classes enhance student knowledge of American government and politics. Coursework may lead students to watch news programs or read about current events online. Students may ask their parents more questions about political affairs.[9] Furthermore, community volunteers, fulfilling a high-school course requirement, may develop a lifetime habit of participation in community organizations and voting.[10]

Schools teach patriotism. In the classroom, students pledge allegiance to the flag, sing patriotic songs, commemorate national holidays, and study the lives of national heroes. Schools may provide ex-

tracurricular activities, including student government organizations. Young people who learn participatory skills in school typically become participatory adults.[11]

Schools teach young people how to work within a power structure. Youngsters inevitably develop attitudes about authority and their roles as participants in a system. Some scholars believe that a primary focus of schools on compliance with rules hinders the development of political participation skills. This phenomenon is particularly true of schools in low-income areas.[12]

College students differ politically from high-school graduates. College life does appear to influence political attitudes as students are exposed to a variety of new ideas and people. As a result, they are less likely than non-college graduates to share their family's political views. However, college-bound youngsters

already tended to vary from non-college peers even before they entered college.

Religious Institutions. People who are active in religious organizations are more likely to be politically engaged as well.[13] This association between religious and political activism is particularly important for African Americans.[14] Historically, the black church has been an important training ground for political leadership.

People tend to join religious organizations that promote their own political beliefs, but these can also influence political views.[15] This is particularly true for religious groups demanding an intense commitment of faith and a belief in religion as a source of truth. Members who accept the religious organization as the authoritative interpreter of the word of God often respect the political pronouncements of religious leaders as well.[16]

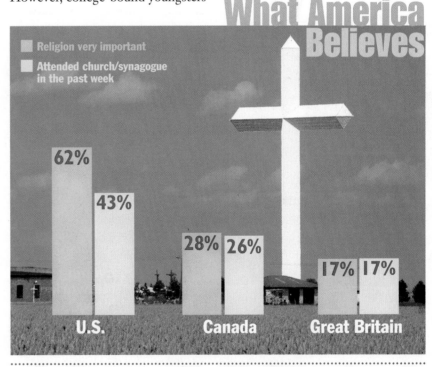

What America Believes

- Religion very important
- Attended church/synagogue in the past week

62% 43% — U.S.
28% 26% — Canada
17% 17% — Great Britain

Americans are more religious than people in most industrial nations. More than 60 percent of Americans tell survey researchers that religion is very important in their lives, and nearly two-thirds belong to a church, synagogue, or other religious body.

Lydia Saad, "Religion Is Very Important to Majority of Americans," December 5, 2003, available at www.gallup.com.

think Should churches and other religious institutions take positions on political issues and candidates?

Peer Groups. Friends and coworkers also shape political attitudes and beliefs. Those who know gays or lesbians are more supportive of gay rights.[17] Studies show that discussions among friends are more important than the media in influencing voter decisions.[18] When adults change jobs or neighborhoods, new peer groups may change their political views as well.[19]

People are more likely to share the values of a group that is important to them. Nonetheless, people may choose to remain in a group even when they disagree with its values. A study of conservative Christian churches found that nearly 40 percent of women members held feminist views contrary to those of their church. The feminist women remained in the church because they perceived little connection between their religious and political views.[20]

Media. Political participation is closely associated with media usage, especially newspaper and newsmagazine readership. Nearly everyone who votes reads a newspaper. Young people who use media frequently understand American government and are more supportive of American values, such as free speech.[21]

The media, especially television, have been shown to determine the importance Americans attach to issues. Television news stories influence Americans' priorities.[22] Media reports also shape public opinion of a president. The more media focus on a policy issue, the more the public incorporates its knowledge of that issue into its overall judgment of a president.[23]

Can Political Attitudes Be Genetically Transmitted?

Researchers compared the political attitudes of monozygotic (identical) and dizygotic (non-identical) twins in the United States and Australia. They found a genetic basis for the way individuals respond to environmental conditions. Political similarities between parents and children, then, may have as much to do with genetics as with socialization. The researchers suggest that the ideological division in American politics may have a genetic basis. They identify two distinct ideological orientations. People with an "absolutist" orientation are suspicious of immigrants, yearn for strong leadership and national

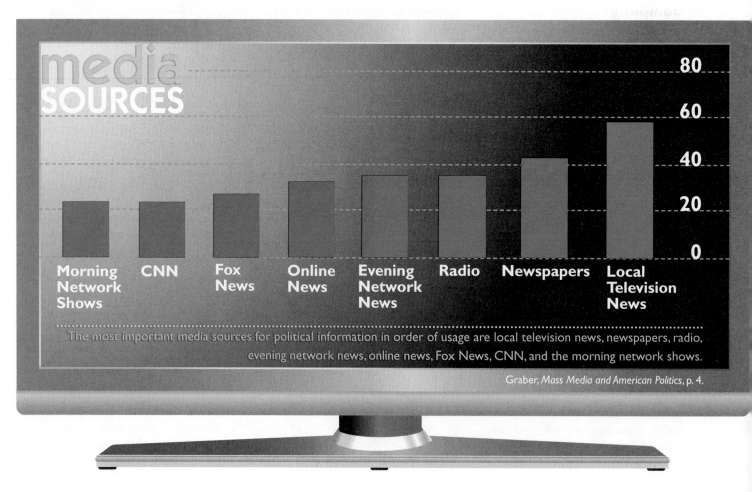

The most important media sources for political information in order of usage are local television news, newspapers, radio, evening network news, online news, Fox News, CNN, and the morning network shows.

Graber, *Mass Media and American Politics*, p. 4.

unity, and seek an unbending moral code. They favor punishment for those who violate society's moral code, tolerate economic inequality, and hold a pessimistic view of human nature. In contrast, people with a "contextualist" orientation are tolerant of immigrants and seek a context-dependent approach to proper social behavior. They dislike predetermined punishments, distrust strong leaders, disapprove of economic inequality, and hold an optimistic view of human nature.[24]

measuring
PUBLIC OPINION

Survey research, the measurement of public opinion, is a familiar part of the American scene. Businesses use market surveys to assess public tastes for their products and services. Political campaigns employ polls to plan strategy. Public officials use surveys to assess public understanding of problems and issues.[25] The media use opinion surveys to gauge public reaction to political events and assess the popularity of officeholders and candidates.

Sampling
In survey research, a **universe** is the population researchers wish to study. It may consist of all adult Americans, or Californians, or likely voters. Survey research enables scholars to examine the characteristics of a large group.

A **sample** is a subset, or smaller part of a universe. It must be chosen carefully to reflect its universe. A sample will allow for a **margin of error** (or **sample error**), a statistical term that refers to the accuracy of a survey. The margin of error's size depends on the size of the sample. The table to the right lists the margins of error for various sample sizes for a large universe. The margin of error decreases as the sample size increases and vice versa. The margin of error for samples of under 100 is so large as to make the survey meaningless. Researchers can reduce the margin of error by increasing the sample size. However, they can never eliminate error unless they survey every member of the universe. In practice, most professional survey research firms aim for a margin of error of plus or minus 3 to 4 percentage points.

The margin of error for a sample of 1,065 persons out of a universe of 500,000 or more is plus or minus 3 percentage points, 95 percent of the time. For example, suppose that we know that 10 percent of all adults are left-handed. Sampling theory tells us that, 95 percent of the time, a randomly selected sample of 1,065 people will include 7, 8, 9, 10, 11, 12, or 13 percent left-handers, that is, plus or minus 3 percentage points from 10, or the true proportion of left-handed people in this universe. Five percent of the randomly selected samples of 1,065 persons will produce an error that is greater than 3 percentage points. In other words, 5 samples out of 100 will contain a proportion of left-handed people less than 7 percent or more than 13 percent.

Survey research is not exact. Suppose one survey shows that Candidate X is leading Candidate Y by a 48 percent to 46 percent margin, while another survey indicates that Candidate Y is leading by 49 percent to 45 percent. The margin of error in each

MARGINS OF ERROR for a Universe Greater than 500,000

margin of error	sample size
+/− 4%	600
+/− 3%	1,065
+/− 2%	2,390
+/− 1%	9,425

survey is a plus or minus 4 percentage points. Statistically, the surveys show the same result—support for the two candidates is within the margin of error. Neither candidate is actually ahead.

Statistical chance dictates that 5 percent of samples taken will have a margin greater than the margin of error. For example, even if two candidates are actually tied in voter support, an occasional sample will show one or the other with a lead greater than the margin of error. Over the course of an election campaign, surveys may show a good deal of small voter movement between candidates, or an occasional major shift in public support even though no actual change in voter support for the two candidates has taken place.

For accuracy, a sample must be representative of its universe. If researchers are interested in the views of all Americans, a sample of a thousand people from Atlanta, a thousand women, or a thousand callers to a radio talk show would not likely be representative. An unrepresentative sample is a **biased sample,** that is, a sample that tends to produce results that do not reflect the true characteristics of the universe because it is unrepresentative of the universe. Internet polls are unreliable because the sample consists of people who choose to participate, sometimes more than once.

A biased sample led to one of the most famous polling mistakes in history. Beginning in 1916, *Literary Digest* conducted presidential polls

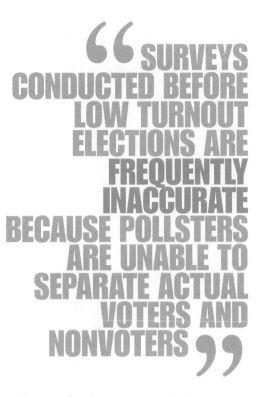

> **SURVEYS CONDUCTED BEFORE LOW TURNOUT ELECTIONS ARE FREQUENTLY INACCURATE BECAUSE POLLSTERS ARE UNABLE TO SEPARATE ACTUAL VOTERS AND NONVOTERS**

every four years. In 1936, the magazine mailed 10 million ballots to names taken from telephone directories and automobile registration lists. About two million people responded, and *Literary Digest* predicted that Republican Alf Landon would defeat Democrat Franklin Roosevelt. In fact, Roosevelt was reelected by the largest landslide in American history!

What went wrong? *Literary Digest*'s sample did not represent the universe of voters. At the height of the Great Depression, the people with telephones and automobiles

biased sample a sample that tends to produce results that do not reflect the true characteristics of the universe because it is unrepresentative of the universe.

random sample a sample in which each member of the universe has an equal likelihood of being included.

were middle- and upper-income, usually Republican, voters. Poor and working-class people could not afford cars and telephones, but they could vote, and they voted for Roosevelt.

The ideal approach is to employ a **random sample**. A random sample gives each member of a universe an equal likelihood of being included; it is unbiased. Researchers could select a random sample by picking names from a student list, for example, if the universe were students of a particular college. It is not always this easy. A random sample of voters in an upcoming election is difficult because no master list exists. Identifying likely voters is especially challenging because people don't like to admit they may not vote. Surveys conducted before low-turnout elections are frequently inaccurate because pollsters are unable to separate actual voters from nonvoters.

National survey research firms generate samples starting from a list

Internet polls are unreliable because the sample consists of people who choose to participate, sometimes more than once. For example, *People* magazine once conducted an online poll to select the Most Beautiful Person of the Year. When Howard Stern, a nationally syndicated radio talk show host, heard about the poll, he encouraged his listeners to vote for Hank, the Angry, Drunken Dwarf. Wrestling fans also flooded the *People* website with votes for Ric "Nature Boy" Flair, a professional wrestler. Hank, the Angry, Drunken Dwarf won the vote as *People*'s Most Beautiful Person and Flair finished second.[26]

of all telephone exchanges in the United States and an estimate of the number of households served by each exchange. A computer creates a master list of telephone numbers and then selects a random sample from its list. The computer creates a list of possible numbers rather than using actual telephone numbers so that unlisted telephone numbers will be as likely to be included as listed numbers. To correct for the possible bias of including only people who are usually home and answer their telephones, polling firms call back repeatedly at different times over several days. Once someone answers, the researchers do not necessarily interview that person. They ask for all the adults in the household and then randomly select a name.

Many people refuse to participate in opinion polls. The response rate for major national surveys is less than 30 to 40 percent. It is even less for snapshot polls taken overnight. Cell phones are another problem for survey researchers. Because wireless carriers charge users by the minute, cell phone users are less likely to participate than people using landlines.[27] Scholars are concerned that low response rates may make surveys inaccurate. Researchers attempt to compensate for differing response rates by adding men, young adults, and other demographic groups, which would otherwise be underrepresented in the sample.[28]

Measuring public opinion on controversial issues is especially difficult. Respondents may not answer questions honestly when they have to do with race, for example, because they do not want to appear prejudiced. Researchers have found voter preferences in contests between African American and white candidates typically overestimate the vote for the African American candidate because white voters may misreport their candidate preferences.[29]

Question Wording

Question wording can affect survey responses because it provides a frame of reference for a question.[30] For example, a majority of Americans say that they oppose gay marriage, yet the nation is evenly divided on whether homosexual couples should be allowed "to legally form civil unions, giving them some of the legal rights of married couples." If the wording mentions "healthcare benefits and Social Security survivor benefits," approval rises to more than 60 percent.[31] Many Americans react negatively to

As an increasing number of young people opt out of landlines, survey researchers must find ways to ensure this demographic group is not underrepresented.

the use of the word *marriage* because it has a religious frame of reference. In contrast, questions that mention healthcare and Social Security benefits frame the issue in a legal rather than a religious context.

btw...

In 1948, Democratic President Harry Truman was running for election against Thomas Dewey, the Republican Party nominee. Throughout the summer and early fall, the polls showed Dewey well ahead and it was generally assumed that Dewey would win. In fact, the major polling firms stopped surveying voters more than a week before the election. They missed a late voter shift in favor of President Truman. Consequently, Truman's election victory was a surprise to many, including the editors of the *Chicago Tribune* who rushed to press on election night with the famous headline: "Dewey Defeats Truman."

Is There a "Bradley Effect"?

REASSESSING THE BRADLEY EFFECT
By DAN WALTERS, PressDemocrat.com

AUGUST 11, 2008

BARACK OBAMA'S HISTORIC BID for the presidency has spawned many political theories, one of which is that he could fall victim to the "Bradley Effect."

Even a cursory media database search finds dozens of recent references to the term, usually in conjunction with Obama's somewhat lackluster standing in the polls vis–à–vis rival John McCain, such as this one from NBC pundit Chris Matthews: "I mean, is this going to be something we can't even interpret through polling? We can talk about the Bradley Effect because of what happened to Tom Bradley when he ran for governor of California and won in the polls twice and lost the governorship twice on Election Day.

"I've seen theories about this, that unless the African American candidate is able to get . . . the election number he needs, he won't get it that day. He has to get it in the polling, and Barack hasn't cracked about 45 percent."

Or this one from a *Wall Street Journal* article on political polling: "Pollsters look for the Bradley Effect, the idea that some white voters are reluctant to say they support a white candidate over a black candidate. The phrase refers to California's 1982 gubernatorial election, when the late Tom Bradley, a black Democratic mayor of Los Angeles, led in exit polls against white Republican George Deukmejian. Mr. Bradley lost the election. The conclusion: Some voters hid their true choice from pollsters."

The effect, which has circulated in California political circles for decades, has gone national. But there's one problem—it probably isn't true.

Did some Californians vote against Bradley because he was black? Of course. But did hidden racism decide one of the closest gubernatorial elections in California history, which Deukmejian won by fewer than 100,000 votes? It's highly unlikely.

The basis for the theory is that Bradley was leading in the polls right up to Election Day, yet lost the election. What Bradley Effect theorists miss is that the polls were actually quite accurate—as far as they went. Bradley won among voters who cast ballots on Election Day, as "exit polling" of voters confirmed. Based on those polls, in fact, many news outlets immediately declared Bradley the winner.

Bradley lost narrowly, however, when absentee votes mailed before the election were counted. The Deukmejian campaign had exploited newly liberalized absentee voting rules and organized a vote-by-mail turnout campaign that was especially effective among gun owners opposed to a gun control measure on the same ballot.

↗CRITICAL THINKING QUESTIONS:

- What is the Bradley Effect?
- Do you know people who voted for or against Obama because of his race?
- The essay above was published before the 2008 presidential election. Do you think the author was correct in his assessment?

>> END

Should public officials use opinion surveys to determine what policies are most popular and then adopt those policies?

Question Sequencing

The order of survey questions may also affect a survey's results. Question order can shape the context of responses. For example, asking about presidential job performance after questions about a particular government policy may affect a president's popularity if that policy is perceived as successful or unsuccessful. Professional researchers try to control this effect by rotating the order in which questions are asked.[32]

Attitudes, Non-Attitudes, and Phantom Opinions

Professional pollsters offer respondents an opportunity to confess that they have not heard of an issue or do not have an opinion. Some survey researchers also ask respondents to indicate the intensity with which they hold their views and take that intensity into account in interpreting survey results.

Phantom opinions are made-up responses from respondents who do not want to appear uninformed.[33] A survey sponsored by the *Washington Post* asked a national sample of Americans this question: "Some people say the 1975 Public Affairs Act should be repealed. Do you agree or disagree that it should be repealed?" The survey found that 24 percent of the sample agreed, while 19 percent said that it should not be repealed. The other 57 percent had no opinion. Ironically, the people with no opinion were the best informed. The Public Affairs Act did not exist. Survey researchers made it up in order to test how many respondents would express an opinion on an issue about which they could obviously have no knowledge.[34]

Interviewer-Respondent Interaction

The race or gender of an interviewer can affect survey results. For example, a survey measuring racial attitudes found black respondents were much more likely to say that white people could be trusted when the interviewer was white than when asked the same question by an African American.[35] Similarly, women are more likely to give pro-choice responses to questions about abortion to female interviewers than they are to male interviewers.[36]

Timing

Even the most carefully conducted survey is only a snapshot of public opinion on the day of the poll. In March 1991, for example, following the American victory in the first Gulf War, the Gallup Poll showed that the approval rating of the first President Bush was 89 percent. Political observers predicted the president would win reelection easily. By August 1992, however, Bush's popularity rating had fallen below 35 percent, and three months later, he was defeated.[37]

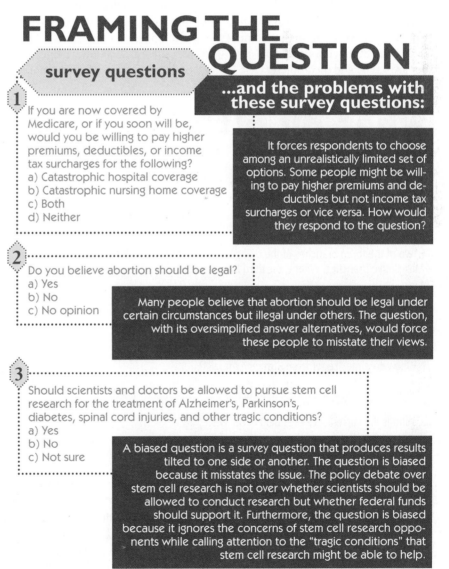

FRAMING THE QUESTION

survey questions

...and the problems with these survey questions:

1 If you are now covered by Medicare, or if you soon will be, would you be willing to pay higher premiums, deductibles, or income tax surcharges for the following?
a) Catastrophic hospital coverage
b) Catastrophic nursing home coverage
c) Both
d) Neither

It forces respondents to choose among an unrealistically limited set of options. Some people might be willing to pay higher premiums and deductibles but not income tax surcharges or vice versa. How would they respond to the question?

2 Do you believe abortion should be legal?
a) Yes
b) No
c) No opinion

Many people believe that abortion should be legal under certain circumstances but illegal under others. The question, with its oversimplified answer alternatives, would force these people to misstate their views.

3 Should scientists and doctors be allowed to pursue stem cell research for the treatment of Alzheimer's, Parkinson's, diabetes, spinal cord injuries, and other tragic conditions?
a) Yes
b) No
c) Not sure

A biased question is a survey question that produces results tilted to one side or another. The question is biased because it misstates the issue. The policy debate over stem cell research is not over whether scientists should be allowed to conduct research but whether federal funds should support it. Furthermore, the question is biased because it ignores the concerns of stem cell research opponents while calling attention to the "tragic conditions" that stem cell research might be able to help.

political
KNOWLEDGE

Political scientist W. Russell Neuman divides the public into three groups based on their knowledge and interest in government and politics. At one end of the spectrum, a large group of people, about a fifth of the population, is indifferent to politics; they have no opinions. At the other end are political junkies, a small group, probably less than 5 percent of the population, who are very interested and informed. The great majority of Americans fits in the middle category. They follow politics halfheartedly. They have opinions on some issues, but their views on many issues are vague and incomplete.[38]

Some groups of Americans are more knowledgeable than others. Men know more about politics than women. Whites are better informed than African Americans. Wealthy people are more knowledgeable than the poor. Republicans know more than Democrats. Well-educated people are better informed than people with less formal schooling.[39]

Knowledgeable Americans vote and cast an informed ballot. In 1994, 70 percent of well-informed survey respondents reported voting in that year's congressional elections. Only 25 percent of less knowledgeable respondents voted. Furthermore, knowledgeable respondents voted for candidates whose views on issues coincided with their own. In contrast, there was almost no relationship between the political issues that low-knowledge voters said mattered to them and the issue positions of the candidates for whom they voted.[40]

Some observers believe political ignorance has led to a "dumbing down" of campaigns, and to negative advertising in particular. Political scientist Samuel Popkin says that candidates now conduct two campaigns: one at informed voters, stressing issues and policy positions, the other directed at less well-informed voters, attacking the character of their opponents.[41]

Support for Democratic Principles

Survey data on gay and lesbian rights raise questions about public support for basic democratic principles of majority rule and minority rights.

what didn't AMERICA KNOW?

	Knew it	Blew it
1. Who delivered the Gettysburg Address?	67%	33%
2. Who was the first president of the U.S.?	92%	8%
3. What is the name of the National Anthem?	58%	42%
4. Two of the three branches of the U.S. government are called the executive and the legislative branches. What is the third branch called?	59%	41%
5. How many U.S. senators are there from each state?	34%	66%
6. In what document are these words found? "We hold these truths to be self-evident, that all men are created equal."	34%	64%
7. Who wrote the "Letter from Birmingham Jail"?	33%	67%
8. What are the first 10 amendments of the U.S. Constitution called?	47%	53%
9. Who is the current vice president of the U.S.?	69%	31%
10. Who is the current chief justice of the U.S. Supreme Court?	17%	83%

Although some Americans are quite knowledgeable about public affairs, a majority of the nation's adults cannot accurately name their own representative in Congress or even one of the U.S. senators from their state. Most Americans are unable to identify the Bill of Rights. Less than a fifth can name the current Chief Justice of the United States.

George H. Gallup, Jr., "How Many Americans Know U.S. History? Part I," October 21, 2003, available at www.gallup.com.

1. Abraham Lincoln 2. George Washington 3. The Star-Spangled Banner 4. Judicial 5. Two 6. Declaration of Independence 7. Martin Luther King, Jr. 8. The Bill of Rights 9. Joe Biden 10. John G. Roberts

Americans believe that "homosexuals should . . . have equal rights in terms of job opportunities" by a substantial 87 percent to 11 percent margin. However, the survey found that 43 percent oppose hiring gays and lesbians as elementary school teachers and 47 percent oppose homosexuals in the clergy.[42]

Do Americans support the democratic principles of majority rule and minority rights? Political scientists have studied this question for decades. During the 1950s, Professor Samuel Stouffer conducted a study to evaluate public opinion toward individual rights. He found a high level of intolerance toward persons with unpopular views. For example, only 27 percent of the persons interviewed would permit "an admitted communist" to make a speech.[43]

In 1960, political scientists James W. Prothro and C. W. Grigg published what has become a classic study of political tolerance. Survey respondents overwhelmingly endorsed the election of public officials by majority vote and stated that people with minority opinions should have the right to express their views. In more specific questions, however, researchers found dramatically less support for minority rights. Respondents said that a communist should not be allowed to take office. Others stated that atheists should not be allowed to speak publicly against religion.[44] Later research has confirmed that Americans are more likely to endorse democratic principles in the

Americans favor civil liberties for groups they like; they oppose civil liberties for groups they dislike. Many Americans dislike Reverend Fred Phelps and the members of his Westboro Baptist Church who picket the funerals of military personnel killed in Iraq and Afghanistan. Phelps and his followers believe that the war is God's punishment for the nation's tolerance of homosexuality.

abstract. One study found that a majority of Americans opposed many of the specific guarantees of individual rights found in the Bill of Rights.[45]

A number of studies conducted in the 1970s concluded that Americans were more tolerant of political diversity. Using questions almost identical to Stouffer's of two decades before, researchers found significantly more Americans willing to tolerate atheists, socialists, and communists. Some concluded that this trend reflected the views of a younger, more urban, and better-educated population.[46]

More recent research contradicts this conclusion. Attitudes toward socialists, communists, and atheists have become more tolerant, but many Americans express intolerant attitudes toward racists and persons advocating military rule. Americans are apparently no more tolerant of persons with unpopular views today than they were in the 1950s. The targets of intolerance have changed, and there are fewer unpopular groups than 50 years ago.[47]

Civil liberties are the protections of the individual from the unrestricted power of government. People may respond to questions about civil liberties based on their perception of a particular group's threat. In the 1950s, many Americans favored limiting free speech for communists. Americans today feel less threatened by communists than by racist groups such as the Ku Klux Klan. When answering survey questions, they express more tolerance for communists than for members of the Klan.[48] In sum, Americans favor civil liberties for groups they like; they oppose them for groups they dislike.

This seeming indifference of many Americans to civil liberties disturbs observers. Tolerance for people of other races, ethnicities, religions, and political beliefs is an

American opinion polls

1824 | The first American poll says Andrew Jackson will defeat John Quincy Adams for the presidency. (He doesn't!)

1932 | George Gallup conducts his first opinion surveys.

1948 | All major opinion polls (including the Gallup Poll) predict that New York Governor Thomas Dewey will defeat Harry Truman. (He doesn't!)

| 1820 | 1830 | 1910 | 1920 | 1930 | 1940 | 1950 |

1916 | The *Literary Digest* prints the first of its presidential polls. Its predictions prove accurate.

1936 | The *Literary Digest* gets it wrong when FDR defeats Landon for reelection.

civil liberties the protection of the individual from the unrestricted power of government.

important underpinning of democracy.[49] Many political theorists believe that a free society requires a high degree of popular support for civil liberties. How, then, can we explain the stability of our democracy when research has often found a lack of support for the fundamental principles of democracy?

Political scientists identify three factors accounting for the preservation of political freedom in the United States. First, the Constitution protects individual rights.[50] These legal guarantees provide an important foundation for individual rights. Second, Americans do not agree on their feared target groups. Some people worry about communists, but others want to silence members of the Klan. Since Americans cannot agree on target groups, they are unable to unite behind undemocratic public policies. Finally, a number of political scientists believe that the attitudes of the general public about civil liberties issues are not nearly as important as the views of **political elites**, the people who exercise a major influence on the policymaking process. Support for democratic principles is stronger among people who are politically active and well-informed than it is among individuals who are politically uninvolved. Democracy endures because those who make policy—political elites—understand and support the principles of majority rule and minority rights.[51]

Political Trust and Political Legitimacy

Political legitimacy is the popular acceptance of a government and its officials as rightful authorities in the exercise of power. Democracy de-

TRUST IN THE GOVERNMENT

Political scientists average the answers to various questions to create a Trust Index. The index fell during the 1960s and 1970s, rose in the 1980s, fell again in the 1990s, increased dramatically after the terrorist attacks on September 11, 2001, and then dropped yet again.

"The NES Guide to Public Opinion and Electoral Behavior," available at www.electionstudies.org

pends on the voluntary cooperation of its citizens. People pay taxes and obey laws because they accept the authority of the government. They seek political change through the electoral process and peacefully accept the outcomes of election contests. If a significant proportion of the population loses trust in the political system, the quality of democracy declines. Tax evasion and disrespect for the rule of law increase. The potential for a revolutionary change in the political order may develop.

Political scientists attempt to measure the level of political trust in society through a set of questions developed by the Center for Political Studies (CPS), a social science research unit at the University of Michigan. The questions probe the degree to which citizens believe that government leaders are honest and competent.

political elites the people who exercise a major influence on the policymaking process.

political legitimacy the popular acceptance of a government and its officials as rightful authorities in the exercise of power.

Political scientists disagree on interpreting the data. Some believe that the figures show Americans have lost confidence in their government. Other political scientists argue that public support for American democracy remains solid. They believe that the survey questions may be poorly worded; they actually measure public approval (or disapproval) of current government officials rather than support for the political system.[52]

Civil Unions in Denmark

In 1989, Denmark became the first country in the world to grant legal recognition to same-sex relationships. The Danish arrangement, which is a form of **civil union**, is known as registered partnership. Since Denmark adopted registered partnerships, five nations (Belgium, Spain, Canada, South Africa, and the Netherlands) have approved same-sex marriage. More than a dozen other countries allow civil unions or registered partnerships, including France, Germany, and the United Kingdom.

The debate over the Danish Registered Partnership Act resembled the current debate over gay marriage in the United States. The proponents of the legislation spoke of the importance of the nation treating all couples equally under the law. They argued that legal recognition of gay unions would promote the development of stable relationships. By discouraging sexual promiscuity, registered partnership would reduce the spread of AIDS and other sexually transmitted diseases. In contrast, opponents of the measure warned that government recognition of same-sex partnerships would weaken support for traditional marriage. The government should protect traditional marriage, they said, by reserving it for traditional couples.

The Danish Registered Partnership Act passed the Danish parliament by a vote of 71 to 47. "Two people of the same sex may have their partnership registered," the law declared. Whenever the word "marriage" or the word "spouse" appears in Danish law, it is construed to include registered partners. For all intents and purposes, then, registered partners are married in the eyes of Danish law.

Nearly 6,000 Danes were classified as registered partners in 2005 compared with more than 2 million married people. Although the number of registered partners has been rising, most gay men and lesbians are not involved in partnerships. About a sixth of same-sex couples are raising children.

Registered partnerships have apparently had no appreciable effect on the marriage rate in Denmark. The long-term trend in countries throughout the region, a trend that predates registered partnerships and same-sex marriage, has been toward lower marriage rates, higher divorce rates, and higher birthrates outside of marriage. In Denmark, the marriage rate was higher in 2000 than it was in 1989 when the registered partnership act was adopted. The divorce rate was roughly the same.

Questions

1. Are registered partnerships (or civil unions) second-class marriages or are they an acceptable compromise between the proponents and opponents of same-sex marriage?

2. Would you expect the adoption of same-sex marriage throughout the United States to have an impact on traditional marriage rates? Why or why not?

3. Why do you think most gay men and lesbians in Denmark are not involved in registered partnerships?

civil union a legal partnership between two men or two women that gives the couple all the benefits, protections, and responsibilities under law that are granted to spouses in a traditional marriage.

Political Efficacy

Political efficacy is the extent to which individuals believe they can influence the policymaking process. Political efficacy is related to participation. People who believe that they can affect government policies are more inclined to participate politically than those who do not.

Internal political efficacy is the assessment by an individual of his or her personal ability to influence the policymaking process. The concept addresses knowledge of the political system and ability to communicate with political decision-makers. Scholars measure internal political efficacy by asking this agree/disagree question: "Sometimes politics and government seem so complicated that a person like me can't really understand what's going on." Agreement with the statement indicates a low level of internal political efficacy. In 2000, 60 percent agreed with the statement compared with 32 percent who disagreed.[53] Internal political efficacy rose during the 1980s and 1990s, when voting turnout was in decline. So it appears that the concept is not related to voter participation. Low levels of internal political efficacy may explain why many Americans do not participate politically in other ways, but they apparently do not account for changes in voter participation rates.

External political efficacy refers to the assessment of an individual of the responsiveness of government to his or her concerns. This concept deals with an individual's evaluation of the willingness of government officials to respond to the views of ordinary citizens. Political scientists have created a Government Responsiveness Index based on responses to questions such as the following: "Over the years, how much attention do you feel the government pays to what the people think when it decides what to do?" The index generally declined from the mid-1960s through the early 1980s, but it has subsequently increased.[54] Scholars believe that external political efficacy is associated with voter participation.[55]

political efficacy the extent to which individuals believe they can influence the policymaking process.

internal political efficacy the assessment by an individual of his or her personal ability to influence the policymaking process.

external political efficacy the assessment of an individual of the responsiveness of government to his or her concerns.

takeaction

FAMILY POLITICS >>

Political scientists believe that families play an important role in the socialization process. Politically active families typically raise children who become politically active adults. Families also pass along their party identification to their offspring, at least initially. Young adults may eventually change their party allegiance to join the party that more closely matches their adult policy preferences.

How did your family impact your political socialization, particularly your level of political involvement and your party identification? Your instructor is going to conduct a class discussion on this topic during an upcoming class session. Prepare to join in the discussion by taking the following steps:

1. Jot down some information about your own level of political involvement and party affiliation. Are you registered to vote? Are you a regular voter? Have you ever joined a political group or participated in a political campaign? How closely do you follow current events? Do you consider yourself a Republican, Democrat, an independent, or a supporter of another political party? Have you always had the same party affiliation?

2. Record your recollections of your family's political involvement and party loyalties. Were your parents or the adults who raised you politically active? What was their political party allegiance?

3. Speak with your parents or other members of your family to verify the accuracy of your recollections. Do their memories match your recollections?

4. Finally, consider the role your family played in your personal political socialization and be prepared to discuss the topic in class.

political
PHILOSOPHY

liberalism the political philosophy that favors the use of government power to foster the development of the individual and promote the welfare of society.

conservatism the political philosophy that government power undermines the development of the individual and diminishes society as a whole.

political right conservatism.

political left liberalism.

right wing conservative.

left wing liberal.

In American politics, the terms *liberalism* and *conservatism* are used to describe political philosophy. **Liberalism** is a political philosophy that favors the use of government power to foster development of the individual and promote the welfare of society. Liberals believe that the government can (and should) advance social progress by promoting political equality, social justice, and economic prosperity. Liberals usually favor government regulation and government spending for social programs. Liberals value social and cultural diversity, and defend the right of individual adult choice on issues such as access to abortion. **Conservatism,** on the other hand, is the political philosophy that government power undermines individual development and diminishes society. Conservatives argue that government regulations and social programs generally harm rather than help. Charities, private businesses, and individuals can solve problems if the government leaves them alone. Conservatives also believe that the government should defend the traditional values of society.

The terms *right* and *left* are also used to describe political ideology. The **political right** refers to conservatism, the **political left** to liberalism. Similarly, **right wing** means conservative; **left wing** means liberal.

Liberals and conservatives approach the problems of the nation differently. Liberals advocate government action to assist disadvantaged groups. They generally support programs such as Social Security, Medicare, and affirmative action programs. In contrast, conservatives argue that government, especially the national government, is too inefficient to solve the nation's social problems. They believe that government should reduce spending on social programs and cut taxes to promote economic growth, which, the conservatives argue, will benefit everyone.

Liberals support government regulation of business. They support environmental-protection laws, consumer-protection regulations, and occupational safety and health standards. Liberals are more likely than conservatives to endorse trade restrictions on foreign companies. Conservatives fear that government reg-

Few issues in the United States are as divisive as the issue of abortion.

ulations will disrupt the market economy. They believe regulations drive up the cost of doing business, increase prices and lower wages.

Consider the issue of the environment. Liberals advocate regulation to ensure clean air and water. They favor government responses to the threat of **global warming,** the gradual warming of the Earth's atmosphere caused by burning fossil fuels and industrial pollutants. In contrast, conservatives want to move slowly on environmental issues to avoid harming economic growth. They prefer market-oriented solutions rather than government mandates.

On social issues, conservatives and liberals trade positions on the role of government. Conservatives favor government intervention, while liberals prefer less government involvement. Conservatives define social issues in terms of their traditional family values. Conservatives generally support rigorous enforcement of pornography laws, the adoption of a constitutional

> **THE TERMS LEFT AND RIGHT COME FROM THE 1789 MEETING OF THE ESTATES GENERAL, THE PARLIAMENT OF PRE-REVOLUTIONARY FRANCE. THE DELEGATES MET IN A HALL AT THE PALACE OF VERSAILLES. THE SEATS ON THE LEFT OF THE HALL WERE RESERVED FOR THE COMMONERS WHO WANTED POLITICAL CHANGE AND REFORM. THE SEATS ON THE RIGHT OF THE HALL WERE USED BY THE NOBILITY, WHO RESISTED CHANGE. THE TERMS LEFT AND RIGHT CAME TO MEAN THE POLITICAL POSITIONS TAKEN BY THE TWO GROUPS.**

amendment against abortion, and the enactment of an amendment permitting school prayer. Conservatives oppose assisted suicide, most stem cell research, and the legalization of same-sex marriage. Liberals prefer that government stay out of these questions except to protect the rights of the individual.

Ironically, both liberals and conservatives criticize government. Liberals say that the government does not act strongly enough to help disadvantaged groups gain economic and political power and that government favors the interests of the rich and powerful. Conservatives, on the other hand, criticize government for interfering with the efficient working of the free enterprise system. Conservatives believe that government economic intervention hurts everyone.

The usefulness of the terms *liberalism* and *conservatism* is limited. Real-life differences between liberals and conservatives are often matters of degree rather than dramatic contrast. In addition, a number of issues do not fit neatly into liberal/conservative divisions. Finally, few Americans are consistently liberal or conservative. Most Americans hold conservative views on some issues, liberal opinions on others.

Are Americans Liberal or Conservative?

Public opinion surveys typically find more self-identified conservatives than liberals. Nonetheless, studies have found that many Americans cannot accurately define liberalism or conservatism. Furthermore, research shows that relatively few people structure their thinking along liberal-conservative lines.[56]

A different way to assess political philosophy is to inquire about the

Liberals believe in the efficacy of government action to solve social problems. President John F. Kennedy phrased the concept in the following terms: "If a free society cannot help the many who are poor, it cannot save the few who are rich."

global warming the gradual warming of the Earth's atmosphere caused by burning fossil fuels and industrial pollutants.

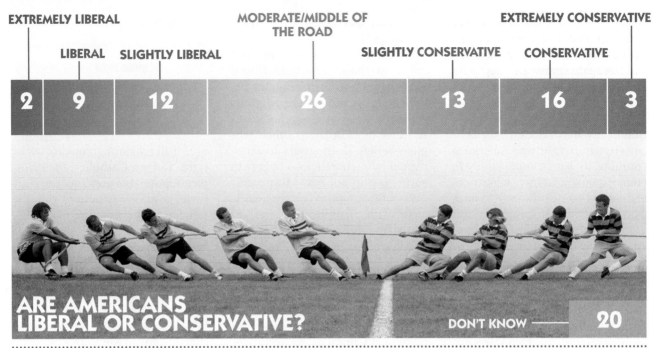

EXTREMELY LIBERAL | LIBERAL | SLIGHTLY LIBERAL | MODERATE/MIDDLE OF THE ROAD | SLIGHTLY CONSERVATIVE | CONSERVATIVE | EXTREMELY CONSERVATIVE

| 2 | 9 | 12 | 26 | 13 | 16 | 3 |

ARE AMERICANS LIBERAL OR CONSERVATIVE?

DON'T KNOW —— 20

According to the National Election Studies (NES), 23 percent of Americans described themselves as slightly liberal, liberal, or extremely liberal in 2004, compared with 32 percent who said they were slightly conservative, conservative, or extremely conservative. Meanwhile, 26 percent described themselves as moderate or middle of the road.

"The NES Guide to Public Opinion and Electoral Behavior," available at www.umich.edu/~nes.

role of government. When asked to choose between "more government services and more spending" or "fewer services to reduce spending," survey respondents favored the former 43 percent to 20 percent, with the rest either in the middle or declaring they don't know.[57]

Surveys show that few Americans favor decreasing or ending federal government involvement in consumer protection, medical research, financing college education, or job training for low-income people.[58]

Survey researchers Albert H. and Susan Davis Cantril's Cantril Index shows that many Americans have mixed feelings about government, but more people support an active government than oppose it. The Cantrils classify 39 percent of adult Americans as steady supporters of government compared to 10 percent who are steady critics. They classify 12 percent of their sample as ambivalent supporters of government and 20 percent as ambivalent critics. Eleven percent of the sample could not be classified.[59]

Opinion Differences Among Groups

Surveys show that political attitudes vary based on factors such as social class, race, and gender. For example, support for gay and lesbian rights is strongest among women, younger adults, people who live on either coast, college graduates, higher-income groups, people who live in urban and suburban areas, Democrats and independents, self-identified liberals, and Catholics. Opposition is greatest among men, older adults, Southerners, people with relatively little formal education, lower-income groups, self-identified conservatives, Republicans, and Protestants.[60]

Social Class. On social welfare issues, lower-income people tend to be more liberal than middle- and upper-income Americans. In contrast, lower-income individuals are often more conservative than other income groups on such non-economic issues as women's rights and the rights of defendants. Lower-income whites are also less support-ive of civil rights for African Americans than are middle-income whites.

Isolationism is the view that the United States should stay away from the affairs of other nations. Lower-income individuals are more isolationist but also more supportive of using military force to deal with other nations. Working-class people often oppose free trade, fearing the loss of jobs to international competition. Middle- and upper-income people are less isolationist, favoring free trade, foreign aid, and negotiated settlements of disputes.[61]

Race & Ethnicity. African Americans and Latinos favor activist government. Members of both minority groups typically support affirmative action, a program designed to ensure equal opportunities in employment and college admissions for racial minorities and women. African Americans, in particular, perceive widespread racial discrimination in

isolationism the view that the United States should stay out of the affairs of other nations.

society and believe that it is the major reason that many African Americans have trouble finding good jobs and adequate housing. They want government to play an active role in the quest for racial equality.

Many whites believe that African Americans have already achieved equality. (In fact, African Americans continue to lag behind whites in employment, income, education, and access to healthcare.) Whites who believe that African Americans are as well off as white Americans are opposed to government programs designed to assist blacks to improve their status.[62]

Although African Americans and Latinos are less likely to support the death penalty than whites, they are more likely to hold conservative views on the issues of abortion and gay marriage. African American and Latino conservatism on these issues reflects relatively high rates of church attendance for both minority groups.[63]

Religion. The **religious left** refers to those who hold liberal views because of their religious beliefs, whereas the phrase **religious right** refers to those who hold conservative views because of their religious beliefs. Both groups feel motivated by their religious beliefs to participate in politics. Most members of the religious left are associated with mainline Protestant Christian churches, such as the Presbyterians, Episcopalians, and Church of Christ (Disciples), or with the Jewish faith. It also includes Buddhists and many people who declare that they are "spiritual" but not associated with organized religion.[64] Christian conservatives tend to be associated with white evangelical Protestant churches, such as Assemblies of God and the Southern Baptist Convention.[65]

religious left those who hold liberal views because of their religious beliefs.

religious right those who hold conservative views because of their religious beliefs.

Not all religious groups are left or right. Roman Catholics, for example, oppose abortion and gay marriage, positions associated with the religious right, but also oppose the death penalty, support civil rights and immigrant rights, and favor government efforts to end poverty.

In contemporary American politics, the religious right has more influence than the religious left. Whereas most mainline Protestant churches have been losing members for years, conservative evangelical churches are growing. Furthermore, church attendance is higher among conservative evangelicals.[66]

African Americans are relatively conservative on the issues of abortion and gay and lesbian rights, reflecting their high rates of church attendance.

Media and Public Opinion

Should the media report the results of their own polls as news? Isn't this the same as "creating" news rather than reporting it?

Should government officials be responsive to public opinion polling?

Overview: The First Amendment was ratified in order to protect free (political) speech, freedom of the press, the right to petition the government for redress of grievances (the right to directly approach and criticize the government), and the right to peaceably assemble. These freedoms are essential if citizens are to engage in the open debate and national discussion necessary for self-rule and democratic politics.

The founders were not blind to the fact that a free and open press (for our purposes, we will use the term "media") would be partisan, at times wrong, and would attempt to mobilize and change public opinion. Contentious and acrimonious public debate is considered to be part of the essence of political freedom. Those at the time of the American founding, however, could not foresee the incredible change in technology and society that today causes citizens to suffer from "information overload." We seek sources of information that can be consumed quickly, accurately, and at little cost.

Historically, the news media has prided itself on providing unbiased and relevant information through which Americans can make informed decisions. Part of this information has been the reporting of political polling, especially in political campaign seasons. A new trend, is developing, though, which has political and media analysts concerned with the quality and bias in reporting public opinion polling data. From Fox News to the *New York Times*, there is concern that editorial positions are being authenticated by self-selected polls which are then reported as "news" in attempts to sway public opinion based on demonstrably false journalism. How is the average, busy citizen to get his or her information? Does this new practice harm the credibility of a necessary, informal political institution?

supporting the use of polling data as news

public opinion polls are a legitimate source of news. In order to make informed decisions, citizens must have access to the same polling data that inform the political and policymaking class.

public opinion polling provides the American people an insight into the politics of the day. Reporting polling data allows individuals to know what their fellow citizens think and desire, where they are in the ideological spectrum, and whether government is adequately addressing these issues.

public opinion polling organizations make their data available on the Internet. Today, most polling organizations make their questions and data available online. This allows citizens to fact-check research and draw conclusions for themselves.

against the use of polling data as news

polling data may be misrepresented to support a media outlet's editorial position. For example, in March 2007, an ABC/BBC poll reported findings on how Iraqis viewed the war in Iraq. In this poll they neglected to mention an oversampling of Sunni Arabs, and this dramatically skewed the poll's result.

polling samples may be skewed to provide a predetermined outcome. Sometimes poll samples determine the outcome of a poll. A case in point would be a poll commissioned by the *Los Angeles Times* in which the sample was heavily skewed toward one political party, with the effective poll result favoring the candidate of that oversampled party.

public opinion polling assumes American democratic government should be responsive to public opinion. The founders designed the constitutional institutions and principles to "slow down" and moderate the effects of public opinion on political institutions with a view to the idea that majority opinion can be unjust. Take, for example, the discriminatory, legal doctrine of "separate but equal."

Because of the growth of conservative Christian churches, active church participation is now associated with political conservatism. At least among whites, the more actively involved people are with religious organizations, the more likely they are to hold conservative political views. For African Americans, the church is a basis for liberal activism on economic issues. Nonetheless, African American churchgoers hold more conservative views on social issues, such as abortion and gay and lesbian rights, than do African Americans who do not participate in a church.[67]

Generation. Younger Americans are more tolerant of ethnic, racial, and social diversity than older adults. People below the age of 30 are more sympathetic to affirmative action and are more likely to favor gay and lesbian rights.[68]

YOUNGER AMERICANS are more *tolerant* of ethnic, racial, and social diversity than OLDER ADULTS

Studies find no evidence that people grow more conservative with age. Instead, age-related differences in political views reflect the impact of socializing events common to a generation.[69] Younger Americans may also be more tolerant because they are better educated than previous generations.[70]

Region. In general, people from the East and West coasts are more liberal than people from the South, Midwest, or Rocky Mountain regions. Most regional differences can be explained by class, race, and religion, but some genuine regional variations based on unique cultural and historical factors may also play a role.

Gender. The phrase **gender gap** refers to differences in party identification and political attitudes between men and women. Women are more likely to vote for Democratic candidates and to favor government programs to provide healthcare and education, and to protect the environment. Women are less likely than men to favor increased defense spending and to support the wars in Afghanistan and Iraq.[71] They hold similar views on the issues of abortion rights, women's equality, and gay marriage.[72]

gender gap differences in party identification and political attitudes between men and women.

CONCLUSION
public opinion
& PUBLIC POLICY

public opinion affects every stage of the policymaking process.

Agenda Building

Candidates and officeholders tend to focus on the issues that interest voters. If polls show that voters are concerned about healthcare, then politicians discuss healthcare. If polls indicate that immigration is a major concern, politicians talk about immigration. Some issues become part of the policy agenda because of the actions of interest groups or public officials. Nonetheless, government officials are unlikely to ignore any issue that is important to a large part of the general public.

Policy Formulation and Adoption

Years ago, political scientist V.O. Key, Jr., introduced the concept of latent opinion to explain the relationship between public opinion and policy formulation and adoption. **Latent opinion** is not what voters think about an issue today, but what public opinion would be by election time if a political opponent made a public official's position on the issue the target of an attack.[73] Elected officials make thousands of policy decisions, and public officials consider public opinion during policy formulation and adoption because they recognize that a future

“PUBLIC OPINION AFFECTS EVERY STAGE OF THE POLICYMAKING PROCESS.”

political opponent could raise the issue during an election campaign.

Contemporary political scientist James A. Stimson introduced the concept of a **zone of acquiescence,** which is the range of policy options acceptable to the public on a particular issue. Stimson says that some policy options are either too conservative or too liberal to be acceptable to a majority of the public. The zone of acquiescence encompasses policy options that lie between the two extremes. The size of the zone varies from issue to issue and may change if public opinion grows more conservative or more liberal. Policymakers tend to choose policy options within the zone of acquiescence; otherwise they risk electoral defeat.[74]

The zone of acquiescence highlights important points about the relationship between public opinion and public policy. First, public opinion affects policy by limiting options. On most issues, the zone of acquiescence is broad enough to include a number of options from which public officials may choose. Public opinion sets this range of acceptable alternatives, but it does not determine which options are selected. Other factors, including the influence of interest groups and political parties, come into play.

Second, the zone of acquiescence does not imply that policies selected will not arouse controversy. The zone of acquiescence is based on majority preferences, but may alarm minorities. Although abortion is legal in the U.S., for example, it remains controversial for many Americans.

Third, the zone of acquiescence is affected by the policymaker's constituency. A **constituency** is the district from which an officeholder is elected. **Constituents** are the people an officeholder represents. A member of Congress elected from a district with a majority of African American constituents, for example, faces a more liberal zone of acquiescence on economic issues than does one whose constituents are mostly upper-income whites. The president, meanwhile, must deal with a nationwide constituency.

Fourth, the zone of acquiescence for an issue changes with public opinion. During the 1980s, public opinion grew more conservative on law and order issues. The range of acceptable policy options available to officials grew more conservative as well. States adopted laws giving harsher sentences to violent criminals, and more states began implementing the death penalty. On other issues, public policy became more liberal as public opinion grew more liberal, especially in large urban areas whose residents are more likely to hold liberal views on the issue than people living in small towns and rural areas.[75]

Policy Implementation and Evaluation

Policymakers consider public opinion, at least indirectly, in policy implementation. Officials enforce

latent opinion what public opinion would be at election time if a political opponent made a public official's position on the issue the target of a campaign attack.

zone of acquiescence the range of policy options acceptable to the public on a particular issue.

constituency the district from which an officeholder is elected.

constituents the people an officeholder represents.

policies that enjoy broad public support. As public sentiment has mounted against drunk driving, officials have adopted tougher DWI laws, and enforced them more aggressively. In contrast, the Supreme Court's decision against state-sponsored prayer in schools enjoys relatively little public support. Many school officials ignore violations until parents complain.

Finally, public opinion influences evaluation. Public officials are more likely to scrutinize policies that have proved unpopular or lack strong public support. Congress and the press are more likely to investigate a program that is perceived as ineffective or that is unpopular with the public, as well.

the THINK SPOT
www.thethinkspot.com

1 The process whereby individuals acquire political attitudes, knowledge, and beliefs is known as which of the following?

A. Political efficacy

B. Political socialization

C. Political trust

D. Political science

2 Which of the following statements about the socialization process is NOT true?

A. Political socialization ends when individuals reach their early 20s.

B. Young children typically identify with the same political party as their parents.

C. Schools historically have taught the children of immigrants to be patriotic Americans.

D. Personal involvement in religious organizations is associated be political participation.

3 Which of the following agents of socialization plays an important role in shaping the party identification of youngsters?

A. Family   B. School

C. Peers   D. Media

4 The universe for a study designed to measure the attitudes of college students would be which of the following?

A. The individuals who are interviewed for the study

B. All college-age adults

C. All college students

D. All Americans

5 How often will a professionally administered survey differ from the universe by more than 3 percentage points merely on the basis of chance?

A. Never. If the sample is truly random, it will never differ by more than the margin of error.

B. One time in 20. Even a perfectly drawn sample will by chance be outside the margin of error 5 percent of the time.

C. 3 percent of the time. The margin of error indicates the error factor built into a survey.

D. One time in five. A well-conducted survey will be wrong 20 percent of the time.

6 A public opinion poll taken a month before the election has a margin of error of 3 percentage points. The poll shows Candidate A ahead of Candidate B 46 percent to 44 percent, with the rest undecided. What is the best analysis of the result of the poll?

A. Candidate A is ahead by at least 2 percentage points but may actually be ahead by 5 percentage points.

B. Candidate A is ahead but it is impossible to know by how much.

C. Candidate B is actually ahead because Candidate A did not reach the 50 percent support level.

D. The candidates are in a statistical tie because the difference in their support is within the margin of error.

7 A major Internet provider regularly conducts online polls. Sometimes tens of thousands of people participate. Would the results of these polls be accurate?

A. Yes. Everyone has a chance to participate.

B. No. The sample size is too small.

C. No. The sample size is too large.

D. Probably not. It is unlikely that the sample is a representative sample of the universe.

8 A survey conducted October 1 shows Candidate A with 55 percent support and Candidate B with 40 percent. What is the best evaluation of the survey?

A. Candidate A is ahead today but surveys can't predict the future.

B. Neither candidate is ahead because the survey is within the margin of error.

C. Candidate A will win by a 15-percentage-point margin.

D. Candidate A will win by a margin of 11 to 19 percentage points.

9 Which of the following statements is NOT true about political knowledge?

A. Only a minority of Americans is especially knowledgeable about politics and government.

B. Knowledgeable Americans are more likely to vote than people who lack political information.

C. Young people are more knowledgeable about politics and government than are older adults.

D. Well-informed voters are more likely to support candidates whose views on issues of importance to them coincide with their own than are voters who are poorly informed.

10 An opinion survey includes this question: "Professor ABC at State University has written that the United States deserved the 9/11 attacks because it supports Israel and undemocratic Arab governments. Should the professor be fired?" What would you expect the survey to show?

A. A majority would oppose firing the professor because most Americans support freedom of speech.

B. A majority would support firing the professor because most Americans oppose freedom of speech.

C. A majority would support firing the professor because they are outraged by his position on 9/11 and aren't considering the civil liberties issue.

D. A majority would oppose firing the professor because they agree with his point of view.

11 Which of the following groups would you expect to express the highest level of support for civil liberties?

A. Low-income people

B. Political elites

C. People who seldom, if ever, vote

D. Recent immigrants

12 The popular acceptance of a government and its officials as rightful authorities in the exercise of power is a good definition of which of the following?

A. Political efficacy   B. Political tolerance

C. Political legitimacy   D. Opinion leaders

13 Which of the following would be a likely result of a low level of political legitimacy in a society?

A. Election turnout would be high.

B. Most people would voluntarily obey laws and regulations.

C. People wanting political change would turn to the electoral system rather than violence to bring about change.

D. None of the above

14 Latent opinion becomes important only if:

A. A voter understands how the government works.

B. A voter thinks that government is not interested in his or her views.

C. Men and women agree on a political position.

D. A political opponent makes an issue of a politician's position.

15 Which of the following statements reflects a high level of internal political efficacy?

A. "I don't believe that government officials care what I think."

B. "I have a good understanding of how the government works."

C. "I think that most of the people running the government are crooks."

D. "Sometimes politics and government seem so complicated that a person like me can't understand it."

16 The assessment of an individual of the responsiveness of government to his or her concerns is a definition of which of the following?

A. Political trust

B. External political efficacy

C. Internal political efficacy

D. Political legitimacy

17 Which of the following positions would be most likely to be taken by a conservative?

A. "Government has a responsibility to ensure that all Americans have access to affordable healthcare."

B. "Government should act aggressively to adopt regulations to slow global warming."

C. "Government has a responsibility to protect the unborn by limiting access to abortion."

D. "Government should address the problem of homelessness by providing more public housing."

18 Which of the following statements reflects a liberal ideology?

A. The government that governs least is best.

B. Government regulations often do more harm than good.

C. The government has no business telling women that they must carry a fetus to term.

D. All of the above

19 Which of the following statements about the gender gap is correct?

A. Woman are more likely than men to vote Republican.

B. Woman are more likely than men to be pro-choice.

C. Woman are more likely than men to favor American military intervention abroad.

D. Women are more likely than men to favor government programs to provide healthcare and education.

20 How would Professor James Stimson explain the relationship between public opinion and the policymaking process?

A. Elected officials can adopt any policy because most Americans are too uninformed to know or care.

B. Policymakers must follow public opinion closely or risk being voted out of office.

C. Public opinion sets limits on policymakers, but within those limits policymakers are free to act.

D. If selected policies turn out badly, voters punish the officials who adopted them by voting them out of office.

KNOW *the* **score**

18–20 correct: Congratulations! You are well informed!

15–17 correct: Your political knowledge is a bit low—be sure to review the key terms and visit TheThinkSpot.

<14 correct: Reread the chapter more thoroughly.

1. B; 2. A; 3. A; 4. C; 5. B; 6. D; 7. D; 8. A; 9. C; 10. C; 11. B; 12. C; 13. D; 14. D; 15. D; 16. B; 17. C; 18. C; 19. D; 20. C

Gender

Women are more likely to vote than men, but men are more likely to engage in other forms of political participation. In 2004, 60 percent of women reported that they voted compared with 56 percent of men.[24] Substantially more men than women are disqualified from voting because of criminal convictions. Women are just as likely as men to participate in election campaigns, but they are less likely to contribute money to political campaigns, contact public officials, or join political organizations.[25]

These data reflect differences in resources and psychological engagement between men and women. Women on average have lower average incomes than men. As you have read, income is closely associated with forms of participation other than voting. Furthermore, surveys indicate that men are more informed about and interested in politics and government than women, even when they have the same level of education.[26]

trends in
VOTER TURNOUT

Political scientists who study election participation measure voter turnout relative to the size of the **voting eligible population (VEP)**, the number of U.S. residents who are legally qualified to vote. The VEP differs from the **voting age population (VAP)**, which is the number of U.S. residents who are 18 years of age or older, because it excludes individuals who are ineligible to cast a ballot. In contrast to the VAP, the VEP does not include non-citizens, convicted criminals (depending on state law), and people who are mentally incapacitated.

The 2004 and 2008 presidential elections suggest that the United States is experiencing a voting revival. After years of declining or flat electoral participation rates, voter turnout has surged to a level not seen in nearly 40 years. The increase reflected the result of massive voter mobilization efforts coupled with high public interest in the

voting eligible population (VEP) the number of U.S. residents who are legally qualified to vote.

voting age population (VAP) the number of U.S. residents who are 18 years of age or older.

election. The two major political parties, supported by their interest group allies, organized sophisti-

think

Should people with prior criminal convictions be permanently disqualified from voting?

cated get-out-the-vote (GOTV) campaigns in 2004 and 2008, focusing on the **battleground states**, which are swing states in which the relative strength of the two major party presidential candidates is close enough so that either candidate could conceivably carry the state. Campaign volunteers and paid organizers telephoned, mailed, e-mailed, or visited millions of potential voters, encouraging them to go to the polls. Exposure to intense campaign activity increases political engagement, especially among low-income voters, a group with typically low voter turnout rates.[27] In the meantime, hot-button issues such as the war in Iraq, the war on terror, gay marriage, healthcare reform, taxes, high gas prices, and the economy energized citizens to go to the polls. According to the ANES, 40 percent of Americans said they were "very much interested" in the 2004 presidential campaign, the highest level of interest in the history of the poll and 14 percentage points higher than the level of interest expressed in 2000.[28] Interest in the 2008 election may have been even higher.

battleground states swing states in which the relative strength of the two major-party presidential candidates is close enough so that either candidate could conceivably carry the state.

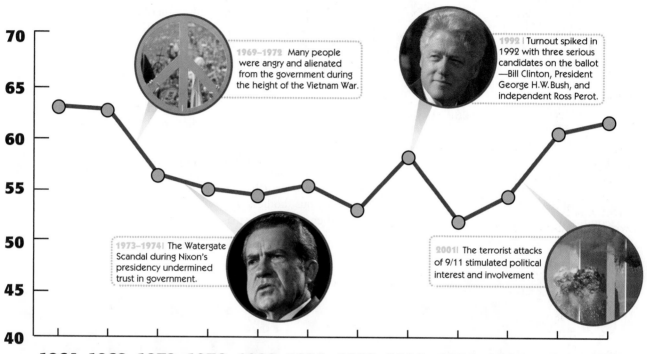

1969–1972 Many people were angry and alienated from the government during the height of the Vietnam War.

1992 Turnout spiked in 1992 with three serious candidates on the ballot —Bill Clinton, President George H.W. Bush, and independent Ross Perot.

1973–1974 The Watergate Scandal during Nixon's presidency undermined trust in government.

2001 The terrorist attacks of 9/11 stimulated political interest and involvement

More than 62 percent of the VEP cast ballots in the 1964 presidential election, capping a steady 36-year rise in voter turnout. For the next 30 years, voter participation rates declined, reaching to a 70-year low in 1996 at 51.7 percent. Election turnout subsequently rebounded to 54.2 percent in 2000, 60.3 percent in 2004, and 61.6 percent in 2008.

participation rates in
COMPARATIVE PERSPECTIVE

Voting turnout in the United States is relatively low compared to other industrialized democracies. According to data collected by the International Institute for Democracy and Electoral Assistance, the United States lags behind most other countries in the world in electoral participation in national legislative elections.[29]

More than a fourth of the potential electorate in the United States is not registered to vote.[30] Political scientists identify three factors that result in the relatively lower American voter turnout rate. First, American election procedures are more cumbersome than they are in most

think Does it really matter that many Americans do not vote?

separation of powers the division of political power among executive, legislative, and judicial branches of government.

other democracies. Before Americans can vote in most states, they must register, usually no later than 30 days before an election. In most other democracies, the government takes the initiative to register eligible voters. American elections traditionally take place on Tuesday, whereas other countries declare a national holiday so citizens can vote without missing work. The United States also holds more frequent elections and elects larger numbers of public officials. Many Americans stay home, confused by the length and complexity of the ballot.[31]

Second, voter participation rates in the United States are lower because American political parties are weaker than those of other democracies. Strong political parties increase voter turnout by educating citizens about candidates and issues, stimulating interest in elections, and mobilizing citizens to vote. Political scientist G. Bingham Powell Jr. estimates that if American political parties were more centralized and had stronger ties to other social organizations, such as labor unions, religious bodies, and ethnic groups, then voter participation would rise by as much as 10 percent.[32]

Finally, many American voters stay home because they do not perceive that elections have much impact on policy. Winning candidates may not be able to keep promises because of **separation of powers**, the division of political authority among the executive, legislative, and judicial branches of government. During the 2006 election campaign, for example, Democratic congressional candidates called for the withdrawal of American troops from Iraq. Even though the Democrats captured majorities in both the House and Senate, they could not keep this promise. Their majority was too slim to pass proposals to bring home the troops, or to override President George W. Bush's veto.

> **"I was just too busy."**
>
> The #1 reason Americans give for not voting is that they couldn't find the time.

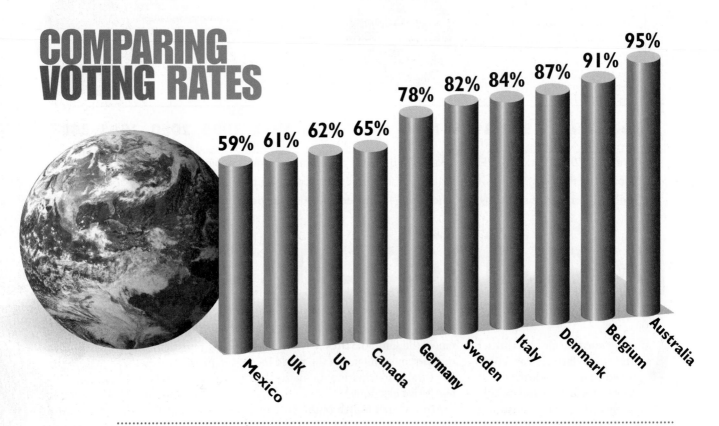

COMPARING VOTING RATES

Mexico 59% | UK 61% | US 62% | Canada 65% | Germany 78% | Sweden 82% | Italy 84% | Denmark 87% | Belgium 91% | Australia 95%

Voting turnout in most recent national election.

108 CHAPTER 5 | political participation

Compulsory Voting in Australia

Compulsory voting is the legal requirement that citizens participate in national elections. It is a low-cost, efficient remedy to the problem of low turnout. Voter participation rates are almost 20 percent higher in nations with compulsory voting than they are in other democracies.[33] Almost everyone votes in Australia, a nation that has had compulsory voting since 1924. For example, voter turnout was 94 percent in the 2004 national election.[34]

The Australian Election Commission (AEC) enforces the nation's compulsory voting law. The AEC sends a "please explain" letter to people who fail to vote in a particular election. Election no-shows can either pay a fine or offer an explanation. If the AEC decides that the explanation is valid, it can waive the fine. The courts settle disputes between the AEC and individual non-voters over the validity of excuses. The proportion of Australians fined for failing to vote never exceeds 1 percent of the electorate.[35]

Political scientists believe that compulsory voting strengthens political parties. Because parties do not have to devote resources to turning out the vote, they can focus on persuasion and conversion. Compulsory voting builds party loyalty. Survey research in Australia finds that most Australian voters express firm and longstanding commitments to a party. You have read that lower-income people are less likely to vote than middle-income citizens. So, compulsory voting also benefits political parties representing the working-class interests more than those representing middle- and upper-income voters because lower-income people are less likely to vote than middle-income citizens.

Questions

1. Does the problem of non-voting need a legal remedy?

2. Do you think compulsory voting in the United States would increase turnout substantially?

3. Do you think that the United States will ever adopt compulsory voting? Why or why not?

compulsory voting the legal requirement that citizens participate in national elections.

Liberal Party lteaders watch election results as their party loses power in the 2007 election.

6 THE

> **WHAT'S AHEAD**

The Media Landscape
Covering the News
Media Biases
Conclusion: The Media
& Public Policy

Even though YouTube has been online only since 2005, it has become a significant media outlet with the capacity to make or break a political campaign. Ask former Virginia Senator George Allen. In 2006, Allen was a heavy favorite to win reelection to the U.S. Senate. Then his campaign unraveled after an incident at a political rally in southwest Virginia. S. R. Sidarth, a 20-year-old college student, was videotaping Allen's remarks. Allen chose to introduce Sidarth to the crowd. "Let's give a welcome to Macaca, here," said the senator. "Welcome to America and the real world of Virginia."[1] Sidarth, a native-born American citizen of Indian descent, was embarrassed and offended by the remark.

The "Macaca Incident" became Allen's undoing. Sidarth quickly posted the tape on YouTube.[2] Allen tried to explain later that he called Sidarth a Macaca because of his Mohawk-style haircut, but bloggers pointed out that some European cultures use Macaca as a racial slur against African immigrants. The extensive coverage of the "Macaca Incident" was probably the single most important factor in Allen's defeat for reelection.[3]

YouTube and other new technologies have changed the political environment for candidates and officeholders. Before camcorders, YouTube, weblogs, and cable TV, the "Macaca Incident" might have gone unreported. At the most, it would have been a one-day newspaper story with little impact on the campaign. Camcorders enable campaign workers, reporters, and even ordinary citizens to tape candidate speeches, campaign rallies, government meetings, and other events that might have gone unrecorded in the past. Videotape is critical for coverage on cable news outlets. Millions of people watched the YouTube video of Allen calling out the young college student and formed their own opinions about the Senator's behavior.

MEDIA

ESSENTIALS...

after studying Chapter 6, students should be able to answer the following questions:

> How would you describe the media landscape in the United States, and what has been the impact of YouTube and other new communication technologies on the policymaking environment?

> How does media consolidation affect news coverage? How do candidates and officeholders attempt to manipulate news coverage?

> Are the news media biased?

> What is the role of the media in the policymaking process?

the media
LANDSCAPE

in contrast to much of the world, there is little direct government ownership of media outlets in the United States. The federal government operates the Armed Forces Radio and Television Service, which provides news and entertainment to members of the U.S. Armed Forces worldwide. Many local entities, including cities, schools, and colleges, operate cable television stations. City governments may use their cable television channels to air city council meetings and other public service programming. Universities and colleges sometimes operate radio stations.

The Public Broadcasting Service (PBS) and National Public Radio (NPR) are private non-profit media services with public and private financial support. PBS is a non-profit private corporation that is owned jointly by hundreds of member tele-vision stations throughout the United States; NPR is a non-profit membership organization of radio stations. The Corporation for Public Broadcasting is a government agency chartered and funded by the U.S. government to promote public broadcasting. It provides some funding for both PBS and NPR. Public radio and television stations also benefit from corporate donations and financial contributions from the general public. PBS and NPR regularly interrupt their programming to ask their viewers and listeners to pledge their financial support.

Private businesses, often large corporations, own and operate most media outlets in the United States. Most **print media** (newspapers and

print media newspapers and magazines.

ARE YOU SIRIUS?

In the final days of the 2008 election campaign, Sirius satellite radio shock jock Howard Stern illustrated how new media contrasts with traditional media. While traditional media espouses objectivity and informed debate, new media has few implicit or explicit rules and begets viral response and participation.

Stern dispatched sidekick Sal to Harlem to interview voters on why they were voting for given candidates. Sal found several Obama supporters, and he then stated John McCain's positions as Obama's and asked supporters if they agreed with those policies. All of them did. One even professed that Sarah Palin was a fine running mate for Obama. (Sal also found a McCain supporter who embraced Obama's policies when they were presented as though they were McCain's.) The interviews were soon up on YouTube, where they were heard more than 300,000 times. Further, they spawned numerous mocking Internet posts, as well as outraged responses from people who thought the bit was racist.

magazines) and **broadcast media** (television, radio, and the Internet) outlets are part of large chains. Consolidation is an important trend in media ownership. The ten largest newspaper groups control a majority of newspaper circulation in the nation. Most television stations belong to national networks, such as CBS, NBC, ABC, Fox, WB, or UPN. Clear Channel Communication and Cumulus Media own hundreds of radio stations, including many in the same city.[4] Cross-media ownership is common as well, in which one corporation owns several types of media. The Tribune Company, for example, owns the *Chicago Tribune* newspaper as well as several radio and television stations in the Chicago area and dozens of other newspapers, television stations, and radio stations around the country.[5]

The media landscape is changing. In terms of circulation and ratings, many mainstream media outlets, especially newspapers, newsmagazines, and the network evening news, have been in decline for years. Between 2001 and 2007, daily newspaper circulation fell by 8 percent; Sunday newspaper circulation dropped by 11 percent. Circulation for the "big three" newsmagazines (*Time*, *Newsweek*, and *U.S. News*) is falling. Ratings for the network evening news and morning news shows are in a long decline as well. Over the past 25 years, the combined audience for the network evening news has fallen on average by a million

SOME OF WHAT NEWS CORPORATION OWNS:

NEWSPAPERS: MORE THAN 175 NEWSPAPERS WORLDWIDE

PROGRAMMING & PRODUCTION: FOX TELEVISION

BOOKS: HARPERCOLLINS

MAGAZINES: NEWS AMERICA MARKETING GROUP

SATELLITE: SKY NEWS

FILM: FOX STUDIOS

INTERNET: INTERMIX

MISC: RECORDS, DIGITAL TECHNOLOGY, SPORTS TEAMS

CEO: Rupert Murdoch
Number of Employees: 44,000

viewers a year.[6] (See figure on the following page.)

Whereas traditional media sources are in decline, the **new media**, a term describing alternative media sources, such as the Internet, cable television, and satellite radio, are in ascendance. Young people in particular are turning away from traditional media sources in favor of the new media.[7] In 1992, newspapers and television network news were the most important reported media sources for news about that year's presidential campaign. By 2004, however, the most important reported sources of information about the presidential contest were newspapers, cable television, network television, radio, and the Internet.[8] Fox News, CNN, and MSNBC offer news coverage around the clock. Radio talk shows offer news and opinion much of the day. In the meantime, anyone with a computer can create a website or write a **weblog or blog**, an online personal journal or newsletter that is regularly updated. Although online news

young people in particular are turning away from traditional media sources in favor of the new media

broadcast media television, radio, and the Internet.

new media a term used to refer to alternative media sources, such as the Internet, cable television, and satellite radio.

weblog or blog an online personal journal or newsletter that is regularly updated.

think

What effect might media consolidation have on the content of the news you consume on television, in newspapers, and on the radio?

Arianna Huffington's blog, the Huffington Post, is a popular online destination for people seeking news and opinion from a liberal perspective.

sources vary considerably in quality and credibility, some have become important sources of information. The Matt Drudge website, the *Drudge Report*, was the first media source to break the news about the relationship between White House intern Monica Lewinsky and President Bill Clinton. Blogs in particular are important opinion outlets. In fact, liberal bloggers have become such an important source of opinion leadership in the Democratic Party that presidential candidates have hired some of them to write blogs for their campaign websites.

Candidates and elected officials have adapted to the new media environment by using the Internet for communication and fundraising. Between 1996 and 2004, the percentage of major party candidates for Congress with campaign websites increased from 22 percent to 81 percent.[9] Although every major presidential candidate has an online presence in 2008, Barack Obama used the Internet more effectively than any of his opponents, raising millions of dollars online.

Network evening news viewership has been steadily declining for years, as more people turn to alternative sources of news.

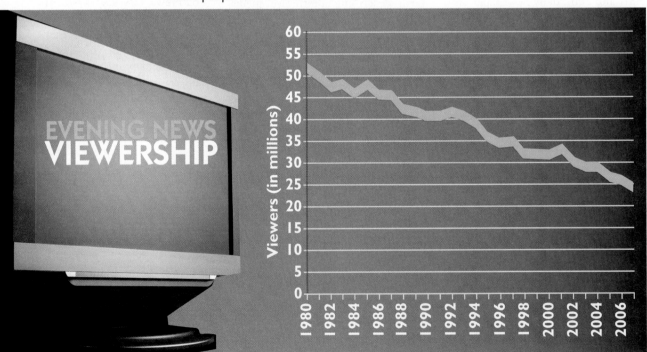

Source: Nielsen Media Research

Government Control of the Media in Cuba

The government tightly controls the media in Cuba. The Cuban government owns the electronic media and controls its content. Foreign news agencies are forced to hire local journalists through government offices if they wish to cover news stories in Cuba. Independent journalists are subject to harassment, detention, and physical attacks. Journalists found guilty of publishing anti-government propaganda or of insulting government officials can be sentenced to long prison terms. According to Reporters Without Borders, an international non-profit organization that advocates freedom of the press, two dozen journalists were held in Cuban prisons in poor conditions in 2008.[10]

The Cuban government attempts to control Internet access by banning private Internet connections. As a result, less than 2 percent of the Cuban population has Internet access. People who want to surf the web or check their e-mail must go to Internet cafés, universities, or other public sites where their activities can be closely monitored. The computers in Internet cafes and hotels have software installed to alert police whenever it spots "subversive" words. Cuban residents who write articles critical of the Cuban government for foreign websites are subject to 20-year prison terms.[11]

The U.S. government attempts to break the Cuban government's monopoly on information with Radio Martí, which broadcasts on shortwave and medium-wave transmitters from Miami, Florida. Miami's most popular Spanish-language AM radio station, powerful enough to be heard throughout Cuba, also carries an hour of news from Radio Martí each night at midnight. The Cuban government jams the shortwave and medium-wave Radio Martí broadcasts throughout the island, and the AM radio station in Havana, so their effectiveness is questionable.

Questions to Consider

1. Can a country be a democracy without a free press? Why or why not?

2. Is it ever appropriate for a government to manage the news media?

3. Should the United States continue to fund Radio Martí?

Young Cubans cheer for a protest singer against Cuban police methods at a rally.

covering
THE NEWS

a major goal of news media outlets is to attract as large an audience as possible. Newspaper advertising rates depend on readership. Arbitron ratings of listeners determine advertising rates for radio stations; Nielsen ratings count television viewers. Online advertising rates depend on website traffic. Even non-profit media outlets such as PBS and NPR want to attract large audience support for their programming, in hopes of having more successful pledge drives.

Media outlets take different approaches to building an audience. Television networks, big city newspapers, and newsmagazines aim to attract as large an audience as possible. They cover mainstream news from a middle-of-the-road perspective with an eye to entertainment value by highlighting dramatic events and celebrities. Stories about Britney Spears get more coverage than in-depth analyses of budget policy. Reports on crime, traffic accidents, and severe weather dominate local news to the near exclusion of serious coverage of local policy issues. In contrast, other media outlets try to build a niche audience by targeting audiences based on political philosophy, issue focus, or religious values. Political activists can find a set of websites, blogs, radio talk shows, magazines, and television shows that reinforce their point of view.

Media consolidation affects news coverage. Because of chain ownership, newspaper stories written for the *New York Times* or *Washington Post* may appear in identical form in local newspapers around the nation. In any given week, all three major newsmagazines may feature the same cover story. Meanwhile, local radio and television stations rely on network news feeds for national news. As a result, news outlets around the country tend to focus on the same handful of national stories each day, often told from the same perspective and sometimes in the same words. Because of staff reductions, local media outlets focus on national election coverage rather than state and local contests.[12]

Campaign organizations attempt to manage news coverage to present their candidates in the most positive light. Indeed, the presidential campaigns of Reagan in 1980 and 1984 and George H. W. Bush in 1988 were the prototype of campaign control of news media coverage. The Reagan-Bush strategy, which most campaigns now attempt to copy, was based on several principles. First, campaign managers choose a single theme to emphasize each campaign day, such as crime, the environment, or defense. If the candidate and the members of the candidate's team address the same issue and only that issue, the news media will be

POLITICS & THE INTERNET

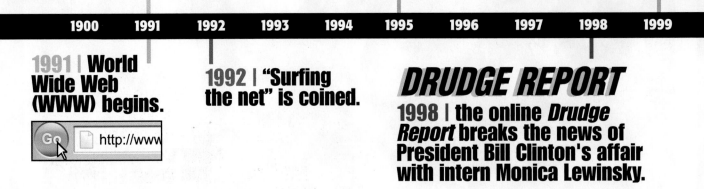

1991 | High Performance Computing and Communication Act of 1991 (sponsored by then Senator Al Gore) leads to the information superhighway.

1996 | equal numbers of voters report getting information from websites and from periodicals.

1999 | Sean Fanning creates NAPSTER; the Blackberry is introduced.

| 1900 | 1991 | 1992 | 1993 | 1994 | 1995 | 1996 | 1997 | 1998 | 1999 |

1991 | World Wide Web (WWW) begins.

Go http://www

1992 | "Surfing the net" is coined.

DRUDGE REPORT

1998 | the online *Drudge Report* breaks the news of President Bill Clinton's affair with intern Monica Lewinsky.

Politics more popular than than "American Idol"? It was in 2008.

World Series	18.8 million viewers
American Idol	24 million viewers
Obama Infomercial	33.6 million viewers
Sarah Palin Convention Speech	37.2 million viewers
Obama Convention Speech	38.4 million viewers
McCain Convention Speech	38.9 million viewers
First Presidential Debate	52.4 million viewers
Third Presidential Debate	56.5 million viewers
Second Presidential Debate	63.2 million viewers
Vice Presidential Debate	69.6 million viewers

The major events of the 2008 presidential campaign consistently received better television ratings than entertainment programs. Even Barack Obama's infomercial, which was a paid 30-minute campaign commercial run a week before the election, had better ratings than the last game of the baseball World Series and the finale of "American Idol."

more likely to focus on that issue in their daily campaign reports.

Second, the campaign selects an eye-catching visual backdrop for its candidate that reemphasizes the theme of the day, such as the Statue of Liberty, a retirement home, or a military base. In 1988, George H. W. Bush even staged a campaign event in a factory that made American flags. Campaign organizers try to ensure that everyone in the audience is friendly so that television images convey the impression of popular support. When President George W. Bush ran for reelection in 2004, he typically appeared at invitation-only rallies to ensure that news reports would be filled with pictures of smiling faces and cheering crowds.

Finally, campaign managers carefully brief the candidate to stick with the campaign script. Each speech includes one or two carefully worded phrases that can be used as

2001 | MoveOn.org is founded as a news source and fundraiser for liberal causes.

2003 | Howard Dean's campaign depends on online giving, bypassing traditional fundraising activities.

2007 | Microsoft is fined $1.3 billion by EU for violating EU free competition rules

2000	2001	2002	2003	2004	2005	2006	2007	2008

2000 | Dot.com bubble bursts.

2002 | 58.5% of U.S. population uses the Internet regularly.

2005 | YouTube is launched.

2008 | Obama's website collects $500 million in political contributions during the 2008 campaign.

WIKIPEDIA
The Free Encyclopedia

Media 6.0 vs. the Typewriter

Does regulation of the Internet media infringe upon Americans' press, speech, and grievance rights? Why or why not?

Does the traditional media itself need a "watchdog," and can the Internet media perform this function to ensure accountability on the part of the press?

Overview: When a gunman opened fire on Virginia Tech's campus in April, 2007, many Americans went straight to their computers for information about the event. From the campus and community, witnesses and victims began sharing cellphone photos and videos, text messages, and e-mails with authorities, friends, and loved ones. This information and the resulting commentary became immediately available on websites like Wikipedia, which reported an average of four visits a second for the first two days after the shooting, dramatically diminishing the authority of traditional media to frame the story.

In addition to the traditional press, politicians are being held accountable and subjected to scrutiny by the In-

ternet media. For example, in the 2004 presidential contest, John Kerry had to address incorrect or false statements he made on the Senate floor in 1986, statements dredged up through Internet research and posted on political blogs. How have elected politicians and traditional media responded to this new reality? By calling for regulation of Internet political speech and media, of course!

Such media luminaries as the *New York Times* editorial page have called for subjecting the Internet media to the same restrictions and standards as the traditional press. Many Internet commentators consider this an attempt to "rein in" or staunch the growing audience and influence

of the new nontraditional media by having government action regulate the increasing crowd of "citizen journalists" who are simply exercising First Amendment rights. The *Times* and others argue that untrained journalists are not capable of providing superior quality and content, but the media marketplace seems to be telling a different story.

Legislation has been introduced to make Internet communication subject to the Bipartisan Campaign Reform Act (BCRA)'s "promote, attack, support, or oppose" rule in which any of those activities can be interpreted as "campaign" speech, and thus become subject to federal regulation.

supporting new media regulation

there is no editorial oversight. A primary reason for the quality enjoyed by traditional news establishments is that there are experienced, educated, and expert editors and producers who can discern whether a source is trustworthy and valid. Untrained journalists typically do not have the requisite experience or education to make that call.

it is difficult for news consumers to determine advocacy from reporting. Many Internet media sites not only report news, but engage in political support as well. It is difficult for the average news consumer to separate news from advocacy, so these sites should be subject to the same restrictions and guidelines as traditional media.

no First Amendment right is absolute. Acrimonious debate and false or misreporting of events harm the quality of the American polity's discourse and knowledge, and government regulation is a proper solution to assuring a well-informed and engaged citizenry.

against new media regulation

a free press is considered a bulwark against governmental corruption and tyranny. All citizens have the right to investigate government corruption or waste and publish their findings. A free press can force government accountability and pressure government and elected officials to act in the public interest.

the new Internet media acts as a watchdog over the traditional press. The Internet media has exposed misreporting by the *New York Times*, CBS News, and the *Los Angeles Times*, among others, and the Internet media are forcing accountability on both journalists and editors/producers alike.

Americans have the First Amendment right for the redress of grievances. Not only does the Internet allow Americans to expose political corruption, but it also allows Americans to opine and discuss government and politics without the filter of editors and producers.

President George W. Bush greets military pilots after landing on their aircraft carrier in 2003. He then used the carrier as a stage from which to deliver a speech proclaiming an end to combat operations in Iraq.

sound bites on the evening news. A **sound bite** is a short phrase taken from a candidate's speech by the news media for use on newscasts. Candidates who lack discipline or who are prone to gaffes distract from their own message.

Once in office, elected officials establish sophisticated communications operations to manage the news. President George W. Bush's communications operation had 63 full-time employees organized among offices of communication, media affairs, speechwriting, global communications, press, and pho-

tography. Other communication employees worked in the offices of the vice president, first lady, and the National Security Council. Altogether, the Bush administration employed more than 300 people full-time to manage and support its communications operation.[13]

The Bush administration's communications strategy attempted to tie policy, politics, and communications together. Professor Bruce Miroff

says that the Bush administration depicted the war in Iraq as if it were a professional wrestling match in

"Brownie, You're doing a heck of a job."

which the audience (the American people) watches the good guy (President Bush) overpower the bad guy (Saddam Hussein). President Bush declared victory on May 1, 2003 after landing a jet on the deck of the aircraft carrier *Abraham Lincoln*. Bush, dressed in a green flight suit, used the aircraft carrier as a stage to announce that combat operations in Iraq were over. A large banner over the president's head read "Mission Accomplished."[14]

sound bite a short phrase taken from a candidate's speech by the news media for use on newscasts.

Katrina flood survivors paint a plea for help on their roof in September 2005. The power and proliferation of these images proved a communications catastrophe for the Bush administration.

Candidates and officeholders do not always succeed in managing the media. The proliferation of media outlets and the emergence of new communications technologies, such as YouTube and blogging, increases the likelihood that candidate bloopers will be caught on tape and broadcast widely. George Allen's "Macaca" remark dominated news about his campaign for months. His campaign's efforts at damage control proved ineffective because of new allegations, reported online and in the broadcast media, that he used racial slurs when he played college football and wore a Confederate flag lapel pin for his high school senior class photo.

Events can also overwhelm an officeholder's communications strategy. Hurricane Katrina, for example, was a communications catastrophe for the George W. Bush administration. Rather than interrupt his vacation, President Bush left Secretary of Homeland Security Michael Chertoff in charge. Television viewers saw thousands of people stranded on roofs and huddled in the New Orleans Superdome, but Chertoff declared his pleasure at the federal response to the disaster. President Bush finally arrived several days after the hurricane, and his rhetoric seemed out of touch with reality in New Orleans. "Brownie," he said to Federal Emergency Management Administration (FEMA) Director Michael Brown, "You're doing a heck of a job."[15]

media BIASES

think

What role should the media play in the dissemination of news, and how important is media objectivity?

Objective journalism is a style of news reporting that focuses on facts rather than opinion, and presents all sides of controversial issues. Major newspapers, broadcast television news, and the major cable news networks pride themselves on their commitment to objective journalism.

The trademark slogan for the Fox News Channel is "fair and balanced." Even though newspapers endorse candidates on their editorial pages, the ideal of objective journalism is that candidate endorsements have no impact on the content or tone of news coverage.

Nonetheless, many political activists believe that the press is biased. Conservatives accuse the media of a liberal bias. For evidence, they cite a survey showing that 44 percent of news journalists identified with the Democratic Party compared with only 16 percent who said they were Republicans. (Another 34 percent were independent.)[16] Conservatives believe that the media slant the news in favor of liberal policy perspectives while ignoring conservative points of view. At the same time, many liberals believe that the media have a conservative bias. Conservative commentators, such as Rush Limbaugh, dominate talk radio and most newspaper editorial endorsements typically go to Republicans. Liberals dismiss talk of a Democratic bias among reporters because the newspapers, television networks, and

> **WE KNOW THAT POLLS ARE JUST A COLLECTION OF STATISTICS THAT REFLECT WHAT PEOPLE ARE THINKING IN 'REALITY.' AND REALITY HAS A WELL-KNOWN LIBERAL BIAS.**
> Stephen Colbert

newsmagazines for which journalists work are large corporations, owned and operated in most cases by conservative Republicans. Management sets editorial policy, they say, not reporters.

Research suggests that media sources may indeed play favorites.

objective journalism a style of news reporting that focuses on facts rather than opinion, and presents all sides of controversial issues.

Stephen Colbert, popular host of the mock-news show, *The Colbert Report.* Colbert coined the term "truthiness," which he uses to describe things that a person claims to know intuitively or "from the gut" without regard to evidence, logic, intellectual examination, or facts.

The network evening news treats Democratic candidates more favorably than it does Republicans. The Democratic candidate for president has enjoyed more favorable coverage on the network evening news than the Republican candidate in three of the last five presidential elections. Coverage was balanced in the other two elections. In 2004, for example, 57 percent of the network news reports on Democratic presidential candidate John Kerry were positive, compared with 37 percent of the news reports on President George W. Bush. Nonetheless, scholars have no evidence that news coverage affects election outcomes. Kerry lost the election despite receiving more favorable network news coverage than Bush. Furthermore, citizens have more news sources available to them than the network news, including newspapers, radio, Internet websites, and cable television. Fox News coverage of the 2004 presidential election was decidedly Bush-friendly. Fifty-three percent of Fox News stories on the president were positive compared with

ARE THE MEDIA BIASED?

A GREAT DEAL **31%**

A FAIR AMOUNT **31%**

NOT TOO MUCH **25%**

NOT AT ALL **9%**

DON'T KNOW/REFUSED **4%**

To what extent do you see political bias in news coverage? Pew Research Center for the People & the Press Political Communications Survey, Dec. 2007, http://people-press.org/questions/?qid=1697968&pid=51&ccid=51#top.

only 21 percent of the Kerry stories.[17] In practice, news consumers often choose media outlets that reflect their particular biases. The CNN and Fox cable news audiences perceive political reality differently. Conservative Republicans watch Fox, while liberal Democrats tune in to CNN.[18] (See figure on the following page.)

Political science research has also identified media biases that are not based on party affiliation or political ideology. Research on Senate races, for example, has found that newspapers tend to slant the information on their news pages to favor the candidate endorsed by the paper on

its editorial page, regardless of that candidate's party affiliation.[19] Furthermore, studies show that the press is biased against presidential incumbents, without regard for party and ideology. An **incumbent** is a current officeholder. All recent presidents, Democrats and Republicans alike, received more negative press coverage than did their opponents when they ran for reelection.[20]

The press has grown increasingly negative. Since the 1960s, bad news has increased by a factor of three and is now the dominant theme of national political news coverage. Thirty years ago, press coverage of public affairs emphasized the words of newsmakers and stressed the positive. The press grew more critical during the 1970s as journalists began to counter the statements of government officials rather than just report them. By the late 1970s, the focus of the Washington, D.C.

incumbent current officeholder.

takeaction
FAVORITE NEWS AND INFORMATION LINKS >>

Do you have a favorite set of online sources of information and opinion? Your assignment is to create an annotated inventory of online sites. For each entry, indicate the name of the site, give its URL, describe it, and explain why you have selected it. Select at least one site in each of the following categories:

- National news source that emphasizes objective journalism;
- State and local news source that emphasizes objective journalism;

- Political commentary, combining news and opinion;
- Issue-oriented website that focuses on a particular issue, either objectively or subjectively;
- Educational or professional website related to your college major or career goals; and
- Personal-interest website that deals with a hobby, sports team, or entertainment that you enjoy.

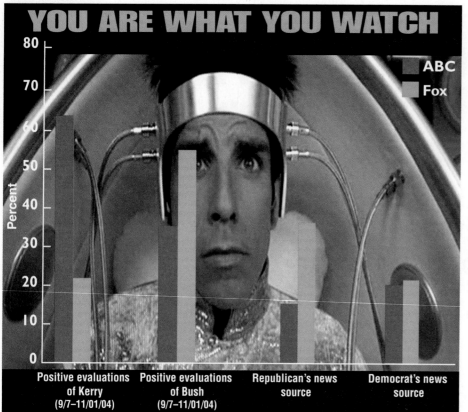

YOU ARE WHAT YOU WATCH

Percent (y-axis): 80, 70, 60, 50, 40, 30, 20, 10, 0

Legend: ABC, Fox

Categories:
Positive evaluations of Kerry (9/7–11/01/04)
Positive evaluations of Bush (9/7–11/01/04)
Republican's news source
Democrat's news source

People tend to seek out viewpoints that reinforce their own. More Republicans prefer news from Fox, and more Democrats seem to prefer ABC.

press corps was **attack journalism**, which is an approach to news reporting in which journalists take an adversarial attitude toward candidates and elected officials. Reporters decided to examine the actions of newsmakers critically, countering the statements of public officials with the responses of their critics and adversaries.[21] As a result, campaign coverage has grown negative. In 1960, 75 percent of press references to both major party presidential candidates (Richard Nixon and John Kennedy) were positive. In contrast, only 40 percent of references to the major party presidential candidates in 1992 (George H. W. Bush and Bill Clinton) were positive.[22]

attack journalism an approach to news reporting in which journalists take an adversarial attitude toward candidates and elected officials.

CONCLUSION
the media
& PUBLIC POLICY

The media play an important role in the policymaking process, especially during the agenda building and policy evaluation stages.

Agenda Building
Political scientists say that the press plays a **signaling role,** the accepted responsibility of the media to alert the public to important developments as they happen. The media may be unable to tell people what to think, but they generally succeed in telling people what to think about. In early 2007, the *Washington Post*

published a series of stories about the poor quality of care injured service personnel had been receiving at Walter Reed Army Medical Center in Washington, D.C. Other media outlets quickly picked up on the coverage and the issue of medical care for Iraq War veterans soon rose to the forefront of the policy agenda. Several congressional committees held hearings on the issue, the Bush administration called for an investigation, and the secretary of defense removed the military commanders in charge of veterans' care at Walter Reed.

signaling role a term that refers to the accepted responsibility of the media to alert the public to important developments as they happen.

Policy Formulation and Adoption
The media play an indirect role in policy formulation and adoption. The media influence policy adoption through **framing,** which is the process by which a communication source, such as a news organization, defines and constructs a political is-

sue or public controversy. The way the media present an issue helps define the approaches that policymakers will take to its resolution. The vivid images of flooded homes and people seeking shelter in the New Orleans Superdome and the accounts of bureaucratic bungling ensured that policymakers would regard Hurricane Katrina as not just a natural disaster, but also the failure of the government to respond effectively to a crisis. The media do not adopt policies, but they do publicize policy adoption by reporting on acts of Congress, Supreme Court decisions, and presidential actions. The press also provides political leaders with a means to communicate with the public, to explain government policies, and ask for support.

Two wounded veterans flank a wounded soldier's wife in 2007, as she testifies at a congressional hearing. They are describing shocking conditions at the Walter Reed Army Medical Center in Washington, D.C.

Policy Implementation and Evaluation

The media have a larger role in policy evaluation than policy implementation. Other than carrying out FCC rules, the media do not implement public policies. They are, however, important participants in policy evaluation, offering both empirical and normative policy analyses. An **empirical analysis** is a method of study that relies on experience and scientific observation, whereas a **normative analysis** is a method of study that is based on certain values. The media are an important source of empirical policy evaluation. In recent years, media outlets have issued a broad range of empirical analyses of government programs and activities, including investigative reports on the conduct of the war in Iraq, the implementation of the Medicare prescription drug program, and the effectiveness of airport luggage screening. The media also publicize empirical reports completed by government agencies and independent groups. In addition to empirical evaluation of policy, the media offer a broad spectrum of normative policy evaluations, ranging from newspaper editorials to radio talk show commentaries and blog postings. Media policy evaluations often set the agenda for policy modifications and the adoption of new policies.

framing the process by which a communication source, such as a news organization, defines and constructs a political issue or public controversy.

empirical analysis a method of study that relies on experience and scientific observation.

normative analysis a method of study that is based on certain values.

TEST yourself

1 Which of the following media outlets is owned by the U.S. government?

A. The *New York Times*

B. CBS Evening News

C. National Public Radio

D. None of the above

2 Which of the following is a set of radio stations?

A. NPR

B. PBS

C. Corporation for Public Broadcasting

D. None of the above

3 Which of the following is a set of television stations?

A. NPR

B. PBS

C. Corporation for Public Broadcasting

D. None of the above

4 Clear Channel Communication is most closely associated with which of the following?

A. Newspapers

B. Internet

C. Radio stations

D. Cable television

5 Cross-media ownership refers to which of the following?

A. A corporation owning several different types of media outlets

B. A corporation owning a chain of television stations in more than one city

C. A corporation owning multiple radio stations in the same city

D. A newspaper jointly owned by several corporations

6 Which of the following have been suffering from a loss of viewers or readers?

A. Daily newspapers

B. Network evening news shows

C. Newsmagazines

D. All of the above

7 Which of the following would be characterized as new media?

A. The *Washington Post*

B. CBS television

C. The *Chicago Tribune*

D. None of the above

8 Matt Drudge is most closely associated with which of the following?

A. An Internet website

B. CNN

C. The *New York Times*

D. *Time* magazine

9 Which of the following media outlets is more important to the Democratic Party than it is to the Republican Party?

A. Talk radio

B. Fox News

C. Internet blogs

D. All of the above

10 A blog would be characterized as which of the following?

A. Print media

B. Attack journalism

C. New media

D. All of the above

11 Which of the following can best be defined as an online personal journal?

A. A blog

B. A sound bite

C. Print media

D. Talk radio

12 Arbitron ratings are the basis for setting advertising rates for which of the following media outlets?

A. Radio

B. Television

C. Newspapers

D. Internet

13 Nielsen ratings are the basis for setting advertising rates for which of the following media outlets?

A. Radio

B. Television

C. Newspapers

D. Internet

14 "Read my lips: No new taxes." This is an example of which of the following?

A. Objective journalism

B. Attack journalism

C. Equal-time rule

D. A sound bite

15 A news editor directs her staff to focus on the facts of the news and avoid interjecting bias or opinion into reporting. The news editor is advocating which of the following?

A. Attack journalism

B. Using sound bites

C. The liberal agenda

D. Objective journalism

16 Rush Limbaugh is most closely associated with which of the following?

A. Talk radio

B. An Internet blog

C. Fox News

D. The *Washington Post*

17 Which of the following pairs do *not* go together?

A. Rush Limbaugh and conservative Republican listeners

B. Fox News and liberal Democrats

C. The *Huffington Post* Internet website and the new media

D. The *New York Times* and print media

18 Which of the following has research on bias in the network evening news discovered?

A. The network evening news treats Democratic candidates more favorably than it does Republicans.

B. The network evening news treats Republican candidates more favorably than it does Democrats.

C. The network evening news treats all candidates equally.

D. The network evening news typically favors incumbent presidents running for reelection regardless of political party.

19 The media have the greatest impact in which of the following stages of the policymaking process?

A. Agenda setting

B. Policy formulation

C. Policy adoption

D. Policy implementation

20 Which of the following is best described as a normative analysis?

A. The U.S. Census Bureau estimates that more than 11 million people are in the country illegally.

B. The General Accountability Office publishes a study on the economic impact of undocumented workers on the American economy.

C. A religious leader writes a blog urging the government to show compassion to people who have lived illegally in the United States for years.

D. All of the above.

KNOW *the* **score**

18–20 correct: Congratulations! You are well informed!

15–17 correct: Your political knowledge is a bit low—be sure to review the key terms and visit TheThinkSpot.

<14 correct: Reread the chapter more thoroughly.

1. D; 2. A; 3. B; 4. C; 5. A; 6. D; 7. D; 8. A; 9. C; 10. C; 11. A; 12. A; 13. B; 14. D; 15. D; 16. A; 17. B; 18. A; 19. A; 20. C

TEST yourself

1 Which of the following organizations is a business federation representing the interests of businesses of all sizes, sectors, and regions?
A. National Federation of Independent Businesses
B. AFL-CIO
C. U.S. Chamber of Commerce
D. NAACP

2 Which of the following organizations would be most likely to favor the repeal of state right-to-work laws?
A. U.S. Chamber of Commerce
B. AFL-CIO
C. Club for Growth
D. LULAC

3 Which of the following statements is true about organized labor?
A. The percentage of the workforce that belongs to labor unions has been in decline for years.
B. Wal-Mart, the nation's largest employer, has successfully resisted unionization efforts.
C. Organized labor is stronger in the Frostbelt and weaker in the Sunbelt.
D. All of the above.

4 Which of the following organizations would be most likely to favor increasing the minimum wage?
A. U.S. Chamber of Commerce
B. American Farm Bureau
C. AFL-CIO
D. AARP

5 Which of the following organizations would be most likely to favor affirmative action in college and university admissions?
A. NAACP
B. AFL-CIO
C. AARP
D. Sierra Club

6 Which of the following pairs of organizations would be most likely to be on the opposite sides of the issue of abortion?
A. Right to Life and NARAL Pro-Choice America
B. U. S. Chamber of Commerce and the AFL-CIO
C. Club for Growth and the NRA
D. Sierra Club and NOW

7 Which of the following organizations would be most likely to celebrate Earth Day?
A. Sierra Club
B. Human Rights Campaign
C. NARAL Pro-Choice America
D. Common Cause

8 Which of the following organizations would be most likely to endorse a Democratic candidate for president in the next election?
A. Right to Life
B. U.S. Chamber of Commerce
C. NRA
D. NARAL Pro-Choice America

9 What are political action committees (PACs)?
A. They are organizations representing the interests of firms and professionals in the same general field.
B. They are organizations whose members care intensely about a single issue or small group of related issues.
C. They are organizations created to raise and distribute money in election campaigns.
D. They are organizations created to seek benefits on behalf of groups of persons who are in some way incapacitated or otherwise unable to represent their own interests.

10 PACs associated with which of the following types of interest groups raise the most money?
A. Business groups
B. Labor groups
C. Racial/ethnic groups
D. Agricultural groups

11 PACs associated with which of the following tend to give most of their campaign contributions to incumbent members of Congress of both political parties?
A. Business groups
B. Labor unions
C. NRA
D. Cause groups

12 Which of the following candidates would you expect to benefit the most from PAC contributions?
A. A Republican challenger
B. A Democratic challenger
C. A candidate from either party running for an open seat
D. An incumbent from either party running for reelection

13 A PAC representing Interest Group A contributed to Congressman B's reelection campaign even though the congressman sides with the interest group's issue positions only about 60 percent of the time. The PAC is acting in accordance with which of the following principles?

A. Friendly Incumbent Rule

B. Common Cause

C. Club for Growth

D. Affirmative action

14 An organization created by individuals and groups to influence the outcomes of elections by raising and spending money that candidates and political parties cannot legally raise is known by which of the following names?

A. Political action committee

B. Interest group

C. Political party

D. 527 committee

15 Which of the following statements about lobbying and lobbyists is true?

A. Groups lobby the legislative branch of government but not the executive branch.

B. Interest group lobbyists frequently focus on the details of legislation rather than votes on final passage.

C. Former members of Congress are prohibited by law from becoming lobbyists.

D. None of the above.

16 What is the best assessment of the relationship between campaign contributions and interest group lobbying?

A. Money buys votes. Members of Congress vote for the causes supported by the groups that give them the most money.

B. Money buys access. Members of Congress are willing to meet with lobbyists representing groups that provide them with campaign contributions.

C. Money and lobbying are unrelated. Members of Congress are open to consider all views regardless of political contributions.

D. Because of campaign finance regulations, interest groups are prohibited from contributing money to help members of Congress run for reelection.

17 Which of the following statements is true about the use of protest demonstrations as a political strategy?

A. Protest demonstrations are a tactic used by groups unable to achieve their goals through other means.

B. Business and trade groups are more likely to use protest demonstrations than are other organizations.

C. Protests are among the more effective approaches interest groups have for achieving their goals.

D. All of the above.

18 Which of the following organizations specializes in the use of litigation to achieve its goals?

A. Chamber of Commerce

B. American Bar Association

C. ACLU

D. Club for Growth

19 Which of the following types of interest groups is typically allied with the Republican Party?

A. Organized labor

B. Environmental organizations

C. African American rights groups

D. Anti-tax groups

20 Which of the following types of interest groups is typically allied with the Democratic Party?

A. Business groups

B. Abortion rights organizations

C. Conservative Christian organizations

D. None of the above

KNOW *the* **score**

18–20 correct: Congratulations! You are well informed!

15–17 correct: Your political knowledge is a bit low—be sure to review the key terms and visit TheThinkSpot.

<14 correct: Reread the chapter more thoroughly.

1. C; 2. B; 3. D; 4. C; 5. A; 6. A; 7. A; 8. C; 9. C; 10. A; 11. A; 12. D; 13. A; 14. D; 15. B; 16. B; 17. A; 18. C; 19. D; 20. B

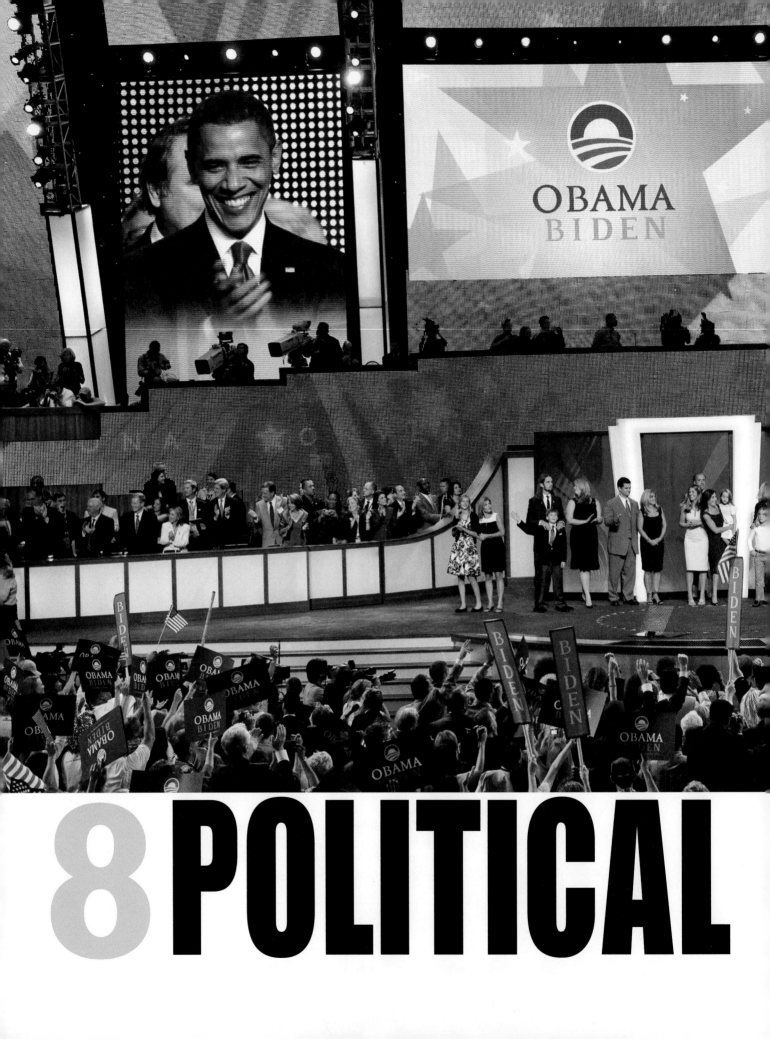

8 POLITICAL

> **WHAT'S AHEAD**

The Party System

Party Organization

The Party Balance: Democrats,
Republicans, and Independents

Voting Patterns

Divided Government

Conclusion: Political Parties
& Public Policy

The Democratic Party won the 2008 election, capturing the presidency for the first time in three elections and strengthening its hold on Congress. In the race for the White House, Democratic presidential candidate Barack Obama defeated Republican John McCain. Obama carried 28 states and the District of Columbia with a total of 365 electoral votes, while McCain took 22 states with 173 electoral votes. Obama also claimed a majority of the popular vote, 53 percent to 46 percent for his Republican opponent. Obama's share of the popular vote was the largest for any Democrat running for president since Lyndon Johnson in 1964.

Democrats did well in other races as well. While Obama was winning the White House, the Democratic Party expanded its majorities in Congress, picking up 8 seats in the Senate and 21 seats in the House. When the new Senate convened in 2009, it contained 59 Democrats and 41 Republicans. The new House included 257 Democrats and 178 Republicans. At the state level, Democrats held the governorships of 29 states compared with 21 state governors who were Republican. In 27 states, Democrats held majorities in both legislative chambers compared with 14 states in which the Republican Party enjoyed full control. The legislatures in eight states were split; the Nebraska legislature is nonpartisan, which means that candidates run for seats without party labels.

PARTIES

ESSENTIALS...

after studying Chapter 8, students should be able to answer the following questions:

> What are the reasons given by political scientists to explain the two-party system in the United States?

> What are the structures of the party organizations, and what tasks do the national party organizations perform for party candidates?

> How do the Democratic and Republican Parties compare in terms of party identification within the electorate?

> How do the Democratic and Republican Parties compare in terms of group support among the voters?

> What are the political philosophies of liberalism and conservatism, and how do they relate to the political parties? How are the platforms of the Democratic and Republican parties different? How are they similar?

> What are the reasons political scientists give to explain divided government?

> What is the role of political parties in the policymaking process?

the party
SYSTEM

a **political party** is a group of individuals who join together to seek government office in order to make public policy. A party differs from an interest group in its effort to win control of the machinery of government. Both parties and interest groups participate in election campaigns, but only parties actually run candidates for office. Candidates for Congress run as Democrats or Republicans, not as representatives of labor unions or corporations.

The number of political parties varies from country to country. The United States has a **two-party system**, which is the division of voter loyalties between two major political parties, resulting in the near exclusion of minor parties from seriously competing for a share of political power. After the 2008 election, 98 of 100 U.S. senators were elected as either Democrats or Republicans. (Bernie Sanders of Vermont and Joe Liebermann of Connecticut won elections as independents, but both caucus with the Democrats and are counted as Democrats for the purpose of committee assignments. Liebermann calls himself an "independent Democrat.") The two major parties held all 435 seats in the U.S. House and all 50 offices of state governor.

A **third party** is a minor party in a two-party system. Third-party candidates and independents may compete for office in a two-party system, but usually with a notable lack of success. The roster of third parties in the United States includes Green, Reform, Libertarian, Natural Law, Official Constitution, Workers World, Socialist, and Socialist Equality parties. The Green and the Libertarians are the most successful, winning a handful of local races.

Why does the United States have a two-party system rather than a system with three or more major

think

Would you vote for a third-party candidate that you liked even if you thought that he or she had no real chance of winning the election?

political parties as in many other democracies? Political scientists offer two sets of explanations—the electoral system and the absence of deep-seated political divisions in American society. Maurice Duverger, a French political scientist, wrote in the 1950s that a **plurality election system**, which is a method for choosing public officials by awarding office to the candidate with the most votes, favors a two-party system.[1] Candidates for executive and legislative office in the

political party a group of individuals who join together to seek government office in order to make public policy.

two-party system the division of voter loyalties between two major political parties.

third party a minor party in a two-party system.

plurality election system a method for choosing public officials that awards office to the candidate with the most votes; it favors a two-party system.

United States run from geographic areas and the candidate with more votes wins the office. Candidates who finish second or third win nothing, no matter how close the race. The **Electoral College**, established in the Constitution for indirect election of the president and vice president, is especially inhospitable to third-party candidates because it awards electoral votes, the only votes that really count, to candidates who win the most popular votes in a state. In 1992, for example, Reform Party candidate Ross Perot won no electoral votes, despite taking 19 percent of the popular vote, because he carried no states. The dilemma for minor parties in the United States is that if they do not quickly develop enough popular support to win elections, the voters will not take them seriously. If voters believe that a party and its candidates are unlikely to win, they often decide to choose between the major party candidates because they do not want to throw away their votes.[2]

Scholars also believe that a nation's party system reflects the fundamental social and political divisions of society. The more intense the divisions, the more likely it is that the nation will have a multiparty system. The United States has a two-party system, they say, because Americans are relatively united. Americans may disagree about the role of government in society, but they generally share the basic values of capitalism and democracy. People with opposing views on some issues can unite under the same party banner because they agree on other issues.

Electoral College the system established in the Constitution for indirect election of the president and vice president.

1992 Popular Vote vs. Electoral Vote

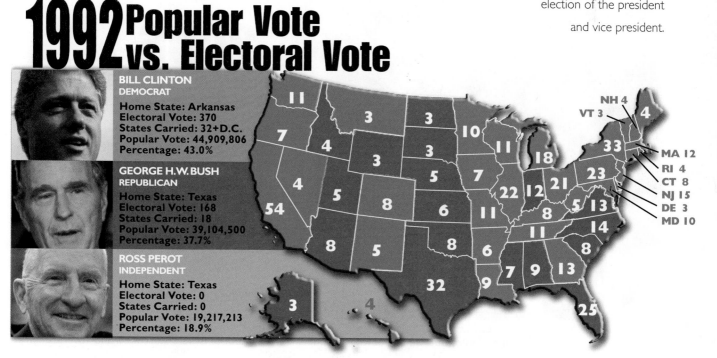

BILL CLINTON
DEMOCRAT
Home State: Arkansas
Electoral Vote: 370
States Carried: 32+D.C.
Popular Vote: 44,909,806
Percentage: 43.0%

GEORGE H.W. BUSH
REPUBLICAN
Home State: Texas
Electoral Vote: 168
States Carried: 18
Popular Vote: 39,104,500
Percentage: 37.7%

ROSS PEROT
INDEPENDENT
Home State: Texas
Electoral Vote: 0
States Carried: 0
Popular Vote: 19,217,213
Percentage: 18.9%

The National Archives and Records Administration

The Israeli Party System

Israel has a **multiparty system,** which is the division of voter loyalties among three or more major political parties. The Knesset, the lower house of the Israeli national legislature, included 12 parties after the 2006 elections. Kadima, the largest party in the Knesset, held 29 of 120 seats. In order to achieve a majority in the Knesset, Kadima had to form a coalition with several smaller parties.

Israel has **proportional representation (PR)**, which is an election system that awards legislative seats to each party approximately equal to its popular voting strength. As long as a party receives at least 2 percent of the total vote, the minimum threshold for gaining representation, the party wins seats in the Knesset in proportion to its share of the vote. In 2006, for example, Kadima won 24 percent of the seats in the Knesset based on 22 percent of the popular vote. Proportional representation is related to multiparty systems because voters know that their votes will count. Unless a party has almost no popular support, each vote it receives will enable it to increase its representation in the Knesset.

Voters in Israel cast their ballots for the party rather than individual candidates by choosing a letter symbol. Before the election, each party prepares a list of candidates for the Knesset and ranks them in order, placing party leaders at the top. If the party wins five seats, the first five candidates on the list become members of the Knesset. If it wins ten seats, the first ten candidates are elected. Candidates are chosen to represent their party in the Knesset rather than individual geographic districts as in the United States.[3]

Democracies with multiparty systems are countries with intense social and political divisions. People who disagree fundamentally about the nature of society and the role of government are less likely to form broad-based coalition parties such as those that exist in the United States. Instead, they create smaller, more narrowly based parties. Societies that are deeply divided are likely to have several political parties.

Many political scientists believe that electoral laws and a nation's social structure interact. Nations with deep social and political divisions create electoral systems based on proportional repre-sentation in order to allow the democratic expression of those divisions at the ballot box. In contrast, countries with fewer divisions establish election procedures that favor a two-party system.[4]

Questions

1. If the United States were to adopt proportional representation, do you think that a multiparty system would soon develop? Why or why not?

2. If Israel were to adopt a plurality election system, do you think a two-party system would eventually emerge in that country? Why or why not?

3. What are the advantages and disadvantages of each type of party system?

multiparty system the division of voter loyalties among three or more major political parties.

proportional representation (PR) an election system that awards legislative seats to each party approximately equal to its popular voting strength.

2006 ISRAELI NATIONAL ELECTION

PARTY	# VOTES	# SEATS
Kadima	690,901	29
Labor-Meimad	472,366	19
Likud	281,996	12
Shas	299,054	12
Yisrael Beitenu	281,880	11
Ichud Leumi - Mafdal	224,083	9
Gil	185,759	7
Torah & Shabbat Judaism	147,091	6
Meretz	118,302	5
United Arab List - Arab Renewal	94,786	4
Hadash	86,092	3
National Democratic Assembly	72,066	3

This menorah sculpture outside of the Knesset building is a symbol of Israel's statehood and sovereignty.

http://www.knesset.gov.il/elections17/eng/Results/main_results_eng.asp

party
ORGANIZATION

The organization of political parties in the United States reflects the federal system, with organizations at both the state and national levels of government. At the state level, the Democratic and Republican party organizations are led by executive party committees, which are elected by party activists who participate in local party meetings, district conventions, and state party conventions. The executive committee usually elects the state party chair.

A national committee and a national chair lead the national party organizations. The national committee consists of a committeeman and committeewoman chosen by the party organizations of each state and the District of Columbia. The national committee elects the national committee chair. When the party controls the White House, the president usually handpicks the national chairperson.

The Republican and Democratic parties raised approximately $1.8 billion for the 2008 election. As a comparison, the gross domestic product (the total value of all goods and services produced) of Greenland in 2007 was $1.7 billion.

The Democratic National Committee (DNC) and Republican National Committee (RNC) work to increase the number of party officeholders. Each party tries to recruit a strong list of candidates for the next election. Although the national party organizations do not control nominations, they can encourage potential candidates to run. They also provide candidates with technical assistance and campaign advice. The DNC and RNC support their candidates with polling data, issue research, media assistance, and advice on campaign strategy. Both national parties offer campaign seminars, teaching inexperienced candidates how to do everything from raising money to dealing with the media. The most important service the national party organizations provide for their candidates is money.

The Republicans have historically enjoyed a significant fundraising advantage over the Democrats because of the socioeconomic status of their support base and because of their fundraising expertise. People who identify with the Republican Party have more money than those who consider themselves Democrats. Moreover, the Republicans have also benefited from a more efficient fundraising operation, especially direct mail. However, the Democrats have closed the fundraising gap, primarily because they have taken better advantage of the Internet than their Republican opponents.[5] In 2008, the Democratic and Republican national campaign organizations raised more than $900 million each to support their candidates with the

A volunteer for Obama reminds voters to go to the polls on Super Tuesday, February 5, 2008.

Democratic Party enjoying a small fundraising advantage.

Political parties take a different approach to campaign finance than do interest groups. Most interest groups contribute primarily to incumbent officeholders because they want to develop positive relationships with influential members of Congress. Their goal is **access**, the opportunity to communicate directly with legislators and other government officials in hopes of influencing the details of policy. In contrast, the goal of political parties is to control the government itself. Consequently, they contribute most of their money to candidates in competitive races, whether incumbents or challengers.[6]

access the opportunity to communicate directly with legislators and other government officials in hopes of influencing the details of policy.

the party balance
DEMOCRATS, REPUBLICANS, AND INDEPENDENTS

Political scientists measure party identification by asking survey respondents if they consider themselves to be Democrats, Republicans, or independents. In 2008, Democrats outnumbered Republicans by 36 percent to 27 percent, with another 36 percent declaring that they were independents. The figures represented a slight gain in party identification for the Democratic Party since 2004 but a sizable decline for the **Grand Old Party (GOP)**, a nickname for the Republican Party. In 2004, the two parties were on nearly equal footing among the electorate.

The Democratic Party has made electoral gains since 2004, not just because the proportion of Republican Party identities has declined, but also because independents are more likely to vote Democratic. In 2004, independents divided almost equally among independents who leaned Democratic, independents who leaned Republican, and true independents. The ratio of Democrats and Democratic-leaning independents to Republicans and Republican-leaning independents was close, 47 percent to 44 percent. (The Republican Party won the 2004 election because Democratic turnout was less than Republican turnout.) In contrast, independents leaning Democratic outnumbered

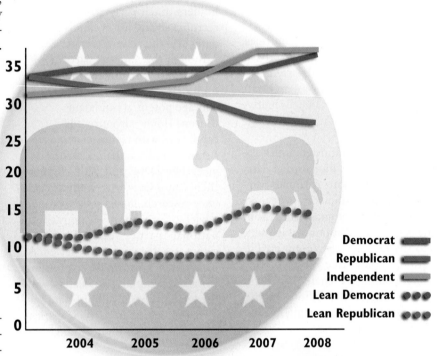

Democrat
Republican
Independent
Lean Democrat
Lean Republican

The Democratic Party has made electoral gains since 2004 not just because the proportion of Republican Party identifiers has declined, but also because independents are more likely to vote Democratic.

http://pewresearch.org/pubs/773/fewer-voters-identify-as-republicans

independents who leaned Republican by a three-to-two margin in 2008. The combination of Democrats and Democratic-leaning independents represented 51 percent of the electorate compared with 37 percent Republican and Republican-leaning independents.[7]

think
Why might a voter choose not to identify with a particular party?

Grand Old Party (GOP) Nickname of the Republican Party.

> **We in America do not have government by the majority. We have government by the majority who participate.**
> Thomas Jefferson

Are Party Conventions Irrelevant?

Are party conventions an anachronism? Are there better means to nominate presidential candidates and develop party platforms?

Do conventions, in fact, help focus voters on the candidates and the issues of election campaigns? Do they serve a purpose in mobilizing the American public for a general election?

Overview: For the greater part of American political history, the primary vehicle for nominating presidential candidates was the party convention. After the first convention was held in 1831, conventions became political forums in which parties not only nominated presidential candidates, but also in which policy and issues were debated by the party faithfuls (that is, delegates selected by their local and state party organizations) to provide both a nominee and platform to offer the American people at election time.

Historically, conventions provided high political drama and a medium through which contentious social and political issues were debated. For example, the Democratic Convention of 1968 was overshadowed by social unrest, the Vietnam War, violence, and protesters, with the result, in part, being a call for reform of the party nominating and convention processes.

With the era of television and reform, the conventions have become ratifying conventions in which the parties present to the country their respective nominees chosen months before the actual convention. Politics and debate have been relegated behind closed doors, so as to offer voters the illusion of party unity. This gives television coverage the quality of an infomercial or advertising. As viewership of conventions has declined, so has network coverage, which again gives the impression that conventions are nothing more than slick, political advertising—why cover something devoid of substance? But is this, in fact, true? Do conventions serve a valid and important purpose? What about the development of the party platform or introduction of a party's nominee, for instance? Are conventions, in fact, irrelevant?

supporting | the increasing irrelevance of party conventions

voters are increasingly disaffected with the current party nomination and convention process. Harvard's John F. Kennedy School of Government's Vanishing Voter Project shows that voters increasingly complain of progressively longer campaign seasons. Voters may now be looking at conventions as a way to rein in this problem.

party conventions are now devoid of substance. In the past, party conventions were used to select presidential nominees, air policy disputes, and debate contentious issues. Now, the nominee is known months in advance and intraparty squabbles are held behind closed doors so as to foster the illusion of party unity.

polling data shows declining public interest in party conventions. On the media aspect of conventions, there is growing consensus that conventions are nothing more than infomercials in which the parties act as political advertising agencies.

against | the increasing irrelevance of party conventions

party conventions give party activists a chance to influence the party platform. A party convention gives party members a forum in which to present their concerns and to aid in writing the party platform.

the essence of a convention happens away from the convention floor. During a convention, there are hundreds of meetings and events that allow party members to exchange ideas, plot strategy, and network—thereby energizing activists for the campaign's final months.

conventions introduce most Americans to a party's candidate. Research shows that the vast majority of Americans do not follow politics or presidential campaigns until the late-summer and autumn of a general election year. Conventions give the parties a chance to present their nominee and policy positions in a favorable light and for an extended length of time before the campaign season begins in earnest.

voting
PATTERNS

Voting patterns reflect differences in income, race and ethnicity, education, gender, age, family and lifestyle status, region, ideology, and religion.

Income

Economic status is one of the most enduring bases for voting divisions in America. Since the 1930s, Republican candidates have typically done better among upper-income voters, whereas Democrats have scored their highest vote percentages among lower-income groups. In 2008, **exit polls**, which are surveys based on random samples of voters leaving the polling place, found that Obama outpolled McCain among voters with family incomes less than $50,000 a year by 60 percent to 38 percent. The two candidates evenly split the votes of people in families with annual incomes greater than $50,000.[8]

> "They will not only try to attack you if you try to point out what's going on in white America—U.S. of KKK..."

Race and Ethnicity

Voting patterns reflect the nation's racial divisions. White voters lean Republican. In 2008, whites backed McCain 55 percent to 45 percent for Obama. In contrast, minority voters support the Democrats. In 2008, African Americans supported Obama over McCain by a lopsided 95 percent to 4 percent. Asian Americans gave Obama 61 percent of their votes compared with 35 percent who supported McCain. Democratic candidates also enjoy strong support from most Latinos. In 2008, Obama won the Latino vote 66 percent to 32 percent for McCain.[9] Latino voters were especially important for Obama because they apparently provided his margin of victory in Colorado, Florida, Nevada, and New Mexico, four hotly contested states that George W. Bush won in 2004.[10] Not all groups of Latinos share the same perspective on party affiliation. Whereas Mexican Americans and Puerto Ricans typically vote Democratic, most Cuban Americans support the GOP because of the Republican Party's strong anti-Castro position.[11]

Education

The Democratic Party is strongest with voters at either end of the education ladder. In 2008, Obama led McCain by 63 percent to 35 percent among voters who had not graduated from high school. Obama won the votes of high school graduates as well by a more modest 52 percent compared to 46 percent for his Republican opponent. The two parties evenly split the votes of college graduates. Among voters with postgraduate degrees, however, Obama led his Republican opponents by 58 percent to 40 percent.[12] For the most part, the relationship between education and party support reflects differences in income. As people move up the education ladder, they also move up the income ladder. Individuals in higher income brackets are more likely to vote Republican than are lower income voters. The pattern holds true

exit polls surveys based on random samples of voters leaving the polling place.

> "The profound mistake of Reverend Wright's sermons is... that he spoke as if... no progress has been made;... [W]hat is called for is nothing more, and nothing less, than what all the world's great religions demand—that we do unto others as we would have them do unto us."

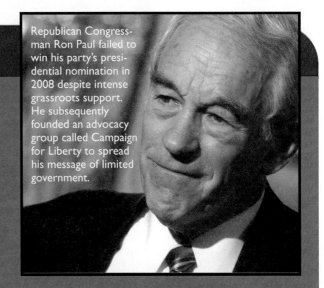
through college but not into graduate and professional school. People who have postgraduate college degrees tend to vote Democratic because many of them hold liberal positions on social issues such as abortion rights, environmental protection, gay and lesbian rights, the war in Iraq, and affirmative action.

Gender

For more than 40 years, American voters have divided along gender lines, producing a gender gap, the differences in party identification and political attitudes between men and women. The **gender gap** has emerged in American politics because men have moved away from the Democratic Party. In 1952, a majority of both men and women

gender gap differences in party identification and political attitudes between men and women.

Tina Fey (l.) and Amy Poehler (r.) satirize Sarah Palin and Hillary Clinton on *Saturday Night Live* during the 2008 presidential campaign.

identified with the Democratic Party. Since then, the percentage of women identifying with the Democrats has risen while the proportion of men has declined. The gender gap was greatest in the 1996 presidential election, at 14 percentage points. Since then, the gap has somewhat narrowed. In 2008, half of male voters supported Obama compared with 56 percent of women voters.[13]

Age

Polling data reveal that younger voters have been moving toward the Democratic Party. In fact, Obama won because of his support from younger voters. He outpolled McCain among voters under the age of 30 by 66 percent to 32 percent. Obama won the 30-to-44 age bracket as well, but by a closer margin of 52 percent to 46 percent. The two candidates split the votes of people age 45 to 64. McCain won a majority of voters over the age of 65, 53 percent to 45 percent for Obama.[14]

Family and Lifestyle Status

People who are members of traditional families tend to vote Republican. In 2008, married voters supported McCain by 51 percent to 47 percent for Obama. In contrast, Obama led his Republican opponent among single people by 65 percent to 33 percent. Voters who identified as gay, lesbian, or bisexual supported Obama by 70 percent to 27 percent for McCain.[15]

Region

Regional voting patterns have changed. Today, Democrats run best in the Northeast and on the West Coast. The GOP is strongest in the South, the Great Plains, and the Rocky Mountain West. The Midwest has become a

2008

" Obama outpolled McCain among voters *under the age of 30* by 66% to 32% "

battleground region between the two parties. In 2008, Obama was strongest in the Northeast, winning 59 percent of the vote and carrying every state in the region. McCain ran best in the South, outpolling Obama 53 percent to 46 percent, and winning every southern state except Florida, North Carolina, and Virginia.[16]

Political Ideology

The Democratic and Republican parties are ideologically polarized.

Conservatives are aligned with the GOP; liberals vote Democratic. In 2008, liberals supported Obama over McCain by a substantial 88

percent to 10 percent. In contrast, conservatives backed McCain by an impressive 78 percent to 20 percent. Moderates tend to be swing voters. Obama captured the votes of moderates, 60 percent, compared to 39 percent for McCain.[17]

The political parties were once more ideologically diverse than they are today. Many conservatives identified with the Democratic Party, especially in the South, whereas the Republican Party had a liberal wing based principally in the Northeast. Important legislation frequently passed Congress with the support of bipartisan coalitions. For example, the Civil Rights Act of 1964 passed Congress because moderate and liberal Republicans joined liberal Democrats to overcome the opposition of southern Democrats.

The political parties are more ideologically distinct today because their coalitions of supporters have changed. The move of Southern white conservatives from the Democratic Party to the GOP has made the Democrats more liberal and the Republicans more conservative. The Democratic Party has adopted liberal positions on a range of social issues in order to appeal to middle-class voters concerned with abortion rights, the environment, and gay and lesbian rights. The Republican Party, meanwhile, has taken conservative positions on social issues to bolster its support among conservative Christians.[18]

Religion

Religion and party support are closely related. During the last party era, voting patterns reflected religious affiliation. Protestants generally supported the Republican Party, Catholics leaned to the Democratic Party, and Jews were strongly Democratic. Today, party divisions based on religion have grown more complex. Although most Jews still vote for Democrats, Catholics have become a swing group. Conservative white evangelical Protestants (including Southern Baptists, Pentecostals, and members of the Assemblies of God) are firmly Republican, as are members of the Church of Jesus Christ of Latter-day Saints (the Mormons). Latinos as a whole typically support the Democrats, but the GOP is stronger among Latino evangelicals than among Latino Catholics, who remain firmly Democratic.[19] White members of mainline Protestant denominations (including Methodists, Episcopalians, and Presbyterians) lean Republican as well, but less so than do evangelicals. Most African Americans are Democrats, regardless of their religious preferences.[20] In 2008, Jews supported Obama over McCain by 78 percent to 21 percent. Catholics backed Obama as well, but the margin was more narrow: 54 percent to 45 percent. Protestants voted for McCain by 54 percent, compared to 45 percent for Obama.[21]

In the current party system, voting patterns are also based on frequency of attendance at religious services. White Protestants and Catholics who attend worship services regularly are more likely to vote Republican than are people in the same group who attend services less frequently.[22] In 2008, McCain led among voters who said that they attended religious services more than once a week by 55 percent to 43 percent for Obama. In contrast, voters who declared that they seldom attended religious services voted for Obama by 59 percent to 40 percent. People who never attended services backed the Democrat by 67 percent to 30 percent.[23]

Place of Residence

Voting patterns reflect place of residence. Generally, Democrats win urban areas, Republicans carry rural areas, and the suburbs are a battleground between the two parties. In 2008, Obama outpolled McCain in large urban areas by 63 percent to 35 percent, whereas the Republican candidate won rural areas by 53 percent to 45 percent. The vote in the suburbs was 50 percent for Obama to 48 percent for McCain.[24]

Issue Orientation

Since 1960, the parties have grown further apart philosophically, with the Democrats generally taking liberal positions and the Republicans expressing conservative views. **Liberalism** is the political philosophy that favors the use of government power to foster the development of the individual and promote the welfare of society. Democrats believe that a strong government is needed to provide essential services and to remedy social inequalities. Democrats make an exception to their endorsement of strong government when it comes to cultural issues, such as abortion and homosexuality. They believe that government should leave decisions on those sorts of issues to the individual. In contrast, the Republican Party embraces **conservatism,** which is the political philosophy that government power undermines the development of the individual and diminishes society as a whole. Republicans believe that a strong government interferes with business and threatens individual freedom. The exception to this approach for Republicans is that they believe that government should enforce traditional values on issues such as abortion.

A **party platform** is a statement of party principles and issue positions. The 2008 Democratic and Republican Party platforms, which are excerpted in the table on the following page, show clear philosophical differences between the parties on many issues. By no means, however, do the parties take opposite sides on all issues. Some differences are nuanced. Consider gun control. Both parties endorse a right of gun ownership, but they disagree on the efficacy of gun regulation. The Democrats endorse "reasonable regulation," while the Republicans declare that gun control penalizes the law-abiding without having an impact on crime. Finally, the two parties take similar positions on some issues. Both the Democratic and the Republican platforms declare support for Israel.

White Protestants and Catholics who attend worship services regularly are more likely to vote Republican than are people in the same group who attend services less frequently.

2008 Party Platforms

Democratic Position   **Republican Position**

	Democratic Position	Republican Position
Healthcare	Declares that every American should be guaranteed affordable, comprehensive healthcare, which should be a shared responsibility between employers, workers, insurers, providers, and government.	Supports health savings accounts that provide tax breaks to individuals who save money to pay for their own health insurance coverage.
Social Security	Opposes Social Security privatization and increasing the retirement age. Promises to raise revenue to support the program by applying the Social Security payroll tax on incomes over $250,000 a year.	Promises that anyone now receiving Social Security benefits will not have their benefits cut or their taxes increased. Calls for partial privatization through the creation of personal investment accounts.
Iraq and Afghanistan	Promises to bring the war in Iraq to a responsible end. Declares that the war in Afghanistan and the fight against the Taliban should be the nation's top military priority.	Says that the waging of war—and the achieving of peace—should never be micromanaged in a party platform. Calls for increasing troop strength in Afghanistan.
Israel	Declares that under all circumstances, the United States must ensure that Israel enjoys a qualitative edge for its national security and its right to self-defense.	Declares support for Israel and pledges that the United States will ensure that Israel enjoy a qualitative edge in defense technologies over any potential adversaries.
Energy	Says that the government should provide incentives to increase domestic production of clean and renewable energy. Declares that the United States must reduce oil consumption by 35 percent by 2030 and calls for more fuel-efficient automobiles.	Advocates the use of free market incentives to promote energy conservation. Calls for drilling in the Arctic National Wildlife Refuge (ANWR), on federal lands in the western United States, and offshore. Supports the construction of new nuclear power plants as well as alternative sources of energy.
Tax policy	Says that families earning more than $250,000 a year will have to give back some of the tax cuts granted them during the Bush administration. Promises to increase the Earned Income Tax Credit (EITC) with the goal of cutting the poverty rate in half in ten years.	Favors making the tax cuts enacted during the early years of the Bush administration permanent. Proposes a major reduction in the corporate income tax rate.
Immigration reform	Calls for securing the nation's borders. Endorses immigration reform that will allow undocumented immigrants the opportunity to become citizens.	Declares that border security is essential to national security. Opposes amnesty. Supports English as the official language of the nation.
Gun control	Promises to preserve the right to own and use firearms, while recognizing the need for reasonable regulation.	Strongly supports the individual right to own and bear arms. Declares that gun control only penalizes law-abiding citizens and is ineffective at preventing crime.
Affirmative action	Supports affirmative action to redress discrimination and achieve diversity in federal contracting and higher education.	Opposes discrimination while rejecting all preferences, quotas, and set-asides based on skin color, ethnicity, or gender.
Abortion	Strongly and unequivocally supports Roe v. Wade and a woman's right to choose a safe and legal abortion, regardless of ability to pay.	Favors a constitutional amendment to prohibit abortion.
Gay and lesbian rights	Endorses federal legislation to prohibit job discrimination based on sexual orientation. Supports equal responsibility, benefits, and protections for same-sex couples. Declares that all men and women should be allowed to serve in the military without regard for sexual orientation.	Endorses a constitutional amendment to define marriage as between one man and one woman. Opposes legal recognition of same-sex relationships or granting benefits to same-sex couples.

divided GOVERNMENT

divided government refers to the phenomenon of one political party controlling the legislative branch of government while the other holds the executive branch. Consider the information shown in the figure on p. 165. During the 24-year period between 1969 and 1993, the Democratic Party controlled both the presidency and Congress for only six years. During the rest of the period, the Republican Party held the White House and the Democrats controlled at least one house of Congress. Political scientists ex-

> **divided government** the phenomenon of one political party controlling the legislative branch of government while the other holds the executive branch.

plained divided government by declaring that the Republican Party enjoyed an advantage in presidential elections, whereas the Democrats had become the party of Congress, especially the House of Representatives. The 1992 and 1994 elections turned this explanation on its head when Democrat Bill Clinton broke the Republican lock on the White House (in 1992) and the GOP captured control of both houses of Congress (in 1994). Consequently, political scientists began to look for explanations of divided government in general.

Historical research shows that divided government is not unique to the late twentieth century, although it has become more frequent. The first instances of divided government occurred before the Civil War. In the nineteenth century, 16 of 50 elections produced divided government, with different parties controlling the White House and at least one chamber of Congress.[25] Between 1900 and 1952, 22 elections produced unified government; 4 resulted in divided government. Divided government has now become commonplace. Between 1952 and 2008, 12 elections resulted in unified government while 17 elections produced divided government.[26] Divided government is common at the state level as well.

The Constitution sets the stage for divided government. In a parliamentary system, the national legislature chooses the chief executive (often called a prime minister) by majority vote. Consequently, the party or coalition of parties that controls the legislature also controls the executive. In contrast, the United States has **separation of powers**, which is the division of political power among executive, legislative, and judicial branches of government. Members of Congress and the president are elected independently from each other. They have different constituencies, serve terms of different length, and stand for election at different times. In particular, midterm elections are more likely to produce divided government than presidential election years. With relatively few exceptions, the president's party loses seats in the House in a midterm election. On nine occasions since 1894, midterm elections have produced divided government or added a second chamber to opposition

control.[27] In 2006, for example, the Democratic Party won control of Congress, producing divided government after a period of unified Republican control. The 2008 election ended divided government because Democrats won control of both the White House and Congress.

Elections for president, Congress, and the Senate usually feature different issues. Whereas candidates for president stress national issues involving foreign policy, defense, and the strength of the nation's economy, candidates for the House of Representatives focus on local issues, such as cleaning up an area waterway or the proposed closure of a regional military base. Local voters may choose the presidential can-

separation of powers the division of political power among executive, legislative, and judicial branches of government.

PARTY CONTROLLING EXECUTIVE AND LEGISLATIVE BRANCHES

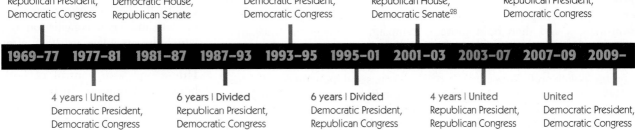

■ United under Democratic Party
■ United under Republican Party
■ Divided Government

8 years | Divided
Republican President,
Democratic Congress

6 years | Divided
Republican President,
Democratic House,
Republican Senate

2 years | United
Democratic President,
Democratic Congress

2 years | Divided
Republican President,
Republican House,
Democratic Senate[28]

2 years | Divided
Republican President,
Democratic Congress

| 1969–77 | 1977–81 | 1981–87 | 1987–93 | 1993–95 | 1995–01 | 2001–03 | 2003–07 | 2007–09 | 2009– |

4 years | United
Democratic President,
Democratic Congress

6 years | Divided
Republican President,
Democratic Congress

6 years | Divided
Democratic President,
Republican Congress

4 years | United
Republican President,
Republican Congress

United
Democratic President,
Democratic Congress

Divided government is not unique to the late twentieth century, but it has become more frequent.

MIDTERM ELECTIONS
CHANGING HORSES
GAINS/LOSSES FOR THE PRESIDENT'S PARTY:

1962 -4 (John F. Kennedy – D)

1966 -47 (Lyndon Johnson – D)

1970 -12 (Richard Nixon – R)

1974 -48 (Gerald Ford – R)

1978 -15 (Jimmy Carter – D)

1982 -26 (Ronald Reagan – R)

1986 -5 (Ronald Reagan – R)

1990 -8 (George H. W. Bush – R)

1994 -52 (Bill Clinton – D)

1998 +5 (Bill Clinton – D)

2002 +5 (George W. Bush – R)

2006 -30 (George W. Bush – R)

didate who they believe will work the hardest to cut taxes while voting for the candidate for Congress who promises to support increased federal spending in the region.[29]

At any given time, Party A may have an advantage on national issues while Party B is perceived by voters as being stronger on local issues. During the 1980s, presidential elections focused on defense, tax rates, and cultural values–issues that favored the Republicans. In contrast, races for Congress focused on more specific policy concerns, such as protecting Social Security, helping farmers or unemployed workers, and promoting local economic development. These were issues that gave Democrats the advantage.[30] Divided government reflects the divided issue preferences of

Americans. Voters want low inflation, a less obtrusive government, and low taxes—positions associated with the GOP. Voters also want the government to ensure a safe environment, promote education, and protect the integrity of the Social Security and Medicare programs—issues that favor the Democratic Party.[31]

Political scientists disagree as to whether divided government is the result of conscious voter choice. Some scholars doubt that the voters choose divided government. Their research shows that few voters literally decide to vote for a Democrat for president and a Republican for Congress, or vice versa, in hopes of producing divided government.[32] In contrast, other research indicates that even though the proportion of voters who split their ticket in order to balance the House with a president of the other party is small, the number is large enough to affect election outcomes.[33]

CONCLUSION
political parties
& PUBLIC POLICY

Political parties are similar to interest groups in that both connect individuals and groups to the government. The concept of democracy is that government policies reflect the policy preferences of citizens. In large, complex societies such as the United States, political parties are a means whereby individuals and groups can make their policy preferences known to government decision-makers and then hold those officials accountable for the adoption and successful implementation of those policy preferences.

Agenda Building

Political parties help set the policy agenda. Individuals and groups work through political parties to identify problems and raise issues for government action. In recent years, for example, religious conservatives have worked within the Republican Party to call attention to what they see as the moral decay of American society. The GOP has articulated their concerns in its party platform, and Republican candidates and elected officials have raised moral issues during election campaigns and while in office. Similarly, the Democratic Party has been a vehicle to advance the cause of groups and individuals concerned with safeguarding the environment, advancing the cause of minority rights, and protecting abortion rights.

Policy Formulation and Adoption

Political parties play an important role in policy formulation and adoption. Parties not only raise issues, but they also develop policy solutions to address the problems they identify. For example, the 2000 Republican Party platform included an outline of a tax cut proposal that eventually became the Economic Growth and Tax Reconciliation Act, which became law in 2001 after Republicans captured the White House and won control of both houses of Congress. In Congress, Democrats and Republicans meet in separate groups to formulate policy proposals and plan strategy for their adoption. The passage of the Economic Growth and Tax Reconciliation Act in 2001 represented a victory for Republicans in Congress over the organized opposition of the congressional Democrats.

Although political parties do not directly adopt policies, they facilitate policy adoption by bridging the separation of powers between the legislative and executive branches. The president works with fellow party members in Congress to pass legislation they support or to defeat legislation favored by the other party. President George W. Bush worked closely with Republican congressional leaders in Congress to pass his tax cut proposal, making compromises when necessary to ensure majority support. In the end, the measure won unanimous Republican support and the votes of a few Democrats, mostly members of Congress from states and districts that voted for Bush in the 2000 presidential election.

Political parties play an especially important role in America's separation of powers system because they reduce the number of political actors necessary to achieve policy compromises. Without political parties, congressional leaders would have to negotiate with dozens, perhaps hundreds, of members of the House and Senate in order to build majority support for policy proposals. In practice, the party leadership in each chamber, along with the White House, negotiates policy compromises on the final version of major legislation.[34]

Policy Implementation and Evaluation

Political parties participate indirectly in policy implementation. Presidential appointees are responsible for administering the agencies and departments of the executive branch of government. Most of the men and

In 2008, the Republican Party's energy platform called for more domestic energy production, including offshore and in the Arctic National Wildlife Refuge (ANWR).

women whom presidents select as department heads and agency administrators are fellow party members. Appointed executive-branch officials typically bring their partisan perspectives with them to the task of policy implementation. For example, Democratic presidents typically appoint administrators who have a background in environmental activism to head the Environmental Protection Agency (EPA). They are committed to aggressively enforcing the nation's environmental laws. They approach enforcement from the perspective of working with business and industry to achieve voluntary compliance with the law whenever possible.

Political parties play a key role in policy evaluation. Every democracy in the world has at least two political parties. The political party or party coalition holding the reins of government in a democracy is the **governing party**. It plays the most

EVERY DEMOCRACY IN THE WORLD HAS AT LEAST TWO POLITICAL PARTIES

important role in policy adoption and implementation. The political party out of power in a democracy is the **opposition party**. The opposition party criticizes the policies of the governing party and offers alternatives. The opposition party ensures that citizens receive more information about government policies and programs than the official statements of government leaders. The opposition party has an incentive to highlight failures and seek out inefficiency and corruption. The opposition also presents alternative policies and offers its leaders to the voters at the next election. Opposition parties help make democracy work by providing information to citizens and offering voters alternative policies and alternative sets of leaders to those put forward by the governing party.

governing party the political party or party coalition holding the reins of government in a democracy.

opposition party the political party out of power in a democracy.

1 Which of the following terms is best defined as a group of individuals who join together to seek government office in order to make public policy?

A. Interest group

B. Political action committee

C. Issue network

D. Political party

2 The Green, Reform, and Libertarian parties are examples of which of the following?

A. Interest groups

B. Party eras

C. Third parties

D. Political action committees

3 Which of the following is not a reason why the United States has a two-party system rather than a multiparty system?

A. The plurality election system awards office to the candidate with the most votes, leaving candidates who finished a strong second or third with nothing.

B. The Electoral College awards electoral votes only to candidates who win the most votes in each state.

C. The United States is not deeply divided along social and political lines.

D. Federal law limits the number of parties on the ballot to two.

4 An election system that awards office to the candidate with the most votes is known by which of the following terms?

A. Proportional representation

B. Party realignment

C. Plurality election system

D. Two-party system

5 Which of the following statements is true about Israel but is not true about the United States?

A. If a political party gets 10 percent of the vote, it will get 10 percent of the seats in the national legislature.

B. Candidates for the national legislature run from geographical areas called districts.

C. Nearly all of the members of the national legislature are members of one of two major political parties.

D. Voters may be reluctant to vote for a smaller party because they do not want to "throw their vote away" on a party that has no chance to gain representation.

6 Which of the following statements is true about political parties and elections in Israel?

A. Candidates are chosen in primaries to run from districts.

B. Voters cast their ballots primarily for political parties rather than for individual candidates.

C. Israel has a two-party system similar to the party system in the United States.

D. All of the above

7 Which of the following statements is true about party fundraising?

A. The Democratic Party has historically raised more money than the Republican Party.

B. The Republican Party closed the fundraising gap with the Democrats in 2006 and especially 2008.

C. The Republican Party has caught up with the Democrats because of Internet fundraising.

D. None of the above

8 The Grand Old Party (GOP) refers to which of the following?

A. Libertarian Party

B. Green Party

C. Democratic Party

D. Republican Party

9 Which of the following statements about party identification is accurate?

A. Since 2004, the proportion of Democrats in the population has increased by at least 5 percentage points.

B. Since 2004, the proportion of independents in the population has decreased by at least 5 percentage points.

C. Since 2004, the proportion of Republicans in the population has decreased by at least 5 percentage points.

D. None of the above

10 Which of the following statements about independents is accurate?

A. Most independents are men.

B. As a group, independents are more religious than are Democrats and Republicans.

C. Most independents are so disinterested in politics that they are not registered to vote.

D. None of the above

11 Among which of the following income groups would you expect the Republican candidate for president to do best in the next presidential election?

A. People making less than $30,000 a year

B. People making between $30,000 and $60,000 a year

C. People making between $100,000 and $150,000 a year

D. People making more than $200,000 a year

12 Which of the following groups would be *least* likely to give a majority of its votes to the Democratic candidate for president in the next election?

A. Asian Americans

B. African Americans

C. Whites

D. Latinos

13 Which of the following statements is true about members of the groups that support each of the two major political parties?

A. Men are more likely than women to vote Democratic.

B. The more education one has, the more likely that person is to vote Republican.

C. White voters are more likely than non-white voters to support Republican candidates.

D. None of the above

14 Which of the following statements is true about voter preferences?

A. Gay and lesbian voters tend to vote Republican.

B. Married voters tend to vote Democratic.

C. Women are more likely to vote Republican than are men.

D. None of the above

15 The Republican Party is strongest in which of the following regions?

A. South

B. West Coast

C. Midwest

D. Northeast

16 Which of the following groups tends to vote Democratic?

A. People who call themselves conservative

B. Gays and lesbians

C. People living in small towns and rural areas

D. Men

17 Which of the following groups tend to vote Republican?

A. People who attend religious services on a weekly basis

B. Women

C. People living in inner-city areas

D. Jews

18 Which of the following groups would be the most supportive of Democratic candidates?

A. Catholics

B. White evangelical Protestants

C. Jews

D. Members of mainline Protestant denominations

19 Political Party A controls both houses of Congress while Political Party B holds the presidency. This situation is an example of which of the following?

A. Divided government

B. Responsible parties

C. Proportional representation

D. Realignment

KNOW *the* **score**

18–19 correct: Congratulations! You are well informed!

15–17 correct: Your political knowledge is a bit low—be sure to review the key terms and visit TheThinkSpot.

<14 correct: Reread the chapter more thoroughly.

---

1. D; 2. C; 3. D; 4. C; 5. A; 6. B; 7. D; 8. D; 9. C; 10. A; 11. D; 12. C; 13. C; 14. D; 15. A; 16. B; 17. A; 18. C; 19. A

deployed small armies of volunteers and paid campaign workers to register voters and get out the vote. Both parties concentrated their efforts on the **battleground states**, the swing states in which the relative strength of the two major-party presidential candidates is close enough that either candidate could conceivably carry the state. The **air war** refers to campaign activities that involve the media, including television, radio, and the Internet. In 2008, campaign professionals focused their television advertising on network shows and cable channels that data analyses showed were popular with people most likely to support the candidates of their party.

battleground states swing states in which the relative strength of the two major-party presidential candidates is close enough so that either candidate could conceivably carry the state.

air war campaign activities that involve the media, including television, radio, and the Internet.

congressional ELECTIONS

In America's representative democracy, citizens elect the Congress. Voters choose members of the House to serve two-year terms. Senators run statewide for six-year terms. Because Senate terms are staggered, voters elect one-third of the Senate every two years.

House Elections

The most striking feature of elections for the U.S. House of Representatives is that most incumbents are reelected. In 2006, only 25 incumbents were defeated for reelection, three in a primary election and 22 in the general election, for a success rate of 94 percent for those members seeking reelection.[26] Since 1986, more than 95 percent of incumbent representatives seeking reelection have won. Furthermore, many races are not close. In 2006, only 58 House races were decided by a margin of 10 percentage points or less.[27]

Incumbency affords sitting members of Congress a number of electoral advantages. Most incumbent House members are much better known than challengers and they are

> In 2006, only 58 House races were decided by a margin of 10 percentage points or less.

almost always better funded. In 2006, the average House incumbent raised $1.3 million compared with $283,000 for the average challenger.[28] Another reason for the high reelection rate for incumbents is that many congressional districts are safe for one party or the other. Incumbents in districts that are safe for their party may face serious challengers in the party primary, but they will probably not be unseated in a general election.

Historically, the political party holding the White House loses seats in the House of Representatives in midterm elections. Between 1920 and 1980, the president's party lost ground in the House in 15 of 16 midterm elections, dropping an average of 35 seats. The phenomenon was so pronounced and appeared so regularly that political scientists de-

"Let's try voting for the greater of the two evils this time and see what happens."

veloped theories to explain it. One set of theories focused on the withdrawal of coattails. The **coattail effect** is a political phenomenon in which a strong candidate for one office gives a boost to fellow party members on the same ballot seeking other offices. Coattails are particularly important in election contests in which voters have relatively little information about either candidate, such as open-seat races for the U.S. House. In presidential election years, some of the people who turn out to cast their ballots for a popular presidential candidate either vote a straight ticket or support candidates from the same party as their presidential choice even though they have no real candidate preference. Two years later, without a presidential race on the ballot, many of the congressional candidates who benefited from the coattail effect lose without it. A second set of theories attempts to explain the tendency of the president's party to lose House seats in the midterm on the basis of ideological balancing. Moderate voters support the opposition party in order to restrain the president from pushing policies that they perceive to be ideologically extreme. Some voters may also use their vote at midterm to punish the president's party for poor performance, especially the performance of the economy.[29]

Senate Elections

Senate races are more competitive than House elections. Incumbency is a factor in Senate contests, but it is not the overwhelming advantage that it is in House races. Furthermore, Senate races are typically closer than House contests, even when the incumbent wins. In 2006, 8 of 33 Senate races were decided by less than 10 percent of the vote.

Political scientists identify a number of differences between Senate and House races that account for the relatively greater vulnerability of Senate incumbents. First, Senate constituencies are more diverse than most House constituencies and, hence, more competitive. Second, incumbent senators generally face stronger challengers than House incumbents. A seat in the Senate is an important-enough prize to attract the candidacies of governors, big-city mayors, members of the House, and well-known figures such as astronauts, war heroes, sports stars, and show business celebrities. Finally, research has found that voters tend to perceive Senate races as national election contests. As a result, national issues often play a prominent role in Senate campaigns and national trends frequently affect Senate election outcomes.

coattail effect a political phenomenon in which a strong candidate for one office gives a boost to fellow party members on the same ballot seeking other offices.

takeaction

IN-PERSON POLITICS >>

Although this is the age of television campaigns and Internet websites, volunteers still have a place in election campaigns. They mail campaign literature to registered voters, telephone supporters to encourage them to vote, and drive citizens to the polls on Election Day. Whereas volunteers augment the work of campaign professionals in races for major office, they are often the backbone of campaigns for local office.

Your assignment is to research campaign activity by volunteering for the candidate of your choice. Contact the local political party organizations to identify local campaigns that are seeking volunteers. Your instructor may be able to assist you in making contact with a campaign as well. To verify your volunteer work, bring your instructor a signed note from the campaign office manager on letterhead stationery indicating the time you spent on the campaign. Also, prepare a written report discussing your volunteer work and your impressions of the campaign. It should cover the following points:

- Identify the candidate and the office the candidate seeks, noting whether the candidate is the incumbent.
- Identify the location and describe the physical layout of the campaign office.
- Describe the other people working in the campaign as to age, gender, race, and ethnicity.
- List the task you completed for the campaign, explaining why you believe your work was important to the campaign's success.
- Assess whether the campaign office was well-organized or disorganized.
- Describe your impression of the experience, discussing whether you had a good time and if you ever plan to volunteer to work for a campaign again.

TEST yourself

1 Luisa Cangelosi voted for the Republican candidate for president, the Democratic candidate for the U.S. Senate, and the Democratic candidate for the U.S. House. Ms. Cangelosi did which of the following?
A. Violated the Voting Rights Act
B. Voted in a presidential preference primary
C. Voted a split ticket
D. Voted in a primary election

2 State A limits primary voting to people who are registered party members. State A has which of the following?
A. A closed primary
B. An open primary
C. A blanket primary
D. A presidential preference primary

3 Which of the following elections is not conducted statewide at-large in most states?
A. Election for governor
B. Election for U.S. House
C. Election for U.S. Senate
D. Election for president

4 How often does reapportionment take place?
A. Every ten years after the U.S. Census
B. Every four years, to coincide with the presidential election
C. Whenever population changes by more than 10 percent
D. None of the above

5 *Baker v. Carr* (1962) and *Wesberry v. Sanders* (1964) dealt with which of the following issues?
A. Gerrymandering
B. Reapportionment
C. Redistricting
D. Voting Rights Act

6 Which of the following statements is true about the role of money in political campaigns?
A. The candidate who spends the most money always wins.
B. Advertising, especially television advertising, is the single largest expenditure in most campaign budgets.
C. Candidates who provide most of their own campaign money usually win because they do not have to spend time fundraising.
D. All of the above.

7 The Swift Boat Veterans for Truth is an example of which of the following?
A. Interest group
B. PAC
C. 527 committee
D. Political party

8 Federal funds are used to partially finance campaigns for which of the following offices?
A. President
B. U.S. House
C. U.S. Senate
D. All federal offices, including Congress and the president

9 Which of the following reasons helps explain why incumbent members of Congress typically win reelection?
A. They usually have more money than their challenges.
B. They are usually better known than their challengers.
C. Many congressional districts are safe for one party or the other.
D. All of the above.

10 Which of **the** following groups officially selected John McCain as the 2008 presidential nominee of the Republican Party?
A. Delegates at the 2008 Republican National Convention by majority vote
B. Electors from each state voting in the Electoral College
C. Voters nationwide in an open primary
D. Voters nationwide in a closed primary

11 How were the delegates to the 2008 Democratic National Convention chosen?
A. They were chosen by the Congress.
B. They were chosen by the Electoral College.
C. They were chosen by each state party, either through a presidential preference primary or a party caucus.
D. They were chosen in a national primary election.

12 Which of the following plays the most important role in selecting the presidential nominees of the Democratic and Republican parties?
A. Party activists and party voters
B. Party bosses
C. Each party's congressional delegation
D. Independent voters

13 Why is doing well in the Iowa Caucus and the New Hampshire Primary important for candidates seeking their party's nomination for president?

A. Candidates who do well in both states benefit from large numbers of convention delegates.

B. Candidates who do well in both states benefit from a large amount of favorable publicity.

C. Candidates who do well in both states benefit from a large number of electoral votes.

D. All of the above.

14 Which of the following statements about presidential electors is true?

A. They choose the party's presidential nominee at the national party convention.

B. They are elected officials, including members of Congress and state legislatures.

C. They are chosen by the state parties.

D. They select the president by a two-thirds vote.

15 Alabama elects seven members of the House. How many electoral votes does Alabama have?

A. 7

B. 8

C. 9

D. 11

16 Assume for the purpose of this question that a Democrat, a Republican, and a major independent candidate are running for president. In California, the Democrat gets 45 percent of the vote, the Republican gets 40 percent, and the independent receives the rest. How many of California's electoral votes will the Democratic candidate receive?

A. All of them

B. 45 percent of them

C. None of them

D. It depends on the outcome of the runoff between the Democrat and the Republican, the two top finishers.

17 Under which of the following circumstances would Candidate A win the 2012 presidential election?

A. Candidate A wins a majority of the popular vote nationwide.

B. Candidate A carries more states than any other candidate.

C. Candidate A wins a plurality of the popular vote nationwide.

D. Candidate A wins a majority of the electoral vote.

18 Which of the following is considered a red state?

A. New York

B. California

C. Texas

D. Illinois

19 Which of the following statements is an expression of retrospective voting?

A. I voted for Candidate A because I like her promises and think she will do a good job in office.

B. I voted for Candidate B because he is a Republican and I am a Republican.

C. I voted for Candidate C because I agree with her on the issues.

D. I voted for Candidate D because I like the way things are going and he is the incumbent.

20 Person A tells survey researchers that she is a committed Democrat who decided to vote for the Democratic nominee for president well before the party's national convention. Person A is an example of which of the following?

A. Base voter

B. Swing voter

C. Retrospective voter

D. Independent voter

KNOW *the* score

18–20 correct: Congratulations! You are well informed!

15–17 correct: Your political knowledge is a bit low—be sure to review the key terms and visit TheThinkSpot.

<14 correct: Reread the chapter more thoroughly.

1. C; 2. A; 3. B; 4. A; 5. B; 6. B; 7. C; 8. A; 9. D; 10. A; 11. C; 12. A; 13. B; 14. C; 15. C; 16. A; 17. D; 18. C; 19. D; 20. A

on all three counts and are in great demand. The money committees in the Senate are Appropriations, Budget, and Finance. In the House, the committees dealing with money are Appropriations, Budget, and Ways and Means. The other Senate committees that are considered prestigious assignments are Foreign Relations, Armed Services, and Judiciary.[21] In the House, members want to serve on the Energy and Commerce Committee because it deals with a broad range of important legislation. The Transportation and Infrastructure Committee is popular as well, because members see it as a way to procure projects for their districts. Senators and representatives frequently request assignments on committees that deal with policy issues particularly relevant to their states and districts. Members of Congress from urban and financial centers are attracted to the banking committees; members from agricul-

tural states favor membership on the agricultural committees. Finally, some members of Congress request particular committee assignments for personal reasons. For example, members of the House with prior military service may seek membership on the Armed Services Committee.[22]

Party committees in each chamber make committee assignments for members of their party. Party leaders control these committees and, in theory, they could use them to reward friends and punish enemies. In practice, however, the party committees try to accommodate the preferences of members. If members are unhappy with a committee assignment, they may request a transfer when openings occur on committees they prefer. Committee switching is not especially common, particularly among senior members, because members who change

committees must start over on the seniority ladder of the new committee. Nonetheless, it is not unusual for members to request transfer to one of the really choice committees.

The majority party controls each committee and subcommittee. Before the 2006 election, the Republican Party was the majority party in the House and Senate. Republicans comprised a majority of the membership of each committee and subcommittee and chaired every committee and subcommittee in both chambers. In 2006, the Democrats won majorities in both houses of Congress and the roles of the parties reversed. Beginning in 2007, Democrats made up a majority of every committee and subcommittee and Democrats chaired every committee and subcommittee.

Each party has its own procedures for selecting committee chairs (for the majority party) and ranking members (for the minority party). Republican Party rules stipulate that the party committee that makes initial committee assignments nom-

think

Which congressional committee would you choose? Explain your answer.

takeaction

IN-PERSON LEARNING >>

Sending E-mail to Your U.S. Representative

Your assignment is to participate in America's democracy by sending an e-mail message about a current policy issue to the man or woman who represents you in the U.S. House. You can find the name and e-mail address of your U.S. representative online at www.house.gov. The following guidelines will help you write an effective letter:

- Know what you are writing about. If you do not understand an issue, your message will have little impact. You may choose an issue discussed in the textbook or another topic in the news. Be sure, however, that you have researched the issue sufficiently to speak about it intelligently.
- Use correct grammar. E-mail messages filled with grammatical errors and misspelled words will not have a positive impact.

- Make your point clearly and succinctly. Present your opinion and give the reasons behind your position in no more than a few paragraphs. Long, rambling messages are ineffective.

Print the e-mail message and submit a copy to your instructor. Your instructor will not grade you on your point of view, but will evaluate your work on the criteria stated above.

inates chairs or ranking members with confirmation by the **party caucus**, which is all of the party members of a chamber meeting as a group. The Republicans select chairs or ranking members based on party loyalty and ability to raise campaign money for party candidates, rather than using seniority as the basis for selection.[23] Each Republican member of the House is expected to contribute money to the party's campaign fund. Party members who fail to meet their financial obligations will be passed over for leadership positions.[24] Democrats, meanwhile, provide for the selection of committee chairs and ranking members by a secret-ballot vote of the party caucus. The Democrat with the most seniority on a particular committee usually wins the vote, except on those rare occasions when a senior member has alienated his or her colleagues. Both parties limit chairs and subcommittee chairs to six-year terms.

In addition to party caucuses, Congress members will join bipartisan caucuses organized around shared agendas and policy goals. Michigan Democrat Carolyn Kirkpatrick is a member of the Congressional Black Caucus.

party caucus all of the party members of the House or Senate meeting as a group.

the legislative
PROCESS

the traditional image of the legislative process is that a member introduces a bill, it is referred to committee, it goes from committee to the floor, from the floor to a conference committee, and, if it passes every step, to the president. Since the early 1990s, the legislative process has not conformed to the traditional to the traditional "bill-becomes-a-law" formula. Congress has adopted modifications in the traditional legislative process to pass major legislation. The key differences between the traditional model and the new model of legislative policymaking are the following:

- Major legislation is often written in the form of **omnibus bills**, which are complex, highly detailed legislative proposals covering one or more subjects or programs. The immigration reform measure that passed the House included border security provisions, criminalization of illegal immigration status, sanc-

tions against people who assist the undocumented, and a tighter worker verification process for employers. The Senate bill contained border security, a guest worker program, employee verification, and a pathway to citizenship for unauthorized residents. Congressional leaders assemble omnibus bills to attract as much support as possible.

- Major legislation is frequently referred to more than one standing committee. Involving several committees in the legislative process provides a measure's supporters with an opportunity to draft legislation that enjoys a broader base of support. Furthermore, the strategy avoids the danger of a hostile committee chair bottling up the bill, which

SINCE THE 1940s, THE LENGTH OF THE AVERAGE BILL HAS INCREASED FROM 2.5 PAGES TO MORE THAN 19 PAGES

sometimes happens to measures referred to only one committee.

- The legislative leadership, especially in the House, coordinates the work of the standing committees and sets timetables to move legislation through the committee stage.

- The legislative leadership, especially in the House, fashions the details of the legislation and develops a strategy for winning passage on the floor. Even after a bill clears committee, the leadership may change its provisions to broaden its base of support.

- A conference committee of dozens, maybe even hundreds, of members works out the final

omnibus bills complex, highly detailed legislative proposals covering one or more subjects or programs.

compromise language of the bill. Once again, the goal is to build a broad-enough coalition of support for the measure to ensure its passage.[25]

Introduction

In 2007, members of Congress introduced 9,227 bills and resolutions—6,194 in the House and 3,033 in the Senate.[26] A **bill** is a proposed law. Except for revenue raising bills, which must begin in the House, any bill may be introduced in either chamber. A **resolution** is a legislative statement of opinion on a certain matter. Resolutions may be introduced in either chamber. A member who introduces a measure is known as its **sponsor**. Bills and resolutions may have multiple sponsors, known as co-sponsors. Over the years, legislative measures have grown longer and more complex. Since

the 1940s, the length of the average bill has increased from 2.5 pages to more than 19 pages.[27] Omnibus bills are far longer. The No Child Left Behind Act, the education reform measure enacted in 2002, was 670 pages long.[28]

Committee and Subcommittee Action

Once a bill or resolution is introduced, it is assigned a number and referred to committee. A measure introduced in the House has the initials "H.R." for House of Representatives, whereas Senate measures begin with the "S." for Senate. The immigration reform measure passed by the House was H.R. 4437. (The number signifies the order in which a measure was introduced.) The sponsors of a bill also give it a popular title designed to put the measure in a favorable light. Representative James F. Sensenbrenner,

Jr., the House sponsor of immigration reform, called his bill the Border Protection, Antiterrorism, and Illegal Immigration Control Act. The chamber parliamentarian, working under the oversight of the Speaker of the House or the Senate majority leader, refers the measure to a committee based on the subject covered by the bill or resolution.

Complex issues such as healthcare, immigration reform, international trade, and homeland security often cut across committee jurisdictions. Sometimes committees develop arrangements to cooperate or

bill a proposed law.

resolution a legislative statement of opinion on a certain matter.

sponsor a member who introduces a measure.

THE GATEKEEPERS

COMMITTEES ARE GATEKEEPERS iN THE LAWMAKiNG PROCESS, KiLLiNG MOST OF THE BiLLS AND RESOLUTiONS REFERRED TO THEM. iN 2007, CONGRESSiONAL COMMiTTEES REPORTED 908 MEASURES TO THE FLOOR OF 9,227 BiLLS AND RESOLUTiONS iNTRODUCED FOR A REPORT RATE OF 9.8 PERCENT. THE FOLLOWiNG MEASURES ARE MOST LiKELY TO RECEiVE DETAiLED COMMiTTEE AND SUBCOMMiTTEE CONSiDERATiON:
- MEASURES THAT COMMiTTEE AND SUBCOMMiTTEE CHAiRS PERSONALLY FAVOR.
- MEASURES THAT HAVE THE SUPPORT OF THE CONGRESSiONAL LEADERSHiP.
- MEASURES THAT ENJOY BROAD SUPPORT iN CONGRESS AS A WHOLE.
- MEASURES THAT BENEFiT FROM THE BACKiNG OF iMPORTANT iNTEREST GROUPS.
- MEASURES THAT DEAL WiTH iSSUES THAT MANY MEMBERS OF CONGRESS AND A LARGE SEGMENT OF THE GENERAL PUBLiC CONSiDER iMPORTANT.
- MEASURES THAT ARE PUSHED BY THE WHiTE HOUSE. iN CONTRAST, MEASURES THAT LACK SUPPORT, OR ARE OPPOSED BY THE COMMiTTEE OR CONGRESSiONAL LEADERSHiP, SELDOM EMERGE FROM COMMiTTEE.

Congressional War Power

Should Congress have more control over U.S. military power? If so, could this harm the United States' ability to act in times of immediate crisis?

Has history run its course in such a way that the executive should keep its increased war-making power? Is it necessary in times when the United States faces an enemy without borders and a conventional military?

Overview: The American founders believed that the predisposition to engage in war lay with the executive power, and that it was through war that nations ended up in tyranny. The founders believed that the decision to go to war should be made by the legislative branch because, in democratic theory, it is the legislative branch that represents the will of the people.

The Constitution does not exactly delineate between congressional and executive war powers. The founders assumed that power would shift between the branches as conditions demanded, but over the course of American history, it is the president's office that has assumed considerable constitutional discretion in how the United States engages in war and diplomacy. For example, James Madison would not go to war with Great Britain in 1812 without a war declaration from Congress, yet the last seven major American conflicts (Korea, Vietnam, First Gulf War, Kosovo, war on terror, Afghanistan, and Iraq War) were and are conducted without declarations of war.

With the September 11, 2001 attacks on American soil, the U.S. government has fundamentally shifted traditional defense policy. The Bush Doctrine holds that the United States will use preemptive military force, if necessary, for national defense. Furthermore, it is undisputed that the United States is now considered the "hyperpower," that is, the sole nation capable of projecting military and economic might anywhere on the globe. This opens up many constitutional and moral questions. What is the proper forum for national debate in regard to this shift in defense strategy? How, then, will future American force be used? For all practical purposes, has the military power of the Congress been assumed by the executive branch? What is to be the role of Congress? These questions promise to be at the forefront of defense policy debate for the foreseeable future.

supporting increased congressional control over military matters

the founders believed the decision to go to war should be left to the American people. With the exception of invasion or extraordinary circumstances, the founders believed Congress is the proper venue to discuss and debate matters of war and peace, as Congress is considered the direct representative of the American people.

some American foreign policy has been harmful to American interests. Executive use of the war power has harmed U.S. interests; take, for example, the Vietnam War. President Johnson used his authority to increase military involvement based on faulty intelligence, and President Nixon used U.S. military force against nations (Cambodia and Laos) with whom America was not at war.

in the post-9/11, post–Cold War world, Congress more than ever needs to supervise U.S. military activity. With the United States' new foreign policy doctrine of preemption, it is imperative that Congress be consulted to ensure that the use of military force is just and absolutely necessary.

against increased congressional control over military matters

declarations of war are a relic of the eighteenth century. With the speed of modern conventional weapons, Congress does not have the time to respond to current military threats. Additionally, the nature of America's enemies has changed—for instance, how does a nation declare war on terrorist organizations whose political and military base transcends borders?

Congress has not abdicated its military power; it has failed to exercise its constitutional prerogatives. The Constitution gives Congress the authority to authorize military expenditures, thus limiting the war-making power of the executive. For example, the new Democratic-controlled House of Representatives passed a war funding bill linking military spending with a timetable to withdraw troops from Iraq.

the Constitution does not explicitly state that a declaration of war is necessary for the use of American Forces. Some constitutional scholars argue that simple congressional resolution is sufficient for Congress to satisfy its Article I obligations.

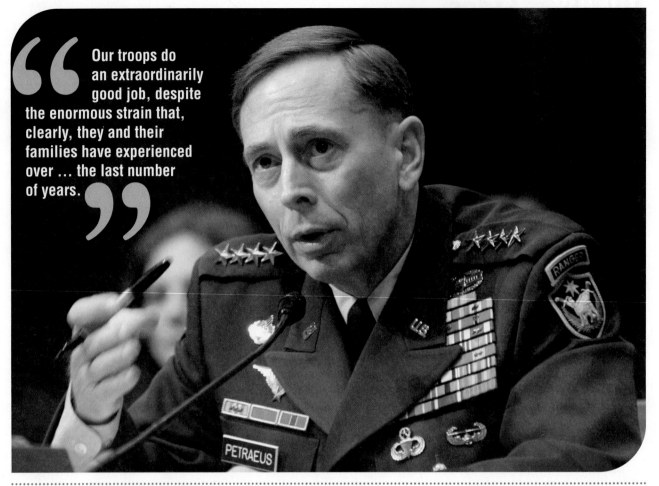

> Our troops do an extraordinarily good job, despite the enormous strain that, clearly, they and their families have experienced over ... the last number of years.

General David Petraeus testifies before Congress in support of continuing operations in the Iraq War. He was confirmed by the Senate as head of the Central military command, directing U. S. forces in East Africa, the Middle East, and Central Asia.

defer to one another.[29] At other times, the leadership employs **multiple referral of legislation,** which is the practice of assigning legislation to more than one committee. The Senate permits joint, sequential, and partial referrals of legislation. House rules allow only sequential and partial referrals, and one committee may be designated the committee of primary jurisdiction. The Speaker makes multiple referral decisions in the House. In the Senate, multiple referral of legislation requires the unanimous agreement of the chamber. Multiple referral of legislation is more common in the House than in the Senate and is more likely to be used for major legislation than routine measures. Although most multiple referrals go to only two committees, complex measures may be referred to several committees. Four com-

mittees considered immigration reform in the House, including Judiciary, Homeland Security, Education and the Workforce, and Ways and Means.

Committees and subcommittees do the detailed work of Congress. Once a measure is sent to committee or subcommittee, the chair and the ranking minority member ask their staffs to prepare separate reports on its merits. For major legislation, the committee or subcommittee chair schedules hearings to allow the measure's supporters and opponents a chance to make their case. Full committees generally conduct Senate hearings; subcommittees hold most hearings in the House.

The next step is **legislative markup**. This is the process in which legislators go over a measure line-by-line, revising, amending, or

rewriting it. In the House, markup usually takes place in subcommittee. Markup in the Senate generally occurs in full committee.

Once markup is complete, the subcommittee, and then the full committee, vote on whether to recommend passage. If the measure is voted down at either stage or members vote to **table** it (that is, postpone consideration), it is probably dead, at least for the session. If the measure is

multiple referral of legislation the practice of allowing more than one committee to consider legislation.
legislative markup the process in which legislators go over a measure line-by-line, revising, amending, or rewriting it.
table to postpone consideration of a measure during the legislative process.

approved in subcommittee and committee, the next step is the floor of the full House or Senate.

The rules of the House provide a mechanism for members to bring to the floor a bill that has been tabled or defeated in committee. However, the procedure is seldom used and almost never successful. A bill's supporters can compel a committee to report a measure to the floor by means of a **discharge petition**, in which a majority of the members of the House of Representatives force a committee to report a bill to the floor of the House. Since 1910, only three measures forced from committee through the use of a discharge petition eventually became law.[30] Most members of Congress are reluctant to sign a discharge petition because they do not want to undermine committee authority. Furthermore, the threat of a discharge petition is sometimes enough to stimulate a committee to act on stalled legislation.

Floor Action

In the House, the process for moving measures from committee to the floor varies, depending on the type of measure involved. The House considers noncontroversial measures of relatively minor importance through a shortcut procedure on designated special days set aside for that purpose. Budget resolutions and **appropriation bills** may go directly from committee to the House floor.

The leadership may bring major pieces of legislation to the floor without committee consideration or with only cursory committee examination. If a measure was carefully studied in committee in the last session of Congress, the leadership may determine that no more committee work is necessary. Sometimes, the leadership wants to move quickly for political reasons. In 2005, the House leadership put legislation on a fast track to provide aid for people affected by Hurricane Katrina, moving it directly to the floor without committee consideration.[31]

Most measures that clear standing committee must go to the Rules Committee before going to the floor. The **House Rules Committee** is a standing committee that determines the rules under which a specific bill can be debated, amended, and considered on the House floor. Because more measures clear committee than the full House has time to consider, the Rules Committee determines which measures go forward. Measures that are not assigned rules are not considered on the House floor and therefore have no chance of passage unless supporters can succeed in forcing the legislation out of the Rules Committee by means of a discharge petition.

When the Rules Committee refers a bill to the floor, it sets a time limit for debate and determines the ground rules for amendments. Debate in the House is defined by the rule under which a measure is considered. The Rules Committee limited debate on the immigration reform bill to two hours, divided equally between proponents organized by the chair of the Judiciary Committee and opponents organized by the committee's ranking member. The Rules Committee also sets the terms for consideration of amendments, including identifying which amendments may be offered, who may propose amendments, and the order in which amendments may be considered. A rule that opens a measure to amendment on the House floor without restriction is an **open rule**. In contrast, a **closed rule** is a rule that prohibits floor consideration of amendments on the House floor. The measure must be voted up or down without amendment. In practice, both open rules and strict closed rules are rare. Nearly two-thirds of rules are at least somewhat restrictive. For most major pieces of legislation, the Rules Committee grants restrictive rules that limit the consideration of amendments to certain specific alternatives. Restrictive rules also determine the order of consideration for amendments.[32]

> **SOMETIMES THE LEADERSHIP WANTS TO MOVE QUICKLY FOR POLITICAL REASONS**

discharge petition a procedure whereby a majority of the members of the House of Representatives can force a committee to report a bill to the floor of the House.

appropriation bill a legislative authorization to spend money for particular purposes.

House Rules Committee a standing committee that determines the rules under which a specific bill can be debated, amended, and considered on the House floor.

open rule a rule that opens a measure to amendment on the House floor without restriction.

closed rule a rule that prohibits floor consideration of amendments on the House floor.

think Does the Rules Committee in the House have too much power?

the legislative process **221**

Rules are a means for structuring debate on the House floor. Rules allowing choice among comprehensive substitute bills focus debate on big choices rather than the details of legislation. Rules can also prevent a measure's opponents from forcing votes on the most unpopular provisions of a bill or offering amendments that the leadership opposes.[33] The Rules Committee is an important element of the Speaker's power. In contrast to other House committees, the Speaker personally appoints the majority party members of the Rules Committee subject to approval by the party caucus, thereby ensuring control. The Speaker uses the Rules Committee not only to determine which measures reach the floor, but also to structure the policy choices available to members on the floor.

In the Senate, a measure typically reaches the floor through the mechanism of a unanimous consent agreement (UCA), which is a formal understanding on procedures for conducting Senate business that requires acceptance by every member of the chamber. UCAs, like rules from the Rules Committee in the House, limit debate and determine the amendments that can be offered. Because a single senator can prevent the adoption of an agreement, UCAs reflect negotiation between the Senate leadership and the membership to consider the needs of every member. A member who objects to a UCA is said to have placed a hold on the measure. Members can work through the Majority Leader's secretary to place holds anonymously, but that approach is rare. Often the purpose of a hold is to force some sort of concession, sometimes on an unrelated piece of legislation. The majority leader may choose to bring the measure to the floor despite the hold, but

The Rules Committee is an important element of the Speaker's power.

> **filibuster** an attempt to defeat a measure through prolonged debate.
>
> **killer amendment** an amendment designed to make a measure so unattractive that it will lack enough support to pass.

the motion to proceed may face a **filibuster,** an attempt to defeat a measure through prolonged debate. If that fails, the bill itself may be filibustered.

Nonetheless, senators usually get their legislation to the floor. A senator can often obtain unanimous consent by accepting policy compromises or by threatening to oppose the legislation favored by the measure's opponents. A senator can also bring a measure to the floor by offering it as an amendment to another bill. Senate rules allow consideration of non-germane amendments, unrelated to the subject matter of the original measure. For example, Senator James N. Imhofe of Oklahoma offered an amendment to the Senate immigration reform bill to declare English the official language of the United States. The amendment passed.[34] Non-germane amendments are not allowed in the House.

Senators may offer a killer amendment, an amendment so unattractive that it will lack enough support to pass. A **killer amendment** is an amendment designed to make a measure Congress considered in 1995, offered an amendment that would count time already served in the calculation.

Prominent southern senators discuss strategy for their filibuster of the 1964 Civil Rights Act. The filibuster failed, and the Civil Rights Act was signed into law by President Lyndon Johnson.

If it passed, many members of Congress would effectively have voted themselves out office.[35] Senators sometimes propose unrelated amendments in order to promote their particular policy views or embarrass their political opponents.

Floor proceedings are more structured in the House than in the Senate. Although House members can delay action through parliamentary maneuvers, the Rules Committee system generally ensures that House proceedings move forward. In contrast, the rules of the Senate maximize the rights of individual senators. One senator or a group of senators may use these rules to produce chaos on the Senate floor.

Jimmy Stewart plays a filibustering senator in the 1939 classic film *Mr. Smith Goes to Washington.*

Indeed, senators sometimes take advantage of the rules to defeat legislation they oppose. Senate rules do not limit the amount of time a senator, or the chamber as a whole, can discuss a measure, so a bill's opponents may filibuster. Under Senate rules, each senator who wishes to speak must be recognized and cannot be interrupted without consent. The Senate cannot vote on a piece of legislation until every senator has finished speaking.[36]

The procedure for ending a filibuster is known as **cloture**. Senators wanting to halt a filibuster must announce their intentions and gather the signatures of a sixth of the Senate, 16 senators, to force a vote on cloture, which, in turn, requires a three-fifths vote of the Senate membership (60 votes) to succeed. Although Senate rules limit post-cloture debate to 30 hours, a measure's opponents often delay action even longer through parliamentary maneuvering.

Filibusters have grown more common. From 1955 to 1960, the Senate experienced only two filibusters.[37] In contrast, recent sessions of Congress have averaged 28

filibusters each, with half of all major pieces of legislation facing a filibuster or a serious threat of a filibuster.[38] The filibuster is a potent weapon. Since 1970, the passage rate for legislation subject to filibuster has been 54 percent compared to a 74 percent passage rate for measures not filibustered.[39]

The nature of the filibuster has changed as well. In the 1950s and 1960s, Senators conducting a filibuster engaged in long-winded debate. Today, classic filibusters are a thing of the past. Senators simply announce their intention to filibuster, and the Senate goes on with other business while the leadership works to gather sufficient support to invoke cloture. Sometimes, Senate leaders file a cloture petition to end debate even before a filibuster materializes. The Senate invoked cloture to end the debate on immigration reform despite the absence of an organized filibuster against the measure.

Conference Committee Action

A measure does not pass Congress until it clears both the House and Senate in identical form. If the House and Senate pass similar, but not identical bills, the chamber that initially passed the measure can

agree to the changes made by the other chamber, or the two houses can resolve their differences by adopting a series of reconciling amendments. When the differences between the two measures are too great for easy resolution, the two chambers create a conference committee. Although Congress resorts to the conference committee process for only about 10 percent of the measures that ultimately become law, conference committees are typical for major legislation.[40]

The Speaker and the Senate majority leader appoint the members of a conference committee (called **conferees**) from lists given to them by committee leaders. Although the Speaker and majority leader can appoint any member, they almost always select members of the standing committee or committees that considered the bill, including the committee chair(s) and ranking member(s). If the Speaker and majority leader are concerned that the conferees may not uphold the position of the majority party, they may also appoint members who are sympathetic to the party's position.[41] Because of omnibus bills, the size of conference committees has grown, sometimes including dozens or even hundreds of members.

A conference committee is sometimes called the third house of Congress because it writes the final version of legislation. The conferees are not bound to stick with the version of the measures passed by either the House or the Senate. The conference committee can delete

Floor proceedings are more structured in the House than in the Senate.

cloture the procedure for ending a filibuster.

conferees members of a conference committee.

President George Bush vetoed the State Children's Health Insurance Program, saying the bill was too costly.

provisions passed by both houses and include provisions passed by neither. In practice, the final version of major legislation reflects a compromise among the party leadership in each chamber, the president, and key interest groups. Each chamber's conferees vote separately. Once a majority agree on a compromise, the revised measure, called the conference report, goes back to the floor of the House and Senate. The first chamber to vote on the conference report has three options: to accept, reject, or return to conference for more negotiations. If the first chamber accepts the measure, the second chamber has two options, to adopt or reject. If both chambers accept the conference report, the measure goes to the president.

SUCCESS RATE OF BILLS IN 2007
INTRODUCED: 9,227
REPORTED: 908
(9.8% OF ALL INTRODUCED)
ENACTED INTO LAW: 138

Presidential Action

If the president signs a measure, it becomes law. If the president does not sign the measure, it becomes law anyway after ten days unless Congress is adjourned, in which case it dies. When a president allows a measure to die without signature after Congress has adjourned, it is known as a **pocket veto.**

If the president opposes a measure he can use his **veto,** the refusal to sign a measure passed by the legislature. A president vetoes a bill by returning it to Congress with a statement of objections. Congress needs a two-thirds vote of each house to override the president's veto and enact the measure into law. Should either house fall short of two-thirds, the veto is sustained, and the measure has failed. Over the last century, presidents have vetoed about 1 percent of the measures reaching their desks, with Congress overriding only about 7 percent of those vetoes.[42]

The president must accept or reject a measure in its entirety. Congress takes advantage of this situation by passing omnibus bills combining provisions the president wants with measures the president would veto were they standing alone. A **rider** is a provision, unlikely to become law on its own merits, which is attached to an important measure so that it will ride through the legislative process. Appropriation bills are favorite vehicles for riders because they are must-pass legislation. For example, Congress enacted a prohibition against smoking on commercial airline flights as a rider attached to an appropriation measure.[43]

Modifications in the legislative process adopted to increase the likelihood that major legislation will become law have been effective. Although the overall success rate for bills is poor, a majority of the major pieces of legislation considered by Congress become law. In 2007, only 138 bills out of 9,227 measures introduced in the House and Senate became law for a success rate of only 1.5 percent.[44] In contrast, major pieces of legislation fare much better. Over the last decade, 59 percent of major bills have become law.[45]

pocket veto the action of a president allowing a measure to die without signature after Congress has adjourned.

veto an action by the chief executive refusing to approve a measure passed by the legislature.

rider a provision, unlikely to become law on its own merits, that is attached to an important measure so that it will ride through the legislative process.

congress
&PUBLIC POLICY

along with the presidency, Congress is the foremost policymaking institution of American national government.

Agenda Building

Congress plays an important role in agenda building. Although many of the issues that Congress addresses were first raised by other political actors, Congress increases an issue's visibility by holding hearings and conducting debates. In recent years, Congress has helped focus attention on such issues as immigration reform, campaign finance reform, global warming, and Internet privacy.

Policy Formulation and Adoption

Congress formulates policy through the legislative process. The policy formulation process in Congress usually involves competition among political interests. The outcome of that process may reflect compromise among those interests or the triumph of one set of interests over other interests, depending on the relative political strength of competing groups.

Congress participates in policy adoption when it passes legislation, ratifies treaties, confirms appointments, and proposes constitutional amendments. In each of these situations, Congress shares policy adoption authority with other political actors. Legislation passed by Congress does not become law unless it is signed by the president or passed by a two-thirds margin over a presidential veto. Treaties cannot be ratified or appointees confirmed unless they are first proposed or nominated by the president. Constitutional amendments must be ratified by three-fourths of the states.

Policy Implementation and Evaluation

Congress uses the authorization process and the budget process to influence policy implementation. Congress typically authorizes the creation of agencies or programs for a limited number of years, after which the agency or program must be reauthorized. Executive branch officials, knowing that their agencies and programs face periodic reauthorization, have an incentive to conform to the wishes of Con-

CONGRESS PARTICIPATES IN POLICY ADOPTION WHEN IT PASSES LEGISLATION, RATIFIES TREATIES, CONFIRMS APPOINTMENTS, AND PROPOSES CONSTITUTIONAL AMENDMENTS

gress as they implement policy.[46] Similarly, Congress uses the budget process to influence policy implementation. Executive officials want to stay on the good side of Congress because Congress controls their budgets.

Finally, Congress evaluates policy. Congress, as a whole, evaluates programs when problems persist or when the media publicize scandals in administration. Standing committees provide legislative oversight. The appropriation committees scrutinize agency spending. Congress sometimes uses the feedback from policy evaluation to formulate and adopt policy revisions.

the THINKSPOT
www.thethinkspot.com

TEST yourself

1 What happens if the House and Senate pass different versions of a bill to address a particular policy issue but cannot agree on compromise legislation?

A. The president creates a conference commission to negotiate a compromise.

B. The measure fails because nothing passes Congress unless both the House and Senate pass it in identical form.

C. The Supreme Court determines which measure becomes law.

D. The House bill goes to the president for signature.

2 Which of the following statements better describes the House than it does the Senate?

A. It makes decisions strictly by majority vote.

B. It has a tradition as a great debating society where members enjoy broad freedom to voice their points of view.

C. It is an individualistic body where one member has considerable influence on the legislative process.

D. All of the above.

3 Which of the following statements better describes the Senate than the House?

A. Every member stands for reelection every two years.

B. A minority of members has the power to bring legislative business to a halt in the chamber.

C. Members of this chamber sometimes run for seats in the other chamber.

D. None of the above.

4 The office of Congresswoman Martinez helps a district resident resolve a problem with the Social Security Administration. The action was an example of which of the following?

A. Filibuster

B. Logrolling

C. Closed rule

D. Constituency service

5 Which of the following statements about congressional turnover is *not* true?

A. Most members of Congress are reelected.

B. The reelection rate for House members is higher than it is for senators.

C. Congress experiences significant turnover because term limits restrict members of the House and Senate to no more than 12 consecutive years in office.

D. Voters typically express a higher level of approval for their representative in Congress than they do for the institution as a whole.

6 In practice, which of the following officials is the most important leader in the U.S. Senate?

A. Speaker of the House

B. Senate president *pro tempore*

C. Senate majority leader

D. Vice president

7 Which of the following officials is the most important leader in the U.S. House?

A. Speaker of the House

B. Senate president *pro tempore*

C. Senate majority leader

D. Vice president

8 How is the Senate majority leader selected?

A. By vote of the members of the majority party in the Senate

B. By popular vote in a national election

C. By the president

D. He or she is the longest served member of the majority party in the Senate

9 What was the party affiliation of the chair of the House Ways and Means Committee in 2008?

A. The chair could have been a Democrat or Republican depending on which member of the committee had the most seniority.

B. The chair would be a Republican because the president was Republican.

C. The chair would be a Democrat because Democrats won a majority in the House in the 2006 election.

D. The chair could be a Democrat or a Republican depending on which member of the committee won a vote of the committee membership.

10 In the current Congress (elected in 2008), which of the following individuals is a Republican?

A. Senate minority leader

B. Speaker of the House

C. Chair of the House Committee on Appropriations

D. Each official could be either Republican or Democrat

11 Why do major legislative measures often take the form of omnibus bills, which are complex, highly detailed legislative proposals covering one or more subjects or programs?

A. Complex problems require complex solutions.

B. Government is so big that legislation must deal with a broad range of policy areas.

C. Congress is in session only part of the year and omnibus bills enable it to get more done in a short period of time.

D. Congressional leaders assemble omnibus bills in order to attract as much support as possible.

12 Which of the following individuals has the authority to introduce a bill in the U.S. Senate?

A. A senator

B. A member of the House

C. The president

D. All of the above

13 The detailed work of Congress takes place at which point in the legislative process?

A. On the floor

B. In committee

C. In conference committee

D. In the Rules Committee

14 Legislative markup occurs at which stage of the legislative process?

A. On the floor

B. In committee

C. In conference committee

D. In the Rules Committee

15 What is the purpose of a discharge petition?

A. It is the process that is used to end a filibuster.

B. It is a demand that a member of Congress be expelled for misconduct.

C. It is a procedure used to force a committee to report a bill to the floor of the House.

D. It is the beginning of the impeachment process.

16 What is the purpose of a closed rule?

A. It prohibits consideration of amendments to a bill on the floor of the House.

B. It is a procedure for ending a filibuster.

C. It is a means of coordinating the work of committees when a bill is multiply referred.

D. It is a procedure used to force a committee to report a bill to the floor of the House.

17 An amendment designed to make a measure so unattractive that it will lack enough support to pass is known as which of the following?

A. Discharge petition

B. Non-germane amendment

C. Killer amendment

D. Cloture petition

18 The Senate is considering a controversial measure. How many votes will the measure's supporters need to ensure passage in the chamber?

A. Legislation passes by majority vote.

B. It takes a two-thirds vote to pass bills in the Senate.

C. It takes 60 votes to invoke cloture and overcome a filibuster.

D. It takes 40 votes to invoke cloture.

19 A conference committee agrees on a conference report. It passes the House, but it fails to pass the Senate. What is the status of the bill?

A. The measure goes to the president.

B. The measure is dead unless Senate reconsiders it and passes it.

C. The House votes again on the measure and if it passes again, it goes to the president.

D. The president convenes a reconciliation committee involving the leadership of both the House and Senate.

20 Congress passes a bill that the president generally favors with the exception of one provision. What are the president's options?

A. The president can ask a conference committee to rewrite the bill.

B. The president can ask the Supreme Court to revise the bill.

C. The president can veto the offensive provision while signing the rest into law.

D. The president can sign or veto the bill in its entirety.

1. B; 2. A; 3. B; 4. D; 5. C; 6. C; 7. A; 8. A; 9. C; 10. A; 11. D; 12. B; 13. B; 14. B; 15. D; 16. C; 17. C; 18. C; 19. B; 20. D

11 THE

> **WHAT'S AHEAD**

The Constitutional Presidency

Presidential Powers

The Organization of the Presidency

Theories of Presidential Leadership

Presidential Popularity

Conclusion: The Presidency & Public Policy

Barack Obama made healthcare a priority of his administration, but he recognized that the enactment of reform legislation would be a challenge. Some of the most powerful groups in the nation have a stake in the issue, including insurance companies, physicians, hospitals, business groups, and labor unions. Any reform plan would need the support or at least neutrality of most if not all of the major groups involved to make it through Congress. After all, the last Democratic administration to make healthcare reform a priority failed miserably. Soon after taking office, President Bill Clinton created the Task Force on National Healthcare Reform chaired by Hillary Clinton, but the effort became the target of intense interest group opposition. Critics attacked the process for being overly secretive and charged that the plan it produced was excessively bureaucratic and too restrictive of patient choice. The proposal died in the Senate without coming to a vote, the victim of a Republican-led filibuster.

Obama, hoping to learn from the mistakes of the Clinton administration, promised an open and inclusive policymaking process. Because his campaign focused heavily on the healthcare issue, he could claim that his election represented a mandate for reform. An **electoral mandate** is the expression of popular support for a particular policy demonstrated through the electoral process. Furthermore, to head off opposition, Obama mobilized his network of supporters to hold house parties to discuss healthcare reform and lobby their representatives in Congress.[1]

President Obama's effort to reform the healthcare system introduces this chapter on the presidency by drawing attention to the factors that affect the ability of the president to accomplish policy goals. The chapter begins by examining the constitutional outline of the office.

PRESIDENCY

the constitutional PRESIDENCY

ESSENTIALS...

after studying Chapter 11, students should be able to answer the following questions:

> What is the constitutional presidency in terms of qualifications and backgrounds, term of office, impeachment and removal, succession, and disability?

> What are the constitutional powers of the presidency, and how have those powers expanded beyond the constitutional outline of the office?

> What is the organization of the White House staff and the Executive Office of the President?

> What are the various perspectives on presidential leadership and presidential power taken by political scientists?

> What factors affect presidential popularity?

> What is the role of the presidency in America's policy process?

think **Should the United States consider amending the Constitution to allow naturalized (foreign-born) American citizens to become president?**

the Constitution describes the office of the presidency in Article II.

Qualifications and Backgrounds

The Constitution declares that the president must be at least 35 years of age, a natural-born American citizen (as opposed to a naturalized citizen), and a resident of the United States for at least 14 years. Before the 2008 election, all the nation's presidents had been white males of Western European ancestry. Two sets of presidents were father and son (John and John Quincy Adams and George and George W. Bush); two were grandfather and grandson (William Henry and Benjamin Harrison); and two were cousins (Theodore and Franklin D. Roosevelt). All but Roman Catholic John Kennedy have been Protestant Christians. Most presidents have been fairly wealthy; the majority of them have been experienced politicians. Most presidents have come from states outside the South. In recent years, however, social barriers have begun to fall as the nation has elected a Roman Catholic (Kennedy), three native Southerners (Jimmy Carter, Clinton, and George W. Bush), and a divorced person (Ronald Reagan) to the White House. The election of Barack Obama, the son of a white woman from Kansas and a black immigrant from Kenya, shattered the barriers of race and ethnicity. Furthermore, Hillary Clinton's strong showing in the race for the Democratic presidential nomination suggested that gender was no longer a major bar-

rier to the White House. The myth that anyone born in the United States could grow up to become president came closer to reality than ever before in the nation's history.

Term of Office

The president's constitutional term of office is four years. The Framers of the Constitution placed no limit on the number of terms presidents could serve, believing that the desire to remain in office would compel presidents to do their best. George Washington, the nation's first chief executive, established a custom of seeking no more than two terms, which every president honored until Franklin D. Roosevelt broke tradition in the early 1940s. After Roosevelt, a Democrat, won election to a third and then a fourth term, unhappy Republicans launched a drive to amend the Constitution to limit the president to two terms. They succeeded with the ratification of the Twenty-second Amendment in 1951.

The proponents of the two-term limit argued that it prevented a president from becoming too powerful. In contrast, critics believed that the two-term limit unnecessarily weakened the office of the presidency by making a second-term president a **lame duck**, an official whose influence is diminished because the official either cannot or

electoral mandate the expression of popular support for a particular policy demonstrated through the electoral process

lame duck an official whose influence is diminished because the official either cannot or will not seek reelection.

You Must Be:
At least 35 years old
A natural-born American citizen
A resident of the United States for at least 14 years

BUT...
Who have our presidents been?
60% were lawyers
80% received higher education
98% (all but one) were Protestant Christian
98% (all but one) were white!
100% were male!

will not seek reelection. The opponents of the Twenty-second Amendment also complained that it was undemocratic because it denied voters the right to reelect a president they admired.

Impeachment and Removal

Impeachment is a process in which an executive or judicial official is formally accused of an offense that could warrant removal from office. The Constitution states that the president may be impeached for "treason, bribery, or other high crimes and misdemeanors." The founders foresaw two broad, general grounds on which a president could be impeached and removed from office. First, impeachment could be used against a president who abused the powers of office, thereby threatening to become a tyrant. Second, it could be employed against a president who failed to carry out the duties of the office.[2] The House has impeached two presidents—Andrew Johnson in 1868 and Bill Clinton in 1998. Impeachment proceedings were begun against President Richard Nixon, but he resigned before the House could act.

The actual process of impeachment and removal involves both houses of Congress. The House drafts **articles of impeachment**, a document listing the impeachable offenses that the House believes the president committed. Technically, *impeach* means to accuse; so when the House impeaches the president by majority vote, it is accusing the president of committing offenses that may warrant removal from office. The Senate then tries the president, with the chief justice of the Supreme Court presiding. The Senate must vote by a two-thirds majority to remove the president from office. The Senate failed to remove either Johnson or Clinton from office.

impeachment a process in which an executive or judicial official is formally accused of an offense that could warrant removal from office.

articles of impeachment a document listing the impeachable offenses that the House believes the president committed.

Impeaching a President

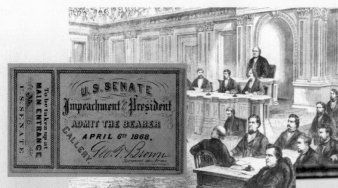

1998 Special Counsel Kenneth Starr began an investigation of a failed land development deal in Arkansas. Subsequently his work expanded, alleging that **CLINTON** had lied under oath about an alleged sexual liaison with White House intern Monica Lewinsky, and that he had obstructed justice in the investigation of his testimony in the sexual harassment lawsuit filed by Paula Jones. The House impeached Clinton in a close vote on strict party lines, with all but five Republicans voting for at least one article of impeachment and all but five Democrats voting against all the articles. The Senate failed to convict the president and remove him from office.

1868 When **JOHNSON** became president after Lincoln's assassination, he quarreled with the Republican Congress over which branch of government would control Reconstruction. Johnson challenged the Tenure of Office Act, which stipulated that any official appointed by the president and confirmed by the Senate could not be removed from office until the Senate had confirmed a replacement. The House of Representatives responded by voting to impeach him, 126 to 47. The Senate voted 35 to 19 for conviction, just one vote short of the two-thirds vote necessary to remove President Johnson from office.

"It depends on what the meaning of the word 'is' is."

Presidential Succession and Disability

The vice president succeeds a president who is removed, resigns, or dies in office. After the vice president, the line of succession passes to the Speaker of the House, president *pro tempore* of the Senate, Secretary of State, and then through the cabinet in order of the creation of the cabinet department. In American history, nine vice presidents have succeeded to the presidency, but no Speakers or Senate presidents *pro tempore*. Furthermore, because of the Twenty-fifth Amendment, the order of succession probably will never extend beyond the office of vice president.

The Twenty-fifth Amendment was ratified in 1967, after President Dwight Eisenhower's heart attack and President Kennedy's assassination focused attention on the issue of presidential succession and disability. The amendment authorizes the president to fill a vacancy in the office of vice president, subject to majority confirmation by both houses of Congress. This procedure was first used in 1973, when President Nixon nominated Gerald Ford to replace Vice President Spiro Agnew, who resigned under accusation of criminal wrongdoing. When Nixon himself resigned in 1974, Ford moved up to the presidency and appointed former governor of New York Nelson Rockefeller to be the new vice president.

Other provisions of the Twenty-fifth Amendment establish procedures for the vice president to become acting president should the president become disabled and incapable of performing the duties of office. The president may declare disability by written notice to the Senate president *pro tempore* and the Speaker of the House. The vice president then becomes acting president until the president declares in writing the ability to resume the responsibilities of office. If the president is unable or unwilling to declare disability, the vice president can declare the president disabled in conjunction with a majority of the cabinet. Should the vice president/ cabinet and president disagree on the question of the president's disability, Congress may declare the president disabled by two-thirds vote of each house.

think

Do you think presidents should be permitted to run for more than two terms?

and WHEN did he know it?"

"I AM NOT A CROOK."

1974 In the Watergate scandal of 1972, five men, employed by the Committee to Reelect the President, broke into Democratic National Committee headquarters to plant electronic eavesdropping devices. **NIXON** called the affair a "two-bit burglary," but as the cover-up began to unravel (culminating in the discovery of tape recordings directly linking Nixon to the cover-up), the House Judiciary Committee recommended impeachment. In August 1974, in the face of these proceedings, Nixon resigned.

The Vice Presidency

The Constitution gives the vice president two duties. The vice president is president of the Senate and votes in case of a tie. The vice president also becomes president of the United States if the office becomes vacant. For most of American history, however, the vice president was the forgotten person of Washington. In 1848, Daniel Webster, a prominent political figure of the time, rejected the vice presidential nomination of his party, by saying "I do not propose to be buried until I am dead."[3] Before the last half of the twentieth century, the vice president had no staff and few responsibilities. The vice president represented the nation at selected ceremonial occasions, such as the funeral of a foreign leader, but had no policy responsibilities.

Today, the vice presidency has become a more visible and important office. The death in office of President Franklin Roosevelt, Eisenhower's heart attack, Kennedy's assassination, Nixon's resignation, and the assassination attempt against Reagan all called attention to the possibility that the vice president could become president at any time. Furthermore, the vice presidency has become the most common path to the office of the presidency, either through succession or election. Since 1950, five presidents (Harry Truman, Lyndon Johnson, Nixon, Ford, and the elder Bush) held office as vice president prior to becoming president. Men and women of stature are now willing to serve as vice president.

Recent presidents have actively involved their vice presidents in their administrations. When George H. W. Bush became president, he appointed his vice president, Dan Quayle, to head a Council on Competitiveness that reviewed proposed regulations for their impact on business and the economy. President Clinton made Vice President Al Gore the chair of the National Performance Review Commission,

RECENT PRESIDENTS HAVE ACTIVELY INVOLVED THEIR VICE PRESIDENTS IN THEIR ADMINISTRATIONS

which was assigned the task of recommending reforms to make government more efficient and cost effective. He assigned Gore the task of debating Ross Perot on the North American Free Trade Agreement (NAFTA), which the administration favored and Perot opposed.

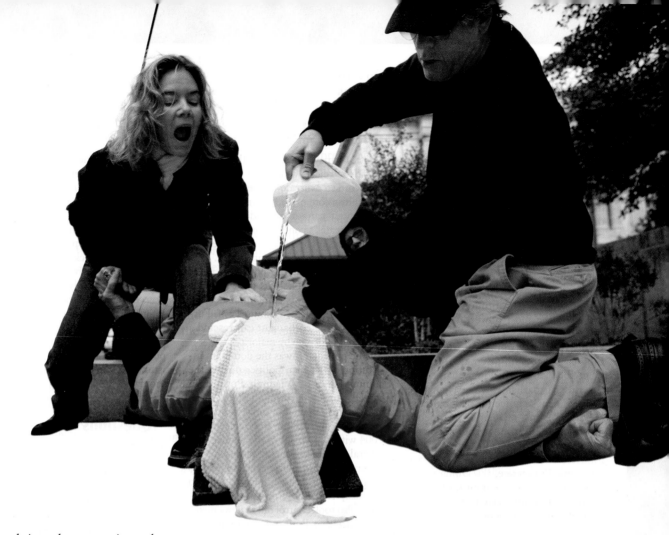

Vice President Dick Cheney and his legal counsel were instrumental in asserting the executive branch's inherent powers to designate enemy combatants and use aggressive interrogation techniques on them. The technique of waterboarding, or simulated drowning, has been banned in multiple countries and even prosecuted in the United States. In the above, human rights activists demonstrate the technique on a volunteer on Capitol Hill.

Roosevelt issued an executive order authorizing the military to relocate all persons of Japanese ancestry from the West Coast to inland relocation centers. More than 120,000 persons were interned, including 70,000 native-born American citizens. The U.S. Supreme Court upheld the constitutionality of the action.[14] After the terrorist attacks of September 11, 2001, President Bush exercised his authority as commander in chief to order the arrest and detention of persons suspected of involvement in terrorist activity.

Congress and the president have frequently quarreled over the authority of the legislative and executive branches to make military policy. Although the president is commander in chief, the Constitution grants Congress sole authority to declare war. The last war that Congress declared, however, was World War II. The president has initiated all subsequent American military actions, including the Korean War and the Vietnam War, without benefit of a congressional declaration of war. Although Congress authorized the use of force in Iraq before the U.S. invasion, it did not issue a declaration of war.

In 1973, during the war in Vietnam, Congress responded to what it considered an infringement of its constitutional power to declare war by enacting the **War Powers Act,** which limited the president's ability to commit American armed forces to combat abroad without consultation with Congress and congressional approval.[15] The measure includes a number of important provisions.

The War Powers Act is probably a less effective check on the president's military power than is public opinion. If a president's actions enjoy broad public support, as was the case with the first war in the Persian Gulf, Congress is unlikely to order a withdrawal of American forces. In contrast, the risk of adverse public reaction may deter some military

War Powers Act a law limiting the president's ability to commit American armed forces to combat abroad without consultation with Congress and congressional approval.

initiatives or cut short others. In 1983, for example, President Reagan ordered American forces withdrawn from Beirut, Lebanon, well in advance of a War Powers Act cutoff date, after several hundred marines were killed in a terrorist bombing. Perhaps more significantly, the ordered withdrawal came well in advance of the 1984 presidential election.

In 2008, a commission recommended that Congress and the president scrap the War Powers Act and replace it with legislation requiring the president and congressional leaders to consult before going to war. The commission, which was headed by two former secretaries of state, Republican James A. Baker III and Democrat Warren Christopher, declared the War Powers Act "ineffective at best and unconstitutional at worst."[16] The commission proposed a law that would create a new committee of congressional leaders and relevant committee chairs, with a full-time staff that would have access to military and foreign policy intelligence information. The president would be required to consult with this committee in advance of military action expected to take longer than a week (except in rare emergencies), and meet with it regularly during an extended conflict. Congress as a whole would be required to vote on an authorization resolution within 30 days of the initiation of hostilities. If the authorization resolution failed, any member of Congress could introduce a resolution of disapproval, which would have to pass both houses of Congress and be signed by the president to go into effect. A presidential veto would have to be overridden by a two-thirds vote before the resolution of disapproval had the force of law.[17]

Inherent Powers

Inherent powers are those powers vested in the national government, particularly in the area of foreign and defense policy, which do not depend on any specific grant of authority by the Constitution, but rather, exist because the United States is a sovereign nation. Consider the **Louisiana Purchase,** which was the acquisition from France of a vast expanse of land stretching from New Orleans north to the Dakotas. President Thomas Jefferson justified his decision to acquire the territory on the basis of inherent powers because the Constitution says nothing about purchasing land from another country. Similarly, Lincoln claimed extraordinary powers to defend the Union during the Civil War on the basis of inherent powers. President George W. Bush used the doctrine of inherent powers to justify the use of military tribunals to try enemy combatants captured in the war on terror, to designate U.S. citizens as enemy combatants, to send terror suspects to countries that practice torture, and to authorize eavesdropping on American citizens by the National Security Agency (NSA).[18]

Presidential assertions of inherent powers are almost invariably controversial because they involve an expansion of government authority and presidential power not authorized by the Constitution. Critics of the Louisiana Purchase, for example, called Jefferson a hypocrite because he had long argued that the authority of the national government was limited to powers clearly delegated by the Constitution. In recent years, critics accused President Bush of not just exceeding his power but violating the Constitution. They challenged his actions in Congress and in the courts.

> **Would you agree that a dunk in the water is a no-brainer if it can save lives?**
> **RADIO SHOW HOST SCOTT HENNEN:**

> **It's a no-brainer for me, but for a while there I was criticized as being the vice president "for torture." WE DON'T TORTURE.**
> **VICE PRESIDENT CHENEY:**

inherent powers powers vested in the national government, particularly in the area of foreign and defense policy, which do not depend on any specific grant of authority by the Constitution, but rather exist because the United States is a sovereign nation.

Louisiana Purchase the acquisition from France of a vast expanse of land stretching from New Orleans north to the Dakotas.

Judicial Powers

The president plays a role in judicial policymaking. The president nominates all federal judges pending majority-vote confirmation by the Senate. The Senate usually approves nominees, but not without scrutiny, especially for Supreme Court selections. The Senate rejected two consecutive Supreme Court appointments by President Nixon before confirming his third choice. Similarly, the Senate rejected President Reagan's nomination of Robert Bork to the Supreme Court.

think

Is the president's authority as commander in chief too broad?

The power of appointment gives a president, especially a president who serves two terms, the opportunity to shape the policy direction of the judicial branch of American government. During his eight years in office, President Clinton appointed 374 federal judges, including two members of the Supreme Court. George W. Bush named more than 300 judges during his two terms in office. His appointments included two Supreme Court justices.[19]

The Constitution empowers the president to grant pardons and reprieves. A **pardon** is an executive action that frees an accused or convicted person from all penalties for an offense. A **reprieve** is an executive action that delays punishment for a crime. With some exceptions, such as President Ford's pardon of former President Nixon, most presidential pardons and reprieves have not been controversial.

Executive Powers

The president is the nation's **chief executive**, that is, the head of the executive branch of government.

The Constitution grants the president authority to require written reports from department heads and enjoins the president to "take care that laws be faithfully executed." As head of the executive branch of government, presidents can issue executive orders to manage the federal bureaucracy. An **executive order** is a directive issued by the president to an administrative agency or executive department. Although the Constitution says nothing about executive orders, the courts have upheld their use based on law, custom, and the president's authority as head of the executive branch.

Presidents have used executive orders to enact important (and sometimes controversial) policies. President Lincoln, for example, used an executive order to issue the Emancipation Proclamation. President Eisenhower issued an executive order to send National Guard troops into Little Rock, Arkansas in 1957 to protect African American youngsters attempting to attend a whites-only public high school. The first President Bush issued executive orders to prohibit abortion counseling at federally funded family planning centers. President Clinton, in turn, used an executive order to reverse the Bush order.

The president's power to issue executive orders is not unlimited. Presidents may issue executive orders only when they fall within the scope of the president's constitutional powers and legal authority. In 1952, for example, during the Korean War, the U.S. Supreme Court overturned an executive order by President Truman seizing the nation's steel mills to head off a strike that would have disrupted steel production and hurt the war effort. The Court declared that the president lacked the legal authority to seize private property and that the

pardon an executive action that frees an accused or convicted person from all penalties for an offense.

reprieve an executive action that delays punishment for a crime.

chief executive the head of the executive branch of government.

executive order a directive issued by the president to an administrative agency or executive department.

Federal troops patrolled the grounds of Central High School in Little Rock, Arkansas after court-ordered integration began.

Judicial Selection and Partisan Politics

Should the judicial nomination process be reformed? If so, why? If not, why not?

Should judicial nominees be selected based on judicial philosophy or political ideology? Is this what the founders intended?

Supreme Court Justice Stephen Breyer, a Clinton appointee, is regarded as one of the more liberal members of the Supreme Court.

Overview: Though the courts have always been a political institution, the increasing polarization of electoral politics over the last four decades has taught political parties and interest groups to view litigation and judicial decisions as tools to circumvent existing law and policy. With this in mind, the two major political parties have turned to further politicization of the federal judiciary in an attempt to shape its ideological leanings.

The 2000 election put the Republican Party in charge of Congress and the presidency for the first time in 40 years. President George W. Bush had promised that he would nominate judges who adhered to the strict-construction philosophy of judicial decision making—that is, he would appoint judges who believed in applying the letter of the law instead of trying to determine its meaning or spirit and attempting to order judicial remedies. The Democratic Party, for its part, instituted a political litmus test for judicial nominees, arguing that a president's nominees should be ideologically mainstream and not selected for their perceived political biases. To prevent President Bush from having his nominees confirmed, the Senate Democrats, in a move used only once in American history, filibustered the president's judicial choices, thus preventing vacant judgeships from being filled.

President Bush avoided the Senate altogether and appointed some of his favored nominees to the federal bench through the process of the recess appointment. Article II of the Constitution gives the president the authority to temporarily appoint judges and officials when the Senate is not in session and, since 1789, over 300 judicial appointments have been made by this method. But questions still remain. Has the Senate's constitutional authority been undermined? What is the best way to ensure an independent and effective judiciary?

supporting reform of the judicial selection process

judicial nominations should be above politics. An independent judiciary is essential to free government. Choosing judicial nominees based on political ideology or litmus tests further makes judges *de facto* tools of political parties and interest groups.

the nature of judicial appointments makes it imperative that judges receive a full hearing. Federal judges may sit on the bench for life, and they can wield considerable clout in determining how the Constitution is interpreted and applied. It follows that judicial appointments merit more open and public deliberation.

Senate obstructionism may deny the judiciary qualified judges. For example, Miguel Estrada was a Bush appointee who graduated with honors from Harvard Law School and clerked for Supreme Court Justice Anthony Kennedy. He withdrew his nomination to sit on the appeals court of the District of Columbia in frustration after two years of obstruction by the Senate.

against reform of the judicial selection process

it is Congress's prerogative to determine its rules of procedure. Article I gives each chamber the authority to "determine the rules of its proceedings" and the historical evolution of Senate rules has provided stability and continuity in the nomination process.

the Senate is an explicitly political institution. Just as the president makes decisions based on political considerations, it is the Senate's appropriate function to ensure judicial nominations will not be too partisan and that judges adhere to moderate ideological and judicial views.

recess appointments are a means for judicial relief. The Constitution states that vacancies may be filled until an intervening midterm or general election. Should the election have a favorable outcome for the president, he may resubmit a nominee for the Senate's consideration.

president's power as commander in chief did not extend to labor disputes.[20] Congress can also overturn an executive order legislatively. Because the president would likely veto a measure reversing an executive order, Congress would need to vote to repeal the order and then to vote again by a two-thirds margin to override the veto.

Legislative Powers

Finally, the Constitution grants the president certain tools for shaping the legislative agenda. From time to time, it says, the president shall "give to Congress information of the state of the Union, and recommend to their consideration such measures as he shall judge necessary and expedient." Traditionally, the president makes a State of the Union address each January before a joint session of Congress and a national television audience. The speech gives the president the opportunity to raise issues and frame the terms of their discussion. In 2005, for example, President George W. Bush used the address to promote his Social Security reform proposal. Although the State of the Union address allows the president the opportunity to present himself or herself as the nation's chief legislator, it may also create unrealistic public expectations. In practice, Congress approves only 43 percent of the policy initiatives included in

the average State of the Union speech, either in whole or in part.[21]

The president can use the veto power to shape the content of legislation. The Constitution empowers the president to return measures to Congress along with objections. A vetoed measure can become law only if both the House and Senate vote to override by a two-thirds margin. The veto is a powerful weapon. In more than 200 years, Congress has overridden less than 1 percent of presidential vetoes.[22] Nonetheless, political scientists consider the actual use of the veto a sign of weakness rather than strength because influential presidents can usually prevent passage of measures they oppose by threatening a veto.[23] A **presidential signing statement** is a pronouncement issued by the president at the time a bill passed by Congress is signed into law. Presidents historically have used signing statements to comment on the bill they are signing, score political points, identify areas of disagreement with the measure, and discuss its implementation. President George W. Bush went further than any of his predecessors in

using signing statements to expand the powers of his office. Bush signing statements identified more than 800 provisions in 500 measures that he signed into law but considered unconstitutional limitations on his authority as president. He asserted his intention to ignore these provisions or treat them as advisory. Bush declared, for example, that legislative provisions establishing qualifications for executive branch officials were advisory rather than mandatory because he believed that they unconstitutionally restricted the presidential power of appointment. He asserted his intention to withhold information from Congress and rejected legislative provisions that he believed would limit his power as commander in chief.

Presidential signing statements are controversial. Political scientist Phillip J. Cooper believes that President Bush used presidential signing statements as a vehicle for revising legislation without issuing a veto, which is subject to congressional override.[24] The American Bar Association (ABA) declares that Bush's use of signing statements is "contrary to the rule of law and our constitutional system of separation of powers" because the Constitution requires that the president sign legislation or veto it in its entirety.[25] In contrast, law professors Curtis A. Bradley and Eric A. Posner argue that signing statements are legal and useful because they provide a way for the president to disclose his or her views about the meaning and constitutionality of legislation.[26]

> THE PRESIDENT CAN USE THE VETO POWER TO SHAPE THE CONTENT OF LEGISLATION

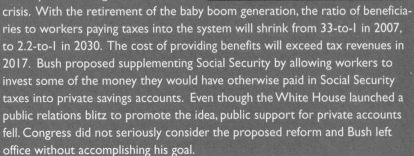

btw...

Reforming Social Security was the foremost priority of President George W. Bush's second term. Social Security faces a long-term financial crisis. With the retirement of the baby boom generation, the ratio of beneficiaries to workers paying taxes into the system will shrink from 33-to-1 in 2007, to 2.2-to-1 in 2030. The cost of providing benefits will exceed tax revenues in 2017. Bush proposed supplementing Social Security by allowing workers to invest some of the money they would have otherwise paid in Social Security taxes into private savings accounts. Even though the White House launched a public relations blitz to promote the idea, public support for private accounts fell. Congress did not seriously consider the proposed reform and Bush left office without accomplishing his goal.

presidential signing statement a pronouncement issued by the president at the time a bill passed by Congress is signed into law.

the organization
OF THE PRESIDENCY

the development of the modern presidency has been accompanied by a significant growth in the size and power of the presidential bureaucracy, that is, the White House staff and the Executive Office of the President. Early chief executives wrote their own speeches and even answered their own mail. They had only a few aides, whom they paid from their own funds. Thomas Jefferson, for example, had one messenger and one secretary. Eventually, Congress appropriated money for the president to hire aides and advisors, and the presidential bureaucracy grew. In the 1920s, the president had a staff of 30. By the 1950s, the number of presidential aides and advisors had grown to 250. Today, the combined staffs of the Executive Office and the White House number more than 2,000, and the president has grown to rely on them more and more.[27] The modern president spends time bargaining with Congress while dealing with the media and the public. Reelection campaigns begin almost from the first day in office. Presidents have responded to the demands of the office by hiring aides with specialized expertise.[28]

The White House Staff

The White House staff consists of personal aides, assistants, and advisors to the president, including a chief of staff, press secretary, speechwriter, appointments secretary, national security advisor, legislative liaison, counselor to the president, and various special assistants. They give the president advice on policy issues and politics, screen key appointments, manage press relations, organize the president's workday, and ensure that the presi-

dent's wishes are carried out. The president selects the White House staff without Senate confirmation. As with most presidential appointees (the exceptions are federal judges and regulatory commissioners), White House staff members serve at the president's pleasure, which means that the president can remove them at will.

Political and personal loyalty is usually the foremost criterion the president uses in selecting a staff. When George W. Bush became

president, he recruited his staff primarily from his father's administration, his own administration as governor of Texas, and his presidential campaign. Andrew H. Card, Jr., the White House chief of staff during Bush's first term, was secretary of transportation in the first Bush administration. Similarly, President Obama selected Rahm Emanuel, a member of Congress from Chicago, Illinois, Obama's political home base, to serve as his chief of staff.

How the
WHITE HOUSE RUNS:
THE EXECUTIVE OFFICE OF THE PRESIDENT

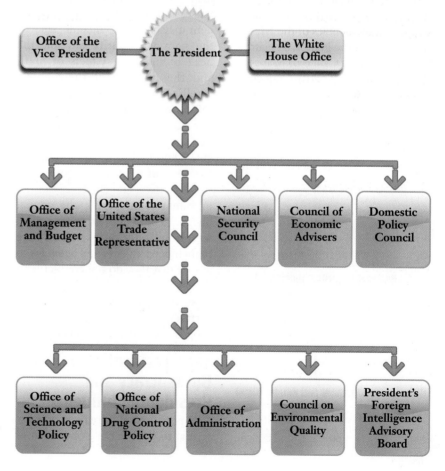

The Executive Office of the President

The **Executive Office of the President** is the group of White House offices and agencies that develop and implement the policies and programs of the president. Congress established the Executive Office in 1939 after a special investigative commission concluded that the responsibilities of the presidency were too great for any one individual. "The president needs help," the commission said. The legislation creating the Executive Office allowed the president to create and disband components without further congressional authorization. Consequently, the size and composition of the Executive Office changes somewhat from administration to administration. During the most recent Bush administration, the Executive Office had 17 units.[29]

The major agencies of the Executive Office are the National Security Council (NSC), Office of Management and Budget (OMB), Council of Economic Advisers (CEA), Council on Environmental Quality, Office of

Executive Office of the President the group of White House offices and agencies that develop and implement the policies and programs of the president.

National Security Council (NSC) an agency in the Executive Office of the President that advises the chief executive on matters involving national security.

Office of Management and Budget (OMB) an agency that assists the president in preparing the budget.

Science and Technology Policy, Office of the United States Trade Representative, and Domestic Policy Council. The first two are the most prominent. The **National Security Council (NSC)** is an agency in the Executive Office of the President that advises the chief executive on matters involving national security. It includes the president, vice president, Secretaries of State and defense, and other officials the president may choose to include, such as the national security advisor, the head of the Joint Chiefs of Staff, and the director of the Central Intelligence Agency (CIA). The **Office of Management and Budget (OMB)** is an agency that assists the president in preparing the budget. The OMB is an important instrument of presidential control of the executive branch. It assists the president in preparing the annual budget to be submitted to Congress, screens bills drawn up by executive branch departments and agencies to ensure that they do not conflict with the president's policy goals, monitors expenditures by executive branch departments, and evaluates regulations proposed by executive agencies.

The Presidential Bureaucracy and Presidential Influence

The presidential bureaucracy is essential to the effective operation of

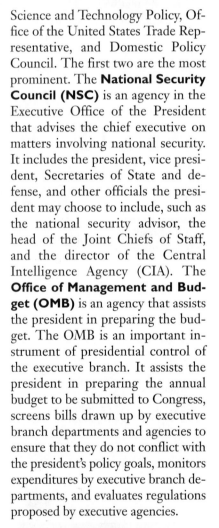

The decision to go to war was based on flawed intelligence interpreted by administration leaders such as Secretary of Defense Donald Rumsfeld (left) and CIA Director George Tenet.

the modern presidency. An efficient, knowledgeable White House staff is an important element of presidential power. Members of the staff not only advise the president on policy issues and political strategy, but they often act on behalf of the president in dealing with Congress, members of the executive branch bureaucracy, and the media. An efficient, professional staff can further the president's policy goals and create an image of presidential competence. A White House staff that is accessible to members of Congress and maintains open lines of communication will help promote the president's policies while keeping the president well-informed enough to prevent surprises.[30] In contrast, an inefficient staff makes the president appear incompetent. During the first two years of the Clinton administration, a disorganized White House staff contributed to the president's penchant for putting off decisions and failing to stick to decisions once they were made. As a result, Clinton developed a reputation for indecision and inconsistency, a reputation that contributed to substantial Democratic losses in the 1994 congressional elections. Leon Panetta, whom Clinton named chief of staff in 1994, brought discipline to the White House, enabling the president to rehabilitate his image and win reelection in 1996.[31]

The tendency of newly elected presidents to select old friends and campaign aides who are unfamiliar with Washington politics to serve in the White House often undermines the president's effectiveness. The problem is made worse if the president is also inexperienced in national politics. Healthcare reform was the foremost goal of Clinton's first term in office. The president appointed a task force chaired by Hillary Clinton to hold hearings and develop a plan to be presented to Congress. Because the task force lacked broad-based representation and conducted much of its work in secret, it failed to develop a plan with enough support to pass Congress, and the effort became an embarrassing failure.

The challenge for a president is to develop a leadership style that delegates neither too little nor too much. Because a president's time, energy, and abilities are limited, the president must delegate some tasks. To be effective, a president must know which tasks can be delegated and which cannot. The president must also have a strong enough grasp of policy issues to recognize when the proposals of subordinates make sense and when they do not.[32]

President George W. Bush's decision to go to war against Iraq was based on a flawed decision-making process within the administration. Bush ordered the overthrow of Saddam Hussein because he believed that Iraq possessed **weapons of mass destruction (WMD)**, nuclear, chemical, and biological weapons designed to inflict widespread military and civilian casualties. The United States had to act, the president declared, before Iraq gave WMD to terrorist groups that could then use them against the United States or its allies. The conclusion that Iraq possessed WMD, however, was wrong. The administration not only misinterpreted some of the intelligence it received, but also attempted to influence the nature of that intelligence to support its position. It sought evidence to prove that Iraq possessed WMD while ignoring information to the contrary. Furthermore, Bush decided to go to war without deliberating with his advisors as to whether war was necessary. The White House shut out Secretary of State Colin Powell from the decision-making process and ignored warnings from the military.[33]

An efficient, professional staff CAN FURTHER THE PRESIDENT'S POLICY GOALS and create an image of presidential competence

Secretary of State Colin Powell made the case for the Iraq invasion in a presentation to the United Nations in New York City.

The Power to Persuade

Political scientist Richard Neustadt believes that presidents succeed or fail based on their skills as political bargainers and coalition builders. Although the presidency is regarded as a powerful office, Neustadt points out that presidents lack authority to command public officials other than the members of the White House staff, some executive branch appointees, and the members of the armed forces. Under America's

POLITICS INVOLVES *NEGOTIATION,* GIVE-AND-TAKE, *AND* COMPROMISE

constitutional system, the members of Congress, federal judges, and state officials do not take orders from the president. Because presidents cannot command, they must convince other political actors to cooperate with them voluntarily. The power of the president, Neustadt says, is the power to persuade.

Presidents must bargain with other political actors and groups to try to win their cooperation. Presidents are brokers, consensus builders. In this task, presidents have several assets: They have a number of appointments at their disposal; they prepare the budget; they can help supporters raise money for reelection; and they can appeal to others on the basis of the national interest or party loyalty. To use these assets to their fullest, presidents must un-

derstand the dynamics of political power.[35]

Neustadt's approach can be used to explain the presidencies of Lyndon Johnson and Jimmy Carter. President Johnson learned as majority leader in the Senate how to build a political coalition to get legislation passed. In the White House, he put those skills to work and won passage for his legislative program, which was known as the **Great Society**. In contrast, President Carter never mastered the mechanics of political power. He ran for president as an outsider, someone who was not tainted by Washington politics. Once in office, Carter appeared standoffish. He had won the Democratic nomination and been elected president without having to bargain with the Washington establishment, and he thought he could govern without bargaining. He was wrong. Politics involves negotiation, give-and-take, and compromise. Carter never understood that and consequently failed to accomplish many of his goals.

Going Public

Political scientist Samuel Kernell has updated the Neustadt approach. Kernell believes that contemporary presidents often must adopt a media-oriented strategy, which he calls "going public," if they are to

achieve their goals in today's political environment. In 1981, for example, President Reagan went on television to ask citizens to contact their representatives in Congress to support his economic program. The public responded and Congress approved the president's budget proposals.

Media-oriented approaches are not new—Franklin Roosevelt was famous for his fireside chats on the radio—but the strategy has become more common. Modern communications and transportation technologies make going public relatively easy. Furthermore, today's presidential selection process tends to favor people who are better at public appeals than political bargaining. Perhaps most important, going public has become an easier

Great Society the legislative program put forward by President Lyndon Johnson.

President Theodore Roosevelt was famous for the use he made of "the bully pulpit"—his ability to use his office to influence debate.

Leadership Style

Some scholars believe that the ability of a president to use the powers of the office effectively depends on leadership style. Political scientist Fred I. Greenstein takes this approach by identifying six qualities associated with effective presidential leadership.

	Public Communicator	Organizational Skills	Political Skills	Vision	Cognitive Skills	Emotional Intelligence
F. ROOSEVELT	✔					
TRUMAN		✔				
EISENHOWER		✔		✔		✔
KENNEDY	✔	✔		✔		
JOHNSON			✔			
NIXON				✔	✔	
FORD		✔				✔
CARTER					✔	
REAGAN	✔			✔		
G. H. W. BUSH		✔		✔		✔
CLINTON	✔					
G. W. BUSH						✔

and more efficient method for achieving political goals than bargaining. In the 1950s, a president pushing a policy agenda had to bargain with a handful of party leaders and committee chairs in Congress. Today, power in Congress is more fragmented and the number of interest groups active in Washington politics has increased. As a result, it has become easier for presidents to go public than to engage in political bargaining.[36]

The George W. Bush administration illustrates both the strengths and limitations of the going public strategy. Bush effectively used the going public strategy to bring the threat of Iraq to the top of the public agenda and put pressure on Congress to approve his war policy. Public concern over Iraq made Democrats in Congress wary about opposing the president on Iraq because Saddam Hussein was a highly unpopular figure. Many Democrats believed that Saddam actually did have WMD and was a threat to national security. Opposing Bush on Iraq could open them to the charge that they were soft on national defense. Nearly 40 percent of House Democrats and 57 percent of Senate Democrats joined nearly every Republican member of Congress in voting in favor of the resolution to authorize the use of military force in Iraq.[37] In contrast, the Bush administration's 60-stops-in-60-days strategy to promote Social Security private accounts was a failure. Although President Bush succeeded in elevating the issue to the top of the policy agenda, he failed to convince a majority of the public that private retirement accounts were a good idea. As a result, it was easy for Democrats in Congress to oppose the president on the issue and difficult for Republicans to support him. Going public is an ineffective strategy if the president's proposed initiative lacks public support.[38]

Unilateral Tools of Presidential Power

Professor Christopher S. Kelley says that presidents have certain "power tools" that allow them to take unilateral action without direct congressional authorization or approval.[39] These tools include the following:

- **Executive orders**. They enable the president to adopt a number of important policies without legislative approval.
- **Executive agreements**. They give the president an important tool that does not require Senate ratification for conducting foreign relations.[40]
- **Presidential signing statements**. They enable the president to define the scope and limitations of legislation passed by Congress.
- **Recess appointments**. By filling vacancies during a period of time when Congress is in recess, the president can temporarily make appointments without the advice and consent of the Senate.[41]

presidential
POPULARITY

presidential popularity influences presidential power. A president's personal popularity affects the position of the president as a political broker and the ability of the president to appeal to the public for policy support. A president who is politically popular can offer more benefits and inducements to other political actors for their cooperation than can an unpopular chief executive. Campaign help from a popular president is more valuable, and support for legislative proposals is more effective. Similarly, a popular president can claim to speak for the national interest with greater credibility.

A popular president enjoys more success with Congress than an unpopular chief executive. After September 11, 2001, President Bush's approval rating soared. Republican members of Congress eagerly associated themselves with the president, whereas Democrats were reluctant to oppose him. Congress passed legislation embodying the president's policy proposals dealing with taxes, the budget, government reorganization, Iraq, and the war on terror. By 2006, however, Bush's approval rating had fallen below 40 percent and members of Congress from both parties found it easy to oppose the president's legislative agenda. Democrats attacked Bush at every opportunity while Republican members of Congress boasted of their independence from the White House.

New presidents are popular, at least for a few months. The tendency of a president to enjoy a high level of public support during the early months of an administration is known as the **honeymoon effect**. In the first few months of an administration, opposition political leaders and the press usually reserve judgment, waiting for the president to act before offering comment. Most voters, regardless of party affiliation, tell poll-takers that they approve of the president's performance in office because they have heard few complaints on which to base disapproval. Once an administration begins making controversial policy decisions, however, opposition leaders and the media begin to

honeymoon effect the tendency of a president to enjoy a high level of public support during the early months of an administration.

Approval Rating of George W. Bush

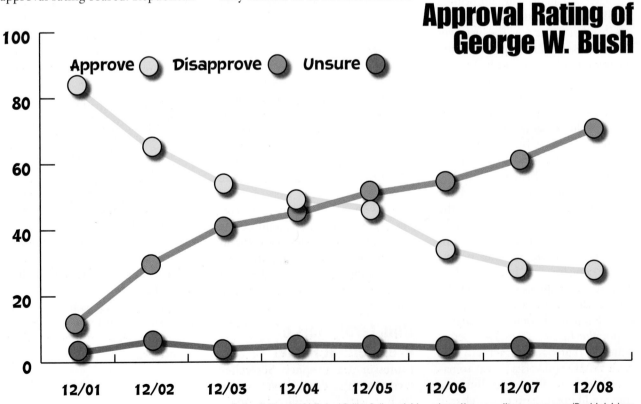

Gallup Poll and USA Today/Gallup Poll, available at http://www.pollingreport.com/BushJob1.htm.

criticize the president's performance. As the criticism mounts, the president's popularity invariably falls, especially among people who identify with the opposition political party.[42]

Presidential approval responds to events. In domestic policy matters, presidential popularity rises with good news and falls with bad news, especially news concerning the economy. Although President Reagan was called the "Teflon President"—regardless of what went wrong, no blame stuck to him—he was an unpopular president during the recession of 1982. Only when the economy began to recover did Reagan's popular standing again exceed the 50-percent approval mark.

Presidential popularity rises dramatically during times of international crisis because of the **rally effect**, which is the tendency of the general public to express support for the incumbent president during a time of international threat. Political scientist John Mueller defines the rally effect as "being associated with an event which 1) is international and 2) involves the United States and particularly the president

directly." Mueller says that the event must be "specific, dramatic, and sharply focused."[43] Mueller found that the "public seems to react to both 'good' and 'bad' international events in about the same way"—with a burst of heightened presidential approval.[44] For example, President George W. Bush's standing in the polls soared after September 11, 2001. The percentage of Americans who told survey researchers that they approved of Bush's performance in office leaped from 51 percent in early September to 90 percent later in the month.[45]

The appearance and size of a rally effect depends on how the crisis is presented to the public in terms of media coverage, comments from opposition political leaders, and statements from the White House.[46] When the nation appears threatened from abroad, the political criticism that generally accompanies presidential action is muted. The White House is able to get its interpretation of events before the public because opposition political leaders do not want to be accused of undermining the president during an international crisis. The public

tends to support the president because the only messages it hears about the president's handling of the crisis are positive messages, usually conveyed by the White House itself or the president's allies in Congress.[47] Even though 9/11 was a national disaster, President Bush's approval rating soared because no one, at least initially, publicly raised questions about the administration's failure to foresee or prevent the terrorist attacks. Instead, the media were filled with images of the president comforting the families of the victims and declaring that the United States would bring to justice the people responsible for the attacks.[48]

The public responds differently to a domestic crisis than it does to an international crisis. Whereas opposition political leaders and the press typically withhold judgment in an international crisis, they are quick to criticize if something goes

rally effect the tendency of the general public to express support for the incumbent president during a time of international threat.

wrong domestically. Consider the reaction to Hurricane Katrina in August 2005 and its impact on President Bush's standing in the polls. Within days of the hurricane's coming ashore, opposition political leaders and the news media were blasting the Bush administration for inadequately responding to the disaster. Between late August and October 2005, the president's popularity rating fell by five percentage points.[49]

Usually, a rally effect has only a short-term impact on presidential popularity. According to a study conducted by the Gallup organization, a president's approval rating reverts to previous levels within seven months of an international crisis unless other factors intervene, such as changing economic conditions.[50] At the beginning of an international crisis, the president enjoys near-unanimous support from members of the president's political party and strong support from independents and members of the other party. As the political climate returns to normal, the press and opposition party leaders begin voicing criticism, initially about domestic policy matters and eventually about foreign affairs, as well. Although members of the president's party usually continue to support the incumbent, members of the other party and independents began to register their displeasure with the president's performance and the president's overall standing in the polls falls.[51]

the presidency
& PUBLIC POLICY

the presidency is a major participant in every stage of the policymaking process.

Agenda Building

No other figure in American politics is better positioned to influence the policy agenda than the president. Because the chief executive is always in the media spotlight, the president has a unique opportunity to direct attention to policy problems. President George W. Bush drew attention to his education reform proposal to require states to implement basic skills testing by visiting schools where similar reforms were already successfully in place. The president can discuss an issue during a State of the Union address, identify a problem during a press conference, or give a major speech to focus attention on an issue.[52] The president also has a number of spokespersons, including the vice president, members of the White House staff, and executive branch department heads, who can raise issues on behalf of the administration.

Research finds that the president has more influence in setting the domestic policy agenda than the agenda in foreign affairs. World events and media coverage of those events set the foreign policy agenda; the president just reacts. George W. Bush did not run for office expecting to fight a war on terror, but after September 11, 2001, the fight against terrorism became the primary focus of his administration. In contrast to foreign policy, the president has the opportunity to operate as an issue entrepreneur in domestic policy. If an issue is not already part of ongoing media coverage or congressional hearings, a president may be able to set the agenda of the television networks and Congress. President Clinton, for example, succeeded in making healthcare reform an important part of the policy agenda in his first term.[53] Furthermore, presidents can sometimes redefine issues already on the policy agenda. When George W. Bush took office, for example, education was already an important part of the nation's policy agenda. Bush succeeded in framing the issue in terms of basic skills testing.[54]

THE PRESIDENT HAS MORE INFLUENCE IN SETTING THE DOMESTIC POLICY AGENDA THAN IN FOREIGN AFFAIRS

Policy Formulation and Adoption

The president is involved in the formulation and adoption of a broad range of policies. Presidents propose legislation to Congress, sometimes drafting the actual bills in the White House or the executive branch. Presidential speeches inform members of Congress of the president's policy priorities.[55] Measures that reach the president for signature often reflect a compromise negotiated between the White House and congressional leaders, especially when the opposition party controls Congress. Because the veto power gives the

president a formal role in legislative policymaking, the president can influence policy formulation. As long as one-third plus one member of either the House or Senate support the president's position on an issue, congressional leaders must negotiate with the White House over the content of legislation. The measure ultimately adopted may not totally reflect the president's policy preferences, but it will likely include some features the president favors and exclude some the president opposes.[56]

The president has the authority to adopt some policies without congressional participation. Presidents make policy when they negotiate executive agreements or issue executive orders. Although Congress has the authority to cancel or repeal an executive agreement or executive or-

der legislatively, the action would be subject to a presidential veto. Over the years, especially during time of war, presidents have exercised extraordinary policymaking power based on their authority as commander in chief of the armed forces.

Policy Implementation and Evaluation

As head of the executive branch, the president plays an important role in policy implementation. Congress frequently allows executive branch agencies a certain degree of discretion in implementing the nation's public policies. For example, the Environmental Protection Agency (EPA) may enforce the Clean Air Act more or less aggressively. President Carter contributed to the aggressive enforcement of environmental laws

by appointing agency administrators who believed strongly in the agency's mission. Carter asked Congress for sufficient funding to support an aggressive enforcement effort. In contrast, President Reagan wanted the EPA to work more positively with the industries it regulates. He appointed critics of the EPA to head the agency and submitted budgets to Congress that cut money for enforcement activities.

The president also evaluates policies. The president can commission policy studies to identify weaknesses with current policies and then propose reforms. President George W. Bush, for example, appointed a commission to evaluate the Social Security system and to recommend changes to ensure its long-term financial stability. The president also engages in policy evaluation during the budgetary process, working primarily through the OMB.

the THINKSPOT

www.thethinkspot.com

TEST yourself

1 After winning reelection in 2004, President George W. Bush was a lame duck. What does that phrase mean?

A. President Bush was unpopular.

B. President Bush was ineligible to run for reelection.

C. President Bush had to deal with a Congress controlled by the opposition party.

D. President Bush was facing impeachment charges.

2 Which of the following is *not* part of the impeachment process?

A. The House drafts articles of impeachment.

B. The House votes to impeach the president by majority vote.

C. The chief justice presides over an impeachment trial in the Senate.

D. The Senate votes to remove the president by majority vote.

3 Which of the following presidents was impeached and removed from office?

A. Andrew Johnson

B. Richard Nixon

C. Bill Clinton

D. None of the above

4 Which of the following statements about the vice presidency is true?

A. The vice president votes in the Senate only to break a tie.

B. The policymaking influence of the vice president today is significantly greater than it was 50 years ago.

C. In case of presidential disability, the vice president can become acting president.

D. All of the above.

5 Who is the chief of state of American government?

A. The Senate president *pro tempore*

B. The president

C. The Speaker of the House

D. The chief justice of the United States

6 What is the difference between an executive agreement and a treaty?

A. Executive agreements do not require Senate ratification.

B. Treaties are more numerous than executive agreements.

C. The president negotiates treaties but members of Congress negotiate executive agreements.

D. None of the above.

7 The Constitution gives the president all but which one of the following powers?

A. To negotiate treaties

B. To appoint ambassadors

C. To declare war

D. To fill judicial vacancies

8 Which of the following is an example of a check and balance on the powers of the presidency?

A. Congress must ratify treaties.

B. Congress must confirm judicial appointments.

C. Congress must confirm ambassadorial appointments.

D. All of the above.

9 Which of the following statements about the War Powers Act is true?

A. It only applies to officially declared wars.

B. It requires the president to consult with Congress whenever possible before committing American forces to combat.

C. It has proved an effective check on the president's authority as commander in chief.

D. None of the above.

10 What constitutional authority does the president have over the Supreme Court?

A. The president can fill vacancies by appointment subject to Senate confirmation.

B. The president can veto Supreme Court rulings subject to possible override by the Court.

C. The president can initiate removal proceedings against justices.

D. None of the above.

11 Suppose that President Obama disagrees with an executive order issued by President George W. Bush. What can he do?

A. Obama can issue an executive order reversing Bush's executive order.

B. Obama can ask Congress to repeal the Bush executive order.

C. Obama can ask the Supreme Court to overturn the Bush order.

D. Nothing.

12 Which of the following constitutional actions can a president take if Congress passes legislation the president opposes?

A. Nothing.

B. The president can veto the measure subject to a possible override.

C. The president can rewrite the legislation subject to a possible override.

D. The president can refuse to enforce the legislation.

13 A pronouncement issued by the president at the time a bill passed by Congress is signed into law is known as which of the following?

A. A veto statement

B. The State of the Union Address

C. A presidential signing statement

D. An executive order

14 Which of the following agencies is part of the Executive Office of the President?

A. Office of Management and Budget (OMB)

B. Department of Justice

C. Federal Communication Commission (FCC)

D. All of the above

15 Which of the following political scientists analyzes presidential performance based on the personality traits of the president?

A. Samuel Kernell

B. Richard Neustadt

C. Fred I. Greenstein

D. James David Barber

16 Which of the following political scientists analyzes presidential performance based on leadership style?

A. Samuel Kernell

B. Richard Neustadt

C. Fred I. Greenstein

D. James David Barber

17 Which of the following political scientists analyzes presidential performance based on the chief executive's skill as a political bargainer and coalition builder?

A. Samuel Kernell

B. Richard Neustadt

C. Fred I. Greenstein

D. James David Barber

18 Which of the following is an example of a unilateral tool of presidential power that does not require congressional approval?

A. Executive agreements

B. Recess appointments

C. Signing statements

D. All of the above

19 Soon after President Barack Obama took office, public opinion polls showed that he enjoyed a high approval rating. Which of the following terms would a political scientist use to describe Obama's high standing in the polls at the very beginning of his administration?

A. Two-presidencies thesis

B. Coat-tail effect

C. Honeymoon effect

D. Rally effect

20 President George W. Bush's approval rating soared after September 11, 2001. Which of the following terms would political scientists use to describe that phenomenon?

A. Two-presidencies thesis

B. Coat-tail effect

C. Honeymoon effect

D. Rally effect

KNOW *the* **score**

18–20 correct: Congratulations! You are well informed!

15–17 correct: Your political knowledge is a bit low—be sure to review the key terms and visit TheThinkSpot.

<14 correct: Reread the chapter more thoroughly.

1. B; 2. D; 3. D; 4. D; 5. B; 6. A; 7. C; 8. D; 9. B; 10. A; 11. A; 12. B; 13. C; 14. A; 15. D; 16. C; 17. B; 18. D; 19. C; 20. D

test yourself   255

12 FEDERAL

> **WHAT'S AHEAD**

Organization of the Bureaucracy

Personnel

Rulemaking

Politics and Administration

Subgovernments and Issue Networks

Conclusion: The Federal Bureaucracy & Public Policy

Hurricane Katrina has become a symbol of bureaucratic failure. Katrina came ashore along the Louisiana, Mississippi, and Alabama coasts in late August, 2005, killing 1,400 people, flooding New Orleans, and leaving thousands of people homeless.[1] The Federal Emergency Management Agency (FEMA) endured criticism for failing to prepare for the storm and respond effectively to its devastation. While FEMA failed to act, thousands took shelter inside the New Orleans Superdome; others perched on rooftops.[2] Furthermore, FEMA's effort to deliver aid was so poorly managed that it cost taxpayers as much as $2 billion.[3]

Why did FEMA fail to respond effectively to the hurricane? The size and scope of Hurricane Katrina may have overwhelmed FEMA.[4] The ability of FEMA to respond to Katrina may also have been undermined by infighting following a bureaucratic reorganization. In 2003, Congress and the president decided to make FEMA part of the Department of Homeland Security, which was created in response to criticism that the government failed to foresee and prevent the terrorist attacks of September 11, 2001. Congress and the president hoped that a single department would be more effective at protecting the nation and responding to threats than the previous bureaucratic structures.

Upon hearing of the reorganization FEMA's director resigned, and his successor, Michael D. Brown, had no emergency management experience. When Katrina struck, Brown was locked in a heated bureaucratic turf battle with Homeland Security Secretary Michael Chertoff and FEMA was an agency in disarray. "People became distracted from the mission," Brown explained, "because we spent so much time and energy fighting for resources and working on reorganization."

BUREAUCRACY

Government Corporations

Government corporations are organizationally similar to private corporations except that the government, rather than stockholders, owns them. Their organizational rationale is that an agency that makes a product or provides a service should be run by methods similar to those used in the private sector. For example, the Postal Service is a government corporation responsible for mail service. An 11-member board of governors appointed by the president to serve 9-year, overlapping terms leads the agency. The board names a postmaster general to manage the day-to-day operation of the service. In addition to the Postal Service, the list of government corporations includes the National Railroad Passenger Corporation (which is known as Amtrak), a federal agency that operates intercity passenger railway traffic; the Federal Deposit Insurance Corporation (FDIC), a federal agency established to insure depositors' accounts in banks and thrift institutions; and the Tennessee Valley Authority (TVA), a federal agency established to promote the development of the Tennessee River and its tributaries.

An important principle behind government corporations is that they should be self-financing, at least to a significant degree. In the case of the Postal Service, users pay most of the cost of operation by purchasing stamps and paying service charges. Not all government corporations, however, are financially self-sufficient. Amtrak requires a subsidy from Congress to keep its trains rolling. Amtrak's critics argue that the agency should be

forced to pay its own way or go out of business. If the demand for passenger rail is not sufficient to support Amtrak's operation, then the service should end. In contrast, the defenders of Amtrak believe that the agency provides an important service that should be continued. Furthermore, they point out that the government subsidizes automobile transportation by building highways and air transportation by constructing airports.

think

If you were a member of Congress, would you vote in favor of government subsidies of AMTRAK?

The FCC fined CBS for a performance by **Justin Timberlake** and **Janet Jackson** at the 2004 Superbowl that included a "wardrobe malfunction" on national television.

Foundations and Institutes

Foundations and institutes administer grant programs to local governments, universities, nonprofit institutions, and individuals for research in the natural and social sciences or to promote the arts. These agencies include the National Science Foundation (NSF), a federal agency established to encourage scientific advances and improvements in science education, and the National Endowment for the Arts (NEA), a federal agency created to nurture cultural expression and promote appreciation of the arts. Foundations and institutes are governed by multimember boards appointed by the president with Senate concurrence from lists of nominees submitted by various scientific and educational institutions.

Independent Regulatory Commissions

An **independent regulatory commission** is an agency outside the major executive departments that is charged with the regulation of important aspects of the economy. The Federal Trade Commission (FTC), for example, is an agency that regulates business competition, including enforcement of laws against monopolies and the protection of consumers from deceptive trade practices. The Federal Communications Commission (FCC) is an agency that regulates interstate and international radio, television, telephone, telegraph, and satellite communications, as well as licensing radio and television stations. The Securities and Exchange Commission (SEC) is an agency that regulates the sale of stocks and bonds as well as investment and holding companies. The Equal Employment Opportunity Commission (EEOC) is an agency that investigates and rules on charges of employment discrimination.

Congress has attempted to insulate independent regulatory commissions

The National Science Foundation supports a wide range of media and museum experiences to engage learners in science education. A recent popular traveling exhibit is "CSI: The Experience" in which participants can enter crime scene rooms and play the role of investigator. They learn scientific principles and real investigative techniques as they try to solve the crime in a given room.

from direct political pressure, especially from the White House. These agencies are headed by boards of three to seven members who are appointed by the president with Senate approval. In contrast to cabinet members and the heads of other executive departments, the president cannot remove regulatory commissioners. Instead, they serve fixed, staggered terms ranging from 3 to 14 years. As a result, a new president must usually wait several years before having much impact on the composition of the boards. Furthermore, the law generally requires that no more than a bare majority of board members be from the same political party.

Congress has designed independent regulatory commissions to provide closer, more flexible regulation than Congress itself can offer through **statutory law**, law written by the legislature. Congress has delegated authority to these agencies to control various business practices using broad, general language. Congress has authorized the FTC, for example, to regulate advertising in the "public convenience, interest, or necessity." It has empowered the EEOC "to prevent any person from engaging in any unlawful employment practice."

independent regulatory commission an agency outside the major executive departments that is charged with the regulation of important aspects of the economy.

statutory law law that is written by the legislature.

Quasi-Governmental Companies

A **quasi-governmental company** is a private, profit-seeking corporation created by Congress to serve a public purpose. For example, Congress created the Federal National Mortgage Association (Fannie Mae) and Federal Home Loan Mortgage Corporation (Freddie Mac) to increase the availability of credit to home buyers. Fannie Mae and Freddie Mac are profit-making corporations run by 18-member boards of governors appointed by the president with Senate confirmation. They are exempt from state and federal taxation and enjoy a line of credit at the U.S. Treasury.

Because of the perception that Congress would bail them out if they got in financial trouble, Fannie Mae and Freddie Mac pay lower interest rates than they would if they were strictly private enterprises. Lower rates benefit home buyers, some of whom would not be able to qualify to purchase a home at all without the lower interest rate.

In 2008, Congress passed, and the president signed, legislation to commit federal funds to Fannie Mae and Freddie Mac to ensure that they would not collapse under the weight of losses incurred in the housing foreclosure crisis. The federal government eventually took over the operation of Fannie Mae and Freddie Mac, at least temporarily, to prevent their financial collapse, which would have been catastrophic for the home mortgage industry. The action kept Fannie and Freddie in business, but potentially put taxpayers on the hook for billions of dollars in bad loans.

quasi-governmental company a private, profit-seeking corporation created by Congress to serve a public purpose.

personnel

the size of the federal civilian bureaucracy has grown dramatically since the early days of the nation. In 1800, only about 3,000 persons worked for the U.S. government. That figure grew to 95,000 by 1881 and half a million in 1925. Today, the federal bureaucracy is the largest civilian workforce in the Western world, with 2.7 million civilian employees stationed in every state and city in the country and in almost every nation in the world.[12]

As the figure on p. 265 indicates, the number of federal civilian employees has generally fallen since the early 1990s. Between 1991 and 2001, the federal payroll decreased from 3.1 million to 2.7 million, a decline of nearly 13 percent. After September 11, 2001, the number of federal employees inched up. Congress passed, and the president signed, legislation to make airport baggage screeners federal employees, adding thousands of people to the federal payroll. Employment in other federal agencies that deal with security issues, including the Border Patrol, increased as well. The post-9/11 surge in federal employment peaked in 2003. Thereafter, the size of the federal workforce began to decline again.

Although the official size of the federal workforce has generally declined since the early 1990s, the actual number of people employed directly and indirectly by the federal government has risen sharply over the same period of time. Political scientist Paul C. Light estimates that the true size of the federal civilian workforce is 14.6 million employees, not the 2.7 million on the official payroll.[13] In addition to civilian employees working directly for the federal government, Light's figure includes millions of contract workers, state and local government employees working on federally funded programs, and federal grant beneficiaries at colleges and universities. The federal government pays their salaries, but their names do not appear on federal personnel rosters. Contract workers collect

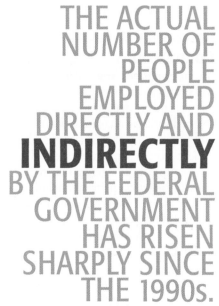

THE ACTUAL NUMBER OF PEOPLE EMPLOYED DIRECTLY AND **INDIRECTLY** BY THE FEDERAL GOVERNMENT HAS RISEN SHARPLY SINCE THE 1990s.

taxes, prepare budget documents, take notes at meetings, and perform hundreds of other governmental functions. The Department of Defense even hires private security guards to protect military bases in the United States.[14] Furthermore, Congress and the president rely on millions of state and local bureaucrats to administer federal programs, such as No Child Left Behind, Medicaid, and the Food Stamp Program.

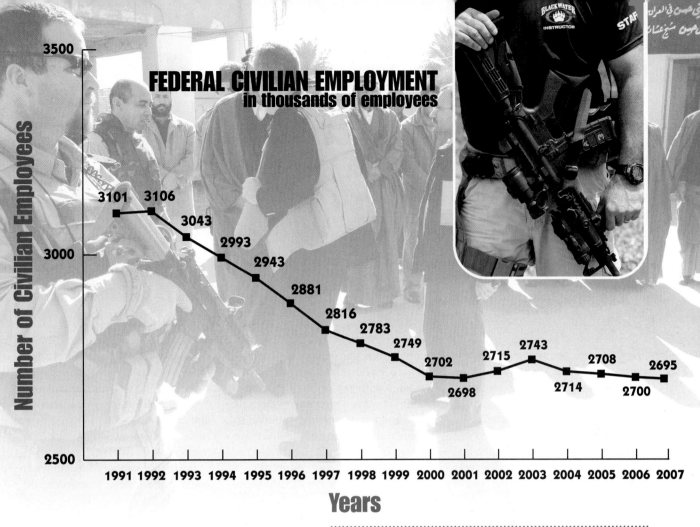

FEDERAL CIVILIAN EMPLOYMENT
in thousands of employees

Number of Civilian Employees

3500

3000

2500

3101 · 3106 · 3043 · 2993 · 2943 · 2881 · 2816 · 2783 · 2749 · 2702 · 2698 · 2715 · 2743 · 2714 · 2708 · 2700 · 2695

1991 1992 1993 1994 1995 1996 1997 1998 1999 2000 2001 2002 2003 2004 2005 2006 2007

Years

The number of federal civilian employees fell during the 1990s and has since leveled off at around 2.7 million.

Employment Practices

Employment practices in the early days of the nation emphasized character, professional qualifications, and political compatibility with the administration in office. Under President Andrew Jackson (1829–1837), political considerations became paramount. A new president would fire many of the employees of the previous administration and replace them with friends and supporters. To the victor belonged the spoils they said, and federal jobs were the spoils. The method of hiring government employees from among the friends, relatives, and supporters of elected officeholders was known as the **spoils system**.

What are the advantages of civil service tests for federal employees?

When a disgruntled office seeker assassinated President James Garfield in 1881, Congress passed, and the new president signed, legislation to reform the federal hiring process. The legislation created a Civil Service Commission to establish a hiring system based on competitive examinations and to protect federal workers from dismissal for political reasons. Initially, the civil service system covered only about

10 percent of federal jobs, but Congress gradually expanded coverage to include more than 90 percent of federal workers.[15] In 1939, Congress enacted another reform, the **Hatch Act** (named after its author, Senator Carl Hatch of New Mexico), which was a measure designed to restrict the political activities of

spoils system the method of hiring government employees from among the friends, relatives, and supporters of elected officeholders.

Hatch Act a measure designed to restrict the political activities of federal employees to voting and the private expression of views.

Where Do Federal Employees Work?

GOVERNMENT AGENCIES	NUMBER OF EMPLOYEES
Postal Service	753,254
Department of Defense	673,722
Veterans Affairs	245,537
Homeland Security	155,397
Department of the Treasury	111,577
Department of Justice	106,946
Social Security Administration	62,769

Source: Federal Civilian Employment by Branch and Agency: U.S. Census Bureau, *The 2008 Statistical Abstract*, available at www.census.gov.

federal employees to voting and the private expression of views. The rationale behind the law was to protect government workers from being forced by their superiors to work for particular candidates.

Although civil service ended the spoils system, it, too, became the target of criticism. Many observers charged that the civil service system was too inflexible to reward merit, punish poor performance, or transfer civil servants from one agency to another without having to scale a mountain of red tape. In 1978, Congress and the president responded to complaints against the civil service system by enacting a package of reforms. The legislation established a Senior Executive Service (SES) composed of approximately 8,000 top civil servants who would be eligible for substantial merit bonuses but who could be transferred, demoted, or fired more easily than other federal employees. The reform measure replaced the old Civil Service Commission with two new agencies: an Office of Personnel Management to manage the federal workforce and a

Evolution of the FEDERAL BUREAUCRACY

1789 | Congress authorizes the creation of the first federal agency, which it later renamed the Department of State.

1881 | A disgruntled federal office seeker assassinates President James Garfield.

1883 | Congress passes the Civil Service Reform Act, also called the Pendleton Act, to reform the federal hiring process on the basis of merit rather than patronage.

| 1780 | 1800 | 1820 | 1840 | 1860 | 1880 | 1900 | 1920 |

1829 | President Andrew Jackson ushers in the spoils system, in which political considerations became paramount in hiring government employees.

1933 | The size of the federal bureaucracy balloons during the New Deal era as President Franklin Delano Roosevelt and Congress create a series of federal agencies to regulate industry and to put Americans back to work during the Great Depression.

Merit Systems Protection Board to hear employee grievances.[16]

Congress and the president have given federal employees limited rights to organize. Federal workers won the right to form unions in 1912. Fifty years later, President John Kennedy signed an executive order giving federal workers the right to bargain collectively over a limited set of issues but not about pay or benefits. **Collective bargaining** is a negotiation between an employer and a union representing employees over the terms and conditions of employment. The civil service reform legislation adopted in 1978 guaranteed federal employees the right to bargain collectively over issues other than pay and benefits, but it prohibited federal workers from striking. In 1981, President Ronald Reagan fired more than 11,000 air traffic controllers for participating in a strike organized by the Professional Air Traffic Controllers Association (PATCO).

Democratic presidents typically have a more positive relationship with federal employee organizations than do Republican presidents. Labor unions in general are allied with the Democratic Party, whereas the GOP has stronger ties to management, and public employee unions are no exception to the pattern. President Bill Clinton, for example, issued an executive order directing federal agencies to develop partnerships with the employee unions. Clinton justified the approach as a means to reform government by making it more efficient. In contrast, President George W. Bush took an adversarial approach toward employee unions. He dissolved the partnership councils created during the Clinton administration and asked

collective bargaining a negotiation between an employer and a union representing employees over the terms and conditions of employment.

Federal employees MAY:

be candidates for public office in nonpartisan elections

express opinions about candidates and issues

contribute money to political organizations

attend and be active in political fundraising functions, political rallies, and political party or club meetings

campaign for or against candidates in partisan elections

Federal employees MAY NOT:

be candidates for public office in partisan elections

use their official authority or influence to affect the outcome of an election

knowingly encourage or discourage the political activity of any person who has business before the agency

engage in political activity while on duty, in any government office, while wearing an official uniform, or while using a government vehicle

Source: U.S. Special Counsel's Office

1939 | Congress authorizes the establishment of the Executive Office of the President (EOP) to assist in managing the bureaucracy, and passes the Hatch Act, which restricts the political activities of federal employees.

SEVERE
SEVERE RISK OF TERRORIST ATTACKS

HIGH
HIGH RISK OF TERRORIST ATTACKS

ELEVATED
SIGNIFICANT RISK OF TERRORIST ATTACKS

GUARDED
GENERAL RISK OF TERRORIST ATTACKS

LOW
LOW RISK OF TERRORIST ATTACKS

2002 | George W. Bush issues an executive order creating an Office of Homeland Security within the EOP, which is later elevated to a full cabinet department.

1940   1960   1980   2000

1965 | Lyndon Johnson's Great Society programs result in the largest expansion of the federal bureaucracy since FDR's New Deal.

1978 | Congress enacts a package of reforms, including the creation of two new agencies: an Office of Personnel Management to manage the federal workforce and a Merit Systems Protection Board to hear employee grievances.

Political scientist Hugh Heclo believes that the concept of issue networks more accurately describes administrative policymaking today than the concept of subgovernments. An **issue network** is a group of political actors concerned with some aspect of public policy. Issue networks are fluid, with participants moving in and out. They can include technical spe-

Environmentalists worried about the effect of highway construction on the environment

cialists, members of Congress, journalists, the president, interest groups, bureaucrats, academic experts, and individual political activists. Powerful interest groups may be involved, but they do not control the process. Instead, policy in a particular area results from conflict among a broad range of political actors both in and out of government.[37]

Consider the fate of the Highway Trust Fund. A subgovernment once dominated federal highway policy, but that is no longer the case. During the 1970s, the number of interest groups concerned with highway construction grew. Environmentalists worried about the effect of highway construction on the environment. Minority rights groups became alarmed about the impact of freeway construction on minority neighborhoods. Groups advocating energy conservation argued that government should divert money from highways to mass transit. In the meantime, congressional committees and subcommittees with jurisdiction over highway programs began to include members of Congress allied to groups opposed to highway spending. As a result, fed-

eral highway policy is now made in a more contentious, uncertain environment than before.[38] In 1991, Congress passed and the president signed the Intermodal Surface Transportation Efficiency Act (ISTEA), granting states considerable leeway in deciding whether to spend federal transportation money for highways or mass transit. The legislation also required that states use a certain amount of money to fund "enhancement programs," which were local transportation-related projects designed to aid a community's quality of life, such as hike and bike trails. The passage of ISTEA reflected the participation of a broad range of interests concerned with transportation policy, not just the traditional set of interest groups involved with highway funding.[39]

issue network a group of political actors that is actively involved with policymaking in a particular issue area.

ISSUE NETWORKS

TECHNICAL SPECIALIST

MEMBERS OF CONGRESS

BUREAUCRATS

POLITICAL ACTIVISTS

JOURNALISTS

ACADEMIC EXPERTS

INTEREST GROUPS

THE PRESIDENT

Issue networks are used to better explain the more complicated relationship among the parties involved in policymaking.

New Offshore Drilling Not a Quick Fix, Analysts Say

BY LISA WANGSNESS, GLOBE STAFF

JUNE 20, 2008

President Bush and Republican presidential candidate John McCain have called this week for lifting a federal moratorium on offshore oil exploration, arguing that taking action to increase domestic oil supplies will help drive down prices.

Americans' anger over $4-a-gallon gasoline apparently has prompted greater public support for renewed offshore drilling. A Gallup poll last month found that 57 percent of respondents favored such drilling while 41 percent were opposed. Democratic candidate Barack Obama supports the moratorium.

In the short term, oil prices could go down slightly if Congress lifts its moratorium on new offshore drilling, which has been in place since 1981, because the market would factor in the prospect of additional oil supplies later on. But the actual oil would not be produced for 10 to 12 years.

And in any case, increased American production from offshore drilling would not necessarily mean lower prices for American consumers because oil is a global commodity whose price is set by global supply and demand.

Robert Kaufmann, director of the Center for Energy and Environmental Studies at Boston University, says in the best-case scenario, the United States could only produce an additional two to four million barrels of offshore oil a day—not enough to shift the global supply-demand balance in a world market that now consumes about 86 million barrels a day and is growing fast. About a quarter of that consumption now occurs in the United States.

"There's nothing on the supply side that we can really do to disrupt OPEC's ability to influence prices," he said.

Environmentalists argue that the pollution caused by drilling could compromise fragile ecosystems for very little economic benefit when the United States should be focusing on conservation—the cheapest barrel of oil, they like to say, is the one we don't have to buy—and developing better renewable energy sources.

But Nancy Rabalais, executive director of the Louisiana Universities Marine Consortium and a scientist who has studied the effects of offshore oil production in the Gulf of Mexico, says that she believes expanding offshore oil exploration would not pose terrible risks to the environment because the effects are relatively contained, and the industry is well-regulated.

Henry Lee, who teaches energy policy at Harvard University's John F. Kennedy School of Government, says he believes there is a middle ground. "There is no panacea," he said, "for solving America's energy problems, so it may be best to lift the prohibitions on offshore drilling, and carefully consider the oil potential and possible environmental costs in different locations on a case-by-case basis."

⬈ CRITICAL THINKING QUESTIONS

- What are the arguments for offshore drilling and the arguments against it?
- Why has support for offshore drilling increased?
- Do you think the United States government should approve offshore drilling now? Why or why not?

>> END

CONCLUSION
the federal bureaucracy
&PUBLIC POLICY

t he federal bureaucracy participates in every stage of the policymaking process.

Agenda Building

The actions of federal agencies sometimes focus public attention on issues. For example, the federal bureaucracy has done more to call public attention to the health risks of tobacco than either Congress or the president. In 1964, the **surgeon general,** an official in the Public Health Service who advises the president on health issues, released a report summarizing research showing a link between smoking and cancer. That document, which was called the *Surgeon General's Report on Smoking and Health*, was the nation's first official recognition that cigarette smoking causes cancer and other serious illnesses. Over the years, the surgeon general has issued additional reports dealing with related issues, such as the effect of second-hand smoke and preventing tobacco use among young people. The initial report and each succeeding report received a good deal of attention, sparking a public debate about the impact of tobacco use on the public health.

Agency reports and official statements can highlight policy issues, especially if the media and the general public perceive that agency officials are acting on the basis of their professional expertise rather than political motives. Even though surgeons general are presidential appointees, they are held in respect because they are physicians who work in an agency dominated by health professionals. The scientific evidence presented in the various reports released by the surgeon general put the tobacco companies on the defensive, making it difficult for them to defeat proposals to restrict tobacco advertising and require health warnings on tobacco products.

Policy Formulation and Adoption

Federal agencies participate in policy formulation. Agency officials work directly with the White House and members of Congress during the legislative process. Agency officials may assist members of Congress in drafting legislation related to their departments. Agencies participate in the budget process by making budget requests to the president and testifying at congressional budget hearings. Officials in the executive branch advise the president on policy decisions.

Executive branch agencies do not directly adopt policy, but they participate in policy adoption by lobbying the president and Congress. Consider the role in policy adoption of the **Joint Chiefs of Staff,** the military advisory body composed of the chiefs of staff of the U.S. Army and Air Force, the chief of naval operations, and sometimes the commandant of the Marine

surgeon general an official in the Public Health Service who advises the president on health issues.

Joint Chiefs of Staff a military advisory body that is composed of the chiefs of staff of the U.S. Army and Air Force, the Chief of Naval Operations, and sometimes the Commandant of the Marine Corps.

The surgeon general has issued a number of reports compiling research showing a direct link between smoking and cancer.

Corps. The Joint Chiefs not only advise the president on defense policy, but they also lobby the White House and Congress on policies that concern the armed forces. When President Clinton attempted to end the policy of excluding gay men and lesbians from military service at the beginning of his first term, members of the Joint Chiefs lobbied Congress to oppose the president's initiative.

Policy Implementation and Evaluation

The federal bureaucracy implements policy. The IRS, for example, enforces the nation's tax laws. The U.S. Armed Forces carry out the nation's military policies. The Department of Homeland Security implements domestic security policies. FEMA responds to natural disasters.

Congress delegates authority to federal agencies to implement policy. Sometimes Congress writes detailed legislation, giving agency administrators little enforcement discretion. At other times, Congress grants agencies broad regulatory discretion. Sometimes Congress gives agencies so much leeway that an argument can be made that the agencies are actually adopting policies themselves, rather than implementing policies adopted by Congress and the president through the legislative process.

Finally, federal agencies evaluate policy. Agencies gather data, conduct research, prepare reports, and recommend policy changes. The

Congress delegates authority to federal agencies to implement policy

Department of Education, for example, conducts and compiles research on the effectiveness of teacher training programs and other educational programs. The Department of Defense researches the effectiveness of weapons systems. After the Katrina disaster, Homeland Security Secretary Chertoff asked Congress to enhance the capacity of FEMA to respond to crises by adding employees and expanding its regional offices.[40]

the THINKSPOT
www.thethinkspot.com

TEST yourself

1 What federal agency was responsible for responding to Hurricane Katrina?
A. Federal Emergency Management Agency (FEMA)
B. Army Corps of Engineers
C. Salvation Army
D. Office of Management and Budget

2 What sort of agency is FEMA?
A. A quasi-government company
B. Part of the Department of Interior
C. Part of the Department of Homeland Security
D. Independent Regulatory Commission

3 Which of the following is *not* a cabinet department?
A. Environmental Protection Agency (EPA)
B. Department of Homeland Security
C. Department of Defense
D. Department of Justice

4 Which of the following cabinet departments has the largest number of civilian employees?
A. Department of Homeland Security
B. Department of Defense
C. Department of Education
D. Department of Justice

5 The attorney general heads which of the following departments?
A. Department of Homeland Security
B. Department of Defense
C. Department of State
D. Department of Justice

6 Which of the following is *not* an example of a government corporation?
A. Amtrak
B. CIA
C. Postal Service
D. FDIC

7 Which of the following agencies is expected to be self-financing?
A. FEMA
B. EPA
C. FDIC
D. Peace Corps

8 Which of the following agencies regulates business competition, including enforcement of laws against monopolies and the protection of consumers from deceptive trade practices?
A. FCC
B. FTC
C. SEC
D. EPA

9 Which of the following agencies regulates interstate and international radio, television, telephone, telegraph, and satellite communications, as well as licensing radio and television stations?
A. FCC
B. FTC
C. SEC
D. EPA

10 The president has the authority to remove all but which one of the following government officials?
A. Attorney general
B. FEMA director
C. SEC commissioner
D. Secretary of transportation

11 Which of the following agencies is an example of a quasi-government company?
A. Postal Service
B. FEMA
C. Amtrak
D. Fannie Mae

12 The spoils system involved which of the following?
A. Hiring friends, relatives, and political supporters to work for the government
B. Giving government contracts to companies owned by friends, relatives, and political supporters
C. Contracting out with private companies to implement government programs
D. Forbidding government employees from engaging in political activities

13 Which of the following rights do federal employees enjoy?
A. The right to form unions
B. The right to vote for candidates of their choice
C. The right to bargain collectively over issues other than pay and benefits
D. All of the above

14 Are private companies legally obligated to follow rules adopted by regulatory agencies?

A. No. Only Congress has the authority to enact legally binding regulations.

B. Yes, but only if the rules are ratified by Congress.

C. Yes. Rules are legally binding.

D. No, although many business follow them voluntarily.

15 Suppose the president disagrees with the policy initiatives of a federal agency. What can the president do to exert control?

A. The president can ask Congress to cut the agency's budget.

B. The president can appoint administrators to head the agency that agree with the president's policy position.

C. The president can ask Congress to reorganize the agency.

D. All of the above.

16 Suppose that a majority of the members of Congress disagree with the policy initiatives of a federal agency. What actions can Congress take to exert control?

A. Congress can cut the agency's budget.

B. Congress can change the legislation under which the agency operates.

C. Congress can reorganize the agency or merge it with another agency.

D. All of the above.

17 Which of the following is an example of fire-alarm oversight?

A. Congress conducts periodic review of an agency's operation.

B. The president conducts periodic review of an agency's operation.

C. Congress responds to complaints about an agency's performance.

D. All of the above.

18 An agency that is accused of working too closely with the interest groups it is supposed to be regulating is known as which of the following?

A. Issue network

B. Captured agency

C. Independent regulatory commission

D. Iron triangle

19 Which of the following political actors is *not* part of a subgovernment or iron triangle?

A. President

B. Congress

C. Interest group

D. Government agency

20 Which of the following is a group of political actors that is concerned with some aspect of public policy?

A. Issue network

B. Captured agency

C. Independent regulatory commission

D. Iron triangle

1. A; 2. A; 3. A; 4. B; 5. D; 6. B; 7. C; 8. B; 9. A; 10. C; 11. C; 12. A; 13. D; 14. C; 15. D; 16. D; 17. C; 18. B; 19. A; 20. A

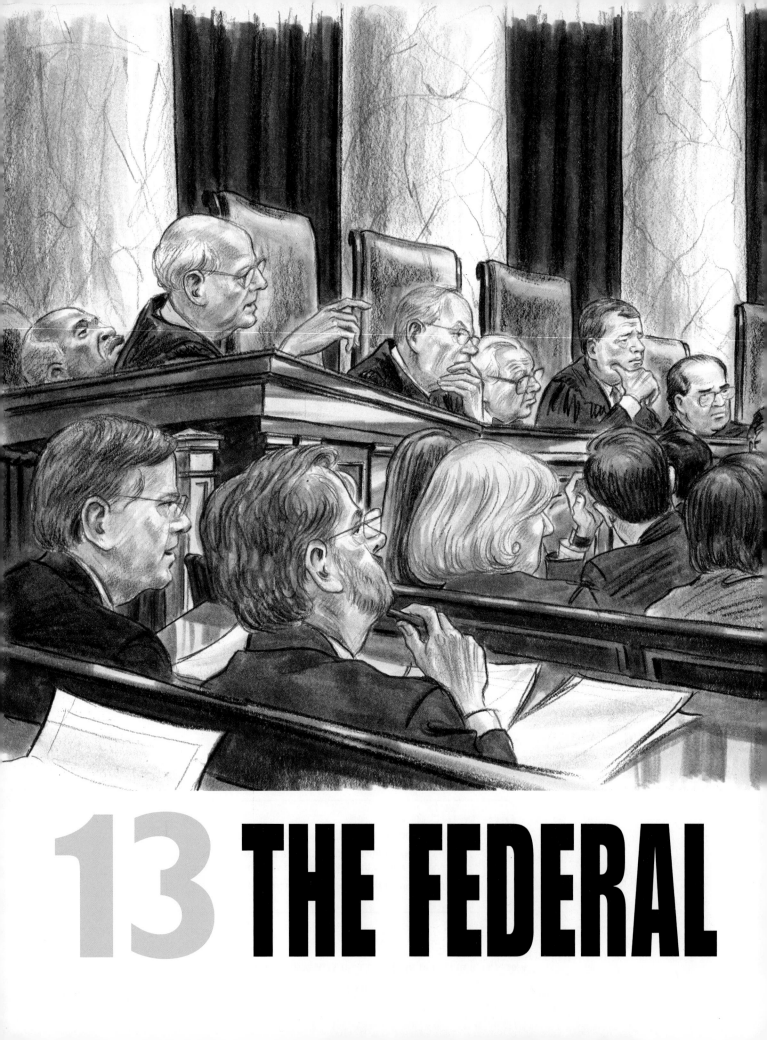

13 THE FEDERAL

> WHAT'S AHEAD

Judicial Policymaking
The Federal Court System
Power, Politics, and the Courts
Conclusion: The Courts
& Public Policy

President Barack Obama may have the opportunity to change the philosophical balance on the U.S. Supreme Court. In January 2009, the average age of the nine justices serving on the Court was 69, with five justices older than 70 years. At 88 years of age, Associate Justice John Paul Stevens is the oldest member of the Court. If Stevens or any other member of the Court dies, retires, or resigns while Obama is in office, Obama will have the opportunity to appoint a replacement, subject to Senate confirmation by majority vote.

Any Obama appointments to the Supreme Court could be critical because the Court is closely divided philosophically. In recent sessions, the Court has decided many cases by the narrowest of margins. In 2007, a third of the Court's decisions came on a vote of 5 to 4. In 2008, the Court decided 17 percent of its cases by a 5–4 vote. In most of these closely decided cases, Justices Stevens, David Souter, Stephen Breyer, and Ruth Bader Ginsburg—the so-called liberal wing of the Court—voted as a bloc. Four other justices—Chief Justice John Roberts and Associate Justices Antonin Scalia, Clarence Thomas, and Samuel Alito—also voted together as the conservative wing of the Court. Associate Justice Anthony Kennedy was the swing vote, siding with the conservative bloc on some issues and with the liberal group on other issues.[1] Depending on which seats on the Court become vacant during his tenure, Obama could maintain the current philosophical balance or move the Court in a more liberal direction on such issues as abortion, gun control, affirmative action, capital punishment (the death penalty), and gay and lesbian rights.[2]

COURTS

Alcee Lamar Hastings is living proof that impeachment does not necessarily end a career in public service. Hastings became a federal judge in 1979 when President Jimmy Carter appointed him as a judge on the U.S. district court for the Southern District of Florida. Hastings's career suffered a setback in 1981 when he was charged with accepting a bribe from a defendant in his court and then lying about it to federal prosecutors. Even though Hastings was acquitted of all charges, the U.S. House impeached him and in 1989 the U.S. Senate removed him from office. Nonetheless, three years later Hastings won election to Congress from the Twenty-third U.S. Congressional District in South Florida. Many of the voters in the district, which is majority African American, apparently believed that Congress had treated Hastings unfairly because he was impeached and removed from his judgeship despite his acquittal. Hastings has subsequently easily won reelection and continues to serve in the U.S. House alongside some of the members who voted to impeach him as a federal judge two decades earlier.

senator shares the president's party affiliation, the White House usually consults state party leaders and/or members of the House for their recommendations.

The Senate Judiciary Committee evaluates district court nominees. After the committee staff conducts a background check, the committee chair schedules a hearing to allow the nominee and interested parties an opportunity to be heard. The confirmation of district court judges is usually a quiet affair, with few nominees rejected. Confirmation is not necessarily speedy, however, especially when the Senate and White House are in the hands of different political parties. Toward the end of a presidential term, the chair of the Senate Judiciary Committee and the Senate majority leader will sometimes delay the confirmation process in hopes that the White House changes parties and the new president can then fill pending vacancies. Even early in a term, the confirmation process takes anywhere from four months to two years, or even longer.[10]

Presidents typically nominate judges whose party affiliation and political philosophy are compatible with their own. Democratic presidents appoint Democratic judges; Republican presidents select Republicans. Some presidents also seek judges with particular political philosophies. In general, Republican presidents choose judges with conservative political philosophies, whereas Democratic presidents select liberal judges. Conservative judges tend to favor government interests over criminal defendants, interpret narrowly the constitutional guarantees of equal rights for women and minorities, support corporate interests against the claims of individual workers or consumers, and rule against federal government involvement in local policy issues. In contrast, liberal judges are more inclined than their conservative counterparts to favor judicial underdogs, such as consumers, workers, criminal defendants, and members of minority groups. They tend to support the federal government in federalism disputes over the relative power of the states and the national government.[11]

Federal judges hold lifetime appointments, with "good behavior," as the Constitution puts it. They may not be retired involuntarily or removed for political reasons, but they are subject to impeachment by the House and removal by the Senate. Although members of Congress occasionally threaten to impeach judges with whom they have policy disagreements, impeachment is rare and always directed against judges who are accused of misconduct. In American history, only seven federal judges have been impeached and removed from office. Most judges who get in trouble resign rather than face the humiliation of impeachment.[12]

Courts of Appeals

The U.S. courts of appeals (also known as circuit courts of appeals) are the primary intermediate appellate courts in the federal system. There are 13 courts of appeals, one

In American history, only seven federal judges have been impeached and removed from office.

for each of the 12 judicial circuits (or regions), and a thirteenth circuit called the U.S. Court of Appeals for the Federal Circuit. The latter court hears appeals in specialized cases, such as patent law, and cases appealed from the Court of International Trade and the Court of Federal Claims. The number of justices for each of the circuits ranges from 3 to 24. Altogether, 179 justices staff the courts of appeals along with another 40 senior justices.

Jurisdiction. The courts of appeals are exclusively appellate courts, usually hearing cases in panels of three justices each. They hear appeals from the U.S. district courts, the Court of International Trade, and the Court of Federal Claims. The courts of appeals also hear appeals on the decisions of the regulatory

DISTRICT COURT JUDICIAL APPOINTEES, BILL CLINTON AND GEORGE W. BUSH (THROUGH JUNE 2007)

Characteristic	Clinton	Bush
White	75%	83%
Black	17	6
Asian	1	–
Latino	6	11
Native American	–	–
Democrat	88	7
Republican	6	85
Independent/Other	6	8
Female	29	20

Sandra Day O'Connor, appointed by President Ronald Reagan in 1981, was the first woman to serve on the Supreme Court.

Harold M. Stanley and Richard G. Niemi, *Vital Statistics on American Politics 2007–2008* (Washington, DC: CQ Press, 2008), p. 290.

commissions, with the rulings of the National Labor Relations Board (NLRB) producing the most appeals. The courts of appeals are generally not required to hold hearings in every case. After reading the legal briefs in a case (a **legal brief** is a written legal argument) and reviewing the trial court record, the appeals court may uphold the lower court decision without hearing formal arguments.

When an appeals court decides to accept an appeal, the court usually schedules a hearing at which the attorneys for the two sides in the dispute present oral arguments and answer any questions posed by the justices. Appeals courts do not retry cases. Instead, they review the trial-court record and consider legal arguments. After hearing oral arguments and studying legal briefs,

appeals court justices discuss the case and eventually vote on a decision, with a majority vote of the justices required to decide a case. The court may **affirm** (uphold) the lower court decision, reverse it, modify it, or affirm part of the lower court ruling while reversing or modifying the rest. Frequently, an appeals court may **remand** (return) a case to the trial court for reconsideration in light of the appeals court decision. The courts of appeals have the final word on more than 95 percent of the cases they hear because the Supreme Court rarely intervenes on appeal.[13]

Selection of Justices. The White House generally takes more care with nominations to the courts of appeals than it does with district court selections. Because the judicial circuits usually include several states, senatorial courtesy does not dictate the selection of justices on the courts of appeals.[14] When a vacancy occurs, a deputy attorney general gathers names of potential nominees, asking party leaders, senators, and members of the House for suggestions. Eventually, the deputy attorney general suggests a name or perhaps a short list of names for the president's consideration, and the president makes a choice. The Senate examines appel-

late court nominees more closely than it considers district court selections, especially when the opposition party controls the Senate. Furthermore, as with district court nominees, delays are not unusual. The length of confirmation delays depends on the size of the president's opposition in the Senate, the proximity of the next presidential election, and whether the nominee is a woman or minority. Appellate court nominees who are women or minorities take twice as long to confirm as do white males.[15] The Senate is more likely to reject nominees when the opposition party controls the Senate, and in the last year of a president's term. Since 1950, the Senate has confirmed 94 percent of district and appellate court appointees when the president's party controls the Senate but only 80

Do you think that federal judges should be periodically subject to reappointment? Why or why not?

legal brief a written legal argument.

affirm the action of an appeals court to uphold the decision of a lower court.

remand the decision of an appeals court to return a case to a lower court for reconsideration in light of an appeals court decision.

Islamic Law in Nigeria

Nigeria is an ethnically and religiously diverse country. Its population includes several major ethnic groups (the Hausa-Fulani, Yoruba, and Igbo) as well as hundreds of smaller groups. The most important religions are Islam, Christianity, Orisha (the traditional Yoruba religion), and Animism, which is the belief that souls inhabit most bodies, including people, animals, plants, and even inanimate objects, such as stones.

After military rule ended in Nigeria in 1999 and the country established a federal system, 12 of the northern states adopted Sharia, Islamic law based on the Koran. Sharia addresses issues of sexual morality and alcohol consumption in addition to other crimes. Punishments under Sharia can be harsh. Adulterers may be stoned to death or flogged. Thieves may suffer the amputation of a hand. Public intoxication is punishable by flogging.

The adoption of Sharia in the northern states of Nigeria has been controversial. Even though Sharia applies only to Muslims, some aspects of it, including banning alcohol and prostitution, apply generally. Critics declare that the use of Sharia violates the principle of separation of state and religion. Furthermore, they charge that the status of women under Sharia and its imposition of harsh punishments cast the nation in an unfavorable light. They point to the 2002 case that provoked international outrage in which a divorced Muslim woman was sentenced to death after having a child out of wedlock. Islamic courts eventually overturned the sentence on the basis of a technicality. Sharia courts have subsequently avoided high-profile controversial cases.[16]

Questions

1. In a country as diverse as Nigeria, is it better for different regions to follow their own legal traditions or would it be preferable for the entire nation to have a uniform system?

2. Should a nation's laws be based on its religious traditions?

3. In what ways, if any, is American law grounded in Judeo-Christian legal traditions?

Amina Lawal and her lawyer appealed Lawal's Sharia sentence of death by stoning for adultery. The court overturned the verdict and Lawal was freed.

percent of nominees when the opposition controls the Senate. The odds of confirmation in any event decline by 25 percent in a presidential election year.[17]

The nomination process for courts of appeals judges is contentious because so many of their decisions are final. In 2007, appellate courts decided more than 30,000 cases compared with fewer than a hundred decided by the U.S. Supreme Court, which agrees to hear relatively few appeals.[18]

Supreme Court

The Supreme Court of the United States is the highest court in the land. Its rulings take precedence over the decisions of other federal courts. On matters involving federal law and the U.S. Constitution, the decisions of the U.S. Supreme Court take precedence over state court rulings as well.

The Constitution says nothing about the size of the Supreme Court, letting Congress and the president set its size legislatively. Through the years, the size of the Court has varied from five to ten justices. The present membership of nine justices has been in effect for more than a century. In the 1930s, President Franklin Roosevelt attempted to enlarge the Court in order to appoint new justices friendly to the New Deal, but his effort was popularly attacked as a court-packing plan and defeated by Congress. Since then, no serious efforts have been made to change the Court's size.

Today's Court includes a chief justice and eight associate justices. The justices are equal and independent, similar to nine separate law firms, but the chief justice is first among them. The chief presides over the Court's public sessions and private conferences. The chief justice can call special sessions of the Court and helps administer the federal court system. The chief justice also assigns justices the responsibility of writing the Court's majority opinion in cases when the chief

Senators John Warner of Virginia and John McCain of Arizona, and their aides, leave a meeting with Majority Leader Bill Frist. The senators represented a group of 14 senators who wanted to avoid the "nuclear option" threatened by Republican senators to force Democratic leadership to bring judicial appointments to the floor of the Senate.

WHEN GEORGE W. BUSH WON the White House in 2000, he was able to appoint judges to fill the vacancies left at the end of Clinton's term. During Bush's first term, Democrats filibustered 10 of 52 appellate court nominees, declaring that the judicial philosophies of the 10 were so conservative that they were outside the judicial mainstream. Republicans responded to the Democrats' tactic by threatening a procedure they labeled the "constitutional option." Democrats called it the "nuclear option." The strategy involved Republican senators asking the presiding officer of the Senate, Vice President Dick Cheney, to rule that it was unconstitutional to filibuster judicial nominees. Because a simple majority would be sufficient to uphold the vice president's ruling, Senate Republicans who outnumbered Democrats 55 to 45 would be able to end the Democratic filibuster and force a vote on Bush's nominations whose appointments had been blocked. Democrats responded to the Republican strategy by threatening to use various parliamentary maneuvers to shut down or at least seriously delay Senate business.[19] Eventually, a group of 14 senators—7 Democrats and 7 Republicans—brokered a compromise to allow the confirmation of some of the filibustered judicial nominees. The compromise defused the crisis temporarily but did not resolve the issue.

votes with the majority. Regular sessions of the Supreme Court run from the first Monday in October until the end of June or early July.

Jurisdiction. Technically, the Supreme Court can be both a trial court and an appellate court. The Constitution gives the Court a limited **original jurisdiction,** which is the set of cases a court may hear as a trial court. The Supreme Court may

try "cases affecting ambassadors, other public ministers and consuls, and those in which a state shall be a party," except for cases initiated against a state by the citizens of another state or nation. In practice, however, the Court does not conduct

original jurisdiction the set of cases a court may hear as a trial court.

THE U.S. SUPREME COURT IN 2009

Justice	Year Born	Appointment Year	Political Party	Law School	Appointing President	Religion	Senate Confirmation Vote
John Paul Stevens	1920	1975	R	Chicago	Ford	Nondenominational	98–0
Antonin Scalia	1936	1985	R	Harvard	Reagan	Roman Catholic	98–0
Anthony Kennedy	1936	1988	R	Harvard	Reagan	Roman Catholic	97–0
David Souter	1939	1990	R	Harvard	G. Bush	Episcopalian	90–9
Clarence Thomas	1948	1991	R	Yale	G. Bush	Roman Catholic	52–48
Ruth Bader Ginsburg	1933	1993	D	Columbia	Clinton	Jewish	96–3
Stephen Breyer	1938	1994	D	Harvard	Clinton	Jewish	87–9
John G. Roberts, Jr.	1955	2005	R	Harvard	G.W. Bush	Roman Catholic	78–22
Samuel A. Alito, Jr.	1950	2006	R	Yale	G.W. Bush	Roman Catholic	58–42

trials. The Court shares jurisdiction with the U.S. district courts on the matters included in its original jurisdiction and leaves most of those cases for the district courts to decide. Even for the few cases of original jurisdiction that the justices consider worthwhile, the Supreme Court does not hold a trial. Instead, the Court appoints a special master to conduct a hearing to determine the facts before it decides the legal issues.

The Court's appellate jurisdiction is set by law and, through the years, Congress has made the Supreme Court of the United States the nation's highest appellate court for both the federal and the state judicial systems. In the federal system, the courts of appeals generate the largest number of appeals by far. Cases may arise from the court of military appeals and special three-judge courts, which Congress has authorized to hear redistricting cases and some civil rights cases. Cases can also be appealed to the Supreme Court from the highest court in each state, usually the state supreme court.

Congress can reduce the jurisdiction of the Supreme Court if it chooses. After the Civil War, Congress removed the authority of the Court to review the constitutionality of Reconstruction legislation. Since then, Congress has been reluctant to tamper with the jurisdiction of the federal courts on grounds that it would interfere with the independence of the judicial branch. In recent years, most attempts to limit the jurisdiction of federal courts in cases involving such controversial issues as abortion, school prayer, busing, and the rights of criminal defendants have failed.[20]

Selection of Justices. Nominating individuals to the Supreme Court is one of the president's most important responsibilities. The formal procedures for appointment and confirmation of Supreme Court justices are similar to those for appellate court justices except that they are generally performed more carefully and receive considerably more publicity. The attorney general begins the task by compiling a list of

possible nominees. The president narrows the list to a few names and the FBI conducts background checks on each.

In selecting individuals to serve on the Supreme Court, presidents look for nominees who share their political philosophy: Conservative presidents prefer conservative justices, whereas liberal presidents want liberal justices. When President Franklin Roosevelt finally had the chance to make appointments to the Supreme Court, he was careful to select nominees sympathetic to the New Deal. In contrast, President Reagan screened nominees to ensure their political conservatism.

The Senate scrutinizes Supreme Court nominations more closely than lower-court appointments. The Judiciary Committee staff and the staffs of individual senators carefully examine the nominee's background and past statements on policy issues. The committee conducts hearings at which the nominee, interest group spokespersons, and other concerned parties testify. The Senate as a whole then debates the nomination on the floor before voting to confirm or reject.

The confirmation process is highly political, with the White House and interest groups conducting public relations campaigns in hopes of putting pressure on wavering senators to confirm or reject the president's choice.[21] For example, the nomination of Clarence Thomas by the first President Bush became a political tug-of-war between women's groups and the White House over

ceived as well-qualified and whose political views are close to those of their constituents. When nominees are less qualified or hold controversial views, the outcome of the confirmation vote depends to a large degree on the political environment.[23] The Senate is most likely to reject Supreme Court nominees when the opposition party controls the Senate and/or when a nomination is made in the last year of a president's term.[24] When both of these conditions apply, the failure

"good behavior," they can serve for life, and many have continued on the bench well past traditional retirement age. Associate Justice Hugo Black, for example, served until age 85; William O. Douglas stayed on the Court until he was 77, despite having had a debilitating stroke. Justices can be impeached and removed from office, but Congress is unlikely to act without clear evidence of misconduct. Politics or old age and ill health are probably not reason enough for Congress to

CAN YOU IDENTIFY THE SUPREME COURT JUSTICES?

According to a December 2005 national survey conducted by FindLaw, only 43 percent of American adults can name at least one justice who is currently serving on the nation's highest court.

SUPREME COURT JUSTICE	% WHO COULD NAME THE JUSTICE
SANDRA DAY O'CONNOR*	27
CLARENCE THOMAS	21
JOHN G. ROBERTS, JR.	16
ANTONIN SCALIA	13
RUTH BADER GINSBURG	12
ANTHONY KENNEDY	7
DAVID SOUTER	5
JOHN PAUL STEVENS	3
STEPHEN BREYER	3

*Sandra Day O'Connor retired in 2005 and was replaced by Samuel A. Alito, Jr., in January 2006.

Incorrect responses from those surveyed as to who is currently serving on the U.S. Supreme Court included George W. Bush, Hillary Clinton, Thurgood Marshall, and Arnold Schwarzenegger.

Source: FindLaw's U.S. Supreme Court Awareness Survey

Thomas's fitness to serve, after Anita Hill, a former employee of Thomas at the Equal Employment Opportunity Commission (EEOC), accused him of sexual harassment. Thomas eventually won confirmation by a narrow margin.

The Senate confirms most Supreme Court nominees. Since 1789, the Senate has approved 122 of 151 nominations. In the twentieth century alone, the rate was 52 of 62.[22] Senators routinely vote to confirm nominees who are per-

rate for Supreme Court nominees is 71 percent. It is 19 percent when one condition applies and only 10 percent when neither condition exists.[25] Some political scientists believe that the frequency of divided government forces the president to nominate politically moderate, cautious justices who accept a rather limited role for the federal judiciary in the political process.[26]

Like other federal judges, members of the Supreme Court enjoy the ultimate in job security. With

initiate impeachment proceedings. Furthermore, because of advances in medicine, life tenure means more today than it did when the Constitution was written. Between 1789 and 1970, the average justice served less than 15 years, with vacancies occurring on average every two years. Since 1970, the average justice serves more than 26 years and a vacancy occurs every three years.[27]

Deciding to Decide. Supreme Court justices set their own agenda. Each year, litigants appeal 7,000 to

Court, which explains and justifies its ruling and serves as a guideline for lower courts when similar legal issues arise in the future. The majority opinion is more important than the outcome of the case because the majority opinion establishes policy.

While the majority opinion is being drafted, other justices may be preparing and circulating concurring or dissenting opinions. A **concurring opinion** is a judicial statement that agrees with the Court's ruling but disagrees with the reasoning of the majority opinion. A justice may write a concurring opinion to point out what the Court did not do in the majority opinion and identify the issues that remain open for further litigation.[34] A **dissenting opinion** is a judicial statement that disagrees with the decision of the court's majority. Justices write dissenting opinions in order to note disagreement with the Court's ruling, to emphasize the limits of the majority opinion, and to express the conscience of the individual justice. Only the majority opinion of the Court has legal force.

The Decision. Eventually, the positions of the justices harden or coalesce, and the Supreme Court announces its decision. The announcement takes place in open court, and the final versions of the majority, concurring, and dissenting opinions are published in the *United States Reports*. The Court decides cases by majority vote—nine to zero, five to four, or anything in between, assuming, of course, that the Court is fully staffed and that every justice participates.

THE MAJORITY OPINION IS MORE IMPORTANT THAN THE OUTCOME OF THE CASE BECAUSE THE MAJORITY OPINION ESTABLISHES POLICY.

Many observers believe that the strength of a Supreme Court decision depends on the level of agreement among the justices. *Brown v. Board of Education* was decided unanimously; the death or resignation of one or two justices was not going to reverse the majority on the issue should a similar case come before the Court in the near future. Furthermore, the Court issued only one opinion, the majority opinion written by Chief Justice Warren. The decision offered no comfort to anyone looking for a weakness of will on the Court. In contrast, the Court's decision in *Furman v. Georgia* (1972) was muddled. In *Furman*, the Court ruled that the death penalty, as then practiced, was discriminatory and hence unconstitutional. The Court did not say, however, that the death penalty, as such, was unconstitutional. The ruling's weakness, perhaps fragility, came from the closeness of the vote, five to four, and the number of opinions—four concurring and four dissenting opinions, besides the majority opinion. The justices could not agree on which facts were

concurring opinion a judicial statement that agrees with the Court's ruling but disagrees with the reasoning of the majority opinion.

dissenting opinion a judicial statement that disagrees with the decision of the Court's majority.

important in the case or what goals the Court should pursue.[35]

Implementation. Political scientists Charles Johnson and Bradley Canon divide the judicial policymaking process into three stages. (see chart below).

Although the implementation of Supreme Court rulings is not automatic, direct disobedience is rare because Court actions enjoy considerable symbolic legitimacy. When the Supreme Court ordered President Nixon to turn over key Watergate tapes to the special prosecutor, for example, Nixon complied. Had the president made a bonfire of them, as some observers suggested, he probably would have been impeached. Instead of defiance, unpopular Supreme Court decisions are often met with delay and subtle evasion. Ten years after the *Brown* ruling, there was not a single state in the Deep South where as many as 10 percent of African American students attended school with any white youngsters.[36] And evasion of the Supreme Court's rulings against government-sponsored school prayers is widespread.[37]

STAGES OF THE JUDICIAL POLICYMAKING PROCESS

FIRST
Higher courts, especially the U.S. Supreme Court, develop policies. Although major policy cases make headlines, the Supreme Court frequently clarifies and elaborates an initial decision with subsequent rulings on related issues.

SECOND
Lower courts interpret the higher court rulings. In theory, lower federal courts apply policies formulated by the U.S. Supreme Court without modification. In practice, however, Supreme Court rulings are often general, leaving room for lower courts to adapt them to the circumstances of specific cases.

THIRD
Relevant government agencies and private parties implement court decisions. For example, state legislatures had to rewrite death penalty statutes to comply with the *Furman* ruling. Local school boards had the task of developing integration plans to comply with the *Brown* decision.[38]

Impact. Supreme Court decisions have their greatest impact when the Court issues a clear decision in a well-publicized case and its position enjoys strong support from other branches and units of government, interest groups, and public opinion.[39] The figure below traces the impact of the Court's rulings on abortion. In 1973, when *Roe v. Wade* was decided, the abortion ratio, the number of abortions out of every hundred pregnancies resulting in an abortion or live birth, was 19.3. (Abortion was already legal in many states.) Four years later, the abortion ratio had risen to 28.6, and it continued climbing until 1983. During the same period, the number of adoptions was falling, apparently because legalized abortion was reducing the number of unwanted infants. In 1970, before *Roe v. Wade*, the total number of adoptions in the nation was 175,000. In 1975, after the decision, the number of adoptions had declined to 129,000.[40]

As the opponents to abortion have grown more aggressive and the Supreme Court has modified its policy position, the impact of *Roe v. Wade* has lessened. Compared with the mid-1970s, fewer physicians are performing abortions, and the number of hospitals and clinics offering abortion services has declined. Pro-life groups such as Operation Save America have picketed not only abortion clinics but also the homes of doctors who perform abortions. Some abortion clinics have been bombed and abortion providers threatened with violence. Several doctors who perform abortions have been shot and killed by abortion opponents. Furthermore, the Supreme Court has somewhat backed away from the *Roe* decision, allowing states more leeway to restrict access to abortion. Declining abortion rates may be due to other factors as well, including better access to contraceptives and pregnancy counseling, and changing attitudes about family size.[41]

HOW THE COURT DECIDES:

- Attorneys for the litigants submit briefs.
- Other parties submit *amicus curiae* briefs.
- Attorneys for the litigants present oral arguments.
- Justices meet in closed conference to discuss and vote.
- Designated justice drafts majority opinion.
- Other justices in the majority may draft concurring opinions.
- Justices in the minority may draft dissenting opinions.
- Decision announced in open court.

ABORTION RATES

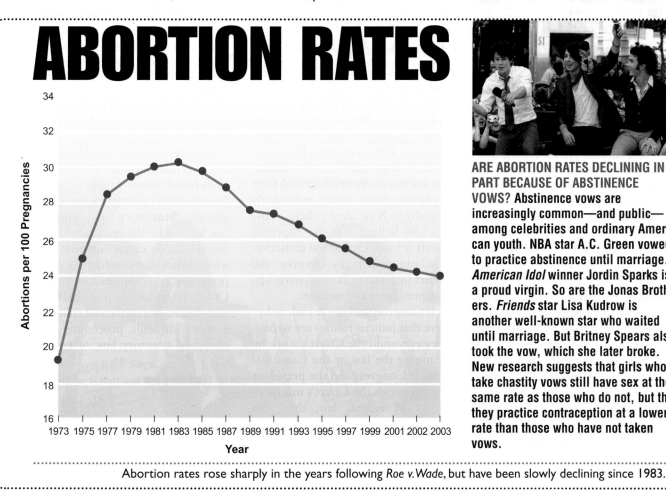

ARE ABORTION RATES DECLINING IN PART BECAUSE OF ABSTINENCE VOWS? Abstinence vows are increasingly common—and public—among celebrities and ordinary American youth. NBA star A.C. Green vowed to practice abstinence until marriage. *American Idol* winner Jordin Sparks is a proud virgin. So are the Jonas Brothers. *Friends* star Lisa Kudrow is another well-known star who waited until marriage. But Britney Spears also took the vow, which she later broke. New research suggests that girls who take chastity vows still have sex at the same rate as those who do not, but that they practice contraception at a lower rate than those who have not taken vows.

Abortion rates rose sharply in the years following *Roe v. Wade*, but have been slowly declining since 1983.

HOW WELL DO SUPREME COURT DECISIONS ON CONTROVERSIAL ISSUES REFLECT PUBLIC OPINION?

Issue:	Case:	SC decision:	Public Opinion at time of decision
Should abortion be legal?	*Roe v. Wade* (1973)	Yes (7-2)	67% support Roe decision
Is the death penalty constitutional?	*Gregg v. Georgia* (1976)	Yes (7-2)	63% favor death penalty
Is flag burning constitutional?	*Texas v. Johnson* (1989)	Yes (5-4)	57% favor amendment to overturn ruling
Should the Boy Scouts be able to ban gay troop leaders?	*Boy Scouts of America v. Dale* (2000)	Yes (5-4)	64% agree with ruling
Should homosexual relations be legal?	*Lawrence v. Texas* (2003)	Yes (6-3)	55% say homosexual relations should be legal
Is affirmative action constitutional?	*Grutter v. Bollinger* (2003)	Yes (5-4)	50% support affirmative action
Should displaying the Ten Commandments on public property be legal?	*Van Orden v. Perry* (2005)	Yes (5-4)	35% agree with school prayer decision

CONCLUSION

the courts and
& PUBLIC POLICY

the federal courts are important participants in the policymaking process.

Agenda Building

The courts play a role in agenda building by tackling issues that might not otherwise be addressed by other levels and branches of government. For example, the U.S. Supreme Court made abortion a national issue in *Roe v. Wade*. Before *Roe*, state governments made abortion policy. Some states, such as New York, permitted abortion; other states, such as Texas, prohibited abortion except to preserve the life of the woman. After *Roe*, abor-

tion became a national policy issue not just for the courts, who continued to hear abortion cases, but also for the president and Congress, because the politics of judicial appointment and confirmation now became the politics of abortion as well. Other issues that have become part of the official policy agenda because of court decisions include legislative redistricting and school prayer.

Policy Formulation and Adoption

The courts play an important role in policy formulation and adoption. Judges formulate policy when they

read legal briefs, listen to oral arguments, and negotiate rulings and opinions among themselves. Furthermore, court decisions affect policy formulation in the other branches and units of government. Members of Congress and state legislators formulating abortion policy, for example, must work within the guidelines established in *Roe* and subsequent abortion decisions or

item veto the power of an executive to veto sections or items of a tax or appropriation measure while signing the remainder of the bill into law.

face the likelihood of having any legislation they pass be overturned in federal courts.

Courts adopt policy when they make rulings and issue opinions. When the Supreme Court issued its decision in *Brown v. Board of Education of Topeka*, for example, it adopted a policy on racial desegregation of public schools. Most judicial policy-making involves civil liberties and civil rights policies. Political scientists concerned with public policies on capital punishment, government-sponsored prayer in public schools, affirmative action, and pornography regulation will spend a good deal of time reading Supreme Court opinions. In contrast, the judicial branch plays a relatively minor role in economic, regulatory, foreign, and defense policymaking.

Policy Implementation and Evaluation

The federal courts play a role in policy implementation. Lower courts implement Supreme Court rulings by applying them to new cases as they arise. The courts also affect policy implementation when they interpret the law. Consider the implementation of the Americans with Disabilities Act (ADA), which is a federal law designed to end discrimination against persons with disabilities and to eliminate barriers to their full participation in American society. The law requires companies to make "reasonable accom-

Supreme Court Justice Antonin Scalia was appointed by President Ronald Reagan in 1986. He is part of the Court's conservative wing.

modation" for otherwise qualified job applicants or current employees who happen to be disabled, unless the business can show that the accommodation would put an "undue hardship" on its operation. When Congress wrote the law, it did not define "reasonable accommodation" and "undue hardship." As a result, the federal courts have been heavily involved with the implementation of the ADA by interpreting its meaning in the context of specific controversies.

Finally, federal courts evaluate policies in light of the Constitution. In theory, at least, judges do not evaluate policies on their effectiveness or wisdom, but only on their constitutionality. In 1996, for example, Congress passed, and Presi-

dent Clinton signed, legislation granting the president the **item veto,** which is the power of an executive to veto sections or items of a tax or appropriation measure while signing the remainder of the bill into law. Two years later, a legal challenge to the policy reached the U.S. Supreme Court. The Court ruled that the law giving the president the item veto was unconstitutional because it legislatively made a fundamental change in the relationship between the executive and legislative branches of government. The Court held that changes of such constitutional significance must be made through the adoption of a constitutional amendment rather than through the legislative process.[48]

the THINKSPOT

www.thethinkspot.com

TEST yourself

1 The power of the courts to declare unconstitutional the actions of the other branches and units of government is known as which of the following?

A. Loose construction

B. Judicial review

C. Strict construction

D. Civil liberties

2 Which of the following statements most closely reflects the philosophy of loose construction of the Constitution?

A. Judges should interpret the Constitution broadly to allow it to change with the times.

B. Judges should recognize that their role is to interpret the law rather than make the law.

C. Judges should stick to the literal meaning of the Constitution.

D. Judges should closely follow the intent of the Framers of the Constitution.

3 A doctrine of constitutional interpretation holding that the document should be interpreted narrowly is known as which of the following?

A. Strict construction

B. Loose construction

C. Civil liberties

D. Judicial review

4 Which of the following federal courts is exclusively a trial court?

A. District court

B. Courts of appeal

C. Supreme Court

D. None of the above

5 How are U.S. district judges selected?

A. They are career civil servants, chosen through a merit hiring process.

B. They are appointed by the president subject to confirmation by the Senate.

C. They are elected by the voters in the states where they serve.

D. They are appointed by the president subject to confirmation by the House and Senate.

6 Which of the following statements most accurately describes the principle of senatorial courtesy?

A. The Senate almost always confirms the president's district court nominees.

B. Senators will always confirm judicial nominees who have the support of the senators from their home states.

C. Senators from the president's party have a veto on the confirmation of district judge nominees from their states.

D. Senators agree not to filibuster judicial nominations.

7 A liberal judge is more likely than a conservative judge to take which of the following policy actions?

A. To rule in favor of the government and against criminal defendants

B. To rule in favor of workers and against corporate interests

C. To rule in favor of state governments in federalism disputes with the federal government

D. All of the above

8 What is the term of a federal district judge?

A. Two years

B. Four years

C. Six years

D. Life, with "good behavior"

9 The "nuclear option" involved which of the following actions?

A. An attempt to increase the size of the Supreme Court

B. An effort to amend the Constitution to restrict the president's authority as commander in chief

C. An effort to eliminate the Senate filibuster for judicial nominees

D. An attempt to limit the jurisdiction of the Supreme Court to prevent it from hearing abortion cases

10 According to the U.S. Constitution, how many justices serve on the Supreme Court?

A. Seven

B. Nine

C. Eleven

D. The Constitution says nothing about the size of the Supreme Court

11 The Supreme Court decides a case by a unanimous vote. Who writes the majority opinion?

A. The chief justice

B. The most senior justice

C. The chief justice either writes the opinion or assigns it to another justice

D. Opinion assignment is done randomly

12 Suppose that Congress passes controversial legislation that some people believe is unconstitutional. When, if ever, will the Supreme Court address the issue?

A. The Supreme Court will decide the issue when and if it accepts a case that involves a challenge to the constitutionality of the legislation.

B. The Supreme Court reviews legislation passed by Congress before it takes effect.

C. The Supreme Court will only review the legislation if Congress requests a review.

D. Never.

13 Why was *Brown v. Board of Education* an example of a test case?

A. The Supreme Court reversed an earlier decision (the *Plessy* case) when it decided *Brown*.

B. The case was prepared, presented, and financed by an interest group.

C. An interest group submitted a legal brief that discussed issues raised by the case.

D. *Brown* is considered a landmark decision in constitutional law.

14 Daryl Renard Atkins was convicted of murder in the state of Virginia and sentenced to death. Under which of the following circumstances would the U.S. Supreme Court hear an appeal of his case?

A. All death penalty cases are automatically appealed to the U.S. Supreme Court.

B. State cases such as the Atkins case cannot be appealed to the federal court system.

C. His attorneys would have to convince a majority of the justices of the Supreme Court that his case is interesting enough to review.

D. His attorneys raise national constitutional issues that at least four justices believe are worth considering.

15 A Supreme Court justice agrees with the outcome of a case but disagrees with the legal reasoning presented in the majority opinion. Which of the following actions would the justice take?

A. File a friend of the court brief

B. Write a concurring opinion

C. Write a majority opinion

D. Write a dissenting opinion

16 What is a friend of the court brief?

A. An opinion written by a member of a court who agrees with the court's ruling but disagrees with the reasoning behind it

B. A judicial order directing the government either to release someone in custody or to justify why the person is being help

C. A court case that is supported financially by an interest group

D. A brief submitted by an interest group not directly involved in a case that is attempting to influence the outcome of the case

17 What is a dissenting opinion?

A. It is a legal brief written by an interest group attempting to influence the outcome of a case.

B. It is an opinion written by a justice on the Supreme Court who agrees with the outcome of a case but disagrees with the reasoning contained in the majority opinion.

C. It is a document written by an interest group that disagrees with a ruling issued by the Supreme Court.

D. It is an opinion written by a justice of the Supreme Court who disagrees with the majority ruling on a case.

18 Suppose that a majority of the members of the Supreme Court believe that a recent action by the president violates the Constitution. What can they do?

A. They can do nothing until a case arises that involves the issue and the case is appealed to the Supreme Court.

B. Nothing. The Supreme Court can review the acts of Congress but not the actions of the president.

C. The Supreme Court can issue an opinion declaring the president's action unconstitutional.

D. The Supreme Court can invite parties to file a challenge against the president's action.

19 What power does the Supreme Court have to enforce its rulings?

A. The Court can order law enforcement personnel to enforce its rulings.

B. The Court must rely on the other branches and units of government to enforce its rulings.

C. None. Court rulings are regularly ignored.

D. None of the above.

20 Which of the following is a check on the power of the Supreme Court?

A. The president can appoint and the Senate can confirm new justices to fill vacancies on the Court.

B. The House and Senate can propose an amendment to the Constitution to overturn a judicial interpretation of the Constitution.

C. Congress and the president can rewrite a law to reverse a judicial interpretation of an act of Congress.

D. All of the above.

KNOW *the* **score**

18–20 correct: Congratulations! You are well informed!

15–17 correct: Your political knowledge is a bit low—be sure to review the key terms and visit TheThinkSpot.

<14 correct: Reread the chapter more thoroughly.

---

1. B; 2. A; 3. A; 4. A; 5. B; 6. C; 7. B; 8. C; 9. D; 10. D; 11. C; 12. A; 13. B; 14. D; 15. B; 16. D; 17. D; 18. A; 19. B; 20. D

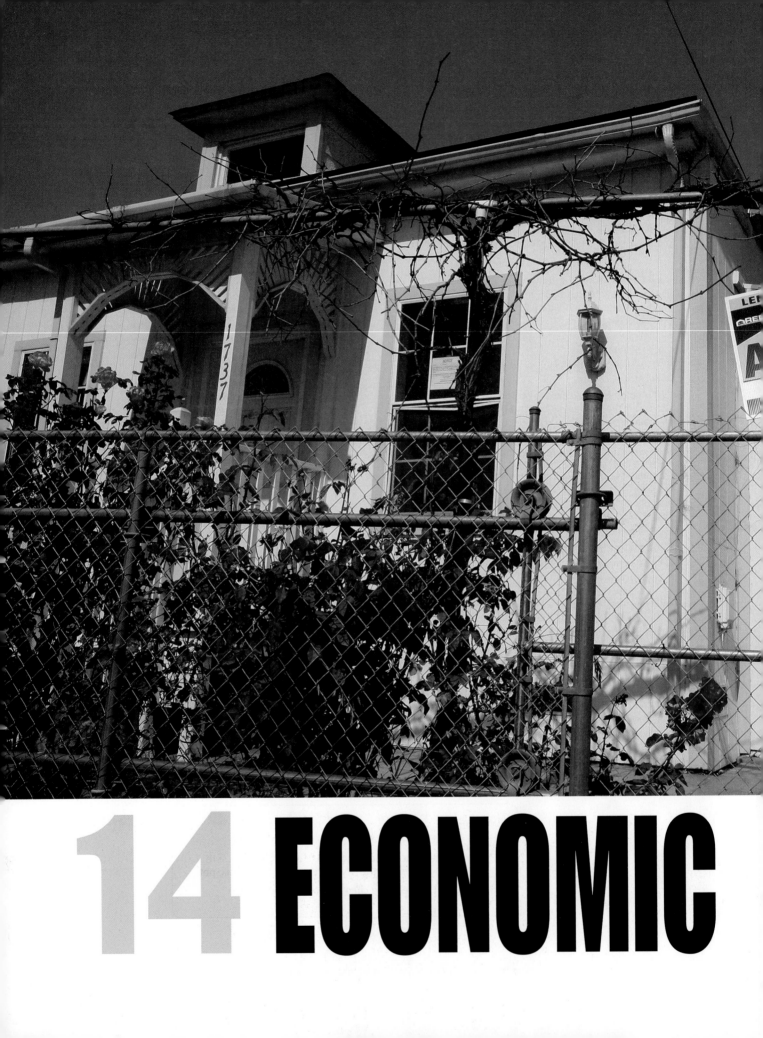

14 ECONOMIC

> **WHAT'S AHEAD**

The Goals of Economic Policy

Tax Revenues

Budget Deficits and Surpluses

Government Expenditures

Fiscal Policymaking

Monetary Policymaking

Conclusion: Economic Policymaking

In late 2008, the National Bureau of Economic Research announced what most Americans had known for months: The U.S. economy was in recession and had been for a year. A recession is an economic slowdown characterized by declining economic output and rising unemployment. During 2008, the American economy lost 2.6 million jobs and the unemployment rate rose from 4.9 percent to 7.2 percent.[1] Moreover, between October 2007 and November 2008, the stock market lost nearly half its value.

Most economists believe that a downturn in the housing market caused the recession. With housing prices falling, some homeowners found themselves owing more on their homes than they were worth. People with adjustable-rate loans no longer had the option of refinancing to reduce their monthly payments. Some of them walked away from their homes, allowing banks and mortgage companies to foreclose. Consequently, many financial institutions found themselves holding properties which were not worth the amount of money loaned on them. A number of financial institutions declared bankruptcy or tightened their loan practices. With auto sales dramatically off, General Motors (GM), Ford, and Chrysler, the "Big Three" of American car companies, warned that they were approaching bankruptcy.[2]

The U.S. government acted to shore up the economy. Early in 2008, Congress passed a $170 billion rebate. The rebate helped stimulate economic growth, but only temporarily. Later in the year, the Bush administration loaned $85 billion to American International Group (AIG), one of the world's largest insurance companies. It loaned more than $17 billion to GM and Chrysler to keep them afloat as well. Meanwhile,

POLICYMAKING

Barack Obama speaks about healthcare reform to a crowd in Texas during his successful campaign for the White House in 2008.

spending programs or provide tax cuts. Strong economic growth in the mid- and late-1990s did at least as much to eliminate the budget deficit as the policy choices of elected officials. In contrast, economic decline reduces the options available to policymakers.

It matters which party controls Congress. Democrats generally back policies designed to assist their traditional support groups: organized labor, inner-city voters, and lower- and middle-income families. Republicans, meanwhile, steer economic policy to benefit their support groups: business people and professionals, suburban voters, and middle- and upper-income families. When Congress and the presidency are in the hands of different parties, economic policy typically reflects compromise between the parties.

Agenda Building

A number of political actors participate in elevating economic issues to the official policy agenda. Candidates often highlight economic issues during election campaigns.

Ross Perot made deficit reduction a major talking point when he ran for president as an independent in 1992 and 1996. Bill Clinton stressed welfare reform when he first ran for president, promising to "end welfare as we know it." George W. Bush promised to cut taxes during his presidential campaign in 2000. Barack Obama stressed healthcare reform.

Interest groups frequently emphasize economic issues. The **AARP**, an interest group representing the interests of older Americans, stresses the need to preserve Social Security and Medicare. Business groups are concerned about tax issues and government regulation. Farm groups, such as the American Farm Bureau, lobby for farm support programs.

Policy Formulation and Adoption

Economic policy formulation takes place in congressional committees, executive branch agencies, and the White House. It involves officials from all levels of government as well as a wide range of interest group participants. The president and the president's staff, department heads, and the OMB prepare detailed budget proposals for submission to Congress. The appropriations committees in each house draft budget legislation; standing committees work on authorization measures. The Ways and Means Committee in the House and the Finance Committee in the Senate deal with tax measures. Conference committees iron out the final details for most appropriation bills, tax measures, and authorization bills. The Federal Reserve Board formulates monetary policy.

Individual members of Congress focus on issues important to their states and districts. Farmbelt senators and representatives pay special attention to legislation affecting agriculture. Members with defense bases or defense industries in their districts are concerned with the defense appropriation. Senators and representatives are also interested in special projects that benefit their states and districts. **Earmarks** are provisions that direct that funds be spent for particular purposes. In 2008, Congress earmarked almost $8 billion for special projects, including money for water resource development, local transportation projects, tourist attractions, and special projects for colleges and universities.[41] The opponents of earmarks charge that they are nothing more than **pork-barrel spending,** expenditures to fund local projects

AARP an interest group representing the concerns of older Americans.

earmarks provisions that direct that funds be spent for particular purposes.

pork-barrel spending expenditures to fund local projects that are not critically important from a national perspective.

that are not critically important from a national perspective. John McCain promised to end earmarking when he ran for president in 2008. Other members of Congress defend earmarks, noting that they have funded many worthwhile projects, including most federal breast cancer research and the Boys & Girls Clubs of America. Moreover, the congressional leadership uses earmarks to win support for appropriation bills that might not otherwise pass.[42]

Interest groups also take part in policy formulation. Corporations lobby Congress to affect the impact of tax policies on their firms. Weapons manufacturers attempt to influence decisions on defense spending. The AARP participates in negotiations over reform of the Medicare program and changes in Social Security.

The executive and legislative branches of American national government are primarily responsible for the adoption of fiscal policy. The judiciary plays a relatively small role. Congress and the president create government programs and appropriate money to fund them. They raise funds through taxation and borrowing. In the meantime, the Fed adopts monetary policies through its rulemaking process.

Policy Implementation and Evaluation

The implementation of economic policy involves nearly the whole of government in America. The Treasury Department, especially the IRS, is responsible for tax collection and borrowing. The Federal Reserve and its member banks implement monetary policy. Money is spent by the agencies of the executive branch and, through federal programs, by an array of state and local governments. State governments, for example, are responsible

economic policy involves nearly the whole of government in America

for implementing federal transportation policies, Medicaid, and most welfare programs.

Congress and the president often leave considerable discretion to officials who implement economic policies. Welfare reform initially allowed states considerable flexibility to design their welfare programs. In general, the legislation set goals and allowed state governments to develop their own strategies for achieving the goals. States which met the goals would receive financial rewards; states falling short of goals would suffer penalties. When Congress reauthorized welfare reform in 2006, however, it tightened the definitions of work and work-related activities, reducing state flexibility.[43]

Both the executive and legislative branches of American government have mechanisms for evaluating economic policy. The OMB assesses the operation of programs within the executive branch for the president, whereas the General Accountability Office (GAO) performs a similar role for Congress, investigating agency activities and auditing expenditures. Outside of the GAO, however, efforts at oversight are haphazard and unsystematic. Furthermore, when they do occur, they tend to focus on nickel-and-dime matters, such as expense accounts and limousine use, or on well-publicized abuses, such as cost overruns on weapons systems purchased by the Pentagon.

the THINK SPOT
www.thethinkspot.com

TEST yourself

1 A financial incentive given by government to an individual or a business interest to accomplish a public objective is known by which of the following terms?
A. Entitlement
B. Welfare program
C. Subsidy
D. Progressive taxation

2 "The nation is suffering a severe economic slump. Many companies have gone out of business and unemployment is at a record high." This statement describes which of the following?
A. Inflation
B. Recession
C. Depression
D. *Laissez-faire*

3 "Prices just keep going up. It sure seems like a dollar doesn't go as far these days as it used to." This statement describes which of the following?
A. Inflation
B. Recession
C. Depression
D. Supply-side economics

4 Which of the following is the most important tax source of revenue for the U.S. government?
A. Sales tax
B. Payroll tax
C. Corporate income tax
D. Individual income tax

5 Which of the following taxes is assessed on wage earnings but not on income generated by stock dividends and interest?
A. Individual income tax
B. Excise tax
C. Corporate income tax
D. Payroll tax

6 Federal payroll taxes fund which of the following government programs?
A. Social Security
B. Medicaid
C. Education
D. All of the above

7 Federal taxes on gasoline, tires, and airplane tickets are examples of which of the following?
A. Progressive tax
B. Excise tax
C. Payroll tax
D. Tax preference

8 The federal income tax is an example of which of the following?
A. Progressive tax
B. Regressive tax
C. Proportional tax
D. Excise tax

9 Which of the following was a goal of the tax reforms associated with President George W. Bush?
A. Increase personal savings and investment
B. Increase taxes on upper income earners
C. Increase the estate tax
D. Make the federal income tax system more progressive

10 Assume that federal government revenues are $2.6 trillion and expenditures are $2.9 trillion. Which of the following statements is accurate?
A. The budget is balanced.
B. The government ran a surplus of $0.3 trillion.
C. The government ran a deficit of $0.3 trillion.
D. The national debt is $0.3 trillion.

11 How does a deficit of $400 billion affect the national debt?
A. It has no impact on the national debt.
B. It increases the national debt by $400 billion.
C. It decreases the national debt by $400 billion.
D. The national debt is $400 billion.

12 Which of the following is *not* one of the top five major expenditure categories in the federal budget?
A. Foreign aid
B. Social Security
C. National defense
D. Healthcare

13 Which of the following is a factor negatively affecting the future of the Social Security program?

A. People are living longer.

B. The baby boom generation is beginning to retire.

C. The generation following the baby boom generation is smaller than its predecessor.

D. All of the above.

14 Which of the following is an example of a means-tested program?

A. Social Security

B. Medicare

C. Medicaid

D. All of the above

15 Which of the following is *not* a result of welfare reform?

A. The number of welfare recipients has fallen.

B. The number of people living in poverty has decreased.

C. Most people leaving welfare have found work.

D. Most people leaving welfare still depend on the government for assistance.

16 Which of the following is an example of an entitlement program?

A. Social Security

B. Medicare

C. Medicaid

D. All of the above

17 Which of the following is *not* an example of mandatory spending?

A. Social Security expenditures

B. Interest on the debt

C. Spending for education

D. Payment for a weapons system contracted for in a prior year

18 Which of the following is primarily responsible for setting monetary policy?

A. Federal Reserve Board

B. Office of Management and Budget

C. Department of the Treasury

D. Congress

19 The Federal Open Market Committee (FOMC) makes decisions that directly impact which of the following?

A. Tax rates

B. Fiscal policy

C. Interest rates

D. Social Security

20 An appropriation bill includes money to fund a mining museum for a small city in Alaska. This provision is an example of which of the following?

A. Entitlement

B. Means-tested program

C. Privatization

D. Earmark

1. C; 2. C; 3. A; 4. D; 5. D; 6. A; 7. B; 8. A; 9. A; 10. C; 11. B; 12. A; 13. D; 14. C; 15. B; 16. D; 17. C; 18. A; 19. C; 20. D

the state. Although the overwhelming majority of private schools chosen by parents for student transfer were religiously affiliated, the U.S. Supreme Court ruled the program constitutional. The Court upheld the program because it had a valid secular purpose (providing educational assistance to poor children in a weak school system), it was neutral toward religion (parents could choose any private school or even another public school), and it provided assistance to families rather than to the schools.[8]

School prayer is perhaps the most controversial Establishment Clause issue. In *Engel v. Vitale* (1962), the Supreme Court ruled that the daily classroom recitation of a prayer written by New York's State Board of Regents violated the First Amendment. "[I]t is no part of the business of government to compose official prayers for any group of the American people to recite as part of a religious program carried on by the government," declared the Court. Furthermore, it was irrelevant that the prayer was voluntary and students were not forced to recite it. "When the power, prestige, and financial support of government [are] placed behind a particular religious belief," the Court said, "the indirect coercive pressure upon religious minorities to conform to the prevailing officially approved religion is plain."[9]

The Supreme Court has consistently ruled against government efforts to introduce religious observances into the public schools. Consider the school prayer controversy in Santa Fe, Texas. The school district allowed students at Santa Fe High School to vote on whether to

have an "invocation" before home football games and then held a second election to select a student to deliver the prayer. Two families—one Mormon and the other Catholic—sued the school district, and the case reached the Supreme Court in 2000. The Court ruled that the invocation was an unconstitutional infringement on the Establishment Clause, rejecting the school district's argument that the student delivering the invocation was exercising her free speech rights. "The delivery of a message such as the invocation here—on school property, at school-sponsored events, over the school's public address system, by a speaker representing the student body, under the supervision of school faculty, and pursuant to a school policy that explicitly and implicitly encourages public prayer—is not properly characterized as 'private' speech."[10]

Free Exercise of Religion. The First Amendment prohibits the adoption of laws interfering with the free exercise of religion. In practice, disputes concerning free exercise fall under two general categories. The first category involves the deliberate effort of government to restrict the activities of small, controversial religious groups. Many localities have also enacted local laws aimed at preventing Jehovah's Witnesses and other religious groups from distributing religious literature door-to-door. The Supreme Court has upheld these sorts of restric-

tions on religious practice only when the government has been able to justify its action on the basis of a compelling or overriding government interest that could not be achieved in a less restrictive fashion. Because the compelling interest test is a high standard, the Supreme Court more often than not has

> School prayer is perhaps the most controversial Establishment Clause issue.

think Do you agree with the Supreme Court's decision in *Engel v. Vitale*? Why or why not?

The First Amendment protects the right of Jehovah's Witnesses, Mormons, and other religious believers to go door-to-door to spread their faith.

Kara Neumann of Weston, Wisconsin died from a treatable form of diabetes after her parents prayed for her healing rather than seek medical treatment. Her parents were charged with reckless child endangerment and a judge ordered them to stand trial despite their claim that the charges violated their constitutional right to religious freedom.

struck down laws and regulations aimed against particular religions or religious practices.[11]

The second category of disputes concerns the impact on religious practice of general laws and government procedures that are otherwise neutral with respect to religion. Prison inmates who are Muslim or Jewish, for example, demand that they be provided meals that do not violate the dietary restrictions imposed by their religious faiths. Amish parents protest school attendance laws. For years, the Supreme Court subjected these sorts of incidental restrictions on religious practice to the compelling government interest test. Since *Employment Division v. Smith* (1990), however, the Supreme Court has held that states can enact laws that have an incidental impact on religious freedom so long as they serve a valid state purpose and are not aimed at inhibiting any particular religion. The *Smith* case involved a decision by the state

of Oregon to deny unemployment benefits to state employees who were fired because they used peyote, which is a hallucinogenic drug, in Native American religious practices. The Court upheld the firing and denial of unemployment benefits because the law under which they were dismissed served a valid state purpose, was not aimed at any particular religion, and had only an incidental impact on religious belief.[12]

Freedom of Expression

The First Amendment guarantees freedom of expression. "Congress shall make no law . . . abridging the freedom of speech, or of the press; or the right of the people peaceably to assemble to petition the government for a redress of grievances."

Anti-Government Speech. Constitutional law holds that the government can restrict political expression only if it has a compelling interest that cannot be achieved by less restrictive means. In practice, the com-

pelling interest standard is so difficult to meet that most laws limiting expression are unconstitutional. Consider the case of Clarence Brandenburg, a Ku Klux Klan leader from Ohio, who was convicted under an Ohio law for making a speech at a Klan cross-burning rally in which he threatened the president, Congress, and the Supreme Court for suppressing the white race. In 1969, the Supreme Court overturned Brandenburg's conviction, saying that the mere advocacy of lawless action was not sufficient to sustain a conviction because the state does not have a compelling interest in outlawing "mere abstract teaching." Instead, the state must prove that the "advocacy is directed to inciting or producing imminent lawless action and is likely to incite or produce such action."[13]

Expression That Threatens the Public Order. Can the government punish expression that may lead to a disruption of public order?

Taking Sides

Flag-Burning Amendment

Can burning a flag be considered proper political speech? What is the intent behind flag burning?

Should the Constitution be amended to alter the Bill of Rights? If this movement is successful, is it likely there will be other attempts to constitutionally limit liberties?

Overview: The business of determining and defining rights is one of the most important functions of government in a liberal, rights-based society. The discovery or determination of rights and liberties is problematic because rights usually come into conflict with other liberties. Take, for example, the debate over whether to amend the Constitution to prohibit flag burning. There are many who argue that burning a flag is a form of political expression. In this instance, the right to political speech comes into conflict with the right of a state to protect political and historical symbols and icons. Indeed, some argue that the patriotism and civic pride encouraged by the flag, the Pledge of Allegiance, the National Anthem, and so on, should have state protection. Furthermore, some hold that flag burning is tantamount to anti-Americanism.

The Supreme Court has held that the right to political expression transcends spoken or written speech. The speech, press, and association clauses of the First Amendment were written to guarantee Americans the constitutional protection to express their displeasure with government policy and law. The Supreme Court struck down flag-protection statutes in 48 states, as well as a 1968 and 1990 federal flag-protection statute in *Texas v. Johnson* (1989) and *U.S. v. Eichman* (1990), but Congress has debated the merits of a flag-burning amendment in almost every session since 1990. In fact, the House of Representatives overwhelmingly passed proposed constitutional amendments to prohibit flag desecration in 1995, 1997, 1999, 2001, 2003, and 2005. And the Senate voted on the proposed amendment in 1995 and 2000, but fell short of the two-thirds vote needed to send the proposed amendment to the state legislatures for ratification.

supporting the flag-burning amendment

the flag represents American values and principles and, as such, should be protected. The flag symbolizes a shared history and common heritage of the pursuit of equal rights, duties, and self-government. A government reserves the right to protect those symbols and artifacts which represent its guiding principles.

veneration of symbols is necessary for good citizenship. At a flag raising at Independence Hall in 1861, Abraham Lincoln expressed his view that honoring the flag helps foster "the spirit [of freedom] that animated" the founders. The flag reminds Americans to respect the rights of others, to behave as good constitutional citizens, and to honor and protect the country in times of turmoil and danger.

an amendment to ban flag burning reflects the will of the majority. Most major public opinion polls show that roughly 63 to 72 percent of all Americans favor an amendment to ban flag burning. Both Democratic– and Republican Party–controlled Congresses have introduced flag-burning amendments.

against the flag-burning amendment

the Constitution should not be amended to prohibit political speech. The First Amendment guarantees freedom of speech and expression, no matter how offensive some may find such speech. Freedom of expression is necessary for vigorous debate and dissent to prevent the abuse of governmental power.

flag burners should be held to the same standard as those who damage their own property. Most flag burners purchase or are given their own flags, and thus they should be subject to the same laws that regulate the burning or destruction of private property. Should people burn a flag that is not their own, they should be held to the same standard to which we hold people when they burn property that is not their own.

flag burning is not a hate crime. Representative Henry Hyde argued during floor debate that flag burning is a hate crime because "burning the flag is an expression of contempt for the moral unity of the American people," but hate crimes can be directed only against individuals, not against symbols or political principles.

abortion except to save the life of a woman. The Court found the Texas statute unconstitutional, declaring that a woman's right to personal privacy under the U.S. Constitution included her decision to terminate a pregnancy. The Court said, however, that a woman's right to privacy was not absolute and must be balanced against the state's interest in protecting health, medical standards, and prenatal life.

The Supreme Court balanced these competing interests by dividing a pregnancy into trimesters. During the first trimester, state governments could not interfere with a physician's decision, reached in consultation with a pregnant patient, to terminate a pregnancy. In the second trimester, the state could regulate abortion, but only to protect the health of a woman. In the third trimester, after

think Should privacy be a constitutional right? Why or why not?

the fetus had achieved viability (the ability to survive outside the womb), the Court ruled that state governments could prohibit abortion except when it was necessary to preserve the life or health of a woman.[20]

Since *Roe*, the Supreme Court has upheld its original decision while allowing states leeway to regulate abortion. In 1989, the Court upheld a Missouri law limiting access to abortion. The statute prohibited the use of public em-

ployees or facilities to perform or assist an abortion except to save a woman's life, and outlawed the use of public funds, employees, or facilities to encourage or counsel a woman to have an abortion not necessary to save her life. Citing recent medical advances, the Court abandoned the trimester system adopted in *Roe* by allowing Missouri to require physicians to perform medical tests to determine fetal viability beginning at 20 weeks.[21] The Court subsequently ruled that a state could regulate access to abortion as long as the regulations did not place an "undue burden" on a woman's right to choose. The Court's majority defined an undue burden as one that presented an "absolute obstacle or severe limitation" on the right to decide to have an abortion. State regulations that simply "inhibited" that right were permissible.

The Court has upheld a number of restrictions on abortion, including the following:

- Women seeking abortions must be given information about fetal development and alternatives to ending their pregnancies.

Abortion Should Be:
Legal in all cases–17%
Legal in most cases–37%
Illegal in most cases–26%
Illegal in all cases–15%
Don't know–5%

An abortion opponent kneels amid mock cemetery crosses to dramatize the loss of life through abortion. Pew Research Center Survey, August 2008.

- Women must wait at least 24 hours after receiving that information before having an abortion.

- Doctors must keep detailed records on each abortion performed.

- Abortion records are subject to public disclosure.

- Unmarried girls under the age of 18 must get the permission of one of their parents or the certification of a state judge that they are mature enough to make the decision on their own.

The only provision in the law that the Court considered an undue burden was a requirement that married women notify their husbands of their plans to have an abortion.[22]

The Supreme Court's most recent application of the right of privacy involved a legal challenge to the Texas sodomy law, which criminalized private, consensual sexual conduct between two adults of the same gender. When police in Houston, Texas, arrived at the home of John Lawrence because of an unrelated call, they found Lawrence and another man engaged in sexual intercourse. They arrested the men and charged them with violating the Texas homosexual conduct law for "engaging in deviate sexual intercourse with another person of the same sex." In *Lawrence v. Texas*, the Court ruled that the Texas law violated the Due Process Clause of the Fourteenth Amendment because it intruded into the personal and private lives of individuals without furthering a legitimate state interest.[23]

Due Process of Law and the Rights of the Accused

Several provisions of the Bill of Rights, including the better part of the Fourth, Fifth, and Eighth Amendments, protect the rights of persons under investigation or accused of crimes. The key constitutional phrase is found in the Fifth Amendment and repeated in the Fourteenth Amendment: No person shall be deprived of "life, liberty, or property, without due process of law." **Due process of law** is the constitutional provision that declares that government must follow fair and regular procedures in actions that could lead to an individual's suffering loss of life, liberty, or property. Neither the national government nor the states may resort to stacked juries, coerced confessions, self-incrimination, denial of counsel, cruel and unusual punishments, or unreasonable searches and seizures.

Searches and Seizures. The Fourth Amendment guarantees the "right of the people to be secure in their persons, houses, papers, and effects, against unreasonable searches and seizures . . . and no warrants shall issue, but upon probable cause . . . and particularly describing the place to be searched, and the persons or things to be seized." In general, this provision means that the police need a **warrant** (that is, an official authorization issued by a judicial officer) for most searches of persons or property. Judges or other magistrates issue warrants after the law-enforcement authorities have shown probable cause that certain

"FREEDOM OF SPEECH SHOULD NOT EXTEND TO GROUPS THAT ARE SYMPATHETIC TO TERRORISTS."
AGREE 45%
DISAGREE 50%
UNSURE 5%
Pew Research Poll, 2008

due process of law the constitutional principle holding that government must follow fair and regular procedures in actions that could lead to an individual's suffering loss of life, liberty, or property.

warrant an official authorization issued by a judicial officer.

Actor Tommy Chong during his "Light Up America" tour, supporting the legalization of marijuana.

"THE POLICE SHOULD BE ALLOWED TO SEARCH THE HOUSES OF PEOPLE WHO MIGHT BE SYMPATHETIC TO TERRORISTS WITHOUT A COURT ORDER."
AGREE 37%
DISAGREE 61%
UNSURE 2%
Pew Research Poll, 2008

Population Policy in China

With a population of more than 1.3 billion people, China is the most populous country in the world. Because of medical advances and nutritional improvements, life expectancy in China has increased dramatically, and the population has more than doubled since 1949. Chinese families have traditionally been large because Chinese couples want children to care for them when they are old. Male children are especially prized because sons traditionally live near their parents, whereas daughters marry and leave home. Chinese couples want to bear sons because their daughters-in-law will care for them in their old age, whereas their daughters will be caring for someone else.[24]

The Chinese government believes that population control is a prerequisite for economic development. Rapid population growth strains the nation's agricultural resources and contributes to the shortage of adequate housing. Substantial economic growth is necessary just to provide jobs for the growing population.

Since the 1980s, the government has implemented a one-child policy. Couples are to bear no more than one child, unless they receive permission from the government based on special circumstances. Some local officials have taken drastic steps to enforce the policy, including forced abortions, sterilization for women who have too many children, and destroying the assets of families that are too large. Because of the cultural preference for male children, some families abort female children. According to Chinese demographic figures, the ratio of male to female children under the age of five in China is 117 to 100. According to the International Planned Parenthood Federation, China aborts seven million fetuses a year and about 70 percent are female. Chinese families apparently abandon millions of other girls to state-run orphanages.[25]

The population policy has worked more effectively in urban centers than in rural areas. In urban areas, women average only one child, whereas rural women have two or more children.[26] Urban couples more readily comply with the policy because they are more subject to government sanctions than are people living in the countryside. Traditional cultural practices are also stronger in rural China than they are in urban centers.

Questions

1. How does China's population policy compare and contrast with America's abortion policy?

2. Would you expect a democracy to adopt a population policy similar to China's policy?

3. Do you believe that the need for economic development is sufficient to justify China's population policy?

A billboard beside a Xining, China, apartment house promotes the official one-child policy.

items will be found. **Probable cause** is the reasonable suspicion based on evidence that a particular search will uncover contraband.

Through the years, the Supreme Court has permitted a number of exceptions to the basic warrant requirement. The police do not need a warrant, for example, to search suspects who consent to be searched or to search suspects after valid arrests. If police officers have a reasonable suspicion of criminal activity, they may stop and search suspicious individuals. The Court has ruled, for example, that the police are justified in searching an individual in a high-crime area who flees when the police appear.[27] The authorities can also search luggage in airports and may fingerprint suspects after arrests.

The Supreme Court has been more willing to authorize searches of automobiles without warrants than it has offices and homes. Consider the 1982 case, *United States v. Ross*. An informant tipped off the District of Columbia police about a narcotics dealer known as Bandit, who sold drugs from the trunk of his purplish-maroon Chevrolet Malibu. When the police spotted a car fitting the description, they pulled it over and searched the trunk, even though they did not have a warrant. Sure enough, they found heroin and cash in the trunk. The car's driver, Albert Ross, Jr., was subsequently tried and convicted of possession of narcotics with intent to distribute. He appealed his case to the Supreme Court. Did the police search of Ross's car trunk without a warrant violate his constitutional rights? The Court said that it did not because the police had legitimately stopped the car and had

CIVIL LIBERTIES AND TERRORISM

In order to curb terrorism in this country, do you think it will be necessary for the average person to give up some civil liberties?

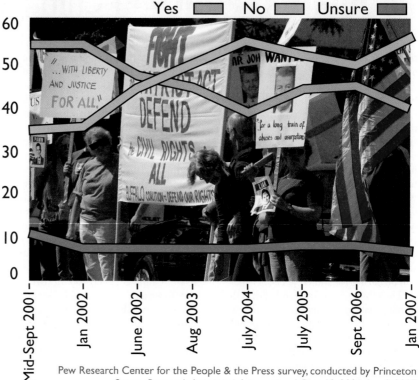

Yes ▢ No ▢ Unsure ▢

Pew Research Center for the People & the Press survey, conducted by Princeton Survey Research Associates International, Dec. 12, 2006–Jan. 9, 2007

probable cause to believe it contained contraband. As a result, the police could search the vehicle as thoroughly as if they had a warrant. The Court added, however, that a search "must be limited by its object," that is, the police cannot conduct a general search to see what might turn up.[28]

The Exclusionary Rule. The **exclusionary rule** is the judicial doctrine stating that when the police violate an individual's constitutional rights, the evidence obtained as a result of police misconduct or error cannot be used against the defendant in a criminal prosecution. In 1914, the Supreme Court estab-

lished the exclusionary rule in federal prosecutions in the *Weeks v. United States* case. The police arrested Fremont Weeks at his place of business and then searched his home. Both of these actions were taken without a warrant. Papers and articles seized in the search were used in federal court against Weeks, and he was convicted. He appealed his conviction, arguing that the judge should not have admitted into

probable cause the reasonable suspicion based on evidence that a particular search will uncover contraband.

exclusionary rule the judicial doctrine stating that when the police violate an individual's constitutional rights, the evidence obtained as a result of police misconduct or error cannot be used against the defendant.

think

If the police obtain evidence in an unlawful search that conclusively proves a defendant guilty, should the evidence be used to prosecute the defendant? Why or why not?

evidence illegally seized materials. The Supreme Court agreed. In 1961, the Supreme Court extended the exclusionary rule to the states in the case of *Mapp v. Ohio*.[29]

The exclusionary rule is controversial. Its defenders say that is a necessary safeguard to ensure that police authorities do not intentionally violate individual rights. In contrast, critics point out that the United States is the only country to take the position that police misconduct must automatically result in the suppression of evidence. In other countries, the trial judge determines whether the misconduct is serious enough to warrant the exclusion of the evidence.[30]

In recent decades, the Supreme Court has weakened the exclusionary rule without repealing it by carving out major exceptions to its application. In 1984, the Court adopted a "good faith" exception to

the exclusionary rule requirement, allowing the use of illegally seized evidence in criminal prosecutions as long as the police acted in good faith.[31] Subsequently, the Court added a "harmless error" exception, allowing a criminal conviction to stand despite the use of illegally obtained evidence when other evidence in the case was strong enough to convict the defendant anyway.[32] In 2009, the Court ruled that evidence obtained from an unlawful arrest based on careless record keeping rather than intentional police misconduct could be used in a prosecution.[33]

The Miranda Warning. Ernesto Miranda was an Arizona man arrested for kidnapping and raping a young woman. Under questioning, Miranda confessed. On appeal, Miranda challenged the use of his confession as a violation of the Fifth Amendment's guarantee against self-

incrimination because the police had not informed him of his constitutional rights to remain silent and consult an attorney.

The Supreme Court reversed Miranda's conviction. The Court's majority held that the prosecution could not use a statement against an accused person in a court of law unless the authorities observe adequate procedural safeguards to ensure that the statement was obtained "voluntarily, knowingly, and intelligently." Before questioning, accused persons must be warned that 1) they have a right to remain silent, 2) that any statements they give may be used against them, and 3) that they are entitled to the presence of an attorney, either retained or appointed.[34]

The Court's *Miranda* ruling has sparked an ongoing debate. Critics say that it makes law enforcement more difficult by preventing police

takeaction

TALKING ABOUT *MIRANDA*

Is the *Miranda* warning a meaningful constitutional safeguard or a technical formality that has no impact on justice? Do police officers take it seriously? Do suspects understand its meaning? The class project is to research the implementation of the *Miranda* warning by interviewing one or more police officers. Some students may know police officers as friends, neighbors, or relatives. Students may also be able to interview members of the campus police at your college.

Before conducting the interviews, prepare a set of questions designed to focus on the following topics:

- Police training. How do police academies cover the topic of *Miranda*? Is it presented as a necessary evil or as an important element of civil liberties in a free society?
- Police supervision. How seriously does management take the *Miranda* warning? Do police supervisors frequently review implementation procedures or is that left to the discretion of individual officers?
- *Miranda* implementation. When, if ever, do officers recite the *Miranda* warning to suspects? Do they read the

warning from a card, or do they have it memorized? What steps, if any, do officers take to ensure that suspects understand the meaning of the warning?

- *Miranda* impact. Do law enforcement officers believe that the *Miranda* warning has an impact on their work? Do they think the warning discourages guilty persons from confessing? Do they believe that *Miranda* plays a positive role in law enforcement by reminding innocent people of their constitutional rights? Or do they believe that the *Miranda* warning is meaningless, a waste of time to satisfy the courts that has no impact in the real world of law enforcement?

from interrogating suspects quickly before they have a chance to concoct an alibi or reflect on the consequences of telling the truth.[35] In contrast, *Miranda*'s defenders call it the "poor person's Fifth Amendment." Educated, middle-class defendants do not need the *Miranda* warning—they know their rights. *Miranda* protects poor, uneducated, and first-time offenders from police coercion.

Singer Michael Jackson leaves a California courthouse after being acquitted of all charges in his child-molestation prosecution. The Sixth Amendment guarantees a fair, speedy, and public trial.

The Supreme Court has weakened the *Miranda* ruling without reversing it. The Court has held that in cross-examining defendants, prosecutors can use statements that do not meet the *Miranda* standard.[36] The Court has also ruled that police need not give the *Miranda* warning before questioning a suspect when the public safety is immediately and directly threatened.[37] The Court even upheld a conviction when the police refused to allow an attorney hired by a suspect's relatives to see

him because the suspect had not asked to see a lawyer.[38]

After the interviews are complete, students should organize their notes and prepare to participate in class discussion. The instructor will ask students not just about the content of the interviews and their reaction to them, but also about the *Miranda* warning in general. In particular, the instructor will invite students to discuss their assessment of the *Miranda* warning. Is it harmful or beneficial, or is it just a meaningless technicality that neither police officers nor criminal suspects take seriously?

Double Jeopardy. The Fifth Amendment prohibits **double jeopardy**, which involves the government trying a criminal defendant a second time for the same offense after an acquittal in an earlier prosecution. No person shall be "twice put in jeopardy of life and limb" for the same criminal offense, the amend-

ment declares. The goal of this provision is to protect individuals from the harassment of repeated prosecutions on the same charge after an acquittal. Because of the Double Jeopardy Clause, no one who has been acquitted of an offense can be retried for the same crime even if incontrovertible evidence of the person's guilt is discovered.

The Supreme Court has held that the Double Jeopardy Clause does not protect persons convicted of child molestation from involuntary commitment to mental hospitals after they have served their prison sentences. Consider the case of *Kansas v. Hendricks*. Leroy Hendricks was a pedophile, an adult who sexually abuses children. He had five convictions for child molestation in the state of Kansas and admitted that he could not stop trying to have sex with children. In 1994, after Hendricks finished serving his most recent sentence for child molestation, the state of Kansas transferred him to a mental health facility, where he was confined indefinitely under provisions of the state's Sexually Violent Predator Act. A state judge ruled that Hendricks was "mentally abnormal" and likely to commit additional crimes. Hendricks and his attorneys filed suit against the state, charging that his continued confinement was a sort of double jeopardy in that he was tried and punished twice for the same crime. The case eventually reached the U.S. Supreme Court, which declared that Hendricks could be confined against his will because he was being held in a mental institution rather than a prison. Technically, he was no longer being punished.[39] Although no one was sympathetic with Hendricks, a number of ob-

double jeopardy the government trying a criminal defendant a second time for the same offense after an acquittal in an earlier prosecution.

think Should child molesters be kept in confinement even after they have served their criminal sentences? Why or why not?

servers worried about the precedent set by the case. "Today we're dealing with sexual predators," said Steven Shapiro of the ACLU. "Who is it tomorrow that we're going to label as abnormal and potentially dangerous?"[40]

Fair Trial. A number of provisions in the Sixth Amendment are aimed at guaranteeing that defendants receive a fair trial. The amendment promises a speedy and public trial. Although the Supreme Court has been reluctant to set timetables for trials, the federal government and many states have adopted "speedy trial laws" to ensure that justice will not be long delayed. As for the public trial requirement, the Supreme Court has held that the public (and the press) may not be excluded from the courtroom except in rare circumstances.[41] Furthermore, the Court has said that states may permit the unobtrusive use of television in a courtroom if they wish.[42]

The Sixth Amendment guarantees trial by an impartial jury. Although juries are traditionally 12 persons, the Supreme Court has said that juries with as few as 6 people are acceptable.[43] The Court has also held that jury selection processes must ensure that the jury pool represents a cross-section of the community, holding, for example, that prosecutors may not systematically exclude racial minorities from jury service.[44]

The Sixth Amendment grants defendants the right to legal counsel. In *Gideon v. Wainwright*, the Supreme Court ruled that states must provide attorneys for indigent defendants charged with serious crimes.[45] The Court has also held that assigned counsel must meet a standard of reasonable competence.[46]

Executions in the United States

Year	Executions
1988	11
1989	16
1990	23
1991	14
1992	31
1993	38
1994	31
1995	56
1996	45
1997	74
1998	68
1999	98
2000	85
2001	66
2002	71
2003	65
2004	59
2005	60
2006	53
2007	42
2008	37

Lethal injection is replacing (clockwise from top left) a firing squad, the electric chair, hanging, or the gas chamber in various U.S. states.

Cruel and Unusual Punishments. Should mentally retarded offenders be held fully accountable for their crimes? Daryl Renard Atkins is a murderer, convicted and sentenced to death by the state of Virginia for the robbery and slaying of a U.S. airman in 1996. Atkins is also severely retarded, at least according to his defense attorneys. Would executing Atkins violate the prohibition against cruel and unusual punishments contained in the Eighth Amendment to the U.S. Constitution? In general, the Supreme Court has interpreted this provision to mean that the punishment must fit the crime. The Court, for example, has held that a life sentence without the possibility of parole for a series of nonviolent petty offenses is cruel and unusual.[47] The Court has also ruled that it is unconstitutional to impose the death penalty on a defendant who rapes a child but does not kill the victim.[48]

No issue has generated more controversy under the Eighth Amendment than the death penalty (**capital punishment**). In 1972, the opponents of capital punishment won a temporary victory in the case of *Furman v. Georgia*. By a 5–4 vote, the Supreme Court declared that the death penalty, *as then applied*, was unconstitutional because it allowed too much discretion, thereby opening the door to discriminatory practices. Which crimes and individuals received the death penalty was so arbitrary, the Court said, that it was similar to being struck by lightning.[49]

Many state legislatures responded to *Furman* by adopting new capital punishment laws designed to satisfy the Court's objections. As the states implemented their new death penalty statutes, cases began to make their way through the court system. In 1976, the U.S. Supreme Court ruled

capital punishment the death penalty.

CONCLUSION
civil liberties
POLICYMAKING

Constitutional law is the most important environmental factor affecting civil liberties policymaking. Civil liberties questions are constitutional questions. Policy debates over prayer in public schools and capital punishment are invariably debates about constitutional law. Did the founders intend for the Establishment Clause to prohibit organized spoken prayer in public schools? Is it cruel and unusual punishment under the Eighth Amendment to execute convicted murderers who are mentally retarded? The Constitution and its interpretation affect every stage of the civil liberties policy process.

Because of the constitutional nature of civil liberties policymaking, judges, especially the men and women who serve on the Supreme Court of the United States, are the most important civil liberties policymakers. Liberal judges are more likely than conservative judges to rule in favor of unpopular litigants, such as atheists, Jehovah's Witnesses, members of the Ku Klux Klan, criminal defendants, and prison inmates. During the 1960s, a liberal bloc of justices led by Chief Justice Earl Warren dominated the Supreme Court. Many of the decisions of that era, including *Engel v. Vitale* and *Miranda v. Arizona*, reflected their policy preferences. In contrast to liberal members of the judiciary, judges with conservative policy preferences tend to decide cases in favor of the police, criminal prosecutors, majority religious preferences, and traditional values. The Supreme Court today is closely divided on civil liberties issues and many cases are decided by the narrowest margin.

Civil liberties policymaking is affected by the presence of interest groups and other organizations capable of participating in the policy process. The American Civil Liberties Union (ACLU) is a frequent participant in civil liberties policymaking. Other interest groups involved with various civil liberties issues include the National Organization for Women (NOW), Planned Parenthood, NARAL Pro-Choice America, the National Rifle Association (NRA), and the National Right to Life Committee.

Public opinion affects the civil liberties policymaking process. Legislatures and executives respond to public demands by enacting death penalty statutes, school prayer requirements, and other measures related to civil liberties. At times, judges seem to respond to public opinion. Historically, the Supreme Court has been more willing to support presidential actions to limit civil liberties during wartime than it is after the war is over.

In the long run, the policy preferences of the president affect civil liberties policymaking because the president appoints judges. Republican presidents tend to select conservative judges, whereas Democratic presidents appoint liberals. Because federal judges enjoy lifetime appointments, a president's influence on judicial policymaking will be slow to materialize but can continue well after the president leaves office.

"It is a fair summary of history to say that the safeguards of liberty have been forged in controversies involving not very nice people."
—Felix Frankfurter, U.S. Supreme Court Justice (1939–1962)

In the early years of the twenty-first century, former Presidents Reagan, Bush, and Clinton continue to affect the judicial branch of government because their appointees still serve on the Court. The survival of the *Roe* precedent depends on future presidential and senatorial elections.

Agenda Building

A number of political actors help set the agenda for civil liberties policymaking. Interest groups and other organizations are particularly important. Conservative groups call on the government to get tough on pornography and crime, and to limit access to abortion. Groups with unpopular views, such as Nazis and members of the Ku Klux Klan, stimulate debate on the First Amendment by attempting to march and demonstrate. A **test case** is a lawsuit initiated to assess the constitutionality of a legislative or executive act. Many of the civil liberties disputes reaching the Supreme Court are test cases initiated by groups such as the ACLU or the Jehovah's Witnesses. The latter have been responsible for more than 50 cases involving religious liberty, winning 90 percent of them.[62] Interest groups ranging from the Chamber of Commerce to B'nai B'rith, a Jewish organization, join other civil liberties cases by means of the *amicus* brief. An **amicus curiae** or **friend of the court brief** is a written legal argument presented by a party not directly involved in a case.

Individuals can add civil liberties issues to the public agenda. Many criminal justice disputes arise from appeals filed by convicted felons, such as Ernesto Miranda. Other individuals raise civil liberties issues on the basis of principle. Madalyn Murray O'Hair, for example, was famous for initiating test cases to challenge what she regarded as unconstitutional government support of religion.

Policy Formulation and Adoption

Many civil liberties policies are formulated and adopted in the executive and legislative branches of government, both at the national level and in the states. After the terrorist attacks of September 11, 2001, for example, Congress passed, and President George W. Bush signed, the USA PATRIOT Act, which makes it easier for federal officials to get wiretapping orders from judges to investigate terrorism, and authorizes nationwide search warrants for computer information in terrorism investigations.[63] State governments adopt policies dealing with the death penalty, state aid to parochial schools, abortion, and other civil liberties issues.

The courts become involved in civil liberties policymaking only when a civil liberties policy adopted by another unit of government is challenged on constitutional grounds. The U.S. Supreme Court has addressed the issue of school prayer because of legal challenges filed against state and local policies. Court rulings then serve as guidelines for other institutions of government.

If the Supreme Court overturns *Roe v. Wade*, the issue of abortion will return to the states. Before *Roe*, states set their own abortion policies. Some states allowed abortion, whereas other states prohibited it except when necessary to protect the life of the woman. In *Roe*, the Supreme Court ruled that women have a constitutional right to an abortion during the first trimester. States could regulate second trimester abortions; they could prohibit late-term abortions. If the Supreme Court overturns the *Roe*

> **THE COURTS BECOME INVOLVED IN CIVIL LIBERTIES POLICYMAKING ONLY WHEN A CIVIL LIBERTIES POLICY IS CHALLENGED ON CONSTITUTIONAL GROUNDS.**

precedent, some states, such as South Dakota, will prohibit abortion except when the woman's life is in jeopardy, whereas others will allow most abortions. Other states will likely take a moderate approach, allowing abortion under certain circumstances but prohibiting abortions otherwise.

Policy Implementation and Evaluation

A broad range of government entities participates in the implementation of civil liberties policy. The Supreme Court's willingness to allow states to enact school voucher programs may not necessarily lead to the adoption of voucher programs, at least not in all states. Some state legislatures will adopt programs, but other legislatures will not. The Supreme Court's decision effectively moves the policymaking arena from the courthouse to the legislature, the governor's mansion, and the school district.

Scholars have completed a number of studies evaluating certain aspects of civil liberties policy. For example, research suggests that the primary impact of the *Miranda* decision has been psychological and that the ruling has had little appreciable effect on confessions and convictions.[64] Another observer concludes that *Miranda* has had no measurable impact on reducing police misconduct.[65] The Liebman study of capital punishment was designed to assess the effectiveness of the death penalty.

test case a lawsuit initiated to assess the constitutionality of a legislative or executive act.

amicus curiae or friend of the court brief written legal arguments presented by parties not directly involved in the case, including interest groups and units of government.

TEST *yourself*

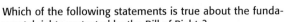

1. The protection of the individual from the unrestricted power of government is the definition for which of the following?
   A. Selective incorporation of the Bill of Rights
   B. Fundamental rights
   C. Civil rights
   D. Civil liberties

2. Where is the Bill of Rights found?
   A. It is the first ten amendments to the Constitution
   B. It is found in Article I, Section 8 of the Constitution
   C. It is part of the Declaration of Independence
   D. It is part of the Articles of Confederation

3. The Bill of Rights initially restricted the power of which of the following levels of government?
   A. Neither the national government nor state governments
   B. Both the national government and state governments
   C. The national government but not state governments
   D. State governments but not the national government

4. The selective incorporation of the Bill of Rights against the states is based on which of the following?
   A. Due Process Clause of the Fourteenth Amendment
   B. First Amendment
   C. Equal Protection Clause of the Fourteenth Amendment
   D. Thirteenth Amendment

5. Which of the following is the reason why China has adopted a one-child policy?
   A. To increase the size of the nation's population
   B. To balance the population between men and women
   C. To limit population growth in order to promote economic development
   D. To force people to move to urban areas

6. Your friend, who works at a local construction company, was fired because his boss disagreed with him over a bumper sticker for a presidential candidate. Does your friend have any legal recourse under the U.S. Constitution or federal law?
   A. Yes, he can sue for his job back based on his boss's violating his freedom of expression.
   B. No, he cannot sue because the First Amendment protects freedom of speech, and bumper stickers are not speech.
   C. No, the First Amendment does not apply to private employers.
   D. Yes, your friend can sue his former boss for age discrimination.

7. Which of the following statements about constitutional rights is true?
   A. All rights are equally important.
   B. Rights are absolute, meaning that government cannot abridge rights guaranteed by the Constitution.

C. State constitutions can guarantee more rights than those found in the federal constitution.
   D. All of the above.

8. Which of the following statements is true about the fundamental rights protected by the Bill of Rights?
   A. They are absolute and may never be abridged by the government.
   B. They are guidelines, but government officials can abridge them when they determine it is in the public interest.
   C. They can be abridged, but only when the government can demonstrate a plausible justification.
   D. They cannot be abridged unless the government can demonstrate a compelling or overriding public interest for so doing.

9. The Parker family is suing the local public school district. The Parkers, who are Mormons, complain that their children's school principal recites prayers over the school intercom and that the prayers are contrary to the family's religious beliefs. Which of the following statements is NOT true about this dispute?
   A. The Parker's lawsuit would be based on the First and Fourteenth Amendments of the U.S. Constitution.
   B. The principal would likely successfully defend against the suit because he has the freedom of religion to express his religious views and that is protected by the Constitution.
   C. The ACLU might be willing to assist the Parkers in their lawsuit.
   D. The Parkers would probably sue in federal court rather than state court.

10. *Engel v. Vitale* dealt with which of the following issues?
    A. Abortion
    B. Freedom of religion
    C. Freedom of speech
    D. Establishment of religion

11. A federal district judge rules that the display of a Ten Commandments monument on the grounds of the county courthouse violates the Establishment Clause. What, if anything, can be done to challenge his decision?
    A. Nothing. Federal court rulings are not subject to reversal because federal judges are appointed for life.
    B. The state legislature and the governor could pass a law to overturn the decision.
    C. Congress and the president could pass a law to overturn the decision.
    D. The county could appeal the decision to a higher court.

12. Which of the following is an example of a hate crime?
    A. A group of white and Latino men break into the home of an Asian family. While robbing the family, they use racial/ethnic slurs, threatening the Asian family with

360   CHAPTER 15 | civil liberties policymaking

violence if they don't move out of the neighborhood.

B. A woman publishes a newsletter in which she attacks homosexuals as "godless pagans who spread disease."

C. A white man who is fleeing from the scene of a crime shoots and wounds a police officer who is African American.

D. All of the above.

13 Which of the following statements is true regarding a right to privacy?

A. The First Amendment guarantees people the right to personal privacy.

B. The Supreme Court has interpreted various provisions of the Bill of Rights to create "zones of privacy."

C. A right to privacy is the basis for *Brown v. Board of Education*.

D. All of the above.

14 Which of the following statements is true about *Roe v. Wade*?

A. It is based on a constitutional right of privacy.

B. It prohibited states from regulating abortion under all circumstances.

C. The Supreme Court has subsequently overturned major parts of *Roe*.

D. All of the above.

15 The constitutional principle that government cannot deprive someone of life, liberty, or property without following fair and regular procedures is known as which of the following?

A. Selective incorporation

B. Parental choice

C. Exclusionary rule

D. Due process of law

16 What is the rationale for the exclusionary rule?

A. If the evidence proves a defendant's guilt, then the evidence should be used against the defendant regardless of how the evidence was obtained.

B. If the government is allowed to use evidence that was obtained illegally, then the government has no incentive to follow the law in collecting evidence.

C. Defendants should be informed of their rights so they can knowingly choose to exercise them or not to exercise them.

D. All of the above.

17 *Mapp v. Ohio* is associated with which of the following?

A. Prior restraint

B. The *Miranda* warnings

C. Double jeopardy

D. Exclusionary rule

18 The right to a counsel is associated with which of the following cases?

A. *Gideon v. Wainwright*

B. *Engel v. Vitale*

C. *Miranda v. Arizona*

D. *Mapp v. Ohio*

19 *Employment Division v. Smith* dealt with which of the following issues?

A. Establishment of religion

B. Freedom of religion

C. School prayer

D. Abortion rights

20 What branch of government has had the greatest impact on civil liberties policy formulation and adoption?

A. Judicial branch

B. Executive branch

C. Legislative branch

D. State governments have been more important than the national government

---

KNOW *the* **score**

18–20 correct: Congratulations! You are well informed!

15–17 correct: Your political knowledge is a bit low–be sure to review the key terms and visit TheThinkSpot.

<14 correct: Reread the chapter more thoroughly.

1. D; 2. A; 3. C; 4. A; 5. C; 6. C; 7. C; 8. B; 9. B; 10. D; 11. D; 12. A; 13. D; 14. A; 15. D; 16. B; 17. D; 18. A; 19. B; 20. A

the
THINKSPOT
www.thethinkspot.com

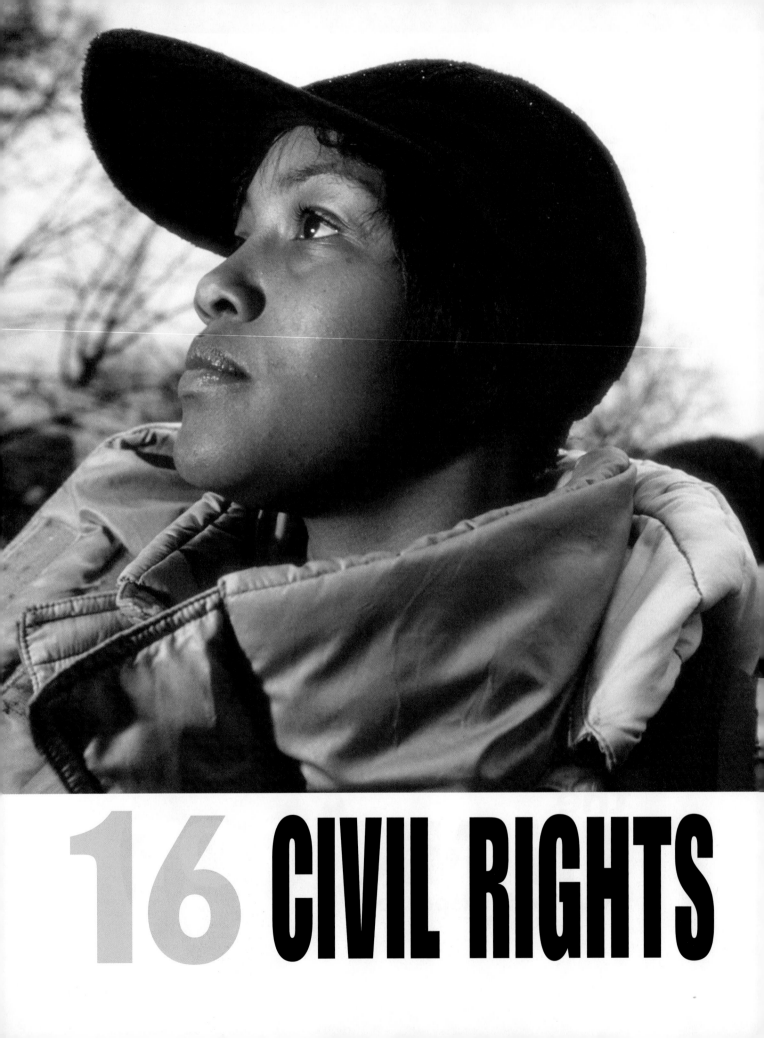

16 CIVIL RIGHTS

T he University of Michigan Law School is one of the most prestigious law schools in the nation. Each year it receives more than 3,500 applications, from which it selects a first-year class of 350 students.

The law school looks for capable students who seem to promise success in the classroom and in the future profession of law. It also strives to admit a mixture of students with varying backgrounds and experiences who will learn from each other. In particular, the law school attempts to ensure that its student body is racially and ethnically diverse by enrolling a critical mass of students from groups that have historically suffered discrimination—especially African Americans, Latinos, and Native Americans. In order to achieve its admissions goals, the law school rejects some academically strong applicants in favor of other applicants who add diversity to its student body. Barbara Grutter was one such student rejected by the law school. Grutter, a white woman, had a college grade point average of 3.8 and a high score on the Law School Admissions Test (LSAT). When the law school rejected her application, Grutter accused it of favoring minority applicants who were less qualified academically. She filed suit, charging that the school discriminated against her on the basis of race in violation of the Fourteenth Amendment and the Civil Rights Act of 1964.[1] Did the University of Michigan Law School illegally discriminate against Barbara Grutter? We will explore the answer to that question as we study civil rights policy in Chapter 16.

POLICYMAKING

ESSENTIALS...

after studying Chapter 16, students should be able to answer the following questions:

> What is the constitutional basis of civil rights policymaking?

> What is the history and current status of constitutional law regarding equality before the law, voting rights and representation, freedom from discrimination, sexual harassment, and affirmative action?

> What are the major factors affecting civil rights policymaking?

both the U.S. Constitution and state constitutions affect civil rights policymaking. The most important provisions dealing with civil rights in the U.S. Constitution are the Fourteenth and Fifteenth Amendments. The Fourteenth Amendment includes the **Equal Protection Clause:** "No State shall . . . deny to any person within its jurisdiction the equal protection of the laws." The Fifteenth Amendment declares that the right to vote "shall not be denied or abridged by the United States or by any State on account of race, color, or previous condition of servitude." Both the Fourteenth and Fifteenth Amendments contain sections granting Congress authority to pass legislation to enforce their provisions.

Most state constitutions include provisions prohibiting discrimination and/or guaranteeing equal protection of the laws. In recent years, a number of state supreme courts have interpreted their state constitutions to require equitable funding for public schools, guarantee equal rights for women, and, in Massachusetts and Connecticut, grant marriage rights to same-sex couples. In each of these cases, state courts adopted policy positions embracing a more expansive interpretation of civil rights than were taken at the time of writing either the U.S. Constitution or federal law.

Equal Protection Clause a provision of the Fourteenth Amendment of the U.S. Constitution that declares that "No State shall . . . deny to any person within its jurisdiction the equal protection of the laws."

Congress has a variety of caucuses, including (from left to right) the Asian Caucus, the Hispanic Caucus (with then-candidate Barack Obama), and the Black Caucus. These groups take a special interest in laws and programs that affect their constituents.

civil rights issues
AND POLICIES

C **ivil rights** is the protection of the individual from arbitrary or discriminatory acts, either by government or by other individuals, based on an individual's group status, such as race or gender. Whereas civil liberties issues involve individual rights, civil rights issues concern group rights. Civil liberties policy issues revolve around the rights of individuals to be free from unwarranted government restrictions on expression, religious belief, and personal liberty. Civil rights policy issues concern the relationship of the government to individuals based on their status as members of a group.

Civil rights issues are similar to civil liberties issues in that they are often constitutional issues. Although executives, legislatures, bureaucracies, interest groups, and political parties are all involved in civil rights issues, the courts, especially the Supreme Court of the United States, usually have the last word on the parameters of policy-making. Consequently, any discussion of civil rights issues focuses heavily on **constitutional law**, that is, law that involves the interpretation and application of the Constitution.

> THE COURT HAS RECOGNIZED THAT MOST DISTINCTIONS ARE NECESSARY AND DESIRABLE, AND HENCE PERMISSIBLE UNDER THE CONSTITUTION.

Equality Before the Law

Although the Fourteenth Amendment guarantees individuals equal protection under the law, the Supreme Court has never required that laws deal with everyone and everything in precisely the same fashion. By their nature, laws distinguish among groups of people, types of property, and kinds of actions. The Court has recognized that most distinctions are necessary and desirable, and hence permissible under the Constitution. Only certain types of classifications that the Court considers arbitrary and discriminatory violate the Equal Protection Clause.

The Supreme Court has ruled that policy distinctions among persons based on their race, ethnicity, and citizenship status are **suspect classifications,** distinctions among persons that must be justified on the basis of a compelling government interest. The Supreme Court has

civil rights the protection of the individual from arbitrary or discriminatory acts by government or by individuals based on that person's group status, such as race and gender.

constitutional law law that involves the interpretation and application of the Constitution.

suspect classifications distinctions among persons that must be justified on the basis of a compelling government interest that cannot be achieved in a less restrictive fashion.

Even though Latinos, African Americans, and Asian Americans together make up 30 percent of the nation's population, only 15 percent of the members of Congress are minority.

Women's Rights in Saudi Arabia

Women in Saudi Arabia have limited legal rights. Under Saudi law, which is based on a conservative interpretation of Islam, women are socially and legally dependent on their male guardians—their fathers at birth and their spouses upon marriage. Women cannot even have their own legal identity cards. Their names are added to their father's identify card when they are born and transferred to their husband's identity card when they marry. As a result, a woman cannot travel, purchase property, or enroll in college without the written permission of a male relative.[34]

The Saudi government encourages women to be stay-at-home mothers. Women must cover themselves fully in public and wear a veil. They cannot attend classes with men or work with men. Women's education is aimed at making women better wives and mothers.

Women cannot study law or become pilots. Instead, they are directed toward occupations deemed suitable for their gender, such as teaching in a girls' school. Women are not allowed to vote or to drive a vehicle. Women who fail to conform to societal norms are subject to harassment by the religious police. They may be arrested, imprisoned, and even caned.

Nonetheless, Saudi Arabia has a women's rights movement. Many Saudi women are aware of the status of women in other countries, including Muslim countries, because of the Internet, satellite TV, and travel abroad, and they are demanding better treatment. Young Saudi women in particular, who are better educated than most of the older women, are challenging their society's conservative interpretation of Islam. They are demanding access to education and employment opportunities.

The Saudi government has made some concessions to women's rights. Women are now permitted to stay in a hotel alone without the presence of a male relative. Even though some leading universities continue to admit only men, women now constitute a majority of university students.[35] The Saudi government is also reportedly considering lifting the ban against women driving.[36]

Questions

1. Is the treatment of women in Saudi Arabia a concern for people around the world, or should it be an internal matter for the Saudis alone to address?

2. Should the United States pressure Saudi Arabia to improve the status of women?

3. Do you think most women in Saudi Arabia are comfortable with their legal and social status?

Although Saudi women cannot drive, they can own cars. These two saleswomen work in a women-only car dealership in Saudi Arabia.

that employers who sexually harass their employees or permit sexual harassment in the workplace are guilty of illegal employment discrimination. Sexual harassment can be male–female, female–male, male–male, or female–female.[37]

The federal courts have identified two categories of sexual harassment: *quid pro quo* harassment and harassment based on a hostile environment. *Quid pro quo* harassment involves a supervisor threatening an employee with retaliation unless the employee submits to sexual advances. "You either sleep with me, or you are fired," is a clear and blatant example of *quid pro quo* sexual harassment. Defining sexual harassment based on a hostile environment is more difficult. Even though no sexual demands are made, an employer may be guilty of sexual harassment if an employee is subjected to sexual conduct and comments that are pervasive and severe enough to affect the employee's job performance. A supervisor who continues to ask a subordinate for a date despite repeated rejections may be guilty of creating a hostile work environment.

Was the CEO in our above example guilty of sexual harassment if, of course, the alleged incident actually occurred? A federal judge threw the case out of court, declaring that the alleged incident, even if true, did not constitute illegal sexual harassment. No threat of retaliation occurred, so the incident could not have constituted *quid pro quo* harassment. Because the alleged incident was an isolated occurrence, the judge ruled that the employee was not subjected to a hostile work environment. The woman appealed the ruling, however, and rather than risk losing on appeal, the CEO agreed to pay her a settlement of $850,000 in exchange for her dropping the lawsuit. Incidentally, the CEO of the large organization was Bill Clinton, who was then governor of Arkansas. The young female employee was Paula Jones.

Affirmative Action

Affirmative action, which refers to steps taken by colleges, universities, and employers to remedy the effects of past discrimination, is controversial. The proponents of race- and gender-based preferences believe they are necessary to remedy the effects of past discrimination. Colleges and universities assert that they benefit from a diverse student body. Employers value a diverse workforce. In contrast, the opponents of racial and gender preferences argue that the only fair way to determine college admissions and employment decisions is merit. It is wrong, they say, to hire or promote someone simply because of race or gender.

Federal government efforts to remedy the effects of discrimination began in the early 1960s. Presidents Kennedy and Johnson ordered affirmative action in federal employment and hiring by government contractors, but their orders had little practical effect until the late 1960s, when the Department of Labor began requiring government contractors to employ certain percentages of women and minorities. For the following decade, affirmative action took on a momentum all its own. For some, affirmative action meant nondiscrimination. For others, it required seeking out qualified women and minorities. For still others, affirmative action stood for hiring set percentages of women and minorities—a quota system. All the while, employers kept careful records of how many women and minority group members were part of their operations.

The election of Ronald Reagan as president in 1980 was a major setback for the proponents of affirmative action. During the Reagan administration, the Equal Employment Opportunity Commission (EEOC), under the leadership of Clarence Thomas, dismantled affirmative action programs and anything that resembled a quota system for women and minorities. In Reagan's view, civil rights laws should offer relief, not to whole

> *colleges and universities* **assert** *that they benefit from a* **diverse student body**

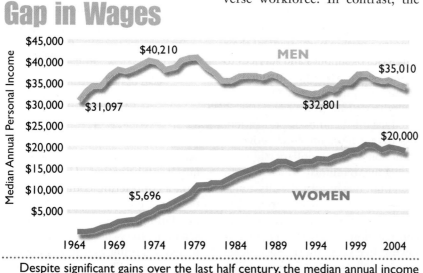

The Gender Gap in Wages

Despite significant gains over the last half century, the median annual income for women is still approximately $15,000 less than that of men.

Isaacs, Julia B. "Economic Mobility Of Men And Women," The Brookings Institution

affirmative action steps taken by colleges, universities, and private employers to remedy the effects of past discrimination.

1 Which of the following constitutional provisions has the greatest impact on civil rights policymaking?

A. Equal Protection Clause of the Fourteenth Amendment

B. First Amendment

C. Second Amendment

D. Due Process Clause of the Fourteenth Amendment

2 Which of the following is a good description of the meaning of civil rights?

A. The right of an individual to be protected from the power of government when it comes to such matters as freedom of expression and freedom of religion

B. The right of an individual not to be harmed or disadvantaged because of the individual's membership in a group based on race, ethnicity, gender, etc.

C. The right of an individual to be protected from the oppressive power of government

D. All of the above

3 Which of the following branches of government plays the greatest role in civil rights policymaking?

A. Legislative branch

B. Executive branch

C. Judicial branch

D. The three branches are equally involved

4 Does the Constitution require that government treat all persons identically, regardless of their race, ethnicity, gender, etc.?

A. Yes. The Equal Protection Clause requires that everyone be treated identically by government.

B. Yes. The Bill of Rights requires that the government not make distinctions among persons on the basis of race, gender, or religion.

C. No. The Supreme Court has long recognized that the government can make distinctions among persons if it can justify the distinctions.

D. No. The Constitution does not address the issue of equal treatment.

5 Under what if any circumstances can the government treat people of different races or ethnicities differently?

A. The government must demonstrate an overriding public interest in making the distinction and prove that it is achieving the compelling public interest in the least restrictive way possible.

B. The government must have a reasonable basis for making the distinction.

C. The government must prove that the distinction is necessary to achieve an important governmental objective.

D. The government must treat all persons identically. The Constitution is color-blind.

6 Which of the following distinctions among persons is not a suspect classification?

A. Ethnicity

B. Race

C. Citizenship status

D. Sexual orientation

7 The judicial decision rule holding that the Supreme Court will find a government policy unconstitutional unless the government can demonstrate a compelling interest justifying the action is known as which of the following?

A. Strict judicial scrutiny

B. Separate but equal

C. Civil liberties

D. Civil rights

8 Under what circumstances would it be constitutionally permissible for the government to deal differently with individuals based on whether they smoke? (For example, the government might prohibit smokers from becoming foster parents.)

A. Under no circumstances—the government must treat everyone alike.

B. The government must demonstrate a compelling government interest to treat people differently.

C. Because smoking status is not a suspect classification, the government need only demonstrate a reasonable basis for making the distinction.

D. The government must offer an exceedingly persuasive justification for making the distinction.

9 The doctrine of "separate but equal" concerned what issue?

A. Separation of powers with checks and balances

B. Affirmative action

C. Voting rights for African Americans

D. Whether laws requiring separate facilities for whites and blacks satisfy the Equal Protection Clause

10 Which of the following statements about *Brown v. Board of Education* is/are true?

A. It was a test case promoted by the NAACP.

B. It overturned *Plessy v. Ferguson*.

C. It outlawed *de jure* segregation but not *de facto* segregation.

D. All of the above.

11 Why is it that many public schools in the United States have student bodies that are all, or almost all, members of the same racial/ethnic group?

A. The Supreme Court overturned *Brown v. Board of Education* in *Parents Involved in Community Schools v. Seattle School District No. 1*.

B. The federal courts no longer enforce the *Brown* decision.

C. Housing patterns in many cities isolate racial and ethnic groups.

D. Public opinion is heavily opposed to racial integration in public schools.

12 Suppose the government reinstates the military draft, but drafts only men and not women. Would it be possible for the government to adopt the policy constitutionally?

A. Yes, but it would have to demonstrate a rational basis for making the distinction.

B. Yes, but it would have to offer an "exceedingly persuasive justification" to make the distinction.

C. Yes, but it would have to demonstrate a compelling government interest in making the distinction.

D. No. Because of the Equal Protection Clause, any draft would have to include both men and women.

13 A state university decides to limit graduate student enrollment in its space physics program to American citizens, excluding permanent residents. Is such an action constitutional?

A. It is, if the university can demonstrate a compelling governmental interest in making the distinction between citizens and non-citizen permanent residents.

B. It is, if the university can state a rational basis for the distinction.

C. Yes. Permanent residents do not have the rights of citizens.

D. No. The Constitution prohibits distinctions based on citizenship status. Everyone must be treated equally.

14 How did the white primary discriminate against African American voters?

A. African Americans were allowed to vote in primary elections but not general elections, thus minimizing their electoral influence.

B. African Americans were prevented from voting in the Democratic primary. Because the South was a one-party Democratic region, the white primary prevented African Americans from voting in the only election that really mattered.

C. African Americans were prevented from voting in the Republican primary. Because the South was a one-party Republican region, the white primary prevented African Americans from voting in the only election that really mattered.

D. African Americans had to pay a tax in order to vote and that discouraged their electoral participation.

15 What was the purpose of a grandfather clause?

A. To exempt white people from voting restrictions placed on African Americans

B. To limit voting to older people

C. To prevent older people from voting

D. To establish different voting requirements based on age

16 What is the current status of deed restrictions that prevent property owners from selling their homes to members of racial and ethnic minority groups?

A. They still apply because they are private agreements, and anti-discrimination laws do not apply to private agreements.

B. They are illegal because of the Voting Rights Act (VRA).

C. The Supreme Court ruled them unenforceable in *Brown v. Board of Education*.

D. The Supreme Court ruled them unenforceable in *Shelley v. Kraemer*.

17 Does the federal government have the authority to outlaw discrimination against racial and ethnic minorities in private businesses such as restaurants and hotels?

A. Yes. The Supreme Court has ruled that Congress can legislate on the basis of its constitutional authority to regulate interstate commerce.

B. Yes. The Supreme Court has ruled that Congress can legislate as part of its authority to enforce the Equal Protection Clause of the Fourteenth Amendment.

C. Yes. The First Amendment gives the federal government the authority to prohibit discrimination.

D. No. These are state issues, not federal issues.

18 What is the basis for sexual harassment law?

A. Federal laws prohibiting gender discrimination in employment

B. First Amendment

C. Equal Protection Clause of the Fourteenth Amendment

D. Voting Rights Act

19 Which of the following cases dealt with affirmative action?

A. *Shelley v. Kraemer*

B. *Brown v. Board of Education*

C. *City of Richmond v. J. A. Croson Company*

D. All of the above

20 Why did the U.S. Supreme Court uphold the admissions program at the University of Michigan law school?

A. The Court ruled that the government has a compelling interest in promoting racial and ethnic diversity in higher education.

B. The admissions program did not establish a quota system for admissions.

C. The admissions program did not award a set number of points to applicants based on their race or ethnicity.

D. All of the above.

1. A; 2. B; 3. C; 4. C; 5. A; 6. D; 7. A; 8. C; 9. D; 10. D; 11. C; 12. B; 13. A; 14. B; 15. A; 16. D; 17. A; 18. A; 19. C; 20. D

17 FOREIGN

> **WHAT'S AHEAD**

The International Community

The Ends and Means of American
Foreign and Defense Policy

Foreign Policy

Defense Policy

Conclusion: Foreign and Defense
Policymaking

S oon after taking office, President George W. Bush declared that Iran, Iraq, and North Korea were an "axis of evil," seeking to develop **weapons of mass destruction (WMD)**, which are nuclear, chemical, and biological weapons designed to inflict widespread military and civilian casualties. The United States went to war against Iraq to overthrow the government of Saddam Hussein and to prevent Iraq from developing nuclear weapons or giving biological or chemical weapons to terrorist groups. American forces quickly defeated the Iraqi military and toppled the government, but, ironically, found no WMD.

Iran and North Korea responded to the American invasion of Iraq by speeding up their own weapons-development programs. Iran has been acquiring the materials and developing the expertise necessary to build nuclear weapons. Furthermore, the Iranian government has failed to cooperate with the International Atomic Energy Agency (IAEA), denying it access to nuclear sites. North Korea is further along in its nuclear program than Iran.

President Bush declared that Iran and North Korea are **rogue states**, nations that threaten world peace by sponsoring international terrorism and promoting the spread of weapons of mass destruction. American policymakers worry that Iran and North Korea, armed with nuclear weapons, would bully their neighbors, perhaps setting off regional arms races as neighboring states rush to acquire nuclear weapons to counter the Iranian or North Korean threat. They might even use a nuclear weapon against the United States or its allies.

The threat of nuclear weapons development in Iran and North Korea is a major foreign and defense policy challenge for the United States. The United States went to war against

AND DEFENSE POLICYMAKING

387

Iraq to defuse a threat that, in retrospect, was less serious than the threats posed by the Iranians and North Koreans. Does the United States have a realistic military option for dealing with either nation now? Can the United States and its allies convince Iran and North Korea to abandon their nuclear ambitions through negotiations? Will the United States simply have to learn to live with a nuclear Iran and a nuclear North Korea?

ESSENTIALS...

after studying Chapter 17, students should be able to answer the following questions:

> What are the most important components of the international community?

> What are the ends and means of American foreign and defense policy?

> What impact did the events of September 11, 2001 have on American foreign and defense policies? What are the internationalist and unilateralist approaches to American foreign policy?

> What are the defense strategies of deterrence and military preemption, and what are the roles of America's strategic and conventional forces?

> What are the roles of the key players in foreign and defense policymaking?

the international COMMUNITY

Since the seventeenth century, the nation-state has been the basic unit of the international community. A **nation-state** is a political community, occupying a definite territory, and having an organized government. Other nations recognize its independence and respect the right of its government to exercise authority within its boundaries, free from external interference. Today, the world's community of nations comprises more than 190 countries.

Political scientists divide the world's nations into three groups based on their level of economic development. The United States, Canada, Japan, and the countries of Western Europe are **postindustrial societies,** nations whose economies are increasingly based on services, research, and information rather than on heavy industry. India, China, South Korea, Brazil, and a number of other countries are modernizing industrial states that are emerging as important economic powers. Finally, many of the countries of Asia, Africa, and Latin America are preindustrial states with an average standard of living well below that in postindustrial societies.[1]

The United States has diplomatic relations with almost all of the world's nations. The term **diplomatic relations** refers to a system

nation-state a political community occupying a definite territory and having an organized government.

postindustrial societies nations whose economies are increasingly based on services, research, and information rather than heavy industry.

diplomatic relations a system of official contacts between two nations in which the countries exchange ambassadors and other diplomatic personnel and operate embassies in each other's country.

Kim Jong-il, the leader of North Korea, commands the fifth-largest standing army in the world. The United States believes that a nuclear North Korea would be a threat to world peace.

of official contacts between two nations in which the countries exchange ambassadors and other diplomatic personnel and operate embassies in each other's country. North Korea, Iran, Cuba, and Libya are among the few nations with which the United States does not have formal diplomatic relations.

In addition to the governments of the world, more than a hundred

bers disagree on how best to approach the problem.

Some of the UN's most important accomplishments have come in the areas of disaster relief, refugee relocation, agricultural development, loans for developing nations, and health programs. The UN has several agencies that carry out these and other tasks, including the International Monetary Fund and the World

ments charged to member nations. The amount of each nation's contribution depends, in general, on the strength of the nation's economy. Although every nation, even small and very poor nations, must support the work of the UN financially, the United States has the largest assessment because the American economy is the world's largest. As a result, the United States is also the

THE NEW AMERICAN EMBASSY IN BAGHDAD, WITH ITS COMPLEX OF 21 BUILDINGS ON 104 ACRES ALONG THE TIGRIS RIVER, IS THE WORLD'S LARGEST EMBASSY. IT ALSO EMPLOYS THE LARGEST STAFF: 5,500 PEOPLE. CRITICS OF THE NEW EMBASSY, ESPECIALLY IRAQIS, SEE IT AS A SYMBOL OF WHO HAS THE REAL POWER IN IRAQ. DEFENDERS SAY THAT THE SIZE OF THE EMBASSY SHOWS THAT THE UNITED STATES IS MAKING A HUGE COMMITMENT TO REBUILD THE WAR-TORN COUNTRY. THE EMBASSY HAS COST ABOUT $730 MILLION AND WILL HAVE ITS OWN POWER AND WATER. IT ALSO HAS REINFORCED WALLS TO PROTECT IT FROM ROCKET ATTACKS IN THE EVENT OF STREET FIGHTING. THE EMBASSY WILL OFFICIALLY OPEN IN 2009.

transnational (or multinational) organizations are active on the international scene. The best known of these is the **United Nations (UN)**, an international organization founded in 1945 as a diplomatic forum to resolve conflicts among the world's nations. In practice, the UN has not always been effective at maintaining the peace. The UN Security Council, the organization charged with maintaining peace and security among nations, has frequently been unable to act because each of its five permanent members (Russia, China, Britain, France, and the United States) has a veto on its actions. The Security Council has been unable to persuade either Iran or North Korea to give up its nuclear weapons program, at least in part, because the permanent mem-

Health Organization. The **International Monetary Fund (IMF)** is an international organization created to promote economic stability worldwide. It provides loans to nations facing economic crises, usually on the condition that they adopt and implement reforms designed to bring long-term economic stability. The World Health Organization (WHO) is an international organization created to control disease worldwide. The WHO is a world clearinghouse for medical and scientific information. It sets international standards for drugs and vaccines and, at government request, helps fight disease in any country. The WHO is in the forefront of the battle against the spread of AIDS in the developing world.

The UN and its affiliated agencies are funded through dues and assess-

UN's most influential member. Nonetheless, the United States has often been highly critical of some UN procedures, especially those associated with budgeting. Congress has sometimes made payment of American dues contingent on the UN agreeing to internal reforms to improve its operations.[2]

United Nations (UN) an international organization founded in 1945 as a diplomatic forum to resolve conflicts among the world's nations.

International Monetary Fund (IMF) the international organization created to promote economic stability worldwide.

Chris Klein (left) and Julian Valentin, members of the Los Angeles Galaxy Major League Soccer team, publicize a UN "Nothing but Nets" workshop at UCLA. The goal of the program is to eradicate malaria in Africa through the distribution and use of mosquito nets.

A number of other international organizations are important to American foreign and defense policies. The **North Atlantic Treaty Organization (NATO)** is a regional military alliance consisting of the United States, Canada, and most of the European democracies. The United States and its allies formed NATO after World War II to defend against the threat of a Soviet attack on Western Europe. With the collapse of the Soviet Union, NATO has expanded to include some of the nations that were once part of the Soviet bloc: Poland, Hungary, the Czech Republic, Bulgaria, Estonia, Latvia, Lithuania, Romania, Slovakia, and Slovenia. The United States, Canada, and the established democracies of Western Europe hope that the inclusion of these nations in the NATO alliance will strengthen their commitment to democratic institutions and capitalist economic structures. In the meantime, NATO has changed its military focus to take into account the changing international environment by creating a multinational force that can be deployed quickly. The United States wants NATO to become a global security organization that is capable either of taking military action or of providing humanitarian relief anywhere in the world. In 2005, for example, NATO gave assistance to earthquake victims in Pakistan and Kashmir.[3]

The **World Trade Organization (WTO)** is an international organization that administers trade laws, and provides a forum for settling trade disputes among nations. It promotes international trade by sponsoring negotiations to reduce tariffs and

Should the United States pull out of the UN?

North Atlantic Treaty Organization (NATO)
a regional military alliance consisting of the United States, Canada, and most of the European democracies.

World Trade Organization (WTO) an international organization that administers trade laws and provides a forum for settling trade disputes among nations.

other barriers to trade. (A **tariff** is a tax on imported goods.) The WTO also arbitrates disputes over trade among its 145 member nations. For example, the WTO has sponsored negotiations to allow modernizing countries to make generic versions of lifesaving drugs for their own use and for export to countries too poor either to make the drugs themselves or to purchase them from pharmaceutical companies. Wealthy nations, led by the United States, want to sharply limit the number of diseases covered by the drugs in order to protect the intellectual property rights of pharmaceutical companies. In contrast, developing nations, such as Brazil, China, and India, argue that governments should have the right to determine which diseases constitute public health crises in their countries.[4]

Nongovernmental organizations (NGOs) are international organizations committed to the promotion of a particular set of issues. Greenpeace, Friends of the Earth, World Wide Fund for Nature, and the Nature Conservancy are NGOs that address environmental issues. Save the Children is an NGO concerned with the welfare of children. Al-Qaeda and other international terrorist organizations are also NGOs.[5] NGOs vary in their relationship to the international community. NGOs such as the International Red Cross and Doctors Without Borders work in partnership with national governments to assist the victims of natural disasters or political turmoil. Other NGOs lobby national governments over policy issues such as the effort to ban the importation of genetically modified foods. Some NGOs encourage consumers to boycott retailers who sell goods produced under exploitative working conditions in developing countries. They organize protests at international meetings of the WTO to push for the incorporation of health and safety conditions in international trade agreements.[6]

tariff a tax levied on imported goods.

nongovernmental organizations (NGOs) international organizations committed to the promotion of a particular set of issues.

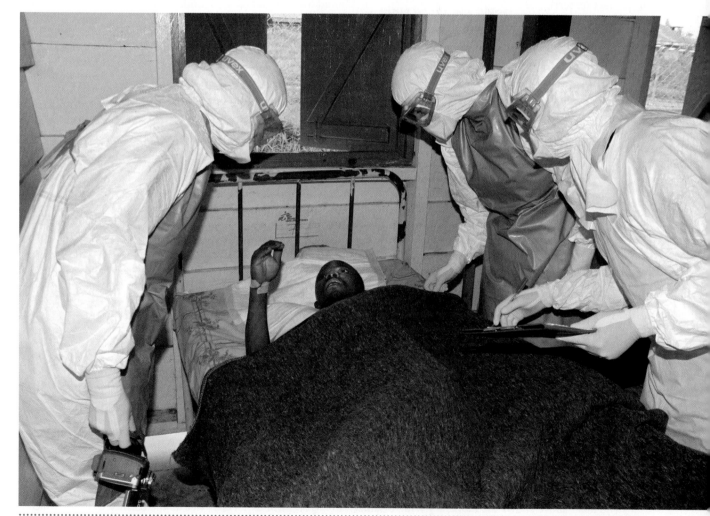

The NGO *Médecins Sans Frontières* (Doctors Without Borders) is an international humanitarian aid organization that provides emergency medical assistance to populations in danger in more than 80 countries. Here MSF doctors in Uganda examine a man thought to be carrying the Ebola virus.

the ends and means of
AMERICAN POLICY

the United States has consistently pursued three foreign and defense policy goals throughout its history: national security, economic prosperity, and the projection of American values abroad.[7] The foremost goal of American foreign and defense policies is national security. A basic aim of the foreign policy of any nation is to preserve its sovereignty and to protect its territorial integrity. No nation wants to be overrun by a foreign power or dominated by another nation. During the **Cold War**, which was the period of international tension between the United States and the Soviet Union lasting from the late 1940s through the late 1980s, American foreign policy was premised on the goal of protecting the nation from communist aggression. Although the United States is today the world's foremost military power, it still has national security concerns. The terrorist attacks of September 11, 2001 demonstrated the vulnerability of the United States to attack by a terrorist group. Although neither Iran nor North Korea would be able to mount a direct attack on the United States, they could threaten American interests in their regions of the world. They could also give or sell nuclear weapons to terrorist groups.

National prosperity is another goal of American foreign and defense policy. This goal includes encouraging free markets, promoting international trade, and protecting American economic interests and investments abroad. Because the American economy is closely entwined with the global economy, it is essential to the nation's economic health that the United States has access both to foreign suppliers of goods and services, and to foreign markets for American products. The nation's military involvement in the Persian Gulf, for example, has been motivated at least in part by a desire by the United States to protect access to the region's oil fields.

think

Do the economic gains from trade outweigh the costs? Would you spend more money to purchase goods that were made in the United States?

INTERNATIONAL TRADE
VALUE IN MILLIONS OF DOLLARS

Period	Total Exports	Total Imports	Balance
1960	25,940	22,432	3,508
1965	35,285	30,621	4,664
1970	56,640	54,386	2,254
1975	132,585	120,181	12,404
1980	271,834	291,241	-19,407
1985	289,070	410,950	-121,880
1990	535,233	616,097	-80,864
1995	794,387	890,771	-96,384
2000	1,070,597	1,450,432	-379,835
2005	1,283,753	1,995,320	-711,567
2007	1,645,726	2,345,983	-700,258

The table above shows the monetary value of American imports and exports as well as the balance of trade, which is the difference between the value of imports and exports. As the table shows, the value of goods and services traded between the United States and other countries has risen dramatically, especially in the last decade. Because imports have risen more rapidly than exports, the United States has a sizable trade deficit.

U.S. Census Bureau, Foreign Trade Division.

International trade has grown increasingly important to the economy of the United States. Trade now accounts for 28 percent of the nation's output of goods and services compared to only 11 percent in 1970. The United States exported $1.6 trillion worth of goods and services in 2007 while importing $2.3 trillion worth. The nation's leading trading partners were, in order of importance, Canada, Mexico, China, and Japan.[8]

An additional goal of **American foreign and defense policy** is the promotion of American ideas and ideals abroad.

Trade is controversial in the United States because it produces winners and losers. Consumers benefit from trade because they have the opportunity to purchase a broad range of goods at competitive prices. American manufacturers of medical instruments, farm equipment, pharmaceuticals, oil drilling equipment, and electronics benefit because they sell their products abroad. In contrast, inefficient small farmers, old steel mills, and the nation's clothing and textile manufacturers suffer because they do not compete effectively against international competition. Some liberal groups in the United States also oppose international trade because they believe it rewards international

corporations that exploit low-wage workers in developing countries and that it leads to environmental degradation around the globe.

Recent administrations of both political parties have favored the growth of trade because they believe that the economic gains from trade outweigh the costs. President Bill Clinton, despite the opposition of a majority of the members of his own political party, won congressional support for the **North American Free Trade Agreement (NAFTA)**, an international accord among the United States, Mexico, and Canada to lower trade barriers among the three nations. The George W. Bush administration negotiated the Central America Free Trade Agreement (CAFTA) with Nicaragua, Honduras, Costa Rica, El Salvador, and Guatemala to phase out tariffs among participating nations on manufactured goods, agricultural commodities, chemicals, and construction equipment.

A final general goal of American foreign and defense policy is the promotion of American ideas and ideals abroad. Historically, American policymakers have justified military interventions as efforts to

protect freedom and promote democracy. Many of the nation's foreign policies today are designed to further the causes of democracy, free-market capitalism, and human rights. For years, the United States has attempted to isolate Cuba economically and diplomatically in hopes of either driving the Castro regime out of power or of forcing Castro to bring democracy and free-market capitalism to the island.

Spreading democracy was at the center of the foreign policy of the George W. Bush administration. When American forces failed to uncover WMD in Iraq, President Bush offered the promotion of democracy as the new justification for the invasion. Democracies are stronger economically and more stable politically than undemocratic governments, he declared. Consequently, their residents have few incentives to join terrorist organizations. Bush also endorsed the theory of the **democratic peace**, which is the concept that democracies do not wage war against other democracies.[9]

North American Free Trade Agreement (NAFTA) an international accord among the United States, Mexico, and Canada to lower trade barriers among the three nations.

democratic peace the concept that democracies do not wage war against other democracies.

THE SELLING OF AMERICAN ARMS

ONE AMERICAN EXPORT that has proved durable is military equipment. In 2006 alone, the U.S. sold more than $21 billion worth of the F-16 fighter jets, mostly to friendly governments in South Asia and the Middle East. The U.S. government must approve all sales of military equipment to prevent unfriendly powers from getting sophisticated technology. In 2006–2007, the U.S. sold $37.2 billion worth of weapons and weapons systems to 174 governments.

Critics of the Bush administration warn that an emphasis on democratization is unrealistic, naïve, and counterproductive. Implanting democracy in countries without a democratic tradition may be impossible because people may be unwilling to make the compromises necessary for democracy to work. The various tribal and religious factions in Iraq fought with each other despite the introduction of democracy after the fall of Saddam. Furthermore, democracy may result in the election of regimes hostile to American interests. In much of the Arab world, including Egypt and Saudi Arabia, free elections would likely produce the selection of distinctly anti-American Islamic regimes. Finally, American pressure to democratize may alienate allies in the war on terror. The United States depends on the cooperation of undemocratic regimes in Egypt and Saudi Arabia to combat terrorism.

The United States pursues its foreign and defense policy goals through military, economic, cultural, and diplomatic means. Since the end of World War II, the Armed Forces of the United States have intervened militarily in Korea, Lebanon, the Dominican Republic, Indochina, Grenada, Panama, Kuwait, Afghanistan, the Serbian province of Kosovo, Iraq, and Liberia. The United States has also given military assistance in the form of arms and advisors to friendly governments fighting against forces hostile to the interests of the United States. For example, the United States has provided military aid to the government of Colombia in its war against guerrilla forces supported by international narcotics traffickers. After September 11, 2001, the United States supplied military aid, including American advisors, to the government of the Philippines in its war against insurgent forces, which may have ties to al-Qaeda.

Besides the actual use of military force, the United States has pursued its policy goals by forming defense alliances and transferring military hardware to other nations. Since the end of World War II, the United States has participated in a number of defense alliances, including NATO and SEATO (the Southeast Asia Treaty Organization). America is also the world's major distributor of weapons, accounting for more than 45 percent of world arms sales. Egypt, Israel, Saudi Arabia, South Korea, and Taiwan are among the major purchasers of American arms.[10] Some international arms sales are private transactions between American firms and foreign governments. Most sales, however, are government-to-government transactions in which the U.S. Department of Defense acts as a purchasing agent for a foreign government wanting to buy American-made weapons.

The United States also attempts to achieve foreign policy goals through economic means, such as trade and foreign aid. Trade can be used to improve international relations. One method the United States employed to improve relations with China was to encourage a trade relationship. In contrast, America has erected trade barriers against foreign governments it wishes to pressure or punish. The United States attempts to isolate Cuba and North Korea economically. In fact, Congress passed, and President Clinton signed, legislation designed to punish third countries that violate the American embargo against Cuba by trading with the island nation. The measure, which was called the Helms-Burton Act, named for former Senator Jesse Helms (R-NC) and Representative Dan Burton (R-IN), provoked accusations of

Trade can be used to improve international relations.

hypocrisy from Canada and Europe. While the United States tries to punish Cuba, they said, it disregards human rights abuses in China, a country that is a major trading partner of the United States.

The United States also uses foreign aid to achieve foreign policy goals. Although the United States is the world's largest donor, its level of giving as a share of national income is among the lowest of the developed nations, less than half that of European countries.[11] The size of the foreign aid budget is also relatively small, less than one percent of the federal budget—and most of this money goes to further the nation's foreign policy aims. The top two recipients of American foreign aid are Israel and Egypt, nations that are close allies of the United States. Both countries receive more money in military aid than they do in economic assistance. Colombia is the third-ranking foreign aid recipient. Furthermore, since September 11, 2001, the United States has increased aid to countries, such as Jordan, Pakistan, Turkey, and postwar Afghanistan, whose assistance America needs in the war on terror.[12] The United States has also made it clear to countries such as

Yemen and the Philippines that their ability to get loans from the IMF depends on their cooperation in the war on terror. Even though the IMF is an international organization, the United States has considerable influence on its loan decisions because it is the organization's largest source of funds.

Foreign policy goals can sometimes be realized through cultural means, including the promotion of tourism and student exchanges, goodwill tours, and international athletic events. The process of improving relations between the United States and China, for example, was facilitated by cultural exchanges. In fact, one of the first contacts between the two nations was the visit of an American table tennis team to China—"ping-pong diplomacy," the pundits called it. The Olympic Games, meanwhile, are not just a sporting event but also a forum for nations to make political statements. The United States boycotted the 1980 Moscow Olympics to protest the Soviet invasion of Afghanistan. The Soviet Union returned the favor in 1984 by staying

home when the games were held in Los Angeles.

Finally, foreign policy goals can also be achieved through **diplomacy,** which is the process by which nations carry on political relations with each other. Ambassadors and other embassy officials stationed abroad provide an ongoing link between governments. The UN, which is headquartered in New York City, offers a forum in which the world's nations can make diplomatic contacts, including countries that may

American soldiers listen intently to a speech by President George W. Bush.

not have diplomatic relations with one another. Diplomacy can also be pursued through special negotiations or summit meetings among national leaders.

diplomacy the process by which nations carry on political relations with each other.

foreign POLICY

the events of September 11, 2001 provide the backdrop for American foreign policy in the post-Cold War world. American policymakers generally agree that the

United States must be closely engaged in world affairs not only to protect its economic interests abroad but also to guard the American homeland against assault by terrorist

groups or rogue states. Policymakers also concur that the United States should exert leadership in international affairs because it is the world's foremost military and economic power. As former Secretary of State Madeleine Albright phrased it, the United States is the world's "indispensable nation" in that its participation is essential to solving the world's military, economic, and humanitarian problems.[13] Policymakers disagree, however, on how closely the United States should work with its allies and the other nations of the world.

Should the United States focus its foreign aid expenditures on humanitarian assistance to poor nations, or should it use aid primarily to further its own foreign policy objectives?

the declaration
OF INDEPENDENCE

In Congress, July 4, 1776

The unanimous Declaration of the thirteen united States of America.

When in the Course of human events, it becomes necessary for one people to dissolve the political bands which have connected them with another, and to assume among the Powers of the earth, the separate and equal station to which the Laws of Nature and of Nature's God entitle them, a decent respect to the opinions of mankind requires that they should declare the causes which impel them to the separation.

We hold these truths to be self-evident, that all men are created equal, that they are endowed by their Creator with certain unalienable Rights, that among these are Life, Liberty and the pursuit of Happiness. That to secure these rights, Governments are instituted among Men, deriving their just powers from the consent of the governed. That whenever any Form of Government becomes destructive of these ends, it is the Right of the People to alter or to abolish it, and to institute new Government, laying its foundation on such principles and organizing its powers in such form, as to them shall seem most likely to effect their Safety and Happiness. Prudence, indeed, will dictate that Governments long established should not be changed for light and transient causes; and accordingly all experience hath shown, that mankind are more disposed to suffer, while evils are sufferable, than to right themselves by abolishing the forms to which they are accustomed. But when a long train of abuses and usurpations, pursuing invariably the same Object evinces a design to reduce them under absolute Despotism, it is their right, it is their duty, to throw off such Government, and to provide new Guards for their future security. Such has been the patient sufferance of these Colonies; and such is now the necessity which constrains them to alter their former Systems of Government. The history of the present King of Great Britain is a history of repeated injuries and usurpations, all having in direct object the establishment of an absolute Tyranny over these States. To prove this, let Facts be submitted to a candid world.

He has refused his Assent to Laws, the most wholesome and necessary for the public good.

He has forbidden his Governors to pass Laws of immediate and pressing importance, unless suspended in their operation till his Assent should be obtained; and when so suspended, he has utterly neglected to attend to them.

He has refused to pass other Laws for the accommodation of large districts of people, unless those people would relinquish the right of Representation in the Legislature, a right inestimable to them and formidable to tyrants only.

He has called together legislative bodies at places unusual, uncomfortable, and distant from the depository of their Public Records, for the sole purpose of fatiguing them into compliance with his measures.

He has dissolved Representative Houses repeatedly, for opposing with manly firmness his invasions on the rights of the people.

He has refused for a long time, after such dissolutions, to cause others to be elected; whereby the Legislative Powers, incapable of Annihilation, have returned to the People at large for their exercise; the State remaining in the mean time exposed to all the dangers of invasion from without, and convulsions within.

He has endeavoured to prevent the population of these States; for that purpose obstructing the Laws for Naturalization of Foreigners; refusing to pass others to encourage their migrations hither, and raising the conditions of new Appropriations of Lands.

He has obstructed the Administration of Justice, by refusing his Assent to Laws for establishing Judiciary Powers.

He has made Judges dependent on his Will alone, for the tenure of their offices, and the amount and payment of their salaries.

He has erected a multitude of New Offices, and sent hither swarms of Officers to harass our people, and eat out their substance.

He has kept among us, in times of peace, Standing Armies without the Consent of our legislatures.

He has affected to render the Military independent of and superior to the Civil Power.

He has combined with others to subject us to a jurisdiction foreign to our constitution, and unacknowledged by our laws; giving his Assent to their acts of pretended Legislation:

For quartering large bodies of armed troops among us:

For protecting them, by a mock Trial, from Punishment for any Murders which they should commit on the inhabitants of these States:

For cutting off our Trade with all parts of the world:

For imposing taxes on us without our Consent:

For depriving us in many cases, of the benefits of Trial by Jury:

For transporting us beyond Seas to be tried for pretended offences:

For abolishing the free System of English Laws in a neighbouring Province, establishing therein an Arbitrary government, and enlarging its Boundaries so as to render it at once an example and fit instrument for introducing the same absolute rule into these Colonies:

For taking away our Charters, abolishing our most valuable Laws, and altering fundamentally the Forms of our Governments:

For suspending our own Legislature, and declaring themselves invested with Power to legislate for us in all cases whatsoever.

He has abdicated Government here, by declaring us out of his Protection and waging War against us.

He has plundered our seas, ravaged our Coasts, burnt our towns, and destroyed the lives of our people.

He is at this time transporting large armies of foreign mercenaries to compleat the works of death, desolation and tyranny, already begun with circumstances of Cruelty and perfidy scarcely paralleled in the most barbarous ages, and totally unworthy the Head of a civilized nation.

He has constrained our fellow Citizens taken Captive on the high Seas to bear Arms against their Country, to become the executioners of their friends and Brethren, or to fall themselves by their Hands.

He has excited domestic insurrections amongst us, and has endeavoured to bring on the inhabitants of our frontiers, the merciless Indian Savages, whose known rule of warfare, is an undistinguished destruction of all ages, sexes and conditions.

In every stage of these Oppressions We have Petitioned for Redress in the most humble terms: Our repeated Petitions have been answered only by repeated injury. A Prince, whose character is thus marked by every act which may define a Tyrant, is unfit to be the ruler of a free people.

Nor have we been wanting in attentions to our British brethren. We have warned them from time to time of attempts by their legislature to extend an unwarrantable jurisdiction over us. We have reminded them of the circumstances of our emigration and settlement here. We have appealed to their native justice and magnanimity, and we have conjured them by the ties of our common kindred to disavow these usurpations which, would inevitably interrupt our connections and correspondence. They too have been deaf to the voice of justice and of consanguinity. We must, therefore, acquiesce in the necessity, which denounces our Separation, and hold them, as we hold the rest of mankind, Enemies in War, in Peace Friends.

We, therefore, the Representatives of the United States of America, in General Congress, Assembled, appealing to the Supreme Judge of the world for the rectitude of our intentions, do, in the Name, and by authority of the good People of these Colonies, solemnly publish and declare, That these United Colonies are, and of Right ought to be Free and Independent States; that they are Absolved from all Allegiance to the British Crown, and that all political connection between them and the State of Great Britain, is and ought to be totally dissolved; and that as Free and Independent States, they have full Power to levy War, conclude Peace, contract Alliances, establish Commerce, and to do all other Acts and Things which Independent States may of right do. And for the support of this Declaration, with a firm reliance of the Protection of Divine Providence, we mutually pledge to each other our Lives, our Fortunes and our sacred Honor.

the constitution
OF THE UNITED STATES OF AMERICA

We the people of the United States, in Order to form a more perfect Union, establish justice, insure domestic Tranquility, provide for the common defence, promote the general Welfare, and secure the Blessings of Liberty to ourselves and our Posterity, do ordain and establish this Constitution for the United States of America.

Article I

Section 1

All legislative Powers herein granted shall be vested in a Congress of the United States, which shall consist of a Senate and House of Representatives.

Section 2

The House of Representatives shall be composed of Members chosen every second Year by the People of the several States, and the Electors in each State shall have the Qualifications requisite for Electors of the most numerous Branch of the State Legislature.

No person shall be a Representative who shall not have attained to the Age of twenty five Years, and been seven Years a Citizen of the United States, and who shall not, when elected, be an Inhabitant of that State in which he shall be chosen.

Representatives and direct Taxes shall be apportioned among the several States which may be included within this Union, according to their respective Numbers, which shall be determined by adding to the whole Number of free Persons, including those bound to Service for a Term of Years, and excluding Indians not taxed, three fifths of all other Persons.* The actual Enumeration shall be made within three years after the first Meeting of the Congress of the United States, and within every subsequent Term of ten Years, in such Manner as they shall by Law direct. The Number of Representatives shall not exceed one for every thirty Thousand, but each State shall have at Least one Representative; and until such enumeration shall be made, the State of New Hampshire shall be entitled to chuse three, Massachusetts eight, Rhode-Island and Providence Plantations one, Connecticut five, New-York six, New Jersey four, Pennsylvania eight, Delaware one, Maryland six, Virginia ten, North Carolina five, South Carolina five, and Georgia three.

When vacancies happen in the Representation from any State, the Executive Authority thereof shall issue Writs of Election to fill such Vacancies.

The House of Representatives shall chuse their Speaker and other Officers; and shall have the sole Power of Impeachment.

Section 3

The Senate of the United States shall be composed of two Senators from each State, chosen by the Legislature thereof, for six Years; and each Senator shall have one Vote.

Immediately after they shall be assembled in Consequence of the first Election, they shall be divided as equally as may be into three Classes. The Seats of the Senators of the first Class shall be vacated at the Expiration of the second Year, of the second Class at the Expiration of the fourth Year, and of the third Class at the Expiration of the sixth Year, so that one third may be chosen every second Year; and if Vacancies happen by Resignation, or otherwise, during the Recess of the Legislature of any State, the Executive thereof may make temporary Appointments until the next Meeting of the Legislature, which shall then fill such Vacancies.†

No Person shall be a Senator who shall not have attained to the Age of thirty Years, and been nine Years a Citizen of the United States, and who shall not, when elected, be an Inhabitant of that State in which he shall be chosen.

The Vice President of the United States shall be President of the Senate, but shall have no Vote, unless they be equally divided.

The Senate shall chuse their other Officers, and also a President pro tempore, in the Absence of the Vice President, or when he shall exercise the Office of the President of the United States.

The Senate shall have the sole Power to try all impeachments. When sitting for that Purpose, they shall be on Oath or Affirmation. When the President of the United States is tried, the Chief Justice shall preside: And no person shall be convicted without the Concurrence of two thirds of the Members present.

Judgment in Cases of Impeachment shall not extend further than to removal from Office, and disqualification to hold and enjoy any Office of honor, Trust or Profit under the United States; but the Party convicted shall nevertheless be liable and subject to Indictment, Trial, Judgment and Punishment, according to Law.

---

*Other persons being black slaves. Modified by Amendment XIV, Section 2.

†Provisions changed by Amendment XVII.

Section 4

The Times, Places and Manner of holding Elections for Senators and Representatives, shall be prescribed in each State by the Legislature thereof; but the Congress may at any time by Law make or alter such Regulations, except as to the Places of chusing Senators.

The Congress shall assemble at least once in every Year, and such Meeting shall be on the first Monday in December, unless they shall by Law appoint a different Day.*

Section 5

Each House shall be the Judge of the Elections, Returns and Qualifications of its own Members, and a Majority of each shall constitute a Quorum to do Business; but a smaller number may adjourn from day to day, and may be authorized to compel the Attendance of absent Members, in such Manner, and under such Penalties as each House may provide.

Each House may determine the Rules of its Proceedings, punish its Members for disorderly Behaviour, and, with the Concurrence of two thirds, expel a Member.

Each House shall keep a Journal of its Proceedings, and from time to time publish the same, excepting such Parts as may in their Judgment require Secrecy; and the Yeas and Nays of the Members of either House on any question shall, at the Desire of one fifth of those Present, be entered on the Journal.

Neither House, during the Session of Congress, shall, without the Consent of the other, adjourn for more than three days, nor to any other Place than that in which the two Houses shall be sitting.

Section 6

The Senators and Representatives shall receive a Compensation for their Services, to be ascertained by Law, and paid out of the Treasury of the United States. They shall in all Cases, except Treason, Felony and Breach of the Peace, be privileged from arrest during their Attendance at the Session of their respective Houses, and in going to and returning from the same; and for any Speech or Debate in either House, they shall not be questioned in any other Place.

No Senator or Representative shall, during the Time for which he was elected, be appointed to any civil Office under the Authority of the United States, which shall have been created, or the Emoluments whereof shall have been encreased, during such time; and no Person holding any Office under the United States shall be a Member of either House during his Continuance in Office.

Section 7

All Bills for raising Revenue shall originate in the House of Representatives; but the Senate may propose or concur with Amendments as on other Bills.

Every Bill which shall have passed the House of Representatives and the Senate, shall, before it become a Law, be presented to the President of the United States;

*Provisions changed by Amendment XX, Section 2.

If he approves he shall sign it, but if not he shall return it, with his Objections, to that House in which it shall have originated, who shall enter the Objections at large on their Journal, and proceed to reconsider it. If after such Reconsideration two thirds of that House shall agree to pass the Bill, it shall be sent, together with the Objections, to the other House, by which it shall likewise be reconsidered, and if approved by two thirds of that House, it shall become a Law. But in all such Cases the Votes of both Houses shall be determined by Yeas and Nays, and the Names of the Persons voting for and against the Bill shall be entered on the Journal of each House respectively. If any Bill shall not be returned by the President within ten Days (Sundays excepted) after it shall have been presented to him, the Same shall be a Law, in like Manner as if he had signed it, unless the Congress by their Adjournment prevent its Return, in which Case it shall not be a Law.

Every Order, Resolution, or Vote to which the Concurrence of the Senate and House of Representatives may be necessary (except on a question of Adjournment) shall be presented to the President of the United States; and before the Same shall take Effect, shall be approved by him, or being disapproved by him, shall be repassed by two thirds of the Senate and House of Representatives, according to the Rules and Limitations prescribed in the Case of a Bill.

Section 8

The Congress shall have Power To lay and collect Taxes, Duties, Imposts and Excises, to pay the Debts and provide for the common Defence and general Welfare of the United States; but all Duties, Imposts and Excises shall be uniform throughout the United States;

To borrow Money on the credit of the United States;

To regulate Commerce with foreign Nations, and among the several States, and with the Indian Tribes;

To establish a uniform Rule of Naturalization, and uniform Laws on the subject of Bankruptcies throughout the United States;

To coin Money, regulate the Value thereof, and of foreign Coin, and fix the Standard of Weights and Measures;

To provide for the Punishment of counterfeiting the Securities and current Coin of the United States;

To establish Post offices and post Roads;

To promote the Progress of Science and useful Arts, by securing for limited Times to Authors and Inventors the exclusive Right to their respective Writings and Discoveries;

To constitute Tribunals inferior to the supreme Court;

To define and punish Piracies and Felonies committed on the high Seas, and Offences against the Law of Nations;

To declare War, grant Letters of Marque and Reprisal, and make Rules concerning Captures on Land and Water;

To raise and support Armies, but no Appropriation of Money to that Use shall be for a longer Term than two Years;

To provide and maintain a Navy;

To make Rules for the Government and Regulation of the land and naval Forces;

To provide for calling forth the Militia to execute the Laws of the Union, suppress Insurrections and repel Invasions;

To provide for organizing, arming, and disciplining, the Militia, and for governing such Part of them as may be employed in the Service of the United States, reserving to the States respectively, the Appointment of the Officers, and the Authority of training the Militia according to the discipline prescribed by Congress;

To exercise exclusive Legislation in all Cases whatsoever, over such District (not exceeding ten Miles square) as may, by Cession of particular States, and the Acceptance of Congress, become the Seat of Government of the United States, and to exercise like Authority over all Places purchased by the Consent of the Legislature of the State in which the Same shall be, for the Erection of Forts, Magazines, Arsenals, dock-Yards, and other needful Buildings;—And

To make all Laws which shall be necessary and proper for carrying into Execution the foregoing Powers, and all other Powers vested by this Constitution in the Government of the United States, or in any Department or Officer thereof.

Section 9

The Migration or Importation of such Persons as any of the States now existing shall think proper to admit, shall not be prohibited by the Congress prior to the Year one thousand eight hundred and eight, but a Tax, or duty may be imposed on such Importation, not exceeding ten dollars for each Person.

The privilege of the Writ of Habeas Corpus shall not be suspended, unless when in Cases of Rebellion or Invasion the public Safety may require it.

No Bill of Attainder or ex post facto Law shall be passed.

No Capitation, or other direct, Tax shall be laid, unless in Proportion to the Census or Enumeration herein before directed to be taken.

No Tax or Duty shall be laid on Articles exported from any State.

No Preference shall be given by any Regulation of Commerce or Revenue to the Ports of one State over those of another; nor shall Vessels bound to, or from, one State, be obliged to enter, clear, or pay Duties in another.

No Money shall be drawn from the Treasury, but in Consequence of Appropriations made by Law; and a regular Statement and Account of the Receipts and Expenditures of all public Money shall be published from time to time.

No Title of Nobility shall be granted by the United States: And no Person holding any Office of Profit or Trust under them, shall, without the Consent of the Congress, accept of any present, Emolument, Office, or Title, of any kind whatever, from any King, Prince, or foreign State.

Section 10

No State shall enter into any Treaty, Alliance, or Confederation; grant Letters of Marque and Reprisal; coin Money; emit Bills of Credit; make any Thing but gold and silver Coin a Tender in Payment of Debts; pass any Bill of Attainder, ex post facto Law, or Law impairing the Obligation of Contracts, or grant any Title of Nobility.

No State shall, without the Consent of the Congress, lay any Imposts or Duties on Imports or Exports, except what may be absolutely necessary for executing its inspection Laws: and the net Produce of all Duties and Imposts, laid by any State on Imports or Exports, shall be for the Use of the Treasury of the United States; and all such Laws shall be subject to the Revision and Control of the Congress.

No State shall, without the Consent of Congress, lay any Duty of Tonnage, keep Troops, or Ships of War in time of Peace, enter into any Agreement or Compact with another State, or with a foreign Power, or engage in War, unless actually invaded, or in such imminent Danger as will not admit of delay.

Article II

Section 1

The executive Power shall be vested in a President of the United States of America. He shall hold his Office during the Term of four Years, and, together with the Vice President, chosen for the same Term, be elected, as follows:

Each State shall appoint, in such Manner as the Legislature thereof may direct, a Number of Electors, equal to the whole Number of Senators and Representatives to which the State may be entitled in the Congress; but no Senator or Representative, or Person holding an Office of Trust or Profit under the United States, shall be appointed an Elector.

The Electors shall meet in their respective States, and vote by Ballot for two Persons, of whom one at least shall not be an Inhabitant of the same State with themselves. And they shall make a List of all the Persons voted for, and of the Number of Votes for each; which List they shall sign and certify, and transmit sealed to the Seat of the Government of the United States, directed to the President of the Senate. The President of the Senate shall, in the Presence of the Senate and House of Representatives, open all the Certificates, and the Votes shall then be counted. The Person having the greatest Number of Votes shall be the President, if such Number be a Majority of the whole Number of Electors appointed; and if there be more than one who have such Majority, and have an equal Number of Votes, then the House of Representatives shall immediately chuse by Ballot one of them for President; and if no Person have a Majority, then from the five highest on the List the said House shall in like Manner chuse the President. But in chusing the President, the Votes shall be taken by States, the Representation from each State having one Vote; a quorum for this Purpose shall consist of a Member or Members from two thirds of the States, and a Majority of all the States shall be necessary to a Choice. In every Case, after the Choice of the President, the Person having the greatest Number of Votes of the Electors shall be the Vice President. But if there should remain two or more who have equal Votes, the Senate shall chuse from them by Ballot the Vice President.*

The Congress may determine the Time of chusing the Electors, and the Day on which they shall give their Votes; which Day shall be the same throughout the United States.

No Person except a natural born Citizen, or a Citizen of the United States, at the time of the Adoption of this Constitution, shall be eligible to the Office of President; neither shall any Person be eligible to that Office who shall not have attained to the Age of thirty five Years, and been fourteen Years a Resident within the United States.

In Case of the Removal of the President from Office, or of his Death, Resignation, or Inability to discharge the Powers and Duties of the said Office, the Same shall devolve on the Vice President, and the Congress may by Law provide for the Case of Removal, Death, Resignation or Inability, both of the President and Vice President, declaring what Officer shall then act as President, and such Officer shall act accordingly, until the Disability be removed, or a President shall be elected.

The President shall, at stated Times, receive for his Services, a Compensation, which shall neither be encreased nor diminished during the Period for which he shall have been elected, and he shall not receive within that Period any other Emolument from the United States, or any of them.

Before he enter on the Execution of his Office, he shall take the following Oath or Affirmation:—"I do solemnly swear (or affirm) that I will faithfully execute the Office of President of the United States, and will to the best of my Ability, preserve, protect and defend the Constitution of the United States."

Section 2

The President shall be Commander in Chief of the Army and Navy of the United States, and of the Militia of the several States, when called into the actual Service of the United States; he may require the Opinion, in writing, of the principal Officer in each of the executive Departments, upon any Subject relating to the Duties of their respective Offices, and he shall have Power to grant Reprieves and Pardons for Offences against the United States, except in Cases of Impeachment.

He shall have Power, by and with the Advice and Consent of the Senate, to make Treaties, provided two thirds of the Senators present concur; and he shall nominate, and by and with the Advice and Consent of the Senate, shall appoint Ambassadors, other public Ministers and Consuls, Judges of the supreme Court, and all other Officers of the United States, whose Appointments are not herein otherwise provided for, and which shall be established by Law: but the Congress may by Law vest the Appointment of such inferior Officers, as they think proper in the President alone, in the Courts of Law, or in the Heads of Departments.

The President shall have Power to fill up all Vacancies that may happen during the Recess of the Senate, by granting Commissions which shall expire at the end of their next Session.

Section 3

He shall from time to time give to the Congress Information of the State of the Union, and recommend to their Consideration such Measures as he shall judge necessary and expedient; he may, on extraordinary occasions, convene both Houses, or either of them, and in Case of Disagreement between them, with Respect to the Time of Adjournment, he may adjourn them to such Time as he shall think proper; he shall receive Ambassadors and other public Ministers; he shall take Care that the Laws be faithfully executed, and shall Commission all the Officers of the United States.

Section 4

The President, Vice President and all civil Officers of the United States, shall be removed from Office on Impeachment for, and Conviction of, Treason, Bribery, or other high Crimes and Misdemeanors.

Article III
Section 1

The judicial Power of the United States, shall be vested in one supreme Court, and in such inferior Courts as the Congress may from time to time ordain and establish. The Judges, both of the supreme and inferior Courts, shall hold their Offices during good Behaviour, and shall, at stated Times, receive for their Services, a Compensation, which shall not be diminished during their Continuance in Office.

Section 2

The judicial Power shall extend to all Cases in Law and Equity, arising under this Constitution, the Laws of the United States, and Treaties made, or which shall be made, under their Authority;—to all Cases affecting

*Provisions superseded by Amendment XII.

Ambassadors, other public Ministers and Consuls;—to all cases of admiralty and maritime Jurisdiction;—to Controversies to which the United States shall be a Party;—to Controversies between two or more States;—between a State and Citizens of another State;—between Citizens of different States;—between Citizens of the same State claiming Lands under Grants of different States, and between a State, or the Citizens thereof, and foreign States, Citizens or Subjects.*

In all Cases affecting Ambassadors, other public Ministers and Consuls, and those in which a State shall be Party, the supreme Court shall have original Jurisdiction. In all the other Cases before mentioned, the supreme Court shall have appellate Jurisdiction, both as to Law and Fact, with such Exceptions, and under such Regulations as the Congress shall make.

The Trial of all Crimes, except in Cases of Impeachment, shall be by Jury; and such Trial shall be held in the State where the said Crimes shall have been committed, but when not committed within any State, the Trial shall be at such Place or Places as the Congress may by law have directed.

Section 3

Treason against the United States, shall consist only in levying War against them, or in adhering to their Enemies, giving them Aid and Comfort. No person shall be convicted of Treason unless on the Testimony of two Witnesses to the same overt Act, or on Confession in open Court.

The Congress shall have Power to declare the Punishment of Treason, but no Attainder of Treason shall work Corruption of Blood, or Forfeiture except during the Life of the Person attained.

Article IV

Section 1

Full Faith and Credit shall be given in each State to the public Acts, Records, and judicial Proceedings of every other State. And the Congress may by general Laws prescribe the Manner in which such Acts, Records and Proceedings shall be proved, and the Effect thereof.

Section 2

The Citizens of each State shall be entitled to all Privileges and Immunities of Citizens in the several States.

A Person charged in any State with Treason, Felony, or other Crime, who shall flee from Justice, and be found in another State, shall on Demand of the executive Authority of the State from which he fled, be delivered up, to be removed to the State having Jurisdiction of the Crime.

No Person held to Service or Labour in one State, under the Laws thereof, escaping into another, shall, in Consequence of any Law or Regulation therein, be discharged from such Service or Labour, but shall be delivered up on Claim of the Party to whom such Service or Labour may be due.

*Clause changed by Amendment XI.

Section 3

New States may be admitted by the Congress into this Union; but no new State shall be formed or erected within the Jurisdiction of any other State; nor any State be formed by the Junction of two or more States, or Parts of States, without the Consent of the Legislatures of the States concerned as well as of the Congress.

The Congress shall have Power to dispose of and make all needful Rules and Regulations respecting the Territory or other Property belonging to the United States; and nothing in this Constitution shall be so construed as to Prejudice any Claims of the United States, or of any particular State.

Section 4

The United States shall guarantee to every State in this Union a Republican Form of Government, and shall protect each of them against Invasion; and on Application of the Legislature, or of the Executive (when the Legislature cannot be convened) against domestic Violence.

Article V

The Congress, whenever two thirds of both Houses shall deem it necessary, shall propose Amendments to this Constitution, or, on the Application of the Legislatures of two thirds of the several States, shall call a Convention for proposing Amendments, which, in either Case, shall be valid to all Intents and Purposes, as Part of this Constitution, when ratified by the Legislatures of three fourths of the several states, or by Conventions in three fourths thereof, as the one or the other Mode of Ratification may be proposed by the Congress; Provided that no Amendment which may be made prior to the Year One thousand eight hundred and eight shall in any Manner affect the first and fourth Clauses in the Ninth Section of the first Article; and that no State, without its Consent, shall be deprived of its equal Suffrage in the Senate.

Article VI

All Debts contracted and Engagements entered into, before the Adoption of this Constitution, shall be as valid against the United States under this Constitution, as under the Confederation.

This Constitution, and the Laws of the United States which shall be made in Pursuance thereof; and all Treaties made, or which shall be made, under the Authority of the United States, shall be the supreme Law of the Land; and the Judges in every State shall be bound thereby, any Thing in the Constitution or Laws of any State to the Contrary notwithstanding.

The Senators and Representatives before mentioned, and the Members of the several State Legislatures and all executive and judicial Officers, both of the United States and of the several States, shall be bound by Oath or Affirmation to support this Constitution; but no religious

Test shall ever be required as a Qualification to any Office or public Trust under the United States.

Article VII

The Ratification of the Conventions of nine States shall be sufficient for the Establishment of this Constitution between the States so ratifying the Same.

Done in Convention by the Unanimous Consent of the States present the Seventeenth Day of September in the Year of our Lord one thousand seven hundred and Eighty seven and of the Independence of the United States of America the Twelfth.* In Witness whereof We have hereunto subscribed our Names.

*The Constitution was submitted on September 17, 1787, by the Constitutional Convention, was ratified by the conventions of several states at various dates up to May 29, 1790, and became effective on March 4, 1789.

amendments
TO THE CONSTITUTION
(The First Ten Amendments Form the Bill of Rights)

Amendment I [1791]

Congress shall make no law respecting an establishment of religion, or prohibiting the free exercise thereof; or abridging the freedom of speech, or of the press, or the right of the people peaceably to assemble, and to petition the Government for a redress of grievances.

Amendment II [1791]

A well regulated Militia being necessary to the security of a free State, the right of the people to keep and bear Arms, shall not be infringed.

Amendment III [1791]

No Soldier shall, in time of peace, be quartered in any house, without the consent of the Owner, nor in time of war, but in a manner to be prescribed by law.

Amendment IV [1791]

The right of the people to be secure in their persons, houses, papers, and effects, against unreasonable searches and seizures, shall not be violated, and no Warrants shall issue, but upon probable cause, supported by Oath or affirmation, and particularly describing the place to be searched, and the persons or things to be seized.

Amendment V [1791]

No person shall be held to answer for a capital or otherwise infamous crime, unless on a presentment or indictment of a Grand Jury, except in cases arising in the land or naval forces, or in the Militia, when in actual service in time of War or public danger; nor shall any person be subject for the same offence to be twice put in jeopardy of life or limb; nor shall be compelled in any criminal case to be a witness against himself, nor be deprived of life, liberty, or property, without due process of law; nor shall private property be taken for public use, without just compensation.

Amendment VI [1791]

In all criminal prosecutions, the accused shall enjoy the right to a speedy and public trial, by an impartial jury of the State and district wherein the crime shall have been committed, which district shall have been previously ascertained by law, and to be informed of the nature and cause of the accusation; to be confronted with the witnesses against him; to have compulsory process for obtaining witnesses in his favor, and to have the Assistance of Counsel for his defence.

Amendment VII [1791]

In Suits at common law, where the value in controversy shall exceed twenty dollars, the right of trial by jury shall be preserved, and no fact tried by a jury, shall be otherwise reexamined in any court of the United States, than according to the rules of the common law.

Amendment VIII [1791]

Excessive bail shall not be required, nor excessive fines imposed, nor cruel and unusual punishments inflicted.

Amendment IX [1791]

The enumeration in the Constitution, of certain rights, shall not be construed to deny or disparage others retained by the people.

Amendment X [1791]

The powers not delegated to the United States by the Constitution, nor prohibited by it to the States, are reserved to the States respectively, or to the people.

Amendment XI [1798]

The Judicial power of the United States shall not be construed to extend to any suit in law or equity, commenced or prosecuted against one of the United States by Citizens of another State, or by Citizens of Subjects of any Foreign State.

Amendment XII [1804]

The Electors shall meet in their respective states and vote by ballot for President and Vice-President, one of whom, at least, shall not be an inhabitant of the same state with themselves; they shall name in their ballots the person voted for as President, and in distinct ballots the person voted for as Vice-President, and they shall make distinct lists of all persons voted for as President, and of all persons voted for as Vice-President, and of the number of votes for each, which lists they shall sign and certify, and transmit sealed to the seat of the government of the United States, directed to the President of the Senate;—The President of the Senate shall, in the presence of the Senate and House of Representatives, open all the certificates and the votes shall then be counted;—The person having the greatest number of votes for President, shall be the President, if such number be a majority of the whole number of Electors appointed; and if no person have such majority, then from the persons having the highest numbers not exceeding three on the list of those voted for as President, the House of Representatives shall choose immediately, by ballot, the President. But in choosing the President, the votes shall be taken by states, the representation from each state having one vote; a quorum for this purpose shall consist of a member or members from two-thirds of the states, and a majority of all the states shall be necessary to a choice. And if the House of Representatives shall not choose a President whenever the right of choice shall devolve upon them, before the fourth day of March next following, then the Vice-President shall act as President, as in the case of the death or other constitutional disability of the President.—The person having the greatest number of votes as Vice-President, shall be the Vice-President, if such number be a majority of the whole number of Electors appointed, and if no person have a majority, then from the two highest numbers on the list, the Senate shall choose the Vice-President; a quorum for the purpose shall consist of two-thirds of the whole number of Senators, and a majority of the whole number shall be necessary to a choice. But no person constitutionally ineligible to the office of President shall be eligible to that of Vice-President of the United States.

Amendment XIII [1865]

Section 1

Neither slavery nor involuntary servitude, except as a punishment for crime whereof the party shall have been duly convicted, shall exist within the United States, or any place subject to their jurisdiction.

Section 2

Congress shall have power to enforce this article by appropriate legislation.

Amendment XIV [1868]

Section 1

All persons born or naturalized in the United States, and subject to the jurisdiction thereof, are citizens of the United States and the State wherein they reside. No State shall make or enforce any law which shall abridge the privileges or immunities of citizens of the United States; nor shall any State deprive any person of life, liberty, or property, without due process of law; nor deny to any person within its jurisdiction the equal protection of the laws.

Section 2

Representatives shall be apportioned among the several States according to their respective numbers, counting the whole number of persons in each State, excluding Indians not taxed. But when the right to vote at any election for the choice of electors for President and Vice President of the United States, Representatives in Congress, the Executive and Judicial officers of a State, or the members of the Legislature thereof, is denied to any of the male inhabitants of such State being twenty-one years of age, and citizens of the United States or in any way abridged, except for participation in rebellion or other crime, the basis of representation therein shall be reduced in the proportion which the number of such male citizens shall bear to the whole number of male citizens twenty-one years of age in such State.

Section 3

No person shall be a Senator or Representative in Congress, or elector of President and Vice President, or hold any office, civil or military, under the United States or under any State, who, having previously taken an oath, as a member of Congress, or as an officer of the United States, or as a member of any State legislature or as an executive or judicial officer of any State to support the Constitution of the United States, shall have engaged in insurrection or rebellion against the same, or given aid or comfort to the enemies thereof. But Congress may by a vote of two-thirds of each House, remove such disability.

Section 4

The validity of the public debt of the United States, authorized by law, including debts incurred for payment of pensions and bounties for services in suppressing insurrection or rebellion, shall not be questioned. But neither the United States nor any State shall assume or pay any debt or obligation incurred in aid of insurrection or rebellion against the United States, or any claim for the loss or emancipation of any slave; but all such debts, obligations and claims shall be held illegal and void.

Section 5

The Congress shall have the power to enforce, by appropriate legislation, the provisions of this article.

Amendment XV [1870]

Section 1

The right of citizens of the United States to vote shall not be denied or abridged by the United States or by any State on account of race, color, or previous condition of servitude.

Section 2

The Congress shall have power to enforce this article by appropriate legislation.

Amendment XVI [1913]

The Congress shall have power to lay and collect taxes on incomes, from whatever source derived, without apportionment among the several States, and without regard to any census or enumeration.

Amendment XVII [1913]

The Senate of the United States shall be composed of two Senators from each State, elected by the people thereof, for six years; and each Senator shall have one vote. The electors in each State shall have the qualifications requisite for electors of the most numerous branch of the State legislatures.

When vacancies happen in the representation of any State in the Senate, the executive authority of such State shall issue writs of election to fill such vacancies: *Provided*, That the legislature of any State may empower the executive thereof to make temporary appointments until the people fill the vacancies by election as the legislature may direct.

This amendment shall not be so construed as to affect the election or term of any Senator chosen before it becomes valid as part of the Constitution.

Amendment XVIII [1919]

Section 1

After one year from the ratification of this article the manufacture, sale, or transportation of intoxicating liquors within, the importation thereof into, or the exportation thereof from the United States and all territory subject to the jurisdiction thereof for beverage purposes is hereby prohibited.

Section 2

The Congress and the several States shall have concurrent power to enforce this article by appropriate legislation.

Section 3

This article shall be inoperative unless it shall have been ratified as an amendment to the Constitution by the legislatures of the several States, as provided in the Constitution, within seven years from the date of the submission hereof to the States by the Congress.

Amendment XIX [1920]

The right of citizens of the United States to vote shall not be denied or abridged by the United States or by any State on account of sex.

Congress shall have power to enforce this article by appropriate legislation.

Amendment XX [1933]

Section 1

The terms of the President and Vice President shall end at noon on the 20th day of January, and the terms of Senators and Representatives at noon on the 3rd day of January, of the years in which such terms would have ended if this article had not been ratified; and the terms of their successors shall then begin.

Section 2

The Congress shall assemble at least once in every year, and such meeting shall begin at noon on the 3rd day of January, unless they shall by law appoint a different day.

Section 3

If, at the time fixed for the beginning of the term of the President, the President elect shall have died, the Vice President elect shall become President. If a President shall not have been chosen before the time fixed for the beginning of his term, or if the President elect shall have failed to qualify, then the Vice President elect shall act as President until a President shall have qualified; and the Congress may by law provide for the case wherein neither a President elect nor a Vice President elect shall have qualified, declaring who shall then act as President, or the manner in which one who is to act shall be selected, and such person shall act accordingly until a President or Vice President shall have qualified.

Section 4

The Congress may by law provide for the case of the death of any of the persons from whom the House of Representatives may choose a President whenever the right of choice shall have devolved upon them, and for the case of the death of any of the persons from whom the Senate may choose a Vice-President whenever the right of choice shall have devolved upon them.

Section 5

Sections 1 and 2 shall take effect on the 15th day of October following the ratification of this article.

Section 6

This article shall be inoperative unless it shall have been ratified as an amendment to the Constitution by the legislatures of three-fourths of the several States within seven years from the date of its submission.

Amendment XXI [1933]

Section 1
The eighteenth article of amendment to the Constitution of the United States is hereby repealed.

Section 2
The transportation or importation into any State, Territory, or possession of the United States for delivery or use therein of intoxicating liquors, in violation of the laws thereof, is hereby prohibited.

Section 3
This article shall be inoperative unless it shall have been ratified as an amendment to the Constitution by conventions in the several States, as provided in the Constitution, within seven years from the date of the submission hereof to the States by the Congress.

Amendment XXII [1951]

Section 1
No person shall be elected to the office of the President more than twice, and no person who has held the office of President, or acted as President, for more than two years of a term to which some other person was elected President shall be elected to the office of the President more than once. But this Article shall not apply to any person holding the office of President when this Article was proposed by the Congress, and shall not prevent any person who may be holding the office of President or acting as President, during the term within which this Article becomes operative from holding the office of President or acting as President during the remainder of such term.

Amendment XXIII [1961]

Section 1
The District constituting the seat of Government of the United States shall appoint in such manner as the Congress may direct:

A number of electors of President and Vice President equal to the whole number of Senators and Representatives in Congress to which the District would be entitled if it were a State, but in no event more than the least populous State; they shall be in addition to those appointed by the States, but they shall be considered, for the purposes of the election of President and Vice President, to be electors appointed by a State; and they shall meet in the District and perform such duties as provided by the twelfth article of Amendment.

Section 2
The Congress shall have power to enforce this article by appropriate legislation.

Amendment XXIV [1964]

Section 1
The right of citizens of the United States to vote in any primary or other election for President or Vice President, for electors for President or Vice President, or for Senator or Representative in Congress, shall not be denied or abridged by the United States or any State by reason of failure to pay any poll tax or other tax.

Section 2
The Congress shall have the power to enforce this article by appropriate legislation.

Amendment XXV [1967]

Section 1
In case of the removal of the President from office or his death or resignation, the Vice President shall become President.

Section 2
Whenever there is a vacancy in the office of the Vice President, the President shall nominate a Vice President who shall take the office upon confirmation by a majority vote of both houses of Congress.

Section 3
Whenever the President transmits to the President pro tempore of the Senate and the Speaker of the House of Representatives his written declaration that he is unable to discharge the powers and duties of his office, and until he transmits to them a written declaration to the contrary, such powers and duties shall be discharged by the Vice President as Acting President.

Section 4
Whenever the Vice President and a majority of either the principal officers of the executive departments or of such other body as Congress may by law provide, transmit to the President pro tempore of the Senate and the Speaker of the House of Representatives their written declaration that the President is unable to discharge the powers and duties of his office, the Vice President shall immediately assume the powers and duties of the office as Acting President.

Thereafter, when the President transmits to the President pro tempore of the Senate and the Speaker of the House of Representatives his written declaration that no inability exists, he shall resume the powers and duties of his office unless the Vice President and a majority of either the principal officers of the executive department or of such other body as Congress may by law provide, transmit within four days to the President pro tempore of the Senate and the Speaker of the House of Representatives their written declaration that the President is unable to discharge the powers and duties of his office. Thereupon Congress shall decide the issue, assembling within 48 hours for that purpose if not in session. If the Congress, within 21 days after receipt of the latter written declaration, or, if Congress is not in session, within 21 days after Congress is required to assemble, determines by two-thirds vote of both houses that the President is unable to discharge the powers and duties of his office, the Vice President shall continue to discharge the same as Acting President; otherwise, the President shall resume the powers and duties of his office.

Amendment XXVI [1971]

Section 1
The right of citizens of the United States, who are 18 years of age or older, to vote shall not be denied or abridged by the United States or any state on account of age.

Section 2
The Congress shall have the power to enforce this article by appropriate legislation.

Amendment XXVII [1992]
No law varying the compensation for the service of Senators and Representatives shall take effect until an election of Representatives shall have intervened.

>glossary

527 committees   Organizations created by individuals and groups to influence the outcomes of elections by raising and spending money that candidates and political parties cannot legally raise.

AARP   An interest group representing the concerns of older Americans (formerly known as the American Association of Retired Persons).

Ability-to-pay theory of taxation   The approach to government finance that holds that taxes should be based on an individual's ability to pay.

Absolute monarchy   A country ruled by one person, usually a king or queen.

Administrative law   Administrative rules adopted by regulatory agencies.

Access   The opportunity to communicate directly with legislators and other government officials in hopes of influencing the details of policy.

Adversary proceeding   A legal procedure in which each side presents evidence and arguments to bolster its position while rebutting evidence that might support the other side.

Advocacy groups   Organizations created to seek benefits on behalf of groups of persons who are in some way incapacitated or otherwise unable to represent their own interests.

Affirm   The action of an appeals court to uphold the decision of a lower court.

Affirmative action   Steps taken by colleges, universities, and private employers to remedy the effects of past discrimination.

Agenda building   The process through which problems become matters of public concern and government action.

Agents of socialization   Those factors that contribute to political socialization by shaping formal and informal learning.

Air war   Campaign activities that involve the media, including television, radio, and the Internet.

American Bar Association (ABA)   An interest group representing the concerns of lawyers.

American Civil Liberties Union (ACLU)   A group organized to protect the rights of individuals as outlined in the U.S. Constitution.

American Federation of Labor-Congress of Industrial Organization (AFL-CIO)   A labor union federation.

American Indian Movement (AIM)   A group representing the views of Native Americans.

American Medical Association (AMA)   An interest group representing the concerns of physicians.

Americans with Disabilities Act (ADA)   A federal law designed to end discrimination against persons with disabilities and eliminate barriers to their full participation in American society.

***Amicus curiae* or friend of the court brief**   Written legal argument presented by parties not directly involved in the case, including interest groups and units of government.

Anti-clericalism   A movement that opposes the institutional power of religion, and the involvement of the church in all aspects of public and political life.

Antifederalists   Americans opposed to the ratification of the new Constitution because they thought it gave too much power to the national government.

Appeal   The taking of a case from a lower court to a higher court by the losing party in a lower-court decision.

Apportionment   The allocation of legislative seats among the states.

Appropriation bill   A legislative authorization to spend money for a particular purpose.

Appropriations process   The procedure through which Congress legislatively allocates money for a particular purpose.

Articles of impeachment   A document listing the impeachable offenses that the House believes the president committed.

At-large election   A method for choosing public officials in which the citizens of an entire political subdivision, such as a state, vote to select officeholders.

Attack journalism   An approach to news reporting in which journalists take an adversarial attitude toward candidates and elected officials.

Authorization process   The procedure through which Congress legislatively establishes a program, defines its general purpose, devises procedures for its operation, specifies an agency to implement the program, and indicates an approximate level of funding for the program but does not actually provide money.

Baby boom generation   The exceptionally large number of Americans born during the late 1940s, 1950s, and early 1960s.

Balance of power   A system of political alignments in which peace and security may be maintained through an equilibrium of forces between rival groups of nations.

Balance the ticket   An attempt to select a vice-presidential candidate who will appeal to different groups of voters than the presidential nominee.

Balanced budget   Budget receipts equal budget expenditures.

Base voters   Rock-solid Republicans or hardcore Democrats, firmly committed to voting for their party's nominee.

Battleground states Swing states in which the relative strength of the two major-party presidential candidates is close enough so that either candidate could conceivably carry the state.

Biased question A survey question that produces results tilted to one side or another.

Biased sample A sample that tends to produce results that do not reflect the true characteristics of the universe because it is unrepresentative of the universe.

Bicameral legislature A two-house legislature.

Bicameralism The division of the legislative branch of government into two chambers.

Bill A proposed law.

Bill of attainder A law declaring a person or a group of persons guilty of a crime and providing for punishment without benefit of a judicial proceeding.

Bill of rights A constitutional document guaranteeing individual rights and liberties.

Bill of Rights The first ten amendments to the U.S. Constitution.

Bipartisan Campaign Reform Act (BCRA) A campaign finance reform law designed to limit the political influence of "big money" campaign contributors.

Bipartisanship The close cooperation and general agreement between the two major political parties.

Blanket primary A primary election system that allows voters to select candidates without regard for party affiliation.

Block grant program A federal grant program that provides money for a program in a broad, general policy area, such as childcare or job training.

Blue states States that vote Democratic, symbolized by the color blue on the electoral college map.

Brady Act A federal gun control law that requires a background check on an unlicensed purchaser of a firearm in order to determine whether the individual can legally own a weapon.

Broadcast media Television, radio, and the Internet.

Budget deficit The amount by which annual budget expenditures exceed annual budget receipts.

Budget surplus The sum by which annual budget receipts exceed annual budget expenditures.

Bundling A procedure in which an interest group gathers checks from individual supporters made out to the campaigns of targeted candidates.

Cabinet departments Major administrative units of the federal government that have responsibility for the conduct of a wide range of government operations.

Capital punishment The death penalty.

Capitalism An economic system characterized by individual and corporate ownership of the means of production and a market economy based on the supply and demand of goods and services.

Captured agencies Agencies that work to benefit the economic interests they regulate rather than serving the public interest.

Categorical grant program A federal grant program that provides funds to state and local governments for a fairly narrow, specific purpose, such as removing asbestos from school buildings or acquiring land for outdoor recreation.

Caucus method of delegate selection A procedure for choosing national party convention delegates that involves party voters participating in a series of precinct and district or county political meetings.

Cause groups Organizations whose members care intensely about a single issue or small group of related issues.

Central Intelligence Agency (CIA) The federal agency that gathers and evaluates foreign intelligence information in the interest of national security.

***Certiorari* or cert** The technical term for the Supreme Court's decision to hear arguments and make a ruling in a case.

Chamber of Commerce A business federation representing the interests of businesses of all sizes, sectors, and regions.

Checks and balances The overlapping of the powers of the branches of government designed to ensure that public officials limit the authority of one another.

Chief executive The head of the executive branch of government.

Chief of state The formal head of a national state as distinguished from the head of the government.

Citizen groups Organizations created to support government policies that they believe will benefit the public at large.

Civil case A legal dispute concerning a private conflict between two parties—individuals, corporations, or government agencies.

Civil liberties The protection of the individual from the unrestricted power of government.

Civil rights The protection of the individual from arbitrary or discriminatory acts by government or by individuals based on that person's group status, such as race and gender.

Civil union A legal partnership between two men or two women that gives the couple all the benefits, protections, and responsibilities under law as are granted to spouses in a traditional marriage.

Civilian supremacy of the armed forces The concept that the armed forces should be under the direct control of civilian authorities.

Class action lawsuits Lawsuits brought by one or more people on behalf of themselves and others who are similarly situated.

Closed primary An election system that limits primary election participation to registered party members.

Closed rule A rule that prohibits floor consideration of amendments on the House floor.

Cloture The procedure for ending a filibuster.

Club for Growth A cause group that favors a low-tax and limited government agenda.

Coattail effect   A political phenomenon in which a strong candidate for one office gives a boost to fellow party members on the same ballot seeking other offices.

Cold War   The period of international tension between the United States and the Soviet Union lasting from the late 1940s through the late 1980s.

Collective bargaining   The negotiation between an employer and a union representing employees over the terms and conditions of employment.

Commerce Clause   The constitutional provision giving Congress authority to "regulate commerce . . . among the several states."

Common Cause   A group organized to work for campaign finance reform and other good-government causes.

Compulsory voting   The legal requirement that citizens participate in national elections.

Concurrent powers   Those powers of government that are jointly exercised by the national government and state governments.

Concurring opinion   A judicial statement that agrees with the Court's ruling but disagrees with the reasoning of the majority opinion.

Confederation   A league of nearly independent states, similar to the United Nations today.

Conferees   Members of a conference committee.

Conference   A closed meeting attended only by the members of the Court.

Conference committee   A special congressional committee created to negotiate differences on similar pieces of legislation passed by the House and Senate.

Conference report   A revised bill produced by a conference committee.

Conservatism   The political philosophy that government power undermines the development of the individual and diminishes society as a whole.

Constituency   The district from which an officeholder is elected.

Constituency service   The action of members of Congress and their staffs attending to the individual, particular needs of constituents.

Constituents   The people an officeholder represents.

Constitution   The fundamental law by which a state or nation is organized and governed, and to which ordinary legislation must conform.

Constitutional amendment   A formal, written change or addition to the nation's governing document.

Constitutional law   Law that involves the interpretation and application of the Constitution.

Constitutional monarchy   A country in which the powers of the ruler are limited to those granted under the constitution and the laws of the nation.

Consumer price index (CPI)   A measure of inflation that is based on the changing cost of goods and services.

Containment   The American policy of keeping the Soviet Union from expanding its sphere of control.

Conventional forces   Non-nuclear forces.

Convergence theory   The view that communism and capitalism were evolving in similar ways, or converging.

Corporation for Public Broadcasting   A government agency chartered and funded by the U.S. government with the goal of promoting public broadcasting.

Cost-benefit analysis   An evaluation of a proposed policy or regulation based on a comparison of its expected benefits and anticipated costs.

Cost-of-Living Adjustment (COLA)   A mechanism designed to regularly increase the size of Social Security benefits to compensate for the effects of inflation.

Criminal case   A legal dispute dealing with an alleged violation of a penal law.

***De facto* segregation**   Racial separation resulting from factors other than law, such as housing patterns.

***De jure* segregation**   Racial separation required by law.

Defense of Marriage Act   The federal law stipulating that each state may choose either to recognize or not recognize same-sex marriages performed in other states.

Defense policy   Public policy that concerns the Armed Forces of the United States.

Delegated or enumerated powers   The powers explicitly granted to the national government by the Constitution.

Democracy   A system of government in which ultimate political authority is vested in the people.

Democratic peace   The concept that democracies do not wage war against other democracies.

Depression   A severe and prolonged economic slump characterized by decreased business activity and high unemployment.

Détente   A period of improved communications and visible efforts to relieve tensions between the two superpowers.

Deterrence   The ability of a nation to prevent an attack against itself or its allies by threat of massive retaliation.

Developing countries   Nations with relatively low levels of per capita income.

Diplomacy   The process by which nations carry on political relations with each other.

Diplomatic relations   A system of official contacts between two nations in which the countries exchange ambassadors and other diplomatic personnel and operate embassies in each other's country.

Direct democracy   A political system in which the citizens vote directly on matters of public concern.

Discharge petition   A procedure whereby a majority of the members of the House of Representatives can force a committee to report a bill to the floor of the House.

Discretionary spending   Budgetary expenditures that are not mandated by law or contract, including annual funding for education, the Coast Guard, space exploration, highway construction, defense, foreign aid, and the Federal Bureau of Investigation (FBI).

Disfranchisement The denial of voting rights.

Dissenting opinion A judicial statement that disagrees with the decision of the court's majority.

District election A method for choosing public officials that divides a political subdivision, such as a state, into geographic areas called districts and each district elects one official.

Divided government The phenomenon of one political party controlling the legislative branch of government while the other holds the executive branch.

Doctrine of natural rights The belief that individual rights transcend the power of government.

Domestic partnership A legal status similar to civil unions in that it confers rights similar to marriage.

Don't ask, don't tell policy The official policy for dealing with gay men and lesbians in the U.S. armed forces. The military would not ask new recruits about their sexual orientation and would stop conducting investigations aimed at identifying and discharging homosexuals, but it would discharge service members who revealed their sexual orientation.

Double jeopardy A procedural defense that forbids a defendant from being tried twice for the same crime using the same set of facts.

Due Process Clause The constitutional provision that declares that no state shall "deprive any person of life, liberty, or property, without due process of law."

Due process of law The constitutional principle holding that government must follow fair and regular procedures in actions that could lead to an individual's suffering loss of life, liberty, or property.

Earmarks Legislative provisions that direct that funds be spent for particular purposes.

Earned Income Tax Credit (EITC) A federal program designed to give cash assistance to low-income working families by refunding some or all of the taxes they pay and, if their wages are low, giving them an additional refund.

Election campaign An attempt to get information to voters that will persuade them to elect a candidate or not elect an opponent.

Electoral College The system established in the Constitution for indirect election of the president and vice president.

Electoral mandate The expression of popular support for a particular policy demonstrated through the electoral process.

Electors Individuals selected in each state to officially cast that state's electoral votes.

Emily's List Emily's list is a PAC, the goal of which is the election of pro-choice Democratic women to office.

Empirical analysis A method of study that relies on experience and scientific observation.

Employment Non-Discrimination Act (ENDA) A proposed federal law that would protect Americans from employment discrimination on the basis of sexual orientation.

Entitlement program A government program providing benefits to all persons qualified to receive them under law.

Environmental Protection Agency (EPA) The federal agency responsible for enforcing the nation's environmental laws.

Equal Employment Opportunity Commission (EEOC) An agency that investigates and rules on charges of employment discrimination.

Equal Protection Clause A provision of the Fourteenth Amendment of the U.S. Constitution that declares that "No State shall . . . deny to any person within its jurisdiction the equal protection of the laws."

Equal Rights Amendment (ERA) A proposed amendment guaranteeing equality before the law, regardless of sex.

Equal-time rule An FCC regulation requiring broadcasters to provide an equivalent opportunity to opposing political candidates competing for the same office.

Estate tax A tax levied on the value of an inheritance.

Ex post facto law A retroactive criminal statute, which operates to the disadvantage of accused persons.

Excise taxes Taxes levied on the manufacture, transportation, sale, or consumption of a particular item or set of related items.

Exclusionary rule The judicial doctrine stating that when the police violate an individual's constitutional rights, the evidence obtained as a result of police misconduct or error cannot be used against the defendant.

Executive agreement An international understanding between the president and foreign nations that does not require Senate ratification.

Executive Office of the President The group of White House offices and agencies that develop and implement the policies and programs of the president.

Executive order A directive issued by the president to an administrative agency or executive department.

Executive power The power to enforce laws.

Exit polls Surveys based on random samples of voters leaving polling places.

External political efficacy The assessment of an individual of the responsiveness of government to his or her concerns.

Externalities Costs or benefits not taken into account by private decision-makers.

Extradition The return from one state to another of a person accused of a crime.

Factions Special interests who seek their own good at the expense of the common good.

Fairness Doctrine An FCC regulation requiring broadcasters to present controversial issues of public importance and to present them in an honest, equal, and balanced manner.

Faith-based initiative A program designed to make federal grant money available to religiously based charitable groups on the same basis as other social service providers.

Federal Communications Commission (FCC)   An agency that regulates interstate and international radio, television, telephone, telegraph, and satellite communications, as well as grants licenses to radio and television stations.

Federal Deposit Insurance Corporation (FDIC)   A federal agency established to insure depositors' accounts in banks and thrift institutions.

Federal Election Commission (FEC)   The agency that enforces federal campaign finance laws.

Federal grant program   A program through which the national government gives money to state and local governments to spend in accordance with set standards and conditions.

Federal mandate   A legal requirement placed on a state or local government by the national government requiring certain policy actions.

Federal Open Market Committee (FOMC)   A committee of the Federal Reserve that meets eight times a year to review the economy and adjust monetary policy to achieving the net goals.

Federal preemption of state authority   An act of Congress adopting regulatory policies that overrule state policies in a particular regulatory area.

Federal Reserve Board (Fed)   An independent regulatory commission that makes monetary policy.

Federal system   *See* Federation or federal system.

Federal Trade Commission (FTC)   An agency that regulates business competition, including enforcement of laws against monopolies and the protection of consumers from deceptive trade practices.

Federalism   The distribution of power in an organization between a central autority and the constituent units.

Federalist Papers   A series of essays written by James Madison, Alexander Hamilton, and John Jay advocating the ratification of the Constitution.

Federalists   Americans who supported the ratification of the Constitution.

Federation or **federal system**   A political system that divides power between a central government, with authority over the whole nation, and a series of state governments.

Feedback   The impact of the results of policy evaluation on the policy process.

Filibuster   An attempt to defeat a measure through prolonged debate.

Fire-alarm oversight   An indirect system of bureaucratic oversight that enables individual citizens and organized interest groups to examine administrative decisions, charge agencies with violating legislative goals, and seek remedies from agencies, courts, and the Congress.

First strike   The initial offensive move of a general nuclear war, aimed at knocking out the other side's ability to retaliate.

First-strike capability   The capacity of a nation to launch an initial nuclear assault sufficient to cripple an adversary's ability to retaliate.

Fiscal policy   The use of government spending and taxation for the purpose of achieving economic goals.

Fiscal year   Budget year.

Flat tax   An income tax that assesses the same percentage tax rate on all income levels above a personal exemption while allowing few, if any, deductions.

Floor   The full House or full Senate taking official action.

Food Stamp Program   A federal program that provides vouchers to low-income families and individuals that can be used to purchase food from grocery stores.

Foreign policy   Public policy that concerns the relationship of the United States to the international political environment.

Formula grant program   A grant program that awards funding on the basis of a formula established by Congress.

Framing   The process by which a communication source, such as a news organization, defines and constructs a political issue or public controversy.

Franking privilege   Free postage provided to members of Congress.

Free-rider barrier   The concept that individuals will have little incentive to join a group and contribute resources to it if the group's benefits go to members and nonmembers alike.

Friendly Incumbent Rule   A policy whereby an interest group will back any incumbent who is generally supportive of the group's policy preferences, without regard for the party or policy views of the challenger.

Frostbelt   The northeastern and midwestern regions of the United States.

Full Faith and Credit Clause   The constitutional provision requiring that states recognize the official acts of other states, such as marriages, divorces, adoptions, court orders, and other legal decisions.

Fundamental right   A constitutional right that is so important that government cannot restrict it unless it can demonstrate a compelling or overriding public interest for so doing.

Gender gap   Differences in party identification and political attitudes between men and women.

General election   An election to fill state and national offices held in November of even-numbered years.

Gerrymandering   The drawing of legislative district lines for political advantage.

Global economy   The integration of national economies into a world economic system in which companies compete worldwide for suppliers and markets.

Global warming   The gradual warming of the Earth's atmosphere reportedly caused by the burning of fossil fuels and industrial pollutants.

Global Warming Treaty   An international agreement to reduce the worldwide emissions of carbon dioxide and other greenhouse gases.

Governing party   The political party or party coalition holding the reins of government in a democracy.

Government   The institution with authority to set policy for society.

Grand Old Party (GOP)   Nickname of the Republican Party.

Grandfather clause   A provision that exempted those persons whose grandfathers had been eligible to vote at some earlier date from tests of understanding, literacy tests, and other difficult-to-achieve voter qualification requirements.

Great Society   The legislative program put forward by President Lyndon Johnson.

Gross domestic product (GDP)   The total value of goods and services produced by a nation's economy in a year, excluding transactions with foreign countries.

Ground war   Campaign activities featuring direct contact between campaign workers and citizens, such as door-to-door canvassing and personal telephone contacts.

***Habeas corpus,* writ of**   A court order requiring that government authorities either release a person held in custody or demonstrate that the person is detained in accordance with law.

Hard money   Campaign funds which are subject to federal contribution and expenditure limitations.

Hatch Act   A measure designed to restrict the political activities of federal employees to voting and the private expression of views.

Hate-crimes law   A legislative measure that increases penalties for persons convicted of criminal offenses motivated by prejudice based on race, religion, national origin, gender, or sexual orientation.

Honeymoon effect   The tendency of a president to enjoy a high level of public support during the early months of an administration.

House majority leader   The second-ranking figure in the majority party in the House.

House Rules Committee   A standing committee that determines the rules under which a specific bill can be debated, amended, and considered on the House floor.

Human Rights Campaign (HRC)   An organization formed to promote gay and lesbian rights.

Impeach   The act of formally accusing an official of the executive or judicial branches of an impeachable offense.

Impeachment   A process in which an executive or judicial official is formally accused of an offense that could warrant removal from office.

Implied powers   Those powers of Congress not explicitly mentioned in the Constitution, but derived by implication from the delegated powers.

In forma pauperis   The process whereby an indigent litigant can file an appeal of a case to the U.S. Supreme Court without paying the usual fees.

Income redistribution   The government taking items of value, especially money, from some groups of people

and then giving items of value, either in cash or services, to other groups of people.

Incumbent   Current officeholder.

Independent executive agencies   Executive branch agencies that are not part of any of the 15 cabinet-level departments.

Independent expenditures   Money spent in support of a candidate but not coordinated with the candidate's campaign.

Independent regulatory commission   An agency outside the major executive departments that is charged with the regulation of important aspects of the economy.

Inflation   A decline in the purchasing power of the currency.

Inherent powers   Those powers vested in the national government, particularly in the area of foreign and defense policy, which do not depend on any specific grant of authority by the Constitution, but rather exist because the United States is a sovereign nation.

Initiative process   A procedure whereby citizens can prepare the adoption of a policy measure by gathering a prerequisite number of signatures. Voters must then approve the measure before it can take effect.

Injunction   A court order.

Inner cabinet   The secretary of state, secretary of defense, secretary of the treasury, and the attorney general.

Interest   Money paid for the use of money.

Interest group   An organization of people who join together voluntarily on the basis of some interest they share for the purpose of influencing policy.

Internal political efficacy   The assessment by an individual of his or her personal ability to influence the policymaking process.

International Monetary Fund (IMF)   The international organization created to promote economic stability worldwide.

Interstate Commerce Clause   The constitutional provision giving Congress authority to "regulate commerce … among the several states."

Isolationism   The view that the United States should stay out of the affairs of other nations.

Issue network   A group of political actors that is actively involved with policymaking in a particular issue area.

Item veto   The power of an executive to veto sections or items of a tax or appropriation measure while signing the remainder of the bill into law.

Jim Crow laws   Legal provisions requiring the social segregation of African Americans in separate and generally unequal facilities.

Joint Chiefs of Staff   A military advisory body that is composed of the chiefs of staff of the U.S. Army and Air Force, the chief of naval operations, and sometimes the commandant of the Marine Corps.

Joint committee   A committee that includes members from both houses of Congress.

Judicial activism   The charge that judges are going beyond their authority by making the law and not just interpreting it.

Judicial power   The power to interpret laws.

Judicial restraint   The concept that judges should defer to the policymaking judgment of the legislative and executive branches of government unless their actions clearly violate the law or the Constitution.

Judicial review   The power of courts to declare unconstitutional the actions of the other branches and units of government.

Jurisdiction   The authority of a court to hear a case.

Killer amendment   An amendment designed to make a measure so unattractive that it will lack enough support to pass.

Laissez-faire   The economic philosophy that government should not interfere with the free-market forces that drive a healthy economy.

Lame duck   An official whose influence is diminished because the official either cannot or will not seek reelection.

Latent opinion   What public opinion would be at election time if a political opponent made a public official's position on the issue the target of a campaign attack.

League of United Latin American Citizens (LULAC)   A Latino interest group.

Left wing   Liberal.

Legal brief   A written legal argument.

Legal writs   Written orders issued by a court directing the performance of an act or prohibiting some act.

Legislative markup   The process in which legislators go over a measure line-by-line, revising, amending, or rewriting it.

Legislative power   The power to make laws.

Libel   False written statements that lower a person's reputation or expose a person to hatred, contempt, or ridicule.

Liberalism   The political philosophy that favors the use of government power to foster the development of the individual and promote the welfare of society.

Limited government   The constitutional principle that government does not have unrestricted authority over individuals.

Literacy test   A legal requirement that citizens demonstrate an ability to read and write before they could register to vote.

Lobbying   The communication of information by a representative of an interest group to a government official for the purpose of influencing a policy decision.

Logrolling   An arrangement in which two or more members of Congress agree in advance to support each other's favored legislation.

Loose construction   A doctrine of constitutional interpretation holding that the document should be interpreted broadly.

Louisiana Purchase   The acquisition from France of a vast expanse of land stretching from New Orleans north to the Dakotas.

Majority-minority district   Legislative district whose population is more than 50 percent African American and Latino.

Majority opinion   The official written statement of the Supreme Court that explains and justifies its ruling and serves as a guideline for lower courts when similar legal issues arise in the future.

Majority whip   The majority leader's first assistant.

Mandamus, writ of   A court order directing a public official to perform a specific act or duty.

Mandatory spending   Budgetary expenditures that are mandated by law, including entitlements and contractual commitments made in previous years.

Margin of error or **sample error**   A statistical term that refers to the accuracy of a survey.

Marshall Plan   The American program that provided billions of dollars to the countries of Western Europe to rebuild their economies after World War II.

Massive retaliation   The concept that the United States will strike back against an aggressor with overwhelming force.

Matching funds requirement   The legislative provision that the national government will provide grant money for a particular activity only on the condition that the state or local government involved supplies a certain percentage of the total money required for the project or program.

Means-tested program   A government program that provides benefits to recipients based on their financial need.

Medicaid   A federal program designed to provide health insurance coverage to low-income persons, people with disabilities, and elderly people who are impoverished.

Medicare   A federally funded health insurance program for the elderly.

Mid-cycle redistricting   The practice of redrawing legislative districts outside the regular redistricting cycle in order to gain political advantage.

Military preemption   The defense policy that declares that the United States will attack nations or groups that represent a potential threat to the security of the United States.

Minimum wage   The lowest hourly wage that an employer can legally pay covered workers.

Minority business set-aside   A legal requirement that firms receiving government grants or contracts allocate a certain percentage of their purchases of supplies and services to businesses owned or controlled by members of minority groups.

Minority leader   The head of the minority party in the House or Senate.

Minority-vote dilution   The drawing of election district lines so as to thinly spread minority voters among several districts, thus reducing their electoral influence in any one district.

Minority-vote packing   The drawing of electoral district lines so as to cluster minority voters into one district or a small number of districts, thus reducing their overall electoral influence.

Minority whip   The minority leader's first assistant in the House or Senate.

Monetary policy   The control of the money supply for the purpose of achieving economic goals.

Monroe Doctrine   A declaration of American foreign policy opposing any European intervention in the Western Hemisphere and affirming the American intention to refrain from interfering in European affairs.

Mothers Against Drunk Driving (MADD)   An interest group that supports the reform of laws dealing with drunk driving.

Moveon.org   An advocacy group that raises money for Democratic candidates.

Multiparty system   The division of voter loyalties among three or more major political parties.

Multiple referral of legislation   The practice of allowing more than one committee to consider legislation.

Mutual assured destruction (MAD)   The belief that the United States and the Soviet Union would be deterred from launching a nuclear assault against each other for fear of being destroyed in a general nuclear war.

NARAL Pro-Choice America   An organization that favors abortion rights.

Nation-state   A political community occupying a definite territory and having an organized government.

National Aeronautics and Space Administration (NASA)   The federal agency in charge of the space program.

National Association for the Advancement of Colored People (NAACP)   An interest group organized to represent the concerns of African Americans.

National debt   The accumulated indebtedness of the federal government.

National Endowment for the Arts (NEA)   A federal agency created to nurture cultural expression and promote appreciation of the arts.

National Organization for Women (NOW)   A group organized to promote women's rights.

National Public Radio (NPR)   A nonprofit membership organization of radio stations.

National Railroad Passenger Service Corporation (AMTRAK)   A federal agency that operates intercity passenger railway traffic.

National Rifle Association (NRA)   An interest group organized to defend the rights of gun owners and defeat efforts at gun control.

National Right to Life Committee   An organization opposed to abortion.

National Science Foundation (NSF)   A federal agency established to encourage scientific advances and improvements in science education.

National Security Council (NSC)   An agency in the Executive Office of the President that advises the chief executive on matters involving national security.

National Supremacy Clause   The constitutional provision that declares that the Constitution and laws of the United States take precedence over the constitutions and laws of the states.

National Voter Registration Act (NVRA)   A federal law designed to make it easier for citizens to register to vote by requiring states to allow mail registration and provide an opportunity for people to register when applying for or renewing driver's licenses or when visiting federal, state, or local agencies, such as welfare offices.

Natural monopoly   A monopoly bestowed by nature on a geographical area, or one that, because of the nature of an enterprise, would make competition wasteful.

Necessary and Proper Clause or **Elastic Clause**   The Constitutional provision found in Article I, Section 8 that declares that "[Congress shall have the power] to make all laws which shall be necessary and proper for carrying into execution the foregoing powers, and all other powers vested by this Constitution in the government of the United States, or in any department or office thereof." It is the basis for much of the legislation passed by Congress because it gives Congress the means to exercise its delegated authority.

New Deal   A legislative package of reform measures proposed by President Franklin Roosevelt for dealing with the Great Depression.

New media   A term used to refer to alternative media sources, such as the Internet, cable television, and satellite radio.

Nixon Doctrine   The corollary to the policy of containment enunciated by President Richard Nixon providing that, although the United States would help small nations threatened by communist aggression with economic and military aid, those countries must play a major role in their own defense.

Non-germane amendments   Amendments that are unrelated to the subject matter of the original measure.

Nongovernmental organizations (NGOs)   International organizations committed to the promotion of a particular set of issues.

Normative analysis   A method of study that is based on certain values.

North American Free Trade Agreement (NAFTA)   An international accord among the United States, Mexico, and Canada to lower trade barriers among the three nations.

North Atlantic Treaty Organization (NATO)   A regional military alliance consisting of the United States, Canada, and most of the European democracies.

Nuclear Non-Proliferation Treaty   An international agreement designed to prevent the spread of nuclear weapons.

Objective journalism   A style of news reporting that focuses on facts rather than opinion, and presents all sides of controversial issues.

Office of Management and Budget (OMB) An agency that assists the president in preparing the budget.

Omnibus bills Complex, highly detailed legislative proposals covering one or more subjects or programs.

One person, one vote The judicial ruling that the Equal Protection Clause of the Fourteenth Amendment to the U.S. Constitution requires that legislative districts be apportioned on the basis of population.

Open primary An election system that allows voters to vote in the party primary of their choice without regard to their party affiliation.

Open rule A rule that opens a measure to amendment on the House floor without restriction.

Opposition party The political party out of power in a democracy.

Original jurisdiction The set of cases a court may hear as a trial court.

Pardon An executive action that frees an accused or convicted person from all penalties for an offense.

Parental choice An educational reform aimed at improving the quality of schools by allowing parents to select the school their children will attend.

Parliament The British legislature.

Parliamentary system A system of government in which political power is concentrated in a legislative body and a cabinet headed by a prime minister.

Party caucus All of the party members of the House or Senate meeting as a group.

Party era A period of time characterized by a degree of uniformity in the nature of political party competition.

Party faction An identifiable subgroup within a political party.

Party-line votes Votes in Congress in which a majority of the members of each party in a chamber vote on opposite sides of an issue.

Party realignment A change in the underlying party loyalties of voters that ends one party era and begins another.

Party platform A statement of party principles and issue positions.

PAYGO A pay-as-you-go budget rule that requires that any tax cut or spending increase be offset by tax increases or spending cuts elsewhere in the budget.

Peace Corps An agency that administers an American foreign aid program under which volunteers travel to developing nations to teach skills and help improve living standards.

Per capita Per person.

Per curium opinion Unsigned written opinion of a court.

Plurality election system A method for choosing public officials that awards office to the candidate with the most votes; favors a two-party system.

Pocket veto The action of a president allowing a measure to die without signature after Congress has adjourned.

Policy adoption The official decision of a government body to accept a particular policy and put it into effect.

Policy evaluation The assessment of policy.

Policy formulation The development of strategies for dealing with the problems on the official policy agenda.

Policy implementation The stage of the policy process in which policies are carried out.

Policymaking environment The complex of factors outside of government that has an impact, either directly or indirectly, on the policymaking process.

Political action committee (PAC) An organization created to raise and distribute money in election campaigns.

Political culture The widely held, deeply rooted political values of a society.

Political campaign An attempt to get information to voters that will persuade them to elect a candidate or not elect an opponent.

Political efficacy The extent to which individuals believe they can influence the policymaking process.

Political elites Persons that exercise a major influence on the policymaking process.

Political left Liberalism.

Political legitimacy The popular acceptance of a government and its officials as rightful authorities in the exercise of power.

Political participation An activity that has the intent or effect of influencing government action.

Political party A group of individuals who join together to seek government office in order to make public policy.

Political patronage The power of an officeholder to award favors, such as government jobs, to political allies.

Political right Conservatism.

Political socialization The process whereby individuals acquire political knowledge, attitudes, and beliefs.

Politics The process that determines who shall occupy the roles of leadership in government and how the power of government shall be exercised.

Poll tax A tax levied on the right to vote.

Pork barrel spending Expenditures to fund local projects that are not critically important from a national perspective.

Postindustrial societies Nations whose economies are increasingly based on services, research, and information rather than heavy industry.

Poverty threshold The amount of money an individual or family needs to purchase basic necessities, such as food, clothing, healthcare, shelter, and transportation.

Power of the purse The control of the finances of government.

Preclearance A requirement of the Voting Rights Act that state and local governments in areas with a history of voting discrimination must submit redistricting plans to the federal Department of Justice for approval *before* they can go into effect.

President's cabinet   An advisory group created by the president that includes the department heads and other officials chosen by the president.

Presidential preference primary   An election in which party voters cast ballots for the presidential candidate they favor and in so doing help determine the number of national convention delegates that candidate will receive.

Presidential signing statement   A pronouncement issued by the president at the time a bill passed by Congress is signed into law.

Primary election   An election held to determine a party's nominees for the general election ballot.

Print media   Newspapers and magazines.

Prior restraint   Government action to prevent the publication or broadcast of objectionable material.

Privatization   A process that involves the government contracting with private business to implement government programs.

Privileges and Immunities Clause   The constitutional provision prohibiting state governments from discriminating against the citizens of other states.

Probable cause   The reasonable suspicion based on evidence that a particular search will uncover contraband.

Progressive tax   A levy that taxes people earning higher incomes at a higher rate than it does individuals making less money.

Project grant program   A grant program that requires state and local governments to compete for available federal money.

Proportional representation (PR)   An election system that awards legislative seats to each party approximately equal to its popular voting strength.

Proportional tax   A levy that taxes all persons at the same percentage rate, regardless of income.

Prospective voting   The concept that voters evaluate the incumbent officeholder and the incumbent's party based on their expectations of future developments.

Public Broadcasting Service (PBS)   A nonprofit private corporation that is jointly owned by hundreds of member television stations throughout the United States.

Public policy   The response or lack of response of government decision-makers to an issue.

Public policy approach   A comprehensive method for studying the process through which issues come to the attention of government decision-makers and through which policies are formulated, adopted, implemented, and evaluated.

Public utility   A privately owned business that performs an essential service for the community.

Quasi-governmental company   A private, profit-seeking corporation created by Congress to serve a public purpose.

Racially restrictive covenants   Private deed restrictions that prohibited property owners from selling or leasing property to African Americans or other minorities.

Rally effect   The tendency of the general public to express support for the incumbent president during a time of international threat.

Random sample   A sample in which each member of a universe has an equal likelihood of being included.

Ranking member   The leader of the minority party on a committee or subcommittee.

Reagan Doctrine   A corollary to the policy of containment enunciated by President Reagan calling for the United States to offer military aid to groups attempting to overthrow communist governments anywhere in the world.

Realignment   A change in the underlying party loyalties of voters that ends one party era and begins another.

Reapportionment   The reallocation of legislative seats.

Recession   An economic slowdown characterized by declining economic output and rising unemployment.

Reconstruction   The process whereby the states that had seceded during the Civil War were reorganized and reestablished in the Union.

Red states   States that vote Republican, symbolized by the color red on the Electoral College map.

Redistricting   The process through which the boundaries of legislative districts are redrawn to reflect population movement.

Regressive tax   A levy whose burden falls more heavily on lower-income groups than on wealthy taxpayers.

Regulatory negotiation   A structured process by which representatives of the interests that would be substantially affected by a rule, including employees of the regulatory agency, negotiate agreement on the terms of the rule.

Religious left   Individuals who hold liberal views because of their religious beliefs.

Religious right   Individuals who hold conservative views because of their religious beliefs.

Remand   The decision of an appeals court to return a case to a lower court for reconsideration in light of an appeals-court decision.

Representative democracy or **republic**   A political system in which citizens elect representatives to make policy decisions on their behalf.

Reprieve   An executive action that delays punishment for a crime.

Republic   A representative democracy in which citizens elect representatives to make policy decisions on their behalf.

Reserved or **residual powers**   The powers of government left to the states.

Resolution   A legislative statement of opinion on a certain matter.

Responsible party   A political party that clearly spells out issue positions in its platform and, when in office, faithfully carries them out.

Retrospective voting   The concept that voters choose candidates based on their perception of an incumbent candidate's past performance in office or the performance of the incumbent party.

Rider   A provision, unlikely to become law on its own merits, that is attached to an important measure so that it will ride through the legislative process.

Right-to-work laws   Statutes that prohibit union membership as a condition of employment.

Right wing   Conservative.

Rogue states   Nations that threaten world peace by sponsoring international terrorism and promoting the spread of weapons of mass destruction.

Rose Garden strategy   A campaign approach in which an incumbent president attempts to appear presidential rather than political.

Rule   A legally binding regulation.

Rule of four   A decision process used by the Supreme Court to determine which cases to consider on appeal, holding that the Court will hear a case if four of the nine justices agree to the review.

Rule of law   The constitutional principle that holds that the discretion of public officials in dealing with individuals is limited by the law.

Rulemaking   The regulatory process used by government agencies to enact legally binding regulations.

Runoff   An election between the two candidates receiving the most votes when no candidate got a majority in an initial election.

Sales tax   A levy assessed on the retail sale of taxable items.

Sample   A subset of a universe.

School Lunch Program   A federal program that provides free or reduced-cost lunches to children from poor families.

Second strike   A nuclear attack in response to an adversary's first strike.

Second-strike capability   The capacity of a nation to absorb an initial nuclear attack and retain sufficient nuclear firepower to inflict unacceptable damage on its adversary.

Securities and Exchange Commission (SEC)   An agency that regulates the sale of stocks and bonds as well as investment and holding companies.

Selective incorporation of the Bill of Rights   The process through which the U.S. Supreme Court interpreted the Due Process Clause of the Fourteenth Amendment of the U.S. Constitution to apply most of the provisions of the national Bill of Rights to the states.

Senate majority leader   The head of the majority party in the Senate.

Senate president *pro tempore*   The official presiding officer in the Senate in the vice president's absence.

Senatorial courtesy   The custom that senators from the president's party have a veto on judicial appointments from their states.

Seniority   Length of service.

Separate but equal   The judicial doctrine holding that separate facilities for whites and African Americans sat-isfy the equal protection requirement of the Fourteenth Amendment.

Separation of powers   The division of political power among executive, legislative, and judicial branches of government.

Shield law   A statute that protects journalists from being forced to disclose confidential information in a legal proceeding.

Sierra Club   An environmental organization.

Signaling role   A term that refers to the accepted responsibility of the media to alert the public to important developments as they happen.

Slander   False spoken statements that lower a person's reputation or expose a person to hatred, contempt, or ridicule.

Small Business Administration (SBA)   The federal agency established to make loans to small businesses and assist them in obtaining government contracts.

Social Security   A federal pension and disability insurance program funded through a payroll tax on workers and their employers.

Social Security Administration (SSA)   The federal agency that operates the Social Security system.

Soft money   The name given to funds that are raised by political parties that are not subject to federal campaign finance regulations.

Solid South   A phrase used to refer to the usual Democratic Party sweep of the electoral votes of the southern states in presidential elections.

Sound bite   A short phrase taken from a candidate's speech by the news media for use on newscasts.

Sovereign immunity   The legal concept that individuals cannot sue the government without the government's permission.

Sovereignty   The authority of a state to exercise its legitimate powers within its boundaries, free from external interference.

Speaker of the House   The presiding officer in the House of Representatives and the leader of the majority party in that chamber.

Special or **select committee**   A committee established for a limited time only.

Split ticket ballot   Voters casting their ballots for the candidates of two or more political parties.

Split ticket voting   Voters casting their ballots for the candidates of two or more political parties.

Spoils system   The method of hiring government employees from among the friends, relatives, and supporters of elected officeholders.

Sponsor   A member who introduces a measure.

Sputnik   The world's first satellite, launched by the Soviet Union.

Standard of living   A term that refers to the goods and services affordable by and available to the residents of a nation.

Standing committee   A permanent legislative committee with authority to draft legislation in a particular policy area or areas.

States' rights   An interpretation of the Constitution that favors limiting the authority of the federal government while expanding the powers of the states.

Statutory law   Law that is written by the legislature.

Straight ticket ballot   Voters selecting the entire slate of candidates of one party only.

Straight ticket voting   Citizens casting their ballots only for the candidates of one party.

Strategic forces   Nuclear forces.

Strict construction   A doctrine of constitutional interpretation holding that the document should be interpreted narrowly.

Strict judicial scrutiny   The judicial decision rule holding that the Supreme Court will find a government policy unconstitutional unless the government can demonstrate a compelling interest justifying the action.

Subgovernment or **iron triangle**   A cozy, three-sided relationship among government agencies, interest groups, and key members of Congress in which all parties benefit.

Subpoena   A legally binding order requiring an individual to appear before a committee to testify and bring requested information.

Subsidy   A financial incentive given by government to an individual or a business interest to accomplish a public objective.

Suffrage   The right to vote.

Sunbelt   The southern and western regions of the United States.

Superdelegates   Democratic Party officials and officeholders selected to attend the national party convention on the basis of the offices they hold.

Supermajority   A voting margin that is greater than a simple majority.

Supplemental Security Income (SSI)   A federal program that provides money to low-income people who are elderly, blind, or disabled who do not qualify for Social Security benefits.

Supply-side economics   The economic theory that tax cuts, especially for business and the wealthy, will lead to savings and investment that will benefit everyone.

Surgeon general   An official in the Public Health Service who advises the president on health issues.

Survey research   The measurement of public opinion.

Suspect classifications   Distinctions among persons that must be justified on the basis of a compelling government interest that cannot be achieved in a less restrictive fashion.

Swing voters   Citizens who could vote for either party in an election.

Table   To postpone consideration of a measure during the legislative process.

Tariffs   Taxes levied on imported goods.

Tax credit   An expenditure that reduces an individual's tax liability by the amount of the credit.

Tax deduction   An expenditure that can be subtracted from a taxpayer's gross income before figuring the tax owed.

Tax exemption   The exclusion of some types of income from taxation.

Tax incidence   The point at which the actual cost of a tax falls.

Tax preference   A tax deduction or exclusion that allows individuals to pay less tax than they would otherwise.

Temporary Assistance for Needy Families (TANF)   A federal program that provides temporary financial assistance and work opportunities to needy families.

Tennessee Valley Authority (TVA)   A federal agency established to promote the development of the Tennessee River and its tributaries.

Term limitation   The movement to restrict the number of terms public officials may serve.

Test cases   Lawsuits initiated to assess the constitutionality of a legislative or executive act.

Test of understanding   A legal requirement that citizens had to accurately explain a passage in the U.S. Constitution or state constitution before they could register to vote.

Third party   A minor party in a two-party system.

Trade associations   Organizations representing the interests of firms and professionals in the same general field.

Triad   The three methods the United States employs to deliver nuclear warheads to their targets. It includes intercontinental ballistic missiles (ICBMs) stored in missile silos and ready for launch, nuclear-powered submarines roaming the world's oceans armed with sea-launched ballistic missiles (SLBMs), and heavy bombers capable of delivering a nuclear payload to targets halfway around the globe.

Trial   The formal examination of a judicial dispute in accordance with law before a single judge.

Truman Doctrine   The foreign policy put forward by President Harry Truman calling for American support for all free peoples resisting communist aggression by internal or outside forces.

Two-party system   The division of voter loyalties between two major political parties.

Two Presidencies Thesis   The concept that the president enjoys more influence over foreign policy than domestic policy.

Tyranny of the majority   The abuse of the minority by the majority.

Unanimous consent agreement   A formal understanding on procedures for conducting business in the Senate that requires the acceptance of every member of the chamber.

Unfunded mandate   A requirement imposed by Congress on state or local governments without providing federal funding to cover its cost.

Unicameral legislature   A one-house legislature.

Unitary government   A governmental system in which political authority is concentrated in a single national government.

United Nations (UN)   An international organization founded in 1945 as a diplomatic forum to resolve conflicts among the world's nations.

United States Postal Service   A government corporation responsible for mail service.

Universe   The population survey researchers wish to study.

Veto   An action by the chief executive refusing to approve a measure passed by the legislature.

Voter activation   The process of inducing particular, finely targeted portions of the electorate to participate in politics.

Voter mobilization   The process of motivating citizens to vote.

Voting age population (VAP)   The number of U.S. residents who are 18 years of age or older.

Voting eligible population (VEP)   The number of U.S. residents who are eligible to vote.

Voting Rights Act (VRA)   A federal law designed to protect the voting rights of racial and ethnic minorities.

War Powers Act   A law limiting the president's ability to commit American Armed Forces to combat abroad without consultation with Congress and congressional approval.

Warrant   An official authorization issued by a judicial officer.

Watergate   A scandal that involved the abuse of the powers of the presidency by President Richard Nixon and members of his administration that led to his resignation in 1974.

Weapons of mass destruction (WMD)   Nuclear, chemical, and biological weapons that are designed to inflict widespread military and civilian casualties.

Weblog or blog   An online personal journal or newsletter that is regularly updated.

Wedge issue   A sharply divisive political issue raised by a candidate or party in hopes of attracting a portion of an opponent's customary supporters.

Welfare programs   Government programs that provide benefits to individuals based on their economic status.

Welfare state   A government that takes responsibility for the welfare of its citizens through programs in public health, public housing, old-age pensions, unemployment compensation, and the like.

Whips   Assistant floor leaders in Congress.

Whistleblowers   Workers who report wrongdoing or mismanagement.

White primary   An electoral system used in the South to prevent the participation of African Americans in the Democratic primary.

World Health Organization (WHO)   An international organization created to control disease worldwide.

World Trade Organization (WTO)   An international organization that administers trade laws and provides a forum for settling trade disputes among nations.

YouTube   A video sharing Internet website where users can upload, view, and share video clips.

Zone of acquiescence   The range of policy options acceptable to the public on a particular issue.

>notes

Introduction

[1]Civil Rights Division, U.S. Department of Justice, "A Guide to Disability Rights Laws," September 2005, available at www.usdoj.gov.

[2]Office of Management and Budget, "Total Government Receipts in Absolute Amounts and as a Percentage of GDP: 1948–2006," *The Budget for Fiscal Year 2008, Historical Tables*, available at www.omb.gov.

[3]David Easton, "Political Science in the United States," in David Easton, John G. Gunnell, and Luigi Graziano, eds., *The Development of Political Science* (London: Routledge, 1991), p. 275.

[4]Thomas A. Birkland, *An Introduction to the Policy Process: Theories, Concepts, and Models of Public Policy Making* (Armonk, NY: M.E. Sharpe, 2001), pp. 4–5.

[5]Thomas A. Birkland, *An Introduction to the Policy Process: Theories, Concepts, and Models of Public Policy Making*, 2nd ed. (Armonk, NY: M. E. Sharpe, 2005), p. 6.

[6]Roger W. Cobb and Marc Howard Ross, "Agenda Setting and the Denial of Agenda Access: Key Concepts," in Cobb and Ross, eds., *Cultural Strategies of Agenda Denial: Avoidance, Attack, and Redefinition* (Lawrence, KS: University of Kansas Press, 1997), pp. 19–20.

[7]David A. Rochefort and Roger W. Cobb, "Problem Definition: An Emerging Perspective," in Rochefort and Cobb, eds., *The Politics of Problem Definition: Shaping the Policy Agenda* (Lawrence, KS: University of Kansas Press, 1994), pp. 1–31.

[8]Jack M. McNeil, *Employment, Earnings, and Disability*, U.S. Bureau of the Census, 2000, available at www.census.gov.

[9]Civil Rights Division, "A Guide to Disability Rights Laws."

[10]U.S. Equal Employment Opportunity Commission, Department of Justice, Civil Rights Division, *The Americans with Disabilities Act: Questions and Answers*, available at www.usdoj.gov.

[11]U.S. Equal Employment Opportunity Commission, "Charge Statistics FY 1997 through FY 2006," available at www.eeoc.gov.

[12]U.S. Equal Employment Opportunity Commission, "Selected Enforcement Guidelines and Other Policy Documents on the ADA," available at www.eeoc.gov.

[13]National Resource Center on AD/HD, "Workplace and Higher Education Issues," available at www.help4adhd.org.

[14]Christine H. Rossell, "Using Multiple Criteria to Evaluate Public Policies: The Case of School Desegregation," *American Politics Quarterly* 21 (April 1993): p. 162.

[15]Jill Smolowe, "Noble Aims, Mixed Results," *Time*, July 31, 1995, p. 55.

[16]U.S. Equal Employment Opportunity Commission, "ADA Charge Data by Impairments/Bases—Merit Factor Resolutions, 1997–2007," available at www.eeoc.gov.

[17]David C. Stapleton and Richard Burkhauser, eds., *Decline in Employment of People with Disabilities: A Policy Puzzle* (Kalamazoo, MI: W.E. Upjohn Institute, 2003).

Chapter 1

[1]U.S. Census Bureau, "Resident Population Projection by Sex and Age: 2010–2050," 2008 Statistical Abstract, available at www.census.gov.

[2]"Vietnam Gears Up for Single-Party Election," May 18, 2002, available at cnn.com.

[3]Michael Slackman, "Testing Egypt, Mubarak Rival Is Sent to Jail," *New York Times*, December 25, 2005, available at www.nytimes.com.

[4]Robert A. Dahl, *Polyarchy: Participation and Opposition* (New Haven, CT: Yale University Press, 1971), p. 3.

[5]Stockholm International Peace Research Institute, "Fifteen Major Spenders in 2006," available at www.sipri.org.

[6]U.S. Census Bureau, "Census Bureau Data Show Key Population Changes Across Nation," available at www.census.gov.

[7]U.S. Citizenship and Immigration Services (USCIS), *Fiscal Year 2004 Yearbook of Immigration Statistics*, available at http://uscis.gov/graphics.

[8]Steven A. Camerota and Karen Jensenius, "Homeward Bound: Recent Immigration Enforcement and the Decline in the Illegal Immigration Population," Center for Immigration Studies, July 2008, available at www.cis.org.

[9]Jeffrey S. Passel, "Unauthorized Migrants: Numbers and Characteristics," Pew Hispanic Center Report, June 2005, available at http://pewhispanic.org.

[10]Christopher Rudolph, *National Security and Immigration: Policy Develops in the United States and Western Europe Since 1945* (Stanford, CA: Stanford University Press, 2006), pp. 126–142.

[11]Mari-Claude Blanc-Chaléard, "Old and New Migrants in France: Italians and Algerians," in Leo Lucassen, David Feldman, and Jochen Oltmer, eds., *Paths of Integration: Migrants in Western Europe (1880–2004)* (Amsterdam: Amsterdam University Press, 2006), p. 54.

[12]Alec G. Hargreaves, *Multi-Ethnic France: Immigration, Politics, Culture, and Society* (NY: Routledge, 2007), p. 201.

[13]U.S. Census Bureau, "Population by Race, Including All Specific Combinations of Two Races, for the United States, 2000," available at www.census.gov.

[14]U.S. Census Bureau, The Population Profile of the United States: 2000, available at www.census.gov.

[15]U.S. Census Bureau, "Resident Population by Region, Race, and Hispanic Origin: 2000," 2001 Statistical Abstract of the United States, available at www.census.gov.

[16]Bureau of Economic Analysis, "Current Dollar and 'Real' Gross Domestic Product," available at www.bea.gov.

[17]Tim Weiner, "Free Trade Accord at 10: Growing Pains Are Clear," *New York Times*, December 27, 2003, available at www.nytimes.com.

[18]Gary Schneider, "Another Kind of Homeland Security," *Washington Post National Weekly Edition*, February 9–15, 2004, p. 16.

[19]Ibid.

[20]David Finkel, "The American Dream, Revisited," *Washington Post National Weekly Edition*, December 22, 2003–January 4, 2004, p. 19.

[21]Robert H. Frank, "Income Inequality and the Protestant Ethic," in Victor Nee and Richard Swedberg, eds., *Capitalism* (Stanford, CA: Stanford University Press, 2007), pp. 73–79.

[22]U.S. Census Bureau, "Income, Poverty, and Health Insurance Coverage in the United States: 2006," available at www.census.gov.

[23]U.S. Department of Health and Human Services, "2008 Annual Update of the HHS Poverty Guidelines," available at www.hhs.gov.

[24]U.S. Census Bureau, "Income, Poverty, and Health Insurance Coverage in the United States: 2006," available at www.census.gov.

[25]U.S. Census Bureau, "Income, Poverty, and Health Insurance Coverage in the United States: 2006," available at www.census.gov.

[26]Ibid.

[27]Passel, "Unauthorized Migrants: Numbers and Characteristics."

Chapter 2

[1]Gordon S. Wood, *The Creation of the American Republic 1776–1787* (Chapel Hill, NC: University of North Carolina Press, 1969), pp. 131–148.

[2]Donald S. Lutz, "The Changing View of the Founding and a New Perspective on American Political Theory," *Social Science Quarterly* 68 (December 1987): 669–686.

[3]Wood, pp. 601–14.

[4]Lutz, p. 677.

[5]Paul Finkelman, "James Madison and the Bill of Rights: A Reluctant Paternity," in Gerhard Casper, Dennis J. Hutchison, and David Strauss, eds., *The Supreme Court Review* (Chicago, IL: University of Chicago Press, 1990), pp. 309–11.

[6]Richard Labunski, *James Madison and the Struggle for the Bill of Rights* (New York: Oxford University Press, 2006), pp. 96–255.

[7]*The Federalist*, no. 51.

[8]Ibid.

[9]Robert A. Dahl, *A Preface to Democratic Theory*, expanded edition (Chicago, IL: University of Chicago Press, 2006), p. 137.

[10]Edward C. Carmines and Lawrence C. Dodd, "Bicameralism in Congress: The Changing Partnership," in Lawrence C. Dodd and Bruce I. Oppenheimer, eds., *Congress Reconsidered*, 3rd ed. (Washington, DC: Congressional Quarterly Press, 1985), pp. 414–436.

[11]Leonard Levy, *Judgments: Essays on American Constitutional History* (Chicago, IL: Quadrangle Books, 1972), p. 17.

[12]*Marbury v. Madison*, 1 Cranch 137 (1803).

[13]Richard H. Fallon, Jr., *The Dynamic Constitution: An Introduction to American Constitutional Law* (New York: Cambridge University Press, 2004), p. 193.

[14]*Plessy v. Ferguson*, 163 U.S. 537 (1896).

[15]*Brown v. Board of Education of Topeka*, 347 U.S. 483 (1954).

[16]Thomas A. Birkland, *An Introduction to the Policy Process: Theories, Concepts, and Models of Public Policy Making* (Armonk, NY: M.E. Sharpe, 2001), p. 39.

[17]Charles A. Beard, *An Economic Interpretation of the Constitution of the United States* (New York: Macmillan, 1913).

[18]James L. Sundquist, *Constitutional Reform and Effective Government*, rev. ed. (Washington, DC: Brookings Institution, 1986), pp. 5–6.

[19]Peter F. Nardulli, "The Constitution and American Politics: A Developmental Perspective," in Peter F. Nardulli, ed., *The Constitution and American Political Development* (Chicago, IL: University of Chicago Press, 1992), p. 12.

[20]Jeffrey M. Jones, "Majority Continues to Consider Iraq War a Mistake," February 6, 2008, available at www.gallup.com.

Chapter 3

[1]Kenneth Wong and Gail Sunderman, "Education Accountability as a Presidential Priority: No Child Left Behind and the Bush Presidency," *Publius: The Journal of Federalism* 37 (Summer 2007): 333–350.

[2]Public Law 107–110.

[3]Claudia Wallis and Sonja Steptoe, "How to Fix No Child Left Behind," *Time*, June 4, 2007, p. 36.

[4]Diana Jean Schemo, "Failing Schools Strain to Meet U.S. Standard," *New York Times*, October 16, 2007, available at www.nytimes.com.

[5]*McCulloch v. Maryland*, 4 Wheaton 316 (1819).

[6]*Dred Scott v. Sandford*, 19 Howard 393 (1857).

[7]*United States v. Lopez*, 514 U.S. 549 (1995).

[8]*Printz v. United States*, 521 U.S. 98 (1997).

[9]*United States v. Morrison*, 529 U.S. 598 (2000).

[10]Larry N. Gerston, *American Federalism: A Concise Introduction* (Armonk, NY: M.E. Sharpe, 2007), p. 69.

[11]Karen Adelberger, "Federalism and Its Discontents: Fiscal and Legislative Power-Sharing in Germany, 1948–1999," *Regional and Federal Studies* 11 (Summer 2000): 43–68.

[12]Jan Erk, *Explaining Federalism: State, Society and Congruence in Austria, Belgium, Canada, Germany, and Switzerland* (New York: Routledge, 2008), pp. 58–70.

[13]Frances E. Lee, "Bicameralism and Geographic Politics: Allocating Funds in the House and Senate," *Legislative Studies Quarterly* 29 (May 2004): 185–214.

[14]Frances E. Lee and Bruce I. Oppenheimer, *Sizing Up the Senate: The Unequal Consequences of Equal Representation* (Chicago: University of Chicago Press, 1999), pp. 203–220.

[15]*Characteristics of Federal Grant Programs to State and Local Governments: Grants Funded 1995* (Washington, DC: Advisory Commission on Intergovernmental Relations, 1995).

[16]David B. Walker, *The Rebirth of Federalism* (Chatham, NJ: Chatham House, 1995), p. 242.

[17]Trinity D. Tomsic, "Managing Medicaid in Tough Times," *State Legislatures*, June 2002, pp. 13–17.

[18]Paul Posner, "The Politics of Coercive Federalism in the Bush Era," *Publius: The Journal of Federalism* 37 (Summer 2007): p. 399.

[19]Gerston, *American Federalism: A Concise Introduction*, p. 20.

[20]Molly Stauffer and Carl Tubbesing, "The Mandate Monster," *State Legislatures*, May 2004, pp. 22–23.

[21]Julia Preston, "Surge in Immigration Laws Around U.S.," *New York Times*, August 6, 2007, available at www.nytimes.com.

[22]Pam Belluck, "Massachusetts Sets Health Plan for Nearly All," *New York Times*, April 5, 2006, available at www.nytimes.com.

[23]Joseph F. Zimmerman, "The Nature and Political Significance of Preemption," *PS: Political Science & Politics* (July 2005): 361.

[24]Jonathan Walters, "Save Us from the States!" *Governing*, June 2001, p. 20.

Chapter 4

[1]Lydia Saad, "Tolerance for Gay Rights at High-Water Mark," May 29, 2007, available at www.gallup.com.

[2]Edward Greenberg, "Orientations of Black and White Children to Political Activity," *Social Science Quarterly* 5 (December 1970): 561–571.

[3]David O. Sears and Nicholas A. Valentino, "Politics Matters: Political Events as Catalysts for Pre-adult Socialization," *American Political Science Review* 91 (March 1997): 45–65.

[4]M. Kent Jennings, "Political Knowledge Over Time and Across Generations," *Public Opinion Quarterly* 60 (Summer 1996): 228–252.

[5]Eric Plutzer, "Becoming a Habitual Voter: Inertia, Resources, and Growth in Young Adulthood," *American Political Science Review* 96 (March 2002): 54.

[6]Richard G. Niemi and Jane Junn, *Civic Education: What Makes Students Learn* (New Haven, CT: Yale University Press, 1998), p. 148.

[7]Cynthia Gordon, "Al Gore's Our Guy: Linguistically Constructing a Family Political Identity," *Discourse and Society* 15 (2004): 607–631.

[8]Paul Allen Beck and M. Kent Jennings, "Family Traditions, Political Periods, and the Development of Partisan Orientations," *Journal of Politics* 53 (August 1991): 742–763.

[9]Niemi and Junn, *Civic Education*, p. 148.

[10]Edward Metz and James Youniss, "A Demonstration that School-Based Required Service Does Not Deter—But Heightens—Volunteerism," PS: *Political Science & Politics* (April 2003): 281–286.

[11]Molly W. Andolina, Krista Jenkins, Cliff Zukin, and Scott Keeter, "Habits from Home, Lessons from School: Influences on Youth Civic Engagement," *Social Education* 67 (October 2003): 278–279.

[12]Edgar Lott, "Civic Education, Community Norms, and Political Indoctrination," *American Sociological Review* 28 (February 1963): 69–75.

[13]Robert Wuthnow, "Mobilizing Civic Engagement: The Changing Impact of Religious Involvement," in Theda Skocpol and Morris P. Fiorina, eds., *Civic Engagement in American Democracy* (Washington, DC: Brookings Institution Press, 1999), p. 352.

[14]Frederick C. Harris, "Something Within: Religion as a Mobilizer of African American-Political Activism," *Journal of Politics* 56 (February 1994): 42–68.

[15]Kenneth D. Wald, Dennis E. Owen, and Samuel S. Hill, Jr., "Churches as Political Communities," *American Political Science Review* 82 (June 1988): 531–548.

[16]Kenneth D. Wald, Dennis E. Owen, and Samuel S. Hill, Jr., "Political Cohesion in Churches," *Journal of Politics* 52 (February 1990): 197–215.

[17]Katharine Q. Seelye and Janet Elder, "Strong Support Is Found for Ban on Gay Marriage," *New York Times*, December 21, 2003, available at www.nytimes.com.

[18]Paul Allen Beck, Russell J. Dalton, Steven Greene, and Robert Huckfeldt, "The Social Calculus of Voting: Interpersonal, Media, and Organizational Influences on Presidential Choices," *American Political Science Review* 96 (March 2002): 57–73.

[19]Herbert P. Hyman, *Political Socialization* (Glencoe, IL: Free Press, 1959), pp. 109–115.

[20]Clyde Wilcox, "Feminism and Anti-Feminism Among Evangelical Women," *Western Political Quarterly* 42 (March 1989): 147–160.

[21]Ibid., p. 185.

[22]Shanto Iyengar and Donald R. Kinder, *News That Matters: Television and American Opinion* (Chicago: University of Chicago Press, 1987), pp. 112–113.

[23]Jon A. Krosnick and Donald R. Kinder, "Altering the Foundations of Support for the President Through Priming," *American Political Science Review* 84 (June 1990): 497–512.

[24]John R. Alford, Carolyn L. Funk, and John R. Hibbing, "Are Political Orientations Genetically Transmitted?" *American Political Science Review* 99 (May 2005): 153–167.

[25]Jeffrey M. Stonecash, *Political Polling: Strategic Information in Campaigns* (Lanham, MD: Rowman & Littlefield, 2003), pp. 141–143.

[26]Richard Morin, "Look Who's Talking," *Washington Post National Weekly Edition*, July 19–25, 1993, p. 37.

[27]Megan Thee, "Cellphones Challenge Poll Sampling," *New York Times*, December 7, 2007, available at www.nytimes.com.

[28]Herbert Asher, *Polling and the Public: What Every Citizen Should Know*, 6th ed. (Washington, DC: CQ Press, 2004), pp. 82–86.

[29]Adam J. Berinsky, "The Two Faces of Public Opinion," *American Journal of Political Science* 43 (October 1999): 1209–1230.

[30]Larry M. Bartels, "Democracy with Attitudes," in Michael B. MacKuen and George Rabinowitz, eds., *Electoral Democracy* (Ann Arbor, MI: University of Michigan Press, 2003), pp. 56–57.

[31]Frank Newport, "Six Out of 10 Americans Say Homosexual Relations Should Be Recognized as Legal," May 15, 2003, available at www.gallup.com.

[32]Asher, *Polling and the Public*, p. 61.

[33]John Zaller and Stanley Feldman, "A Simple Theory of the Survey Response: Answering Questions versus Revealing Preferences," *American Journal of Political Science* 36 (August 1992): 579–616.

[34]Richard Morin, "What Informed Public Opinion?" *Washington Post National Weekly Edition*, April 10–16, 1995, p. 36.

[35]Howard Schuman and Jean Converse, "The Effects of Black and White Interviewers on Black Response in 1968," *Public Opinion Quarterly* 35 (Spring 1971): 44–68; and Shirley Hatchett and Howard Schuman, "White Respondents and Race of Interviewer Effects," *Public Opinion Quarterly* 39 (Winter 1975): 523–528.

[36]Asher, *Polling and the Public*, p. 96.

[37]*Gallup Poll Monthly*, July 1992, pp. 8–9.

[38]W. Russell Neuman, *The Paradox of Mass Politics: Knowledge and Opinion in the American Electorate* (Cambridge, MA: Harvard University Press, 1986), ch. 1.

[39]Richard Morin, "Tuned Out, Turned Off," *Washington Post National Weekly Edition*, February 5–11, 1996, p. 6.

[40]Morin, "Tuned Out, Turned Off," p. 7.

[41]Quoted in Morin, "Tuned Out, Turned Off," p. 8.

[42]"Homosexual Relations," available at www.gallup.com.

[43]Samuel A. Stouffer, *Communism, Conformity, and Civil Liberties: A Cross Section of the Nation Speaks Its Mind* (Garden City, NY: Doubleday, 1955), pp. 28–42.

[44]James W. Prothro and C. W. Grigg, "Fundamental Principles of Democracy: Bases of Agreement and Disagreement," *Journal of Politics* 22 (Spring 1960): 276–294.

[45]Robert Chandler, *Public Opinion: Changing Attitudes on Contemporary Social and Political Issues*, A CBS News Reference Book (New York: R. R. Bowker, 1972), pp. 6–13.

[46]Clyde Z. Nunn, Harry J. Crockett, Jr., and J. Allen Williams, Jr., *Tolerance for Nonconformity: A National Survey of Americans' Changing Commitment to Civil Liberties* (San Francisco: Jossey-Bass, 1978); James A. Davis, "Communism, Conformity, Cohorts, and Categories: American Tolerance in 1954 and 1972–73," *American Journal of Sociology* 81 (November 1975): 491–513.

[47]Jeffrey J. Mondak and Mitchell S. Sanders, "Tolerance and Intolerance, 1976–1998," *American Journal of Political Science* 47 (July 2003): 492–502.

[48]Donald Philip Green and Lisa Michele Waxman, "Direct Threat and Political Tolerance," *Public Opinion Quarterly* 51 (Summer 1987): 149–165.

[49]James L. Gibson, "Enigmas of Intolerance: Fifty Years after Stouffer's *Communism, Conformity, and Civil Liberties*," *Perspectives on Politics* 4 (March 2006): 21–34.

[50]David G. Barnum and John L. Sullivan, "The Elusive Foundations of Political Freedom in Britain and the United States," *Journal of Politics* 52 (August 1990): 719–739.

[51]Dennis Chong, "How People Think, Reason, and Feel about Rights and Liberties," *American Journal of Political Science* 37 (August 1993): 867–899.

[52]Timothy E. Cook and Paul Gronke, "The Skeptical American: Revisiting the Meanings of Trust in Government and Confidence in Institutions," *Journal of Politics* 67 (August 2005): 784–803.

[53]"The NES Guide to Public Opinion and Electoral Behavior," available at www.electionstudies.org

[54]Ibid.

[55]Ruy A. Teixeira, *Why Americans Don't Vote: Turnout Decline in the United States 1960–1984* (New York: Greenwood Press, 1987), p. 78.

[56]William G. Jacoby, "The Sources of Liberal-Conservative Thinking: Education and Conceptualization," *Political Behavior* 10 (Winter 1988): 316–332.

[57]"The NES Guide to Public Opinion and Electoral Behavior," available at www.electionstudies.org

[58]Albert H. Cantril and Susan Davis Cantril, *Reading Mixed Signals: Ambivalence in American Public Opinion About Government* (Washington, DC: Woodrow Wilson Center Press, 1999), pp. 10–14.

[59]Ibid., p. 20.

[60]The Gallup Poll, available at www.gallup.com.

[61]Eugene R. Wittkopf and Michael R. Maggiotto, "Elites and Masses: A Comparative Analysis of Attitudes Toward America's World Role," *Journal of Politics* 45 (May 1983): 303–334.

[62]Richard Morin, "It's Not as It Seems," *Washington Post National Weekly Edition*, July 16–22, 2001, p. 34.

[63]Frank Newport, "Blacks as Conservative as Republicans on Some Moral Issues," *Gallup Poll*, December 3, 2008, available at www.gallup.com.

[64]Caryle Murphy and Alan Cooperman, "Seeking to Reclaim the Moral High Ground," *Washington Post National Weekly Edition*, May 29–June 4, 2006, p. 12.

[65]James L. Guth, John C. Green, Corwin E. Smith, and Margaret M. Poloma, "Pulpits and Politics: The Protestant Clergy in the 1988 Presidential Election," in Guth and Green, eds., *The Bible and the Ballot Box* (Boulder, CO: Westview Press, 1991), pp. 73–93.

[66]Allen D. Hertzke and John David Rausch, Jr., "The Religious Vote in American Politics: Value Conflict, Continuity, and Change," in Craig, *Broken Contract?*, p. 191.

[67]Steven A. Peterson, "Church Participation and Political Participation: The Spillover Effect," *American Politics Quarterly* 20 (January 1992): 123–139.

[68]Amy Goldstein and Richard Morin, "The Squeaky Wheel Gets the Grease," *Washington Post National Weekly Edition*, October 28–November 3, 2002, p. 34.

[69]Nicholas L. Danigelis and Stephen J. Cutler, "Cohort Trends in Attitudes about Law and Order: Who's Leading the Conservative Wave?" *Public Opinion Quarterly* 55 (Spring 1991): 24–49.

[70]Thomas C. Wilson, "Trends in Tolerance Toward Rightist and Leftist Groups, 1976–1988," *Public Opinion Quarterly* 58 (Winter 1994): 539–556.

[71]Laurel Elder and Steven Greene, "The Myth of 'Security Moms' and 'Nascar Dads,' Parenthood, Political Stereotypes, and the 2004 Election," *Social Science Quarterly* 88 (March 2007), p. 11.

[72]Karen M. Kaufmann, "The Gender Gap," *PS: Political Science & Politics* (July 2006): 447–453.

[73]V. O. Key, Jr., *Public Opinion and American Democracy* (New York: Alfred Knopf, 1961), p. 499.

[74]James A. Stimson, *Public Opinion in America: Moods, Cycles, and Swings* (Boulder, CO: Westview Press, 1991), pp. 19–21.

[75]Kenneth D. Wald, James W. Button, and Barbara A. Rienzo, "The Politics of Gay Rights in American Communities: Explaining Antidiscrimination Ordinances and Policies," *American Journal of Political Science* 40 (November 1996): 1152–1178.

Chapter 5

[1]David Mark, "2008 Could See Turnout Tsunami," March 24, 2008, available at www.politico.com.

[2]Michael P. McDonald, United States Election Project, available at http://elections.gmu.edu.

[3]"The ANES Guide to Public Opinion and Electoral Behavior," available at www.electionstudies.org.

[4]John R. Petrocek and Daron Shaw, "Nonvoting in America: Attitudes in Context," in William Crotty, ed., *Political Participation and American Democracy* (New York: Greenwood Press, 1991), p. 83.

[5]McDonald, United States Election Project.

[6]Sidney Verba, Kay Lehman Schlozman, and Henry E. Brady, *Voice and Equality: Civic Volunteerism in American Politics* (Cambridge, MA: Harvard University Press, 1995), p. 51.

[7]André Blais, *To Vote or Not to Vote?* (Pittsburgh: University of Pittsburg Press, 2000), pp. 12–13.

[8]Henry E. Brady, Sidney Verba, Kay Lehman Schlozman, "Beyond SES: A Resource Model of Political Participation," *American Political Science Review* 89 (June 1995): 3.

[9]Andrea Louise Campbell, "Self-Interest, Social Security, and the Distinctive Participation Patterns of Senior Citizens," *American Political Science Review* 96 (September 2002): 565–574.

[10]Ibid.

[11]Verba, Schlozman, and Brady, *Voice and Equality: Civic Volunteerism in American Politics*, p. 354.

[12]Michael Luo, "Obama Hauls in Record $750 Million for Campaign," *New York Times*, December 4, 2008, available at www.nytimes.com.

[13]Thomas M. Holbrook and Scott D. McClurg, "The Mobilization of Core Supporters: Campaigns, Turnout, and Electoral Composition in the United States Presidential Elections," *American Journal of Political Science* 49 (October 2005): 689–703.

[14]Donald P. Green, Alan S. Gerber, and David W. Nickerson, "Getting Out the Vote in Local Elections: Results from Six Door-to-Door Canvassing Experiments," *Journal of Politics* 65 (November 2003): 1083–1096.

[15]Alan S. Gerber and Donald P. Green, "The Effects of Canvassing, Telephone Calls, and Direct Mail on Voter Turnout: A Field Experiment," *American Political Science Review* 94 (September 2000): 653–63.

[16]Blais, *To Vote or Not to Vote?* p. 13.

[17]U.S. Census Bureau, "Voting and Registration in the Election of November 2004," available at www.census.gov.

[18]APSA Task Force Report, "American Democracy in an Age of Rising Inequality," p. 656.

[19]U.S. Census Bureau, "Voting and Registration in the Election of November 2004."

[20]Verba, Schlozman, and Brady, *Voice and Equality: Civic Volunteerism in American Politics*, pp. 332–38.

[21]U.S. Census Bureau, "Voting and Registration in the Election of November 2004."

[22]Jeff Manza and Christopher Uggen, *Locked Out: Felon Disenfranchisement and American Democracy* (NY: Oxford University Press, 2006), pp. 76–80.

[23]Matt A. Barreto, "¡Sí Se Puede! Latino Candidates and the Mobilization of Latino Voters," *American Political Science Review* 101 (August 2007): 425–441.

[24]U.S. Census Bureau, "Voting and Registration in the Election of November 2004."

[25]Verba, Schlozman, and Brady, *Voice and Equality: Civic Volunteerism in American Politics*, p. 255.

[26]Richard Morin, "Tuned Out, Turned Off," *Washington Post National Weekly Edition*, February 5–11, 1996, p. 6.

[27]James G. Gimpel, Karen M. Kaufmann, and Shanna Pearson-Markowitz, "Battleground States Versus Blackout States: The Behavioral Implications of Modern Presidential Campaigns," *Journal of Politics* 69 (August 2007): 786–797.

[28]U.S. Census Bureau, "Voting and Registration in the Election of November 2004."

[29]International Institute for Democracy and Electoral Assistance, available at www.idea.int.

[30]U.S. Census Bureau, "Voting and Registration in the Election of November 2004," available at www.census.gov.

[31]Gary W. Cox, "Electoral Rules and the Calculus of Mobilization," *Legislative Studies Quarterly* 24 (August 1999): 387–419.

[32]G. Bingham Powell, Jr., "American Voter Turnout in Comparative Perspective," *American Political Science Review* 80 (March 1986): 17–43.

[33]Mark N. Franklin, "Electoral Engineering and Cross-National Turnout Differences: What Role of Compulsory Voting?" *British Journal of Political Science* 29 (January 1999): 205.

[34]International Institute for Democracy and Electoral Assistance, "Voter Turnout," available at www.idea.int/vt.

[35]M. Mackerras and I. McAllister, "Compulsory Voting, Party Stability, and Electoral Advantage in Australia," *Electoral Studies*, 18 (June 1999): 217–33.

[36]Petrocek and Shaw, "Nonvoting in America: Attitudes in Context," pp. 71–72.

[37]Gary C. Jacobson, *A Divider, Not a Uniter: George W. Bush and the American People* (New York: Pearson Longman, 2007).

[38]Peter L. Francia, Rachel E. Goldberg, John C. Green, Paul S. Herrnson, and Clyde Wilcox, "Individual Donors in the 1996 Federal Elections," in John C. Green, ed., *Financing the 1996 Election* (Armonk, NY: M. E. Sharpe, 1999), p. 128.

[39]Theda Skocpol, *Diminished Democracy: From Membership to Management in American Civic Life* (Norman, OK: University of Oklahoma Press, 2003), pp. 6–13, 224–244.

[40]APSA Task Force Report, "American Democracy in an Age of Rising Inequality," p. 657.

[41]*Adarand Constructors v. Pena*, 515 U.S. 200 (1995).

Chapter 6

[1]Tim Craig and Michael D. Shear, "Allen Quip Provokes Outrage, Apology," *Washington Post*, August 15, 2006, p. A01.

[2]www.youtube.com/watch?v=r90z0PMnKwI.

[3]Claude R. Marx, "The Media and Campaign 2006," in Larry J. Sabato, ed., *The Sixth Year Itch: The Rise and Fall of the George W. Bush Presidency* (New York, NY: Pearson, 2008), pp. 159–160.

[4]Project for Excellence in Journalism, available at www.stateofthenewsmedia.org.

[5]"2006 Annual Report," available at www.tribune.com.

[6]"The State of the News Media 2006," available at www.stateofthenewsmedia.org.

[7]Pew Center for the People & the Press, available at http://people-press.org.

[8]Stephen J. Farnsworth and S. Robert Lichter, *The Nightly News Nightmare: Television's Coverage of U.S. Presidential Elections, 1988–2004*, 2nd ed. (Lanham, MD: Rowman & Littlefield, 2007), p. 25.

[9]Philip N. Howard, *New Media Campaigns and the Managed Citizen* (New York, NY: Cambridge University Press, 2006), p. 27.

[10]"Cuba—Annual Report 2007," available at www.rsf.org.

[11]Ibid.

[12]Erika Franklin Fowler and Kenneth M. Goldstein, eds., "Free Media in Campaigns," in Stephen C. Craig, ed., *The Electoral Challenge: Theory Meets Practice* (Washington, DC: CQ Press, 2006), pp. 112–115.

[13]Martha Joynt Kumar, "Managing the News: The Bush Communications Operation," in George C. Edwards III and Desmond S. King, eds., *The Polarized Presidency of George W. Bush* (New York, NY: Oxford University Press, 2007), pp. 353–354.

[14]Bruce Miroff, "The Presidential Spectacle," in Michael Nelson, ed., *The Presidency and the Political System*, 8th ed. (Washington, DC: CQ Press, 2006), p. 277.

[15]White House Press Release, "President Arrives in Alabama, Briefed on Hurricane Katrina," September 2, 2005, available at www.whitehouse.gov.

[16]S. Robert Lichter, Linda S. Lichter, and Stanley Rothman, *The Media Elite: America's New Powerbrokers* (Bethesda, MD: Adler and Adler, 1986), pp. 54–71.

[17]Farnsworth and Lichter, *The Nightly News Nightmare*, pp. 118–161.

[18]Jonathan S. Morris, "Slanted Objectivity? Perceived Media Bias, Cable News Exposure, and Political Attitudes," *Social Science Quarterly* 88 (September 2007): 707–728.

[19]Kim Fridkin Kahn and Patrick J. Kenney, "The Slant of the News: How Editorial Endorsements Influence Campaign Coverage and Citizens' Views of Candidates," *American Political Science Review* 96 (June 2002): 381–394.

[20]Tim Groeling and Samuel Kernell, "Is Network News Coverage of the President Biased?" *Journal of Politics* 60 (November 1998): 1063–1087; Larry Sabato, "Is There an Anti-Republican, Anti-Conservative Media Tilt?" *Campaigns and Elections*, September 1993, p. 16.

[21]Thomas E. Patterson, "Bad News, Period," *PS: Political Science and Politics* (March 1996): 17–20.

[22]Elizabeth A. Skewes, *Message Control: How News Is Made on the Presidential Campaign Trail* (Lanham, MD: Rowman & Littlefield Publishers, 2007), p. 13.

Chapter 7

[1]Jeffrey M. Jones, "Public Believes Americans Have Right to Own Guns," March 27, 2008, available at www.gallup.com.

[2]Anthony J. Nownes, *Total Lobbying: What Lobbyists Want (and How They Try to Get It)*, (New York, NY: Cambridge University Press, 2006), p. 13.

[3]Center for Responsive Politics, available at www.opensecrets.org.

[4]"Labor Union Membership by Sector," *2009 Statistical Abstract*.

[5]*Dukes v. Wal-Mart, Inc.*, 04-16688 (9th Cir. Feb. 6, 2007).

[6]Peter L. Francia, "Protecting America's Workers in Hostile Territory: Unions and the Republican Congress," in Paul S. Herrnson, Ronald G. Shaiko, and Clyde Wilcox, eds., *The Interest Group Connection: Electioneering, Lobbying, and Policymaking in Washington*, 2nd ed. (Washington, DC: CQ Press, 2005), p. 214.

[7]Amy Joyce, "Divided Unions," *Washington Post National Weekly Edition*, August 1–7, 2005, p. 20.

[8]Caryle Murphy and Alan Cooperman, "Seeking to Reclaim the Moral High Ground," *Washington Post National Weekly Edition*, May 29–June 4, 2006, p. 12.

[9]John C. Green and Nathan S. Bigelow, "The Christian Right Goes to Washington: Social Movement Resources and the Legislative Process," in Herrnson, Shaiko, and Wilcox, eds., *The Interest Group Connection*, pp. 191–206.

[10]John C. Green, Mark J. Rozell, and Clyde Wilcox, eds., *The Values Campaign? The Christian Right and the 2004 Election* (Washington, DC: Georgetown University Press, 2006), p. 4.

[11]Roderi Ai Camp, *Politics in Mexico: The Democratic Consolidation* (New York, NY: Oxford University Press, 2007), p. 89.

[12]Ibid., pp. 144–145.

[13]Daniel C. Levy and Kathleen Bruhn, *Mexico: The Struggle for Democratic Development*, 2nd ed. (Berkeley, CA: University of California Press, 2006), pp. 123–124.

[14]Camp, Politics in Mexico, p. 146.

[15]Center for Responsive Politics, available at www.opensecrets.org.

[16]Federal Election Commission, "PAC Financial Activity, 2005–2006," available at www.fec.gov.

[17]Professor James A. Thurber, quoted in Jeffrey H. Birnbaum, "Mickey Goes to Washington," *Washington Post National Weekly Edition*, February 25–March 2, 2008, p. 6.

[18]Ronald G. Shaiko, "Making the Connection: Organized Interests, Political Representation, and the Changing Rules of the Game in Washington Politics," in Herrnson, Shaiko, and Wilcox, eds., *The Interest Group Connection*, p. 32.

[19]Rogan Kersh, "The Well-Informed Lobbyist: Information and Interest Group Lobbying," in Ciglar and Loomis, ed., *Interest Group Politics*, pp. 390–406.

[20]John R. Wright, "Contributions, Lobbying, and Committee Voting in the U.S. House of Representatives," *American Political Science Review* 84 (June 1990): 417–38.

[21]Thomas B. Edsall, "A Chill but Not the Cold Shoulder," *Washington Post National Weekly Edition*, January 16–22, 2006, p. 15.

[22]Dan Clawson, Alan Neustadtl, and Mark Weller, *Dollars and Votes: How Business Campaign Contributions Subvert Democracy* (Philadelphia: Temple University Press, 1998), pp. 67–69.

[23]Ruth Markus and Charles R. Babcock, "Feeding the Election Machine," *Washington Post National Weekly Edition*, February 17, 1997, p. 7.

[24]*District of Columbia v. Heller*, 07-290 (2008).

[25]Richard Monastersky, "Protesters Fail to Slow Animal Research," *Chronicle of Higher Education*, April 18, 2008, pp. A1, A26–A28.

[26]Diana Evans, "Before the Roll Call: Interest Group Lobbying and Public Policy Outcomes in House Committees," *Political Research Quarterly* 49 (June 1996): 287–304.

[27]Marcella Ridlan Ray, *The Changing and Unchanging Face of U.S. Civil Society* (New Brunswick, NJ: Transaction Publishers, 2002), pp. 2–3.

[28]Richard M. Skinner, *More Than Money: Interest Group Action in Congressional Elections* (Lanham, MD: Rowman & Littlefield, 2007), pp. 165–167.

[29]Lydia Saad, "Public Divided on 'Pro-Choice' versus 'Pro-Life' Abortion Labels," Gallup News Service, May 21 2007, available at www.gallup.com.

[30]Americans for Tax Reform, available at www.atr.org.

Chapter 8

[1]Maurice Duverger, *Political Parties* (New York: Wiley, 1954), p. 217.

[2]A. James Reichley, "The Future of the American Two-Party System at the Beginning of a New Century," in John C. Green and Rick Farmer, eds., *The State of the Parties: The Changing Role of Contemporary American Parties*, 4th ed. (Lanham, MD: Rowman & Littlefield, 2003), pp. 20–21.

[3]Asher Arian, *Politics in Israel: The Second Republic*, 2nd ed. (Washington, DC: CQ Press, 2005), p. 203.

[4]Octavio Amorim Neto and Gary W. Cox, "Electoral Institutions, Cleavage Structures, and the Number of Parties," *American Journal of Political Science* 41 (January 1997): 149–74.

[5]Michael Toner, "The Impact of the New Campaign Finance Law on the 2004 Presidential Election," in Larry Sabato, ed., *Divided States of America: The Slash and Burn Politics of the 2004 Presidential Election* (New York, NY: Pearson Longman, 2006), p. 197.

[6]Timothy P. Nokken, "Ideological Congruence versus Electoral Success: Distribution of Party Organization Contributions in Senate Elections, 1990–2000," *American Politics Research* 31 (January 2003): 3–26.

[7]Pew Center for the People & the Press, "Fewer Voters Identify as Republicans," March 20, 2008, available at http://pewresearch.org.

[8]Exit poll data, available at www.cnn.com.

[9]Ibid.

[10]Juan Castillo, "Latinos Deliver on Potential, Turn Out Big for Obama," *Austin American-Statesman*, November 6, 2008, available at www.statesman.com.

[11]David L. Leal, Stephan A. Nuño, Jongho Lee, and Rodolpho O. de la Garza, "Latinos, Immigration, and the 2006 Midterm Election," *PS: Political Science & Politics* (April 2008): 312.

[12]Exit poll data.

[13]Ibid.

[14]Ibid.

[15]Ibid.

[16]Ibid.

[17]Exit poll data.

[18]Morris P. Fiorina, *Culture War? The Myth of a Polarized America*, 2nd ed. (New York, NY: Pearson Education, 2006), pp. 61–70.

[19]Jongho Lee and Harry P. Pachon, "Leading the Way: An Analysis of the Effect of Religion on the Latino Vote," *American Politics Research* 35 (March 2007): 252–272.

[20]John C. Green, Lyman A. Kellstedt, Corwin E. Smidt, and James L. Guth, "How the Faithful Voted: Religious Communities and the Presidential Vote," in David E. Campbell, ed., *A Matter of Faith: Religion in the 2004 Presidential Election* (Washington, DC: Brookings Institution Press, 2007), pp. 1–28.

[21]Exit poll data.

[22]Frank Newport, "Church Attendance and Party Identification," Gallup News Service, May 18, 2005, available at www.gallup.com.

[23]Exit poll data.

[24]Ibid.

[25]Joel H. Silbey, "Divided Government in Historical Perspective, 1789–1996," in Peter F. Golderisi, ed., *Divided Government: Change, Uncertainty, and the Constitutional Order* (Lanham, MD: Rowman & Littlefield, 1996), pp. 9–34.

[26]Morris Fiorina, *Divided Government*, 2nd ed. (Cambridge, MA: Harvard University Press, 1996), p. 7.

[27]Andrew E. Busch, *Horses in Midstream: U.S. Midterm Elections and Their Consequences, 1894–1998* (Pittsburgh: University of Pittsburgh Press, 1999), pp. 15–22.

[28]After the 2000 election, the Senate was evenly divided between the two parties and the vote of Republican Vice President Richard Cheney enabled the GOP to claim majority status. In 2001, however, Republican Senator James Jeffords of Vermont switched his party allegiance from Republican to independent to allow the Democrats to claim the majority.

[29]John R. Petrocik and Joseph Doherty, "The Road to Divided Government: Paved Without Intention," in Golderisi, ed., *Divided Government: Change, Uncertainty, and the Constitutional Order*, p. 105.

[30]Gary C. Jacobson, "The Persistence of Democratic House Majorities," in Gary W. Cox and Samuel Kernell, eds., *The Politics of Divided Government* (Boulder, CO: Westview, 1991), pp. 57–84.

[31]Gary C. Jacobson, "Divided Government and the 1994 Elections," in Golderisi, ed., *Divided Government: Change, Uncertainty, and the Constitutional Order*, p. 62.

[32]Barry C. Burden and David C. Kimball, "A New Approach to the Study of Ticket Splitting," *American Political Science Review* 92 (September 1998): 533–44.

[33]Walter R. Mebane, Jr., "Combination, Moderation, and Institutional Balancing in American Presidential Elections," *American Political Science Review* 94 (March 2000): 37–57.

[34]Richard D. Forgette, *Congress, Parties, and Puzzles: Politics as a Team Sport* (New York, NY: Peter Lang, 2004), p. 176.

Chapter 9

[1]Robert E. Cushman and Robert F. Cushman, *Cases in Constitutional Law*, 3rd ed. (New York: Appleton-Century-Crofts, 1968), p. 42.

[2]*Baker v. Carr*, 369 U.S. 186 (1962) and *Wesberry v. Sanders*, 376 U.S. 1 (1964).

[3]Mark Monmonier, *Bushmanders and Bullwinkles: How Politicians Manipulate Electronic Maps and Census Data to Win Elections* (Chicago, IL: University of Chicago Press, 2001), p. 62.

[4]David Lublin and D. Stephen Voss, "Racial Redistricting and Realignment in Southern State Legislatures," *American Journal of Political Science* 44 (October 2000): 792–810.

[5]David T. Canon, *Race, Redistricting, and Representation: The Unintended Consequences of Black Majority Districts* (Chicago, IL: University of Chicago Press, 1999), p. 257.

[6]*Reno v. Bossier Parish School Board*, 528 U.S. 320 (2000).

[7]*Georgia v. Ashcroft*, 539 U.S. 461 (2003).

[8]Thomas L. Wyrick, "Management of Political Influence: Gerrymandering in the 1980s," *American Politics Quarterly* 19 (October 1991): 396–416.

[9]Michael P. McDonald, "Redistricting and Competitive Districts," in Michael P. McDonald and John Samples, eds., *The Marketplace of Democracy: Electoral Competition and American Politics* (Washington, DC: Cato Institute, 2006), p. 225.

[10]Richard G. Niemi and Laura R. Winsky, "The Persistence of Partisan Redistricting Effects in Congressional Elections in the 1970s and 1980s," *Journal of Politics* 54 (May 1992): 565–72.

[11]Ibid.

[12]John Mintz and Ruth Marcus, "Bush's Bucks Have a High Burn Rate," *Washington Post National Weekly Edition*, March 6, 2000, p. 11.

[13]Ken Herman, "Campaigns Spend Millions to Seek Yet More Millions," *Austin American-Statesman*, August 22, 2004, available at www.statesman.com.

[14]Center for Responsive Politics, available at www.opensecrets.org.

[15]Federal Election Commission, available at www.fec.gov.

[16]Richard A. Oppel, Jr., "Campaign Documents Show Depth of Bush Fund-Raising," *New York Times*, May 5, 2003, available at www.nytimes.com.

[17]Wayne Slater, "Elite Donors Lifted Bush," *Dallas Morning News*, May 5, 2003, available at www.dallasnews.com.

[18]Kirsten A. Foot and Steven M. Schneider, *Web Campaigning* (Cambridge, MA: MIT Press, 2006), pp. 197–198.

[19]Center for Responsive Politics.

[20]Michael J. Malbin, *The Election After Reform: Money, Politics, and the Bipartisan Campaign Reform Act* (Lanham, MD: Rowman & Littlefield, 2006), pp. 3–4.

[21]Glen Justice and Jim Rutenberg, "Advocacy Groups Step Up Costly Battle of Political Ads," *New York Times*, September 25, 2004, available at www.nytimes.com.

[22]Kerwin C. Swint, *Mudslingers: The Top 25 Negative Political Campaigns of All Time* (Westport, CT: Praeger, 2006), p. 47.

[23]Richard R. Lau and Gerald M. Pomper, "Effectiveness of Negative Campaigning in U.S. Senate Elections," *American Journal of Political Science* 46 (January 2002): 47–66.

[24]David E. Damore, "Candidate Strategy and the Decision to Go Negative," *Political Research Quarterly*, 55 (September 2002): 669–685.

[25]Stephen Ansolabehere and Shanto Iyengar, "Winning Through Advertising: It's All in the Context," in James A. Thurber and Candice J. Nelson, eds., *Campaigns and Elections American Style* (Boulder, CO: Westview, 1995), p. 109.

[26]Paul R. Abramson, John H. Aldrich, and David Rohde, *Change and Continuity in the 2004 and 2006 Elections* (Washington, DC: CQ Press, 2007), pp. 265–266.

[27]Center for Responsive Politics.

[28]Ibid.

[29]Robert S. Erikson and Gerald C. Wright, "Voters, Candidates, and Issues in Congressional Elections," in Lawrence C. Dodd and Bruce I. Oppenheimer, eds., *Congress Reconsidered*, 7th ed. (Washington, DC: CQ Press, 2001), p. 72.

[30]David J. Samuels, "Incentives to Cultivate a Party Vote in Candidate-Centric Electoral Systems: Evidence from Brazil," *Comparative Political Studies* 32 (June 1999): 487–518.

[31]Barry Ames, "Electoral Rules, Constituency Pressures, and Pork Barrel: Bases of Voting in the Brazilian Congress," *Journal of Politics* 57 (May 1995): 324–343.

[32]Secretary of State of New Hampshire, available at www.sos.nh.gov.

[33]John S. Jackson, Nathan S. Bigelow, and John C. Green, "The State of Party Elites: National Convention Delegates, 1992–2000," in John C. Green and Rick Farmer, eds., *The State of the Parties: The Changing Role of Contemporary American Parties* (Lanham, MD: Rowman & Littlefield, 2003), pp. 54–78.

[34]Paul R. Abramson, John H. Aldrich, Phil Paolino, and David W. Rohde, "Sophisticated Voting in the 1988 Presidential Primaries," *American Political Science Review* 86 (March 1992): 55–69.

[35]"State-by-state Election Results," available at www.govote.com.

[36]John M. Bruce, John A. Clark, and John H. Kessel, "Advocacy Politics in Presidential Politics," *American Political Science Review* 85 (December 1991): 1091–1105.

[37]Barbara Norrander, "Nomination Choices: Caucus and Primary Outcomes, 1976–88," *American Journal of Political Science* 37 (May 1993): 343–64.

[38]Federal Election Commission.

[39]Mark Z. Barabak, "How Obama Went from Underdog to Alpha," *Los Angeles Times*, June 4, 2008, available at www.latimes.com.

[40]Jackie Calmes, "Clinton Braces for Second Loss; Union, Senators May Back Obama," *Wall Street Journal*, January 8, 2008, available at www.wsj.com.

[41]Gerald M. Pomper, "Parliamentary Government in the United States: A New Regime for a New Century?" in Green and Farmer, eds., *The State of the Parties*, p. 273.

[42]Exit Poll Data, available at www.cnn.com.

[43]Ibid.

[44]David W. Abbott and James P. Levine, *Wrong Winner: The Coming Debacle in the Electoral College* (New York, NY: Praeger, 1991), p. 32.

[45]Lawrence D. Longley and Neal R. Peirce, *The Electoral College Primer 2000* (New Haven, CT: Yale University Press, 1999), p. 24.

[46]George C. Edwards III, *Why the Electoral College is Bad for America* (New Haven, CT: Yale University Press, 2004), p. 150.

[47]Ann N. Crigler, Marion R. Just, and Edward J. McCaffery, *Rethinking the Vote: The Politics and Prospects of American Electoral Reform* (New York: Oxford University Press, 2004).

[48]Daron R. Shaw, *The Race to 270: The Electoral College and the Campaign Strategies of 2000 and 2004* (Chicago: University of Chicago Press, 2006), p. 143.

[49]Kim J. Fridkin, Patrick J. Kenney, Sarah Allen Gershon, Karen Shafer, and Gina Serignese Woodall, "Capturing the Power of a Campaign Event: The 2004 Presidential Debate in Tempe," *Journal of Politics* 69 (August 2007): 770–785.

[50]Michael Dimock, April Clark, and Juliana Menasce Horowitz, "Campaign Dynamics and the Swing Vote in the 2004 Election," in William G. Mayer, ed., *The Swing Voter in American Politics* (Washington, DC: Brookings Institution, 2008), p. 58.

[51]Exit Poll Data.

[52]Mayer, ed., *The Swing Voter in American Politics*, p. 19.

[53]Ibid.

[54]Exit Poll Data.

[55]Warren E. Miller, "Party Identification, Realignment, and Party Voting: Back to the Basics," *American Political Science Review* 85 (June 1991): 557–68.

[56]John R. Petrocik, "Reporting Campaigns: Reforming the Press," in Thurber and Nelson, eds., *Campaigns and Elections American Style*, p. 128.

[57]Stephen Ansolabehere, Jonathan Rodden, and James M. Snyder, Jr., "The Strength of Issues: Using Multiple Measures to Gauge Preference Stability, Ideological Constraint, and Issue Voting," *American Political Science Review*, 102 (May 2008): 215–232.

[58]Scott J. Basinger and Howard Lavine, "Ambivalence, Information, and Electoral Choice," *American Political Science Review* 99 (May 2005): 169–184.

[59]Thomas M. Holbrook, "Do Campaigns Matter?" in Craig, ed., *The Electoral Challenge: Theory Meets Practice*, pp. 12–13.

[60]Edward Roeder, "Not Only Does Money Talk, It Often Calls the Winners," *Washington Post National Weekly Edition*, September 26–October 2, 1994, p. 23.

[61]Brian F. Schaffner, "Priming Gender: Campaigning on Women's Issues in U.S. Senate Elections," *American Journal of Political Science* 49 (October 2005): 803–817.

[62]Alan I. Abramowitz, "Can McCain Overcome the Triple Whammy?" May 29, 2008, Larry J. Sabato's Crystal Ball 2008, available at www.centerforpolitics.org.

[63]Exit Poll Data.

[64]David Karol and Edward Miguel, "The Electoral Cost of War: Iraq Casualties and the 2004 U.S. Presidential Election," *Journal of Politics* 69 (August 2007): 633–648.

[65]Exit Poll Data.

[66]Brad Lockerbie, "Prospective Voting in Presidential Elections, 1956–1988," *American Politics Quarterly* 20 (July 1992): 308–325.

[67]Michael B. MacKuen, Robert S. Erikson, and James A. Stimson, "Peasants or Bankers? The American Electorate and the U.S. Economy," *American Political Science Review* 86 (September 1992): 597–611.

[68]Tracy Sulkin, *Issue Politics in Congress* (New York, NY: Cambridge University Press, 2005), pp. 168–175.

[69]Evan J. Ringquist and Carl Dasse, "Lies, Damned Lies, and Campaign Promises? Environmental Legislation in the 105th Congress," *Social Science Quarterly* 85 (June 2004): 400–419.

[70]James A. Stimson, Michael B. McKuen, and Robert S. Erikson, "Dynamic Representation," *American Political Science Review* 89 (September 1995): 543–65.

[71]Lawrence J. Grossback, David A. M. Peterson, and James A. Stimson, *Mandate Politics* (New York, NY: Cambridge University Press, 2007), pp. 179–192.

[72]Jeffrey E. Cohen, "The Polls: Presidential Referendum Effects in the 2006 Midterm Elections," *Presidential Studies Quarterly* 37 (September 2007): 545–557.

Chapter 10

[1]Charles B. Cushman, Jr., *An Introduction to the U.S. Congress* (Armonk, NY: M.E. Sharpe, 2006), p. 5.

[2]Robert V. Remini, *The House: The History of the House of Representatives* (New York, NY: HarperCollins, 2006), p. 496.

[3]Mildred Amer and Jennifer E. Manning, "Membership in the 111th Congress: A Profile," Congressional Research Service, December 31, 2008, available at http://assets.opencrs.com.

[4]Donald R. Matthews, *U.S. Senators and Their World* (New York, NY: Vintage Books, 1960), pp. 116–117.

[5]Burdett Loomis, *The New American Politician: Ambition, Entrepreneurship, and the Changing Face of Political Life* (New York, NY: Basic Books, 1988), pp. 233–244.

[6]Brandice Canes-Wrone, David W. Brady, and John F. Cogan, "Out of Step, Out of Office: Electoral Accountability and House Members' Voting," *American Political Science Review* 96 (March 2002): 127–140.

[7]Sally Friedman, *Dilemmas of Representation: Local Politics, National Factors, and the Home Styles of Modern U.S. Congress Members* (Albany, NY: State University of New York Press, 2007), pp. 223–225.

[8]Richard F. Fenno, *Home Style* (Boston, MA: Little, Brown, 1978), p. 18.

[9]Richard G. Forgette, *Congress, Parties, and Puzzles: Politics as a Team Sport* (New York, NY: Peter Lang, 2004), p. 174.

[10]Robert A. Bernstein, "Determinants of Differences in Feelings Toward Senators Representing the Same State," *Western Political Quarterly* 45 (September 1992): 701–725.

[11]George Serra, "What's in It for Me? The Impact of Congressional Casework on Incumbent Evaluation," *American Politics Quarterly* 22 (October 1994): 403–420.

[12]Roger H. Davidson and Walter J. Oleszek, *Congress and Its Members*, 8th ed. (Washington, DC: CQ Press, 2004), p. 60.

[13]John R. Hibbing and Christopher W. Larimer, "What the American Public Wants Congress to Be," in Lawrence C. Dodd and Bruce I. Oppenheimer, eds., *Congress Reconsidered*, 8th ed. (Washington, DC: CQ Press, 2005), p. 63.

[14]"Membership of the 110th Congress: A Profile."

[15]Robert Pear, "House's Author of Drug Benefit Joins Lobbyists," *New York Times*, December 16, 2004, available at www.nytimes.com.

[16]Kristin Kanthak, "Crystal Elephants and Committee Chairs: Campaign Contributions and Leadership Races in the U.S. House of Representatives," *American Politics Research* 35 (May 2007): 389–406.

[17]Gary W. Cox and Mathew D. McCubbins, *Setting the Agenda: Responsible Party Government in the U.S. House of Representatives* (New York, NY: Cambridge University Press, 2005), pp. 1–9.

[18]Library of Congress, available at http://thomas.loc.gov.

[19]Gary W. Cox and Mathew D. McCubbins, *Legislative Leviathan: Party Government in the House*, 2nd ed. (New York, NY: Cambridge University Press, 2007), pp. 256–257.

[20]Eric S. Heberlig and Bruce A. Larson, "Party Fundraising, Descriptive Representation, and the Battle for Majority Control: Shifting Leadership Appointment Strategies in the U.S. House of Representatives, 1990–2002," *Social Science Quarterly* 88 (June 2007): 404–421.

[21]Laura W. Arnold, "The Distribution of Senate Committee Positions: Change or More of the Same?" *Legislative Studies Quarterly* 26 (May 2001): 227–248.

[22]Scott A. Frisch and Sean Q. Kelly, *Committee Assignment Politics in the U.S. House of Representatives* (Norman, OK: University of Oklahoma Press, 2006), pp. 328–330

[23]Paul R. Brewer and Christopher J. Deering, "Musical Chairs: Interest Groups, Campaign Fund-Raising, and Selection of House Committee Chairs," in Paul S. Herrnson, Ronald G. Shaiko, and Clyde Wilcox, eds., *The Interest Group Connection: Electioneering, Lobbying, and Policymaking in Washington*, 2nd ed. (Washington, DC: CQ Press, 2005), pp. 141–146.

[24]Jeff Zeleny, "Of Party Dues and Deadbeats on Capitol Hill," *New York Times*, October 1, 2006, available at www.nytimes.com.

[25]Barbara Sinclair, *Unorthodox Lawmaking: New Legislative Processes in the U.S. Congress*, 3rd ed. (Washington, DC: Congressional Quarterly Press, 2007), pp. 5–8.

[26]Congressional Record, Daily Digest, "Résumé of Congressional Activity, 110th Congress," available at www.senate.gov/reference/resources/pdf/110_1.pdf.

[27]Roger H. Davidson and Walter J. Oleszek, *Congress and Its Members*, 7th ed. (Washington, DC: CQ Press, 2000), p. 31.

[28]Public Law 107–110, January 2002.

[29]John Baughman, *Common Ground: Committee Politics in the U.S. House of Representatives* (Stanford, CA: Stanford University Press, 2006), pp. 175–179.

[30]Davidson and Oleszek, *Congress and Its Members*, 7th ed. p. 242.

[31]Sinclair, *Unorthodox Lawmaking*, p. 19.

[32]Ibid., p. 22.

[33]Ibid., p. 32.

[34]Library of Congress, available at http://thomas.loc.gov.

[35]John D. Wilerson, "'Killer' Amendments in Congress," *American Political Science Review* 93 (September 1999): 535–552.

[36]Gregory J. Wawro and Eric Schickler, *Filibuster: Obstruction and Lawmaking in the U.S. Senate* (Princeton, NJ: Princeton University Press, 2006), pp. 13–14.

[37]Christopher J. Deering, "Leadership in the Slow Lane," *PS: Policy and Politics* (Winter 1986): 37–42; Bruce I. Oppenheimer, "Changing Time Constraints on Congress: Historical Perspectives on the Use of Cloture." in Lawrence C. Dodd and Bruce I. Oppenheimer, eds., *Congress Reconsidered*, 4th ed. (Washington, DC: Congressional Quarterly Press, 1989), pp. 393–413.

[38]Sinclair, *Unorthodox Lawmaking*, p. 69.

[39]Barbara Sinclair, "The '60-Vote Senate': Strategies, Process, and Outcomes," in Bruce I. Oppenheimer, ed., *U.S. Senate Exceptionalism* (Columbus, OH: Ohio State University Press, 2002), pp. 258–259.

[40]Sinclair, *Unorthodox Lawmaking*, p. 76.

[41]Jeffrey Lazarus and Nathan W. Monroe, "The Speaker's Discretion: Conference Committee Appointments in the 97th through 106th Congresses," *Political Research Quarterly* 60 (December 2007): 593–606.

[42]Samuel B. Hoff, "Saying No: Presidential Support and Veto Use, 1889–1989," *American Politics Quarterly* 19 (July 1991): 317.

[43]Dan Morgan, "Along for the Rider," *Washington Post National Weekly Edition*, August 19–25, 2002, p. 15.

[44]"Résumé of Congressional Activity, 110th Congress."

[45]Sinclair, *Unorthodox Lawmaking*, p. 272.

[46]James H. Cox, *Reviewing Delegation: An Analysis of the Congressional Reauthorization Process* (NY: Praeger, 2004), p. 124.

Chapter 11

[1]Robert Pear, "At House Party on Health Care, the Diagnosis Is It's Broken," *New York Times*, December 23, 2008, available at www.nytimes.com.

[2]Michael J. Gerhardt, *The Federal Impeachment Process: A Constitutional and Historical Analysis* (Princeton, NJ: Princeton University Press, 1995), p. 105.

[3]Quoted in Michael Nelson, "Choosing the Vice President," *PS: Political Science and Politics* (Fall 1988): 859.

[4]Joseph A. Pike, "The Vice Presidency: New Opportunities, Old Constraints," in Michael Nelson, ed., *The Presidency and the Political System*, 5th ed. (Washington, DC: Congressional Quarterly Press, 1998), pp. 548–54,

[5]Jody C. Baumgartner, *The American Vice Presidency Reconsidered* (Westport, CT: Praeger, 2006), p. 133.

[6]Barton Gellman and Jo Becker, "A 'Surrogate Chief of Staff,'" *Washington Post National Weekly Edition*, July 9–15, 2007, pp. 6–12.

[7]Harold J. Krent, *Presidential Powers* (New York, NY: New York University Press, 2005), pp. 215–216.

[8]Ryan J. Barilleaux, "Venture Constitutionalism and the Enlargement of the Presidency," in Christopher S. Kelley, *Executing the Constitution: Putting the President Back Into the Constitution* (Albany, NY: State University of New York, 2206), pp. 40–42.

[9]"Learning About the Senate: Treaties," available at www.senate.gov.

[10]Ibid.

[11]*Korematsu v. United States*, 323 U.S. 214, (1944).

[12]M. Steven Fish, *Democracy Derailed in Russia: The Failure of Open Politics* (New York, NY: Cambridge University Press, 2005), pp. 30–80.

[13]Clifford J. Levy, "With Tight Grip on Ballot, Putin Is Forcing Foes Out," *New York Times*, October 14, 2007, available at www.nytimes.com.

[14]*Korematsu v. United States*, 323 U.S. 214 (1944).

[15]Public Law 93–148 (1973).

[16]James A. Baker III and Warren Christopher, "Put War Powers Back Where They Belong," *New York Times*, July 8, 2009, available at www.nytimes.com.

[17]John M. Broder, "Report Urges Overhaul of the War Powers Law," *New York Times*, July 9, 2008, available at www.nytimes.com.

[18]Louis Fisher, "The Scope of Inherent Powers," in Edwards and King, *The Polarized Presidency of George W. Bush*, p. 53.

[19]Administrative Office of the U.S. Courts, "Federal Judicial Vacancies," available at www.uscourts.gov.

[20]*Youngstown Sheet and Tube Co. v. Sawyer*, 343 U.S. 579 (1952).

[21]Donna R. Hoffman and Alison D. Howard, *Addressing the State of the Union: The Evolution and Impact of the President's Big Speech* (Boulder, CO: Lynne Rienner, 2006), p. 194.

[22]Andrew Rudalevige, "The Executive Branch and the Legislative Process," in Joel D. Aberbach and Mark A. Peterson, eds., *The Executive Branch* (New York, NY: Oxford University Press, 2005), p. 373.

[23]Rebecca A. Deen and Laura W. Arnold, "Veto Threats as a Policy Tool: When to Threaten?" *Presidential Studies Quarterly* 32 (March 2002): 30–45.

[24]Phillip J. Cooper, "George W. Bush, Edgar Allan Poe, and the Use and Abuse of Presidential Signing Statements," *Presidential Studies Quarterly* 35 (September 2005): 515–532.

[25]Robert Pear, "Legal Group Faults Bush for Ignoring Parts of Bills," *New York Times*, July 24, 2006, available at www.nytimes.com.

[26]Curtis A. Bradley and Eric A. Posner, "Presidential Signing Statements and Executive Power," *Constitutional Commentary* 23 (Winter 2006): 307–364.

[27]John P. Burke, "The Institutional Presidency," in Michael Nelson, ed., *The Presidency and the Political System*, 8th ed. (Washington, DC: CQ Press, 2006), p. 386.

[28]Matthew J. Dickinson and Matthew J. Lebo, "Reexamining the Growth of the Institutional Presidency, 1940–2000," *Journal of Politics* 69 (February 2007): 206–219.

[29]The Executive Office of the President, available at http://first.gov/Agencies/Federal/Executive/EOP.shtml.

[30]Dickinson and Lebo, "Reexamining the Growth of the Institutional Presidency, 1940–2000," pp. 206–219.

[31]Paul J. Quirk, "Presidential Competence," in Nelson, *The Presidency and the Political System*, 8th ed. pp. 156–158.

[32]Ibid., pp. 179–89.

[33]James. P. Pfiffner, "Intelligence and Decision Making Before the War with Iraq," in Edwards and King, *The Polarized Presidency of George W. Bush*, p. 235.

[34]Michael Nelson, "The Psychological Presidency," in Nelson, ed., *The Presidency and the Political System*, 8th ed., pp. 170–194.

[35]Richard E. Neustadt, *Presidential Power: The Politics of Leadership* (New York, NY: Wiley, 1980).

[36]Samuel Kernell, *Going Public: New Strategies of Presidential Leadership*, 3rd ed. (Washington, DC: Congressional Quarterly Press, 1997).

[37]Scott B. Blinder, "Going Public, Going to Baghdad: Presidential Agenda-Setting and the Electoral Connection in Congress," in Edwards and King, eds., *The Polarized Presidency of George W. Bush*, pp. 336–344.

[38]Brandice Canes-Wrone, *Who Leads Whom? Presidents, Policy, and the Public* (Chicago, IL: University of Chicago Pres, 2006), p. 185.

[39]Kelly, *Executing the Constitution*, pp. 4–5.

[40]Steven A. Shull, *Policy by Other Means: Alternative Adoption by Presidents* (College Station, TX: Texas A&M University Press, 2006), pp. 30–35.

[41]Ryan C. Black, Anthony J. Madonna, Ryan J. Owens, and Michael S. Lynch, "Adding Recess Appointments to the President's 'Tool Chest' of Unilateral Powers," *Political Research Quarterly* 60 (December 2007): 645–654.

[42]Raymond Tatalovich and Alan R. Gitelson, "Political Party Linkages to Presidential Popularity: Assessing the 'Coalition of Minorities' Thesis," *Journal of Politics* 52 (February 1990): 241.

[43]John E. Mueller, *War, Presidents, and Public Opinion* (New York, NY: Wiley, 1973), p. 208.

[44]Ibid., p. 212.

[45]Jeffrey M. Jones, "Bush's High Approval Ratings Among Most Sustained for Presidents," *Gallup Poll Monthly*, November 2001, p. 32.

[46]William D. Baker and John R. O'Neal, "Patriotism or Opinion Leadership? The Nature and Origins of the 'Rally 'round the Flag' Effect," *Journal of Conflict Resolution* 45 (October 2001): 661–687.

[47]Richard Brody, "International Crises: A Rallying Point for the President?" *Public Opinion*, December/January 1984, pp. 41–43, 60.

[48]Marc J. Hetherington and Michael Nelson, "Anatomy of a Rally Effect: George W. Bush and the War on Terrorism," *PS: Political Science and Politics* (January 2003): 37–42.

[49]Gallup Poll, "Presidential Job Approval in Depth," available at www.gallup.com.

[50]*Gallup Poll Monthly*, June 1991, p. 27.

[51]Frank Newport, "Bush Job Approval Update," Gallup News Service, July 29, 2002, available at www.gallup.com.

[52]Roger T. Larocca, *The Presidential Agenda: Sources of Executive Influence in Congress* (Columbus, OH: Ohio University Press, 2006), pp. 5–6.

[53]George C. Edwards III and B. Dan Wood, "Who Influences Whom? The President, Congress, and the Media," *American Political Science Review* 93 (June 1999): 327–344.

[54]Jeffrey E. Cohen and Ken Collier, "Public Opinion: Reconceptualizing Going Public," in Steven A. Shull, *Presidential Policymaking: An End of the Century Assessment* (Armonk, NY: M.E. Sharpe, 1999), p. 43.

[55]Matthew Eshbaugh-Soha, *The President's Speeches: Beyond "Going Public"* (Boulder, CO: Lynne Rienner, 2006), p. 157.

[56]David W. Brady and Craig Volden, *Revolving Gridlock: Politics and Policy from Jimmy Carter to George W. Bush*, 2nd ed. (Boulder, CO: Westview Press, 2006), pp. 32–33.

Chapter 12

[1]Michael Grunwald, "The Katrina Disaster Was Par for the Corps," *Washington Post National Weekly Edition*, May 22–28, 2006, p. 21.

[2]Eric Lipton, "Republicans' Report on Katrina Assails Response," *New York Times*, February 13, 2006, available at www.nytimes.com.

[3]Eric Lipton, "'Breathtaking' Waste and Fraud in Hurricane Aid," *New York Times*, June 27, 2006, available at www.nytimes.com.

[4]Spencer S. Hsu, "Pondering FEMA's Future," *Washington Post National Weekly Edition*, February 20–26, 2006, p. 13.

[5]Michael Grunwald and Susan B. Glasser, "FEMA's Failure," *Washington Post National Weekly Edition*, January 16–22, 2006, pp. 11–13.

[6]"Federal Civilian Employment by Branch and Agency," *Statistical Abstract of the United States*, available at http://www.census.gov.

[7]G. Calvin MacKenzie, "The Real Invisible Hand: Presidential Appointees in the Administration of George W. Bush," *PS: Political Science & Politics* (March 2002): 28.

[8]Paul C. Light, "Late for Their Appointments," *New York Times*, November 16, 2004, available at www.nytimes.com.

[9]Nolan McCarty and Rose Razaghian, "Advice and Consent: Senate Responses to Executive Branch Nominations, 1885–1996," *American Journal of Political Science* 43 (October 1999): 1122–1143.

[10]Shirley Anne Warshaw, "The Formation and Use of the Cabinet," in Phillip G. Henderson, ed., *The Presidency Then and Now* (Lanham, MD: Rowman & Littlefield, 2000), p. 137.

[11]Joseph A. Pika and John Anthony Maltese, *The Politics of the Presidency*, 6th ed. (Washington, DC: CQ Press, 2004), p. 230.

[12]"Federal Civilian Employment, by Branch and Agency: 1990 to 2006," *Statistical Abstract of the United States 2000*.

[13]Paul C. Light, "The New True Size of Government," Robert F. Wagner Graduate School, New York University, available at http://wagner.nyu.edu.

[14]Scott Shane and Ron Nixon, "In Washington, Contractors Take on Biggest Role Ever," *New York Times*, February 4, 2007, available at www.nytimes.com.

[15]O. Glenn Stahl, *Public Personnel Administration*, 8th ed. (New York, NY: Harper & Row, 1983), p. 42.

[16]Joel D. Aberbach and Bert A. Rockman, "Senior Executives in a Changing Political Environment," in James P. Pfiffner and Douglas A. Brook, eds., *The Future of Merit: Twenty Years After the Civil Service Reform Act* (Washington, DC: Woodrow Wilson Center Press, 2000), pp. 81–97.

[17]James R. Thompson, "Federal Labor-Management Relations Under George W. Bush: Enlightened Management or Political Retribution?" in James S. Bowman and Jonathan P. West, eds., *American Public Service: Radical Reform and the Merit System* (Boca Raton, FL: RC Press, 2007), p. 240

[18]Christopher Lee, "An Overhaul, Not a Tune-Up," *Washington Post National Weekly Edition*, June 16–22, 2003, p. 30.

[19]Ann Gerhart, "Homeland Insecurity," *Washington Post National Weekly Edition*, April 4–10, 2005, pp. 6–7.

[20]Cornelius M. Kerwin, *Rulemaking: How Government Agencies Write Law and Make Policy*, 3rd ed. (Washington, DC: CQ Press, 2003), p. 21.

[21]Terry M. Moe, "The Presidency and the Bureaucracy: The Presidential Advantage," in Michael Nelson, ed., *The Presidency and the Political System*, 6th ed. (Washington, DC: CQ Press, 2000), pp. 465–468.

[22]Alan B. Morrison, "Close Reins on the Bureaucracy: Overseeing the Administrative Agencies," in Herman Schwartz, ed., *The Burger Years* (New York, NY: Viking, 1987), pp. 191–205.

[23]Ron Duhl, "Carter Issues an Order, But Is Anybody Listening?" *National Journal*, June 14, 1979, pp. 1156–1158.

[24]Robert Pear, "Bush Directive Increases Sway on Regulation," *New York Times*, January 30, 2007, available at www.nytimes.com.

[25]Edward Wyatt, "House Panel Challenges Smithsonian," *New York Times*, May 11, 2006, available at www.nytimes.com.

[26]Michael D. Reagan and John G. Salzone, *The New Federalism*, 2nd ed. (New York: Oxford University Press, 1981), chap. 3.

[27]Schlozman and Tierney, *Organized Interests and American Democracy*, pp. 341–346.

[28]Terry M. Moe, "Control and Feedback in Economic Regulation: The Case of the NLRB," *American Political Science Review* 79 (December 1985): 1094–1116; Jeffrey E. Cohen, "The Dynamics of the 'Revolving Door' on the FCC," *American Journal of Political Science* 30 (November 1986): 689–708.

[29]Steven P. Croley, *Regulation and Public Interests: The Possibility of Good Regulatory Government* (Princeton, NJ: Princeton University Press, 2008), pp. 214–230.

[30]Colin Campbell, "The Complex Organization of the Executive Branch: The Legacies of Competing Approaches to Administration," in Joel D. Aberbach and Mark A. Peterson, eds., *The Executive Branch* (New York, NY: Oxford University Press, 2005), p. 254.

[31]Dennis D. Riley and Bryan E. Brophy-Baermann, *Bureaucracy and the Policy Process* (Lanham, MD: Rowman & Littlefield Publishers, 2006), p. 98.

[32]Jeffrey Kluger, "Space Pork," *Time*, July 24, 2000, pp. 24–26.

[33]Jeffrey M. Berry, "Subgovernments, Issue Networks, and Political Conflict," in Richard A. Harris and Sidney M. Milkis, *Remaking American Politics* (Boulder, CO: Westview Press, 1989), pp. 239–260.

[34]Hugh Heclo, "Issue Networks and the Executive Establishment," in Anthony King, ed., *The New American Political System* (Washington, DC: American Enterprise Institute, 1978), pp. 87–124.

[34]Jamil E. Jreisat, *Politics Without Process: Administering Development in the Arab World* (Boulder, CO: Lynne Rienner, 1997), pp. 97–101.

[35]Monte Palmer, Ali Leila, and El Sayed Yassin, *The Egyptian Bureaucracy* (Syracuse, NY: Syracuse University Press, 1988), p. 151.

[36]Jreisat, *Politics Without Process*, p. 110.

[37]Hugh Heclo, "Issue Networks and the Executive Establishment," in Anthony King, ed., *The New American Political System* (Washington, DC: American Enterprise Institute, 1978), pp. 87-124

[38]John R. Provan, "The Highway Trust Fund: Its Birth, Growth, and Survival," in Theodore W. Taylor, ed., *Federal Public Policy* (Mt. Airy, MD: Lomond Publications, 1984), pp. 221–258.

[39]Jonathan Walters, "Revenge of the Highwaymen," *Governing*, September 1997, p. 13.

[40]Hsu, "Pondering FEMA's Future," p. 13.

Chapter 13

[1]Jeffrey Rosen, "Supreme Agreement," *Time*, July 14, 2008, pp. 36–37.

[2]Robert Barnes, "It 'Sits on a Knife's Edge,'" *Washington Post National Weekly Edition*, July 7–13, 2008, p. 33.

[3]Richard L. Pacelle, Jr., *The Role of the Supreme Court in American Politics: The Least Dangerous Branch* (Boulder, CO: Westview, 2002), p. 35.

[4]Harold W. Stanley and Richard G. Niemi, *Vital Statistics on American Politics 2007–2008* (Washington, DC: Congressional Quarterly Press, 2008), p. 301.

[5]Kermit Roosevelt III, *The Myth of Judicial Activism: Making Sense of Supreme Court Decisions* (New Haven, CT: Yale University Press, 2006), p. 3.

[6]Thomas M. Keck, *The Most Activist Supreme Court in History: The Road to Modern Judicial Conservatism* (Chicago, IL: University of Chicago Press, 2004), pp 286–289.

[7]Carp, Stidham, and Manning, *Judicial Process in America*, pp. 43–44.

[8]Ibid., p. 52.

[9]Ibid., p. 53.

[10]Karl Derouen, Jr., Jeffrey S. Peake, and Kenneth Ward, "Presidential Mandates and the Dynamics of Senate Advice and Consent, 1885–1996," *American Politics Research* 33 (January 2005): 106–131.

[11]Cass R. Sunstein, David Schkade, Lisa M. Ellman, and Andres Sawicki, *Are Judges Political? An Empirical Analysis of the Federal Judiciary* (Washington, DC: Brookings Institution, 2006), pp. 147–149.

[12]Ibid., p. 141.

[13]Joan Biskupic, "Barely a Dent on the Bench," *Washington Post National Weekly Edition*, October 24–30, 1994, p. 31.

[14]Ashlyn Kuersten and Donald Songer, "Presidential Success through Appointments to the United States Courts of Appeal," *American Politics Research* 31 (March 2003): 119.

[15]David C. Nixon and David L. Gross, "Confirmation Delay for Vacancies on the Circuit Courts of Appeal," *American Politics Research* 29 (May 2001): 246–274.

[16]John N. Paden, Muslim Civic Cultures and Conflict Resolution: The Challenge of Democratic Federalism in Nigeria (Washington, DC: Brookings Institution Press, 2005), pp. 139–174.

[17]Sarah A. Binder and Forrest Maltzman, "Congress and the Politics of Judicial Appointments," in Lawrence C. Dodd and Bruce I. Oppenheimer, *Congress Reconsidered*, 8th ed. (Washington, DC: CQ Press, 2205), pp. 302–305.

[18]R. Jeffrey Smith, "Back-Bench Politics," *Washington Post National Weekly Edition*, December 15-21, 2008, p. 7.

[19]Helen Dewar and Mike Allen, "GOP May Target Use of Filibuster," *Washington Post*, December 13, 2004, p. A01.

[20]Charles Gardner Geyh, *When Courts and Congress Collide: The Struggle for Control of America's Judicial System* (Ann Arbor, MI: University of Michigan Press, 2006), p. 19.

[21]Quoted in Henry J. Abraham, *Justices and Presidents: A Political History of Appointments to the Supreme Court* (New York, NY: Oxford University Press, 1974), p. 246.

[22]Timothy R. Johnson and Jason M. Roberts, "Presidential Capital and the Supreme Court Confirmation Process," *Journal of Politics* 66 (August 2004): 663–683.

[23]Updated data, based on Lawrence Baum, *The Supreme Court* (Washington, DC: CQ Press, 1981), p. 25.

[24]Charles M. Cameron, Albert D. Cover, and Jeffrey A. Segal, "Senate Voting on Supreme Court Nominees: A Neoinstitutional Model," *American Political Science Review* 84 (June 1990): 525–34.

[25]Keith E. Whittington, "Presidents, Senates, and Failed Supreme Court Nominations," *2006 The Supreme Court Review* (Chicago, IL: University of Chicago Press, 2006), pp. 412–421.

[26]John Massaro, *Supremely Political: The Role of Ideology and Presidential Management in Unsuccessful Supreme Court Nominations* (Albany, NY: State University of New York Press, 1990), p. 136.

[27]Mark Silverstein, "Bill Clinton's Excellent Adventure: Political Development and the Modern Confirmation Process," in Howard Gillman and Cornell Clayton, eds., *The Supreme Court in American Politics: New Institutional Interpretation* (Lawrence, KS: University of Kansas Press, 1999), p. 145.

[28]Linda Greenhouse, "New Focus on the Effects of Life Tenure," *New York Times*, September 10, 2007, available at www.nytimes.com.

[29]U.S. Supreme Court, "2007 Year-End Report on the Federal Judiciary," available at www.supremecourtus.gov.

[30]Ibid.

[31]*Baker v. Carr*, 369 U.S. 186 (1962).

[32]Lee Epstein and Jack Knight, "Mapping Out the Strategic Terrain: The Informational Role of *Amici Curiae*," in Cornell W. Clayton and Howard Gillman, *Supreme Court Decision-Making, New Institutional Approaches* (Chicago, IL: University of Chicago Press, 1999), p. 229.

[33]Timothy R. Johnson, "Information, Oral Arguments, and Supreme Court Decision Making," *American Politics Research* 29 (July 2001): 331–351.

[34]David O. Stewart, "A Chorus of Voices," *ABA Journal* (April 1991): 50.

[35]*Furman v. Georgia*, 408 U.S. 238 (1972).

[36]Harrell R. Rodgers, Jr., and Charles S. Bullock III, *Law and Social Change* (New York, NY: McGraw-Hill, 1977), p. 75.

[37]H. Frank Way, Jr., "Survey Research on Judicial Decisions: The Prayer and Bible Reading Cases," *Western Political Quarterly* 21 (June 1968): 189–205.

[38]Charles A. Johnson and Bradley C. Canon, *Judicial Policies: Implementation and Impact* (Washington, DC: Congressional Quarterly Press, 1984), ch. 1.

[39]Gerald N. Rosenberg, *The Hollow Hope: Can Courts Bring About Social Change?* (Chicago, IL: University of Chicago Press, 1991), pp. 336–338.

[40]*Statistical Abstract of the United States, 1991*, 111th ed. (Washington, DC: U.S. Department of Commerce, 1991), p. 71.

[41]Naseem Sowti, "Fewer Abortions," *Washington Post National Weekly Edition*, July 25–31, 2006, p. 29.

[42]*Tennessee Valley Authority v. Hill*, 437 U.S. 153 (1978).

[43]*Oregon v. Mitchell*, 400 U.S. 112 (1970).

[44]Carp, Stidham, and Manning, *Judicial Process in America*, p. 371.

[45]Robert Dahl, "Decision-Making in a Democracy: The Supreme Court as a National Policy-Maker," *Journal of Public Law* 6 (Fall 1957): 279–295.

[46]Johnson and Canon, *Judicial Policies*, pp. 231–232.

[47]Rosen, *The Most Democratic Branch*, pp. 7–8.

[48]*Clinton v. City of New York*, 524 U.S. 417 (1998).

Chapter 14

[1]Bureau of Labor Statistics, available at www.bls.gov.

[2]Chris Isidore, "It's Official: Recession Since Dec. '07," available at www.cnnmoney.com.

[3]Office of Management and Budget, *Fiscal Year 2009, Mid-Session Review*, available at www.omb.gov.

[4]Chris J. Dolan, John Frendreis, and Raymond Tatalovich, *The Presidency and Economic Policy* (Lanham, MD: Rowman & Littlefield, 2008), p. 3.

[5]Office of Management and Budget, *The Budget for Fiscal Year 2009, Historical Tables*, available at www.omb.gov.

[6]U.S. Census Bureau, "Gross Public Debt, Expenditures, and Receipts by Country: 1990–2006," *The 2008 Statistical Abstract*, available at www.census.gov.

[7]Anthony J. Cataldo II and Arline A. Savage, *U.S. Individual Federal Income Taxation: Historical, Contemporary, and Prospective Policy Issues* (Oxford, UK: Elsevier Science, 2001), pp. 39–40.

[8]Wojciech Bienkowski, Josef C. Brada, and Mariusz-Jan Radto, *Reaganomics Goes Global: What Can the EU, Russia, and Other Transition Countries Learn from the USA?* (New York, NY: Palgrave MacMillan, 2006), p. 69.

[9]Lori Montgomery, "The Bush Tax Cuts, Revisited," *Washington Post National Weekly Edition*, April 7–13, 2008, p. 23.

[10]Larry Rohter and Michael Cooper, "3 Candidates with 3 Financial Plans, but One Deficit," *New York Times*, April 27, 2008, available at www.nytimes.com.

[11]Congressional Budget Office, available at www.cbo.gov.

[12]Matthew Benjamin, "Cost of U.S. Crisis Action Grows, Along with Debt," October 10, 2008, available at www.bloomberg.com.

[13]Michael E. Bradley, "The Inexorable Rise of the National Debt," in Phillip John Davies, ed., *An American Quarter Century: U.S. Politics from Vietnam to Clinton* (Manchester, UK: Manchester University Press, 1995), pp. 59–61.

[14]Office of Management and Budget, *Fiscal Year 2009, Mid-Session Review*.

[15]Congressional Budget Office, "CBO's March 2008 Baseline: Medicare," available at www.cbo.gov.

[16]Robert Pear, "Medicare Costs to Increase for Wealthier Beneficia-ries," *New York Times*, September 11, 2006, available at www.nytimes.com.

[17]Centers for Medicare and Medicaid Services, available at www.cms.hhs.gov.

[18]Health Canada, available at www.hc-sc.gc.ca.

[19]Gerard W. Boychuk, National Health Insurance in the United States and Canada (Washington, DC: Georgetown University Press, 2008), pp. 3–21.

[20]Congressional Budget Office, "Budget Options," available at www.cbo.gov.

[21]Edmund L. Andrews, "Sharp Increase in Tax Revenue Will Pare U.S. Deficit," *New York Times*, July 13, 2005, available at www.nytimes.com.

[22]*Social Security and Medicare Boards of Trustees 2008 Annual Reports*, available at www.ssa.gov.

[23]Congressional Budget Office, "Fact Sheet for CBO's March 2008 Baseline: Medicaid," available at www.cbo.gov.

[24]Donald B. Marron, "Medicaid Spending Growth and Options for Controlling Costs," Testimony before the Senate Select Committee on Aging, available at www.cbo.gov.

[25]Social Security Administration, available at www.ssa.gov.

[26]Jesse J. Holland, "Raise Retirement Age to Save Social Security?" *Business Week*, August 1, 2008, available at www.businessweek.com.

[27]*Social Security and Medicare Boards of Trustees 2008 Annual Reports*.

[28]Social Security Administration, Trust Fund Data, available at www.ssa.gov.

[29]*Social Security and Medicare Boards of Trustees 2008 Annual Reports*.

[30]June O'Neill, "The Trust Fund, the Surplus, and the Real Social Security Problem," in Michael D. Tanner, ed., *Social Security and its Discontents: Perspectives on Choice* (Washington, DC: CATO Institute, 2004), pp. 37–38.

[31]William A. Kelso, *Poverty and the Underclass: Challenging Perceptions of the Poor in America* (New York, NY: New York University Press, 1994), p. 4.

[32]Robert Pear, "Welfare Spending Shows Huge Shift from Checks to Services," *New York Times*, October 13, 2003, available at www.nytimes.com.

[33]U.S. Department of Health and Human Services, Office of Family Assistance, Temporary Assistance for Needy Families, *Sixth Annual Report to Congress*, November 2004, available at www.acf.hhs.gov.

[34]Congressional Budget Office, "The Budget and Economic Outlook: An Update," available at www.cbo.gov.

[35]Jonathan Walters, "Is Welfare Working?" *Governing*, February 2008, pp. 28–33.

[36]Bureau of the Public Debt, available at www.treasurydirect.gov.

[37]Roger H. Davidson and Walter J. Oleszek, *Congress and Its Members*, 7th ed. (Washington, DC: CQ Press, 2000), p. 372.

[38]Office of Management and Budget, *Budget of the United States Government, Fiscal Year 2009*.

[39]Ibid.

[40]Alan I. Abramowitz, "Can McCain Overcome the Triple Whammy?" May 29, 2008, Larry J. Sabato's Crystal Ball 2008, available at www.centerforpolitics.org.

[41]Carl Hulse, "Congress is Still Pursuing Earmarks," *New York Times*, December 20, 2007, available at www.nytimes.com.

[42]Jonathan Weisman, "Bush Puts the Kibosh on Lawmakers' Pet Projects—Later," *Washington Post National Weekly Edition*, February 4–10, 2008, p. 7.

[43]Sheri Steisel and Jack Tweedle, "TANF Rules Tough on States," *State Legislatures*, March 2006, p. 23.

Chapter 15

[1]CNN.com, "U.S. Authorities Capture 'Dirty Bomb' Suspect," June 10, 2002, available at cnn.com.

[2]Quoted in Ted Bridis, "Bush Promises More Terror Arrests," June 11, 2002, available at http://foi.missouri.edu/terrorandcivillib/bushpromises.html.

[3]Josh Tyrangiel, "And Justice for..." *Time*, November 26, 2001, pp. 66–67.

[4]*Pruneyard Shopping Center v. Robins*, 447 U.S. 74 (1980).

[5]Richard H. Fallon, Jr., *The Dynamic Constitution: An Introduction to American Constitutional Law* (New York, NY: Cambridge University Press, 2004), pp. 60–61.

[6]Patrick M. Garry, *Wrestling with God: The Court's Tortuous Treatment of Religion* (Washington, DC: Catholic University of America Press, 2006), pp. 70–72.

[7]*Everson v. Board of Ewing Township*, 330 U.S. 1 (1947).

[8]*Zelman v. Simmons-Harris*, 536 U.S. 639 (2002).

[9]*Engel v. Vitale*, 370 U.S. 421 (1962).

[10]*Santa Fe School District v. Doe*, 530 U.S. 290 (2000).

[11]*Cantwell v. Connecticut*, 310 U.S. 296 (1940) and *Martin v. Struthers*, 319 U.S. 141 (1943).

[12]*Employment Division, Oregon Department of Human Resources v. Smith*, 493 U.S. 378 (1990).

[13]*Brandenburg v. Ohio*, 395 U.S. 444 (1969).

[14]*Cohen v. California*, 403 U.S. 15 (1971).

[15]"Hate is Not Speech: A Constitutional Defense of Penalty Enhancement for Hate Crimes," *Harvard Law Review* 106 (April 1993): 1314–31.

[16]*Wisconsin v. Mitchell*, 508 U.S. 47 (1993).

[17]*Texas v. Johnson*, 491 U.S. 397 (1989).

[18]*United States v. Eichman*, 396 U.S. 310 (1990).

[19]*Griswold v. Connecticut*, 381 U.S. 479 (1965).

[20]*Roe v. Wade*, 410 U.S. 113 (1973).

[21]*Webster v. Reproductive Health Services*, 492 U.S. 490 (1989).

[22]*Planned Parenthood of Southeastern Pennsylvania v. Casey*, 505 U.S. 833 (1992).

[23]*Lawrence v. Texas*, 539 US 558 (2003).

[24]Alan Hunter and John Sexton, *Contemporary China* (London: MacMillan Press, 1999), pp. 59–60.

[25]Beth Nonte Russell, "The Mystery of the Chinese Baby Shortage," *New York Times*, January 23, 2007, available at www.nytimes.com.

[26]Cecilia Nathansen Milwertz, *Accepting Population Control: Urban Chinese Women and the One-Child Family Policy* (Richmond Surrey, UK: Curzon Press, 1997), p. 11.

[27]*Illinois v. Wardlow*, 528 U.S. 119 (2000).

[28]*United States v. Ross*, 456 U.S. 798 (1982).

[29]*Mapp v. Ohio*, 367 U.S. 643 (1961).

[30]Adam Liptak, "U.S. Alone in Rejecting All Evidence if Police Err," *New York Times*, July 19, 2008, available at www.nytimes.com.

[31]*Massachusetts v. Shepherd*, 468 U.S. 981 (1984) and *United States v. Leon*, 468 U.S. 897 (1984).

[32]*Arizona v. Fulminante*, 499 U.S. 270 (1991).

[33]*Herring v. United States*, 7-513 (2009).

[34]*Miranda v. Arizona*, 384 U.S. 436 (1966).

[35]Gary L. Stuart, *Miranda: The Story of America's Right to Remain Silent* (Tucson, AR: University of Arizona Press, 2004), p.100.

[36]*Harris v. New York*, 401 U.S. 222 (1971).

[37]*New York v. Quarles*, 467 U.S. 649 (1984).

[38]*Moran v. Burdine*, 475 U.S. 412 (1986).

[39]*Kansas v. Hendricks*, 521 U.S. 346 (1997).

[40]Quoted in *Time*, July 7, 1997, p. 29.

[41]*Globe Newspaper Co. v. Superior Court*, 457 U.S. 596 (1982).

[42]*Chancler v. Florida*, 449 U.S. 560 (1981).

[43]*Williams v. Florida*, 399 U.S. 78 (1970).

[44]*Snyder v. Louisiana*, No. 06-10119 (2008).

[45]*Gideon v. Wainwright*, 372 U.S. 335 (1963).

[46]*Tollett v. Henderson*, 411 U.S. 258 (1973).

[47]*Solem v. Helm*, 463 U.S. 277 (1983).

[48]*Kennedy v. Louisiana*, No. 07-343 (2008).

[49]*Furman v. Georgia*, 408 U.S. 238 (1972).

[50]*Gregg v. Georgia*, 428 U.S. 153 (1976).

[51]Bureau of Justice Statistics, "Capital Punishment Statistics," available at www.ojp.usdoj.gov.

[52]James S. Leibman, *A Broken System: Error Rates in Capital Cases, 1973-1995*, available at www.thejusticeproject.org.

[53]Ibid.

[54]Bureau of Justice Statistics, "Capital Punishment 2005," available at www.ojp.usdoj.gov.

[55]"Supreme Court Bars Executing Mentally Retarded," June 20, 2002, available at cnn.com.

[56]*Atkins v. Virginia*, 536 U.S. 304 (2002).

[57]Otis H. Stephens, Jr., "Presidential Power, Judicial Deference, and the Status of Detainees in an Age of Terrorism," in David B. Cohen and John W. Wells, eds., *American National Security and Civil Liberties in an Era of Terrorism* (New York, NY: Palgrave MacMillan, 2004), p. 82.

[58]*Ex parte Quirin*, 317 U.S. 1 (1942).

[59]*Hamdi v. Rumsfeld*, 542 U.S. 507 (2004).

[60]*Hamdan v. Rumsfeld*, 548 U.S. 557 (2006).

[61]*Boumediene v. Bush*, 553 U.S. ___ (2008).

[62]Henry J. Abraham and Barbara A. Perry, *Freedom and the Court*, 7th. ed. (New York, NY: Oxford University Press, 1998), p. 236.

[63]Ranata Lawson Mack and Michael J. Kelly, *Equal Justice in the Balance: America's Legal Responses to the Emerging Terrorist Threat* (Ann Arbor, MI: University of Michigan Press, 2004), p. 238.

[64]Otis H. Stephens, Jr., *The Supreme Court and Confessions of Guilt* (Knoxville, TN: University of Tennessee Press, 1973).

[65]Donald L. Horowitz, *The Courts and Social Policy* (Washington, DC: Brookings Institution, 1977), p. 223.

Chapter 16

[1]*Grutter v. Bollinger*, 539 U.S. 306 (2003).

[2]Elder Witt, *The Supreme Court and Individual Rights*, 2nd ed. (Washington, DC: Congressional Quarterly Press, 1988), pp. 223–26.

[3]*Plessy v. Ferguson*, 163 U.S. 537 (1896).

[4]*Missouri ex rel Gaines v. Canada*, 305 U.S. 337 (1938).

[5]*Sweatt v. Painter*, 399 U.S. 629 (1950).

[6]*McLaurin v. Oklahoma State Regents*, 339 U.S. 637 (1950).

[7]*Brown v. Board of Education of Topeka*, 347 U.S. 483 (1954).

[8]*Brown v. Board of Education of Topeka*, 349 U.S. 294 (1955).

[9]Gerald Rosenberg, "Substituting Symbol for Substance: What Did *Brown* Really Accomplish?" *P.S. Political Science & Politics* (April 2004): 205.

[10]*Alexander v. Holmes County Board of Education*, 396 U.S. 19 (1969).

[11]Rosenberg, "Substituting Symbol for Substance," p. 206.

[12]*Swann v. Charlotte-Mecklenburg Board of Education*, 402 U.S. 1 (1971).

[13]*Keyes v. School District #1, Denver, Colorado*, 413 U.S. 189 (1973).

[14]Greg Winter, "Schools Resegregate, Study Finds," *New York Times*, January 21, 2003, available at www.nytimes. com.

[15]"School Segregation on the Rise," *Harvard Gazette News*, July 19, 2001, available at www.new.harvard.edu/gazette.

[16]*Millikin v. Bradley*, 418 U.S. 717 (1974).

[17]*Missouri v. Jenkins*, 515 U.S. 70 (1995).

[18]*Parents Involved in Community Schools v. Seattle School District No. 1*, 551 U.S. ___ (2007).

[19]*In re Griffiths*, 413 U.S. 717 (1973); *Examining Board of Engineers, Architects and Surveyors v. de Otero*, 426 U.S. 572 (1976); *Bernal v. Fainter*, 467 U.S. 216 (1984).

[20]Philippa Smith, "The Virginia Military Institute Case," in Sibyl A. Schwarzenbach and Patricia Smith, eds., *Women and the Constitution: History, Interpretation, and Practice* (New York, NY: Columbia University Press, 2003), p. 343.

[21]*United States v. Virginia*, 518 U.S. 515 (1996).

[22]*Rostker v. Goldberg*, 453 U.S. 57 (1981).

[23]*Romer v. Evans*, 517 U.S. 620 (1996).

[24]*Smith v. Allwright*, 321 U.S. 649 (1944).

[25]*Guinn v. United States*, 238 U.S. 347 (1915).

[26]*Louisiana v. United States*, 380 U.S. 145 (1965).

[27]*Harper v. State Board of Elections*, 383 U.S. 663 (1966).

[28]Quoted in Alfred H. Kelley and Winfred A. Harbison, *The American Constitution: Its Origins and Development* (New York, NY: Norton, 1970), p. 460.

[29]Quoted in Witt, *The Supreme Court and Individual Rights*, p. 247.

[30]*Civil Rights Cases*, 109 U.S. 3 (1883).

[31]*Shelley v. Kraemer*, 334 U.S. 1 (1948).

[32]*Heart of Atlanta Motel v. United States*, 379 U.S. 241; and *Katzenbach v. McClung*, 379 U.S. 294 (1964).

[33]Augustus B. Cochran III, *Sexual Harassment and the Law* (Lawrence, KS: University of Kansas Press, 2004), p. 114.

[34]Stephen Schwartz, "Shari'a in Saudi Arabia, Today and Tomorrow," in Paul Marshall, ed., *Radical Islam's Rules: The Worldwide Spread of Extreme Shari'a Law* (Lanham, MD: Rowman & Littlefield, 2005), pp. 33–34.

[35]Mai Yamani, "Muslim Women and Human Rights in Saudi Arabia," in Eugene Cotran and Mai Yamani, eds., *The Rule of Law in the Middle East and the Islamic World: Human Rights and the Judicial Process* (London, UK: I. B. Tauris, 2000), pp. 137–145.

[36]Damien McElroy, "Saudi Arabia to Lift Ban on Women Drivers," Daily Telegraph, January 21, 2008, available at www.telegraph.co.uk.

[37]*Oncale v. Sundowner Offshore Services, Inc.*, 523 U.S. 75 (1998).

[38]*City of Richmond v. J. A. Croson Co.*, 488 U.S. 469 (1989).

[39]*Regents of the University of California v. Bakke*, 438 U.S. 265 (1978).

[40]*Grutter v. Bollinger*, 539 U.S. 306 (2003).

[41]*Gratz v. Bollinger*, 539 U.S. 244 (2003).

[42]Gallup, "Race Relations," available at www.gallup.com.

[43]The Pew Center for the People & the Press, "The Black and White of Public Opinion," October 2005, available at www.people-press.org.

[44]Peter Schmidt, "Michigan Overwhelmingly Adopts Ban on Affirmative-Action Preferences," *Chronicle of Higher Education*, November 17, 2006, p. A23.

[45]*Grove City College v. Bell*, 465 U.S. 555 (1984).

[46]*Time*, June 23, 1997, p. 34.

Chapter 17

[1]Robert Cooper, *The Postmodern State and the World Order* (London: Demos, 2000), p. 22.

[2]Courtney B. Smith, *Politics and Process at the United Nations: The Global Dance* (Boulder, CO: Lynne Rienner, 2006), p. 28.

[3]Jim Hoagland, "A Transformative NATO," *Washington Post National Weekly Edition*, December 12–18, 2005, p. 5.

[4]Elizabeth Becker, "Trade Talks Fail to Agree on Drugs for Poor Nations," *New York Times*, December 21, 2002, available at www.nytimes.com.

[5]Michael E. Brown, ed., *Grave New World: Security Challenges in the 21st Century* (Washington, DC: Georgetown University Press, 2003), p. 307.

[6]Jonathan P. Doh and Hildy Teegan, *Globalization and NGOs: Transforming Business, Government, and Society* (Westport, CT: Praeger, 2003), pp. 3–9, 206–219.

[7]Terry L. Deibel, *Foreign Affairs Strategy: Logic for American Statecraft* (New York, NY: Cambridge University Press, 2007), p. 271.

[8]"United States Foreign Trade Highlights," International Trade Administration, U.S. Department of Commerce, available at www.ita.doc.gov.

[9]Marvin Zonis, "The 'Democracy Doctrine' of President George W. Bush," in Stanley A. Renshon and Peter Suedfeld, eds., *Understanding the Bush Doctrine: Psychology and Strategy in an Age of Terrorism* (New York, NY: Routledge, 2007), p. 232.

[10]Congressional Research Service, *Conventional Arms Transfers to Developing Nations, 1996–2003*, August 26, 2004, available at www.fas.org/man/crs.

[11]Celia W. Dugger, "U.S. Challenged to Increase Aid to Africa," *New York Times*, June 5, 2005, available at www.nytimes.com.

[12]Budget of the United States Government, Fiscal Year 2003, available at www.omb.gov.

[13]Robert J. Lieber, *Eagle Rules? Foreign Policy and American Primacy in the Twenty-First Century* (Upper Saddle River, NJ: Pearson, 2002), pp. 5–6.

[14]Joseph S. Nye, Jr., *The Paradox of American Power: Why the World's Only Superpower Can't Go it Alone* (New York, NY: Oxford University Press, 2002), p. 156.

[15]Quoted in G. John Ikenberry, "Is American Multilateralism in Decline?" *Perspectives on Politics* 1 (September 2003): 534.

[16]Robert S. Litwak, *Regime Change: U.S. Strategy Through the Prism of 9/11* (Baltimore, MD: Johns Hopkins University Press, 2007), pp. 2–10.

[17]Steven Lee Myers and Elaine Sciolino, "North Koreans Bar Inspectors at Nuclear Site," *New York Times*, September 25, 2008, available at www.nytimes.com.

[18]Isaiah Wilson III, "What Weapons Do They Have and What Can They Do?" *PS: Political Science & Politics* (July 2007): 473.

[19]Willie Curtis, "Illusionary Promises and Strategic Reality: Rethinking the Implications of Strategic Deterrence in a Post 9/11 World," in Renshon and Suedfeld, eds., *Understanding the Bush Doctrine*, pp. 133–143.

[20]Ibid.

[21]Steven Mufson, "Rogue States: A Real Threat?" *Washington Post National Weekly Edition*, June 12, 2000, p. 15.

[22]John Dumbrell, "The Bush Doctrine," in George C. Edwards III and Philip John Davies, *New Challenges for the American Presidency* (New York: Longman, 2004), pp. 232–234.

[23]Thomas E. Ricks, "A New Way of War," *Washington Post National Weekly Edition*, December 10–16, 2001, p. 6.

[24]David S. Cloud, "Navy to Expand Fleet with New Enemies in Mind," *New York Times*, December 5, 2005, available at www.nytimes.com.

[25]Ann Scott Tyson, "A Road Map for Resources," *Washington Post National Weekly Edition*, February 13–19, 2006, p. 29.

[26]David Albright, "Securing Pakistan's Nuclear Weapons Complex," Institute for Science and International Security," October 2001, available at www.isisonline.org/publications/terrorism/stanleypaper.html.

[27]Farzana Shaikh, "Pakistan's Nuclear Bomb: Beyond the Non-Proliferation Regime," *International Affairs* 78 (January 2002): 29–48.

[28]Richard Morin, "A Gap in Worldviews," *Washington Post National Weekly Edition*, April 19, 1999, p. 34.

[29]Cecil V. Crabb, Jr., Glenn J. Antizzo, and Leila E. Serieddine, *Congress and the Foreign Policy Process* (Baton Rouge, LA: Louisiana State University Press, 2000), p. 189.

[30]James Meernik, "Presidential Support in Congress: Conflict and Consensus on Foreign and Defense Policy," *Journal of Politics* 55 (August 1993): 569–87.

[31]Litwak, *Regime Change*, p. 48.

[32]Richard J. Stoll, "The Sound of the Guns," *American Politics Quarterly* 15 (April 1987): 223–37.

[33]Jeffrey M. Jones, "Bush's High Approval Ratings Among Most Sustained for Presidents," *Gallup Poll Monthly*, November 2001, p. 32.

[34]Evelyn Nieves and Ann Scott Tyson, "'Don't Tell' Because We Need You Now," *Washington Post National Weekly Edition*, February 21–27, 2005, p. 29.

>credits

TEXT CREDITS

Agee, Mark. From "Small Texas school district lets teachers, staff pack pistols" by Mark Agee, *Star-Telegram*, August 15, 2008. Courtesy of the Fort Worth Star-Telegram.

Flaherty, Ann. From "Study: Congress Should Repeal, 'Don't Ask, Don't Tell'" by Ann Flaherty, July 7, 2008. Used with permission of The Associated Press Copyright © 2008. All rights reserved.

Gallup, George H. "How Many Americans Know U.S. History? Part I" by George H. Gallup, Jr. October 21, 2003, www.gallup.com. Courtesy of Gallup News Service.

Holland, Jesse J. From "Raise retirement age to save social security" by Jesse J. Holland. Reprinted from the August 1, 2008 issue of *Business Week* by permission. Copyright © 2008 by The McGraw-Hill Companies.

Isaacs, Julia B. From "Economic Mobility of Men and Women" by Julia B. Isaacs, www.brookings.edu. Reprinted by permission of The Brookings Institution.

Maloney, Jennifer. From "College presidents want drinking age lowered to 18" by Jennifer Maloney, *Newsday*, August 19, 2008. Copyright © 2008 Newsday. Used by permission.

Martin, Courtney E. Reprinted with permission from Courtney E. Martin, "Why American Youth Will Vote," *The American Prospect Online*: November 04, 2008. www.prospect.org. The American Prospect, 1710 Rhode Island Avenue NW, 12th Floor, Washington, DC 20036. All rights reserved.

The National Entertainment State. From "10th Anniversary The National Entertainment State." Reprinted with permission from the July 3, 2006 issue of *The Nation*. For subscription information, call 1-800-333-8536. Portions of each week's *Nation* magazine can be accessed at http://www.thenation.com.

Ramstack, Tom. "Justice Kennedy casts decisive vote" by Tom Ramstack, *The Washington Times*, June 27, 2008. Copyright © 2008 The Washington Times LLC. This reprint does not constitute or imply an endorsement or sponsorship of any product, service, company or organization. Reprinted by permission.

Saad, Lydia. From "Religion is Very Important to Majority of Americans" by Lydia Saad, December 5, 2003, www.gallup.com. Courtesy of Gallup News Service.

Trends in Higher Education Series: Trends in Student Aid, 2007, www.collegeboard.com. Used by permission of The College Board.

Walter, Dan. "Reassessing the 'Bradley Effect'" by Dan Walter, *Sacramento Bee*, August 11, 2008. Copyright © 2008 by The Sacramento Bee. Reprinted by permission.

Wangsness, Lisa. From "New offshore drilling not a quick fix, analysts say" by Lisa Wangsness, *The Boston Globe*, June 20, 2008. Copyright © 2008, Globe Newspaper Company. Republished with permission.

PHOTO CREDITS

Front Matter

iv (l): Cedric Joubert/AP Photo; (c):Afton Almaraz/AP Photos; (r): vario images GmbH & Co.KG/Alamy; **v** (l): Mark Peterson/CORBIS; (c): Tammie Arroyo/AP Photo; (r): ROBERT GALBRAITH/Reuters/Corbis; **vi** (l): The Everett Collection; (c): Amy Sancetta/AP Photo; (r): Reuters/CORBIS; **vii** (l): David Maung/AP Photo; (c): Bettmann/CORBIS; (r): Tim Sloan/AFP/Getty Images; **viii** (l): LUC GNAGO/Reuters/Landov; (c): Lara Porzak Photography via Getty Images; (r): Jim West/The Image Works; **ix** (l): Susan Steinkamp/CORBIS; (c): Emilio Morenatti/AP Photo; (r): NatalieHelbert/istockphoto.com.

Introduction

2–3 UPI Photo/Michael Kleinfield/Newscom; **3** (tr): James Pinsky/U.S. Navy/ZUMA/CORBIS; **4** (t): UPI Photo/Michael Kleinfield/Newscom; (b): James Pinsky/U.S. Navy/ZUMA/CORBIS; (inset): Jerry Grayson/Helifilms Australia PTY Ltd/Getty Images; **5** Sascha Burkard/Used under license from Shutterstock; **7** Gerald Herbert/AP Photo; **8** Bill Fritsch/Brand X/Corbis; **9** Alfred Eisenstaedt/Time & Life Pictures/Getty Images.

Chapter 1

14–15 Mike Theiler/Reuters; **15** (tr): Solus-Veer/Corbis; **16** (t): Mike Theiler/Reuters; (b): Judy Ben Joud/Used under license from Shutterstock; **17** Molly Riley/Reuters/Landov; **18** Greg Baker/AP Photo; **19** Solus-Veer/Corbis; **20** Justin Sullivan/Getty Images; **21** Cedric Joubert/AP Photo; **22** *Reagan, Nixon, Johnson:* Bettmann/CORBIS; *George H.W. Bush:* Bachrach/Getty Images; *George W. Bush:* Brooks Kraft/Corbis; *Clinton:* Alex Wong/Getty Images; *Carter:* Wally McNamee/CORBIS; **23** (t): VisionsofAmerica/Joe Sohm/Getty Images; (b): Michael Silver Editorial/Alamy; **24** (t): Koji Sasahara/AP Photo; (b): magicoven/Used under license from Shutterstock; **25** (t): Sherwin Crasto/Reuters/CORBIS; (b): Tim Boyle/Getty Images; **26** Damian Dovarganes/AP Photo; **27** (l): EMMANUEL DUNAND/AFP/Getty Images; (r): Chip Somodevilla/Getty Images; **28** HANS DERYK/Reuters/Landov; **29** (t): Leah Nash/The New York Times/Redux Pictures; (b): Rolf Haid/dpa/Landov; **31** Amy Sancetta/AP Photo.

Chapter 2

34–35 Eduardo Munoz/Reuters; **35** (tr): Craig Brewer/Photodisc/Getty Images; **36** (t): Eduardo Munoz/Reuters; (b): Colonial Williamsburg Foundation; **37** (t): Mike Bentley/istockphoto.com; (b): David Frazier/PhotoEdit; **38** Courtesy, PETA; **39** COLUMBIA TRISTAR/ANDREW COOPER/THE KOBAL COLLECTION/Picture Desk; **41** Laurie Asseo/Bloomberg News/Landov; **42** Craig Brewer/Photodisc/Getty Images; **43** (l): Hulton Archive/Getty Images; (r): AP Photo; **44** Stock Montage/Getty Images; **45** Bob Daemmrich/The Image Works; **47** (bkgd): Toby Melville/WPA rota/PA Wire URN:5316105/AP Photos; (inset): REUTERS/Suzanne Plunkett/Landov; **48** Afton Almaraz/AP Photos; **49** Joe Fudge/Daily Press/AP Photo; **50** Bettmann/CORBIS; **51** culligan-photo/Alamy; **52** Ken James/UPI Photo/Landov; **53** Bettmann/CORBIS; **54** AP Photos; **55** Ron Edmonds/AP Photos.

Chapter 3

58–59 STEPHEN McGEE/The New York Times/Redux Pictures *This photo has been altered slightly from the original. Writing on the blackboard has been removed.*; **59** (tr): vario images GmbH & Co.KG/Alamy; **60** STEPHEN McGEE/The New York Times/Redux Pictures (detail); **61** vario images GmbH & Co.KG/Alamy; **62** Greg Wahl-Stephens/AP Photo; **64** Tom Grill/CORBIS; **65** Eric Draper/AP Photo; **66** (t): A. Radzkou/Used under license from Shutterstock; (bl):Photos.com; (br): Yellowj/Used under license from Shutterstock; **68** quaxelc/Used under license from Shutterstock; **69** Kuttig-People/Alamy; **70** Pakhnyushcha/Used under license from Shutterstock; **72** Kapu/Used under license from Shutterstock.

Chapter 4

76–77 Mike Segar/Reuters; **77** (tr): Paul Tomas; **78** (tl): Mike Segar/Reuters; (b): Mark Peterson/CORBIS; **79** John Sundlof/Alamy; **82** (l): Jeff Siner/The Charlotte Observer/AP Photo; (r): Dan Wagner; **83** (t): Stockbyte/Getty Images; (b): Clifford K. Berryman/The National Archives and Records Administration; **84** Bonnie Schiffman/CORBIS; **87** (t): Baltimore Sun, Jed Kirschbaum/AP Photo; (bl): Library of Congress Prints and Photographs Division Washington, D.C. [LC-USZCN4-189]; (br): AP Photo; **88** Izzy Schwartz/Photdisc/Getty Images; **89** David Hoffman Photo Library; **90** Michael Newman/Photo Edit; **91** (b): Paul Tomas; (tl): KAREN BLEIER/AFP/Getty Images; (cr): Kimberly White/Reuters; **92** Bettmann/CORBIS; **93** Pete Stone/CORBIS; **94** Digital Vision/Getty Images; **95** Gene Blevins/LA Daily News/CORBIS.

Chapter 5

100–101 Terry Gilliam/AP Photo; **101** (tr): Mike Wintroath/AP Photo; **102** (t): Terry Gilliam/AP Photo; (b): Matt Rourke/AP Photo; **103** (l): Matt Stroshane/Getty Images; (r): Tammie Arroyo/AP Photo; **104** Paul Hawthorne/Getty Images; **105** (t): MR. MONOPOLY © 1935, 2009 Hasbro. All rights reserved. (b): Andresr/Used under license from Shutterstock; **106** Chuck Burton/AP Photo; **107** (tl): Wally McNamee/CORBIS; (tr): Alex Wong/Getty Images; (bl): Bettmann/CORBIS; (br): Sean Adair/Reuters/Landov; **108** suravid/Used under license from Shutterstock; **109** Mick Tsikas/Reuters; **110** Mike Wintroath/AP Photo; **111** Andrew Lichtenstein/Sygma/Corbis; **112** B.S.P.I./CORBIS; **113** Jeff Greenberg/The Image Works.

Chapter 6

116–117 Matthew Cavanaugh/epa/CORBIS; **117** (tr): Damian Dovarganes/AP Photo; **118** (t): Matthew Cavanaugh/epa/CORBIS; (b): REUTERS/Ethan Miller/CORBIS; **119** Roger Ressmeyer/CORBIS; **120** (t): Lynn Goldsmith/Corbis; (b): Dell/Dreamstime.com; **121** Jose Goitia/AP Photo; **122** (tl): Robert Maass/CORBIS; (bl): James A Isbell/Shutterstock; (tr): Lou Dematteis/REUTERS; (br): Courtesy, The Drudge Report; **123** (t): Mark Mainz/AP Images for Fox; (cl): Keyur Khamar/Bloomberg News/Landov; (c): Reuters/CORBIS; (cr): Ted S. Warren/AP Photo; (bc): Philippe Wojazer/REUTERS; (br): Cafe Press/AP Photo; **124** © 2008 Wikimedia Foundation Inc.; **125** (t): Damian Dovarganes/AP Photo; (b): ROBERT GALBRAITH/Reuters/Corbis; **126** Comedy Central/Courtesy the Everett Collection; **127** (t): Shutterstock; (b): Courtesy, ESPN; **128** Paramount Pictures/Photofest; **129** CHUCK KENNEDY/MCT/Landov.

Chapter 7

132–133 Reuters/CORBIS; **133** (tr): The Everett Collection; **134** Reuters/CORBIS; **135** *montage* Joshua Lott/AP Photo; Peter M. Fredin/AP Photo; John Russell/AP Photo; Peter Cosgrove/AP Photo; Brandon Thibodeaux/Dallas Morning News/Corbis; Nam Y. Huh/AP Photo; Mark Gilliland/AP Photo; Scott Olson/Getty Images; PRNewsFoto/Mothers Against DrunkDriving/newscom; **136** (t): J.D. Pooley/Getty Images; (b): Jerry S. Mendoza/AP Photo; **137** Amy Sancetta/AP Photo; **138** (l): Alex Wong/Getty Images; (r): Patti Longmire/AP Photo; **139** Gregory Bull/AP Photo; **140** (l): Chuck Savage/Corbis; (r): Peter Hvizdak/The Image Works; **141** Brendan Smialowski/AFP/Getty Images; **142** Matt Rourke/AP Photo; **143** (t): Gerald Herbert/AP Photo; (b): Scott Maxwell/LuMaxArt 2008/Used under license from Shutterstock.com;

144 Tatiana Popova 2008/Used under license from Shutterstock.com; 145 Richard Lord/The Image Works; 146 (t): Jason Kempin/WireImage/Getty Images; (b): The Everett Collection; 147 Rick Wilking/Reuters/Corbis; 148 Diane Bondareff/AP Photo.

Chapter 8

152–153 Lynn Goldsmith/CORBIS; 153 (tr): Cory Ryan/Getty Images; 154 Lynn Goldsmith/CORBIS; 155 (tr): Jason Kirk/Getty Images; (tl): Cynthia Johnson/Getty Images; (cl): Dirck Halstead/Time Life Pictures/Getty Images; (bl): Justin Sullivan/Getty Images; 156 Shai Ginott/CORBIS; 157 Cory Ryan/Getty Images; 159 Wally McNamee/CORBIS; 160 (l): Chip Somodevilla/Getty Images; (r): Chip Somodevilla/Getty Images; 161 (t): Dennis Van Tine/Abaca Press/MCT/Newscom; (b): NBC-TV/THE KOBAL COLLECTION/EDELSON DANA/The Picture Desk; 162 Courtney Perry/Dallas Morning News/Corbis; 163 Stephen Saks Photography/Alamy; 165 David Coleman/Alamy; 167 Joshua Roberts/Bloomberg News/Landov.

Chapter 9

170–171 Gabriel Buoys/AFP/Getty Images; 171 (tr): John Moore/Getty Images; 172 (t): Gabriel Buoys/AFP/Getty Images; b Probate Court Jefferson County, AL; 173 UPI Photo/A.J. Sisco/Landov; 175 Eric Gay/AP Photo; 176 North Wind Picture Archives; 177 Obama Campaign/AP Photo; 178 (l): SwagHouse Media/Getty Images; (r): Reuters/CORBIS; 179 Jim McIsaac/Getty Images; 180 Randy Faris/Corbis; 181 Courtesy, Matthew Sheldon; 182 Vahan Shirvanian/Cartoonstock.com; 183 John Moore/Getty Images; 184 J. Scott Applewhite/AP Photo; 185 Silvia Izquierdo/AP Photo; 187 Dave Weaver/AP Photo; 188–189 (bkgd): Daniel Mandic/Used under license from Shutterstock; *Edwards:* Ethan Miller/Getty Images; *Biden:* Alex Wong/Getty Images; *Giuliani:* Moose/AdMedia/Newscom; *Romney:* Soren McCarty/WireImage/Getty Images; *Clinton:* Chris Fitzgerald/CandidatePhotos/Newscom; *McCain:* Yoan Valat/epa/Corbis; *Paul:* David McNew/Getty Images; *Obama:* Stefan Zaklin/epa/Corbis; *Huckabee:* TOSHIFUMI KITAMURA/AFP/Getty Images; *Gravel:* Alex Wong/Getty Images; 190 (tl): Brooks Kraft/Corbis; (tr): Steve Pope/epa/Corbis; (bl): Brendan Smialowski/Getty Images; (br): Rick Friedman/Corbis; 191 (l): Jiri Moucka/Shutterstock; (r): Jiri Moucka/Shutterstock; 192 The Granger Collection, New York; 194 BETH A. KEISER/AP Photo; 195 Bettmann/CORBIS; 197 Richard Drew/AP Photo; 198 Namir Noor-Eldeen RCS/AH/Reuters.

Chapter 10

202–203 David Maung/AP Photo; 203 (tr): Lauren Victoria Burke/AP Photo; 204 (t): David Maung/AP Photo; (b): MANDEL NGAN/AFP/Getty Images; 205 Tim Sloan/AFP/Getty Images; 206 Craig Lassig/epa/Corbis; 207 Doug Mills/The New York Times/Redux Pictures; 209 Seth Perlman/AP Photo; 210 Dana Edelson/NBCU Photo Bank via AP Images; 211 (t): Jeff Gentner/AP Photo; (tr): Lauren Victoria Burke/AP Photo; (cl): Brendan Hoffman/Getty Images; (cr): Susan Walsh/AP Photo; (bl): Dennis Cook/AP Photo; (br): Susan Walsh/AP Photo; 212–213 Diane Cook and Len Jenshel/Getty Images; 213 (t): LM Otero/AP Photo; 214 AP Photo; 215 (l): Scott Cohen/Reuters; (r): Jim Mone/AP Photo; 216 Michael Hall Photography Pty Ltd/Corbis; 217 Ron Edmonds/AP Photo; 218 The Everett Collection; 219 istera/Used under license from Shutterstock; 220 Susan Walsh/AP Photo; 222 Bettmann/CORBIS; 223 SuperStock Inc.; 224 Pat Bagley/www.caglecartoons.com.

Chapter 11

228–229 Matthew Holst/The New York Times/Redux Pictures; 229 (tr): Bettmann/CORBIS; 230 Matthew Holst/The New York Times/Redux Pictures; 231 *T. Roosevelt, Eisenhower, Kennedy:* Bettmann/CORBIS; *Reagan:* Wally McNamee/CORBIS; *Clinton:* Alex Wong/Getty Images; 232 (tl): David J. & Janice L. Frent Collection/CORBIS; (t): CORBIS; (bl): Martin H. Simon/Corbis; (br): AFP/Getty Images; 233 Popperfoto/Getty Images; 234 (t): Paul Szep; (b): Reuters/CORBIS; 235 AP Photo; 236 (l): Seattle Post-Intelligencer Collection; Museum of History and Industry/CORBIS; (r): U.S. Navy, Shane T. McCoy/AP Photo; 237 Alexander Natruskin/Pool/epa/Corbis; 238 Matthew Cavanaugh/epa/Corbis; 240 Bettmann/CORBIS; 241 Shawn Thew/epa/Corbis; 242 Brendan Smialowski/AFP/Getty Images;. 244 (bkgd): AP Photo; (l): Reuters/CORBIS; (r): Alex Wong/Getty Images; 245 Frank Franklin II/AP Photo; 246 (tl,bl): Bettmann/CORBIS; (tr): Popperphoto/Getty Images; (br): AP Photo; 247 Frank Micelotta/Getty Images; 248 Bettmann/CORBIS; 251 Mary Ellen Matthews/NBCU Photo B via AP Images; 253 Nick Ut/AP Photo.

Chapter 12

256–257 JAMES NIELSEN/AFP/Getty Images; 257 (tr): Library of Congress Prints and Photographs Division Washington D.C. [LC-USZC4-1587]; 258 JAMES NIELSEN/AFP/Getty Images; 259 UPI Photo/Anne Ryan/Newscom; 260 David Scharf/Peter Arnold Inc.; 261 (both): Courtesy of the Peace Corps; 262 Jeff Kravitz/FilmMagic/Getty Images; 263 (l): National Science Foundation; (r): © CBS/Courtesy: Everett Collection.; 265 (bkgd): Scott Peterson/Getty Images; (inset): Gerry Broome/AP Photo; 266 (t): David R. Frazier/The Image Works; (b): Bettmann/CORBIS; (br): Library of Congress Prints and Photographs Division Washington D.C. [LC-USZC4-1587]; 267 Joe Marquette/AP Photo; 268 (t): SETH WENIG/Reuters/Landov; (b): Mario Tama/Getty Images; 269 AP Photo/David J. Phillip; 270 Library of Congress.

Washington D.C. [LC-USZC4-3859]; 271 (l): AP Photo/Portland Police Department; (cl): David Toase/Getty Images; (cr): Juergen Becker/zefa/Corbis; (bl): Steven Puetzer/Getty Images; bc dkey/A.collection/Getty Images; (br): George Doyle/Getty Images; 273 Jack Kurtz/ZUMA/Corbis; 274 Ron Sachs/CNP/Sygma/Corbis; 275 Carlos Osorio File/AP Photo; 276 AP Photo/Damian Dovarganes; 277 Reza/Webistan/Corbis; 278 (l): Cindy Charles/PhotoEdit; (cl): Congressional Quarterly/Getty Images; (c): Eric Rowley/AP Photo; (cr): MANDEL NGAN/AFP/Getty Images; (b): Tony Gutierrez/AP Photo; 280 David Young-Wolff/PhotoEdit.

Chapter 13

284–285 © Art Lein 2008; 285 (tr): LUC GNAGO/Reuters/Landov; 286 (t): © Art Lein 2008; (b): Ed Fischer/Cartoonstock.com; 287 (bkgd): Bettmann/CORBIS; (inset): Time & Life Pictures/Getty Images; 288 Travelpix Ltd/Getty Images; 289 ROBERT GALBRAITH/Reuters/Landov; 290 SERGEI KARPUKHIN/Reuters/Corbis; 291 Jack Kurtz/ZUMA/Corbis; 292 LUC GNAGO/Reuters/Landov; 293 Joe Raedle/Getty Images; 295 (bkgd): AP Photo/J. Scott Applewhite; (fgd): Roslen Mack/Used under license from Shutterstock; 296 (t): Time & Life Pictures/Getty Images; (b): Charles Dharapak/AP Photo; 297 (t): CORBIS; (b): AFP/Getty Images; 301 Mark Blinch/Reuters/Corbis; 302 Comstock/Jupiter Images; 303 Mario Tama/Getty Images; 304 Joe Raedle/Newsmakers/Getty Images; 305 Lara Porzak Photography via Getty Images; 306 Tony Savino/Corbis; 307 Bob Daemmrich/Corbis.

Chapter 14

310–311 Justin Sullivan/Getty Images; 311 (tr): Ryan Donnell/The New York Times/Redux; 312 (t): Justin Sullivan/Getty Images; (b): Rick Lew/Getty Images; 313 Brian Snyder/Reuters/Corbis; 314 (l): Doug Hyun © F/X Network/Everett Collection; (r): MTV/THE KOBAL COLLECTION/Picture Desk; 315 Bonnie Kamin/PhotoEdit; 316 Commercial Eye/Getty Images; 317 Robert Llewellyn/Jupiter Images; 318 Marc Asnin/CORBIS SABA; 319 (t): Matthew Cavanaugh/epa/Corbis; 320 Richard Baker/Corbis; 321 Kathy Willens/AP Photo; 323 DOG EAT DOG FILMS/WEINSTEIN COMPANY/THE KOBAL COLLECTION/Picture Desk; 325 (bkgd): Bettman/Corbis; (inset): NBC-TV/THE KOBAL COLLECTION/Picture Desk; 326 (t): Ryan Donnell/The New York Times/Redux; (b): Getty Images; 329 Jim West/The Image Works; 330 (both): Gerald Herbert/AP Photo; 331 Wilfredo Lee/AP Photo; 333 J. Scott Applewhite/AP Photo; 334 Tony Gutierrez/AP Photo.

Chapter 15

338–339 J. Pat Carter/AP Photo 339 (tr): Susan Steinkamp/CORBIS; 340 J. Pat Carter/AP Photo; 341 PRNewsFoto/Newsweek/Newscom; 342 John Gress JG/CCK/Reuters; 343 Ron Edmonds/AP Photo; 344 Jeff Greenberg/PhotoEdit; 345 Wausau Daily Herald Butch McCartney/AP Photo; 346 (t): Andy Wong/AP Photo; 348 HIROKO MASUIKE/AFP/Getty Images; 349 Susan Steinkamp/CORBIS; 350 Tim Mosenfelder/Corbis; 351 Bohemian Nomad Picturemakers/CORBIS; 352 AP Photo/Don Heupel; 353 © NBC/Courtesy: Everett Collection.; 354 Kimberly White/CORBIS; 355 (tl): Douglas C. Pizac/AP Photo; (tr): Nati Harnik/AP Photo; (bl): Mark Jenkinson/Corbis; (br): Jeffrey Coolidge/Ionica/Getty Images; 357 Northwestern University Library [http://www.library.northwestern.edu/govpub/collections/wwii-posters/img/ww1646-72]; 358 Christina Dicken/Chronicle-Tribune/AP Photo.

Chapter 16

362–363 Najlah Feanny/CORBIS SABA; 363 (tr): Emilio Morenatti/AP Photo; 364 (t): Najlah Feanny/CORBIS SABA; (bl): Alex Brandon/AP Photo; (br): Lawrence Jackson/AP Photo; 365 Manuel Balce Ceneta/AP Photo; 366 Time & Life Pictures/Getty Images; 367 Bettman/Corbis; 368 Flying Colours Ltd/Getty Images; 369 David Churchill/Arcaid/Corbis; 370 James Dawson/Jupiter Images; 371 F. Carter Smith/Sygma/Corbis; 372 Emilio Morenatti/AP Photo; 373 (t): Bettman/Corbis; (tr,br): Hulton Archive/Getty Images; (bl): North Wind Picture Archives; 374 Bettman/Corbis; 375 (t): Jean Claude Revy ISM/Phototake; (b): FOCUS FEATURES/THE KOBAL COLLECTION/Picture Desk; 376 Donna Abu-Nasr/AP Photo; 378 Henry Griffin/AP Photo; 379 (t): Michael Newman/PhotoEdit; (bl): Don Hammond/Design Pics/Corbis; (bc): AFP/Getty Images; (br): Tomas Van Houtryve/Corbis; 381 Andy Mead/Icon SMI/Corbis; 382 Michael Ventura/Alamy.

Chapter 17

386–387 Nikoo Harf Maher/Document Iran/Corbis; 387 (tr): Transtock/Corbis; 388 (t): Nikoo Harf Maher/Document Iran/Corbis; (b): STR/AFP/Getty Images; 389 AP Photo; 390 (bkgd): AP Images for U.N. Foundation; (inset): Andy Crump TDR WHO/Photo Researchers Inc.; 391 Claude Mahoudeau/AFP/Getty Images; 392 Diego Lezama Orezzoli/Corbis; 393 Alejandro Ernesto/epa/Corbis; 394 Transtock/Corbis; 395 LARRY DOWNING/Reuters/Corbis; 397 Javed Khan/AP Photo; 398 Phil Walter/Getty Images; 399 epa/Corbis; 401 Natalie Helbert/istockphoto.com; 402 UNIVERSAL PICTURES/THE KOBAL COLLECTION/DUHAMEL FRANCOIS/Picture Desk; 403 Les Stone/Zuma/Corbis; 404 Courtesy, The Point Foundation; 405 RIZWAN TABASSUM/AFP/Getty Images; 407 Connecticut Post Brian A. Pounds/AP Photo; 408 Doug Mills/AP Photo.

>index

AARP (formerly the American Association of Retired Persons), 140, 144, 334

ABA (American Bar Association), 136, 242

ABC network, 119

ability to pay theory of taxation, 318

Ableman v. Booth, 66

abortion
cause groups, 140
in party platforms, 164
political philosophy and, 91
privacy rights, 349
protest demonstrations, 110
public opinion, 306
religion and, 94
Supreme Court and, 287, 301, 359

abortion rates, 301

Abramoff, Jack, 143

abstinence vows, 301

academic experts, 278

access, 142, 157

ACLU (American Civil Liberties Union), 138, 299, 354, 358–359

ActBlue, 141–142

activists, 278

ADA. *See* Americans with Disabilities Act (ADA)

Adams, John, 51, 230

Adams, John Quincy, 87, 193, 230

ADAPT (Americans Disabled for Attendant Programs Today), 6

Administration, Office of, 243

administrative law, 342

advertising, 176–177

Advice and Consent, 62

advocacy groups, 138. *See also* cause groups

AEC (Australian Election Commission), 109

affirm, 291

affirmative action, 137, 164, 306, 377–379

Afghanistan, 394, 395, 397, 405

Afghanistan War, 35, 164, 219, 236, 330, 372

AFL-CIO (American Federation of Labor-Congress of Industrial Organization), 136, 140–141, 144

Africa, 19, 261, 386, 388

African Americans
civil rights movement, 378
college admissions, 383
in Congress, 206–207
demographics of, 28, 379
discrimination in public accommodations, 373–374
equality, 366–370
immigration and, 212
income distribution and, 26
interest groups, 137
opinion differences and, 94, 96
party affiliation, 27

political knowledge, 86
political socialization and, 78
population diversity, 22
poverty and, 29–30
public school enrollment, 368–369
redistricting and, 175
religion and, 163
segregation, 50, 52, 366–370
suffrage, 370, 372, 373
voter turnout, 105
voting patterns, 160

age, 104, 162. *See also* aging of population

Agee, Mark, 149

agenda building
civil liberties policy-making, 359
civil rights, 380–382
Congress, 225
constitutional environment and, 55
cultural, international, and socio-economic context and, 30
definition, 6
economic policymaking, 334
elections, 198
federal bureaucracy, 280
federal courts, 306
federal system, 73
foreign and defense policymaking, 406
interest groups, 147–148
media, 128
political participation, 111
political parties, 166
presidency, 252
public opinion, 96

agents of socialization, 78–80

aggressive interrogation techniques, 238

aging of population, 15, 16, 23

Agnew, Spiro, 232

agricultural industry, 312

Agriculture, Department of, 258–259, 273, 313

AIDS patients, 261

AIG (American International Group), 311

AIM (American Indian Movement), 137

Air Force, U.S., 280

air traffic controller strike, 267

air war, 182

airport screening/screeners, 271

Alabama, 257

Alaska, 173, 191, 195

Alaskan Natives, 22, 28

Albright, Madeleine, 395

Alexander, Lamar, 141

Algeria, 21

Alito, Martha-Ann, 296

Alito, Samuel A., Jr., 285, 294, 295, 296

Allen, George, 116–117, 126

al-Qaeda, 236, 339, 394, 397, 404

AMA (American Medical Association), 136, 144

Amendment Two (Colorado), 370

amendments, 41, 50. *See also specific amendments*

America, changes in, 14–31
demographic environment, 18–23
economic environment, 24–30
international environment, 18
political culture, 16–17

American Academy of Actuaries, 328

American Association of Retired Persons (now known as AARP), 140, 144, 334

American Bankers Association, 135

American Bar Association (ABA), 136, 242

American Center for Law and Justice, 146

American Civil Liberties Union (ACLU), 138, 299, 354, 358–359

American Coming Together, 142

American Federation of Government Employees, 268

American Federation of Labor-Congress of Industrial Organization (AFL-CIO), 136, 140–141, 144

American Federation of State/County/Municipal Employees, 142

American Federation of Teachers, 141, 142

American Hospital Association, 144

American Idol, 123, 301

American Indian Movement (AIM), 137

American Indians, 22, 28, 207, 368

American International Group (AIG), 311

American Medical Association (AMA), 136, 144

American National Election Studies (ANES), 102, 107

American political thought, 39–40

American Prospect, The, 11

American Samoa, 204

Americans Disabled for Attendant Programs Today (ADAPT), 6

Americans with Disabilities Act (ADA)
civil rights and, 382
definition, 3, 374
evaluation of, 10
implementation of, 9, 307
as public policy, 6, 7

Amgen Inc., 144

amicus curiae, 298, 359

Amish, 345

Amtrak (National Railroad Passenger Service Corporation), 262

Anderson, Pamela, 38

ANES (American National Election Studies), 102, 107

Animal Liberation Front, 146

Anthony, Susan B., 381

anti-clericalism, 139

Antifederalists, 43

anti-government speech, 345

ANWR (Arctic National Wildlife Refuge), 134, 167

appeal, 288

appeals, courts of, 290–291, 293

Appeals, U.S. Court of, 288

Appeals Court of the District of Columbia, 241

appellate courts, 288

apportionment, 174

appropriation bills, 221

Appropriations Committee, 216, 272

appropriations process, 68, 331

approval ratings, 209, 250–252

Arabic translators, 404

Arbitron ratings, 122

Arctic National Wildlife Refuge (ANWR), 134, 167

Arizona, 22

Arkansas, 184, 240

Arkansas State Capitol, 110

Armed Forced Radio and Television Service, 118

armed forces, civilian supremacy of, 236

Armed Services Committee, 216, 408

Army, U.S., 280

Article I of Constitution, 41, 49, 61, 241

Article II of Constitution, 49, 62, 235, 241

Article III of Constitution, 62

Articles of Confederation, 36, 37–38, 40, 50

articles of impeachment, 231

Asbestos Hazard Emergency Response Act, 73

Ashcroft, John, 62, 339, 357

Asia, 19, 388

Asian Americans
in Congress, 207
demographic shifts, 28
income distribution and, 26
interest groups, 137
population diversity, 22
poverty and, 29–30
public school enrollment, 368
voter turnout, 105
voting patterns, 160

Asian Caucus, 364

Assault Weapons Ban, 133

Assemblies of God, 94, 163

Associated Press, 409

association, freedom of, 17

AT&T Inc., 144

Atkins, Daryl Renard, 49, 355

at-large election, 173

attack journalism, 128

attitudes, 85

Australia, 108, 109, 396

Australian Election Commission (AEC), 109

authorization process, 68, 331

axis of evil, 385

baby-boom generation, 18, 28, 30–31, 322, 326
Baker, James A. III, 239
Baker v. Carr, 174
Bakke, Allan, 379
balance of trade, 392
balance the ticket, 190
balanced budget, 321
Bali, Indonesia, 399
Bank of America, 135
Baptists, 207
Barber, James David, 246–247
Barton, Joe, 141
base voters, 195
battleground states, 107, 182, 194
BCRA (Bipartisan Campaign Reform Act), 124, 145, 178–179
Beard, Charles, 54
Beck, Glenn, 313
Beirut, Lebanon, 239
Belgium, 89, 108
Benjamin, Stephen, 404
Berkshire Hathaway, 319
Bernanke, Ben, 332, 333
Beslan, Russia, 399
bias, 110–111, 126–128
bias questions, 85
biased sample, 82
bicameralism, 38, 46, 48, 204–206
Biden, Joe, 188, 190, 210–211, 259
bill of attainder, 42, 43
Bill of Rights, 39, 42–43, 340–341
bills, 218
Bin Laden, Osama, 339, 405
binge drinking, 71
Bipartisan Campaign Reform Act (BCRA), 124, 145, 178–179
bipartisanship, 406
Black, Hugo, 295
Black Caucus, 364
Blackberry, 122
Blagojevich, Rod, 209
Blair, Tony, 47
blanket primary, 173
block grant programs, 68, 70
blog, 119–120
blue states, 195, 196
Blunt, Roy, 211
Boasso, Walter, 173
Boehner, John, 211
Bolivia, 397
Bonds, Barry, 289
book banning, 342
Border Protection, Antiterrorism, and Illegal Immigration Control Act, 218
Bork, Robert, 240
Boy Scouts, 306
Boy Scouts of America v. Dale, 306
Bradley, Curtis A., 242
Bradley, Tom, 84
Bradley Effect, 84
Brady Act, 66
Brady Handgun Violence Prevention Act, 66
Brandenburg, Clarence, 345
Brazil, 19, 185, 388, 391
Brennan, William, 296, 347
Breyer, Stephen, 241, 285, 294, 295
bridge collapse, 215
British parliamentary system, 47
broadcast media, 118

Brodhead, Richard, 71
Bronfman, Edgar, 318
Brown, Gordon, 47
Brown, Linda, 297, 368, 381
Brown, Michael D., 126, 257
Brown v. Board of Education, 50, 52, 287, 297, 300, 307, 368–369
Buddhists, 94
budget agreements, 330
Budget Committees, 216
budget crisis, 52
budget deficits, 321
budget resolutions, 221
budget surpluses, 321
budget year, 314
budgeting, 329–332
Buffett, Warren, 319
Bulgaria, 390
bully pulpit, 248
Bureau of Justice Statistics, 356
bureaucracy, federal. *See* federal bureaucracy
bureaucracy, in Egypt, 277
bureaucracy, presidential, 244–245
bureaucratic agencies, 276
bureaucrats, 273, 278
Burma, 236
"Burning Down the House: What Caused Our Economic Crisis," 181
Burton, Dan, 394
Bush, George H.W.
    1992 election, 155, 193
    affirmative action, 378
    appointments, 332
    approval ratings, 85
    budget agreements, 330
    character of, 247
    judicial appointments, 294, 295
    leadership style of, 249
    media coverage of, 128
    midterm elections, 166
    presidency and, 230
    presidential campaign, 122, 123
    Sunbelt and, 22
    vice presidential selection, 233
Bush, George W.
    agenda building and, 252
    appointments, 332, 333
    cabinet appointments, 258
    campaign fundraising, 177–178
    campaign strategy, 179
    civil rights, 375
    as commander in chief, 236, 238
    communications operation, 125
    congressional relations, 213
    decision-making process, 245
    economic policy, 311
    election of, 113, 155, 160, 192, 195, 199
    enemy combatants and, 357
    executive authority, 339
    executive office of, 244
    executive orders, 240, 267
    federal employees and, 267, 268
    federal financing and, 188
    foreign and defense policy, 385, 398
    Hurricane Katrina, 126
    inherent powers and, 239
    Iraq War, 108, 125, 396–397
    judicial appointments, 240, 291, 293, 294, 359

    leadership style of, 249
    media coverage of, 127
    midterm elections, 166
    military preemption, 402–403
    No Child Left Behind (NCLB), 55, 59
    offshore drilling, 279
    popularity of, 251
    portrayals of, 251
    power to persuade, 249
    presidency and, 230
    presidential campaign, 123
    presidential signing statements, 242
    rulemaking and, 271
    Social Security reform and, 253
    staff of, 243
    State of the Union, 242
    Sunbelt and, 22
    Supreme Court appointments, 241
    tax policy, 167, 317–318, 334
    tax reductions, 26
    trade and, 393
    USA PATRIOT Act, 359
    vetoes and, 35, 224
    vice presidential selection, 234
Bush Doctrine, 219
business groups, 134–135
Business Week, 328
Byrd, James, 371
Byrd, Robert, 211
cabinet departments, 258–260
cable television, 119
CAFTA (Central America Free Trade Agreement), 393
California
    2000 election, 192
    budget crisis, 52
    electoral votes, 191, 194
    gay and lesbian rights, 48, 375
    global warming policy, 65
    highway system, 276
    NASA and, 273
    nomination process, 184, 189, 190
Cambodia, 397
campaign budget, 176–177
campaign finance reform, 178–179
Campaign for Liberty, 161
campaign fundraising, Internet and, 180
campaigns. *See* election campaigns
Campbell, Foster, 173
Canada
    civil unions, 89
    Great Britain and, 36
    healthcare in, 323
    immigration and, 19
    NAFTA and, 234
    as post-industrial society, 388
    purchasing power, 24
    religious beliefs, 79
    trade with, 393
    voter turnout, 108
Canon, Bradley, 300
Cantril, Albert H., 93
Cantril, Susan Davis, 93
Cantril Index, 93
capital punishment, 94, 300, 306, 355–356, 359 *See also* death penalty

capitalism, 16–17
Capitol, U.S., 204
captured agencies, 272
Card, Andrew H., Jr., 243
Caribbean, 25
Carter, Jimmy
    character of, 247
    China and, 235
    enforcement of environmental laws, 253
    leadership style of, 249
    midterm elections, 166
    power to persuade, 248
    rulemaking and, 271
    Sunbelt and, 22, 230
Castro, Fidel, 393
Castro, Raúl, 393
categorical grant programs, 68, 70
Cato Institute, 145
caucus method of delegate selection, 186–187
caucuses, congressional, 364
cause groups, 140. *See also* advocacy groups
CBO (Congressional Budget Office), 324
CBS network, 119, 341
CEA (Council of Economic Advisers), 243, 244
cell phones, 83
census, national, 174
Census Bureau, 15, 28, 104
Center for Energy and Environmental Studies, 279
Center for Immigration Studies, 19
Center for Political Studies (CPS), 88
Central America Free Trade Agreement (CAFTA), 393
Central High School (Little Rock), 240, 367
Central Intelligence Agency (CIA), 244, 260, 261, 407, 408
Certiorari (cert.), 297
Chamber of Commerce, U.S., 135, 144
checks and balances, 44–46, 60
Cheney, Richard, 234, 238, 239, 293
Chertoff, Michael, 126, 257, 281
Chicago Tribune, 83, 119
chief executive, 165, 240
chief of state, 235
Children's Defense Fund, 138
China
    defense spending, 18
    human rights abuses, 393
    immigration and, 19
    Iran and, 396
    as modernizing industrial state, 388
    outsourcing and, 25
    population policy, 351
    public health, 391
    relations with, 235
    Summer Olympics 2008, 346
    trade with, 393
    UN Security Council, 389
Chisholm v. Georgia, 303
Chong, Tommy, 350
Christopher, Warren, 239
Chrysler, 311–312
Church of Christ (Disciples), 94
Church of England, 47

Church of Jesus Christ of Latter-day Saints, 163
church/state relations in Mexico, 139
CIA (Central Intelligence Agency), 244, 260, 261, 407, 408
cigarettes, 280, 320
citizen, advocacy, cause groups, 138, 140
City of Richmond v. J.A. Croson Co., 378–379
civil case, 288
civil liberties policymaking, 339–359
   constitutional basis of, 340–341
   definition, 87–88
   due process of law, 350, 352–356
   executive authority, 356–357
   freedom of expression, 345–347
   government and religion, 342–345
   privacy rights, 347, 349–350
   rights of the accused, 350, 352–356
   summary of, 358–359
civil rights, 363–383. *See also* civil rights movement; gay and lesbian rights
   affirmative action, 137, 164, 306, 377–379
   constitutional basis of, 364
   definition, 365
   equality before the law, 365–370
   freedom from discrimination, 373–375
   issues and policies, 365–379
   racial equality, 366–370
   Roman Catholics and, 94
   sexual harassment, 375, 377
   summary of, 380–383
   voting rights and representation, 370, 372
Civil Rights Act of 1875, 373
Civil Rights Act of 1964, 136, 162, 222, 363, 368, 373, 374
Civil Rights Act of 1991, 374–375
Civil Rights Cases, 373, 374
civil rights movement, 368, 378. *See also* civil rights
Civil Service Commission, 265–266
Civil Service Reform Act, 266
civil unions, 89, 375. *See also* marriage rights; same-sex marriage
Civil War, 48, 239, 294, 296, 357
civilian employment, 265–266
civilian supremacy of the armed forces, 236
clash of civilization, 399
Class Action Fairness Coalition, 135
class action lawsuit, 136
Clausewitz, Karl von, 400
Clean Air Act, 140, 253
Clean Water Act, 9
cleaning occupations, 20
Clear Channel Communication, 119
Clemens, Roger, 289
Cleveland, Grover, 181, 192
Clinton, Bill
   appointments, 332
   budget agreements, 330, 331
   cabinet members and, 260
   divided government and, 165
   election of, 155, 193
   executive orders, 240

federal employees and, 267
foreign policy, 394
gays in the military and, 281, 409
harassment charges, 377
healthcare and, 229, 245, 252
Hillary Clinton and, 171
impeachment, 199, 231, 232
judicial appointments, 240, 291, 294, 359
leadership style of, 249
Lewinsky scandal, 120, 122
media coverage of, 128
midterm elections and, 166
presidency and, 230
staff of, 244–245
Sunbelt and, 22
Supreme Court appointments, 241
tobacco regulation, 320
trade and, 393
vice presidential selection, 233–234
voter turnout and, 107
welfare reform, 327, 334
Clinton, Hillary
   as cabinet appointee, 259
   campaign fundraising, 176
   federal matching funds and, 188
   healthcare and, 229, 245
   nomination phase, 184, 186–187, 189–190
   portrayals of, 161
   presidency and, 230
   as presidential candidate, 170–171
closed primary, 173
closed rule, 221
cloture, 223
Club for Growth, 140
Clyburn, James E., 211
CNN network, 80, 119, 127
Coalition for the Homeless, 138
Coast Guard, 326
coattail effect, 183
Code of Federal Regulations, 269
cognitive skills, 249
Cohen, Jeffrey E., 199
Cohen, Paul, 346
COLA (cost-of-living adjustment), 324
Colbert, Stephen, 126
The Colbert Report, 126
Cold War, 357, 392, 400, 403, 406
collective bargaining, 267
college admissions, 379, 383
college graduates, 160
"College Presidents Want Drinking Age Lowered to 18" (Maloney), 71
Colombia, 394, 395, 397
colonial period, 36–37
Colorado, 160, 195, 370
commander in chief, 62, 236, 238
commerce, 49
Commerce Clause, 66
Commerce Committee, 216
Commerce, Department of 258–259
committee system, 49, 215–217, 218, 220–221, 276
Committee to Reelect the President, 233
Common Cause, 138
Community Development Program, 70
community involvement, 104

compulsory voting, 109
computer programming occupations, 26
concurrent powers, 63
concurring opinion, 300
Confederation Congress, 37
conferees, 223
conference, 297
conference committee, 212, 213, 223–224
Congress, 202–225. *See also* House of Representatives; Senate
   approval ratings, 209
   bicameralism, 204–206
   caucuses, 364
   committee/subcommittee organization, 49, 215–217, 218, 220–221, 276
   communication with, 216
   compensation of members, 207
   control of judiciary, 305
   federal bureaucracy and, 271–272
   financial industry bailout, 311–312
   home style of members, 208–209
   issue networks and, 278
   legislative process. *See* legislative process
   membership, 206–210
   membership turnover, 209–210
   minority members, 365
   organization, 210–215
   partisanship, 208
   personal style of members, 207–208
   profile of membership, 206–207
   public policy, 225
   war power, 219, 238
Congressional Black Caucus, 217
Congressional Budget Office (CBO), 324
congressional elections, 182–183
Connecticut, 364
Connecticut Compromise, 46
conservatism, 91–93, 163
conservative Christians, 162
Conservative Party, 47
consolidation, of media, 119, 122
constituency, 97
constituency services, 205, 272
constituents, 97
Constitution, U.S., 34–55. *See also specific amendments*
   amendments, 41, 50
   American political thought, 39–40
   Article I, 41, 49, 61, 241
   Article II, 49, 62, 235, 241
   Article III, 62
   background of, 36–40
   as basis for civil rights, 364
   as basis for federal system, 60–66
   as basis of civil liberties policymaking, 340–341
   changes through amendment, 50
   changes through judicial interpretation, 51–52
   changes through practice and experience, 49–50
   constitutional principles, 40–48
   historical setting, 36–38
   as a living document, 49–52
   location of original, 382
   natural rights interpretation, 53

organization of the floor, 210–213
politics and public policy, 52, 54
ratification of, 43–44
role in policymaking, 35
constitutional law, 302, 342, 365
constitutional principles, 40–48
   bicameralism, 48, 60, 108, 165, 305
   checks and balances, 44–46
   federalism, 46, 48
   limited government, 43–44
   natural rights interpretation, 53
   representative democracy, 40–41
   rule of law, 41–43
   separation of powers, 44–46
construction occupations, 20
consumer price index (CPI), 324
Continental Congress, 37
contraception, 301
contractual commitments, 329
conventional forces, 400, 403–404
conventions, political, 102, 152–153, 159, 184, 190
Cooper, Phillip J., 242
corporate income tax, 315, 316
Corporation for Public Broadcasting, 118
corruption, 209, 290
Costa Rica, 393
cost-benefit analysis, 269
cost-of-living adjustment (COLA), 324
Council of Economic Advisers (CEA), 243, 244
Council on Competitiveness, 233
Council on Environmental Quality, 243, 244
County of Allegheny v. ACLU, 299
Court of Appeals, U.S., 288
Court of Federal Claims, U.S., 287, 288, 290
Court of International Trade, U.S., 287–288, 290
courts of appeals, 290–291, 293
CPI (consumer price index), 324
CPS (Center for Political Studies), 88
criminal case, 288
Crisis at Central High, 367
Croley, Steven, P., 272
cruel and unusual punishment, 49, 355
"CSI: The Experience," 263
Cuba, 121, 389, 393, 394–395
Cuban, Mark, 269
Cuban Americans, 160
Cuban Missile Crisis, 54
Cumulus Media, 119
Cuyahoga River, 9
Czech Republic, 390
Dahl, Robert A., 16, 17, 303–304
Dallas Mavericks, 269
Damletta, Egypt, 277
Dancing with the Stars, 269
Danish Registered Partner Act, 89
Davis, Rick, 178
de facto segregation, 368
de jure segregation, 368–369
Dean, Howard, 123, 180
death penalty, 94, 300, 306, 355–356, 359 *See also* capital punishment
Death With Dignity Law, 62

debates, 194
Declaration of Independence, 39
deduction, 315
defense and foreign policymaking, 387–409
  defense forces and strategy, 400–404
  defense policy, 400–404
  defense spending, 400
  ends and means of American policy, 392–395
  foreign policy, 395–398
  international community, 388–391
  summary of, 406–408
Defense Department, 258–259, 266, 281, 326, 394, 408
Defense Language Institute, 404
Defense of Marriage Act, 305
deficits, 321, 334
Delaware, 173, 191
DeLay, Tom, 175
delegated powers, 60
delegate-selection process, 184, 186–187
democracy, 16, 17, 40
Democratic Convention of 1968, 159
Democratic National Committee (DNC), 157
Democratic National Convention, 152–153, 184
Democratic Party
  2006 midterm elections, 35, 203
  age and, 162
  changes in, 27
  civil rights, 381–382
  demographic shifts, 27
  divided government and, 164
  education and, 160
  gender and, 161
  income and, 160
  Iraq War and, 108
  nomination phase, 186–187
  party identification, 158
  political ideology and, 162
  regional voting patterns, 162
  religion and, 163
  voter turnout and, 110
democratic peace, 393
democratic principles, support for, 86–88
demographic environment, 18–23
  economy and, 325
  effect on political parties, 27
  illegal immigration, 19–20, 31
  immigration, 19
  population diversity, 22
Denmark, 89, 108
depression, 314
detainment camps, 236
deterrence, 402
Deukmejian, George, 84
developing countries, 25, 388
Dewey, Thomas, 83, 87
"Dewey Defeats Truman" (*Chicago Tribune*), 83
diabetes, 345
dietary restrictions, 345
diplomacy, 395
diplomatic powers, 235
diplomatic relations, 388
direct democracy, 40, 111
direct election of the president, 194

direct mail, 178
dirty bomb, 339
disability rights, 6
Disability Rights Education and Defense Fund (DREDF), 6
discharge petition, 221
discretionary spending, 331
discrimination, freedom from, 373–375
discrimination, gender, 370, 381
disfranchisement, 372
dissenting opinion, 300
district courts, 287, 288–290
district election, 174
District of Columbia, 37, 204
districts and redistricting, 173–176
divided government, 164–166
DNC (Democratic National Committee), 157
Dobson, James, 138
Doctors Without Borders, 391
Dodd, Chris, 188
domestic partnership, 375
Domestic Policy Council, 243–244
Dominican Republic, 394
"don't ask, don't tell" policy, 404
dot.com bubble, 123
Douglas, William O., 295
Dred Scott v. Sanford, 64, 66, 303
DREDF (Disability Rights Education and Defense Fund), 6
drinking age, 140
Drudge, Matt, 120
Drudge Report, 120, 122
Due Process Clause, 42–44, 299, 340, 347, 350
due process of law, 42–44, 299, 350, 352–356
Dukes v. Wal-Mart Stores, Inc., 136
Duma, 237
Durbin, Dick, 207, 211
Duverger, Maurice, 154
earmarks, 334
Earned Income Tax Credit (EITC), 326
Earth Day, 140
eavesdropping on American citizens, 239
ebola virus, 391
economic environment, 24–30
  global economy, 25–26
  income distribution, 26, 29
  poverty, 29–30, 327
economic growth, 314
Economic Growth and Tax Reconciliation Act, 166–167
economic policymaking, 310–333
  budget deficits and surpluses, 321
  fiscal policymaking, 329–332
  goals of, 312–314
  government expenditures, 322, 324–329
  healthcare, 322–324
  income security, 322, 326–327, 329
  interest on the debt, 329
  monetary policymaking, 332–333
  national defense, 322, 326
  Social Security, 324–326
  summary of, 333–335
  tax revenues, 314–319
economic recovery plan, 312, 321

Education, Department of, 68, 258–259, 273, 281, 408
education, voting patterns and, 160–161
Education Amendments of 1972, 374
Education and the Workforce Committee, 220
education policy, in Germany, 69
education tax credits and deductions, 67
Edwards, John, 179, 184, 187, 188, 189, 192
EEOC (Equal Employment Opportunity Commission), 9, 10, 263, 295, 377, 383
effectiveness, evaluation of, 9
Egypt, 17, 277, 394–395, 397
Eighth Amendment, 42, 49, 350
Eisenhower, Dwight
  cabinet members and, 260
  character of, 246
  civil rights and, 368
  executive orders, 240
  heart attack, 232–233
  judicial appointments, 296
  leadership style of, 249
EITC (Earned Income Tax Credit), 326
El Salvador, 19, 393
Elastic Clause, 61
election campaigns. *See also* elections
  budget, 176–177
  cost of, 176
  fall campaign, 194–195
  funding sources, 177–179
  Internet and, 180
  money, role of, 176–179
  nomination phase, 184, 186–187, 189–190
  organization and strategy, 179, 181–182
  voters and, 196–197
election turnout. *See* voter turnout
electioneering, 140–142
elections. *See also* election campaigns
  of 2000, 193
  of 2008, 14, 84, 100, 153, 170–171, 195, 196–197, 199, 230
  in Brazil, 185
  congressional, 182–183
  districts and redistricting, 173–176
  Electoral College, 155, 191–194
  fall campaign, 194–195
  general election phase, 172, 191–195
  gerrymandering, 176
  issues, 196
  party identification, 196
  presidential, 184, 186–190
  reapportionment, 174
  retrospective and prospective voting, 197
  summary of, 198–199
  types of, 172–173
  voters decide, 196–197
  Voting Rights Act (VRA), 137, 175, 206, 373
elections, free and fair, 17
Electoral College, 155, 191–194
electoral mandate, 198, 229–230
electoral vote, 155, 192–193
electors, 191

electric chair, 355
electronic voting, 113
Elementary and Secondary Education Act (ESEA), 68
Eleventh Amendment, 63, 303
Emancipation Proclamation, 240
Emanuel, Rahm, 243
EMILY's List, 141, 142
eminent domain, 41
emotional intelligence, 249
empirical analysis, 10, 129
Employment Division v. Smith, 345
employment practices, 265–268
Endangered Species Act, 140, 302
ends and means of American policy, 392–395
enemy combatants, 238, 239, 339
energy, 164, 167
Energy, Department of, 258–259, 326
Energy Committee, 216
Engel v. Vitale, 344, 358
entitlement program, 329
enumerated powers, 60, 63
environment, 92
EOP (Executive Office of the President), 244, 267
EPA (Environmental Protection Agency), 9, 167, 253, 260, 261, 273
Episcopalians, 94, 163, 207
Equal Employment Opportunity Commission (EEOC), 9, 10, 263, 295, 377, 383
Equal Protection Clause, 52, 174, 303, 363–364, 365, 367, 370
equal protection of the law, 44
equality before the law, 365–370
ESEA (Elementary and Secondary Education Act), 68
Establishment Clause, 343–344
establishment of religion, 342–344
estate tax, 318
Estonia, 390
Estrada, Miguel, 241
Ethiopia, 397
Europe, 19
European Union, 123
evening network news, 80
Everson v. Board of Ewing Township, 343
ex post facto law, 42, 43
excise taxes, 316
exclusionary rule, 352–353
executions, 49
executive agencies, independent, 260–261
executive agreement, 235, 249
executive authority, 356–357
executive branch, powers of, 61–62
executive cabinet, 49
Executive Office of the President (EOP), 244, 267
executive orders, 9, 238, 240, 249, 357
executive power, 44, 61, 240, 242
exemption, 315
exit polls, 160, 190
expenditures, 321, 322, 324–329
exports, 390
expression, freedom of, 17, 345–347
external political efficacy, 90
Extradition, 62
Exxon Mobil Corporation, 134, 144

leadership style of, 249
media coverage of, 128
midterm elections and, 166
pardon of, 240
resignation of, 231, 233
Sunbelt and, 22
Supreme Court and, 300
Supreme Court appointments, 240
vice presidential candidate selection, 232
Watergate scandal, 107, 233
NLRB (National Labor Relations Board), 291
No Child Left Behind (NCLB), 55, 59, 67–68, 72–73, 218, 265
Nogales, Arizona, 213
Nogales, Mexico, 213
nomination phase, of presidential elections, 184, 186–190
Iowa and New Hampshire, 188–189
national party conventions, 190
post-Super Tuesday contests, 189–190
pre-primary positioning, 188
Super Tuesday, 189
non-attitudes, 85
Nongovernmental organizations (NGO), 391
nonvoters, characteristics of, 110
Normandy invasion, 236
normative analysis, 9–10, 129
North Africa, 21
North American Free Trade Agreement (NAFTA), 234, 235, 393
North Atlantic Treaty Organization (NATO), 390, 394
North Carolina, 195, 374, 397, 398
North Korea, 387, 388–389, 392, 394, 396, 398, 403
Northeast, 162, 195
Norway, 396
"Nothing but Nets," 390
NOW (National Organization for Women), 135, 140, 141, 358, 381
NPR (National Public Radio), 118, 122
NRA (National Rifle Association), 102, 133, 134, 140, 141, 142, 144, 146, 358
NSA (National Security Agency), 239
NSC (National Security Council), 243, 244
NSF (National Science Foundation), 70, 263
"nuclear option," 293
nuclear weapons, 405
Nunn, Sam, 408
OASI (Social Security Old Age and Survivors Insurance Trust Fund), 329
Obama, Barack
2008 election, 14, 170–171
advertising, 178
cabinet appointments, 259
campaign fundraising, 176, 179
convention and, 152–153
economic recovery plan, 312, 321
election of, 84, 195, 196–197, 199, 230
endorsements, 140

federal matching funds and, 188, 194
first-time voters and, 105
healthcare, 334
infomercial, 123
Joe the Plumber and, 313
nomination phase, 184, 186–187, 189–190
offshore drilling, 279
presidency and, 229
Social Security and, 328
supporters of, 118, 160, 162, 163
Supreme Court appointments, 285
tax policy, 318–319
use of Internet, 120
vice presidential selection, 190
Warren and, 343
website, 123
objective journalism, 126
obstruction of justice, 289
obstructionism, 241
O'Connor, Sandra Day, 291, 295
Odessa, Texas, football team, 304
The Office, 325
Office of Administration, 243
Office of Homeland Security, 267
Office of Management and Budget (OMB), 243, 244, 269, 330–331, 335
Office of National Drug Control Policy, 243
Office of Personnel Management, 266, 267
Office of Science and Technology Policy, 243, 244
Office of the United States Trade Representative, 243, 244
office workers, 325
Official Constitution Party, 154
offshore drilling, 279
O'Hair, Madalyn Murray, 359
Ohio, 189, 194, 195, 273, 327, 343
Oklahoma, 276
Oklahoma City bombing, 356
"An Older and More Diverse Nation by Midcentury," 28
Olympic Games, 395
OMB (Office of Management and Budget), 243, 244, 269, 330–331, 335
omnibus bills, 217
one person, one vote, 174, 287
one-child policy, 351
online news sources, 80
open primary, 173
open rule, 221
Operation Save America, 301
opinion polls, 87
opposition party, 167
Oregon, 62, 345
Oregon v. Mitchell, 303
organizational skills, 249
original jurisdiction, 293
Osborne, Tom, 181
outsourcing, 25
PAC (political action committee), 141, 211, 276
Pacific Islanders, 22, 26, 28
Padilla, Jose, 339, 357
Pakistan, 395, 397, 399, 405
Palin, Sarah, 103, 123, 138, 161, 179, 190
Panama, 394

Panama Canal Treaty, 407
Panetta, Leon, 245
pardon, 240
parental choice, 343
Parents Involved in Community Schools v. Seattle School District No. 1, 370
Parliament, 47
parliamentary system, 47
parochial schools, 343
partisan politics, and judicial selection, 241
partisanship, 208
party affiliation, 27
party balance, 158
party caucus, 217
party identification, 158, 196
party organization, 157
party platform, 163–164, 167, 190
party system, 154–155
PATCO (Professional Air Traffic Controllers Association), 267
The Patriot, 39
Paul, Ron, 161, 189
PAYGO, 330
payroll taxes, 315, 316
PBS (Public Broadcasting Service), 118, 122
Peace Corps, 260, 261
Pearl Harbor, 236
Pederson, Jim, 177
peer groups, as agent of political socialization, 80
Pell grants, 67
Pelosi, Nancy, 141, 203, 211
Pendleton Act, 266
Penn, Sean, 375
Pennsylvania, 22, 189, 194, 273
Pentecostals, 163
People for the Ethical Treatment of Animals (PETA), 146
People magazine, 82
People's Republic of China. See China
Pepper, Claude, 181
per curiam opinion, 298
perjury, 289, 290
Perot, Ross, 155, 193, 234, 334
Perry, Rick, 175
Persian Gulf didn't fitWar. See Gulf War
personal resources, 103
personal style of congressional members, 207–208
Personnel Management, Office of, 266, 267
Peru, 397
PETA (People for the Ethical Treatment of Animals), 146
Petraeus, David, 220
Pettite, Andy, 289
Pew Internet and American Life study, 180
Pew Research, 27
peyote, 345
phantom opinions, 85
Pharmaceutical Research and Manufacturers of America, 144, 210
Philip Morris, 134
Philippines, 19, 395
physician-assisted suicide, 62, 66
Pioneers, 177

place of residence, voting patterns, 163
Planned Parenthood, 358
Plessy v. Ferguson, 52, 366–367
Plumbers/Pipefitters Union, 142
plurality election system, 154
pocket veto, 224
Poehler, Amy, 161
Pol Pot, 399
Poland, 20, 390
policy adoption, 8–9
policy deadlocks, 54
Policy Development, Office of, 243
policy evaluation, 9–10
policy formation, 7–8
policy formulation and adoption
civil liberties policymaking, 359
civil rights, 382
Congress, 225
constitutional environment and, 55
cultural, international, and socio-economic context and, 30–31
economic policymaking, 334–335
elections, 198–199
federal bureaucracy, 280–281
federal courts, 306–307
federal system, 73
foreign and defense policymaking, 406–408
interest groups, 148
media, 128–129
political participation, 111–112
political parties, 166–167
presidency, 252–253
public opinion, 96–97
policy implementation and evaluation, 9
civil liberties policymaking, 359
civil rights, 382–383
Congress, 225
constitutional environment and, 55
cultural, international, and socio-economic context and, 31
economic policymaking, 335
elections, 199
federal bureaucracy, 281
federal courts, 307
federal system, 73
foreign and defense policymaking, 408
interest groups, 148
media, 129
political participation, 112
political parties, 167
presidency, 253
public opinion, 97
policy stability, 54
policymaking environment, 6, 55
political action committee (PAC), 141, 211, 276
political contributions, 123
political conventions, 159
political culture, 16–17
political efficacy, 90, 103
political elites, 88
political expression, 348
political ideology, 162
political knowledge, 86–90
political left, 91–92
political legitimacy, 88, 193
political participation, 100–113

age and, 104
bias in, 110–111
community involvement and, 104
compared to other countries,
    107–108
factors in, 103–104
forms of, 102–103
gender and, 106
income and, 104–105
patterns of, 104–106
personal resources and, 103
psychological engagement and,
    103
race/ethnicity and, 105
summary of, 111–112
voter mobilization, 103–104
voter turnout trends, 106–107
political parties, 152–167
    conventions, 159
    divided government, 164–166
    participation rates and, 108
    party balance, 158
    party organization, 157
    party system, 49, 154–155
    platforms, 164
    summary of, 166–167
    voting patterns, 160–164
political philosophy, 91–96
    of judicial appointments, 294
    liberal vs. conservative, 92–93
    opinion differences among
        groups, 93–94, 96
political right, 91–92
political skills, 249
political socialization, 78–81
political thought, 39–40
political tolerance, 87
political trust, 88
political violence, 146
politicians, reasons for running, 247
politics, 5, 52, 54
poll tax, 372, 373
polling data, 145
Pollock v. Farmers' Loan & Trust Co.,
    303
pollution, 9, 279, 398
Popkin, Samuel, 86
popular vote, 155, 192–193
population, aging of, 15, 16, 23
population, growth rate of, 19
population diversity, 22, 23
population policy, 351
population shifts, 22
pork-barrel spending, 185, 334
Portugal, 21
Posner, Eric A., 242
Postal Service, 262, 266, 272
postindustrial societies, 388
post-Super Tuesday contests,
    189–190
poverty, 29–30, 327
poverty threshold, 29
Powell, Colin, 245
Powell, G. Bingham, Jr., 108
power of the purse, 60
power to persuade, 248
PR (proportional representation),
    156, 185
prayer in public schools, 303, 304,
    344
pre-industrial states, 25, 388
pre-primary positioning, 188
Presbyterians, 94, 163, 207

prescription drugs, 72, 324
presidency, 228–253. See also
    presidential leadership;
    presidential powers
    bureaucracy and influence,
        244–245
    constitutional basis of, 230–234
    Executive Office of the
        President, 244, 267
    federal bureaucracy and, 270–271
    gender and, 230
    impeachment and removal, 49,
        205, 231–233, 290
    issue networks and, 8, 275–276,
        278
    organization of, 243–245
    popularity, 250–252
    qualifications and background,
        230
    in Russia, 237
    succession and disability,
        232–233
    summary of, 252–253
    term of office, 230–231
    vice presidency, 232, 233–234
    White House staff, 243
presidential campaigns, media and,
    122
presidential character, classification
    of, 246–247
presidential debates, 123
presidential election, 2000, 193
presidential election, 2008, 14, 84,
    95, 100, 153, 170–171,
    196–197, 199, 230
presidential elections. See elections
presidential leadership, 246–249
presidential powers, 235–242
    diplomatic powers, 235
    executive powers, 44, 61, 240,
        242
    inherent powers, 239
    judicial powers, 240
    legislative powers, 242
    military powers, 236, 238–239
presidential preference primary, 184
presidential signing statements, 242,
    249
presidential vetoes, 41, 224, 242
president's cabinet, 259
Presidents' Foreign Intelligence
    Advisory Board, 243
press freedom, 346
price stability, 314
price-support loans, 313
Primary Constituency, 208
primary election, 172, 372
prime minister, 237
print media, 118
Printz v. United States, 66
privacy rights, 347, 349–350
private sector economic activity, 313
Privileges and Immunities Clause,
    62
probable cause, 352
Professional Air Traffic Controllers
    Association (PATCO), 267
professional associations, 136
progressive tax, 317
Prohibition, 50
project grant programs, 70
pro-life groups, 301
proportional representation (PR),
    156, 185
proportional tax, 317

Proposition 209, 383
prospective voting, 197
protest demonstrations, 102, 110,
    144, 146, 346, 368, 374
Protestantism, 53, 139, 163
Prothro, James W., 87
psychological engagement, 103
Public Affairs Act, 85
Public Broadcasting Service (PBS),
    118, 122
public communicator, 249
public education, 59
public good, 40
Public Health Service, 273, 280
public opinion, 76–97
    on affirmative action, 380
    attitudes, non-attitudes and
        phantom opinions, 85
    interviewer-respondent
        interaction, 85
    measurement of, 81–85
    media and, 95
    political knowledge, 86–90
    political philosophy, 91–96
    political socialization, 78–81
    question sequencing, 85
    question wording, 83
    sampling, 81–83
    summary of, 96–97
    timing, 85
public order, 346
public policy, 6, 52, 54
public policy approach, 6–9
    agenda building, 6
    definition, 6
    policy adoption, 8–9
    policy evaluation, 9–10
    policy formation, 7–8
    policy implementation, 9
    policymaking environment, 6
public policy institutions, 17
public pressure, creating, 144
public school enrollment, by
    race/ethnicity, 368–369
public schools, prayer in, 303, 304,
    344
Puerto Ricans, 160
Puerto Rico, 204
purchasing power, 24
Putin, Vladimir, 237
Qatar, 399
quasi-governmental companies, 264
Quayle, Dan, 233
Queen Elizabeth II, 47
question sequencing, 85
question wording, 83
quid pro quo harassment, 377
Rabalais, Nancy, 279
race and ethnicity
    of Congressional members, 207
    minority rights groups, 137
    opinion differences and, 93–94
    political participation and, 105
    public school enrollment by, 368
    voting patterns, 160
racial equality, 366–370
racial segregation, 50, 52, 366–370
racially restrictive covenants, 374
radio, 80
Radio Martí, 121
"Raise Retirement Age to Save
    Social Security" (Holland),
    328

Rajya Sadha, 214
rally effect, 251
Ramstack, Tom, 299
random sample, 82
Rangers, 178
ratification, 43–44, 50
ratifying convention, 159
Reagan, Ronald
    affirmative action, 377–378
    appointments, 332
    assassination attempt, 233
    character of, 246–247
    as commander in chief, 239
    defense spending, 400
    enforcement of environmental
        laws, 253
    federal employees and, 267
    judicial appointments, 193, 291,
        294, 299, 359
    leadership style of, 249
    midterm elections, 166
    popularity of, 251
    power to persuade, 248
    presidency, 230
    presidential campaign, 122
    Sunbelt and, 22
    Supreme Court appointments,
        240
    tax reductions, 26
Reagan Democrats, 27
reapportionment, 174
"Reassessing the Bradley Effect"
    (Walters), 84
rebellions, 38
receipts, 321
recess appointments, 241, 249
recession, 311, 314
Reconstruction, 294, 303
recount, Florida, 193–194
recruiting center, 61
Red Cross, 391
red states, 195, 196
redistribution of income, 313–314
redistricting, 173–176
Reelection Constituency, 208
Reform Party, 154
Regents of the University of California
    v. Bakke, 379
regional voting patterns, 162
regions, opinion differences and, 96
regressive tax, 317
regulations, 9
regulatory commissions,
    independent, 263
Reid, Harry, 141, 211
religion
    of Congressional members, 207
    establishment of, 342–344
    free exercise of, 344–345
    government and, 342–345
    opinion differences and, 94, 96
    Supreme Court and, 299
    voting patterns, 163
religious beliefs, 79
religious groups, 137–138
religious institutions, as agent of
    political socialization, 79
religious leaders, 48
religious left, 94, 138
religious right, 94, 137–138
remand, 291
remote order-taking, 25

Reporters Without Borders, 121, 346
representation, 370, 372
representative democracy, 40–41, 111
reprieve, 240
republic, 41, 62
Republican National Committee (RNC), 157
Republican National Convention, 102, 184
Republican Party
  2006 midterm elections, 35, 203
  changes in, 27
  civil rights, 381–382
  demographic shifts, 27
  divided government and, 164
  family and lifestyle status, 162
  fundraising advantage, 178
  income and, 160
  nomination phase, 186–187
  party identification, 158, 196
  political ideology and, 162
  regional voting patterns, 162
  religion and, 163
  voter turnout and, 110
reserved powers, 63
residual powers, 63
resolution, 218
retirement income security, 30
retrospective voting, 197
revolution, theory of, 39
Revolutionary War, 37
Rice, Susan, 259
Richardson, Bill, 188
Richmond, Virginia, 378
Ricketts, Pete, 177
rider, 224
right of political leaders to compete for support and votes, 17
right to be elected, 17
right to vote, 17
right wing, 91
rights of the accused, 350, 352–356
right-to-work laws, 135
RNC (Republican National Committee), 157
Roberts, John G., Jr., 285, 294, 295
Rockefeller, Nelson, 232
Rocky Mountain West, 162, 195
Roe v. Wade, 140, 287, 301, 306, 349, 359
rogue states, 385
Rolling Stone magazine, 18
Roman Catholics, 94, 139, 163, 207
Romania, 390
Romer v. Evans, 370
Romney, Mitt, 184, 186–187, 189
Roosevelt, Franklin
  character of, 246–247
  as commander in chief, 236
  death of, 233
  election of, 82
  internment of Japanese Americans, 236, 305, 357, 371
  judicial appointments, 294
  leadership style of, 249
  New Deal, 64, 266–267, 302
  power to persuade, 248
  presidency, 230
  Supreme Court and, 293
  World War II, 236, 238
Roosevelt, Kermit, III, 287

Roosevelt, Theodore, 181, 230, 248
Rosen, Jeffrey, 304
Ross, Albert, Jr., 352
Ross case, 352
rule, 269
Rule of Four, 297
rule of law, 41–43
rulemaking, 269–270
Rumsfeld, Donald, 244, 404
runoff, 172
rural areas, 29, 163
Russia, 25, 237, 389, 398
Rutgers University women's basketball team, 341
safe districts, 208
salmonella infection, 260
same-sex marriage, 48, 65, 83, 89, 94, 305, 375. *See also* civil unions
sample error, 81
sample size, 81
sampling, 81–83
San Francisco County Board of Supervisors, 375
Sanders, Bernie, 154
Santorum, Rick, 176
satellite radio, 118–119
Saturday Night Live, 161, 206, 210, 251
Saudi Arabia, 17, 376, 392
SBA (Small Business Administration), 260, 261
Scalia, Antonin, 285, 294, 295
SCHIP (State Children's Health Insurance Program), 224
Schobel, Bruce, 328
school, as agent of political socialization, 79
school attendance, 345
school desegregation, 287, 307. *See also* segregation
School Lunch Program, 70
school prayer, 304, 307, 344
school vouchers, 343
Schumer, Charles, 207
Schwarzenegger, Arnold, 52
Science and Technology Policy, Office of, 243, 244
searches and seizures, 350, 352
SEATO (Southeast Asia Treaty Organization), 394
Seattle, 370
SEC (Securities and Exchange Commission), 263, 269
Second Amendment, 42, 133
Second Bank of the United States, 64
Second Treatise on Government (Locke), 39
second-strike capability, 401
secretary of state, 232
Securities and Exchange Commission (SEC), 263, 269
Security Council, UN, 389, 397. *See also* United Nations (UN)
Sedition Act, 357
segregation, 50, 52, 366–370
select committee, 215
selection of justices, 291, 293, 294–295
selective incorporation of Bill of Rights, 340
self-incrimination, 353
Senate, 46, 183, 203, 205, 235, 240. *See also* Congress

Senate Commerce Committee, 210
Senate Environment and Public Works Committee, 276
Senate Environmental Protection Agency (EPA), 9, 167, 253, 260, 261, 273
Senate Foreign Relations Committee, 210
Senate majority leader, 210, 211, 213, 223, 290
Senate majority whip, 211
Senate minority leader, 211, 213
Senate minority whip, 211
Senate president *pro tempore*, 210, 211, 232
senatorial courtesy, 289
senators, direct election of, 46
Senior Executive Service (SES), 266
seniority, 210
Sensenbrenner, James F., Jr., 218
separate but equal, 52, 366–367
separation of powers, 44–46, 60, 108, 165, 305
September 11 terrorist attacks. *See also* terrorism
  agenda building and, 30, 31
  Bush and, 238, 250, 251, 252, 402
  clash of civilization theory, 399
  Congressional war power and, 219
  defense spending, 400
  Department of Homeland Security, 257
  effect on voter turnout, 107
  foreign and defense policymaking, 390
  9/11 Commission, 274
  shaping foreign policy, 406
  Trust Index, 88
  USA PATRIOT Act and, 359
Service Employees International Union, 141, 142
service learning, 45
SES (Senior Executive Service), 266
Seventeenth Amendment, 46
Seventh Amendment, 42
sexual discrimination lawsuit, 136
sexual harassment, 375, 377
Shanahan, Jack, 409
Shapiro, Steven, 354
shared powers, 63
Sharia, 292
Shas Party, 156
Shay, Daniel, 38
Shay's Rebellion, 38
Shelley v. Kraemer, 374
Shepard, Matthew, 346, 371
Showtime Network, 271
SICKO, 323
Sidarth, S.R., 117
Sierra Club, 138, 140
signaling role, 128
Silverstone, Alicia, 38
Simmons, Russell, 104
Sirius satellite radio, 118
sit-ins, 374
Sixteenth Amendment, 303
Sixth Amendment, 42, 355
Sky News, 119
slavery, 66
Slovakia, 390
Slovenia, 390

Small Business Administration (SBA), 260, 261
"Small Texas School District Lets Teachers, Staff Pack Pistols" (Agee), 149
Smathers, George, 181
Smith, Gordon, 62
Smithsonian Institution, 271
smoking, 280
snail darter, 302
social class, 93
social conservatives, 65
social issues, 92
social liberals, 65
social policy, 65
Social Security
  definition, 15
  government expenditures, 324–326
  in party platforms, 164
  payroll taxes, 316
  reform of, 242, 249, 321–322, 328
Social Security Administration (SSA), 5, 260, 261, 266
Social Security Old Age and Survivors Insurance (OASI) Trust Fund, 329
Socialist Equality Party, 154
Socialist Party, 154
sodomy, 350
soft money, 145, 178–179
Sojourners, 138
sound bite, 125
Souter, David, 285, 294, 295
South, 162, 195
South Africa, 89
South Dakota, 359
South Korea, 388, 394, 398
Southeast Asia Treaty Organization (SEATO), 392
Southern Baptist Convention, 94, 163
Southwest, 195
sovereignty, 46
Soviet Union, 18, 399, 402, 403
Spain, 89, 396
Sparks, Jordin, 301
Speaker of the House, 210, 211, 213, 223, 232
Spears, Britney, 122, 178, 301
special committee, 215
special education programs, 72
split ticket ballot, 172
spoiled ballots, 113
spoils system, 265, 266
sponsor, 218
Spurlock, Morgan, 314
SSA (Social Security Administration), 5, 260, 261, 266
SSI (Supplemental Security Income), 326
Stalin, Joseph, 399
Stamp Act, 36
standard of living, 24–25
standing committee, 215
Standing Conference of Ministers of Culture (KMK), 69
Starr, Kenneth, 232
Star-Telegram, 149
State Children's Health Insurance Program (SCHIP), 224
state constitutions, 341
State Department, 258–259, 266, 408

State of the Union, 242
state powers, 63
states, 62–63, 63, 65, 165
states' rights, 63, 64, 66
statistical chance, 81
statutory law, 263, 302, 342, 373
steel mills, seizure of, 240
Stern, Howard, 82, 118
steroid use in baseball, 289
Stevens, John Paul, 285, 294, 295, 297
Stewart, Jimmy, 223
Stiller, Ben, 128
Stimson, James A., 96–97
stock market, 197
Stop Animal Exploitation Now, 146
Stouffer, Samuel, 87
straight ticket ballot, 172
strategic forces, 400–401
strict construction, 286
strict judicial scrutiny, 366
strict-constructionist philosophy, 241
strong national government, 40, 45
student discipline, 340
"Study: Congress Should Repeal 'Don't Ask, Don't Tell'" (Associated Press), 407
subgovernments, 275–276, 278
subsidy, 312, 313
suburbs, 163
Subversive Activities Control Act, 357
Sudan, 397
Sudeikis, Jason, 210
suffrage, 370
Summer Olympics 2008, 346
Sunbelt, 22, 136, 174
Sundquist, James, 54
Super Tuesday, 189
superdelegates, 187
Superdome, 257
supermajority, 41
Supplemental Security Income (SSI), 326
supply-side economics, 319
Supreme Court, U.S., 293–301
    2000 election, 193
    abortion, 287, 301, 359
    acceptance of cases, 295–298
    on affirmative action, 379
    on anti-government speech, 345
    appointments to, 240, 241, 285
    Bush election and, 113
    on capital punishment, 356
    case decisions, 298, 300
    on civil liberties, 341
    civil rights, 373
    decision implementation, 300
    demographics of justices, 294
    on enemy combatants, 357
    equality before the law, 365–370
    on establishment of religion, 343–344
    on executive orders, 240
    on fair trials, 355
    federal system and, 63–64, 66
    gay and lesbian rights, 306, 370
    on hate-crimes legislation, 347, 371
    impact of, 301
    on internment of Japanese Americans, 236, 238

judicial review, 51–52
jurisdiction, 293–294
    national supremacy vs. states' rights, 66
    powers of, 62
    public opinion and, 306
    on reapportionment, 174
    on right of privacy, 347
    on search and seizures, 352
    selection of justices, 294–295
    on Voting Rights Act, 175
    white primary, 372
surgeon general, 280
Surgeon General's Report on Smoking and Health, 280
surpluses, 321
survey research, 81
suspect classifications, 365
Sutton v. United Airlines, 7
Swann v. Charlotte-Mecklenburg Board of Education, 369
Sweatt v. Painter, 367
Sweden, 108, 394
Swift Boat Veterans for Truth, 145, 179
swing vote, 299
swing voters, 195
symbolic expression, 347
table, 220
Taiwan, 394
Talent, James, 176
Taliban, 236, 396, 404, 405
TANF (Temporary Assistance to Needy Families), 70, 326
tariff, 391
Task Force on National Healthcare Reform, 229
Tauzin, Billy, 210
tax breaks for college students, 316
tax burden, 316–317
tax deduction, 315
tax exemption, 315
tax fairness, 317–318
tax incidence, 317–318
tax policy, 164
tax preference, 315
tax revenues, 314–319
    Bush tax reforms, 318–319
    corporate income tax, 315, 316
    individual income tax, 26, 314–316
    issues in government finance, 316–318
    payroll taxes, 315, 316
    sources of, 315
taxation without representation, 37
Teamsters Union, 142, 275
technical specialists, 278
technology, use of, 25
"Teflon President," 251
Tejada, Miguel, 289
television ratings, 122–123
Temporary Assistance to Needy Families (TANF), 70, 326
Ten Commandments, 306
Tenet, George, 244, 274
Tennessee Valley Authority (TVA), 262
Tenth Amendment, 42, 62, 63, 65
Tenure of Office Act, 232
terrorism, 30, 352, 399. *See also* September 11 terrorist attacks

terrorist suspects, 299
test cases, 297, 359, 367
test of understanding, 372
Texas
    2000 election, 192
    2008 election, 189
    civil rights, 367
    death penalty, 356
    electoral votes, 194
    federalism and, 65
    highway system, 276
    NASA and, 273
    nomination phase, 190
    privacy rights, 350
    redistricting, 175
    school prayer, 344
    Sunbelt, 22
Texas v. Johnson, 306, 348
The End of History and the Last Man (Fukuyama), 397
Third Amendment, 42, 347
third party, 154, 161
Thirteenth Amendment, 64
Thomas, Clarence, 285, 294, 295, 377
Thompson, Fred, 188
Thweatt, David, 149
Tilden, Samuel, 192
Timberlake, Justin, 262
Time, 119
timing, and public opinion measurement, 85
Title II, 374
Title IX, 374, 381, 383
tobacco regulation, 320
Torah and Shabatt Judaism Party, 156
Torrenueva, Joseph, 179
torture, 238
trade associations, 135
trade embargo, 391
traditional families, 162
traditional media, 124
Traficant, James, 206
transit strike, 268
Transportation, Department of, 112, 258–259
Transportation and Infrastructure Committee, 216
Treasury Department, 258–259, 264, 266, 312, 329
treaties, 41, 235
trial, 287
Tribune Company, 119
Truman, Harry, 83, 87, 233, 240, 249
Trump, Donald, 26
Trump, Ken, 149
Trust Index, 88
Turkey, 395, 397, 399
TVA (Tennessee Valley Authority), 262
Twenty-fifth Amendment, 204, 232
Twenty-first Amendment, 50
Twenty-second Amendment, 230–231
Twenty-sixth Amendment, 303
two-party system, 154
tyranny of the majority, 41
UAW (United Auto Workers Union), 136, 142, 275
UCA (unanimous consent agreement), 222

Uganda, 397
UN (United Nations), 245, 389, 397
unanimous consent agreement (UCA), 222
Unemployment Insurance, 70
unemployment rate, 326
unicameral legislature, 37
unilateral tools of presidential power, 249
United Arab Emirates, 399
United Arab List-Arab Renewal Party, 156
United Auto Workers Union (UAW), 136, 142, 275
United Kingdom. *See* Great Britain
United Nations (UN), 245, 389, 397
United States Reports, 300
United States Trade Representative, Office of the, 243, 244
universal healthcare, 73, 323
universe, 81
University of Michigan, 88
University of Michigan Law School, 363, 379, 381
University of Oklahoma, 367
unreasonable search and seizure, 49
UPN network, 119
urban areas, 29, 163
USA PATRIOT Act, 357, 359
U.S. Air Force, 280
U.S. Army, 280
U.S. Chamber of Commerce, 144
U.S. News, 119
U.S. v. Eichman, 348
U.S. v. Morrison, 66
USDA. *See* Agriculture, Department of
Valentin, Julian, 390
Van Orden v. Perry, 306
Vanishing Voter Project, 159
VAP (voting age population), 106
VEP (voting eligible population), 106, 107
veterans, wounded, 330
Veterans Affairs, Department of, 258–259, 266
veto, 41, 224, 242
vice presidency, 190, 232, 233–234
Vietnam, 17
Vietnam War, 54, 107, 159, 219, 238, 346, 400
Violence Against Women Act, 66
Virgin Islands, 204
Virginia, 195, 355
Virginia Military Institute (VMI), 370
Virginia Tech attack, 124
"virtual" child pornography, 299
vision, 249
VMI (Virginia Military Institute), 370
volunteers, campaign, 183
voter mobilization, 103–104
voter turnout. *See also* voting patterns
    2008 election, 101
    by age, 11, 104
    factors in, 107–108
    internationally, 108
    by race/ethnicity, 105
    trends in, 106–107
voters, 196–197
voting, registration for, 106

voting age, 303
voting age population (VAP), 106
voting eligible population (VEP), 106, 107
voting patterns. *See also* voter turnout
   age and, 162
   education and, 160–161
   family and lifestyle status, 162
   gender and, 161–162
   income and, 160
   issue orientation, 163
   place of residence, 163
   political ideology, 162
   political parties and, 160–164
   race and ethnicity, 160
   region, 162
   religion, 163
voting rights, 370, 372
Voting Rights Act (VRA), 137, 175, 206, 373
VRA (Voting Rights Act), 137, 175, 206, 373
Wagram Air Base, 372
Wall Street Journal, 84
Wallace, George, 193
Wallis, Jim, 138
Wal-Mart, 25, 135, 136
Walter Reed Army Medical Center, 128, 129

Walters, Dan, 84
Wangsness, Lisa, 279
war, civil liberties and, 357
War on Terror, 219, 236, 239, 356–357, 357, 394, 399
war power of Congress, 219
War Powers Act, 238–239, 303
Warner, John, 293
warrant, 350
Warren, Earl, 287, 296, 300, 358, 368
Warren, Rick, 343
Washington, D.C., 299
Washington, George, 37, 230
Washington Post, 85, 122, 128
Washington Times, 299, 328
waterboarding, 238
Watergate scandal, 107, 233
Ways and Means Committee, 216, 220, 332, 334
WB, 119
weapons, exportation of, 394
weapons of mass destruction (WMD), 245, 249, 387
weblog, 119–120
Webster, Daniel, 233
Weeks, Fremont, 352
Weeks case, 352
welfare reform, 326–327, 329, 334
Wesberry v. Sanders, 174

West Coast, 162, 195
Westboro Baptist Church, 87
Western Europe, 388
White House staff, 243
white primary, 372
WHO (World Health Organization), 389
"Why American Youth Will Vote" (Martin), 11
Wilson, Charlie 400
Wichita, Kansas, 371
Wilson, Woodrow, 296
Winfrey, Oprah, 103
winner-take-all election system, 191
Wisconsin, 371
Wisconsin v. Mitchell, 371
WMD (weapons of mass destruction), 245, 249, 387
women in military, 372
women's rights, in Saudi Arabia, 376
women's suffrage, 303, 370
Worcester v. Georgia, 66
Workers World Party, 154
working-class whites, immigration and, 212
World Health Organization (WHO), 389
World Series, 123
World Trade Center, 31

World Trade Organization (WTO), 390
World War I, 357
World War II, 54, 236, 238
World Wide Fund for Nature, 391
World Wide Web (WWW), 122
Wright, Jeremiah, 160
writ of *habeas corpus*, 41–42, 236, 289, 357
writ of *mandamus*, 51
WTO (World Trade Organization), 390
Wurzelbacher, Joe, 313
WWW (World Wide Web), 122
www.mypoliscilab.com, 97
Wyoming, 173
X, Malcolm, 378
Yemen, 395
Yisrael Beitenu Party, 156
youth, 11, 27, 29
YouTube, 117, 118, 123, 181
zone of acquiescence, 97
zones of privacy, 347